Gringras: The Laws of the Internet

Third Edition

Gringras: The Laws of the Internet

Third Edition

Elle Todd
Olswang

Contributing Editors

Competition
Alasdair Balfour
Olswang

Tax
Stephen Hignett
Olswang

Trade Marks, Domain Names and Passing Off
Phillip Johnson
Barrister, 7 New Square

Tottel
publishing

Published by
Tottel Publishing Ltd
Maxwelton House
41–43 Boltro Road
Haywards Heath
West Sussex
RH16 1BJ

Elle Todd, Clive Gringras, Alasdair Balfour, Stephen Hignett and Phillip Johnson have asserted their right to be identified as the authors of this work in accordance with the Copyright, Designs and Patents Act 1988.

British Library Cataloguing-in-Publication Data.
A catalogue record for this book is available from the British Library.

ISBN: 978 1 84592 243 6

Typeset by Phoenix Photosetting, Chatham, Kent
Printed and bound in Great Britain by Antony Rowe, Chippenham, Wilts.

Dedication

For Corrin and Tom who I miss.

'Bless the darkness around you
That's why you're a poet
As the night presses inward
you radiate beams of light.'

Andrei Voznesenskiĭ

Foreword to the Third Edition

When the first edition of this book appeared in 1997 the task of producing a definitive book on Internet law could best be described as ambitious. Ten years later, the task looks (charitably) immense or (less charitably) foolhardy, depending on one's viewpoint. Elle Todd, Clive Gringras and the contributors are to be commended for even taking on such a task. That they have managed to repeat the success of the 1997 effort, is still more laudable.

The incessant and increasing pace of technological and service development in the Internet world has meant that laws and regulations aimed at controlling, or at least managing this new world have often been hastily adopted or obsolete even before adoption. It is the conventional wisdom that the development of the Internet is moving so fast that laws and regulations cannot keep up. If one digs deeper, however, as this book does, the picture is somewhat more nuanced. Certainly, there are numerous examples of offshore, cross-border services cocking a snook at national laws which attempt to restrict their activity locally. At the same time, however, there are as many examples of existing legal frameworks coping admirably with the new challenges of the digital world.

Indeed, the most striking thing about this book is how familiar the chapter titles will be to any lawyer: Contract, Tort, Intellectual Property, Crime, Data and Data Protection, Taxation, Competition Law, and Elle's new chapter, Regulation and Regulated Activities. The book manages to demystify the Internet (at least for legal purposes) and presents findings in a clear and straightforward way. At the same time, however, the text does not shy away from addressing the more difficult issues the Internet throws up for which there are no immediate answers and where legal history provides little or no guide.

The free flow of information and services around the world via the Internet creates genuinely new issues and problems. This is true for rules of jurisdiction and applicable law. It is also true for how novel new products and services should be regulated; from my personal perspective, think about Internet communications and legacy telephony regulation. Should a PC-residing piece of peer-to-peer software such as that provided by Skype – with its online voice, video, chat, file transfer, money transfer, presence and other functionality – be regulated along the lines of a traditional telephony service? The answer seems obvious, but confusion and doubt, certainly facilitated by powerful and monied interests, continues to reign among many governments and regulators around the world.

The Internet does, too, allow for the emergence of a few new crimes, though most of what is deemed cybercrime by the media and, sadly, many government agencies, is neither cybernetic nor new.

In general, governments and courts continue to struggle to come to terms with the speed of technological change and the obvious erosion of sovereign borders which the Internet brings. At the same time, however, traditional law and its local application has certainly not collapsed, as many predicted towards the end of the last century. The real strength of Gringras: The Laws of the Internet is that it captures perfectly the tension between old and new and offers solid, practical advice which can be used by the practitioner and the student as well as the interested bystander.

Robert Miller
General Counsel, Skype
January 2008

Foreword to the First Edition

Judging by some of the stuff one reads – particularly from journalists – the Internet will throw laws, or many of them, into chaos. The suggestion seems to be the law cannot cope with the breakdown of national barriers, the cross-border implications of the interlinking of computers world-wide. The scenario painted is that the Internet will be a lawless dimension, with lawyers and clients having no idea what to do or how to control the activities of others. Clive Gringras is to be congratulated on not only debunking this myth but by doing so in a constructive (and readable) way. What he has done here is to consider, subject by subject, what rules the courts will develop and apply. As always what the law will do is develop appropriate rules by analogy. Contract, tort (including special variants of old torts, eg negligently allowing a virus to spread and new ways of defaming people), intellectual property (particularly trade marks and copyright), questions of jurisdiction, crime, data protection, and so on all have passed under his intelligent consideration. Of course there are, as yet, few actual cases on most points. So he has used his imagination to create problems and indicate how the law is likely to answer them. Because he understands the Internet and how it works well, his imaginary problems are realistic. Moreover he has up-to-date intelligence of case law from other countries (particularly the US) which supplement his fictional examples. Anyone with an Internet problem will find this book a first port of call – and in many cases may well find an answer, or a reasonable prediction of the answer. In one area where he obviously does not feel entirely at home, namely tax (who would blame him?), he has sought assistance from Conrad McDonnell of Gray's Inn Chambers.

There is something of a spate of books which carry the names of firms of solicitors. Many (but not all) are rather slight works, rushed out after some new piece of legislation and not telling you much that is not in the Act. This is far from such a work. Nabarro Nathanson are to be congratulated on allowing Mr Gringras to put in what must have been a vast amount of work.

Hon Sir Robin Jacob
January 1997

Preface to the Third Edition

Five years on from the second edition, double that since the first and 'Laws of the Internet' almost takes on a whole different meaning. There are some, for starters.

And yet, surprisingly, such changes have not required a whole new structure for this book. Each body of law which needed consideration at the beginning remains relevant and are still considered here. But the application of these areas of law to the multifarious scenarios and developments the Internet throws up has moved on. In many ways there is less need for conjecture. Governments appear less nervous in drawing up rules covering online activities whilst existing legislation and precedent from a pre-Internet era has proven more able to expand to fit a virtual, non-premises based arena than many expected (albeit with a little helping hand here and there). In other areas speculation continues. I have needed to add a chapter to keep up with the developments and from the increasing size of this volume a reader will see that it is now even more relevant to speak of Internet laws in the plural.

The Internet remains the most exciting of challenges for legal analysis. Its significance and reach are simultaneously complicated, unnerving and empowering. We hear in the press the horror stories of an Internet rife with cyber-stalking, identity theft and kiddie porn. But, as I finished this edition in late 2007, the Internet was also fixing the world's eyes on thousands of buddhist monks marching defiantly against the Burmese military regime; a gaze and witness which had not been there in 1988. The Internet can also give hope and bring new opportunities.

Consideration of the limits of control which, after all, is what laws are about, demands more attention and thought in the context of the Internet than perhaps ever before. I fear a text book can do little justice to this and yet a little understanding will hopefully inspire more.

Thank you to Alasdair Balfour (with generous assistance from Tomos Jones) and Stephen Hignett for updating the Competition and Tax chapters respectively, and to Phillip Johnson for his contribution on trade marks, domain names and passing off in the chapter on Intellectual Property. Thank you also to Clive for trusting me with this task and accepting my need to make it my own: I hope you recognise respect and not just scars in its content.

To Penny, Jan, Bonny and particularly Marco, for your support and understanding of my too numerous absences.

Elle Todd
January 2008

Contents

Foreword to the Third Edition   vii

Foreword to the First Edition   ix

Preface to the Third Edition   xi

Table of Cases   xxi

Table of Statutes   xxxi

Table of Statutory Instruments   xxxvii

1   Introduction   **1**

    1.1   Language and networks   2

    1.2   InterNetworking   2

    1.3   The Internet   3

    1.4   The cost   4

    1.5   Internet concepts   4

        1.5.1   IP addresses and domain names   5

        1.5.2   Email   5

        1.5.3   Pseudo-anonymity   6

        1.5.4   Instant messaging   6

        1.5.5   Bulletin boards   7

        1.5.6   Forums   7

        1.5.7   User-Generated Content   8

        1.5.8   File Transfer Protocol   8

        1.5.9   World Wide Web   8

    1.6   This book   10

2   Contract   13

    2.1   Formation of contract   14

        2.1.1   Contracting via the Internet   15

        2.1.2   Pre-contract information   17

        2.1.3   Offers and invitations to treat   23

        2.1.4   Acceptance   30

        2.1.5   Consideration   47

        2.1.6   Intention   48

2.2	Performance: payment		50
	2.2.1	Internet payment	50
	2.2.2	Credit card non-payment	50
	2.2.3	Digital cash non-payment	51
2.3	Type of contract		52
	2.3.1	Exhaustion of rights	53
	2.3.2	Retention of title	53
	2.3.3	Using is copying	53
	2.3.4	Implied licence	54
	2.3.5	Express licence	54
	2.3.6	Auctions	55
2.4	Jurisdiction		56
	2.4.1	Brussels regulation and Lugano convention	57
2.5	Choice of law		71
	2.5.1	The Rome convention	72
	2.5.2	Express choice of law	73
	2.5.3	Absence of choice	79
3	**Tort**		**85**
3.1	Negligence		86
	3.1.1	Constituent parts	87
	3.1.2	Application to Internet cases	93
3.2	Trespass/wrongful interference with goods		105
	3.2.1	Physical interference with goods	105
	3.2.2	Possession	106
	3.2.3	Damage	106
3.3	Other tortious actions		107
	3.3.1	Occupiers' liability	108
	3.3.2	Product liability	108
	3.3.3	Rylands v Fletcher	109
	3.3.4	Economic torts	110
3.4	Negligent misstatement		110
	3.4.1	Hedley Byrne v Heller	110
3.5	Contracts and disclaimers		115
	3.5.1	Exclusions	116
	3.5.2	Effectiveness of exclusions	118
3.6	Defamation		120
	3.6.1	Technicalities	121
	3.6.2	The Defamation Act 1996	122

	3.6.3	Defences	125
	3.6.4	Damages	137
	3.6.5	Strategy	139
3.7	Jurisdiction		141
	3.7.1	Brussels Regulation and Lugano Convention	142
	3.7.2	Brussels Regulation Jurisdiction over torts	142
	3.7.3	Common law jurisdiction over torts	148
3.8	Choice of law		155
	3.8.1	Common law choice of law	155
	3.8.2	Statutory choice of law	156

4 Intellectual property **159**

4.1	Trade marks, domain names and passing off		160
	4.1.1	Technical rights v legal rights	160
	4.1.2	The nature of trade mark protection	162
	4.1.3	Domain names	162
	4.1.4	Trade marks v domain names	163
4.2	Registration of trade marks		164
	4.2.1	Signs that can be registered as trade marks	165
	4.2.2	Absolute grounds of refusal	165
	4.2.3	Registering in relation to goods and services	167
	4.2.4	Classification	167
	4.2.5	Opposition and registration	170
4.3	Registration of domain names		171
	4.3.1	Trying to identify the domain name owner	171
4.4	Trade mark infringement		172
	4.4.1	Use of a sign in the course of trade	173
	4.4.2	Use as a trade mark	179
	4.4.3	In relation to goods or services	180
	4.4.4	Identical sign to registered trade mark	180
	4.4.5	Similar or identical sign with similar or identical goods or services	181
	4.4.6	Dilution protection	183
	4.4.7	Metatags	186
	4.4.8	Defences	189
	4.4.9	Trade mark infringement remedies	191
4.5	Passing off		192
	4.5.1	Goodwill of plaintiff	192
	4.5.2	Misrepresentation by defendant	193

	4.5.3	Damage	195
	4.5.4	Instrument of fraud claim	196
	4.5.5	Passing off remedies	199
4.6		Protective domain name measures	200
	4.6.1	Check availability of domain name	200
	4.6.2	Register domain name	200
	4.6.3	Clear use of domain name	201
	4.6.4	Protect domain name with trade mark registration	201
	4.6.5	Consider domain name dispute rules	202
4.7		Uniform resolution dispute policy	202
	4.7.1	Formal issues	203
	4.7.2	Factual issues	203
	4.7.3	Legal issues	204
	4.7.4	Timing of the arbitration	211
	4.7.5	Domain names and registration companies	212
4.8		Jurisdiction over infringement	212
	4.8.1	Jurisdiction	212
	4.8.2	Jurisdiction and EC domiciles	213
	4.8.3	Jurisdiction and non-EC domiciles	215
	4.8.4	Applicable law	216
4.9		Copyright	217
	4.9.1	Copyright protection	218
	4.9.2	Protected works	219
	4.9.3	Scope of copyright protection	222
	4.9.4	Qualification requirements	223
	4.9.5	Term of protection	226
	4.9.6	Internet examples	227
	4.9.7	Databases	240
4.10		Moral rights and the Internet	243
	4.10.1	Paternity	244
	4.10.2	Integrity	245
	4.10.3	Waiver of rights	247
	4.10.4	Copyright and database right infringement	247
4.11		Copyright prohibited acts	247
	4.11.1	Copying	248
	4.11.2	Issuing copies to the public	249
	4.11.3	Renting or lending to the public	249
	4.11.4	Performing, showing or playing in public	249

	4.11.5	Communication to the public	250
	4.11.6	Making or acts in relation to an adaptation	250
4.12	Database infringement		251
	4.12.1	A substantial part	251
	4.12.2	Secondary infringement	253
	4.12.3	Dealings	253
	4.12.4	Licences and defences	256
4.13	Copyright infringement and the Internet: examples		265
	4.13.1	Email	265
4.14	Search engines and web links		272
4.15	Websites		273
	4.15.1	Backup copies	274
	4.15.2	Framing	275
	4.15.3	Making an unlicensed article	276
	4.15.4	Deep links and spiders	277
4.16	Jurisdiction over infringement		278
	4.16.1	Infringement of UK copyright abroad	278
	4.16.2	Enforcement of copyright abroad	281

5 Crime | | | **283** |
5.1	computer misuse		285
	5.1.1	Introduction	285
	5.1.2	Section 1: unauthorised access	287
	5.1.3	Section 2: hacking to offend further	302
	5.1.4	Section 3: unauthorised acts to impair or to prevent or hinder access	304
	5.1.5	Section 3A: making, supplying or obtaining articles for use in computer misuse	312
	5.1.6	Jurisdiction and extradition	314
5.2	Internet fraud		320
5.3	Obscene and indecent material		321
	5.3.1	Publication over the Internet	321
	5.3.2	Indecent material	324
	5.3.3	Transmission, retrieval and downloading	325
	5.3.4	Liability of Internet service providers	326
5.4	Anti-terrorism and terrorist materials		328
	5.4.1	Threat to electronic systems	329
	5.4.2	Liability for terrorist material	329
5.5	Cyberstalking/harassment		333

	5.5.1	The Protection From Harassment Act	334
	5.5.2	Malicious Communications Act	335
	5.5.3	Section 127 Communications Act	336
5.6	Evidence		337
	5.6.1	Common law presumption	337
	5.6.2	The evidential burden	338

6   Data and data protection   **341**

6.1	The legislative landscape		342
	6.1.1	The Data Protection Act 1998	343
	6.1.2	The Privacy and Electronic Communications (EC Directive) Regulations 2003	343
	6.1.3	The Regulation of Investigatory Powers Act 2000	343
	6.1.4	Anti-Terrorism, Crime and Security Act 2001	344
	6.1.5	Directive 2006/24/EC on data retention	345
6.2	Data protection		345
	6.2.1	Personal data	345
	6.2.2	Processing	351
	6.2.3	Processors and controllers	354
	6.2.4	Data protection notification	360
	6.2.5	Principles of data protection	362
	6.2.6	Enforcement	399
6.3	Direct marketing		400
	6.3.1	Transparency requirements	400
	6.3.2	Consent requirements	400
	6.3.3	Penalties and enforcement	403
6.4	Data retention and disclosures for law enforcement		405
	6.4.1	Restrictions on interception of communications	405
	6.4.2	Obligations to provide access to data	406
	6.4.3	Obligations to retain data	407

7   Taxation   **411**

7.1	UK tax – General	412
7.2	Sole trader, partnership or company?	414
7.3	Business profits	415
7.4	UK Residence	416
7.5	The source of profits and taxable presence	417
7.6	UK permanent establishment	418
7.7	Withholding taxes	418

	7.8	VAT	420
		7.8.1	Introduction	420
		7.8.2	Exempt and zero-rated supplies	421
		7.8.3	The VAT system in the UK	422
		7.8.4	VAT and supplies made via the Internet	422
		7.8.5	ESS and the VAT on Electronic Commerce Directive	427
		7.8.6	Further changes to the place of supply of ESS	428

8	**Competition law and the Internet**		**431**
	8.1	Introduction to competition law	432
	8.2	The legal framework	433
		8.2.1	Anti-competitive agreements and abuse of a dominant position	433
		8.2.2	UK cartel offence	434
		8.2.3	Market investigations	434
		8.2.4	Merger control	434
		8.2.5	Sector-specific legislation	434
	8.3	Anti-competitive agreements	435
		8.3.1	Undertakings	435
		8.3.2	Agreements and concerted practices	436
		8.3.3	Decisions of associations of undertakings	436
		8.3.4	May affect trade	437
		8.3.5	Jurisdiction	437
		8.3.6	Object or effect	438
		8.3.7	Prevention, restriction or distortion of competition	438
		8.3.8	Appreciability	440
		8.3.9	Market definition	441
		8.3.10	Convergence	444
		8.3.11	Exemptions	447
	8.4	Anti-competitive conduct	449
		8.4.1	Dominance	449
		8.4.2	Abuse	452
	8.5	Enforcement procedure	460
		8.5.1	Complaints	460
		8.5.2	Investigation	461
		8.5.3	Interim measures	461
		8.5.4	Orders to terminate infringements	461
		8.5.5	Commitments	461

		8.5.6	Fines	462
		8.5.7	Whistleblowing/leniency	462
	8.6	Cartel offence		463
	8.7	Merger control		464
		8.7.1	EC Merger Regulation	464
		8.7.2	UK Enterprise Act	465
	8.8	Market investigations		466

9   Regulation and regulated activities   469

	9.1	Internet access and administration		470
		9.1.1	Introduction	470
		9.1.2	Ofcom regulation of ISPS	470
		9.1.3	Voice over Internet protocol	471
		9.1.4	Self-regulation	472
	9.2	Financial products and services		472
		9.2.1	The Electronic Commerce (Financial Services and Markets) Directive and Financial Promotions	473
		9.2.2	Electronic money	475
		9.2.3	Financial contracts over the Internet	476
	9.3	Advertising		480
		9.3.1	Voluntary advertising codes	480
		9.3.2	Unfair commercial practices	481
	9.4	Online gambling		484
		9.4.1	Gambling	484
	9.5	Contracting with consumers		488
		9.5.1	Introduction	488
		9.5.2	Selling goods and services at a distance	488
	9.6	Audiovisual media		500
		9.6.1	The Communication Act	500
		9.6.2	The Audiovisual Media Services Directive	501

Index   503

Table of Cases

PARA

1-800 Contacts v WhenU.com 414 F 3d 400 (2005) 4.4.7.2
1-800 Flowers [2002] FSR 12 .... 4.4.1.1, 4.4.2.2
800-JR Cigars v GoTo 437 F Supp 2d 273 (DNJ 2006) 4.4.7.2

A

A & M Records v Napster Inc 239 F 3d 1004 (2001) 4.13.1.4.1
ABKCO Music and Records Inc v Music Collection International Ltd [1995] RPC
   657 .... 4.16.1
ACLU v Reno (No 3) [2000] F3d 162 .... 5.3.1.2
AMF v Sleekraft Boats 599 F 2d 341 .... 4.7.3.2
A-G's Reference (No 1 of 1991) [1992] 3 All ER 897, [1993] QB 94 ... 5.1.2.1.3, 5.1.4.2.1
Abidin Daver, The [1984] 1 All ER 470 .... 2.4.1.8.2; 3.7.3.2
Adam Opel (Case 48/05) [2007] ETMR 33 .... 4.4.1, 4.4.3, 4.4.8.2
Adams v Lindsell (1818) 1 B & Ald 681 .... 2.1.3.5.1, 2.1.4.2.1
Adidas v Fitnessworld (Case 408/01) [2004] ETMR 10 .... 4.4.6, 4.4.6.2
Agnew v Länsförsakringsbolagens AB [2000] 1 Lloyd's Rep 317 .... 3.7.2.1
Ahlstrom v EC Commission (Cases 114, 125-129/85) [1988] ECR 5193 .... 8.3.5
Aiken v Stewart Wrightson Members' Agency Ltd [1995] 3 All ER 449 .... 3.1.1.2
Airbus Industrie GIE v Patel [1999] 1 AC 119 .... 2.4.1.8.2; 3.7.3.2
Airtours v EC Commission (Case T-342/99) [2002] 5 CMLR 317 .... 8.4.1.3
Alcock v Chief Constable of South Yorkshire [1991] 4 All ER 907 .... 3.8.2.1
Allied Marine Transport Ltd v Vale do Rio Doce Navigacao SA [1985] 1 WLR
   925 .... 2.1.4.1.1
America Online Inc v IMS 24 F Supp 24 .... 3.2.3.1
Anacon Corpn Ltd v Environmental Research Technology Ltd [1994] FSR 659 ... 4.9.6.2.2
Anderson v New York Telephone Co 361 NYS 2d 913 (NYCA 1974) 3.6.2.5
Anderton v Ryan [1985] AC 560 .... 5.1.3.4
Anheuser-Busch Inc v Budejovicky Budvar Narodni Podnik (Case C-245/02)
   [2005] ETMR 27 .... 4.4.2, 4.4.3, 4.4.8.2
Anns v London Borough of Merton [1977] 2 All ER 492 .... 3.1.1.1
Anvil Jewellery Ltd v Riva Ridge Holdings Ltd (1985-1987) 4.12.4
Arsenel v Reed (Case C-206/01) [2003] ETMR 19 .... 4.4.1, 4.4.2, 4.4.3, 4.5.2
Atkins v DPP [2000] 2 All ER 425 .... 5.3.2
Attock Cement Co Ltd v Romanian Bank for Foreign Trade [1989] 1 All ER
   1189 .... 2.4.1.8.1; 3.7.3.1
Autospin (Oil Seals) Ltd v Beeline Spinning (a firm) [1995] RPC 683 .... 4.9.2.4
Avery Dennison v Jerry Sumpton 189 F3d 868 .... 4.4.6.2.2
Avnet Inc v Aviation Network Inc (WIPO D2000-0046) 4.2.4.1
Avnet Inc v Isoact Ltd [1997] ETMR 562 .... 4.2.4.1, 4.4.7

B

BMW v Deenik [1999] ETMR 339 .... 4.4.8.2
BREIN v Techno Design "Internet Programming" BV [2006] ECDR 21 .... 4.14
BT v One-in-a-million [1999] 1 WLR 903, CA; [1998] FSR 265 ... 4.4.1.3, 4.4.6.2.2, 4.4.9,
                                             4.5.2.1, 4.5.3, 4.5.4.1, 4.5.4.3
Badger v MoD [2006] 3 All ER 173, QB 3.1.2.1.5
Bailey v Derby Corpn [1965] 1 All ER 443 .... 3.1.1.4.1

PARA

Bal v Van Staden [1902] TS 128 . . . . 2.1.4.2.2
Bank of Credit & Commerce International SA (No 8), Re [1996] 2 All ER 121 . . .   2.2.2
Barclays Mercantile Business Finance v Mawson [2005] STC 1 . . . .   7.2
Barnett v Chelsea & Kensington Hospital Management Committee [1969] 1 QB
   428 . . . . 3.1.2.1.4
Barry v Bradshaw & Co (a firm) [2000] CLC 455, CA 2.4.1.5
Bauman v Fussell [1978] RPC 485 . . . . 4.9.6.3.2
Beaumatic v Mitchell [1999] ETMR 912 . . . .   4.4.4.1
Beguelin Import v GL Import Export (Case 22/71) [1972] CMLR 81 . . . .   8.3.1
Ben & Jerry's Homemade Inc v Ben & Jerry's Ice Cream Ltd (unreported, 19
   January 1995) 4.5.4.1
Berezovsky v Michaels [2000] 2 All ER 986 . . . .   3.7.3.3
Beta Computers (Europe) v Adobe Systems Europe 1996 SLT 604 . . . . 2.1.4.1.1
Bier BV v Mines de Potasse D'Alsace (Case 21/76) (1976) ECR 1735 . . . .   4.8.3.2
Biotrading & Financing OY v Biohit Ltd [1998] FSR 109 . . . .   4.12.1
Blair v Osbourne & Tomkins [1971] 2 QB 78 . . . .   4.12.4
Blunt (John) v David Tilley, Paul Hancox, Christopher Stephens, AOL UK Ltd,
   Tiscali UK Ltd & British Telecommunicationsplc [2006] EWCH 407, QB . . . 3.6.3.2.1,
                                                                                            3.6.3.2.2
Blyth v Birmingham Waterworks Co (1856) 11 Ex Ch 781 . . . .   3.1.1.2
Bodil Lindqvist v Kammaraklagaren (Case C-101/01) (2003), ECJ 6.2.2, 6.2.5.8
Bonnier Media v Smith [2002] ETMR 86 . . . .   4.4.1.1
Bostik v Sellotape GB Ltd [1994] RPC 556 . . . .   4.5.2.2
Bowerman v Association of Travel Agents Ltd [1995] NLJR 1815 . . . . 2.1.3.2.2, 2.1.3.3
Boys v Chaplin? 3.7.3.1.1
Bravado Merchandising Services v Mainstream Publishing [1996] FSR 205 . . . . . .   4.4.3
Brinkibon Ltd v Stahog Stahl und Stahlwarenhandelshcaft mbH [1983] 2 AC
   34 . . . . 2.1.4.2.1, 2.1.4.2.2, 2.1.4.2.3, 2.4.1.8.1
Britannia Building Society v Prangley (unreported 12 June 2000) 4.4.1.3, 4.5.4.2
British Gas Trading Ltd v Data Protection Registrar [1998] Info TLR 393 . . . . 6.2.5.1.2
British Horseracing Board v William Hill [2001] 2 CMLR 215 . . . .   4.9.8.1
British Leyland v Armstrong [1896] RPC 279 . . . .   2.3.4
British Northrop Ltd v Texteam Blackburn Ltd [1974] RPC 57 . . . .   4.9.4.1
British Road Services Ltd v Arthur V Crutchley Ltd [1967] 2 All ER 785 . . . .   2.1.4.3
British Sugar v James Robertson [1997] ETMR 118 . . . .   4.4.3
British Telecommunications v Nextcall Telecom [2000] FSR 679 . . . .   4.5.2
Brogden v Metropolitan Rly (1877) 2 App Cas 66 . . . . 2.1.4.1.1
Bronner (Oscar) v Mediaprint (Case C-7/97) [1998] ECR I-7791 . . . .   8.4.2.7
Butler Machine Tool Co Ltd v Ex-Cell-O Corpn (England) Ltd [1979] 1 WLR 401:   2.1.4.3
Byrne v Deane [1937] 1 KB 818 . . . .   3.6.2.5

C
CBS Songs Ltd v Amstrad Consumer Electronics plc [1998] AC 1013 . . . . 4.13.1.4.3,
                                                                                            4.14, 4.16.1
CDW Graphic Design TM App [2003] RPC 30 . . . .   4.4.6
Cala Homes (South) Ltd v Alfred McApline Homes East Ltd [1995] FSR 818 . . . .   4.9.6.3.9
Cambridge Water Co Ltd v Eastern Counties Leather plc [1994] 1 All ER 53 . . . . .   3.3.3
Campbell v MGN Ltd [2003] QB 633 . . . .   6.2.2
Candler v Crane Christmas & Co [1951] 1 All ER 426 . . . .   3.4.1.4
Canon v MGM [1999] ETMR 1 . . . . 4.4.5, 4.4.5.2
Cantor Fitzgerald International v Tradition (UK) Ltd [2000] RPC 95 . . . .   4.12.1
Caparo Industries plc v Dickman (Case C-39/97) [1990] 1 All ER 568 . . . . . 3.4.1, 3.4.1.4.2
Carlill v Carbolic Smoke Ball Co [1893] 1 QB 256 . . . .   2.1.3.1
Celine Sarl v Celine SA (Case C-17/06) [2007] ETMR 80 . . . . 4.4.2, 4.4.3, 4.4.8.2
Celltech R & D Ltd v Medimmune (2005) FSR 21 . . . .   4.8.4

PARA

Chadha & Discom Technologies Inc v Dow Jones & Co Inc [1999] EMLR 724 ... 3.7.3.3
Charge Card Services Ltd, Re [1989] Ch 497 .... 2.2.2, 2.2.3.1
Chemco Leasing SpA v Rediffusion Ltd [1987] 1 FTLR 201 .... 2.1.3.5.1
Christoffer v Poseidon Film Distributors [2000] ECDR 487 .... 4.10.1
Clock v Clock House Hotel (1936) 53 RPC 269 .... 4.5.2
Coin Control Ltd v Suzo International (UK) [1997] FSR 660 .... 4.8.3
Compass Publishing BV v Compass Logistics [2004] EWHC 520, [2004] RPC
 41 .... 4.2.2.2, 4.4.4
Compuserver Inc v Cyber Promotions Inc? 3.2.3.1
Computer Associates v Altar 982 F 2d 693 .... 4.9.6.3.7
Concentration between Worldcom Inc & MCI Communications Corpn [1999] 5
 CMLR 876 .... 8.3.9
Conelly v RTZ Corpn plc [1998] AC 854 .... 2.4.1.8.2; 3.7.3.2
Cook v Lewis [1952] 1 DLR 1 .... 3.1.2.1.4
Cooper v Universal Music Australia Pty Ltd [2006] FCAFC 187 .... 4.14
Cowden v Bear Country Inc 382 F Supp 1321 (DSD 1974) 3.1.2.1.1
Cox v Riley (1986) 83 Cr App Rep 54 .... 3.1.2.1.3; 5.1.4
Crédit Chimique v James Scott Engineering Group Ltd 1982 SLT 131 .... 2.4.1.8.2; 3.7.3.2
Crescent Tool v Kilborn & Bishop 247 F 299 (1917) 4.5.2.2
Cubby Inc v Compuserve Inc 776 F Supp 135 (SDNY 1991) 3.6.3.1.3
Custom Made Commercial Ltd v Stawa Metallban GmbH (Case C-288/92) [1994]
 ECR I-2913 .... 2.4.1.5
Cyber Promotions Inc v America Online Inc 948 F Supp 456 (ED Pa 1996) 8.4.2.7

D
Daimler Chrysler v Alavi [2001] ETMR 98 .... 4.4.6.2.1, 4.4.8.2
Dann v Hamilton [1939] 1 All ER 59 .... 3.1.1.5.2
Davidoff v Goffkid (Case C-292/00) [2003] ETMR 42 .... 4.4.6
Davies v Sumner [1984] 3 All ER 831 .... 4.12.3.3
Dearlove v Combs [2007] EWHC 375 (Ch) 4.4.1.1
De Beers Consolidated Mines Ltd v Howe [1906] AC 455, 5 TC 198, HL 7.5
Definitely Maybe (Touring) Ltd v Marek Lieberberg Kanzertagentur GmbH [2001]
 4 All ER 283 .... 2.5.3.1
Def Lepp Music v Stuart-Brown [1986] RPC 273 .... 4.16.1
Delaware Mansions Ltd v Westminster City Council [2002] 1 AC 321 .... 3.1.1.4.3
Denco v Joinson [1992] 1 All ER 463 .... 5.1.4.1.1
Designers' Guild Ltd v Russell Williams Textile Ltd [2001] 1 All ER 700, [2000] 1
 WLR 2416, [2001] FSR 113 .... 4.9.6.3.8, 4.12.1
Dicks v Brooks (1880) 15 Ch D 22 .... 4.9.6.4
Direct Line Group Ltd v Direct Line Estate Agent Agency Ltd [1997] FSR 374 ... 4.5.4
Director General of Fair Trading v First National Bank plc [2002] 1 All ER 97 .... 3.5.2.2.2
Director of Public Prosecutions v Bignell [1998] 1 Cr App Rep 1 .... 5.1.2.2.4
Director of Public Prosecutions v Collins [2006] UKHL 40 .... 5.5.2, 5.5.3
Director of Public Prosecutions v David Lennon [2006] EWCH 1201 .... 5.1.4
Distillers Co (Biochemicals) Ltd v Thompson [1971] All ER 694 .... 3.7.3.1.1
Dodd Properties (Kent) Ltd v Canterbury City Council [1980] 1 All ER 928 ...... 3.1.1.4.1
Doe v MySpace Inc, No A-06-CA983-SS (WD Tax 2/13/2007) 3.1.2.2.5
Douglas v USDC Central District (DC No. CV-06-03809-GAF) 2.1.4.1.1
Duke of Brunswick v Harmer (1849) 14 QB 185 .... 3.7.3.3
Draw-Tite Inc v Plattsburgh Spring 4.7.3.2.2, 4.7.3.4
Dumez France v Hessische Landesbank (Helaba) [1990] ECR 49 .... 3.7.2.2.2; 4.8.3.4
Dunlop Pneumatic Tyre Co Ltd v Selfridge Ltd [1915] AC 847 .... 2.1.5
Durant v Financial Services Authority [2003] EWCA Civ 1746 .... 6.2.1.1, 6.2.1.2.1

E
Easygroup IP Licensing v Sermbezis [2003] All ER (D) 25 (Nov) 4.5.4.2

PARA

Ebay Inc v Bidder's Edge Inc (ND Cal 2000) 100 F Sepp 2d 1058 . . . . 3.2.3.1
Edwards v Skyways Ltd [1964] 1 WLR 349 . . . . 2.1.6.1
Edward Wong Finance Co Ltd v Johnson Stokes & Master [1984] AC 296 . . . . 3.1.1.2
Ellenbogen v Pearson (WIPO D-00-001) 4.7.3.4
Ellis v DPP [2001] EWHC Admin 362, [2001] All ER (D) 190 (May) 5.1.2.1.3
Ellis v Home Office [1953] 2 All ER 149 . . . . 3.1.2.1.1
Entores Ltd v Miles Far East Corpn [1951] 2 QB 327 . . . . 2.1.4.2.1, 2.1.4.2.3, 2.4.1.8.1
Erich Gasser GmbH v MISAT SRL [2003] All ER (D) 148 (Dec) 2.4.1.7
Erven Earnink v Townend ("Advocaat") [1979] AC 731 . . . . 4.5, 4.5.2
Esso Petroleum v C & E Commrs [1976] 1 WLR 1 . . . . 2.1.3.3
Esso Petroleum Co Ltd v Mardon [1975] 1 All ER 203 . . . . 3.4.1.2
Estée Lauder v Fragrance Counter [2002] RTMR 843 . . . . 4.4.7.1
Etablissements A de Bloos SPRL v Societes en Commandité par Actions Bayer
  (Case C-14/76) [1976] ECR 1497 . . . . 2.4.1.5
Euromarket Designs v Peters Crate & Barrel [2000] ETMR 1025, [2001] FSR 20 . 4.4.1.1
Ewing v Buttercup Margarine [1917] 2 Ch 1 . . . . 4.5.2
Express Newspapers v News (UK) [1990] FSR 359 . . . . 4.9.6.2.1
Exxon Corpn v Exxon Insurance Consultants International Ltd [1982] Ch 119 . . . 4.5.4

F
Feist Publications Inc v Rural Telephone Service Co 499 US 330 (1991) 4.9.2.4
Ferreo v Kindercare [2005] ETMR 6 . . . . 4.4.6.2.2
Fletcher v Rylands (1866) LR 1 Ex 265 . . . . 3.2, 3.2.3.1, 3.3.3
Fletcher Challenge Ltd v Fletcher Challenge Pty Ltd [1982[FSR 1 . . . . 4.5.4
Flethouse v Brindley (1862) 11 CBNS 869 . . . . 2.1.4.1.1
Fort Dodge Animal Health Ltd v Akzo Nobel [1998] FSR 222 . . . . 4.8.3.2
Francis, Day & Hunter Ltd v Twentieth Century Fox Corpn Ltd [1940] AC 112 . . . 4.9.6.4
Frank v Wright (1937) OPQD 113 . . . . 2.1.4.1.1
Froom v Butcher [1975] 3 All ER 520 . . . . 3.2.1.5
Fylde Microsystems Ltd v Key Radio Systems Ltd [1998] FSR 449 . . . . 4.9.6.3.6, 4.9.6.3.9

G
GAT v Luk (Case C-4/03) [2006] FSR 45 . . . . 4.8.3.3
GEICO v Google 300 F Supp 2d 700 (ED Va 2004) 4.4.7.2
GIE Groupe Concorde v Master Vessel Suhadiwarno Panjan (Case C-440/97)
  [1999] ECR I-6307 . . . . 2.4.1.5
GOTO.com v Disney 202 F 3d 1199 . . . . 4.4
GTE New Media Services Inc v Ameritech Corpn (6 October 1997) 8.3.7.3
Geographia Ltd v Penguin Books [1985] FSR 208 . . . . 4.9.6.2.2
Gencor Ltd v Commission [1999] ECR II-753 . . . . 8.4.1.3
General Motors v Yplon (Case C-375/97) [1999] ETMR 950 . . . . 4.4.6
Gerolsteiner Brunnen (Case 100/02) [2004] RPC 39 . . . . 4.4.8.2
Gilette v LA Laboratories (Case C-228/03) [2005] ETMR 67 . . . . 4.4.8.2
Glaxo plc v Glaxo WellcomeLtdm Cullen & McDonald [1996] FSR 388 . . . . 4.5.4
Global Projects Management v Citigroup [2005] EWHC 2663 (Ch), [2006] FSR 39: 4.5.4.2
Godfrey v Demon Internet [2001] QB 201 . . . . 3.6.2.5, 3.6.3.1, 3.6.3.2.1
Gold Star Publications Ltd v DPP [1981] 2 AlL ER 257 . . . . 5.3.1.2
Griggs & others v Evans & others (2004) FSR 48 . . . . 4.8.4, 4.9.2.2
Groppera Radio AG v Switzerland (1990) 12 EHRR 321 . . . . 5.3.1.2
Grossman v Canada [1901-4] Mac CC 36 . . . . 4.9.4.1
Guttrick v Dow Jones & Co Inc [2001] VSC 305 . . . . 3.7.3.3

H
HIB Ltd v Guardian Insurance Co [1997] 1 Lloyd's Rep 412, QB 2.5.3.1
Habib Bank Ltd v Habib Bank AG Zurich [1981] 2 All ER 650 . . . . 4.5.4
Hall v Cognos (unreported, 1997) 2.1.1.1, 2.1.4.5.1

PARA

Hall-Brown v Iliffe & Sons Ltd (1928-35) Macq Cop Ca 88 . . . . 4.12.4
Halley, The (1868) LR 2 PC 193 . . . . 3.8.1.1
Handelswekerij GJ Bier v Mines de Potasse d'Alsace SA [1978] QB 708 . . . . 3.7.2.2
Harrods (Buenos Aires) Ltd, Re [1992] Ch 72 . . . . 2.4.1.8.1; 3.7.3.1.2
Harrods v Schwartz-Sackin [1986] FSR 490 . . . . 4.4.3
Hartog v Colin & Shields [1939] 3 All ER 566 . . . . 2.1.4.4
Harvela Investments Ltd v Royal Trust Co of Canada (CI) Ltd [1986] AC 207 . . . . 2.1.3.3
Hawkes & Son v Paramount Film Service [1934] Ch 593 . . . . 4.12.1
Hedley Byrne & Co Ltd v Heller & Partners Ltd [1963] 2 All ER 575 . . . . 3.4.1, 3.4.1.2,
3.5.1.2
Hendrickson v Ebay Inc 2001 WL 1078981, CD Cal, 4 Sept 2001 . . . . 3.1.2.2.5,
3.6.3.2.1; 4.12.4.4.1
Hodgkinson & Corby Ltd v Wards Mobility Ltd [1995] FSR 169 . . . . 4.5.2.2
Hollier v Rambler Motors (AMC) Ltd [1972] 1 All ER 399 . . . . 3.5.2.1
Holwell Securities Ltd v Highes [1974] 1 WLR 155 . . . . 2.1.4.2.1
Home Office v Dorset Yacht Co Ltd [1970] 2 All ER 294 . . . . 3.1.1.4.3
Household, Fire & Carriage Accident Insurance Co Ltd v Grant (1879) 4 Ex D
216 . . . . 2.1.4.2.2, 2.4.1.8.1
Houston (Angelica) v Turner Entertainment [1992] ECC 334 . . . . 4.10.2
Howard Marine & Dredging Co Ltd v A Ogden & Sons (Excavations) Ltd [1978] 2
All ER 1134 . . . . 3.4.1.3
Hudson v Nicholson (1839) 5 M & W 437 . . . . 3.1.2.1.3

I

IMS Health GmbH & Co OHG v NDC Health GmbH & Co KG (Case C-418/01)
[2004] ECR I-5039 . . . . 8.4.2.8.1
IRC v Muller & Co's Margarine Ltd [1901] ADC 217 . . . . 4.5.1
Ibcos Computers Ltd v Barclays Mercantile Highland Finance Ltd [1994] FSR
275 . . . . 4.9.2.4, 4.9.6.3.7, 4.12.1
Indofood International Finance Ltd v JP Morgan Chase Bank NA [2006] STC 1195: 7.8
Industrie Tessili Italiana Corpn v Dunlop (Case C-12/76) [1976] ECR 1473 . . . . . . 2.4.1.5
Information Services Inc v Maclean Hunter Market Reports Inc 44 F 3d 61 (1994): 4.9.2.4
Innovations (Mail Order) Ltd v Data Protection Registrar (DA/92/31/49/1) 6.2.5.1.1
Intel Corpn v CPM UK [2007] ETMR 59 . . . . 4.4.6.2
Intel Corpn v Kourosh Kenneth Hamidi (2003, Sup Ct Cailf. No 103781) 3.2.3.1
Inter Corpn v Sihra [2004] ETMR 44 . . . . 4.4.6.2
Interlego v Tyco Industries [1989] AC 217 . . . . 4.9.2.3

J

Jameel v Dow Jones & Co Inc [2005] EWCA Civ 75 . . . . 3.6.4.1
John v MGN Ltd [1996] 2 All ER 35 . . . . 3.6.4.2, 3.6.4.3
John Richardson Computers v Flanders [1993] FSR 497 . . . . 4.9.6.3.7
Johnson v Medical Defence Union [2007] EWCA Civ 262 . . . . 6.2.2, 6.2.5.1.3
Jolley v Sutton London Borough Council [2000] 3 All ER 409, HL 3.1.14
Jonatham Wren & Co Ltd v Microdec plc (unreported, 5 July 1999) 2.1.4.1.1
Joy Music Music v Sunday Pictorial [1960] 2 QB 60 . . . . 4.12.1
Jurisdiction in Tort & Contract, Re (1988) ECC 415 . . . . 4.8.3.2

K

KODAK Trade Mark (No 2) [1990] FSR 49 . . . . 4.4.2
Kalfelis v Schroeder, Munchmayer [1988] ECR 5565 . . . . 3.7.2.1
Kelly v Metropolitan Rly Co [1895] 1QB 944 . . . . 3.1.1.1
King v Lewis & others [????] EWCA Civ 1329 . . . . 3.7.3.1.1
Kleinwort Benson Ltd v Glasgow City Council [1999] 1 AC 153 . . . . 3.7.2.1
Kroch v Rossell [1937] 1 All ER 725 . . . . 3.7.3.3

PARA

Kuwait Airways Corpn v Iraqi Airways Co (No 3) [2002] UKHL 19, [2002] 3 All
ER 209 .... 3.8.1.1

L

LA Gear v Gerald Whelan & Sons (1991) FSR 671 .... 4.8.4
LA Gear Inc v Hi-Tec Sports plc [1992] FSR 121 .... 4.12.3.3, 4.12.3.5
LTJ Diffussion SA v Sadas Vertbaudet SA (Case C-291/00) [2003] ECR I-2799,
[2003] ETMR 83 .... 4.4.4
Ladbroke (Football) Ltd v William Hill (Football) Ltd [1964] 1 WLR 273 . . . 4.9.6.4, 4.12.1
Lamb v Camden London Borough Council [1981] 2 All ER 408 .... 3.1.1.4.3
Laurence John Wrenn & Integrated Multi-Media Solutions Ltd v Stephen
Landamore [2007] EWHC 1833 .... 4.9.6.3.6
Law Society v KPMG Peat Marwick [2000] 1 All ER 515 .... 3.4.1
Law Society of England & Wales v Griffiths [1995] RPC 16 .... 4.5.2.1
Leathertex Divisione Sinitetici SpA v Bodetex BVBA (Case C-420/97) [1999] 2 All
ER (Comm) 769 .... 2.4.1.5
Levene v IRC [1928] AC 217, HL 7.5
Liesbosch, Dredger v Edison, *sub nom*, The Edison [1933] All ER Rep 144 ..... 3.1.1.4.1
Lloyd Schufabrick Mayer v Kliysen Handel (Case C-342/97) [1999] ETMR 690 .. 4.4.5,
4.4.5.3
Lloyds Bank Ltd v Railway Executive [1952] 1 All ER 1248 .... 3.1.12
L'Oreal SA v Bellure NV [2007] EWCA Civ 968, [2008] ETMR 1 ... 4.4.2, 4.4.7.2, 4.4.8.2
Lourho plc v Fayed [1992] 1 AC 448 .... 3.7.3.1.1
Loutchansky v Times Newspapers Ltd (No 2) [2001] EMLR 876 .... 3.6.1.3, 3.6.2.4
Lubbe v Cape plc [2001] 1 Lloyd's Rep 139, CA 2.4.1.8.2
Lucas BAS [1976] IIC 420 .... 4.4.6.1
Lukowiak v Unidad Editorial SA [2001] EMLR 1043 .... 3.8.1
Luttges v Sherwood (1895) 11 TLR 233 .... 2.2.3.2

M

MBM Frabri Clad Ltd v Eisen Und Huntle werke Thale AD (unreported, 3
November 1999), CA 2.4.1.4, 2.4.1.5
MBNA America Bank NA v Stephen Freeman [2001] EBLR 13 .... 4.5.2.1, 4.5.4.2
MTV Networks v Adam Curry 867 F Supp 202 (SDNY 1994) 4.1.1
McFarlane v Hulton [1899] 1 Ch 884 .... 4.9.4.1
McLoughlin v O'Brian [1982] 2 All ER 298, [1983] 1 AC 410 .... 3.1.2.1.1
Murray v King (1983) 2 IPR 99 .... 4.9.6.3.9
Macmillan & Co v Cooper (1923) 40 TLR 186 .... 4.9.6.2.1
Mango Sports v Diknah [2005] ETMR 5 .... 4.4.6.2.1
Manta Line v Sofianites (1984) 1 Lloyd's Rep 14 .... 4.8.4
Marcic v Thames Water Utilities Ltd [2002] 2 All ER 55 .... 3.3.3
Marengo v Daily Sketch (1948) 65 RPC 242 .... 4.5.2.1
Marinari v Lloyds Bank plc (Zibadi Trading Co intervening) [1996] All ER (EC) 84: 3.7.2.2.3
Mecklermedia v DC Congress [1997] FSR 627 .... 4.4.1.2, 4.8.3.4
Melluish (Inspector of Taxes) v BMI (No 3) Ltd [1996] AC 454 .... 3.6.3.1.4
Merck v Mediplan Health 425 F Supp 2d 402 (SDNY 2006) 4.4.7.2
Mercury Communications Ltd v Mercury Interactive (UK) Ltd [1995] FSR 850 ... 4.2.4,
4.2.4.1, 4.4.8.2
Metall und Rohstoff AF v Donaldson, Lufkin & Jenrette Inc [1989] 3 All ER 14 .. 3.7.3.1.1
Metalrax Group v Vanci [2002] EWHC 167 .... 4.5.4.2
Metro Goldwyn Mayer Studios Inc v Grokster Ltd 545 US 913, 125 SCt 2764
(2005) 4.13.1.4.3
Microsoft v EC Commission (Case T-201/04) 8.4.1.2.1
Microsoft Corpn v Paul Fox ? 3.2.1
Midlands Bank Trust Co Ltd v Hett, Stubbs & Kemp [1978] 3 All ER 571 .... 3.4.1.4
Midlands Electricity plc v Data Protection Registrar (20 July 1999) 6.2.5.1.1

PARA

Minories Finance Ltd v Afribank Nigeria Ltd [1995] 1 Lloyd's Rep 134 . . . . 2.1.4.1.1
Modus Vivendi v British Products Sanmex Co Ltd [1996] FSR 790 . . . . 4.8.3.4
Molnlycke v Procter & Ganble (No 4) (1992) 1 WLR 1112 . . . . 4.8.3.2
Morphitis v Salmon [1990] Crim LR 48 . . . . 3.1.2.1.3
Morris v Murray [1990] 3 All ER 801 . . . . 3.1.1.5.2
Morris v West Hartlepool Steam Navigation Co Ltd [1956] 1 All ER 385 . . . . 3.1.1.2
Mother Bertha Music Ltd v Bourne Music Ltd [1997] EMLR 457 . . . . 4.16.2
Motorola v New Gate Internet (WIPO D-2001/0449) 4.7.3.2
Mutual Life & Citizens Assurance Co Ltd v Evatt [1971] 1 All ER 150 . . . . 3.4.1.2
My Kinda Town v Soll [1983] RPC 407 . . . . 4.5.2

N
NBTY Europe Ltd (formerly Holland & Barrett Europe Ltd) v Nutricia International
   BV [2005] All ER (D) 415 (Apr) 2.1.1.1, 2.1.4.1.2
Napp Pharmaceuticals v Director General of Fair Trading [2002] Comp AR 13 . . . 8.4.2.1
Nationwide News v Copyright Agency (1996) 136 ALR 273 . . . . 4.14
Navitaire Inc v Easyjet Airline Co & Bulletproof Technolgies Inc [2004] EWHC
   1725 (Ch), [2006] RPC 111 . . . . 4.9.2.2, 4.9.6.3.8
Newspaper Licending Agency Ltd v Marks & Spencer plc [2001] 3 All ER 977 . . . 4.9.6.3.7
Nilesh Metha v J Pereira Fernandes SA [2006] 1 All ER (Comm) 885 . . . . 2.1.4.5.1
Norman v Ricketts (1886)3 TLR 182 . . . . 2.2.3.2
Northern Foods plc v Focal Foods Ltd [2001] EWCA Civ 1262, [2001] All ER (D)
   306 (Jul) 2.1.4.1.1
Norwich Pharmacal Co v C & E Commrs [1974] AC 133 . . . . 3.6.5.3
Nova Productions Ltd v Mazooma Games Ltd & others [2007] EWCA Civ 219 . . . 4.9.2.2

O
OTM Ltd v Hydranautics [1981] 2 Lloyd's Rep 211 . . . . 2.1.4
Oasis Stores's TM [1999] ETMR 531 . . . . 4.4.6.2.1
Ogden v Association of the United States Army (a corpn) 177 F Supp 498 . . . . 3.7.2.2.4
Oldendorff (Egon) v Liberia Corpn [1996] 1 Lloyd's Rep 380, QBD 2.5.2.1
Olley v Marlborough's Court [1949] 1 All ER 127 . . . . 3.5.2.1
Overseas Tankship (UK) Ltd v Morts Dock & Engineering Co Ltd, The Wagon
   Mound (No 1) [1961] 1 All ER 404 . . . . 3.1.1.4

P
Palsgraf v Long Island Railroad 162 NE 99 (1928) 3.1.2.1.1
Parfums Christian Dior SA v Evora BV (Case C-337/95) [1998] ETMR 26 . . . . . . 4.4.2
Pearce v Ove Arup Partnership (1997) Ch 293, (2000) Ch 403 . . . 4.8.3.2, 4.8.4, 4.8.5, 4.16.2
Pensher Security Doors Ltd v Sunderland City Council [1999] EWCA Civ 1223,
   [2000] RPC 249 . . . . 4.12.3.3
Pepper (Inspector of Taxes) v Hart [1993] 1 All ER 42 . . . . 3.6.3.1.4
Perfect 10 Inc Google Inc 416 F Supp 2d 828 (CD Cal 2006) 4.14
Pharmaceutical Society of Great Britain v Boots Cash Chemists Ltd [1953] 1 QB
   401 . . . . 2.1.3.1, 2.1.3.2.1
Phillips v Eyre (1870) LR 6 QB 1 . . . . 3.8.1.1
Phones4U v Phones4U.co.uk [2006] EWCA Civ 244, [2007] RPC 5 . . . . 4.5.4.2
Pierce v Promco SA [1999] ITCLR 233 . . . . 4.9.6.3.6
Pillai v Sarkar (The Times, 21 July 1994) 3.7.3.3
Pitman Training Ltd v Nominet UK [1997] FSR 797 . . . . 4.1.3
Pitts v Hunt [1990] 3 All ER 344 . . . . 3.1.1.5.1
Playboy Enterprises Inc v Chuckleberry Publishing Inc 939 F Supp 1032 (SDNY
   1996) 4.16.1
Playboy Enterprises v Terri Welles 279 F3d 796 . . . . 4.4.7.1
Playboy Enterprises Inc v George Frena 839 F Supp 1552 (MD Fla 1993) 4.12.4.4.6
Premier Brands v Typhoon [2000] ETMR 1071 . . . . 4.4.6, 4.4.6.1

PARA

Print Concept GmbH v GEW (EC) Ltd [2001] ECC 36, CA 2.5.3.1
Prior v Lansdowne Press Pty Ltd [1977] RPC 511 .... 4.9.6.3.9

Q
Quenerduaine v Cole (1883) 32 WR 185 .... 2.1.3.5.1

R
R v Arnold [1997] 2 All ER 548 .... 5.3.1, 5.3.1.1
R v Brown [1996] 1 All ER 545 .... 6.2.2
R v Cochrane [1993] Crim LR 48 .... 5.6.2.1.1
R v Cropp (transcript of shorthand notes, p 7G) 5.1.2.2.4, 5.1.3.1
R v Cuthbert (unreported, 7 October 2005) 5.1.2.2
R v Debnath [2005] EWCA Crim 3472 .... 5.5
R v Department of Health , ex p Source Infomatics [1999] 4 All ER 185 .... 6.2.1.3
R v Director of Public Prosecutions (unreported, 8 October 2000) 5.3.2.1
R v Fellows [1997] 2 All ER 548 .... 5.3.1.1, 5.3.3
R v Gold & Shifreen [1988] 2 All ER 186 .... 5.1.1
R v Governer of Brixton Prison, ex p Adeniyi Momudu Allison [1999] QB 847 ... 5.1.2.2.4
R v Governor of Brixton Prison, ex p Levin [1997] QB 65; aff'd [1997] 3 All ER
    289, HL 5.1.6.2
R v Hardy (unreported, November 1992) 5.1.4.2.1
R v Jayson [2002] EWCA Civ 683, CA 5.3.3
R v Johnstone [2003] UKHL 28 .... 4.4.2
R v Jonathan Bowden [2001] QB 88 .... 5.3.2
R v Joseph McElroy (unreported, 3 February 2005) 5.1.4.2.1
R v Land [1998] 1 All ER 403, CA 5.3.4.2
R v Mould (unreported, 6 November 2000) 5.3.2
R v Pearce, Farquharson (unreported, 9 December 1993) 5.1.2.2.4
R v Pecciarich (1995) 22 OR (3d) 748 .... 5.3.1.1
R v Perrin [2002] EWCA Crim 747, [2002] All ER (D) 359 (Mar) 5.3.1.2
R v Pile (unreported, May 1995) 5.1.4.1.1
R v Pryce (unreported, 21 March 1997) 5.1.6.1.1
R v Rymer (unreported, December 1993) 5.1.4.1.1
R v Shivpuri [1987] AC 1 .... 5.1.3.4
R v Spielman (unreported, March 1995) 5.1.4.1.1
R v Waddon (unreported, 30 June 1999) 5.3.1.2, 5.6.2.1.1
R v Whitely (1991) 93 Cr App 25 .... 3.1.2.1.3, 3.2.1; 5.1.4
R & B Customs Brokers Ltd v United Dominions Trust Ltd [1998] 1 WLR 321 ... 4.12.3.3
Radio Telefis Eireann (RTE) & Independent Television Publications Ltd (ITP) v
    Commission (Magill) [1995] ECR 743 .... 8.4.2.8.1
Raiffeisen Zentralbank Österreich AG v Five Star General Trading LLC [2001] 3 All
    ER 257 .... 2.5.1
Ray v Classic FM [1998] FSR 622 .... 4.9.2.2, 4.9.6.3.6
Read v J Lyons & Co Ltd [1946] 2 All ER 471 .... 3.3.3
Reckitt & Coleman v Borden ("Jiff Lemon") [1990] RPC 341 .... 4.5
Red Sea Insurance Co Ltd v Bouygues SA [1995] 1 AC 190 .... 3.7.3.1.1, 3.8.1.1
Reed Executive v Reed Business Information [2004] EWCA Civ 159, [2004] RPC
    40 .... 4.2.2.2, 4.4.4.1, 4.4.5.3, 4.4.7.1, 4.4.8.2
Register com Inc v Verio Inc 126 F Supp 2d 3.2.3.1
Religious Technology Center v Netcom Online Communications Services Inc 907 F
    Supp 1361 (ND Cal 1995) 4.12.4.4.3
Rich (Marc) v Societa Italiana (No 2) (1992) 1 Lloyd's Rep 624 .... 4.8.4
Road Tech Computer Systems v Mandata [2000] ETMR 970 .... 4.4.7.1
Roberts v Candiware [1980] FSR 352 .... 4.12.4
Robophone Facilities v Blank [1966] 1 WLR 1428 .... 2.1.4.1.1
Roerig v Valiant Trawlers Ltd [2002] 1 All ER 961 .... 3.8.2.2

S

S v KD 1983, J146, Tribunal de Grande Instance de Paris 2.5.3.1
St Albans' City & District Council v International Computers Ltd [1996] 4 All ER
   481 .... 2.5.2.2.3; 3.5.1.1
Sabel v Puma (Case C-251/95) [1998] ETMR 1 .... 4.4.5
Sallen (Jay D) v Corinthians Licenciamentos 273 F 3d 14 (2001) 4.7.4
Schapira v Ahronson [1999] EMLR 735 .... 3.7.3.1.1, 3.7.3.3
Schenipp-Hirth Kommandit-Gesellschaft (owners of the Glider Standard Austria
   SH 1964) v Persons Having Possession of The Glider Standard Austria SH
   1964 [1965] 2 All ER 1022 .... 4.3.1
Scottish Provident Institution v Commrs of Inland Revenue [2005] STC 15 ...... 7.2
Seaconsar v Bank Merkazi Jomhouri Islami Iran [1994] 1 AC 438 ...... 2.4.1.8.1; 3.7.3.1
Second Sight Ltd v Novell Inc & Novell UK Ltd [1995] RPC 423 .... 4.2.4.1
Shetland Times Ltd v Dr Jonathan Wills [1997] FSR 604 .... 4.9.6.4
Shevill v Presse Alliance SA [1995] All ER (EC) 289 .... 3.7.2.2.4, 3.7.3.3; 4.8.3.2
Sieckmann (Case C-273/00) [2003] EMTR 37 .... 4.2.1
Sierra Leonne Telecommunications Co Ltd v Barclays Bank plc [1998] 2 All ER
   821 .... 2.5.3.1
Sim v Strectch [1936] 2 All ER 1237 .... 3.6.2.1
Singer Manufacturing Co v Loog (1882) 8 App Ca 15 .... 4.5.2.2, 4.5.4.3
Slater v Swann (1730) 2 Stra 872 .... 3.2.3
Smith v Hughes (1871) LR 6 QB 597 .... 2.1.6.1
Smith Kline & French Laboratories, Re [1990] 1 AC 64 .... 4.9.2.4
Snow v Eaton Centre Ltd (1982) 70 CPR (2d) 105 .... 4.10.2
Societa Italiano Vetro v EC Commission [1992] ECR II-1403 .... 8.4.1.3
Solar Thomson Engineering Co Ltd v Barton [1977] RPC 537 .... 4.12.4
Sony v Pacific Game Technology (2006) EWHC 2509 .... 4.4.1.1
Sony Corpn v Universal City Studios Inc 464 US 417 (1984) 4.13.1.4.3
Spartan Stell & Alloys v Martin & Co (Contractors) Ltd [1972] 3 All ER 557 ..... 3.1.2.1.3
Specht v Netscape Communications Corpn & America Online Inc (US Dist Ct NY,
   3 July 2001) 2.1.4.1.1
Spiliada Maritime Coprn v Cansulex Ltd [1987] AC 460 .... 2.4.1.8.2; 3.7.3.2
Springfield v Thame (1903) 89 LT 242 .... 4.12.4
Stewart v West African Terminals Ltd [1964] 2 Lloyd's Rep 371 .... 3.1.1.4.2
Stratton Oakmount Inc v Prodigy Services Co 1995 WL 323710 .... 3.6.3.1.3

T

Taittinger v Allbev [1993] FSR 641 .... 4.4.6.2.2, 4.5.2, 4.5.2.2, 4.5.3
Takenaka (UK) Ltd v David Frankl (unreported, 11 October 2000) 3.6.1.2
Television Broadcasts Ltd v Madarin Video Holdings [1984] FSR 111 .... 4.9.4.1
Tesco Stores v Elogicom [2006] EWHC 403 (Ch), [2007] FSR 4 .... 4.5.4.2
Thomas v Thomas (1842) 2 QB 851 .... 2.1.5
Thompson v Smiths Shiprepairers (North Shields) Ltd [1984] 1 All ER 881 ...... 3.1.1.2
Thomson Holidays v Norweigan Cruise Lines [2003] RPC 32 .... 4.4.5
Thorley v Lord Kerry (1812) 4 Taunt 355 .... 3.6.2.1
Thornton v Shoe Lane Parking [1971] 2 QB 163 .... 2.1.6.1
Ticketmaster Corpn v Microsoft Corpn (CV-97-3055) RAP (CD Cal 1997) 4.15.4,
                                                                         4.15.4.1
Tidy v Trustees of the Natural History Museum (1995) 39 IPR 501 .... 4.10.2
Totalise plc v Motley Fool Ltd [2002] 1 WLR 1233 .... 3.6.5.3
Trade Indemnity v Försäkrings AV Njord [1995] 1 All ER 796 .... 3.7.2.1
Trieste e Venezia Assicurzzioni Genertel v Crowe Italia [2001] ETMR 66 .... 4.4.7.1
Tropical Resorts Management Ltd v Morgan [2001] All ER (D) 38 (Jul) 4.4.1.3
Turner v Grovit [2004] All ER (EC) 485 .... 2.4.1.7
Tutton v AD Walter Ltd [1986] QB 61 .... 3.1.2.1.2
Tyburn Productions v Conan Doyle (1991) Ch 75 .... 4.8.4

PARA

U

Unidor v Marks & Spencer plc [1988] RPC 275 .... 4.4.2
Union Transport plc v Continental Lines SA [1992] 1 WLR 15 .... 2.4.1.5
United Brands v EC Commission [1978] ECR 207 .... 8.4.1
United States v Dupont 351 US 377 (1956) 8.3.9
United States v Microsoft (Civil Action No 98-1232) 8.4.1.2.2, 8.4.2.6,
8.4.2.7, 8.4.2.8.1, 8.4.2.8.3
United States v Morris 928 F 2d 504 (2nd Cir) (1991) 5.1.4.2.1
United States v Thomas 74 F 3d 701 (1996) 5.3.2.1
University of London Press v University Tutorial Press [1916] 2 Ch 601 .. 4.9.2.4, 4.9.6.2.1

V

V & S Vin & Spirit Aktiebolag v Absolut Beach [2002] IP & T 203 .... 4.4.1.1
VNU Business Publications v Monster Board [2002] ETMR 111 .... 4.4.7.1
Verizon Related Reduction Claim, Re 2003 Me, PUC Lexis 181 .... 3.1.2.1.2
Viaticum v Google France [2004] ETMR 63 .... 4.4.7.1
Virgin Net v Adrian Paris ? 3.2.1
Volk v Vervaecke (Case 5/69) [1969] ECR 295 .... 8.3.8
Volvo v Heritage [2000] FSR 253 .... 4.4.8.2

W

Walter v Lane [1900] AC 539 .... 4.9.6.2.1
Warlow v Harrison (1859) 1 E & E 309 .... 2.1.3.2.1
Warwick Film Productions Eisinger [1967] 3 All ER 367 .... 4.12.1
Washington Post Co v Total News Inc 97 Civ 190 (PKL) (1997) 4.15.2
Weatherby v Banham (1832) 5 C & P 228 .... 2.1.4.1.1
Wegmann v Elsevier Science (1997) IlPr 760 .... 4.8.3.2
Weller & Co v Foot & Mouth Disease Research Institute [1965] 3 All ER 560 .... 3.1.2.1.1
Westminster City Council v Croyalgrange Ltd [1986] 2 All ER 353 .... 5.1.2.2.4
Wood v Holden [2006] STC 443 .... 7.5
Wooldridge v Sumner [1962] 2 All ER 978 .... 3.1.1.5.2

Y

Yarmouth v France (1887) 19 QBD 647 .... 7.4
Youssoupoff v Metro-Goldwyn-Mayer Pictures Ltd (1934) 50 TLR 581 .... 3.6.2.1
Yuen Jun Yeu v A-G of Hong Kong [1988] AC 175 .... 3.1.2.1.1

Z

ZYX Music GmbH v Chris King [1997] 2 All ER 129, CA 4.12.3.5
Zezev & Yarimaka v Governor of HM Prison Brixton & Government of the United
    States of America [2002]EWHC 589 (Admin), [2002] 2 Cr App Rep 515 ... 5.1.4.2.1,
5.1.6.2

Table of Statutes

PARA

Administration of Justice Act 1956 .   4.3.1
Anti-terrorism, Crime and Security
   Act 2001 . . . . 5.4; 6.1.5, 6.1.6,
                     6.4.3.1, 6.4.3.2
Betting, Gaming and Lotteries Act
   1963 . . . . 9.4.1.1
British Nationality Act 1981 . . . . . . 4.9.4.2
Business Names Act 1985 . . . 2.1.2, 2.1.2.2,
                          2.1.2.2.1
Child Protection Act 1999 . . . . 5.3.1.2
Civil Jurisdiction and Judgments Act
   1982 . . . . 2.4.1.2, 2.4.1.2.1
   s 8(1), (2) 2.4.1.6
     41(2), (6), (7) 2.4.1.2.1
     42(2)–(4) 2.4.1.2.2
     49 . . . . 2.4.1.8.1; 3.7.3.1.2
Civil Jurisdiction and Judgments Act
   1991 . . . . 2.4.1.2.1
Communications Act 2003 . . . . . 5.5; 9.1.2,
                          9.1.3, 9.6.1
   s 127 . . . .   5.5.3
       (1)(a) 5.5.3
       (2) 5.5.3
     232–234 . . . .   9.6.1
Companies Act 1985 . . . . 2.1.2, 2.1.2.2,
                          2.1.2.2.1
   s 349, 351 . . . .   2.1.2
     725 . . . .   4.8.4
Companies Act 2006 . . . .   2.1.2
Competition Act 1998 . . . . 8.6, 8.7
   Pt I Ch I (ss 1–16) 8.2.1, 8.3, 8.3.1,
                     8.3.2, 8.3.3, 8.3.5,
                     8.3.6, 8.3.7, 8.3.7.5,
                     8.3.8, 8.3.11,
                     8.3.11.1, 8.3.11.2,
                     8.4, 8.4.1, 8.4.2,
                     8.4.2.4, 8.5.1, 8.5.6,
                     8.7.1, 8.7.2
   s 2(1) 8.3
     (3) 8.3.5
   Pt I Ch II (ss 17–24) . . 8.2.1, 8.4, 8.4.1.3,
                     8.4.2, 8.4.2.2, 8.5.1,
                     8.5.6, 8.7.1, 8.7.2
   s 18(3) 8.4
     19 . . . .   8.4.2
     31 . . . .   8.5.4
     31A 8.5.5

PARA

Competition Act 1998 – contd
   s 32 . . . .   8.5.4
     35 . . . .   8.5.3
     36(8) 8.5.6
     60 . . . . 8.3, 8.4.1
Computer Misuse Act 1990 . . . . 5.1.1, 5.1.2,
                     5.1.2.1, 5.1.2.1.1,
                     5.1.2.1.3, 5.1.4,
                     5.1.6, 5.1.6.1, 5.4;
                     6.2.5.1.2
   s 1 . . . . 5.1.1, 5.1.2.1,
                     5.1.2.1.1, 5.1.2.1.2,
                     5.1.2.1.3, 5.1.2.2,
                     5.1.2.2.4, 5.1.2.3,
                     5.1.3, 5.1.3.1,
                     5.1.3.2, 5.1.3.3,
                     5.1.3.4, 5.1.4.1.1,
                     5.1.4.2, 5.1.4.2.1,
                     5.1.5.1, 5.1.6.1.1,
                     5.1.6.1.2
       (1) 5.1.2.1.2, 5.1.2.2.4
         (a) 5.1.2.1.3, 5.1.2.2.4
         (b), (c) 5.1.2.2.2
       (3) 5.1.2.3
       (3) 5.1.3.3
       (4) 5.1.3.4
       (5) 5.1.3.5
     3 . . . . 5.1.1, 5.1.2.2.4,
                     5.1.2.3, 5.1.4,
                     5.1.4.1.1, 5.1.4.2.1,
                     5.1.5.1, 5.1.6.1.3,
                     5.1.6.2
       (1)(a) 5.1.4.1.1
         (b) 5.1.4.2, 5.1.4.2.1
       (2) 5.1.4.2
         (a)–(d) 5.1.4.2.1, 5.1.4.2.2
       (3) 5.1.4.2.2
         (a), (b) 5.1.4.2.1
         (c) 5.1.4.2
       (4) 5.1.4.2.1
       (5) 5.1.4.1.1, 5.1.4.2
         (a), (b) 5.1.4.1.1
         (c) 5.1.4.2.1
       (6) 5.1.4
     3A 5.1.5, 5.1.5.4
       (5) 5.1.5.4
     4 . . . . 5.1.6.1

PARA

Computer Misuse Act 1990 – *contd*

s 4(2) 5.1.6.1.1, 5.1.6.1.3
  (4) 5.1.6.1.2
  5 . . . . 5.1.6.1
  (2) 5.1.6.1.1
  (3) 5.1.6.1.3
  6, 7 . . . . 5.1.6.1
  8(1), (4), (5), (9) 5.1.6.1.2
  12(1)(a) 5.1.3.2
  17 . . . . 5.1.2.2.4
  (1)(d) 5.1.2.1.3
  (2) 5.1.2.1.3
  (a)–(c) 5.1.2.1.3, 5.1.2.2.4
  (d) 5.1.2.2.4
  (3) 5.1.2.1.3
  (a) 5.1.2.1.3
  (4)(a), (b) 5.1.2.1.3
  (5) 5.1.2.2.3, 5.1.2.2.4,
                                          5.1.2.3
  (6) 5.1.2.1.1
  (7) 5.1.4.1.1, 5.1.4.2.1
  (a), (b) 5.1.4.1.1

Consumer Credit Act 1974 . . . . 2.1.1.1,
                                          2.5.2.1
s 75 . . . . 2.2.2

Consumer Protection Act 1987 . . . . 3.3.2
  Pt III 9.3.2
  s 2 . . . . 3.3.2
  3(2) 3.3.2
  4(1)(e) 3.3.2

Contracts (Applicable Law) Act 1990 . . . . 2.5.1
s 3(3)(a) 2.5.1

Copyright, Designs and Patents Act 1988 . . . . 2.3.3, 2.3.5, 2.5.2.1;
                                 4.9, 4.9.2.1, 4.9.4,
                                 4.9.4.2, 4.9.6.3.2,
                                 4.9.6.4, 4.9.7, 4.10,
                                 4.10.1; 5.1.2.1.1

  Pt II 4.10
  s 1(1) 4.9.2.1
  (a) 4.9.6.3.5
  (b) 4.9.6.2.1
  (c) 4.9.6.3.7
  3(1) 4.9.6.1
  (b) 4.9.6.3.7
  (c) 4.9.6.3.2
  (2) 4.9.2.2
  3A(1) 4.9.6.2.1, 4.9.7.1
  (2) 4.9.7.1
  4(1)(a) 4.9.6.3.2
  (2)(a), (b) 4.9.6.3.2
  5(2), (10) 4.9.6.3.5
  8 . . . . 4.9.6.3.7
  9 . . . . 4.9.2.2
  (3) 4.9.6.2.1

PARA

Copyright, Designs and Patents Act 1988 – *contd*

s 10(1) 4.9.6.3.9
  11(1) 4.9.2.2
  (2) 4.9.2.2, 4.10
  12–14 . . . . 4.9.5
  15 . . . . 4.9.5, 4.9.6.3.7
  16(1) 4.11, 4.13.1.4.2,
                                          4.16.1
  (a) 2.3.3
  (e) 4.9.6.4
  (2) 2.3.3; 4.10.4, 4.12.4,
                               4.13.1.4.2, 4.16.1
  (3)(a) 2.3.3; 4.9.6.3.6,
                                   4.9.6.3.7, 4.9.6.4,
                                          4.12.1
  (b) 4.11.1.2
  17 . . . . 4.16.1
  (2) 2.3.3, 4.11.1.2
  (6) 4.11.1.2
  18 . . . . 4.11.2, 4.16.1
  (2) 4.16.1
  18A 4.11.3
  19 . . . . 4.11.4, 4.16.1
  (2)(b) 4.10.4, 4.16.1
  (4) 4.11.4
  20 . . . . 4.11.5
  21 . . . . 4.11.6
  22 . . . . 4.10.4, 4.12.3
  23 . . . . 3.6.3.1.5; 4.10.4,
                                          4.12.3
  (a) 4.12.3.4
  (c) 4.16.1
  (d) 4.12.3.3, 4.16.1
  24 . . . . 4.10.4, 4.12.3
  (1)(a) 4.15.3
  25, 26 . . . . 4.10.4, 4.12.3
  27(2) 4.12.3.2
  (3) 4.12.3.6
  (4) 4.12.3.2
  (5) 2.3.1
  28A 4.12.4.1
  30(1) 4.9.6.4
  50 . . . . 4.12.4.1
  50A 4.12.4
  (1) 4.15.1
  50B 4.11.2, 4.12.4
  50C 4.11.2, 4.12.4,
                                          4.12.4.1
  77(1) 4.10.1
  (2)(a) 4.10.1
  (4)(a) 4.10.1
  (7)(c) 4.10.1
  78(1), (2) 4.10.1
  (3)(a) 4.10.1
  79(3) 4.10

PARA

Copyright, Designs and Patents Act
1988 – *contd*
s 80(1) 4.10.2
  (2)(a), (b) 4.10.2
  (4)(a) 4.10.2
  81(1)(a) 4.10
  87(1) 4.10.2, 4.10.3
  (3) 4.10.3
    (b) 4.10.3
  89(1) 4.10.1
  (2) 4.10.2
  90 . . . . 2.1.4.5
  97A 4.12.4.3
  153 . . . . 4.9.4
    (1)(b) 4.9.4.1
  154 . . . . 4.9.4.1
    (1), (2) 4.9.4.2
  155 . . . . 4.9.4.1
    (3) 4.9.4.1
  156 . . . . 4.9.4.3
  157 . . . . 4.9.4.1
  175(1) 4.9.4.1
    (a) 4.9.4.1
    (2)(a) 4.9.4.1
  178 . . . . 4.10.1, 4.12.3.3
  180 . . . . 4.9.2.1
Courts and Legal Services Act 1990: 3.6.4.3
  s 8 . . . . 3.6.4
Criminal Attempts Act 1981 . . . . . . 5.1.3.4
Criminal Damage Act 1971 . . . . . 3.1.2.1.3,
                                3.2.1; 5.1.4
  s 1(1) 3.1.2.1.3
  10(1) 3.1.2.1.3
Criminal Justice Act 2003 . . . .   5.3
Criminal Justice and Police Act 2001
  s 43, 127 . . . . 5.5.2
Criminal Justice and Public Order
  Act 1994 . . . . 5.3.2, 5.3.2.1
  s 168 . . . . 5.3.1
  Sch 9 . . . . 5.3.1
Criminal Procedure and Investiga-
  tions Act 1996 . . . .   5.6
Data Protection Act 1984 . . .6.1.2, 6.2.5.1.1,
                         6.2.5.1.5, 6.2.5.3,
                         6.2.5.4.2, 6.2.5.6.1,
                         6.2.6
Data Protection Act 1988 . . 5.6; 6.1.2, 6.1.3,
                         6.2, 6.2.1.2, 6.2.1.2.1,
                         6.2.1.2.2, 6.2.1.3,
                         6.2.3, 6.2.3.2, 6.2.4,
                         6.2.5.1.2, 6.2.5.2.1,
                         6.2.5.3, 6.3, 6.3.3.1,
                         6.4
  s 1(1) 6.2.1.1, 6.2.1.2,
                         6.2.2, 6.2.3.1,
                         6.2.3.2, 6.2.4.1

PARA

Data Protection Act 1988 – *contd*
  s 1(3) 6.2.1.2.3
  2(3) 6.2.5.7.1
  5 . . . . 6.2.3.1.3
  7 . . . . 6.2.5.6.1
    (1)(a) 6.2.5.6.1, 6.2.5.6.3
    (3) 6.2.5.6.1
    (7), (8), (10), (11) 6.2.5.6.1
  11(1)–(3) 6.2.6.6.2
  12 . . . . 6.2.5.6.3
    (1) 6.2.5.6.3
    (2)(a), (b) 6.2.5.6.3
    (3), (6)–(8) 6.2.5.6.3
  14 . . . . 6.2.5.4.1
  17(1) 6.2.3.2
    (4) 6.2.4.1
  18(1) 6.2.3.2
  21(1) 6.2.3.2
  33(3) 6.2.5.5.2
  36 . . . . 6.2.4.1
  Pt V (ss 40–50) 6.3.3.2
  s 40 . . . . 6.2.5.8.4
    (2) 6.2.5.8.4
  47 . . . .   6.2.6
  68 . . . . 6.2.1.1
  70 . . . . 6.2.4.1
  Sch 1 . . . .   6.2.5
  Pt II
    para 1(1) 6.2.5.1, 6.2.5.1.1
    2 . . . . 6.2.5.1.1, 6.2.5.1.4
      (2) 6.2.5.1.1
        (a) 6.2.5.1.1
      (3) 6.2.5.1.1
    5(a), (b) 6.2.5.2.1
    6 . . . . 6.2.5.2.1
    7 . . . . 6.2.5.4.1
      (a) 6.2.5.4.1
    9(a), (b) 6.2.5.7.1
    11(a), (b) 6.2.5.7.1
    12(a), (b) 6.2.5.7.1
  Sch 2 . . . . 6.2.5, 6.2.5.1.4
  Sch 3 . . . .   6.2.5
  Sch 4 . . . . 6.2.5.8.4
Defamation Act 1996 . . 3.1.2.2.5, 3.6, 3.6.2,
                         3.6.2.6, 3.6.3,
                         3.6.3.1.3, 3.6.3.1.4,
                         3.7.2.2.4; 4.12.4.4.1;
                         5.3.4.2
  s 1 . . . . 3.6.2.6, 3.6.3,
                         3.6.3.1, 3.6.3.2.2,
                         3.6.3.1.2
    (1) 3.6.3.1.4
      (b), (c) 3.6.3.1.3, 3.6.3.1.5,
                         3.6.3.2.1
    (2) 3.6.3.1.2, 3.6.3.1.3
    (3)(c) 3.6.3.1.3

PARA

Defamation Act 1996 – *contd*
s 1(3)(e) 3.6.3.1.3; 5.3.4.2
   (5)(a) 3.6.3.1.4, 3.6.3.1.5
   (b) 3.6.3.1.4, 3.6.3.1.5
   (c) 3.6.3.1.4, 3.6.3.1.5
2–4 .... 3.6.2
8–11 .... 3.6.2
17(1) 3.6.2.3, 3.6.3.1.2
Electronic Communications Act
   2000 .... 2.1.4.5, 2.1.4.5.1,
                  2.1.4.5.2; 4.10.1
s 7(1), (3) 2.1.4.5, 2.1.4.5.1
Employment Rights Act 1996 .... 2.5.2.2.1
Enterprise Act 2002 ...... 8.2.2, 8.2.3, 8.6,
                      8.7.2
Extradition Act 1989 .... 5.1.6.2
s 1(3) 5.1.6.2
Extradition Act 2003 .... 5.1.6.2
Fair Trading Act 1973 .... 8.2.3, 8.2.4
Financial Services and Markets Act
   2000 .... 9.2, 9.2.1.1
Forgery and Counterfeiting Act
   1981 .... 5.1.1
Fraud Act 2006 .... 5.2, 5.4
Gambling Act 2005 .... 7.1; 9.4, 9.4.1,
                9.4.1.1, 9.4.1.2,
                      9.4.1.4
Pt I (ss 1–18) 9.4.1.2, 9.4.1.3,
                      9.4.1.5
s 5(1) 9.4.1.5
6 .... 9.4.1.2
14 .... 9.4.1.3
Sch 2 .... 9.4.1.2
Gaming Act 1968 .... 9.4.1.2
Gaming Duties Act 1981 .... 9.4.1.1
Human Rights Act 1998 .. 5.3.2; 6.2.5.1.4,
                      6.2.5.1.5
art 10 .... 3.6.4.1
Income Tax Act 2007 .... 7.2
Income Tax (Earnings and Pensions)
   Act 2003 .... 7.2
Income Tax (Trading and other
   Income) Act 2005 .... 7.2
Indecent Displays (Control) Act
   1981 .... 5.3
Interpretation Act 1978 .... 2.1.1.1
Sch 1 .... 2.1.1.1; 4.10.1
Law Commissions Act 1965
s 3(1)(e) 2.5.2.2.3
Law of Property Act 1925
s 40 .... 4.10.1
Law Reform (Contributory Negli-
   gence) Act 1945 .... 3.1.1.5.1
s 1(1) 3.1.1.5.1
London Olympic Games and Para-
   lympics Games Act 2006 .... 4.2

PARA

Malicious Communications 1988 ..   5.5,
                     5.5.1.2, 5.5.2
Obscene Publications Act 1959 .. 5.3, 5.3.1,
                   5.3.1.2, 5.3.4.2
s 1(3) 5.3.1, 5.3.1.1
   (b) 5.3.1
   (5) 5.3.1
2 .... 5.3.1
Occupiers' Liability Act 1957 ..... 3.3.1
s 1(3) 3.3.1
Occupiers' Liability Act 1984 ..... 3.3.1
Olympic Symbols etc (Protection)
   Act 1995 .... 4.2
Police and Criminal Evidence Act
   1984 .... 5.6
s 69 .... 5.1.6.2, 5.6.1
72 .... 5.1.6.2
Police and Justice Act 2006 .. 5.1.1, 5.1.2.1,
               5.1.2.1.1, 5.1.2.1.3,
                   5.1.2.2.1, 5.1.4,
                   5.1.4.2.2, 5.1.4.3,
                   5.1.5, 5.1.6.1.1,
                      5.1.6.1.3
s 3 .... 5.1.4, 5.1.4.1.1
53 .... 5.1.1
Post Office (Amendment) Act 1955: 5.5.3
Private International Law (Miscellaneous Provisions) Act 1995 ..3.7.3.1.1,
                   3.7.3.2, 3.8.1, 3.8.2
Pt III (ss 9–15) 4.8.4
s 9(1) 4.8.4
10 .... 3.7.3.1.1
11 .... 3.7.3.1.1, 3.8.2.2
   (1) 3.7.3.1.1, 3.8.2.1;
                      4.16.2
   (2) 3.8.2.1
   (a) 3.8.2.1
   (b) 3.8.2.1; 4.16.2
   (c) 3.8.2.1
   (3) 3.8.2.1
12 .... 3.7.3.1.1, 3.8.2.2
13 .... 3.7.3.1.1, 3.7.3.1.1
   (1) 3.8.1, 3.8.2.1
   (2) 3.8.1
Protection from Harassment Act
   1997 .... 5.5, 5.5.1
s 2, 3 .... 5.5.1.1
4 .... 5.5.1.2
Protection of Children Act 1978 ... 5.3.4.2
s 1(1) 5.3.2, 5.5.1.1
   (c) 5.3.4
   (2) 5.5.1.1
4(1) 5.5.1.1
5 .... 5.5.1.1
7(2) 5.3.3
   (4)(b) 5.3.2.1

PARA

Protection of Children Act 1978 –
  contd
  s 7(7) 5.3.2.1
  15 .... 5.3
Regulation of Investigatory Powers
  Act 2000 .... 5.6; 6.1.4, 6.4.1,
                          6.4.3, 6.4.3.2
  Pt I (ss 1–25) 6.4.1
  Pt I Ch I (ss 1–20) 6.4.2
  s 9, 10 .... 6.4.1
  Pt I Ch II (ss 21–25) 6.4.2
Sale and Supply of Goods Act
  1994 .... 3.5.1.1
Sale of Goods Act 1979 ..... 2.3.6, 3.5.1.1;
                          9.5.2.4.8
  s 57(2) 2.3.6
Sexual Offences Act 2003 ..5.3, 5.3.2, 5.3.3
Statute of Frauds (1677)
  s 4 .... 2.1.4.5.1
Supreme Court Act 1981 .... 4.3.1; 6.3.3.1
Taxes Management Act 1970 ..... 7.2
Telecommunications Act 1984 .... 5.5.3
  s 43 .... 5.3
Terrorism Act 2000 .... 5.4, 5.4.1
  s 1(1)(b), (c) 5.4.1
    (2)(e) 5.4.1
    (4)(c) 5.4.1
Terrorism Act 2006 ... 5.3.4.2, 5.4, 5.4.2.1,
                          5.4.2.3.2, 5.6
  s 1 .... 5.4.2.1, 5.4.2.2,
                    5.4.2.3.1, 5.4.2.3.2
  2 .... 5.4.2.1, 5.4.2.2,
                    5.4.2.3.1, 5.4.2.3.2
    (1) 5.4.2.2
  3 .... 5.4.2.3.2
    (4) 5.4.2.3.1
    (5)(a) 5.4.2.3.1
    (7) 5.4.2.3.1
  4 .... 5.4.2.3.1
Theft Act 1968 .... 5.1.3.4, 5.1.6.2, 5.2
  s 15A 5.1.3.1
  17(1)(a) 5.1.3.1
Theft Act 1978 .... 5.2
Torts (Interference with Goods) Act
  1977 .... 3.2
Trade Descriptions Act 1968 ...... 9.3.2
Trade Marks Act 1938 .... 4.4.2
Trade Marks Act 1994 .... 4.1.3, 4.2
  s 1(1) 4.2.1
  2 .... 4.4.8.2
  3 .... 4.2.2
    (1) 4.2.2.2
  5(5) 4.4.8.1
  9(3) 4.2.5
  10 .... 4.4
    (3) 4.2.3

PARA

Trade Marks Act 1994 – *contd*
  s 10(4) 4.4.1
  11 .... 4.4.8.2
    (1) 4.4.8.2, 4.8.5
    (2) 4.4.8.2
      (a) 4.4.8.2
      (C) 4.8.5
  12 .... 4.4.1
  14 .... 4.4.9
    (1) 4.8.5
    (2) 4.4.9
  15 .... 4.4.9
  16 .... 4.4.9
    (1) 4.4.9
  17 .... 4.4.9
    (4) 4.4.9
  18–20 .... 4.4.9
  21 .... 4.5.4.2
  38(1) 4.2.5
  40 .... 4.2.5
    (3) 4.2.5
  46 .... 4.2.4.1
  56–59 .... 4.2
  95 .... 4.6.4
Unfair Contract Terms Act 1977 ... 2.3.6,
                    2.5.2.2.3; 3.5.2.2,
                    3.5.2.2.1, 3.5.2.2.2,
                    3.5.2.2.2; 4.12.3.3;
                          9.5.1
  s 1(3) 3.5.2.2.1
  2(2) 3.5.2.2.1
  11 .... 3.5.2.2.1
  12(1)(a), (b) 3.5.2.2.1
  26 .... 2.5.2.2.3
    (1), (3), (4) 2.5.2.2.3
  27(2) 2.5.2.2.1
    (a) 2.5.2.2.1
Value Added Tax Act 1994 .... 7.9.2
  Sch 5 ....7.9.3.2, 7.9.4
Youth Justice and Criminal Evidence
  Act 1999 .... 5.6.1

UNITED STATES
Anti Cybersquatting Statute 4.3.1
California Civil Code
  § 1798.29, 1798.82 .... 3.1.2.1.1
Communication Act 2006
  s 527 .... 9.6.1
Communications Decency Act ... 3.1.2.2.5
Computer Fraud and Misuse Act . 5.1.4.2.1
Digital Millennium Copyright Act: 3.1.2.2.5,
                    3.6.3.2.1; 4.12.4.4.1;
                          5.3.4.2
  § 512(c)(1)(C) 3.1.2.2.5, 3.6.3.2.1;
                          4.12.4.4.1

PARA

Digital Millennium Copyright Act –
  contd
  § 512(i)(1)(A) 3.1.2.2.5, 3.6.3.2.1;
                                    4.12.4.4.1

PARA

Information Practices Act 1977 ... 3.1.2.1.1
Lanham Trademark Act
  s 43(d)(2)(A) 4.3.1

Table of Statutory Instruments

PARA

Civil Jurisdiction and Judgments
Order 2001, SI 2001/3929 ...... 2.4.1.2,
2.4.1.2.1, 2.4.1.2.2,
2.4.1.6
Civil Procedure Rules 1998, SI
1998/3132
r 6.2 .... 2.4.1.8
6.5 .... 4.8.4
6.18(g) 2.4.1.2
6.19(1) 2.4.1.2
6.20 .... 4.8.4
(1) 2.4.1.8.1
(2) 3.7.3.1.1
(5), (6) 2.4.1.8.1
(8) 2.4.1.8.1; 3.7.3.1.2;
4.8.4
(a), (b) 3.7.3.1, 3.7.3.1.1
6.21(1) 2.4.1.8.1
(1A) 3.7.3.1.2
(2A) 2.4.1.8.1; 3.7.3.1
7.2, 7.4 .... 4.8.4
Pt 11 .... 2.4.1.8.1
Community Trade Mark Regulations
2006, SI 2006/1027
reg 5 .... 4.4.9
Companies (Registrar, Languages
and Trading Disclosures) Regulations 2006, SI 2006/3429 ..... 2.1.2
Consumer Credit Act 1994 (Electronic Communications) Order
2004, SI 2004/3236 .... 2.1.1.1
Consumer Credit (Enforcement,
Default and Termination Notices)
(Amendment) Regulations 2004,
SI 2004/3237 .... 2.1.1.1
Consumer Protection (Distance Selling) Regulations 2000, SI 2000/
2334 .... 2.1, 2.3.6; 9.2, 9.3.2.1,
9.5.1, 9.5.2, 9.5.2.4
reg 3(1) 9.5.2.1.2, 9.5.2.1.3
5(1) 9.5.2.1.1
(a)–(c), (f) 9.5.2.1.1
7(1) 9.5.2.2
(a)(i)–(vi) ... 9.5.2.2.1, 9.5.2.3.1
(vii)–(ix) 9.5.2.2.1
(b), (c) 9.5.2.2.1
(2) 9.5.2.2.2

PARA

Consumer Protection (Distance Selling) Regulations 2000 – contd
reg 8(1) 9.5.2.3.4
(2)(a)–(e) 9.5.2.3.1
10(1), (3) 9.5.2.4.3
(4)(a), (b) 9.5.2.4.3
(5)(a) 9.5.2.4.3
13(1) 9.5.2.4.1
(b), (c), (e), (f) 9.6.2.3
14(1), (3) 9.5.2.4.9
(5) 9.5.2.4.8
15 .... 9.5.2.4.9
17(2) 9.5.2.4.1
(3) 9.5.2.4.8
Sch 1 .... 9.5.2.1.2
Sch 2 .... 9.5.2.1.2
Consumer Protection from Unfair
Trading Regulations 2007 (not yet
in force) 9.3, 9.3.1.1, 9.3.2,
9.3.2.1, 9.3.2.6
reg 3 .... 9.3.2.2
5–7 .... 9.3.2.4
Sch 1 .... 9.3.2.3
Copyright and Performances (Application to other Countries) Order
2007, SI 2007/273 .... 4.9.4.2
Copyright and Related Rights
Regulations 2003, SI 2003/2498 . 4.9.4.3
Copyright and Rights in Databases
Regulations 1997, SI 1997/3032 . 4.9.7
reg 12 .... 4.9.8.1, 4.12
13(1) 4.9.8.1
16 .... 4.12
(1) 4.12
19(1) 4.12
Copyright (Computer Programs)
Regulations 1992, SI 1992/3233
reg 8 .... 2.3.4
Data Protection (Notification and
Notification Fees) Regulations
2000, SI 2000/188
Schedule
para 1–4, 15 .... 6.2.4.1
Electronic Commerce Directive
(Racial and Religious Hatred Act
2006) Regulations 2007, SI 2007/
2497 .... 5.4.2.3.2

PARA

Electonic   Commerce   Directive
(Terrorism Act 2006) Regulations
2007, SI 2007/1550 .... 5.4.2.3.2
reg 3(1) 5.4.2.3.2
Electronic Commerce (EC Directive) Regulations 2002, SI 2002/
2013 .... 2.1, 2.1.2.1.1,
2.1.2.1.2, 2.1.2.2.1,
2.1.2.2.2, 2.1.2.3.1,
2.1.3.2.1, 2.1.4.2,
2.1.4.5.1, 2.4.1.8.1,
2.5, 2.5.2.2.2; 3.1.1.5,
3.1.1.5.3, 3.1.2.1.5,
3.1.2.2.5, 3.6.2.5,
3.6.2.6, 3.6.3, 3.6.3.2,
3.6.3.2.1, 3.6.3.2.2,
3.6.5, 3.7; 4.8.3.1, 4.9,
4.12.4.3, 4.12.4.4,
4.12.4.4.6, 4.14;
5.3.4.2, 5.4.2.3.2;
6.2.5.1.1, 6.3, 6.3.1;
9.1.4, 9.2.1.1, 9.5.1,
9.5.2.2.2
reg 2(1) 2.1.2.1.1, 2.1.2.1.2
4(1), (4) 4.8.3.1
5 .... 2.4.1.8.1
6(1) 2.1.2.2.2; 3.7.2.2.4
(a)–(g) 2.1.2.2.1
(2) 2.1.2.2.1
7 .... 4.8.3.1
9 .... 2.1.3.3
(2) 2.1.2.3.1
(3) 2.1.2.3.1
11 .... 2.1.2.3.1
(1)(a) 2.1.4.1.1
(2) 2.1.3.5.1, 2.4.1.8.1
(b) 2.1.4.1.1
13 .... 2.1.2.2, 2.1.2.3,
2.1.4.1.1
15 .... 2.1.2.3
(1) 3.1.2.2.5
17 .... 3.6.3.2
18 .... 3.6.3.2
(a)................... 4.12.4.3.1
(b)(i)............... 4.12.4.3.2
(b)(ii)–(iv) 4.12.4.3.3
19 .... 3.6.2.6, 3.6.3.2;
4.12.4.4, 4.13.1.2;
5.3.4.2
(a).................. 4.12.4.4.2
(i) 3.6.3.2.1; 5.3.4.2
(ii) 3.6.3.2.1; 4.12.4.4.5,
4.12.4.4.6; 5.3.4.2
(b) 3.6.3.2.1; 4.12.4.4.1;
5.3.4.2
22 .... 4.12.4.4.3; 5.3.4.2

PARA

Electronic Money (Miscellaneous
Amendments) Regulations 2002,
SI 2002/765 .... 2.2.1
Electronic Signatures Regulations
2002, SI 2002/318 .... 2.1.4.5, 2.1.4.5.2
Financial Services and Markets Act
2000 (Financial Promotion) Order
2001, SI 2001/1335 .... 9.2.1.2
Financial Services and Markets Act
2000   (Regulated   Activities)
(Amendment) Order 2002, SI
2002/682 .... 2.2.1; 9.2.2
Financial   Services   (Distance
Marketing) Regulations 2004, SI
2004/2095 .... 9.2, 9.2.3, 9.2.3.1,
9.2.3.1.1, 9.2.3.1.2,
9.2.3.1.3, 9.2.3.2,
9.2.3.2.1, 9.2.3.3,
9.2.3.3.1, 9.2.3.3.2,
9.2.3.3.3, 9.2.3.4
Privacy and Electronic Communications (EC Directive) Regulations 2003, SI 2003/2426 ..... 3.1, 3.2.1;
6.1.3, 6.2.1.2,
6.2.5.1.1, 6.2.5.1.4,
6.3, 6.3.2, 6.3.2.1,
6.3.2.3, 6.3.3,
6.3.3.1, 6.3.3.2
reg 22(2) 6.3.2.1
(3) 6.3.2.2
Regulation of Investigatory Powers
(Maintenance   of   Interception
Capability) Order 2002, SI 2002/
2323 .... 6.1.4
Representation   of   the   People
(England and Wales) (Amendment)   Regulations   2002,   SI
2002/1871 .... 6.2.5.1.1
Rules of the Supreme Court 1965, SI
1965/1776
Order 11 .... 2.4.1.8.1
Sale   and   Supply   of   Goods   to
Consumers Regulations 2002, SI
2002/3045 .... 2.3.6
Stop Now Orders (EC Directive)
Regulations 2001, SI 2001/1422
reg 2(3)(i) 9.5.2.5.2
Sch 1
para 9 .... 9.5.2.5.2
Telecommunications (Data Protec-
tion and Privacy) Regulations
1999, SI 1999/2093 .... 6.1.3, 6.3.2
Telecommunications   (Lawful
Business Practice) (Interception
of Communications) Regulations
2000, SI 2000/2426 .... 6.1.4, 6.4.1

PARA

Trade Marks (International Registration) Order 1996, SI 1996/714 .... 4.2

Trade Marks (Proof of Use etc) Regulations 2004, SI 2004/946 .. 4.4.6

Trade Marks (Amendment) Rules 2006, SI 2006/3039 .... 4.2.4

Trade Marks Rules 2000, SI 2000/136

  r 7 .... 4.2.4

  8(2)(b) 4.2.4.1

PARA

Unfair Terms in Consumer Contracts Regulations 1999, SI 1999/2083 .... 2.1.4.1.1, 2.5.2.2.1, 2.5.2.2.3; 3.5.2.2, 3.5.2.2.2; 9.5.1

  reg 2(1) 3.5.2.2.2

  3(3) 3.5.2.2.2

  Sch 3

    para 1(i) 3.5.2.2.2

Value Added Tax Regulations 1995, SI 1995/2518 .... 7.9.2

CHAPTER ONE

Introduction

'The Lord came down to look at the city and tower that man had built, and the Lord said: "If, as one people with one language for all, this is how they have begun to act, then nothing that they propose to do will be out of their reach.". . . That is why it was called Babel, because there the Lord confounded the language of all the earth. . .'

Genesis 11: 6–7

Few people now living have not heard of or used the Internet. Some may even wonder how they coped before it existed or, indeed, don't even recall such a time. To determine how laws may apply to the Internet one needs to have more than merely an observer's appreciation; a working knowledge is required. Fortunately, the Internet can be easily explained.

The Internet is a global network of computers all speaking the same language. To understand the Internet, therefore, it is useful first to appreciate computers. Computers are simple machines: they understand only the numbers zero and one. The reason that computers are able to show colours on a screen, play sounds and process data is that they are very accurate and quick translators. With incredible speed they are able to convert a full-length movie into a long stream of zeros and ones. And with the same speed they can convert a similar stream of zeros and ones into a sound, or a document, or a program. Everything passing into and out of a computer will, at some point, be reduced to binary: two numbers, zero and one.

It is not difficult to connect two computers, say by a wire, and send a stream of these binary numbers from one computer to the other. Each number one in the stream is represented by an 'on' electrical pulse; each zero by an 'off' pulse. These pulses last for a fraction of a second allowing the numbers describing a picture to be transmitted in minutes. A difficulty arises in ensuring that the computer receiving such a stream translates the zeros and ones correctly. As a simple example, the receiving computer may be ready to receive a binary description of a picture, but is instead sent a binary translation of a document. The receiving computer will attempt to translate the zeros and ones, actually a document, into a picture; there will be confusion. It is evidently crucial that to connect computers successfully they both must speak the same language. This 'digital Esperanto' is the key to the Internet.

1.1   LANGUAGE AND NETWORKS

The many variations of this digital Esperanto are called 'protocols'. As long as the sending and receiving computers are using the same protocols, they will be able to share information, in a raw binary form, with absolute accuracy.

A 'network' is a group of computers connected together using the same protocols; they are using the same phrase book. Information stored on one computer on the network can be readily sent, or accessed, by any other computer on the network. In a company this allows one individual to access a file that has been created on somebody else's machine across a network, or 'intranet'. The connection between these computers on a network is not always a simple copper wire. A set of wireless radio devices can be used as a link; they convey information using pulses across the radio spectrum rather than electricity. Links between computers do not even have to be in the same building. 'Wide area networks', or WANs, can stretch across many hundreds of miles.

The key is to ensure that each of the computers connected to the network uses the same protocols. If they do, it will not matter greatly whether a stream of ones and zeros has come from across the corridor or from across the Atlantic Ocean. The receiving computer will be able to translate them appropriately, no matter the length of their journey. The Internet builds on this technology.

1.2   INTERNETWORKING

In 1969 America's Department of Defense commissioned the construction of a super-network, called ARPANET: the Advanced Research Projects Agency Network. This military network was intended to connect computers across the American continent, with one special feature. If one part of this great network was destroyed, the communications system would remain operative. The information passing through the system was required to detour around the damaged part and arrive at its destination by another route.

In 1972 the ARPANET was demonstrated. The network consisted of 40 computers connected by a web of links and lines. The detouring feature was accomplished by allowing a stream of binary information from one computer to pass through other computers on the network, rather than always having to flow directly from A to B.

One example will illustrate this: three computers, A, B and C, are connected in a triangle. A can communicate directly with both B and C. Similarly, B has a line of communication with A and C. If A has to send information to B it has a direct route. But if this route is damaged, or blocked, it can send the information to C with an instruction to pass it on to B: A to B through C. On a larger scale, this allows every computer connected to a network to send information to any other computer on the network. The information simply has to be passed from one computer to another, gradually nearing its destination.

One further advance was made to secure the information being sent from A to B. Instead of sending the information as one long stream, the sending computer splits the data into discrete packets. Each packet, like an envelope, contains the information being sent and has an address of where it must arrive. The packet also has a number that denotes its place in the whole data stream. If any packets are lost, or blocked, they can be re-sent. When all the packets have arrived, the receiver assembles the chunks of digital data into the continuous data stream. This so-called 'packet-switched' network allows many computers to use the same communication lines and allows one data stream to travel by different routes to speed delivery over congested lines.

The demonstration of packet-switched networks and routing in 1972 was such a success that the InterNetworking Working Group was created. The Internet was born. *The New York Times* wrote on 15 April 1972: '[the] experimental network ... may help bring to realization a new era in scientific computation'.

1.3   THE INTERNET

The 40 or so computers on the late 1970s' ARPANET, each using the same protocols, were added to: by 1981, over 200 computers were connected, from all around the world. When the first edition of this book was published, in May 1997, this number of hosts had reached about 20 million. Now, worldwide usage figures are in the billions and connections are increasing. This vast collection of computers is the Internet, the largest network of computers in the world.

The majority of the links and connections between computers are permanent and allow digital streams to be sent back and forth extremely quickly. In addition, each *host* computer connected to the Internet has a unique numeric address or Internet Protocol address. This means that a digital stream can be directed from any computer connected to the Internet to any other computer connected to the Internet, anywhere in the world. The impact of this is great when one appreciates that almost the whole of modern culture can now be reduced to a digital form. Digital information includes colour pictures, animations and movies, high-quality music and sound, text with typefaces and layout, even three-dimensional images.

The real power of today's Internet is that it is available not only to anyone with a computer and a telephone line, but now through various different devices (phones and PDAs) and access mediums (wireless, cable, satellite, dial-up).

By connecting a piece of hardware called a modem to a personal computer, any information can be converted into a digital stream of ones and zeros. The modem can then send this translation down a telephone or cable line to one of the computers already connected to the Internet. The two computers can then pass information between themselves, using a common protocol. Alternatively, some devices now already come wi-fi enabled, allowing connection to the Internet via radiowaves in special wi-fi 'hotspots'.

Because a device connected to the Internet can connect with any other device on the Internet, a personal computer or even a pocket-sized device can now connect with any of the millions of computers on the Internet.

Like human languages, computer protocols work in both directions. They allow information to be easily sent from a home or office computer, or even a mobile phone, to any other such device on, or with access to, the Internet. What is more important is that they allow any computer to gain access to information from any other computer on the Internet: libraries are now literally at our fingertips; a shop simply needs to connect to the Internet to advertise to the world. One language allows the world of computers to share a world of information. The law, in contrast with this transnational system, operates within defined jurisdictional boundaries. The practical resolution of these opposites forms a common thread through each of the following chapters.

1.4   THE COST

Sharing a world of information sounds expensive, but it is not. To connect to the Internet, one needs only to connect to a computer already connected. The first cost is therefore the price of the connection, often a telephone call or subscription to allow connection to that connected computer, or credit payment made via a web browser log-in for intermittent wi-fi usage. The user is not charged for the cost of sending or receiving information *beyond* that first computer unless a particularly quick or secure route is chosen. What is levied, however, is a price to connect to this computer.

The companies controlling these first-port-of-call computers are known as Internet service providers (ISPs). Their computers are called 'servers', as is any computer permanently connected to the Internet. The computers that pay for the connection charges, the users' computers, are called 'clients'.

Some ISPs provide more than purely a connection to the Internet through their server: they provide materials and services on their own servers. This has the advantage of being quicker to view, safer to access and more focused on the needs of the users. These companies provide more than simply an email address and a ramp to the Internet: they commission, license and provide their own services tailored for their members. And they are paid for these value-added services either directly through a subscription, a share of the connection charges paid by their users, or indirectly through selling advertising or 'space' on their pages. On top of connection charges, some websites may charge for membership or other access to their services – whether that be a forum, community or chatroom. Others provide their services for free and rely on advertising revenue to fund their activities.

These companies are often the targets for litigation. They are blamed for the copyright infringing material that other people leave on their computers; some say that they should be culpable for facilitating the transmission of obscene images and movies; there are even suggestions that they should be responsible for publishing others' defamatory statements. Each chapter raises the question of how the law treats these piggies-in-the-middle, as well as the individual primarily responsible.

1.5   INTERNET CONCEPTS

Using several different protocols, the Internet has been able to provide various services to its connected computers. In the similar way that the word 'chat' has a different meaning in French from its meaning in English, so can two protocols used across the Internet allow servers to pass different information to clients. Different uses of protocols give the Internet its utility. What follows is a tour of the different features of the Internet. To appreciate the tour it may help to remember that the information being shunted around the network is still that digital stream of ones and zeros. The various features are produced by simply applying a different protocol to this stream before and after it is sent between computers. The method of conversing is largely the same; what changes is the language being used.

1.5.1   IP addresses and domain names

Every server permanently connected to the Internet has a unique identification number, or Internet Protocol address. To make it easier for humans to remember, these numbers have a unique literary equivalent called a domain name that is allocated by one of the Internet Registries. Commercial entities tend to use .com or their national domain name suffix, such as .co.uk. Academic institutions use the suffix 'ac'. Often the suffix includes information relating to where the domain has been registered. For example, the University of Oxford has the domain, 'oxford.ac.uk'. Scuffles arise because there are a limited number of domain names and they are usually allocated on a first-come first-served basis. The chapter on intellectual property considers the legal implications of this.

1.5.2   Email

'Email' is short for electronic mail. The word 'mail' should be understood at its widest: the electronic mail system over the Internet can carry more than simple messages and letters. A picture, a sound, in fact anything that can be created and stored on a computer can be sent as electronic mail to any other computer connected to the Internet.

First, the item is digitally packed into an appropriate parcel. Like physical items sent by the post, items require suitable packaging. The equivalent of a vase sent through the conventional post is a picture, or a sound or a movie sent over the Internet. These require a digital 'padded envelope'; the common one is called Multipurpose Internet Mailing Extensions (MIME). MIME, and its more secure sister S/MIME have special ways of treating every eighth fragile one or zero that make up multimedia objects. Plain old text does not need each eighth one or zero so does not need to be parcelled up in any special way: the standard Internet protocols are adequate to cope with this simple text. Most email programs automatically choose the correct type of encoding to ensure that the object survives the electronic transmission to its recipient.

It is vital to realise that standard electronic mail copies the contents of the digital envelope; it does not actually send the material from the creator's machine. So, electronic mail, unlike its terrestrial equivalent, does not touch the original created by the sender; instead it provides an identical copy to each recipient. This has its advantages: copies are automatically retained of all outgoing mail. However, it also has some disadvantages: malicious code that piggy-backs electronic messages may also be copied onto the recipient's computer. And, of course, in the eyes of copyright law, a copy is being made of a copyright work.

Once the text or multimedia object is appropriately encoded, the sender simply needs to tack on an address for the email. All email addresses are in the format: username@domain. To receive electronic mail, one needs to have an agreement with the controller of the domain. Some domains are controlled by employers, and they provide email addresses to their staff like direct telephone numbers. Members of staff will have their name, or other reference, before the '@' symbol.

Controllers of other domains, like ISPs, rent out user names on their domains and also provide access to the Internet or other services.

1.5.3   Pseudo-anonymity

Sending a postcard anonymously is easy: simply do not sign it. Sending an email anonymously is more difficult: it is 'signed' by it being sent from you. The way that Internet users have attempted to remain anonymous is either to lie about who they are when they establish their own email address, or to send their emails via an 'anonymous remailer'. This is a computer on the Internet which runs a special program. This program strips any incoming emails of their headers: this removes the identification of from where the email originated. The program then sends this stripped email to the intended recipient, purporting to be from someone else. If the anonymous remailer keeps a log of who is the actual author of a message, they may be ordered by a court to reveal who is the actual sender of the message. If the remailer automatically deletes a log, or never even kept one, of course no court order can then restore the identification of the email sender.

A stronger method of remaining anonymous is to send an email via more than one anonymous remailer and to scramble or 'encrypt' all but the next email in the chain. In this way, even if a court were to order a remailer to reveal the sender's identity they would only have access to the details of the remailer who sent them the message and to the next in the chain. To reveal the identity, therefore, all the remailers would have to co-operate with the court order, and all the remailers would have had to maintain logs. This said, problems of identifying defendants over the Internet should not be exaggerated; it is far easier to send a truly anonymous postcard than a truly anonymous email.

1.5.4   Instant messaging

Instant messaging is just that. Email is a 'store and forward' system for exchanging information. When the email is sent from your computer, its first destination is your Internet service provider or email provider. From there it is hurried across the Internet to an inbound mail server and finally into the recipient's mailbox. If the recipient is not connected to the Internet at the moment of receipt in their mailbox, they may not know it has arrived. Worse still, it is difficult for you to know that they weren't there.

Instant messaging addresses these two deficiencies of the email system: it is instant and you can tell whether someone is connected or not. Like email, messages can consist of more than mere text: pictures, documents and even, because of its instantaneous nature, video and audio can be sent using instant messaging.

1.5.5 Bulletin boards

Digital bulletin boards are similar to their physical counterparts. Anyone with access to the board can pin up a message or question, and any other person can leave a reply on the board. Also like a physical bulletin board, someone is ultimately responsible for it. Someone must remove old messages; perhaps even remove rude or defamatory messages. On the Internet that person is often called a moderator, or is simply the provider 'hosting' the bulletin board. This means that the provider stores the messages on equipment under their control; it is a moot point whether the messages left by their users are also under their control. This will be considered later in the book, but particularly in relation to defamation and copyright.

When a message is posted onto a digital bulletin board, what is technically occurring is that the person is sending an email to the board. This is reproduced in a readable format for any user of the board to see. If a reader wishes to reply to the message, they have a choice. They may either send an email directly and privately to the person who left the message, or they can send a reply that will be stored on the bulletin board itself. It will be listed just below the first message for all to see. This process of replying to a message can occur many times, thus creating a 'conversation thread'.

As explained earlier, an email does not need to be a written note; it may be a digitised picture, a digitised sound recording or even a digital movie. These families of emails can also be left on bulletin boards not for people to reply to, but for people to download, to view or hear. Obscene and indecent pictures and copyright infringement are rife on unmoderated bulletin boards. The issue of when the operator of the board becomes liable for such illegal postings is a vital point that is addressed in this book.

1.5.6 Forums

Many service providers run bulletin boards only for access by their members. These are called 'forums'. Each forum has a title that indicates the sorts of conversation threads and files that can be found on the board. An ISP may host a legal forum. Within the forum there may be many different sections, some dealing with family law, others with recent cases. Occasionally these forums will be unmanned, or 'unmoderated'; anything posted on the board will remain for a certain time. It is more usual to find that forums have a moderator who vets and deletes offensive messages. This book tackles the vexed question of whether by doing this, the ISP becomes legally responsible for the messages left on the system.

1.5.7 User-generated content

The last few years have witnessed an astonishing increase in websites relying on content produced and uploaded by users themselves. Forums and bulletin boards based on text are now surpassed by services, allowing users to view other users' photos, films, videos and hear their sound recordings. YouTube is a prime example. This clearly presents challenges for the service provider, as the risk of unlawful content being posted increases, and judgments must be made as to when to intervene, when and if to monitor, what to restrict and how to act in the event of a complaint. A wrong decision can have far-reaching legal ramifications, even though the content may not be the site owner's.

1.5.8 File transfer protocol

File transfer protocol, or 'ftp' for short, is what it purports to be: a language that allows files to be transferred from one computer to another. For ftp there are usually two significant computers: the ftp server and the client. The ftp server is simply a computer connected to the Internet that stores the files to be transferred. The client is the computer that receives the files stored, and transferred by, the server. To access an ftp site, unlike a website, one usually is required to enter a password. This should not indicate that an ftp site is particularly secure: the majority of ftp sites are termed 'anonymous ftp' meaning that anyone may gain access simply by using the word 'anonymous' or 'guest' as a password.

When a client has gained access to a site it is rather like seeing the contents of a computer's hard disk. There are directories or folders and within those directories there are files. Each of the files may be retrieved, usually by double-clicking on the file name or icon. In addition to retrieving files though, rather like a bulletin board, it is possible to upload a file from one's computer to the ftp server. This lack of control over the content of a site can cause legal problems for the owner of the ftp site. If copyright materials are uploaded by an anonymous depositor, the owner may be a secondary infringer of the copyright in the works. And because the primary defendant may be difficult to trace, the ftp site owner is an obvious alternative choice.

1.5.9 World Wide Web

When most people refer to the 'Internet', they are really talking about a large aspect of it called the World Wide Web. The World Wide Web, or 'the web', is the most user-friendly use for the Internet. But it is not the Internet, and the Internet is not the World Wide Web.

The web, like all the technologies described so far, is merely a common language that allows one computer to understand another when they communicate across telecommunications lines.

Accessing a computer on the web allows a user, or viewer, to do many things. Viewers can see colourful images and graphics, hear sounds and music, see animations and short movies. They can also interact with the accessed computer, or server, in such a way as to allow the viewer to download any material in digital form to his own computer. They can share files across peer-to-peer networks. But these superficial aspects of the web do not explain where it got its name. This explanation reveals the most powerful aspect of the web and the source of the main legal issues involved in its use.

1.5.9.1 Links

Computers connected to the World Wide Web mainly store their information in a special form; it is called Hypertext Markup Language, or HTML. This common language is primarily a language of layout and design. It allows the owner of a computer to format some information, say a table, and store it on their website or 'home page'. Anyone who accesses that site will see the table as intended. The same goes for graphics, animations and so on. The web therefore offers, for the first time, an opportunity for the owner of a server computer to control exactly what is seen by a person accessing that computer. HTML also offers hypertext.

Hypertext is a way of designing a document with links to other documents. It is most easily understood with an example. Some of the footnotes in this book refer the interested reader to other materials, often a case. But if that interested reader wanted actually to read the referred case, they would have to go to their law library, pick the book from the shelf and turn to the appropriate page. A hypertext version of this book would work as follows. A reader who was interested in the case would merely position an on-screen arrow over the footnote, where the case was mentioned, and press a button on their mouse. The case would then appear on the screen replacing or neighbouring the page of the digitised book. So hypertext is a way of connecting one document to another by means of a link. Links on web pages are usually shown by the word denoting the link being underlined and coloured blue. Pictures, animations, in fact anything you can 'click' on, can also serve as links.

The real power of a link on a website can be understood when one appreciates that the link may be to a document held on any other computer anywhere else on the World Wide Web. So, an Internet version of this book could just as easily link a reader to an American case stored on a web server in the United States as to an English case stored on a web server somewhere in England. And having followed a link to another web page, one can just as easily follow a link from that page to another page on the web. These vast numbers of links, criss-crossing between digital pages across the planet, warrant the title 'World Wide Web'.

1.5.9.2 Browsers

Like other aspects of the Internet, the web only works while all the computers that use it understand a common language. The web's main language is HTML. To allow a viewer's computer to interpret this language into a collection of text, pictures and sound, the computer must use a 'browser'. This is a program that not only shows the web page on the viewer's screen as was intended but also it helps the viewer navigate around the World Wide Web. All browsers have a core of common features. They all allow a user to visit a particular site on the web by typing in the site's address. All browsers also have a set of navigation buttons.

These are vital if one is to get back to where one came from. In a sense, the browser lays down digital string through the maze of the web so allowing one to click the 'back' icon to the last turning. As a final aid to navigation, browsers will store a collection of the addresses of favourite pages or sites, so that one can return to a favourite place without having to retrace one's steps each time.

1.5.9.3   Navigation aids

Of course, having millions of pages of information at one's fingertips is useful only if it is easy to find the information needed. However well-stocked a library, there will be few visitors if the books are in an uncatalogued random order. Portals and search engines bring order to the chaotic layout of the web.

Portals are, at their most basic, simply a collection of links under a particular topic. For example, a law firm may wish to advertise its clients. To do this it could have a page on its website that features a list of links to its clients' web pages. An academic may use a website to collect a series of links to useful websites for research purposes. Link lists bring to the Internet what the Dewey decimal system brings to our randomly stocked library.

Search engines are websites that find every site on the web that mentions a particular term. Google, a search engine, can trawl its record of two *billion* documents for one word in under a second. For example, in 0.19 seconds the Google search engine found over 1,360,000 instances of the phrase 'needle in a haystack' on the web.

1.6   THIS BOOK

This book tackles the legal issues arising from the Internet under chapter headings appropriate to a law textbook. This does not mean that the book is for lawyers only. Where possible, the law is explained in plain English; it is envisaged that someone in an e-commerce business or from the Internet industry will use this book as a first port of call. To help these clients and their advisers, the text is highlighted with hundreds of fictional scenarios and their legal effect. For some basic questions, a glance at one of these may be all that is needed to appreciate the law on a point. This said, readers should always seek specific legal advice, rather than rely entirely on the text and scenarios in this book. It should be noted that these scenarios, and the names used, are fictitious, and any resemblance to real persons or companies, alive or operating, now or in the past, is purely coincidental.

The author appreciates that even legal readers who use the Internet regularly will be unfamiliar with its use of technical Internet terms. For this reason two policies have been adopted. The first policy is never to assume technical knowledge; whenever required, this book explains the technology. The second policy adopted is never to use a technical term where a simplified one will suffice. It is more important that lawyers who advise about the Internet truly understand it, rather than simply repeat the latest Internet jargon.

There are many excellent general texts on contract, tort, crime and the topics of the other chapters of this book. This book is not intended to replace these works; the intention is that it will supplement them. This book, therefore, only refers to laws when it is apparent that the Internet raises unique issues about the legal area that may not be covered in existing general literature. One of the many interesting aspects of practising in this area is that so many unique and new issues are constantly raised. The Internet and the laws which define it are always changing, and inevitably at different speeds. Case law in many areas considered in this chapter remains in surprisingly short supply; this fact necessitates the formation of opinions and beliefs based in part on conjecture, on assumptions about how past and new laws may be interpreted, and always with an eye to future developments at home and abroad. As Clive before me, I have not shied from offering my interpretations and opinions, while recognising these may be open to change and challenge.

Finally, a disclaimer. This book examines the English laws that apply to the Internet. The Internet is a transnational beast, however. It will therefore often be prudent to consult the laws of other jurisdictions to check what they have to say on any particular issue. Similarly it is hoped that this book will serve those from abroad who wish to know English law's approach to an Internet issue.

CHAPTER TWO

Contract

'The customer pays his money and gets a ticket. He cannot refuse it. He cannot get his money back. He may protest to the machine, even swear at it. But it will remain unmoved. He is committed beyond recall. He was committed at the very moment when he put his money into the machine.'

Lord Denning, *Thornton v Shoe Lane Parking*[1]

Electronic commerce, or e-commerce, is now part of our daily lives. Whatever financial reasons are given for this, whatever 'paradigm shifts' are held responsible, one fact is certain. If consumers and businesses did not believe that the commerce they were transacting was enforceable, they would not enter the digital marketplace provided by the Internet. The Internet, built for and used as a means of communication, provides a vast arena for agreements. This chapter will consider the English law of contract, so far as it relates to consumer and business contracts entered into using the Internet.

The Internet gives businesses access to a vast number of consumers, gives businesses access to each other and, increasingly, opportunities for individuals to meet each other and even to create, publicise and share their own content. The first large-scale consumer and business use that was made of the web was the erection of websites for marketing and advertising purposes. These sites promoted companies and products. Initially, they did not offer the possibility of selling those products and services. Sales took place in parallel through more traditional means of communication.

A majority of websites now offer international and cost-effective opportunities for selling goods and services to consumers. Businesses too are benefiting from transacting with other businesses over the Internet. A website is rapidly and easily accessible. It can include static or moving graphics, it can be interactive, it is easily updated and purchases can be made immediately, and consumers can be given an infinite amount of browsing and 'window shopping' time. A website can operate like a shop window and also as the cashier and till. Where appropriate, a website can send digital products directly to the consumer and transact services between businesses.

---

1   [1971] 2 QB 163 at 169.

These commercial benefits create new issues for contract law. This chapter considers the following:

1.   What are the requirements for a binding contract to be made over the Internet?

2.   How do you decide when a contract formed over the Internet is made?

3.   What are, and do we need, digital signatures?

4.   How can digital forms of payment be used to bind agreements?

5.   What type of contract should be used to provide digital information over the Internet?

6.   Which country's courts will resolve the disputes arising out of an e-commerce contract?

7.   Which country's law will apply to an e-commerce contract?

2.1   FORMATION OF CONTRACT

In the main this chapter does not consider the *terms* of a contract made over the Internet; the main concern is to analyse the validity of contracts made over the Internet. This is an important distinction. Under English common law, an agreement becomes legally binding when four elements of formation are in place: offer, acceptance, consideration and intention to create legal relations. Usually, a number of discrete chronological stages will also be identifiable, including, an invitation to treat, offer, acceptance and performance, although the four elements for contract formation may be found without necessarily going through each of these.

For contracts entered into over the Internet (or other 'information society service', therefore including mobile services as well as interactive television offerings), the UK's Electronic Commerce (EC Directive) Regulations 2002 ('Electronic Commerce Regulations')[2] and Consumer Protection (Distance Selling) Regulations 2000 ('Distance Selling Regulations'),[3] together with certain other content-specific regulations, introduce new pre-contract formalities, in particular for consumers and, in the case of the Electronic Commerce Regulations, businesses which do not agree otherwise. Along with these formal requirements, law, statute and a body of regulatory and self-regulatory codes and guidance prescribe the content of a contract. For example, an e-commerce contract may be validly formed, but one of its terms may be ineffective under other

---

2   These Regulations implement Directive 2000/31/EC of the European Parliament and of the Council of 8 June 2000 on Certain Legal Aspects of Information Society Services, in particular electronic commerce, in the Internal Market, OJ L179/1 ('Electronic Commerce Directive').

3   This Regulation implements Directive 97/7/EC on the protection of consumers in respect of distance contracts. See Chapter 9 for analysis.

rules. This section focuses on the formation of a contract, examining each of the four elements and key stages in turn, and highlights those additional features specific to the Internet of which businesses and their advisers should be aware.

2.1.1 Contracting via the Internet

It is worth noting that there will usually be no reason why a contract may not be formed over the Internet, whether via a website or email, provided that each of the four elements required to form a valid contract is satisfied. Indeed, the Electronic Commerce Directive requires all member states to ensure that their legal systems allow contracts to be concluded by electronic means and that any legal obstacles to the process are removed.[4] Steps have been taken by the UK government to provide for this, as considered below.

There are, however, exceptions to this principle that contracts may equally be made using digital means as with more traditional (tangible) mediums. These exceptions are: (i) where the parties have agreed that a contract (or amendments to it) must be formed otherwise (in which case there will not be requisite intention to be bound if this is not followed); and (ii) where there is a statutory requirement that a document or agreement must be in a specific format. Each is considered below.

2.1.1.1 Stipulation by the parties

There may be various reasons, public policy or otherwise, why parties may choose to contract or amend contracts in a format other than the Internet. In most situations this will be because parties desire evidence and a physical record of the contract. In others, it will simply be because this is the way they 'have always done things'. Although the use of technical means (such as a pdf to seek to prevent a document from being amended, and digital signatures – see section 2.1.4.5)), and the fact that email communications are now commonplace in disclosure, have gone a long way towards assuring parties that they will have evidence in the event of a dispute, some still prefer to seek reliance on paper contracts and records.[5]

Whatever the parties' choice, it is essential that this be made clear. Those who draft and review contracts are urged to consider references to 'writing' carefully, to ensure that email correspondence is included or removed as required, and clearly exclude electronic contracting or amendments if this is intended. The case of *Hall v Cognos*[6] provides a useful warning on this point. In this case, Mr Hall missed a company deadline for submission of an expenses claim. In response to an email requesting an extension, Mr Hall was told 'okay' by his manager. The company subsequently refused to grant the extension and Mr Hall brought a claim against them. The court held that the claims policy which formed

---

4   Recitals 34 to 38 and art 9.
5   Indeed this may be a stipulation of some companies' insurance policies.
6   *Hall v Cognos Ltd* (unreported, 1997).

a part of Mr Hall's contract of employment (which stated that any variations had to be 'in writing and signed by the parties') *had* been varied by the email. The email constituted writing and the printed name of the sender at the top of the email was judged a signature. This case sends out a further warning to parties on the use of email for making binding contractual statements since, in this case, the manager who emailed back the confirmation did not even have authority to agree the variation. However, he was held to have ostensible authority sufficient to bind the company.

In another case, email communications were held *not* to bind the parties to a contract, since the emailed statement said that 'I hope we now have a deal. I look forward to your confirmation and receiving a deal memo by fax.' Although the other party said that the 'deal is now approved' and that he would send the contract by email, the judge held that there was no binding contract. This was because the common intention of the parties was that the contract would only become binding when each signed some form of memorandum or other paper copies to be given or exchanged, or if the contract were amended to provide for electronic signing, communication or delivery (see section 2.1.4.5 below for further details in relation to digital signatures).

2.1.1.2   Statutory requirement

The Electronic Communications Act 2000 gives Parliament the right to amend old statutes which specifically require the use of ink and paper, in order to facilitate electronic commerce. Some statutes have already been changed through regulation in this was. An examples is the Consumer Credit Act 1994 (Electronic Communications) Order 2004, which amends the Consumer Credit Act 1974, to enable consumer credit agreements to be concluded and most notices and documents[7] to be provided by electronic means. This removes the prior requirement that they must be in paper form.

However, the Electronic Communications Act still requires that each statute be amended in turn. With this piecemeal approach, some statutes still remain unamended. It remains important that parties consider whether there may be any statutes that apply to the subject matter of such contract and its form which would require that specific requirements be followed.

It should be noted that, where legislation simply refers to a requirement that something be 'in writing', without any other requirement (i.e. the statutory context is neutral as to the medium and does not, for example, refer to the need for paper copies), the Interpretation Act 1978 states that:

> 'Writing includes typing, printing, lithography, photography and other modes of representing or reproducing works in a visible form, and expressions referring to writing are construed accordingly.'[8]

---

7   Note that default, enforcement and termination notices have been singled out (by way of the Consumer Credit (Enforcement, Default and Termination notices) (Amendment) Regulations 2004) as a special case and still retain a requirement that they be provided in paper format since such notices are deemed to have significant impact on the rights of debtor and hired. The assumption is that default is likely to be due to financial hardship which in turn means that the individual may no longer have access to electronic communications.

8   Sch 1, Interpretation Act 1978.

The Law Commission's interpretation of this is that:

> 'Writing includes its natural meaning as well as the specific forms refrerred to.
> The natural meaning will include any updating of its construction; for example,
> to reflect technological developments.'[9]

In this way, the Law Commission's view, as is this author's, is that electronic communications such as emails or website order processes will constitute 'writing'.

Of course, in the majority of contracts, particularly in the electronic commerce arena, there will be no statutory requirement providing for specific formats, whether in writing or otherwise. To this extent, general common law principles will apply and it is clear from a number of cases, that there is no reason why a contract may not be concluded via electronic means, provided that the requisite elements are met.[10]

2.1.2 Pre-contract information

The Electronic Commerce Directive and its implementing legislation oblige almost every owner of a website established in the EEA to provide certain information to its visitors, whether the website permits transactions or not, and regardless of whether users of the website are acting in a consumer or business capacity. These requirements fall outside the established elements of contract formation in requiring an additional layer of information to be provided for Internet services.

In the UK, further information requirements apply pursuant to the Companies Act 1985 (as amended pursuant to the Companies Act 2006[11]), and the Business Names Act 1985. These require that a company (and in respect of the Business Names Act 1985, also a partnership or other trading entity) registered in England and Wales place certain key contact and other particulars regarding the company on all of its websites and in official business correspondence. Companies are generally advised to include it in all email correspondence by default to avoid the need to determine whether it is actually a business email or not.

We examine the Electronic Commerce Directive requirements in this chapter by first assessing where a website owner is 'established'. We then consider the manner of provision and nature of the information which EEA-established entities must make available to all visitors to a website. Finally we analyse the nature of the additional 'transactional' information that may need to be provided prior to orders being taken.

2.1.2.1 Establishment of providers

The Electronic Commerce Directive does not have extraterritorial reach; it binds only member states, meaning here, those established within the EEA (therefore

---

9   Para 3.7, 'Electronic Commerce: Formal Requirements in Commercial Transactions, advice from the Law Commission, December 2001'.

10   See, for example, *Hall v Cognos Ltd* (unreported, 1997) and *NBTY Europe Ltd (Formerly Holland & Barrett Europe Ltd) v Nutricia International BV* [2005] All ER (D) 415 (Apr).

11   Amendments have been made to ss 349 and 351 of the Companies Act 1985 pursuant to the Companies Act 2006 and the Companies (Registrar, Languages and Trading Disclosures) Regulations 2006.

including Iceland, Liechtenstein and Norway as well as European Community members). With websites and servers, the concept of establishment, however, is not so straightforward. Popular websites are hosted simultaneously on many so-called duplicating 'mirror servers'. These increase resilience. But they may be situated anywhere on the planet. Consequently, they may be many thousands of miles from the headquarters of those who control them.

2.1.2.1.1   Location of servers not conclusive

The Electronic Commerce Regulations which implement the Directive take a pragmatic view of where a provider is established:

> '"established service provider" means a service provider who is a national of a Member State or a company or firm as mentioned in Article 48 of the Treaty and who effectively pursues an economic activity using a fixed establishment for an indefinite period, but the presence and use of the technical means and technologies required to provide the service do not, in themselves, constitute an establishment of the provider . . .'[12]

In effect, therefore, moving one's servers around the world does not change where one is established. To determine establishment one must look first to an economic activity being pursued from a fixed establishment. Having located this, one must determine whether or not the use of the fixed establishment is for an indefinite period. Employees working in a leased building are the sort of situation envisaged here. One cannot conclude anything from the mere fact that servers are, or are not, inside the building.

2.1.2.1.2   Multiple establishments

Complications arise where more sophisticated companies have multiple locations providing support to a particular website. Imagine the following. A website company's headquarters is in Japan but a team based in California handles technical control of the website. Meanwhile, all the text on the website is written by a group of Irish freelance journalists which posts finished articles to an editor in a small office in Dublin, and customer support is handled from the UK. The site's credit card processing is conducted in Germany and all goods are shipped from local distribution centres around the world. Where is this company established?

The Electronic Commerce Regulations and Electronic Commerce Directive clearly envisage such a scenario. We are told, 'in cases where it cannot be determined from which of a number of places of establishment a given service is provided, that service is to be regarded as provided from the place of establishment where the provider has the centre of his activities relating to that service'.[13]

In the scenario above, therefore, the place of establishment on this basis may well be considered to be Japan because this is where the main base is. However, there is a concern associated with this definition being used to interpret where a multiple-state-located service provider is established for the purposes of the Electronic Commerce Directive and Electronic Commerce Regulations. The

12   Reg 2(1), part definition.
13   Reg 2(1). Recital 19 is similar.

recital and definition would seem to suggest that different services may have different centres of activities relating to them. What follows from this is the possibility that the service of, say, ordering a product from a website is centred within the UK but the service of delivering it is centred in the US. In other words, one service is EU-centred; the other, from the same website, may not be. In such circumstances, the service provider may be unsure whether the legislation applies. In the first scenario, therefore, the management services undertaken in Japan may be viewed as separate to the Irish editorial service and UK customer support. As will be explained, the contractual sanctions for not complying with the Electronic Commerce Regulations are potentially severe enough that any UK service provider is advised to assume that they are established in the EEA, for the purposes of the Electronic Commerce Regulations.

2.1.2.2 General information to all

If a service provider is established in the EEA, they must make available certain general information about themselves. This information must be made available to the recipients of their service (i.e., a website) 'in a form and manner which is easily, directly and permanently accessible'. If a service provider fails to do this, they may be liable in damages by their visitors for breach of statutory duty[14].

Alongside this, the information requirements contained in the Companies Act 1985 (as amended) and the Business Names Act 1985 in relation to websites and emails duplicate the requirements previously required in respect of business stationery and other documents. Such information must be legible. Failure to comply with these non-Electronic Commerce Regulations requirements is a criminal offence carrying a fine of up to £1,000.

2.1.2.2.1 Information to be made available

The scope of the information to be made available pursuant to the Companies Act 1985 consists of the company name, place of registration (i.e., England and Wales), registered number and registered address. The Business Names Act 1985 requires that, in the case of a partnership, the name of each partner, in the case of an individual, his or her name and, in the case of a company, the corporate name, is given clearly and legibly.

The information required under the Electronic Commerce Regulations (discussed below) is straightforward. It is[15]:

1. the name of the service provider;

2. the geographic address at which the service provider is established;

3. the details of the service provider, including his electronic mail address, which make it possible to contact him rapidly and communicate with him in a direct and effective manner;

---

14   The Electronic Commerce (EC Directive) Regulations 2002, reg 13.
15   The Electronic Commerce (EC Directive) Regulations 2002, regs 6(1)(a)–(g) and 6(2).

4.   where the service provider is registered in a trade or similar register avail-able to the public, the register in which the service provider is entered and his registration number, or equivalent means of identification in that register;

5.   where the provision of the service is subject to an authorisation scheme, the particulars of the relevant supervisory authority;

6.   where the service provider exercises a regulated profession:

(i)   the details of any professional body or similar institution with which the service provider is registered;

(ii)   his professional title and the member state where that title has been granted;

(iii)   a reference to the professional rules applicable to the service provider in the member state of establishment and the means to access them;

7.   where the service provider undertakes an activity that is subject to value added tax, the VAT number; and

8.   where prices are referred to, these shall be indicated clearly and unambigu-ously and, in particular, shall indicate whether they are inclusive of tax and delivery costs.

Again it should be stressed that this information must be provided regardless of whether the website in question is transactional or not.

2.1.2.2.2   Form and manner of information

The above information must be 'made available to the recipient of the service . . . in a form and manner which is easily, directly and permanently accessible'.[16] Unlike specific transactional information mentioned below, the above informa-tion may be made available *at any time* during the encounter with the website visitor. This said, one should note that this information must be 'easily' accessi-ble. Burying the information after numerous other pages on a website is unlikely to satisfy this requirement. A link from the homepage to a list of this information is probably the most obvious way to make the information available. Some web-site operators may choose to include this information within their standard 'Terms and Conditions'. This too is likely to be acceptable but with one caveat. This information must be made available 'permanently'. Consequently, websites must not be designed so that the information is, say, only available while one is conducting a particular activity or about to finish placing an order. The informa-tion must be able to be accessed even *after* a visitor has enjoyed the site. Another common place to position this information on non-transactional sites is in an 'About Us' or 'Contact and Legal Details' section.

16   Reg 6(1).

1. An online news service has a subscription service: individuals pay £15 each month to access the service's database of past news articles. The Electronic Commerce Regulations' 'General Information' is made available through a link to the right of the search area on the site. The link is called 'About Us', but the page on which it is housed is only accessible during the course of a paid month and not afterwards. It is therefore arguable that the information is not 'permanently' accessible and so is non-compliant.

2.1.2.3   Transactional information prior to order

If a service provider is established in the EEA and is soliciting orders from visitors to its website, it must provide specific information about its transactions to potential consumers and businesses (additional requirements specific to consumer-only transactions are considered separately in this chapter) who do not agree otherwise. This information must be provided to the recipients of their service 'in a clear, comprehensible and unambiguous manner'.

If a service provider fails to do this, they may be held liable by their visitors for damages in breach of statutory duty.[17] In addition, they must allow a consumer to identify and correct input errors prior to placing their order. If the service provider does not make this facility available, the consumer may rescind the contract.[18] Should the customer so cancel, the service provider may apply to the court to order that the consumer may not rescind the contract.'[19]

Website owners and their advisors are therefore strongly advised to pay particular attention to the following section. An owner of a website may well choose to ignore the requirement to make available the general information. If they do so, they are taking the low-cost risk of an action for damages for breach of statutory duty. Few website owners, in contrast, can afford to run the risk that any of their contracts could simply be rescinded by the customer at any time.

2.1.2.3.1   Provision of information in clear, comprehensible and unambiguous manner

The scope of the information to be provided in a 'clear, comprehensible and unambiguous manner' prior to the order being placed is simple to understand.[20] It nevertheless may be complex to implement and include on certain websites. The six headings below detail the information required and special concerns of each requirement.

Technical steps to conclude contract

The clearest and most comprehensive manner to provide the different technical steps to conclude a contract is to use a 'crumb trail' at the top of the ordering section of the site. What is meant by this is a line of text showing all the steps needed to enter the contract with the current step highlighted. Having, say, 'Choose – Provide Credit Card – Confirm' at the top of the screen certainly does go some

---

17   Reg 13.
18   Reg 15.
19   Reg 15.
20   Reg 11.

way to be clear and comprehensive. What is needed in addition, however, is some explanation of the meaning of each of these steps. A link from each with a short description would ensure that the 'crumb trail' is not ambiguous as to, for example, when the order is complete.

Filing of concluded contract

This rather bizarre requirement obliges website owners to provide information before the order is placed whether or not the concluded contract will be filed and, if so, whether it will be accessible. Although it is obviously trivial to state this in such a way as to comply with the Electronic Commerce Regulations, it may be more difficult to comply with the actual statement itself.

Many well-built websites allow a user to access at any time in the future their previous fulfilled orders. This, of course, is only one aspect of the concluded contract. The other aspect is the text of the contract itself; usually, the Terms and Conditions from the website. The common difficulty with providing a link to the Terms and Conditions is that they are usually in constant flux. The Terms and Conditions used to sell an item in January may differ to those used to sell the same item in the following May. To comply with the filing requirement, therefore, one would need not only to provide customers with access to their completed orders but also to the potentially historical Terms and Conditions used to conclude each order.

The complexity of achieving this will tend to persuade most websites to take the easy and legal way out and not state that they file the contract!

How to identify and correct input errors

This aspect of the Electronic Commerce Regulations obliges websites to provide in a clear, comprehensible and unambiguous manner information about how customers may identify and correct input errors before they place an order. In addition, the website is obliged to make available 'appropriate, effective and accessible' technical means to identify and correct input errors.

Again, best practice would suggest that the easiest way to comply with this is to allow a user either to confirm an order, or adjust it. There is unlikely to be a problem so long as the customer is left in no doubt that the order details on the confirmation page of the ordering procedure may be rejected, and then altered, or accepted.

---

2. CD410.co.uk is a website which sells music CDs for no more than £10 each. Its designers cannot be bothered to alter their ordering pages to allow individuals to correct input errors. Instead, by the 'Confirm' button, they state: 'Don't worry if you've made a mistake and have ordered the wrong thing, simply pop it back unsealed in the post to us with 30 days and we'll credit the money back to you!' CD410.co.uk has not complied with the requirement to allow individuals to correct errors before they place their order; each customer will be able to rescind the contract at any time not only within their stipulated 30 days.

Languages offered for contract

Websites must provide details of the languages that are offered for conclusion of the contract. So that there is no misunderstanding: websites are not obliged to *offer* any particular language or languages; they are simply required to let visitors know what languages they do offer.

Relevant codes of conduct

Many website operators are members of voluntary or mandatory codes of conduct. Where this is the case, a list of these must be provided prior to the order being placed, together with information about how to consult the codes electronically.[21]

Terms and conditions for storage and reproduction

It is sensible for most websites to allow each customer to see the site's terms and conditions before they can place an order. If they cannot see the terms and conditions, there is a risk that a court will deem that the terms and conditions have not been 'incorporated' into the contract with the customer. This is discussed below.

Where terms and conditions are provided, the Directive and Regulations impose a further obligation on the website operator. The website operator must make the contract available to the recipient in such a way that allows him to 'store and reproduce' it.[22] The obvious way to comply with this requirement is to include a 'print' button next to the terms and conditions.

Bearing in mind a court may require the service provider to comply, this author is of the opinion that websites should go further than merely permitting printing. They should allow the user to send the terms and conditions to themselves or be sent them automatically by email. This is recommended because websites are increasingly being accessed using devices other than computers. Interactive television allows websites to be viewed. Personal digital assistants connected to a mobile phone, and some mobile phones, allow websites to be visited. But these devices rarely are connected to a printer. Consequently, by sending the contract to an email address, the website should be in a strong position to argue that they have complied with reg 9(3).

2.1.3 Offers and invitations to treat

Having provided visitors with the requisite information described above, websites can (finally) get on with the formalities required to bind their visitors to contracts – should they so wish – to make them customers.

It is discussed below that an offer, met with suitable acceptance, consideration and an intention to create legal relations can form a contract binding both parties. An owner of a website may not want to contract with every party who gains access to their site. For example, the owner may want to contract with parties from the locale rather than from any country.[23] They may also want to provide

---

21 Reg 9(2).
22 Reg 9(3).
23 This is happening increasingly where a supplier wishes to create geographical price differentials or where the supplier wishes to avoid the laws (often mandatory consumer protection in nature) of a particular jurisdiction.

protection against becoming automatically bound to a contract where there is an error (such as in pricing) in the website or otherwise until they have had an opportunity to approve or confirm the order. Owners of websites should therefore ensure that the advertising aspect of the site is construed as an 'invitation to treat', not as an offer and, as proposed here, that the customer will usually be the one making the offer in submitting an order, then subject to the owner's acceptance at its discretion.

2.1.3.1 Webvertisements

One fundamental of e-commerce is that suppliers use websites to conduct business. Like a billboard, a website advertises products and services, but unlike a billboard it can also assist the supplier to complete the sale. In doing so, a website can be designed to advertise the features of a product or services; it can even allow a viewer to examine the product in a restricted form.[24] After examining the product or the advertising, a viewer may then select the part of the website or follow other prompts to enter a contract to acquire the product or services. The Internet in effect fuses the advertising and the shop. The law, in contrast, has distinguished between advertising and shop displays.[25] This unique commercial situation has legal ramifications.

2.1.3.2 Shops and adverts

2.1.3.2.1 Shop invitations

Old and much-considered authority explains that the display of goods and their prices in a shop window or on shop shelves are not offers to sell those goods; they are merely invitations to any customer to make an offer to make the purchase.[26] The mechanics are that a customer makes an offer to the retailer, which the retailer may choose to accept or reject. Website owners should desire the same legal mechanics, whether they are supplying to businesses or, in particular, to consumers. Indeed, by doing so, those website owners contracting with consumers will be more easily able to comply with the 'placing of the order' rules of the Electronic Commerce Directive.[27]

2.1.3.2.2 Advertisement offers

For the purposes of offers, the law distinguishes shop displays from certain advertisements. It is therefore essential that those who wish to contract over the Internet

---

24 Software can be downloaded from a website in a 'crippled' form. For example, a word processor may be downloaded but may be prevented from printing or saving: it provides a 'test drive'. If the user is content with the product he may then re-access the website to form a contract to receive the uncrippling key.

25 *Pharmaceutical Society of Great Britain v Boots Cash Chemists Ltd* [1953] 1 Q.B.401; cf *Carlill v Carbolic Smoke Ball Co* [1893] 1 QB 256.

26 See *Warlow v Harrison* (1859) 1 E & E 309 and its more modern equivalent, *Pharmaceutical Society of Great Britain v Boots Cash Chemists Ltd* [1953] 1 Q.B.401.

27 Art 11.

understand this difference. The law assesses advertisements in two categories: those which promote unilateral contracts and those promoting bilateral contracts. A unilateral contract is one in which money, generally, is offered to another party to perform some act without that person promising anything in return. A person accepting the offer does not need to communicate this fact to the offeror or to complete the contract; he simply needs to do what is required of him.

This legal notion has been confirmed by the Court of Appeal.[28] A travel agent's physical premises displayed the standard ABTA scheme of protection notice. This included the statement: 'ABTA [a travel agent association] arranges for you to be reimbursed the money that you have paid for your holiday [if there are financial difficulties with the agent].' The travel agent became insolvent and the claimant sought to recover the cost of the holiday from ABTA. The Court of Appeal held that this published statement would constitute an offer and, as such, was accepted and formed a contract with the claimant and any customer doing business with the travel agent.

---

3. A website that offers advertising space to vendors runs a promotion. Its site advertises, 'If you visit our pages three times this month and don't buy anything from our advertisers, we'll credit £10 to your bank account!' This site risks creating a unilateral contract, which the entire Internet community may accept.

A bilateral contract, in contrast, has both parties making a promise. Each offer is usually accepted by a communication of the other's promise.

2.1.3.3 Web invitations

The owner of a website has little reason to prefer a unilateral contract to a bilateral contract, and where possible should seek to be viewed by the courts as a shopkeeper. The main point to make is that the law looks not simply at the words used for a contract, but the objective intention behind them. This means that if a website would induce a reasonable person into viewing statements on the pages as offers, so will a court. In *Bowerman*, Hobhouse, LJ states this succinctly:

'The document as reasonably read by a member of the public would be taken to be an offer of a legally enforceable promise. . . It suffices that ABTA intentionally published a document which had that effect. A contracting party cannot escape liability by saying that he had his fingers crossed behind his back.'

An owner of a website therefore must err on the side of caution in creating a web invitation.

One method is for the owner of the website to state that it will not be bound by any communication or 'order' from a user, but the site owner will inform that party if it accepts the communication or order. This creates three factors in favour of the site owner. First, it goes some way to preventing the reasonable person from thinking the owner has made an offer which can be accepted automatically.

---

28 *Bowerman v Association of Travel Agents Ltd* [1995] NLJR 1815.

The second point relates to the first: it provides evidence to a court that the site owner did not *intend* to make an offer. Simply using indicative words above a link such as 'make an offer' may not be enough.[29] Third, by explaining the stages to conclude the contract, the website will comply with art 10 of the Electronic Commerce Directive and reg 9 of the Electronic Commerce Regulations as discussed above. This legislation states that, prior to an order being placed by *a consumer* or a business not having agreed otherwise, the service provider must 'clearly, comprehensively and unambiguously' provide[30]:

'(a) the different technical steps to follow to conclude the contract;

(b) whether or not the concluded contract will be filed by the service provider and whether it will be accessible;

(c) the technical means for identifying and correcting input errors prior to the placing of the order;

(d) the languages offered for the conclusion of the contract.'

In addition, the following information must also be made available:

'[an indication of] any relevant codes of conduct to which [the website owner] subscribes and information on how these codes can be consulted electronically.'

These pre-contractual consumer formalities may not be contracted out of by a supplier's contract. And, as described above, the sanctions for ignoring these requirements include not only damages but rescission of the contract.[31]

If such an option is taken by the website owner, then it is of course necessary that (not least to comply with the requirements listed above), particularly with consumers, the contractual process and the point at which a binding contract is made, is clear. This will involve not only ensuring that the statements made pre-order are transparent at this point, but also those made to confirm it (as considered below).

---

4. A retailer advertises its products on a website. To process an order, the consumer must provide certain information and then click the button labelled 'Submit'. Before the consumer submits this information the website clearly states that their information is to allow the site owner to decide whether to accept their offer. This allows the site owner to check the product type and cost entered and reject, for example, any offer for a television less than £30 as a minimum price for any television. This application of 'backstop logic' reduces the cost of mistakes. It will be important however that the site owner is clear in subsequent communications or confirmations of this order, as to at what point in time acceptance occurs.

It is mentioned above that the courts view a shop's shelves as invitations to treat and not offers. A website owner may therefore attempt to argue that the site is more like a shop's shelves than anything else, and that it should be viewed

---

29   E.g. *Harvela Investments Ltd v Royal Trust Co of Canada (CI) Ltd* [1986] AC 207.
30   Art 9(1).
31   See 'Transactional information prior to order' at p 21.

accordingly. While this analogy appears reasonably accurate, it may not withstand the strain of a court's detailed scrutiny.

A justification for not holding shops as making offers is to ensure that, if the shop's stock is depleted, a willing consumer cannot sue the shopkeeper for damages.[32] Where a website is offering not physical but digital goods for 'sale'[33] it is difficult to assert that supplies can be exhausted. One of the features of digital products distributed over the Internet is that they are, in effect, in infinite supply. It may therefore be that the primary justification for the rule that shops do not offer but invite to treat is based in part on a commercial factor that is absent from a digitally distributing website.[34] Whatever the common law justification, the Electronic Commerce Directive is concerned with a consumer (or business that has not agreed otherwise) 'placing the order'. It follows, therefore, that to have known of the possibility of being able to place an order, the website displayed an invitation to treat.[35]

2.1.3.4 Misrepresentations

The distinction between an invitation to treat and an offer is that an offer, met with acceptance, may form a contract. An invitation to treat does not serve as an offer: the courts construe that taking up the invitation is an offer (or possibly 'order' in the language of the Electronic Commerce Directive). The distinction does not entitle a website to induce a consumer to enter a contract by using misleading statements. If a factual statement prior to a contract being formed is classified as misleading, the induced party may be entitled to claim damages, rescind the contract, or even both. If an individual is concerned that an invitation to treat or statement on a website may constitute such a misrepresentation, he should take proper legal advice. It is worth noting that the established law and statute on misrepresentation are equally and fully applicable to a contract formed over the Internet as to one formed in other ways. Website owners who simply use their sites as a 'billboard' for contracts that are formed in other ways must therefore consider that the content of their site may induce someone to enter a contract.[36] It makes no legal difference to the law of misrepresentation that the misrepresentation is on a website but that the contract is not formed over the Internet. They must also ensure that they provide the general information as described in section 2.1.2 above.

2.1.3.5 Timing and location of offers

That an offer was made provides two useful pieces of information: when the offer was made and where it was made. When a court deems an offer is made is

---

32 See *Esso Petroleum v Customs and Excise Comrs* [1976] 1 WLR 1 at 11.
33 See 'Type of contract', at p 52.
34 Of course, a limited licence may have been imposed on the supplier restricting the number of digital products he can supply.
35 Art 11(1).
36 There may also be a misrepresentation by the viewer, say, as to the means of payment or the country of his residence.

often vital. At any moment up to acceptance, an offer can be retracted. Where an offer was made has some relevance to the applicable law for a contract, in the absence of choice, and the relevant section of this chapter will consider this in greater depth.[37]

2.1.3.5.1   When an offer is made

It is often relevant for the purposes of a contract dispute to determine when an offer is made. Under the Electronic Commerce Directive (for consumers) or otherwise (not for consumers), any offer can be revoked before acceptance. Therefore the first question to answer is when was an offer made. The need for discussion arises because electronic communications are often delayed in transmission and a court will have to decide whether a revocation of the communication will be deemed to take effect before the conclusion of the contract. In short, the court has a choice: offers may be deemed to be made at the time of sending or at some time later.

Consumer's offers

The Electronic Commerce Directive appears, at first glance, to simplify greatly when a consumer's Internet offer is deemed received: 'the [offer]. . . [is] deemed to be received when the part[y] to whom [it is] addressed [is] able to receive [it]'.[38]

This, however, leaves open the undergraduate law exam chestnut of a delayed or garbled offer.

Delayed offers

Adams v Lindsell[39] is old and approved authority as to when an offer is deemed to take effect. In the case, wool was offered for sale by a letter sent to the claimants. Because of a mistake made by the offerors the letter arrived two days late, at which time it was promptly accepted. The court held that the contract was formed on acceptance, despite the offer being delayed. The court indicated, more than once, that its decision was partially founded on the reason for delay being the offeror's mistake. If the offeror had included a time limit on the efficacy of the offer, however, a late acceptance would not have bound them.

Despite the technology, email can suffer from the same delays and problems as experienced by the defendants in *Adams v Lindsell*. People wrongly consider email and even website offering to be a quick method of communication and compare it to a fax, or perhaps even a telephone.

Post, faxes and emails

An email is more like a posted letter being delivered to a pigeon-hole ready for collection. Emails are not instantaneous, unlike faxes and telephone calls. An

---

37   See 'The Rome Convention', at p 72.
38   Art 11(1) and reg 11(2).
39   (1818) 1 B & Ald 681.

email message is sent to an Internet service provider (ISP) who, like the Royal Mail, attempts to deliver it as quickly and accurately as possible. But as with the Royal Mail, mistakes can occur and emails can arrive garbled, late or even not arrive at all. The similarities with the Royal Mail go further: the Royal Mail does not usually deliver post abroad; that is left to the local postal system of the foreign country. The Royal Mail delivers the mail to only the 'first stop' outside England. The same applies to emails: they are passed between many different carriers to arrive at their final destination.

Unlike a telephone call and fax, some emails are delivered not to the recipient's desk, but to an electronic pigeon-hole for collection. This pigeon-hole is the 'inbox'. Many users of email must log into their ISP account to check on the arrival of an email; often users must collect their email, it is not 'delivered' to them. This technical framework serves as a useful backdrop for the discussion which now follows on when an offer is deemed to have been made. It will also be useful when acceptances are considered later.[40]

Emails can be misaddressed, delayed by any server or router on the way, and worse than ordinary mail, they may not be 'collected' for some time after delivery. This is a situation comparable to sending an offer to a pigeon-hole abroad. Many parties are involved in the transmission of the message, and even on arrival the recipient must act to retrieve it.

Before dealing with the English and European legal resolutions to this situation, a technical point must be made. Certain email systems permit a 'read' and a 'receive' receipt to be automatically returned to a sender of an email. The 'receive' receipt usually informs the sender that the email has not been received by the individual, but by his ISP; if analogies are useful, the receipt informs senders when the mail arrives in the inbox. The 'read' receipt informs when the individual retrieves the email from the ISP. Even there, like a letter in an unopened envelope, the email may not be read for some time.

Deemed receipt of emails

A sent and received email offer will be deemed received because it is able to be accessed but this will not necessarily apply in the case of businesses, who may agree otherwise (for example an agreement that the un-accessed offer is not deemed as being received).[41]

Consequently (assuming no other agreement has been made in the case of non-consumers), if a sender improperly addresses the email and it does not arrive, no order has been placed, no offer made. If the sender properly addresses the email, or properly uses the website, but the supplier is unable to access the order, the order is not deemed received. This will be the situation if it is the 'sender's ISP that is at fault. It is even the conclusion if it is the supplier's website that is at fault. In short, a problem in transmission outside the sender's control will affect the sender's legal position in making an offer before a particular date.

---

40 See 'Timing of acceptances', at p 37.
41 The Electronic Commerce Directive, art 11(1), second indent; Electronic Commerce (EC Directive) Regulations 2002, reg 11(2).

Practically, where it is possible to agree otherwise in business relationships, the best practice is to make any electronic offer subject to a date on which the offer will lapse. Specifying this date in relative terms, for instance, five days after receipt, poses problems unless the offeror provides a definition of exactly what is 'receipt'. A simpler and more certain method is to specify an objective date and time.[42]

---

5. A consumer places an order for a wine box from the 'Swig It' website which is delayed by two days owing to the 'site's Internet Service Provider having a computer fault. Unlike *Adams v Lindsell* the delay was out of the control of the offeror; a court will deem the order as being deemed received when it is accessible to the website owner – i.e., not until the two days have passed.

2.1.4 Acceptance

There is little special about the terms of an acceptance made over the Internet, as opposed to one made in any other way. The acceptance must unequivocally express assent to all the terms of the offer. Much has been written about what constitutes such an acceptance. It is useful here to draw out the special methods of accepting over the Internet and so this section is divided into consideration of acceptances via websites and via email. The section then goes on to consider timing of acceptances, authentication and mistake.

It has been mentioned that an email can have a 'read' and a 'receive' receipt.[43] Receiving one of these will not constitute an acceptance of an emailed offer. An automatically generated receipt of an offer (or order) is not an acceptance of the terms of an offer. Even an email sent in reply that states the recipient's intention to reply in due course will not be an acceptance.[44]

2.1.4.1 Means of acceptance

2.1.4.1.1 Websites

An acceptance needs to assent to an offer. It does not, in general, need to be in any particular form (although see section 2.1.1 above for a more detailed discussion on formats and Internet contracting generally). For this reason, where a website is established to make or complete contracts, its owner should be aware of what conduct may bind him. This is of paramount importance. Contracts made over the web are rarely completed by two humans: a website operates automatically according to a set of instructions, often called a script. In this respect, it is crucial that the owner of a website understands how a contract can be completed

---

42 If no mention is made of the lifespan of the offer the courts will imply a lapse after a reasonable time. See *Chemco Leasing SpA v Rediffusion Ltd* [1987] 1 FTLR 201. To assess what is reasonable the courts will take into account many factors including the subject matter of the contract and the method of communicating the offer. Clearly with an email offer, the expiration will be implied sooner than an offer made by post. See *Quenerduaine v Cole* (1883) 32 WR 185.

43 See 'Delayed offers', at p 28.

44 See *OTM Ltd v Hydranautics* [1981] 2 Lloyd's Rep 211.

because, generally, a website operates without supervision. This section examines two scenarios: first where, as advised, a website accepts an offer and second, where it makes one.

(A) Website acceptance and acknowledgement

Having discussed when and how offers can be made it is now relevant to determine how and when acceptances are made. The general rule is that an acceptance must be communicated to the person making the offer. The Electronic Commerce Directive also obliges offerees to acknowledge the receipt of an offer (order) 'without undue delay and by electronic means' unless agreed otherwise in the case of non-consumers.[45] An acknowledgement of receipt may well also be the acceptance of the offer. Fortunately the two may be dealt with separately. Otherwise this would then bind the supplier into accepting the offer 'without undue delay and by electronic means'. The supplier is entitled first to acknowledge receipt of the offer, and then (potentially later) to accept the offer. If a supplier does not acknowledge receipt of the order, they may be sued for damages for breach of statutory duty.[46]

Suppliers should take care over the language used in any acknowledgement. They should ensure that it does not act as an acceptance and so, inadvertently, form a contract earlier than intended.

---

6. A young school child orders a birthday present from a website to arrive for her father the next day. The website, on receiving the order, immediately sends an email to the child stating: 'Thank you for your order. This is now being processed.' Such ambiguous language could be deemed as being an acceptance and not a mere acknowledgement. The website may now be unable to refute the order.

Any person making any *offer* may waive the general rule that acceptance must be communicated and can instead permit acceptance by conduct. This general rule is examined in the light of e-commerce transactions.

Communication of acceptance

The acknowledged rule is that acceptance of an offer must be communicated to the offeror[47]. This must not be confused with the Electronic Commerce Directive's rule that *acknowledgement* of a consumer's offer must also be communicated. In addition, as the Court of Appeal has stated[48]:

> 'We have all been brought up to believe it to be axiomatic that acceptance of an offer cannot be inferred from silence, save in the most exceptional circumstances. . .'

---

45 Electronic Commerce Directive, art 11(1), first indent; Electronic Commerce Regulations, reg 11(1)(a).
46 Reg 13.
47 [1974] 1 WLR 155 at 157.
48 *Allied Marine Transport Ltd v Vale do Rio Doce Navegacao SA* [1985] 1 WLR 925 at 927.

The question is, what are the 'most exceptional circumstances' when it is appropriate for an acceptance to be silent? These exceptional circumstances stem from the reasons for the rule: to protect both offeror and offeree.

The rule protects the offeror from being bound by a contract without knowing that the offer is accepted. An exception to this may be, therefore, where the offeror expressly or impliedly waives the requirement of communication. For example, an offer to sell goods may be made by sending goods to an offeree who can accept the offer by using them.[49] Here there is not mere silence or inactivity; there is conduct indicating acceptance.

Conversely before the Electronic Commerce Directive, offerees were also protected by this rule. If they did not wish to accept an offer, it was not felt undesirable that offerors could put them to the trouble of communicating a refusal.[50] Indeed, authority from an established precedent, *Felthouse v Bindley*,[51] indicates that the offeror can waive communication of acceptance, but not waive an unequivocal external manifestation of acceptance so as to bind the offeree. Communication of acceptance may also be deemed 'waived' by the 'custom and practice' of the area of commerce.[52] The Electronic Commerce Directive alters these common law rules for consumers and businesses who do not agree otherwise. Service providers must acknowledge offers/orders, whether they intend to accept them or not.

That the above is good law is not doubted; its bearing on standard practice for electronic commerce, is. For the most part it is suppliers who draft the offers being made over the Internet, particularly on the web. In this situation it is difficult to see any unfairness in holding an acceptor, i.e. the supplier, bound despite making no contact to that effect: it would appear that the onus is on the owner of a website to state categorically what will constitute acceptance.[53] For transactions unless otherwise agreed in the case of non-consumers, this is stipulated by art 10(1)(a), but for all business transactions, it is surely best practice. Contracting over the Internet may therefore reverse the court's assumptions in *Felthouse v Bindley* because the offeree generally drafts the offer. If that party does not specify the method of acceptance, and also does not reply to a submitted offer it risks the serious possibility of being bound by numerous contracts without having made explicit approval. Even if a stipulation as to the method of acceptance is made in the email or on the website, if the offeree drafted these terms and accepts by another method, the offeree can be viewed as having waived that specified method. A court will look to whether the offeror has been prejudiced by the changed method of acceptance.[54] Of course, readers will recall that consumer-

49   *Weatherby v Banham* (1832) 5 C & P 228. Interestingly, the Electronic Commerce Directive, recital 34 and the Electronic Commerce Regulations, reg 11(2)(b), clearly envisage that acknowledgement of the order may only be by the provision of the *service* ordered.
50   *Chitty on Contracts* vol 1 at §2-063 (29th ed.) Sweet & Maxwell, 2004.
51   (1862) 11 CBNS 869.
52   *Minories Finance Ltd v Afribank Nigeria Ltd* [1995] 1 Lloyd's Rep 134 at 140.
53   See *Jonathan Wren & Co Ltd v Microdec plc* (5 July 1999, unreported) Technology and Construction Court.
54   See generally *Robophone Facilities v Blank* [1966] 1 WLR 1428.

locused transactions are required to state the steps necessary to follow to conclude the contract.[55]

Acceptance by conduct

The website can accept an offer, 'on behalf' of its owner, by certain conduct. For example, a viewer can click a button on a web page to send a request for some software and the software may then begin to download to the viewer's computer. This positive action can be viewed as an acceptance of the offer made by the viewer without the owner (or offeree) having expressly assented to the offer itself.[56] But, our courts commonly apply an 'objective' test to interpret the actions of the offeree. Conduct will therefore be regarded only as acceptance if the reasonable person would be induced into believing that the offeree has unequivocally accepted the offer.

Completing an order by downloading a file to the consumer is likely to be construed as acceptance by the reasonable person.[57] Owners must therefore carefully construct their websites. The owner must ensure that the website is able to validate the terms of the offer from the viewer. Generally this is achieved by the website having a contract or order page that the viewer is encouraged to complete, submit, or offer, by clicking a link or button. On receiving this notification the website will automatically start the downloading of digital material to the viewer. But the automation of this acknowledgement of receipt and acceptance places a burden on the site owner: he must ensure that the terms of the offer submitted are the terms of the offer expected. It is essential that a viewer cannot submit an offer with an adjustment to the terms, say lowering the price. This would be a counter-offer which may, unwittingly, be accepted by downloading the requested material to the viewer.

There is a technical method to achieve this certainty. The web page should clearly state the terms of the order. Included within these terms should be a clause to the effect that an acceptance will only be valid where an offer is received through the website.[58] This, to some extent, prevents an adjusted offer being sent by email and automatically accepted.

Controllers of sites should pay much attention to their automatic checking programs: an error may result in the owner being bound to a contract that would have been unacceptable (see also section 2.1.4.4 on mistakes).

---

7. A website provides the terms of an offer to download software from the site at a cost of £60. The site is structured so that the viewer must type the words, 'I Agree' in a box, at which point the website acknowledges and accepts the offer by downloading to the viewer the requested software. One viewer types 'I agree to pay £30'. Because the

---

55 Electronic Commerce Directive, art 10(1)(a).
56 See *Brogden v Metropolitan Rly* (1877) 2 App Cas 666.
57 See *Northern Foods plc v Focal Foods Ltd* [2001] EWCA Civ 1262, [2001] All ER (D) 306 (Jul), in which Focal supplied goods to Northern and later disputed that such supply deemed their acceptance of the loss-making price for the goods. The Court of Appeal held that a letter sent by Focal to Northern was accepted by the conduct of supplying the goods. See also Electronic Commerce Regulations, reg 11(2)(b) in relation to 'acknowledgement by providing services'.
58 See *Frank v Wright* (1937) OQPD 113 where acceptance was specified to be received in writing, but was not valid where made orally.

> automatic checking program looks simply for the words 'I Agree', but not exclusively, the software is downloaded to the viewer in error. A contract may have been formed at the lower price.

(B)   Consumer acceptance

This chapter advises against websites making offers. Nevertheless, for the sake of completeness, rather than recommendation, this section examines this method of contracting.[59] Many of the same legal considerations are applicable here as for when the website accepts an offer.

Acceptance by conduct

It has been explained that conduct can constitute acceptance.[60] In the scenario where a website makes an offer, it will be the conduct of the consumer, or viewer, which the courts will examine to check for acceptance. It is in the interests of the website to ensure that the conduct by the consumer is therefore as unequivocal and unambiguous as possible.

> 8. A web page has a scrollable window headed 'Licence'. Below this window is a button labelled 'download software'. A viewer clicks on this button to download the software and is later accused of breaching the licence provisions. The viewer may have an arguable case that his conduct was not in relation to the terms of the licence, but in relation, simply, to gaining access to the software. A more thoughtful page design may have removed this problem.

Conduct is regarded as acceptance, and, for services, acknowledgement of receipt of the order, only if the reasonable person would be induced into believing the offeree has accepted. This 'objective' test can create difficulties for the operator and designer of a web page. Many digital consumers using the web for commerce view it like a shop, only a 'virtual' one. They may therefore be surprised, and not aware, that to acquire a product they must not only provide payment but also then consent to a licence. Their more usual tangible purchases involve simply paying in exchange for receiving the product. On this basis it is difficult to fathom how a court could objectively construe as acceptance the clicking of a button that denotes downloading the product rather than accepting the licence. Under Scottish law, a case concerning 'shrink-wrapped' computer software showed the court's readiness to construct two contracts out of the supply of computer software transaction.[61] First, the retail sale of the physical box of software containing the product. This contract is between the retailer and consumer. The second is purported by the software publisher to be between them and the consumer; the so-called 'shrink-wrap licence'. In this case, the consumer did not break the 'shrink-wrapping' and so was decreed not to have a contract with the software publisher. Bearing in mind this case, owners of websites should not

---

59   See 'Shop invitations', at p 24.
60   See 'Acceptance by conduct', at p 33.
61   *Beta Computers (Europe) v Adobe Systems Europe* 1996 SLT 604.

shy from explaining that clicking a button will bind that person to obligations regarding the material that they will acquire. This provides the background for the final issue pertaining to the acceptance by the conduct of a consumer – ignorance of offer.

Ignorance of offer: lack of intention

It can be appreciated that, even with provision of the information required by the Electronic Commerce Directive, consumers could click on a button labelled 'download' without envisaging that they may be entering an explicit, rather than implied, contract: consider the eagerness to acquire some new software or material and consider the typical ignorance that the acquisition is subject to an explicit licence. It is also possible to press the wrong button. In such a situation, Electronic Commerce Directive or not, the courts may be reluctant to bind unwitting offerees simply because they have performed an action[62] that purportedly indicates acceptance. A further reason that the courts may not hold consumers bound by their action is that, in not knowing of the offer, the consumers have no intention to be legally bound by their actions.

The solution to these possible problems is for any website that seeks to bind users to be explicit, avoid uncertainty and 'go further' than merely 'make available' the 'Terms and Conditions'. One method is to prevent the viewer being able to perform the conduct before they have scrolled, or paged, through the entire contract. True, an individual may simply click on a 'next page' link without actually reading the text of the contract; but, at least they then have a weaker argument that their conduct does not objectively indicate acceptance and that they were ignorant of the offer.

Conduct also becomes relevant in terms of amendments to terms and conditions. Increasingly, websites seek to provide that updates to the terms and conditions are deemed accepted by a website user by conduct if they use the website after the amended terms and conditions have been uploaded to the site. Even some offline providers have sought to direct customers to check their website regularly for amendments to their terms to which they are bound. There has been no case law on this issue in the UK to date but any provider who uses such techniques should be alert to the problems this presents, particularly when dealing with consumers. The key issue is that this of course places the entire burden on the user to proactively check the site terms, plough through them for changes and then take the decision whether to continue to use the services or exercise any cancellation rights on this basis. Not even the fanatical, alert to this requirement, in the first place would do so! It is unlikely that a unilateral amendment in this way, particularly where it relates to changes which impose new obligations on the consumer or reduce the comfort they have, will be enforceable (being unfair under The Unfair Terms in Consumer Contracts Regulations 1999) unless something more is done to bring it to the consumer's attention to indicate their acceptance to it. In the case of registered users, sending an email with updated changes is one option, another would be drawing the new terms or changes to

---

62   For example, clicked on a link or icon. See *Specht v Netscape Communications Corpn and America Online Inc* US District Court of Southern District of New York, 3 July 2001.

their attention when they next log onto the site. For non-registered users where no contact details or log-in are available, this will not be possible. With such user terms, there may already be problems with proving that they are enforceable contractually (although as considered in Chapter 3, the main point of such terms is usually to provide a disclosure for tortious purposes and an intellectual property notice). A prominent notice placed on the home page (particularly where major changes have been made) may assist.[63]

---

9. The home page of a website features only one line of legal text to avoid looking too ominous. It states, 'By proceeding you agree to be bound by our terms.' The word 'terms' is underlined on the site to indicate a link to the terms of the website. This may not bind the viewer, but if it does, there is a likelihood that onerous exclusions of liability will not operate against the viewer. The website owner should find other ways of ensuring that those onerous terms are definitely read by the viewer, for example, by inclusion of a tick box confirming acceptance and which must be 'ticked' if the viewer wishes to continue.

2.1.4.1.2   Email acceptance

Email is increasingly being used by parties to enter into contracts to ensure speed of communication and agreement and avoid the need for acquiring physical signatures. Identifying the point of 'acceptance' is often trickier with emails than with a website order process however since there is less likely to be a clearly identifiable 'act' that occurs equivalent to the clicking of an 'I accept' or the sending of an order confirmation. It is more likely with email communications that the medium will have been used alongside other offline communications, for negotiations and therefore isolating the final point at which the parties are bound will more frequently come down to an interpretation of the words used.

Issues may easily arise where parties are seeking to reach agreement as to a variation of an existing arrangement or to settle a dispute with each party taking a different interpretation of the other's position or their own proposals.

In some cases a party may try to seek reliance on the principle set out in *Chitty on Contracts*, General Principles that 'where parties are genuinely at cross-purposes as to the subject matter of the contract and the terms of the offer and acceptance are so ambiguous that it is not possible to point to one or the other of the interpretations as the more probable, the court must necessarily hold that no contract exists.'[64] However, as recent cases such as that of *NBTY Europe Ltd (Formerly Holland & Barrett Europe Ltd)*[65] indicate, a finding of 'impossibility'

---

63   The US Court of Appeals case for the Ninth Circuit in the case of *Douglas v USDC Central District* (DC number CV-06-03809-GAF) provides some guidance on this topic, albeit from the US. In that case, the court held that a telecommunications company could not enforce updated terms and conditions placed on its website against a user. However, in this case, the user never used the website, paying via credit card separately. The initial terms also failed to draw attention to how such changes would be notified – both aspects which clearly worked against the provider.

64   *Chitty on Contracts*, General Principles vol I at 5-060.(29th ed.) Sweet & Maxwell, 2004.

65   *NBTY Europe Ltd (Formerly Holland & Barrett Europe Ltd) v Nutricia International BV* [2005] All ER (D) 415 (Apr).

is a high threshold. Again, parties are therefore here urged to treat email communications with as much certainty and precision and with such clarity as to whether something is agreed and accepted, as they would with more traditional paper correspondence. As considered above in section 2.1.1.1, it is also essential that such caution is passed down to employees and managers to guard against the risk of a party becoming bound through their more lax correspondence.

One further point to note is that, as mentioned earlier, an email can have a 'read' and a 'receive' receipt. Receiving one of these will not constitute an acceptance of an emailed offer. An automatically generated receipt of an offer (or order) is not an acceptance of the terms of an offer. Even an email sent in reply that states the recipient's intention to reply in due course will not be an acceptance. Issues of acceptance with email contracting is therefore heavily bound up with intention (see section 2.1.6). The problems of timing and non-receipt are considered in further detail in the next section.

2.1.4.2 Timing of acceptances

Because an offer may normally be revoked at any point until acceptance, it is obviously vital to appreciate when acceptance is deemed to have taken place over the Internet. Unlike for offers, the Electronic Commerce Directive and Electronic Commerce Regulations do not specify when acceptance is deemed to be received.

---

10. Onepotatotwo.com sells seeds to consumers through its website. During July, a consumer selects some seeds through the site and confirms his order by clicking an icon labelled 'I accept'. The moment he does this he receives an email from onepotatotwo.com thanking him for the order and confirming the seeds are on their way. Before reading the email, he sees the seeds being sold at seedyseedsmart.com at a reduced price. Even though he has not read the email, as he was able to, the contract was concluded. (However, as a consumer, he may be able to take advantage of the cooling-off period under the Distance Selling Regulations in order to cancel the contract and obtain a refund (for which, see Chapter 9)).

One person may make an offer which is acknowledged as being received and is accepted immediately by the other person. But if that offer is withdrawn before the acceptance is received by them there may be a conflict. The possible legal outcomes are that the contract was made when the acceptance was sent; or when, and if, it arrives at the recipient.

English law does not resolve or offer guidance on this critical timing issue, nor does the Electronic Commerce Directive (although it is interesting to note that early drafts did contemplate the inclusion of sections clarifying the moment at which the contract is concluded). In this respect, English and European law (unlike that of the US) has not equivocally followed in statute the approach set down in the UNCITRAL Model Law approach.[66] This states that, unless otherwise agreed between the originator and the addressee, the time of receipt of a

---

66 UNCITRAL Model Law on Electronic Commerce (1996) with additional art 5 bis as adopted in 1998 Guide to Enactment.

data message is the time at which it enters the designated information system or, if a designated information system has not been selected, the time at which the data message is retrieved by the addressee.[67]

Nor does English case law to date cover this timing point in relation to email or website acceptances. It is therefore necessary to extrapolate from the law relating to acceptance by post, telephone and telex.

When a viewer reads or views a website, packets of digital information pass between the site and the client. An acceptance by either party will, generally, be immediately received by the other. The more difficult questions of timing of acceptances are therefore seldom pertinent for web communication or for 'instant' messages such as MSN Messenger. For emails the issues are more complex.

This discussion is therefore in halves: the first considers acceptance by email where it is reasoned that the 'postal rule' will usually apply; the second considers acceptance over a website where it is submitted the more general rule will apply that the contract is formed when the acceptance is received. Again, readers should note that the Electronic Commerce Directive addresses only timing of 'orders' and not acceptances.

2.1.4.2.1   Acceptance by post, telephone and telex

Where acceptances are sent by post there is a generally applicable rule that the English courts have used to determine the deemed time of acceptance.[68] Acceptance takes place when that letter is posted. Where acceptances are made by an instantaneous form of communication, such as telephone or telex, another rule has been generally applied.[69] Acceptance is deemed to take place when the acceptance is communicated to the offeror.

It is a moot point whether these rules should be mechanically applied, or whether they are, as is more likely, a starting point to assess what is fair between the parties. Certainly the courts have stated that the posting rules should not be applied where it would lead to 'manifest inconvenience or absurdity'.[70] And there are occasions where this would be the case: it would be absurd for an acceptance to be deemed accepted at the time of posting if it is delayed in the post because the offeree wrongly addressed it. It is perhaps as much as can be hoped, therefore, that this chapter explains what would not be manifestly inconvenient or absurd for email acceptances. It is essential that those who would seek to rely on the following section for email acceptances are aware that it is simply guidance. Even after almost 200 years of examination of the postal rule, there is no universally applicable rule; there are merely pointers for the parties and the court.[71]

---

67   Ibid, art 15(2).
68   See *Adams v Lindsell* (1818) 1 B & Ald 681.
69   See *Entores Ltd v Miles Far East Corpn* [1955] 2 QB 327, and *Brinkibon Ltd v Stahag Stahl und Stahlwarenhandelgesellschaft mbH* [1983] 2 AC 34.
70   *Holwell Securities Ltd v Hughes* [1974] 1 WLR 155 at 161.
71   This is not to say that organisations have not lobbied to clarify and harmonise the position: the UN Convention on Contracts for the International Sales of Goods (adopted in Vienna, 1980) contains provisions dealing with acceptance, offer and withdrawal of an offer (Articles 14–24); see also, the EC Communication from the Commission to the Council and the European Parliament on European Contract Law, Com (2001) Final, 11 July 2001.

2.1.4.2.2 Acceptances by email

As mentioned earlier, email is not quite like the post and it is certainly not like instantaneous communication by the telephone.[72] It is sometimes slower than the post, and the arrival of the acceptance by email is far more reliant on the recipient than the sender. It is not like a fax or telephone for two reasons. First, there is no direct line of communication between sender and receiver. Instead, the email is broken into chunks and sent as a collection of packets, each with an 'address' for the recipient. The arrival of an email is therefore far more fragmented than a telephone call. The second, and central, difference between the two is that with a telephone call it is possible to check that the intended recipient has heard the acceptance. With email this is near to impossible but is often quite necessary. Emails are sent using protocols, precise languages, which allow one computer to pass on information accurately to another. But sometimes these protocols are used incorrectly and an email may arrive entirely garbled or missing a few important characters such as zeros and pound signs. This problem must be combined with the issue that an email requires its recipient to collect it, rather like collecting mail from a pigeon-hole. It is therefore difficult, unlike a phone call, to check that the offeror has received the acceptance and to check that it is unequivocal.

Reasonableness of email acceptance

Like the posting rules, the first issue to consider in relation to an acceptance is whether it is reasonable to use email to accept. A rule of thumb applied in postal cases has been that if an offer is made by post, it is reasonable to accept by post. This, at first blush, appears applicable to email; it may not be. Some email users are permanently connected to their Internet Service Provider: as soon as an email arrives for them, they are notified and can immediately view the message. What is more common, however, is that a user's email arrives to a server which the user must contact by modem to access any messages: the connection is not permanent. These users are rarely notified that an email awaits them. They must simply log-on on the off-chance that an email is ready for them. For these remote email users, a period of days may elapse before they check for any email. It may therefore be less reasonable that an important *acceptance* is emailed to one of these remote users, than for an offer to be sent from one of these users. That said, it is submitted that the senders have at least some responsibility to inform their recipients not to reply by email if they collect their email infrequently.

Priority over subsequent communications

Because an email is not instantaneous, if it is reasonable to use email to accept,[73] it is not absurd to deem the time of making the contract as the time of sending the email where otherwise a later acceptance sent would act prejudicially. A later

---

72 Readers should note that since the first edition of this text *Chitty* has now altered its view on this issue to confirm this point. See *Chitty on Contracts* (Sweet & Maxwell, 29th ed., 2004) Volume 1 at §2-046; cf § 2-031 (27th ed.).
73 See 'Reasonableness of email acceptance', above.

posting or email should not 'beat' the earlier acceptance sent by email. Of course, convenience and policy have a role to play in balancing the interests of the two competing offerees.[74] It would not be reasonable to prefer the earlier sent email if it was addressed incorrectly, or was sent in full knowledge that the offeror's email server had crashed.[75]

Accepted but not received

Emails can be delayed in their transmission, sometimes through no fault of the offeree. As one early example (there are many more), on 13 April 1998, software flaws crippled an AT&T data network for about 24 hours. This affected millions of consumers who tried to send, and hoped to receive, emails during the period.[76] Less often an email will not be received at all. There are three possible reasons for this. First, the sender sends the acceptance to an incorrect email address: it is extremely unlikely that a court will grant such carelessness with the benefit of the doubt; the email will not be acceptance. A second reason that the email may not be received is owing to a fault at some point in the transmission process. As another example, on 17 July 1997 hundreds of thousands of email messages sent to known addresses simply 'bounced back' as though the addresses did not exist. The cause of this was an employee of Network Solutions Inc (who at the time maintained the 'master' address list) who was working the night shift and failed to react to an alarm.[77] Like a loss in the Royal Mail, a court must weigh the fairness to the offeree against the unfairness to the offeror, who may have already contracted with another party. Even so, it is still likely that the contract will have been formed at the time of sending the email.[78] The third, and most common, reason that an email acceptance will not be received is that its recipient does not retrieve it. This may be because the person no longer checks their email inbox, or because the person sees who the message is from and deletes it without reading it. In both of these situations, the email would constitute acceptance; an offeror's recklessness will not prevent the formation of a contract.

It follows from the above that an email acceptance sent, but not yet received, cannot be 'beaten' by a later sent revocation of the offer. This rule is well established under rules of postal acceptance and there seems little justification to adjust it for acceptances over the Internet.[79]

Inaccurate transmission

It has been mentioned that an email may arrive missing, or including, certain characters and it may even be entirely illegible. The legal significance of a flawed

---

74   *Brinkibon Ltd v Stahag Stahl und Stahlwarenhandelgesellschaft mbH* [1983] 2 AC 34 at 41.
75   See *Bal v Van Staden* [1902] TS 128 in which it was held unreasonable to insist that an acceptance be deemed accepted where the sender knew of postal delays.
76   *USA Today*, 23 April 1998.
77   *The Times*, 19 July 1997.
78   See *Household, Fire and Carriage Accident Insurance Co Ltd v Grant* (1879) 4 Ex D 216.
79   Offerors over the Internet must not forget that to revoke an offer the withdrawal must actually reach the offeree. A reversal of the postal rule will not apply. See *Re London and Northern Bank* [1900] 1 Ch 220.

email is that its sender may never know. In this way email differs to a large extent from a telephone acceptance, and to a smaller extent to a fax acceptance. During a telephone call one can check that an acceptance has been heard; fax machines will report an error if a fax cannot be sent with sufficient quality, or there is no paper at the receiver's end. In contrast, if an email is garbled, it is impossible for the offeree to know before it is too late. For this reason, it would be both inconvenient and absurd for any other rule to apply other than making the offeror bound by a garbled email. The offeror, having not specified an alternative method of acceptance, is not at liberty to presume it is a counter-offer.

This rule is not purely based on technical realities and policy; it is also based on evidential matters. As with a fax, the sender retains a copy of that which is sent. On the other hand, it is often possible, using digital translators, to unscramble the received email to establish whether it was an unequivocal acceptance.[80]

---

11. An insurance firm establishes a website and allows potential customers to submit details of their works of art for insurance. All valuations and contracts are formed over the Internet. The firm sends by email to a customer an offer of insurance for a painting; this customer types his acceptance by email but, unfortunately, this is not sent across the Internet as the customer has not paid his monthly fee to his Internet Service Provider. The painting is then stolen. The customer will not be able to benefit from the delay in the post, as the delay was attributable to his fault.

2.1.4.2.3 Acceptances over the web

Unlike email communications, on the web the client and server are in simultaneous communication for most purposes. The communication between the two has the quality of a telephone conversation between computers rather than humans. Either party will be immediately aware if the other party 'goes offline'. This is because when one party sends digital data to the other, these data are sent together with a checksum which allows the receiving computer to check that the correct information has been received. A checksum is almost the equivalent of someone saying 'Okay?' after asking a question over the telephone; it is a way of checking that the silence is due to acquiescence rather than absence.

If the client loses contact with the server, the server will 'know' of this situation within seconds, as its checksums and 'received data' will not arrive; if the server loses contact from the client very often a message will appear to the effect of 'server not responding'. In law this 'knowledge' of non-transmission makes a crucial difference. In *Entores Ltd v Miles Far East Corpn* Lord Denning considered for the first time when an acceptance sent by telex should be considered as making a contract.[81] It is instructive to follow closely Denning LJ's reasoning in this case: this will demonstrate that a website acceptance greatly differs to an email acceptance and should be treated like a telephone, or telex, acceptance.

---

80   A binary document, say a word processing document, which is emailed as text, may be irreversibly scrambled. Other types of modification, however, such as a '£' becoming a '#', can be reversed to indicate to the court the true nature of the acceptance.

81   [1955] 2 QB 327. Applied by the House of Lords in *Brinkibon Ltd v Stahag Stahl GmbH* [1983] 2 AC 34.

First, Denning LJ considered the hypothetical case where one person, in the earshot of another, shouts an offer to the other person.[82] The person hears the offer and replies, but his reply is drowned by noise from an aircraft flying overhead. Denning LJ was clear that there is no contract at the moment of the reply. The accepting person must wait until the noise has gone and repeat the acceptance so the other can hear it. Next, Lord Denning took the case of a contract attempted to be made over the telephone. An offer is made but in the middle of the reply of acceptance the line goes 'dead'. Denning LJ was again clear that there is no contract at this point because the acceptor will know that the conversation has abruptly been broken off. Finally, Lord Denning considered use of telex to form a contract. Again, if the line goes dead in the middle of the sentence of acceptance, the teleprinter motor will stop. If the line does not go dead, but, say, the ink dries up, the clerk at the receiving end will send back a message 'not receiving'. In all Denning's examples the person sending the acceptance knows that it has not been received or has reason to know it.

Parallels with acceptance over a website are now obvious: if a communication of acceptance is sent from or to a website, it will become immediately obvious if a problem has occurred which blocks the communication. Like a telephone acceptance, a server will always 'know' whether a message has been received by its intended recipient; it is waiting for received data to signify that the message has been received. And like a telex acceptance, if a client sends a message to the server but there is some problem preventing transmission, the client will receive, not unlike the telex clerk's message, a 'server not responding' message. It is therefore submitted that communications over the web differ from those by email. The contract is complete when the acceptance is received by the offeror.

---

12. A company which sells ties establishes a website that allows viewers to select a pattern and length for a tie. After selecting the tie, the viewer is asked to click the 'I want to buy' icon. The company's web server then sends an automatic receipt of offer and acceptance of offer. The server is notified that this acceptance does not reach the viewer. No contract is formed because the non-delivery of the acceptance was known to the company before the viewer left its site. It should have retransmitted the acceptance, maybe by email.

2.1.4.3   Battle of the forms

The rapidity of email and automatic confirmations of receipt lend the Internet to contractual negotiations where previously faxes had been used. This may allow a 'battle of the forms' to commence. This is where two standard-form email contracts are exchanged, each differing slightly to the other but claiming to govern the legal relationship entirely. The situation may be resolved by no contract being formed; there is no agreement. What can be more problematic is that a contract is formed on one party's terms when that was not expected. Except for the issues

---

82   [1955] 2 QB 327 at 332.

of location and timing already mentioned, there is little that the Internet will add to established methods of judging the result of a battle of the forms[83].

2.1.4.4 Mistake

Given the tendency for websites to provide automatic acceptances of orders placed, there is a risk that mistakes will arise which could lead to the formation of a contract on terms that the website owner does not anticipate. We have discussed above some of the safeguards that website owners may put in place, including ensuring that there is a space between acknowledgement and acceptance and that the terms of any offer made by a user are checked. It is worth considering here, however, the circumstances in which a party may have redress due to a mistake, and how such risks may be further mitigated with some examples.

A common scenario for mistakes is where a pricing error on a website leads to goods being advertised at a lower price than the website owner is willing to accept.

The risk of website pricing errors was first brought to public attention in September 1999, when a Sony television was offered for £2.99 on the Argos website. The correct price was in fact £299. Argos initially refused to honour the orders; proceedings against them were later abandoned due to costs. In 2002, another well-known retail name, Kodak, advertised a 'special deal' package comprising camera, docking station, memory card and paper for just £100. The true figure was over £329. Customers placing orders received automated email confirmations, but on spotting the mistake, Kodak wrote to these customers, withdrawing the offer. County court proceedings were initiated by several customers, and under increasing media scrutiny Kodak agreed to fulfil the confirmed orders.

In *Hartog v Colin and Shields*[84] the court held that a buyer should have known that a price per pound rather than per item offer was a mistake, and that the seller did not mean to sell at that price. The buyer's acceptance of the offer did not form a binding contract. Although it was not in the end tested before the courts, Kodak may have had a difficult time in seeking to rely on this case, given the labelling of the package as a 'special deal' and given that the low price was advertised during sale time. This contrasts with the Argos situation where the £2.99 was more obviously a mistake more akin to *Hartog*.

A later incident, again involving Argos, demonstrates how simple changes made to a website ordering process can greatly assist. In this later case, Argos advertised a television valued at £349 on its website for just 49p. However, in the interim since the previous pricing mistake, Argos had amended its terms and conditions (accepted and incorporated when orders were placed). These now stated that, if errors in the price of goods were identified, customers would be informed and given an opportunity to reconfirm the order at the correct price or to cancel it or, where the customer could not be contacted, the order would be

---

83   *British Road Services Ltd v Arthur V Crutchley Ltd* [1967] 2 All ER 785 and *Butler Machine Tool Co Ltd v Ex-Cell-O Corpn (England) Ltd* [1979] 1 WLR 401.

84   *Hartog v Colin and Shields* [1939] 3 All ER 566.

cancelled by Argos. Steps were also taken to ensure that it was clear to customers that an email acknowledgement of an order was not the same as a confirmation that it would be fulfilled without condition.

2.1.4.5 Authentication and digital signatures

The signature is a familiar way of an individual making apparent on paper that he or she is who they say they are and that, often, they agree to be bound by whatever they are signing below. The signature, therefore, generally provides 'authentication' of the signatory. It is also an indication of 'acceptance' or 'consent' to a legally binding commitment. Sometimes, legislation and statute demands that a signature is provided, for example, in assignments of copyright.[85] Sometimes individuals decide that, for a particular contract, a signature will be their agreed sign of acceptance.

In both examples, the use of a computer, software and the Internet to provide, generate and deliver these signatures is an important issue. As outlined in section 2.1.1 above, if legislation insists on ink and paper (as opposed to just any type of signature) for certain transactions, then e-commerce's benefits will not be felt in areas of commerce simply because of this bureaucracy. Similarly, if individuals do not feel comfortable in relying upon digital signatures, they too may not derive benefits from electronic commerce's speed and geographical reach. The European Union and the UK have implemented legislation to facilitate digital signatures being usable and relied upon in commerce.

The EC Directive on a Community Framework for Electronic Signatures[86] attempts, among other issues, to create a common understanding across Europe as to what constitutes an 'electronic signature'. Clearly, electronic commerce across Europe would be hampered if member states differed on what an acceptable 'technical' standard is for an electronic signature. Further, the Directive requires that member states ensure that an electronic signature is not denied legal effectiveness in legal proceedings merely because it is in an electronic form and has not been created by a secure electronic device or by a particular third party.[87] In short, basic electronic signatures (as opposed to advanced ones, considered below), like paper ones, need not be generated in any particular way nor need they be created (read 'witnessed') by any particular person. As with paper signatures, it is open to a court to call into question the reliability, and possible forgery, of an electronic signature. Even so-called 'advanced signatures' are not beyond the rules applicable to proper signatures.[88]

The UK's Electronic Communications Act 2000 and Electronic Signatures Regulations 2002 introduce the key element of the Electronic Signatures Directive, being that, merely because a signature is electronic does not prevent a court from relying upon its veracity in a dispute.[89] The UK statutory framework

---

85 Copyright, Designs and Patents Act 1988, s 90.
86 OJ No L13, 19 January 2000, p 12.
87 Art 5.
88 Arts 2 and 5 and recital 20.
89 S 7(1).

for electronic communications does however contain some important departures from the Directive as considered below in the context of basic and advanced signatures.

2.1.4.5.1 Basic electronic signatures

A basic electronic signature would cover all manner of sign or signature.

However, unlike the Directive, for the purpose of evidencing such electronic signature in legal proceedings, the Electronic Communications Act states that both this signature and 'the certification by any person of such signature, shall each be admissible in evidence in relation to any question as to the authenticity of the communication or data or as to the integrity of the communication or data.' This means that, although in many cases just having some kind of electronic signature (such as an 'I accept' or 'I confirm' button, or the typing in of a user's name) will be sufficient to form the contract, if there is a question over the validity or authenticity, certain additional certification criteria will be relevant when put before the court. 'Certification' to this extent, means that a person should have made a statement (whether before or after making the communication) that[90]:

'(a) the signature;

(b) a means of producing, communicating or verifying the signature; or

(c) a procedure applied to the signature;

is (either alone or in combination with other factors) a valid means of establishing the authenticity of the communication or data, the integrity of the communication or data, or both.'

What this means is that if one wishes to utilise a basic electronic signature to conclude a contract, one might also be required to produce a statement, technical in nature, which is a valid means of proving the signature and document are not forged and are reliable.

There is no prescribed form for any such statement, and in most cases, whether or not a signature is in fact authentic will come down to a matter of evidence gleaned after the event.

It is interesting that, in relation to the few English cases that we have had on electronic signatures, the courts have not considered the issues of certification, or indeed the ECA at all. This is presumably because, in the few cases we have had, the focus has been on what constitutes a signature in the context of an email communication, rather than on whether or not the signatures in question were genuine or not. In the cases of both *Hall v Cognos*[91] and *Nilesh Metha v Fernandes*,[92] the question arose as to whether the sending of an email constituted a signed document. Different judgments emerged. In *Hall v Cognos*, as considered earlier in this chapter, variations to a company policy could only be made where they were signed in writing. The Industrial Tribunal held that the presence of the name of

---

90   S 7(3).
91   *Hall v Cognos Ltd* (unreported, 1997)
92   *Nilesh Metha v J Pereira Fernandes SA* [2006] 1 All ER (Comm) 885.

the sender at the top of the email was a sufficient signature. In *Nilesh Metha v Fernandes*, the question arose as to whether an email relating to a guarantee constituted a sufficient signature for the purposes of s 4 of the Statute of Frauds. This statute refers to the need for documents to be 'in writing and signed by the party charged therewith'. The email in question contained only the name of the sender in the header and the judge held that, given that this had been inserted automatically and not deliberately, on an objective basis, the email or document had not been signed. He went on to state (again without consideration of the ECA) that a party could have signed the email for the purposes of the statute in question had they typed in their name or last name prefixed by some or all of his initials or using his initials and possibly by using a pseudonym or a combination of letters and numbers. However, the fact that the document in question was an email, as opposed to being in paper form, was immaterial.

The outcome of these cases demonstrates that the approach of the courts to the use of emails and signatures is still unclear, although a signature is more likely to be found where the person 'signing' has had to actively do something to affirm their consent or agreement (as opposed to just sending an email). However, in each of these cases, no arguments were made that the 'signatures' were forgeries or otherwise inauthentic. Rather the basis for contesting them was that the marks were not signatures at all. In this respect, key legal issues associated with the Electronic Communications Act and Regulations and basic signatures did not arise. On this basis, readers should be aware that, although a signature may be found in email communications, website owners and contracting parties may still wish to consider the insertion of statements fulfilling the criteria of the Electronic Communications Act and Regulations or to use an advanced electronic signature in order to provide evidence in the event that it is contested.

2.1.4.5.2   Advanced electronic signatures

The Electronic Signature Regulations also provide for a regulated regime for the development of advanced or qualified electronic signatures. The advantage of such signatures is that they do not need accompanying statements to be admitted for evidence purposes, since they are already deemed to incorporate such tests.[93] These super-strength electronic signatures would satisfy any legal requirement for a signature in respect of the signed data. However, one must consider that UK legislation usually twins the word 'signature' with another, 'writing'. Every piece of legislation that refers to both these words remains impervious to digitalisation: the legislation itself will need amending to bring it into the binary age.

A further crucial issue about the Electronic signatures legislation is it does not 'fast-forward' existing legislation into the electronic world in this respect. It does not 'search and replace' the word 'signature' in legislation with the words 'signature, digital or otherwise'. If old legislation states currently that 'writing' and 'signatures' are required for a particular legal instrument, the grand-sounding Electronic Communications Act 2000 does nothing to change this requirement.

---

93   Technically, these must meet the hurdles of Annexes I, II and III of the Directive.

Advisors should therefore ensure that their clients, while eager to embrace electronic commerce, do not misread the European Directive and the Electronic Communications Act 2000 and Electronic Signatures Regulations 2002. Old legislation may still insist upon paper signatories, or the parties may themselves choose this too, as explained in more detail in section 2.1.1, and all too frequently references are made by parties to using a 'digital signature' without proper understanding or clarification as to whether this is basic (with or without statement) or advanced.

2.1.5   Consideration

As an oversimplification, perhaps, it can be stated that the English law of contract distinguishes breakable promises from enforceable contracts.[94] Consideration given in return for a promise is the main ingredient that turns promises into contracts. Consideration has been variously defined as 'something of value in the eye of the law'[95]; '[d]etriment to the promisee'[96]; 'the price for which the promise is bought'[97]; and there is much academic debate as to its exact ambit.

English law has always recognised that mutual promises may be adequate consideration for each other, thus forming a contract. If a builder promises to repair a roof and the unfortunate homeowner promises to pay on completion of the repair, a binding contract is formed. No services have been provided yet and no money has been given.[98] Similarly, promises to pay over the Internet are enough to form the consideration to create a contract.

---

13. A video shop with a website offers DVDs for sale. A viewer selects a DVD for £15 from the website and types 'I Agree' in the requisite box together with a credit card number. The DVD is shipped immediately at which point the shop discovers that the credit card number is fictitious. That the agreement has been completed over the Internet is of no legal consequence: the viewer's promise to provide the £15 will be 'valuable' (i.e. of value) consideration for the shop to enforce the contract.

It is only important for this chapter to assess whether the factual reality of contracting using the Internet affects the doctrine of consideration. For general statements, readers are advised to look to specialist texts. One contractual situation is particular to the Internet: the consideration needed to cement a web-wrap

---

94   Although, a promise made in a deed may be enforceable. This is considered out of the scope of this chapter, but it may be noted that there appears little preventing a deed being made using electronic methods.

95   *Thomas v Thomas* (1842) 2 QB 851 at 859.

96   Holdsworth W, *History of English Law*, Vol 8, at p 11.

97   *Dunlop Pneumatic Tyre Co Ltd v Selfridge Ltd* [1915] AC 847 at 855.

98   If this was not the law, there could never be an action in contract for non-payment. The defendant would argue that, having not paid, no consideration has been provided, no contract therefore subsists.

contract.[99] These are agreements at the 'front' of a website which purport to bind their viewers to a contract should they proceed to view the rest of the site.

2.1.5.1   Web-wrap consideration

It is now common that to enter a website one must click a link labelled, 'I Agree to the terms above'. These terms are generally divided into two sections: the top section expresses the intellectual property rights that the site owner licenses to viewers; the bottom section attempts to exclude liability for any damage caused by the site. This section will not address the *terms* of these contracts, but merely whether there is consideration for the licence.

If a web-wrap contract is properly constructed it seems likely that there is consideration to form a binding contract with the viewer. What the developer of the website must attempt to create is a set of mutual promises that will form the consideration for the contract. One method of achieving this is to *actually prevent* a viewer who does not click the 'I Agree' link or icon from entering the site itself. Promising the viewer access to the site if the 'I Agree' link is selected then forms one of the promises to bind the contract. The other promise must come from the viewer. This, of course, is to promise to abide by the terms of licence. This prevention can then be classed as a promise to allow the viewer into the website if he agrees to the terms on the screen. Such a legally robust suggestion would have no commercial support unless the site was very worried about exposing itself to liability.

Website designers and legal advisers should work together to ensure that the contract is formed at the correct time. The contract will not work retroactively; if a website owner is concerned to exclude liability for material on his home page a contract should appear before the home page. From a designer's perspective, foisting a legal document on a new viewer may not be appropriate.[100] Ultimately the disciplines of law, design and IT must meet in the middle: the greater the risk of liability and infringement (outside an implied licence) the greater the need for a lawyer to ensure the site binds visitors to a contract. Many sites may well decide it is better to run the risk of there being no valid contract than to risk losing an annoyed visitor to a competing site.

2.1.6   Intention

The fourth and final ingredient to create a binding contract is an intention to create legal relations. The reason that this is a factor in resolving a contractual issue over the Internet is that often only one human is involved. When a person makes an agreement with a website, the site accepts or rejects the communication by the person according to a computer program being run at the time. A human does not

---

99   The use of 'digital cash' in exchange for goods or services raises issues not of consideration but of performance of a contract. For this reason the legal issues involved with digital cash are examined under 'Performance: Payment' at p 50.

100   A contract in a frame and a simple home page can be an acceptable compromise.

sit on the server side of the website. This raises the issue of how the contract can be formed without this direct intention. It is not complicated, nor unique to the Internet, but is a factor which advisers should not overlook: bugs in these programs will not negative the owner's intention.

2.1.6.1 Programmed intention

In *Thornton v Shoe Lane Parking*[101] Mr Thornton accepted a contract by driving a car into a car park. In that case, Lord Denning stated that the automatic reaction of the car park turning a light from red to green and thrusting a ticket was enough to create a contract.[102] All the ingredients were present. It is of no legal consequence that the contract was physically completed by a machine. The court looks objectively to whether a contract can be said to have been made: has the user been induced reasonably to believe that a contract was being made or offered? In comparison, it is of no legal consequence that a computer program completes the contract over the Internet; many contracts are 'made' with machines. That a computer program is being relied upon, however, can be of commercial significance to its owner.

Usually web-wrap contracts and automated email contracts use an express agreement. If, as a result of a bug in the contracting program, the viewer's offer is accepted in error, the court will presume that there was the requisite intention. The offeror has the heavy burden to prove that there was no intention to have a legal consequence.[103] The subjective opinion of, say, the owner of the website is of little consequence to the court,[104] unless the viewer knew of the lack of intention.

---

14. For the payment of £10 a website allows its viewers to download pictures of a certain quality. An additional payment of £2 allows viewers to download the pictures at a higher resolution, which are more appropriate for professional use in brochures and magazines. An error in the Java script permits viewers to download any of the pictures for £10. The website owner will be hard pressed to claim the extra £2: the viewers are unlikely to know of the private intention.

Owners of websites who seek to use them for forming contracts should be aware that an error in their automated program may be of great financial consequence, as can be taken from the Kodak and Argos examples given in section 2.1.4.4 above. Such validation programs should be carefully checked and, where possible, the owner should seek to obtain an indemnity from the programmer against such loss or, if not, insurance.

---

101   [1971] 2 QB 163.
102   [1971] 2 QB 163 at 169.
103   *Edwards v Skyways Ltd* [1964] 1 WLR 349 at 355.
104   See *Smith v Hughes* (1871) LR 6 QB 597.

2.2   PERFORMANCE: PAYMENT

2.2.1   Internet payment

It has been discussed that the Internet can be used to make an offer and accept that offer. What has not been explained is how the Internet can be used to pay for the goods or services that may be the subject of the offer.

The introduction to this book explains in detail that everything passing through the Internet consists of digital ones and zeros. What varies is the way that digital stream is translated into an item at the end of its journey. The same can be said for methods of payment: unless the payment is made outside the confines of the Internet, the payment must be converted into zeros and ones.[105] There are two problems with this that do not concern us, but which are mentioned for completeness. The first problem is associated with the way the Internet moves digital streams between computers: they do not move directly; they can pass through many different computers on their way to a destination. Passing money through unknown computers is clearly unsafe. The second problem is that if digital money consists of only ones and zeros in a long string, it may be easy to duplicate the money. Any computer could potentially become a forgery for digital bank notes.

The technical solutions to both these problems are being addressed by many companies across the world. There are many companies using sophisticated encryption methods to secure the payment technically. Internet browsers and website servers allow credit card details to be sent over the Internet securely; some companies issue what is, in effect, a digital travellers' cheque that can also be sent securely across the Internet. To the banking industry, the European Central Bank, the Bank of England and banking lawyers this issue of cash is obviously both interesting and important. Indeed, it has prompted the Electronic Money Directive and requisite UK legislation.[106] For the seller, buyer and their lawyers these new 'forms' of payment do not have any dramatic impact on contract law.

2.2.2   Credit card non-payment

That there is a contract must be distinguished from who should pay for the goods or services, and what happens if that payment does not arrive. With a charge or credit card, the customer, by presenting a valid card, or by issuing a valid set of numbers, honours his obligations under the contract. Of course, at this point, a further contract comes into existence between the card company and the user to pay to the card company the full sum under the vendor's con-

---

105   A contract could be made over the Internet and a cheque sent by conventional mail.
106   Directive 2000/46/EC on the taking up, pursuit of and prudential supervision of the business of electronic money institutions (and to a lesser extent, Directive (2000/28/EC)); The Financial Services and Markets Act 2000 (Regulated Activities) (Amendment) Order 2002; The Electronic Money (Miscellaneous Amendments) Regulations 2002.

tract. If the card company does not pay the vendor, *and the card was valid*, the vendor's right of action is against the card company, not the individual.[107] One justification for this is that if the vendor was entitled to pursue the customer for payment in cash, the customer would lose the benefit of the payment by credit and, often, the insurance over the goods.[108] This would therefore increase the burden on the customer.

The commercially safest way of trading over the Internet is for vendors to insist on receiving and then validating payment *before* providing their side of the bargain. Terms to this effect should be incorporated into any standard form electronic commerce contract.

2.2.3 Digital cash non-payment

Digital cash has two species. The first, more primitive, is like a charge card. The issuing bank provides the payment to the vendor on presentation of appropriate authority. The sum is then withdrawn from the user's account and transferred to the vendor's. Over the Internet this appropriate authority will be no more than the card number and, perhaps, its expiry date. This species can be called 'third party digital cash'. The second species of digital money is close to actual cash and will be called 'pure digital cash'. A customer has an agreement with a digital cash provider[109] who allows the customer to send encrypted messages which represent sums of money. Once a customer sends one of these encrypted messages to a vendor, it can then be subsequently used by the vendor without having to go to the issuing bank for exchange into cash. The only time when the message will be exchanged into more regular currency is when someone seeks to deposit it in their bank. This new form of payment does not greatly strain existing contractual principles of payment.

2.2.3.1 Third party digital cash

As with a credit card, it is likely that a court will find that the issuing company is liable for the payment, rather than the user.[110] This view is carefully stated as being 'likely'. Both vendor and user should consider that the Court of Appeal has concluded that, merely because a third party has agreed to make payment to a vendor does not automatically mean that the risk of non-payment is removed from the user.[111]

---

107 *Re Charge Card Services Ltd* [1989] Ch 497, generally approved by the Court of Appeal in *Re Bank of Credit and Commerce International SA (No 8)* [1996] 2 All ER 121 at 133.

108 See, for example, the Consumer Credit Act 1974, s 75 which makes the credit card company liable for the vendor's misrepresentations and breaches of contract.

109 Or so-called Electronic Money Issuer pursuant to the Financial Services and Markets Act 2000 (Regulated Activities) (Amendment) Order 2002 and as discussed further in Chapter 9.

110 See 'Credit card non-payment', at p 50.

111 See *Re Charge Card Services Ltd* [1988] 3 All ER 702 at 707.

2.2.3.2   Pure digital cash

Paying by the second species of digital money can be thought of as sending cash for most legal purposes. If the encrypted sum is lost on the Internet, or perhaps intercepted, the intended receiver will, no doubt, claim that payment has not been made. To some extent this is the general rule: sending a banknote in the post, which is lost, will not constitute payment.[112] However, this appears inequitable where the intended receiver expressly permits payment to be made by such a method. Indeed, there is followed authority that if the intended receiver impliedly, or as will be the situation over the Internet, expressly, authorises transmission of payment in a particular way, the sender is discharged of liability if he follows the guidelines of transmission.[113]

---

15. A website offers two methods for its viewers to pay to gain access to its materials: by credit card and by digital cash. A viewer sends by email the digital cash, accesses the materials, but the cash is never received. The viewer may not be liable to pay again. The site impliedly authorises its customers to pay using the Internet as the conduit: the owner may not be able to transfer this risk to its customers having so authorised them.

If a website seeks to allow payment to be made using digital cash, in either species, it must face the reality that the sum may not arrive. It should therefore incorporate into its contracts a term stipulating that its performance under the contract will be honoured only after receipt of the digital cash. Customers, in anticipation of this, should be wary of sending uninsured digital cash over the Internet. If the contract is suitably worded and held enforceable, the customer may lose the money and not benefit from the contract.

2.3   TYPE OF CONTRACT

Many owners of websites do not only make contracts over the Internet, but also try to perform them over the Internet. Software companies distribute software from websites; information and picture libraries provide digital copies of their information. Movies and music are sent across the Internet for payment. The various intellectual property rights that may vest in these items are discussed in the chapter on intellectual property. What is important here is to examine what should be the nature of the contract with the receiver of the digital information. The answer is a licence, and certainly not a sale, but justification for this is provided below. The first justification is to attempt to sidestep the principle of exhaustion of rights; the second, peculiar to digitised material, is to grant a licence to the user of the material.

---

112   See *Luttges v Sherwood* (1895) 11 TLR 233.
113   *Norman v Ricketts* (1886) 3 TLR 182.

2.3.1 Exhaustion of rights

If digitised copyright goods are *sold*, rather than licensed, within the EC there is a risk that the exhaustion of rights principle will apply. This principle is broadly that once goods protected by intellectual property rights are sold in any member state with the consent of the owner, national intellectual property laws cannot be used to block the goods' entry into another member state. The Copyright, Designs and Patents Act 1988 states this explicitly at s 27(5).

2.3.2 Retention of title

Partially as an attempt to avoid the application of this principle, many producers of digital material do not sell it; they license it. To avoid being viewed as selling the material many manufacturers include a 'shrink-wrap' licence which explicitly retains title in the goods being passed to the consumer and states words to the effect, often in emboldened capitals, 'This software is not sold to you; we are licensing it to you'.

2.3.3 Using is copying

The material downloaded over the Internet is likely to be given legal recognition and protection as a copyright work under the Copyright, Designs and Patents Act 1988. It is this intellectual property right that forms the foundation for any transaction.

For digital material to be used, it must first be transferred into a computer's memory.[114] This transfer exactly reproduces in the memory of the computer the words and characters of the material sent from the server. The material on the server remains unchanged and intact; two copies of the material now exist. An obvious comparison is that when one views a painting, the painting remains on the canvas and there is no need to copy the work. A digital version of the same painting can only be viewed by being copied.

The Copyright, Designs and Patents Act 1988 grants certain rights to the owner of a copyright work. In particular, s 16(1)(a) states that the owner has the exclusive right to copy the work. Thus, without a licence from the owner, under s 16(2), copying the work can constitute infringement of the copyright in the work. Copying any copyright work is defined widely as reproducing the work as a whole, or any substantial part, in any material form. This includes storing the work in a medium by electronic means.[115]

The viewer of the actual painting, like the viewer of the digitised version, is able to enjoy viewing an artistic work which attracts copyright protection. However, the viewing of the canvas does not involve a reproduction of the work

---

114   This transfer is called 'loading'. This should not be confused with 'running' a program when a computer carries out the instructions specified by a program that has already been loaded.
115   Copyright, Designs and Patents Act 1988, ss 16(3)(a) and 17(2).

in a material form. It can be seen, therefore, that normal use of a painting does not copy the copyright work. Conversely, an accurate application of the Copyright, Designs and Patents Act 1988 suggests that normal usage of any downloaded material will be regarded as a copy of the copyright work. This is because the digitised material is necessarily reproduced by downloading it from the server into the computer's memory.

2.3.4   Implied licence

The above analysis may appear to indicate that if the owner of a website does not give an express licence to each viewer of the site, each viewer is an infringer. This is not the case: copying a copyright work is not infringement if there is a licence permitting that copying. In the situation of the Internet there is undoubtedly a licence for authorised viewers and downloaders of material to copy the work.

First, the law is likely to imply a licence into the actions of the website owner for reasons of business necessity. Second, a court could apply the so-called 'rule of non-derogation from grant' to prevent the publisher, having supplied the material, then alleging infringement.[116] Third, but specifically for computer programs, the Directive on the Legal Protection of Computer Programs at art 5.1 specifies that the 'lawful acquirer' of a computer program shall not require authorisation by the copyright owner to run a computer program in the absence of specific contractual provisions. Fourth, temporary copies of works other than new programs or databases will be permitted for lawful use of the work.[117]

2.3.5   Express licence

For programs, therefore, the Copyright, Designs and Patents Act 1988 expressly provides that a user has a right to copy the program into memory for its use. Until the implementation of the Copyright Directive, art 5.1, viewers of graphics and sound, movies and music, must rely on implications by the common law to legitimise their activities. Even after the implementation of art 5.1, non-temporary use will rely on common law. And for programs, graphics and sound alike, the supplier of those materials may have to accept a court's wide understanding of what type of licence is implied. For example, a designer of a graphic image used as a backdrop for a website frame may not want its viewers to copy the image onto their own publications. To expressly prevent these unwanted uses, owners of copyright material used on the Internet are advised to use on-screen licences that leave no non-temporary uses of the material to doubt or disagreement.

In providing a licence over the copyright material some publishers go further to attempt to exclude liability for certain damage caused by the material. The

---

116   See *British Leyland v Armstrong* [1986] RPC 279.
117   See the Copyright, Designs and Patents Act 1988, ss 50A, 50B, 50C, inserted by the Copyright (Computer Programs) Regulations 1992, SI 1992/3233, reg 8. Also, art 5.1 of the EC Copyright Directive 2001.

efficacy of these exclusion clauses is examined in the chapter on tort, but one point is worth noting here. The English courts will not uphold every exclusion clause. This is particularly true where the clause excludes liability to a consumer.

The conclusion from this section is simple: publishers should include express licences over their digital work to avoid exhaustion of rights and disagreements over acceptable use of the work.

2.3.6 Auctions

There is no comprehensive definition of 'auction' in English statute, and yet determining whether or not a transaction has been conducted by one remains important in terms of contract law and certain consumer protection regulations.

The significance stems from the Sale of Goods Act 1979, which states that:

> 'A sale by auction is complete when the auctioneer announces its completion by the fall of the hammer, or in other customary manner; and until the announcement is made any bidder may retract his bid.'[118]

In effect, this sets when acceptance takes place and a binding contract formed, and the point up to which the bid or offer may be retracted.

This presents obvious problems for Internet auction processes. Not only is a virtual hammer hard to pinpoint, but there is a real risk that individuals have to be given an opportunity to retract bids at any stage, requiring fast readjustments to current highest bid prices which simply may not be possible. Further, the running of traditional auctions involves consideration of various restrictions and obligations on the auctioneer which have been developed through case law, the establishment of a fiduciary duty to the vendor, and certain information and potential licence conditions that certain London boroughs impose on auctions conducted in their locale.

It is little wonder then that the 'auctions' we see in the Internet arena, have sought to deviate from the traditional auction model, for example through the removal of an identifiable auctioneer, replacing this with a model that introduces vendors to potential buyers directly.

However, not being an auction presents its own problems. Auctions (again undefined) with business buyers are currently excluded from the implied terms requirements of the Unfair Contract Terms Act 1977 as to description, quality and fitness (provided there is a notice put up to this purpose and exclusions satisfy the reasonableness test.[119] The Consumer Protection (Distance Selling) Regulations 2002 also currently exempt auctions entirely and therefore the consequent prior and post contract information requirements and the need to provide a cooling-off period to buyers (see Chapter 9 for more details), do not apply.

---

118   Sale of Goods Act 1979, s 57(2).
119   Note that the Sale and Supply of Goods to Consumers Regulations 2002 amended the Unfair Contract Terms Act 1977 to apply protections to consumer buyers in respect of new goods and second-hand goods auctioned over the Internet or by phone where the consumer cannot attend in purpose. See reg 14 of these Regulations amending s 12 of the Act.

Not only is there no statutory definition of an auction, but there has also been no case law on what constitutes an 'auction' for the purposes of references to them in English statutes (such as those listed above) to date. This leaves the position of such remodelled Internet auctions somewhat unclear. In Germany, some clarity has been given in a judgment of the German Federal Court of Justice which held that a consumer buying from a business through eBay is granted a right to revocation of such contract,[120] even though the exemption for auctions has also been incorporated into Germany's implementing legislation of the Distance Selling Directive. eBay was not deemed by it to be an auction.

It is becoming increasingly evident that further consideration of the status of such trading models is needed and this is, at the time of writing, a subject of discussion in the European Commission. It is reasonable that online auction models involving competitive bidding but following very different contractual structures to traditional auctions should be treated differently from their offline, physical counterparts however. Providing a right to renege on a deal made through an online auction at will potentially renders the outcome and indeed the involvement of genuine bid-placers in it, a farce.

2.4   JURISDICTION

Every contract may form the basis of a dispute. Because the Internet allows an owner of a website to conduct transactions with consumers and businesses from anywhere on the planet it is convenient for that owner to know where he can rightfully sue and be sued. The question over where a contract should be litigated is a question of private international law, or the conflict of laws. It should also be remembered of course that the question as to where proceedings may be brought must be considered separately from questions of enforcement and the law which will govern such proceedings (issues covered in subsequent sections).

For the purpose of jurisdiction, it is important to consider first whether or not the parties to the contract made express provision as to which courts will hear a dispute and to establish the geographical elements relevant to the dispute in question in order to determine which rules need to be looked at and will determine the jurisdiction where no such binding choice was made. The Brussels Regulation on Jurisdiction and the Enforcement of Judgments in Civil and Commercial Matters is the appropriate starting place for any contract formed over the Internet involving other European member states (Denmark signing up in 2007).[121] For European Free Trade Association (EFTA) countries, Switzerland, Iceland and Norway (with the exception of Liechtenstein), similar rules under the Lugano Convention regulate jurisdiction and enforcement issues. If outside of these, then English common law rules will apply.

First, therefore, one must assess whether the Brussels Regulation or Lugano Convention apply or whether it 'transfers' jurisdiction to the English common

---

120   BGH Utreil v. 3 November 2004 – VIII ZR 375/03.
121   This entered into force, replacing the Brussels Convention, on 1 March 2002 (2001 OJ L012, 16.01.2001).

law and then to assess, accordingly what rules apply which will largely depend on whether the parties made an express choice and on the nature of the contract itself.

2.4.1 Brussels regulation and Lugano Convention

2.4.1.1 Civil and commercial matter

Most contracts made over the Internet will fall within art 1, that is, the resulting dispute is a civil and commercial matter. Before deciding that the Regulation applies, litigants are advised to consider specialist texts and cases from the European Court which highlight the broad scope of art 1 under the previous 1968 Brussels Convention.

2.4.1.2 Domicile of defendant

Subject to articles outside the scope of this chapter, the fundamental issue for the purposes of the Regulations and Lugano Convention is where the defendant is domiciled. Article 2 establishes that persons domiciled in a member state[122] can be sued in the courts of that state, sometimes with the claimant having a choice of another forum. Articles 59 and 60 direct the English courts to consider the domicile of the defendant with reference to the UK's 'internal law'.[123] Even for e-commerce contracts, jurisdiction hinges on 'domicile', an essentially static concept which is mostly unrelated to the complex factors such as where a server is based.[124]

For Regulation purposes, a defendant can be domiciled in one of two types of state: a member state or a non-member state. If the defendant is domiciled within a member state, the Regulation rules apply; if outside, the common law rules or the rules of the Lugano Convention will apply. These two outcomes are decided, currently, with reference to the Civil Jurisdiction and Judgments Act 1982, as amended.

2.4.1.2.1 Individual's domicile

UK domicile

An individual is domiciled within the UK only if he is resident in the UK and the nature and circumstances of his residence indicate that he has a substantial connection with the UK.[125] It is presumed, unless proved otherwise, that being resident for the last three months or more will constitute the requisite substantial

---

122 I.e. any member state and excluding Switzerland, Iceland and Norway which (as EFTA countries) apply the rules of the 1988 Lugano Convention.

123 The Civil Jurisdiction and Judgments Act 1982 (as amended by both the Civil Jurisdiction and Judgments Act 1991 and the Civil Jurisdiction and Judgments Order 2001), ss 4 and 42.

124 Prescribed as being relevant tests by the Civil Procedure Rules 1998, rr 6.18(g) and 6.19(1).

125 Civil Jurisdiction and Judgments Act 1982 (as amended by both the Civil Jurisdiction and Judgments Act 1991 and the Civil Jurisdiction and Judgments Order 2001), s 41(2).

connection.[126] The ownership, control or access to a website anywhere in the world is wholly irrelevant for the purposes of jurisdiction over an individual under the Regulation. If an individual is a UK resident nothing will be gained for jurisdiction purposes by locating a web server 'offshore'.

Member state or EFTA state domicile

If an individual is not domiciled in the UK for the purposes of the Regulation, one must decide whether the individual is domiciled within another member state. If he is not domiciled in a member state, the Regulation will not apply to the dispute.

An individual is domiciled in a state other than the UK if that other state would view him as domiciled in that state. Therefore, to determine whether a defendant in an Internet contract dispute is domiciled within a member state that person's domicile must be assessed from that state's legal perspective.[127] Failing this, the Civil Jurisdiction and Judgments Act 1982 (as amended), s 41(7) establishes the test to determine whether a defendant is domiciled outside member states. For those domiciled in EFTA countries (other than Liechtenstein), the Lugano Convention applies similar rules.

Non-member state or EFTA state domicile

An individual is domiciled outside all the EFTA and EU member states if none of those states would deem him to be domiciled within their jurisdiction and if a further two-part test is satisfied. First, the individual must be resident in the non-member state, and second, the nature and circumstances of his residence indicate that he has a substantial connection with that state.[128] One is not required to consult the non-member state's law on domicile.

---

16.   An English programmer who lives in England allows downloads of his shareware programs to be made from an American web server. Another programmer, also from England, appropriately transfers his digital cash payment for the software but does not receive a working copy of the software and so litigates. Without a jurisdiction clause in the contract, the English courts will have jurisdiction over the dispute as the defendant is domiciled in England. The location of the server is of no relevance for jurisdiction over the programmer in the English courts.

If the result of the domicile tests is that an individual defendant is domiciled within a member state, the Regulation will apply to any other questions of jurisdiction. If the result is that the defendant is domiciled outside the member states, the English common law rules on jurisdiction will apply.[129] These are described after the Regulation regime.[130]

---

126   Civil Jurisdiction and Judgments Act 1982 (as amended by both the Civil Jurisdiction and Judgments Act 1991 and the Civil Jurisdiction and Judgments Order 2001), s 41(6).
127   Brussels Regulation, art 59 (2).
128   Civil Jurisdiction and Judgments Act 1982 (as amended by both the Civil Jurisdiction and Judgments Act 1991 and the Civil Jurisdiction and Judgments Order 2001), s 41(7).
129   Art 4.
130   See 'Common law jurisdiction over contracts', at p 66.

2.1.1.2.2. Company's or other legal person's domicile

A company or other legal person has its domicile in the state where it has its statutory seat, or central administration, or principal place of business.[131] A sole trader or partner in a business being sued on his own can be sued where his principal residence is (see the rules for individuals above).

UK domicile

A company or other legal person is domiciled within the UK if it was incorporated or formed under a law of a part of the UK, and its registered office or other official address is in the UK; or if its central administration or principal place of business is in the UK.[132] Again, the ownership, control or access to a website anywhere in the world is mostly irrelevant for the purposes of jurisdiction under the Regulation. A corporation which is, in effect, based in the UK will not be able to avoid the jurisdiction of the English courts simply by using an offshore server.

Member state or EFTA state domicile

If a company or other legal person is not domiciled in the UK for the purposes of the Regulation, one must decide whether it is domiciled within another member state or EFTA state. If it is not, the Regulation or Lugano Convention will not apply to the dispute; questions of jurisdiction are decided with recourse to the common law. A company or other legal person is domiciled in a state other than the UK if it satisfies two tests.

First, the English courts must be satisfied that the company or other legal person was incorporated or formed under the law of that other member state, or, its central management and control is exercised in that state.[133]

The second test that must also be affirmatively answered, is that the entity shall not have been incorporated or formed under the law of a part of the UK, or, shown not to be regarded by the courts of the other member state or EFTA state to have its seat within that member state.[134] If either test is not satisfied, the common law rules on jurisdiction will apply[135]; these are discussed after the Regulation rules.

---

17. A health-food company is incorporated and operates from England. It sells edible flowers across the world. Its server is physically based in New Zealand and the domain name has a suffix indicating a New Zealand firm. A French supplier of health food enters into a contract, over the Internet, for a large shipment of particular sweet edible flowers. The contract does not have a jurisdiction clause. The flowers do not arrive and the health-food company claims it is not at fault. The French supplier tries to sue the

---

131   Art 60(1).
132   Civil Jurisdiction and Judgments Act 1982 (as amended by both the Civil Jurisdiction and Judgments Act 1991 and the Civil Jurisdiction and Judgments Order 2001), s 42(2).
133   Civil Jurisdiction and Judgments Act 1982 (as amended by both the Civil Jurisdiction and Judgments Act 1991 and the Civil Jurisdiction and Judgments Order 2001), s 43(3).
134   Civil Jurisdiction and Judgments Act 1982 (as amended by both the Civil Jurisdiction and Judgments Act 1991 and the Civil Jurisdiction and Judgments Order 2001), s 43(4).
135   Art 4.

company in the English courts. The use of an offshore server will have no bearing on the court's jurisdiction over the company. The English courts will have jurisdiction over the company at least for the reason that it would consider the company as having its seat within England.

Non-member state or EFTA state domicile

If both of the previous tests fail to establish the defendant as domiciled in the UK or another member state or EFTA state, the common law rules on jurisdiction will apply.

2.4.1.3   Regulation jurisdiction over contract

Having decided that the Regulation or Lugano Convention applies (all involving 'contracting states'), unless the contract is classed as a consumer, insurance or employment contract or unless the contract has a jurisdiction clause, the defendant may be sued in the courts of his domicile[136] or 'in the courts for the place of performance of the obligation in question'.[137]

2.4.1.4   Place of performance for sale of goods or supply of services

For sales of goods and supplies of services unless agreed otherwise, there are two presumptions as to the place of their performance. Where goods are sold (or should have been sold) under contract, the relevant court is in the place in a contracting state where the goods were delivered or should have been delivered. In the case of services, a similar approach must be followed. The relevant court is the one in the contracting state where the services were provided or should have been provided.[138] If neither presumption applies, one must look to resolve the more general question of where was the 'place of performance of the obligation in question'.[139]

18. A website called StockTaken.de operates from and is based in Germany. It allows business users to specify what industrial equipment they need and at what price. Once sufficient numbers of buyers have pledged an interest in particular equipment, an invoice is issued to the buyers and the equipment shipped to them. There is no jurisdiction clause in the agreements between StockTaken.de and its buyers. A business in England receives the equipment it ordered, faulty. Despite StockTaken.de being based in Germany, it may be sued in the English courts as its principal obligation, breached, must have been to deliver non-defective equipment in England.[140]

---

136   Art 2(1).
137   Art 5(1)(a).
138   Art 5(1)(b).
139   Art 5(1)(c).
140   See *MBM Fabri Clad Ltd v Eisen Und Huntle werke Thale AG* (3 November 1999, unreported), CA.

19. OurFastParts.com operates an EU business-to-business website allowing its members to barter parts for vehicles. No money changes hands. One member, the Seller, lists the parts he wants to 'sell' and other members, the Buyers, will bid for those parts using their own parts which they want to sell. After a certain period, the Seller may conclude his barter with a Buyer. To avoid disputes about which is the relevant court for this bilateral delivery of goods, the member agreement states that 'the Parties irrevocably agree that for the purposes of the Brussels Regulation, Article 5, the place of performance of the obligation to trade the Parts shall be the place in the Member State where the Seller delivered or should have delivered his Parts'.

2.4.1.5 Other obligations

Where the contract does not relate to sales of goods or supplies of services, one must concentrate on the 'obligation in question'. Lord Goff puts this as 'regard must be had to the contractual obligation under consideration and not to the contract as a whole'.[141] This may result in a court which does not have the closest connection with the dispute being seized of the action. It should therefore be obvious that the pleading of the contractual claim, or rather, the principal contractual obligation, is critical to any question of jurisdiction. Further, advisers should note that to determine what is the principal obligation, they might rely on what law would apply to the obligation.[142]

Europe-based owners of websites who are concerned about being sued outside their home state should therefore be concerned to have jurisdiction clauses in their contracts if their principal obligations must be performed outside their home state[143] or if their e-commerce agreements are with consumers. As will be discussed, consumers can sue and can only be sued in their home state.[144] As many of the users of the Internet are consumers but the majority of website owners are suppliers or professionals, this application of jurisdiction will frequently occur. Those who own websites, therefore, may find themselves having to litigate and be sued away from home.

---

141 *Union Transport plc v Continental Lines SA* [1992] 1 WLR 15 at 19H, referring to *Etablissements A de Bloos SPRL v Societes en Commandité par Actions Bayer* (Case 14/76) [1976] ECR 1497. Also see *Custom Made Commercial Ltd v Stawa Metallban GmbH* (C–288/92) [1994] ECR I–2913, paras 14–23 and *Barry v Bradshaw and Co (a firm)* [2000] CLC 455, CA. Note the reluctance of Lord Justice Pitt to accept that: 'When a professional man is instructed to perform services in one jurisdiction he becomes liable to another Brussels Convention jurisdiction if the services include dealing with a public authority in that other jurisdiction.'

142 *Industrie Tessili Italiana Corp v Dunlop* (Case 12/76) [1976] ECR 1473, para 13; *Custom Made Commercial Ltd v Stawa Metallban GmbH* (C–288/92) [1994] ECR I–2913, para.26; *GIE Groupe Concorde v Master of Vessel Suhadiwarno Panjan* (C–440/97) [1999] ECR I–6307, para 32; *Leathertex Divisione Sinitetici SpA v Bodetex BVBA* (C–420/97) [1999] 2 All ER (Comm) 769.

143 See *MBM Fabri Clad Ltd v Eisen Und Huntle werke Thale AG* (3 November 1999, unreported), CA.

144 Arts 15, 16 and 17.

2.4.1.6   Consumer contracts

At first glance it may appear there is a straightforward answer to the question of which is the correct forum for a dispute over a contract made with a consumer. The Brussels Regulation contains rules to protect consumers in relation to consumer contracts, from being sued, or having to sue, otherwise than in the member state of their domicile.[145] What is important is that art 15 of the Brussels Regulation defines a 'consumer contract', inter alia, as one concluded which can be regarded as being outside the consumer's trade or profession[146] where the contract is:

(a)   for the sale of goods on instalment credit terms; or[147]

(b)   for a loan repayable by instalments, or for any other form[148] of credit, made to finance the sale of goods; or

(c)   in all other cases, the contract has been concluded with a person who pursues commercial or professional activities in the member state of the consumer's domicile, or, by any means, directs such activities to that state or the several states including that state, and the contract falls within the scope of such activities.[149]

Article 15(1)(c) was introduced into the Brussels Regulation. It broadened the definition of a consumer contract which existed under art 13 of the Brussels Convention and which still exists in the Lugano Convention. These refer to the conclusion of the contract being preceded by a specific invitation addressed to the consumer or by advertising and where the consumer took steps necessary for the conclusion of that contract. The reason for the new concept of 'consumer contract' was to ensure that consumers who transact, for example, over the Internet are protected by the special rules on jurisdiction[150].

Articles 15(1)(a) and (b) are self-explanatory and not 'Internet' specific. The same is not true for art 15(1)(c). This new addition to the Brussels rules of jurisdiction was meant to provide certainty to consumer and to businesses. As the following discussion will illustrate, it does not. Fortunately there are steps that businesses can take to minimise the risk of being sued in a member state other than their own or one acceptable to them.

---

145   Brussels Convention, arts 13 and 14, and the Brussels Regulation, arts 15 and 16. The Civil Jurisdiction and Judgments Act 1982, s 8(1) and 8(2) (as amended by the Civil Jurisdiction and Judgments Order 2001) specifies that, in the UK, the courts where a consumer must be sued and can sue are those in the 'part' of the UK where they are domiciled. At the time of writing the three parts are: England and Wales, Scotland and Northern Ireland.

146   Brussels Regulation, art 15(1).

147   Brussels Regulation, art 15(1)(a).

148   Brussels Regulation, art 15(1)(b).

149   Brussels Regulation, art 15(1)(c).

150   See, for example, the various speakers reported in the Department of Trade and Industry's Consumer Affairs Report on the Revision of the Brussels Convention and the Proposals for a Community Regulation (2 November 1999).

The express right of a consumer to bring an action in their home jurisdiction under art 15(1)(c) of the Brussels Regulation can apply in two situations. First, where the supplier 'pursues commercial or professional activities in the member state of the consumer's domicile and the contract falls within the scope of such activities'. The second situation is where the supplier 'by any means directs commercial or professional activities to the member state of the consumer's domicile or to several States including that member state and the contract falls within the scope of such activities'. These two situations will be examined separately.

2.4.1.6.1 Pursuing activities in consumer's member state

A key aspect to this situation is that the contract being litigated must fall within the scope of the activities being pursued in the member state of the consumer's domicile. This is important. Many businesses conduct a great number of commercial and professional activities abroad. A website may promote employment opportunities for individuals living in the member state. Glossy advertisements in financial newspapers within that member state may also promote the business in a wider sense. On paper, the business may appeal to current and potential shareholders and stakeholders in the business. The business may also regularly attend trade fairs and exhibitions in the member state to illustrate the business's success, almost as a way to ward off competitors. And all these activities may be actively pursued within the consumer's member state.

What art 15(1)(c) requires, however, is something more. The pursuit of the activities within the consumer's member state *must relate* to the consumer's contract under dispute.[151]

---

20. Ratty-Ionise is an Italian company that operates a website selling its biochemical, free-standing, air-conditioning unit. The unit is expensive but is very popular in small offices in London. Ratty-Ionise regularly attend trade shows in the UK where it communicates with its local distributors. Without any other activity in the UK, consumers who order a unit for their home will not benefit from the additional protection afforded by the Brussels Regulation.

Many European businesses will wish to be selective as to which member states' jurisdictions they are subject. These businesses must examine *all* of their activities within each particular contracting member state of concern. They will need to ensure that any contracts entered into with consumers in that contracting member state are not related to any other commercial or professional activities pursued in those member states.

---

151 The European Council and Commission's Joint Statement on arts 15 and 68 states that 'for Article 15.1(c) to be applicable it is not sufficient for an undertaking to target it's [*sic*] activities at the member state of the consumer's residence, or at a number of member states including that member state; a contract must also be concluded within the framework of it's [*sic*] activities'.

2.4.1.6.2   By any means directs activities to several member states

This second leg of art 15(1)(c) begs the obvious question: when is a website 'directed' to several member states? Ultimately, it will be for the courts to decide this on a case-by-case basis. In the meantime, however, readers will not be helped by consulting the European Council, European Commission and DTI's musings on the issue. The Joint Statement issued by the European Council and Commission states:

> 'the mere fact that an Internet site is accessible is not sufficient for Article 15 to be applicable, although a factor will be that this Internet site solicits the conclusion of distance contracts and that a contract has actually been concluded at a distance, by whatever means. In this respect, the language or currency which a website uses does not constitute a relevant factor.'

One takes from this that it is the conduct of commerce in the member state that determines whether or not activities are directed to that member state. If those from the UK, for instance, cannot *transact* with the site (but can still view it) it would seem that the Council and Commission deem this not to be 'directed' at the UK. And this is even the case if the site is written in English and uses pounds sterling and not euros. This can be contrasted with the DTI's more e-commerce-friendly interpretation:

> 'We believe that [to determine whether a website falls within Article 15(1)(c)]:
>
> • it would be necessary to look at the nature of any given website;
>
> • websites giving information in different Community languages and currencies and offering to deliver to EU countries might well be covered by Article 15;
>
> • some websites (e.g. a site in English with prices in pounds and confining orders to UK customers) might be hard to describe as directed anywhere but the UK.'

The DTI here appears to be taking a narrower view than the European Council and Commission. It is essentially concluding that the mere fact that a transaction takes place on a site does not mean that the site has been directed at any particular member state. It is the 'nature' of the website that determines where, if anywhere, it is directed.

These are very different approaches. The Council and Commission explain that one must avoid *transacting* with consumers in a particular member state; the DTI explains that one must avoid *appealing* to consumers in a particular Member State. This author sides with the DTI. Its interpretation is likely to be closer to a court's. The article speaks of 'commercial and professional activities' being directed to the member state. It therefore is focused not particularly on the *contract* but on the *pre*-contractual enticement.

On this basis, how does one structure a website to avoid the bite of art 15(1)(c)? It is not trivial. Nevertheless, steps can be taken to reduce a business's chance of transacting over the Internet with consumers within a particular member state. First, the business can operate a website which requests the user's jurisdiction from a 'drop-down' menu or a series of flags. This allows the business to shield out a consumer from a particular country. More sophisticated still, a business can make technical checks of the user's computer and connecting server. For example, the business can check for the server time zone and the language setting of the user's browser. In addition, the business can conduct a 'reverse DNS lookup' where the domain name of the user's service provider is used to locate the server. Not one of these steps is foolproof. Combined, however, these checks can provide a reasonable approximation of whether the user is based in a 'friendly' member state. If they are not based in the 'friendly' member states make sure not to transact with them after they access the site.

---

21 'NotWeeMen' is a company arranging adventure activities in the Scottish Highlands. The company has two main types of clientele: businesses conducting 'away days' in the UK and men arranging stag nights in Glasgow city centre. It ensures that all of its advertising outside the UK is about 'corporate bonding' and is contained in business journals. Its website, in contrast, solely describes the stag activities, is written only in English and features a price list of 'stag activities' in pounds sterling. It also details the various trains and planes that fly from around the UK to Glasgow. The company does not pursue the 'stag' activities in the EU by virtue of its advertising.

2.4.1.7 Jurisdiction clauses: express choice

Parties to a contract are generally free to choose which court(s) will consider any disputes arising under the contract. An English court will usually regard a court in a member state or an EFTA state as having exclusive jurisdiction over a dispute where the parties to a contract have prescribed it in the contract.[152] However, there are a few twists and exceptions to parties' right to choose.

Contracts involving consumers, or even employees or in rare cases, where a local court is deemed to have special expertise for the matter in question, may have a different outcome regardless of what the parties have agreed. The position in relation to consumer contracts where a ''jurisdiction clause can only add to but not derogate from the protection afforded to consumers[153] is set out below.

In addition, two recent European Court of Justice (ECJ) cases have cast a significant shadow on the comfort that exclusive jurisdiction clauses may previously have given, even where the exceptions set out above do not apply. Both cases concerned the application of art 27 of the Brussels Regulation, which provides that, where proceedings regarding the same cause of action are brought in the courts of different contracting states, any court other that the court first seized of the action should stay proceedings until the first court has established jurisdiction, following which the other court must decline it. In the case of *Erich Gasser GmbH v MISAT SRL*,[154] MISAT brought proceedings in the Italian courts against Erich Gasser despite the inclusion of an exclusive jurisdiction clause in the contract between them in respect of the Austrian courts. Gasser brought proceedings

---

152   Brussels Regulation, art 23(1).
153   Brussels Regulation, art 17. Also see *Benincasa v Dentalkit Srl* [1998] All ER (EC) 136.
154   *Erich Gasser GmbH v MISAT SRL* [2003] All ER (D) 148 (Dec).

seven months later in the Austrian courts claiming exclusive jurisdiction pursuant to art 23 of the Brussels Regulation. The ECJ held that the Austrian courts had to stay proceedings whilst the Italian courts decided whether or not they had jurisdiction, despite the parties' previous express choice.

This decision was endorsed in the case of *Turner v Grovit*,[155] in which the ECJ held that anti-suit injunctions (interim orders preventing another party from pursuing parallel proceedings in a foreign court) were incompatible with the Brussels Convention as relates to contracting states.

The conclusion from these two cases is that parties may now bring proceedings quickly in a foreign court for tactical reasons, despite being bound to a contractual agreement only to bring an action in another court in order to frustrate actions being brought there. Even though the initial proceedings may ultimately fail, this requires the other party to contest it and will, at the very least, lead to increased cost and wasted time.

---

22. A UK consumer downloads some software from a French website after selecting an icon labelled 'I Agree' at the bottom of a set of terms and conditions. The contract makes clear that no goods are being sent to the consumer and that, anyway, no title passes to the consumer; the consumer is gaining only a licence to use the software. The final clause of the contract, in capitals, is 'By clicking "I Agree", you submit to the French courts to resolve any dispute arising under or related to this licence'. The consumer at a later date seeks to sue in an English court the owner of the website for breach of contract as the software is defective. The French website owner may have some success in preventing the English courts from accepting jurisdiction because the contract was a licence of software not a contract for a sale of goods or supply of services. As a result the jurisdiction clause may apply despite the contract being with a consumer.

2.4.1.8   Common law jurisdiction over contracts

If the defendant to an Internet contract is not domiciled within a contracting state,[156] the court must apply its domestic laws to determine jurisdiction.[157] The main method is considered below: service out of the jurisdiction with permission. The aspect of this is jurisdiction to serve out the next, the application of the courts' discretion.[158] Service by presence in England is not considered in any detail[159]; readers are advised to consult more general texts on private international law.

2.4.1.8.1   Service out

There are two separate and distinct aspects to serving out of the jurisdiction.[160] The first aspect is jurisdiction: does the claimant's claim fall within one of the

---

155   *Turner v Grovit* [2004] All ER (EC) 485.
156   See 'Domicile of defendant', at p 57.
157   Art 4.
158   See 'Discretion under service out', at p 69.
159   See CPR, r 6.2
160   See *Seaconsar v Bank Merkazi Jomhouri Islami Iran* [1994] 1 AC 438, which applied, and it is suggested remains applicable, under the old Rules of the Supreme Court, Ord 11.

sub-rules of CPR r 6.20(5) and (6). Although not yet deeply analysed by the courts, it is likely that this test does not need to be satisfied to any high degree of proof: a good arguable case that the claim is covered by one of the sub-rules is probably sufficient.[161] The second aspect, which will not be covered here in great detail, is one of discretion: no permission to serve a claim out of the jurisdiction will be given unless the court is satisfied that England and Wales is the proper place in which to bring the claim. This is specified by CPR r 6.21(2A).

Jurisdiction under a contract sub-rule

The most common sub-rules that will apply in certain cases for e-commerce contracts entered over the Internet is CPR r 6.20(5). This is where[162]:

> 'a claim is made in respect of a contract where the contract. . .'

The rule then goes on to describe a number of contracts which will fall for consideration under this rule. These include: a contract made within the jurisdiction; a contract made by or through an agent trading or residing within the jurisdiction; a contract containing a term that the court shall have jurisdiction to determine any claim made in respect of a breach of contract within the jurisdiction. For the purposes of Internet contracts, however, the most contentious rule is where the contract was made within the jurisdiction.

Where a contract is made

The earlier part of this chapter focuses on when a contract is deemed to have been made when formed by email or over the web. It is now appropriate to consider *where* such a contract is formed. The implications of where a contract is formed are great. For example, if contracts made over the web are made at the place of the server it will be simple for an organisation always to ensure that their contracts are formed outside Europe, or any other jurisdiction they wish to avoid. A server can be physically located anywhere in the world despite its owner and clients being elsewhere. Conversely, if a contract is deemed to be formed wherever a consumer is situated at the time of making a contract the owner of a website may find himself making contracts throughout the world.

There is no case law on this area although by analogy it is submitted that contracts made using email will be viewed as being made where the acceptance (not acknowledgement) email is sent and contracts made over the web will be viewed as being made where the client is located.

Email contracts

It has been suggested that an emailed acceptance is very like a posted acceptance in the eyes of the law: it can go astray and it depends on the actions of a third party for proper delivery without the sender necessarily knowing of its arrival.[163]

---

161 See *Attock Cement Co Ltd v Romanian Bank for Foreign Trade* [1989] 1 All ER 1189, which applied, and it is suggested remains still applicable, under the old Rules of the Supreme Court, Ord 11.
162 Of course, CPR r 6.20(1) and r 6.20(8) may be more appropriate in some circumstances.
163 See 'Acceptances by email', at p 39.

In such circumstances this chapter has suggested that the exception should apply to the general rule of 'communication of acceptance': the so-called 'postal rule' should apply deeming the time of making the contract the time of its posting, not its receipt. It follows that the contract is completed when the letter is posted, or for our purposes, when the email is sent. This author's view is that the Electronic Commerce Regulations add little to the private international law question of where a contract is formed.[164]

The 'postal rule' also applies if an acceptance is not simply delayed in the post but if the acceptance never reaches the offeror.[165] It must therefore be true that the contract is also made at that place of posting; if this were not the case, a letter which becomes lost in the post may be deemed to form a contract at a place where it was meant to arrive at a time before it could have arrived and, in fact, at a place where it never arrives. To avoid such fictions, the rule applied by the English courts has been that 'acceptance is complete as soon as the letter is put into the letter box, and that is the place where the contract is made'.[166]

For a contract made purely using email, it is submitted that the place where the contract is made is the place from where the acceptor sent the email; it is not from where the server which sends the email is located. Just as a postal contract is made from the place at which the acceptor no longer has control over the letter, i.e. the letterbox, so the place where an email contract is made is at the acceptor's computer.

---

23.   An American, who uses a German Internet Service Provider, sends an email to an English property developer. The email contains a certain offer to buy the individual's holiday home in Florida. The English property developer firmly accepts the offer by sending an email from his London offices. Technically, this email acceptance is sent from London, to a French server and then on to the American's inbox located in Germany. The American reads the email using a laptop computer and a mobile phone while in Mexico. If the contract is deemed to be formed when the English email was sent, it will be formed at the place where it was sent: London.

Website contracts

Contracts made over the web, as previously examined, differ considerably from email contracts.[167] On the assumption made earlier that the general rule applies, and that there is no binding contract until notice of acceptance is able to be accessed by the offeror, the contract is made at the place where the offeror could receive notification of the acceptance; where the offeror is.[168]

---

164   See Electronic Commerce Regulations 2002, reg 5 and Electronic Commerce Directive, art 1(4).
165   See *Household Fire and Carriage Accident, Insurance v Grant* (1879) 4 Ex D 216.
166   *Entores Ltd v Miles Far East Corpn* [1955] 2 QB 327 at 332, per Denning LJ. See also *Benaim v Debono* [1924] AC 514. This common law rule should be contrasted with the Electronic Commerce (EC Directive) Regulations 2002, reg 11(2) which specifies *when* an order (which may be the acceptance) is deemed to be received.
167   See 'Acceptances over the Web', at p 41.
168   See *Entores v Miles Far East Corpn* [1955] 2 QB 327 at 336 per Parker LJ; also *Brinkibon Ltd v Stahag Stahl GmbH* [1983] 2 AC 34 at 41 and 43 respectively, per Lord Wilberforce and Lord Fraser.

24. A bookseller based in Chicago establishes a website within a portal which is based in New York. The portal uses a standardised online order form which ensures users make offers which are then accepted, if appropriate, by the individual stores. A teacher in England orders two books by American authors and the website responds with an acceptance notice that the books would be delivered to the teacher's address. This contract is made in England because the notification of acceptance, to the teacher, is received in England.

The conclusion that a website 'makes' contracts wherever its customers are, assuming the website accepts and properly acknowledges acceptance, accords with the case law and also accords with the business reality of the web. The web, more than any other medium, allows vendors from around the world to sell easily to English consumers. For a vendor, it is akin to having an agent in every town in the world who can visit every customer at home. A user only needs to make a local phone call to and receive acceptances from foreign vendors at home. The contracts being formed have every indication that they are being made in England.

The reason for discussing where a contract is made, it will be recalled, was to demonstrate that an English consumer could serve a claim form out of England to a foreign website owner in respect of a contract. However, even if a dispute falls within one of the sub-rules under CPR r 6.20 a court has discretion whether to permit the service out.

Discretion under service out

It is not sufficient simply to satisfy a court of a good arguable case under one of the sub-rules under CPR r 6.20. The claim must also be a proper case for service out under CPR r 6.21(1). The discretion to serve out includes as a main factor, an assessment, perhaps not overtly, of whether England is the *forum conveniens*, the most suitable forum in which to hear the dispute. This will be considered briefly in the following section on staying actions.[169] This discretionary factor should not be overlooked by legal advisers: for a contract made over the Internet it may be difficult to persuade a court to serve out. If the defendant, in contrast, is domiciled in Europe, the court has far less discretion over jurisdiction.[170]

2.4.1.8.2 Staying actions

It is always open to a putative defendant to apply to stay the common law jurisdiction of the English courts by pleading that it is not the most suitable forum in which to resolve the dispute.[171] Whether a court stays an action is decided with recourse to the principle of *forum non conveniens*. This principle is impressively

---

169 The court's assessment is the same, although for service out, the claimant must ask the court to exercise discretion; for staying service as of right, the defendant must persuade the court to stay the action.
170 See the Court of Appeal's interpretation of the Civil Jurisdiction and Judgments Act 1982, s 49 in *Re Harrods (Buenos Aires) Ltd* [1992] Ch 72.
171 CPR, Pt 11 provides the necessary procedure.

explained and stated in the House of Lords decision in *Spiliada Maritime Corpn v Cansulex Ltd.*[172] In a later case Lord Goff explains *forum non conveniens* as 'a self-denying ordinance under which the court will stay (or dismiss) proceedings in favour of another clearly more appropriate forum'.[173] A full discussion of this case is beyond the scope of this chapter, but an appreciation of its implications is worthwhile. Until courts approach electronic commerce and Internet disputes with the familiarity and understanding that they approach, say the telephone and telex, litigators must be prepared to argue that despite the transnational nature of the Internet, some forums are more suitable than others.

Lord Goff provided the leading judgment given in *Spiliada*. He set out a number of guidelines[174] that may guide a court as to whether England is a suitable and appropriate forum: the court must, in effect, balance the suitability of England against that of another forum. This forum must be clearly and distinctly more appropriate: one 'with which the action [has] the most real and substantial connection'.[175] At this point, 'the court may nevertheless decline to grant a stay if persuaded by the claimant, on whom the burden of proof then lies, that justice requires that a stay should not be granted'.[176]

This discretion, unlikely to be disturbed on appeal,[177] may be of paramount importance in an Internet dispute. In contrast to most other means of communication, the Internet can make it appear that a defendant has little connection with any country. A server may be in a country far away from the defendant's domicile. Worse than this, a defendant may be using a hosting company situated on the other side of the world. The contract and possibly digital product that is the root of the dispute may have passed through as many as one hundred countries. Worse still, it is a question of technical semantics to resolve whether the digital product moved from the server to the claimant or whether the claimant 'collected' the digital product from the server.

These issues, and many more like them, may be used to cloud the answer to which is the forum conveniens for the dispute. The pivotal question before the courts should be: which is the suitable forum in the interests of all the parties and the ends of justice?

The answering of this question involves examining the mechanics of hearing the dispute as well as its geographical basis. In illustration, often it is important to know where the relevant evidence is held and where the relevant witnesses live.[178] For many Internet disputes, however, such factors may not be weighty enough to disturb the jurisdiction of the court. Computer files will often be the main evidence and often the party in England will be the sole human witness to the contract itself. So, for an Internet dispute, the jurisdiction of the English court

---

172   [1987] AC 460.
173   *Airbus Industrie GIE v Patel* [1999] 1 AC 119 at 132C.
174   The necessary details of these guidelines can be found in specialist texts but readers are also directed to the very full judgments in *Lubbe v Cape plc* [2001] 1 Lloyd's Rep 139, CA.
175   *The Abidin Daver* [1984] 1 All ER 470, at 478 per Lord Keith.
176   *Conelly v RTZ Corpn plc* [1998] AC 854 at 872A, per Lord Goff for the House of Lords restating the second stage of the *Spiliada* test.
177   [1986] 3 All ER 843 at 846–847 per Lord Templeman.
178   See [1986] 3 All ER 843 at 855.

may be less easily upset. As a further illustration, the issue of convenience, often a factor for the court, may be less convincing when all of the actual evidence is in a digital format. Such evidence can be sent to England, over the Internet, cheaply, quickly and accurately. Again, the actual nature of the Internet may lead to the conclusion that little is lost by hearing the dispute in England.

The court must consider all the relevant factors, such as where the defendant and claimant are and which law will apply to this dispute. It is discussed in the next section that, without a choice of law clause, English law will generally apply to contracts made over the web with English consumers. Even with a choice of law clause, protection for English consumers will apply in addition to the stated law. And Lord Goff in *Spiliada* notes that the law of the dispute will often be a relevant factor.[179] What can be concluded from all this is that presence of the Internet in a contract dispute will never create the situation where no court is appropriate to hear the case.

2.5   CHOICE OF LAW

Even as long ago as 1980, debates were commencing around the problems of examining the choice of law over computer networks such as the Internet[180]:

> '[T]he question of choice of law. . . is particularly difficult in the case of international computer networks where, because of dispersed location and rapid movement of data, and geographically dispersed processing activities, several connecting factors could occur in a complex manner involving elements of legal novelty.'

The following section is included because the Internet makes the questions of choice of laws more prevalent. As e-commerce expands, more contracts will be formed between parties in different jurisdictions.[181] It is essential that the law which applies to a contract is established before applying the reasoning in this chapter. Readers must not be confused into concluding that the Electronic Commerce Directive, and its implementing Electronic Commerce (EC Directive) Regulations 2002, address these questions of private international

---

179   With reference *to Crédit Chimique v James Scott Engineering Group Ltd* 1982 SLT 131. In this Scottish case, Lord Jauncy goes further and asks that a court look not simply at the fact that foreign law will be applied, but to look deeper at the nature of the foreign law. It may be that it is trivial for an English court to turn its mind to the foreign law, but it also may be that the law is so alien that the most appropriate court to consider the legal issues is a court which regularly deals with them.

180   Organisation for Economic Co-operation and Development, Explanatory Memorandum, Guidelines on the Protection of Privacy and Transborder Flows of Personal Data, 13, 36 (1980).

181   It is, of course, correct to state that the telephone, telex and fax also allow transnational contracts to be made. The significant difference between the Internet and these other means of communication is that there are no temporal, financial or logistical problems with contacting a website abroad. The site is permanently switched on, time differences are not a relevant factor; the cost may be no more than that of a local phone call, and there is no increase in marginal cost, unlike fax, telex and telephone.

law. First, they only apply to those Information Service Providers which are established within the EEA. Second, the statutes certainly do not determine which country's *law* will apply in a given situation. They merely prevent an Information Service Provider established in a member state outside the UK being restricted from conducting activities inside the UK which would have been legal in their member state.[182] This section therefore describes nothing wider than the application of English law to a contract.

2.5.1   The Rome Convention

Where the litigation over a dispute takes place in England, and its substance is a contractual obligation made over the Internet, the Rome Convention[183] will generally apply.[184] This section is concerned mainly with those contracts where one party contracts using a website. Before considering the Convention in greater detail one must address the obvious, and logically, first question: what is a contract? The answer is not merely that which English law considers to be a contract. The laws of some other Convention countries do not demand 'consideration' or 'privity'. As a consequence, courts (and litigants before them) 'must clearly strive to take a single, international or "autonomous" view of the concept of contractual obligations ...'[185] and not merely rely on an English-law view of a contract.

For the purposes of the Rome Convention, and therefore English law, there are two possible types of contract that can be made over the Internet: one in which the law that will govern the contract is agreed, and one in which it is not. These two possibilities will be dealt with, but it is worthwhile noting here that there is little justification for not including an applicable law in a contract. It provides more certainty, and some insurance policies will only protect claims under contracts governed by English law.

---

182   Reg 4.
183   The Rome Convention is incorporated into the Contracts (Applicable Law) Act 1990. References to articles within the Convention can be located in the Schedules to the domestic statute. The Convention can be interpreted by recourse to the Giuliano and Lagarde report (OJ 1980, C282/10), see the Contracts (Applicable Law) Act 1990, s 3(3)(a).
184   The justification for this bold statement is that the Convention applies to contracts made after 1 April 1991 (art 17). In view of the youth of widespread electronic commerce it is presumed that contracts made using the Internet were made after this date. Attention is drawn to art 1(2) which lists the exceptions of its application. These include, among others, contractual obligations relating to wills and succession (art 1(2)(b)) obligations arising under negotiable instruments to the extent that the obligations arise out of their negotiable character (art 1(2)(c)) questions governed by the law of companies such as creation, legal capacity, and personal liability of officers and members (art 1(2)(e)) and questions as to whether an agent is able to bind a principal (art 1(2)(f)). To give definitive advice, therefore, advisers should consult a specialist text.
185   *Raiffeisen Zentralbank Österreich AG v Five Star General Trading LLC* [2001] 3 All ER 257, at 26, para 33.

2.5.2 Express choice of law

The first issue to understand is that although an e-commerce contract may contain an agreed choice of law, other laws may be applicable in addition. It will be seen below that certain mandatory laws of England will be applied despite choice, and that consumers benefit from certain other protections.

It is significant that no special words are required to choose a law for a contract. The Convention states that a choice can be express, or demonstrated with reasonable certainty by the terms of the contract or the circumstances of the case.[186] Both parties should be aware, therefore, that an express choice may be deemed to have been made even where a contract does not express 'The Law governing this contract will be the laws of England'. Where a contract entered into over the Internet does express the choice in such unambiguous terms, that law will apply to the contract. In certain circumstances a chosen law will be modified by English mandatory laws and consumer protective measures.[187]

2.5.2.1 Demonstration of choice

The Giuliano and Lagarde report provides some guidance of what is a demonstration with reasonable certainty that a contract is governed by a particular law.[188] Where a standard form is used, such as Lloyd's policy of marine insurance, it can be taken that a choice of English law has been made. However, this does not suggest that a standard form of a lesser known company can suffice as a reasonably certain demonstration. This is especially the case when contracting over the Internet where it is possible, for example, unknowingly, to enter a contract to buy an American piece of software but from a French distributor. In this scenario there will not be sufficient certainty to demonstrate any choice of law for the contract.

Other indicators within the terms of the contract may demonstrate this certainty. For example, references to the courts of England. In a shipping dispute, an arbitration clause in favour of England provided a 'strong indication of the parties' intention to choose English Law as the applicable law'.[189] References to English statutes are also indicative. References to the Copyright, Designs and Patents Act 1988 or the Consumer Credit Act 1974, may leave a court in no doubt that English law was always intended to apply despite the lack of its expression.

---

25. A web-wrap contract expresses that the jurisdiction of California shall apply for all disputes but that this will not exclude the application of any consumer protection laws applicable in the consumer's place of residence. No express choice of law is made. This confusion over jurisdiction and choice of law, and the lack of other indicators, will be unlikely to demonstrate the reasonable certainty required that a particular law was deliberately chosen.

---

186 Art 3(1).
187 See 'Modifications to express or demonstrated law', at p 74.
188 OJ 1980, C282/10 at C282/17.
189 *Egon Oldendorff v Libera Corpn* [1996] 1 Lloyd's Rep 380, QBD, per Clark J.

2.5.2.2 Modifications to express or demonstrated law

2.5.2.2.1 Mandatory rules

Even though an e-commerce contract may expressly state that the law of France should apply, if all the other relevant factors to the situation at the time of choice are connected with one country only, the mandatory rules of that country will remain applicable.[190] A mandatory rule is one that cannot be derogated from by contract.[191] Examples from English law include the Employment Rights Act 1996. The most relevant example for contracting over the Internet is the Unfair Terms in Consumer Contracts Regulations 1999 and the Unfair Contract Terms Act 1977 (UCTA), s 27(2).[192] This particular Act is discussed below.

A mandatory law will apply in the limited circumstances that all relevant factors are connected with one country. This is a high burden and one which will be difficult to satisfy where the parties reside in different countries. In such a situation, clearly not all the relevant factors are connected with solely one country. And where downloading, or shipment, occurs from a country other than that of the purchaser's residence the mandatory rules will be unlikely to operate.

One more point must be made about mandatory rules. The mandatory rules that may apply need not be those from England. The first test is to establish a country with which all the elements of the situation are connected. This country may be somewhere other than England. And if the second aspect of the test is satisfied, that the laws are mandatory, the English court must apply them in addition to the chosen or demonstrated law of the contract.

---

26. A website, based in England and controlled by an English company, uses the same contract for all those who wish to download its software. The contract specifies that the law of New York will apply. If an American contracts with the website and is then sued in England, it is unlikely that English mandatory rules will apply. In contrast, if an English consumer contracts with the site, it may appear that all the relevant elements relate to England so that the mandatory rules will apply.

This difference in application depending on who makes a contract with a website can pose certain difficulties: the main one is that, if the same contract is used for all jurisdictions, its effect will differ for different consumers (as opposed to businesses). Web owners should be conscious that using one standard form contract, and allowing a person from any jurisdiction to complete that contract, may result in an unforeseen situation. Where possible a website should use a contract that is, at the least, predictable for each of the possible locations from where a consumer may contract. Some website owners have a home page where their viewers must select their residence from a list before a contract is presented for their acceptance.

---

190   Rome Convention, art 3(3).
191   A statute may state that it applies only to contracts governed by English law. If it does not, it is a matter of statutory construction to establish whether the statute is a mandatory law.
192   Unfair Contract Terms Act 1977, s 27(2)(a) states that the Act will apply also if a term in a contract appears to have been included 'wholly or mainly' to avoid the operation of the Act.

2.5.2.2.2 Modifications by the Electronic Commerce Directive?

Some readers may be confused by the paragraph above: do the Electronic Commerce Directive and Regulations not do away with this issue? The Electronic Commerce Directive does introduce, within the EU, a so-called 'country of origin rule'. This can be summed up as: 'what is legal at home should be legal abroad'.[193] The Directive does, however, specifically avoid 'trumping' the Rome Convention. Article 4 states that 'this Directive does not establish additional rules on private international law nor does it deal with the jurisdiction of the courts'. And for consumer contracts, the 'country of origin' rule or 'internal market' is weakened further. Indeed, the Directive clearly avoids suggesting that any member state's law could trump the law that would otherwise apply to a consumer contract. For example, 'contractual obligations concerning consumer cont[r]acts'.[194] The Electronic Commerce Directive does not, therefore, eliminate the need to look first to the law governing the contract under the Rome Convention and then to any mandatory laws that may be 'layered' on top of the applicable law.

2.5.2.2.3 Application of UCTA

Where a court deems that the mandatory laws of England do apply to a contract it is necessary to check whether UCTA applies. The Act will apply to certain contracts governed by non-English law, where either or both:

> 'the [choice of law] term appears to the court. . . to have been imposed wholly or mainly for the purpose of enabling a party imposing it to evade the operation of this Act; or in the making of the contract one of the parties dealt as consumer, and he was then habitually resident in the United Kingdom, and the essential steps necessary for the making of the contract were taken there, whether by him or by others on his behalf.'

It is important to realise that the operation of this does not strike down the choice of foreign law; it merely makes the operation of that law subject to the effect of UCTA.

Despite the above, not all the protection that UCTA provides to consumers and businesses will be applicable to certain contracts made over the Internet. This is because, if the contract is an 'international supply contract', UCTA's rules on 'excluding or restricting' liability[195] will not apply. There is no such similar exclusion in the Unfair Terms in Consumer Contracts Regulations.

An international supply contract has three features.[196] First, it must be either a contract for the sale of goods or one under or in pursuance of which the possession or ownership of goods passes. Second, it must be made between parties whose places of business or residences are in territories of different states. The third feature is that there must be an international aspect to the contract: the

---

193   Art 3(1) and 3(2).
194   Art 3(3), Annex, sixth indent.
195   Unfair Contract Terms Act 1977, s 26(1).
196   Unfair Contract Terms Act 1977, s 26(3) and (4).

goods must be carried from one territory to another; or, the acts constituting offer and acceptance must have been done in different states; or, the contract must provide for the goods to be delivered to a place other than where these acts are done.

So, although an English court may decide that UCTA applies to regulate a foreign contract, a foreign seller of goods who forms contracts over the Internet will not be bound by UCTA's restraints on exclusion of liability clauses. Applying the same reasoning, the operation of UCTA can prevent a foreign supplier of services from unreasonably excluding liability.

---

27. An American wine seller sets up a website with its standard form contract expressing no jurisdiction clause but an express choice that the law of New York shall apply to any disputes. A UK consumer is made ill by some corked wine delivered and understands that under the Unfair Contract Terms Act 1977 the supplier's contract could not exclude its liability. This Act will not apply to prevent this exclusion of liability because the contract is for the international supply of goods.

This contrast between the application of the Act to goods and services may be crucial to the supply of digital information over the Internet. The supply of software over the Internet is likely not to be classified as a sale of goods, indeed no title passes and there is no physical possession. Certainly, if the obiter dictum of Sir Iain Glidewell is followed,[197] supplies of software made over the Internet will not be international supply contracts for the purposes of UCTA. As a result these contracts will be subject to UCTA's rules on the exclusions and restrictions of liability.

It is worth noting that the Law Commission and the Scottish Law Commission have advocated in the course of their report and proposals on UCTA that s 26 should not be replicated in any reform of the legislation and that express provisions in new legislation are needed to prevent attempts to evade the consumer protections offered by art 5 of the Rome Convention by means of a choice of foreign law. The Commissions had specific concerns that art 5 would not in and of itself necessarily protect consumers only temporarily resident in a member state with which the contract is most closely connected.[198] It is hoped that such recommendations will be taken into account in the context of the current review by the DTI and European Commission of the eight EU consumer *Acquis* minimum harmonisation directives and their implementation in the UK.

---

28. Two American software suppliers set up websites to provide software to English consumers. Both suppliers utilise an on-screen contract which excludes all liability and choose the contract to be governed by 'the Laws of the State of New York to the extent that all non-American consumer protection provisions will be inapplicable'. One supplier provides the software by shipping it on a CD-ROM to the English consumer. UCTA will

---

197   See *St Alban's City and District Council v International Computers Ltd* [1996] 4 All ER 481 at 492–494.
198   The Law Commission and the Scottish Law Commission Unfair Terms in Contracts, Report on a reference under s 3(1)(e) of the Law Commissions Act 1965, February 2005.

not operate to restrict the application of the exclusion clause because this is an international supply contract. The other supplier decides to download the software to consumers using the Internet. UCTA will operate to restrict the application of the exclusion clause because the contract is not an international supply contract as no goods are passed.

2.5.2.2.4 Consumer contracts

Far more common than the application of a mandatory rule to a contract is the application of a particular mandatory rule, consumer protection laws. Article 5(2) expresses that in certain circumstances a choice of law made by the parties shall not deprive the consumer of the protection afforded by the mandatory rules from the law of his country of habitual residence. It was once thought that this provision will have very limited effect because English consumers generally buy from English suppliers under contracts governed by English law. This certainly was the case even for goods manufactured abroad. The Internet alters this though; the digital landscape is covered with foreign suppliers contracting directly with local consumers, missing out the domestic supplier. It is now relevant for these manufacturers to appreciate the effect of art 5. It will affect their decision whether to sell over the Internet and what legal advice they should take.[199] It should be repeated here that the Electronic Commerce Directive expressly does not reduce the applicability of the Rome Convention. It also does not reduce the mandatory protection afforded to consumers by the laws of their domicile.

Before considering these circumstances, which are usually satisfied over the web, one must address what is a consumer contract. The courts may not consider a licence over copyright material to be a consumer contract as it is neither for the supply of goods or supply of services. The German Bundesgerichtshof held that a timeshare contract was neither a contract for the supply of goods nor services within the meaning of art 5.[200] On the basis that such a licence is classified as a consumer contract, parties contracting over the Internet should appreciate the conditions that must prevail for the consumer protection to apply.

Websites and consumers

Article 5(2) specifies that there are three ways in which the mandatory consumer protective laws will apply to a contract where a choice of law has been made or demonstrated appropriately. One of these ways directly concerns a contract made over the Internet:

> 'if in that country the conclusion of the contract was preceded by a specific invitation addressed to him or by advertising, and he had taken in that country all the steps necessary on his part for the conclusion of the contract. . .'

This chapter has explained that a court may view a website as a form of advertising. This is very likely where the website does not even attempt to block

---

199   It may not be enough simply to seek the advice of a domestic lawyer; to understand fully the possible effect of a web contract, legal advice should be solicited from other jurisdictions where potential contracting parties may reside.

200   VIII ZR 316/96, RIW 1997, 875, 19 March 1997.

viewers from specified countries, either technically or by consent. It has also been explained that clicking a download button, or simply agreeing to a contract, will be sufficient to show that the consumer has taken all the necessary steps[201] in the country of his habitual residence. This provision will therefore often act to introduce consumer protective laws into a contract that a website owner never envisaged.

The fact that the similar provisions of the Brussels Convention have been amended in the Brussels Regulation begs one simple question: Does the current Rome Convention have a more narrow application than the Brussels Regulation? The answer to this question is found below under 'Avoiding certain consumers'.

Avoiding certain consumers

Avoiding the ambit of art 5 is difficult both technically and legally because it remains impossible to 'block' totally all access to a website from one particular jurisdiction. The website owner must make a decision: is he happy to contract with a consumer from every country in the world? If there is a jurisdiction that the owner seeks to avoid there are two methods to employ. First, technical solutions. Ensure that the web pages that precede the contract stress that the site is not intended for those consumers from the unwanted jurisdiction. This may be effective. The Giuliano and Lagarde report advises that[202]:

> '[i]f. . . the German replies to an advertisement in American publications, even if they are sold in Germany, the [art 5(2)] rule does not apply unless the advertisement appeared in special editions of the publication intended for European countries.'

One can also ensure that a web server establishes what language is 'set' for the consumer's Internet browser. This will allow the filtering of some jurisdictions by the unique languages spoken there. A further refinement of those filtered can be achieved by running a 'reverse DNS look-up'. This resolves the domain name of the Internet Service Provider being used by the consumer. A domain name ending in '.com' may indeed give little indication of the jurisdiction of the consumer. In contrast, an Internet Service Provider with a domain name ending in '.co.uk' gives a fair indication that the consumer using it is from the UK. Then the actual server being used to access the Internet can be located on the planet with a high degree of accuracy. Of course, the server may not be local to the consumer for a number of reasons. Although also not precise, one further check can be made of the consumer's time zone. Collectively these solutions can weed out consumers from unsought territories.

The second method is to ensure, as is suggested, that the contract is not accepted by the consumer, but rather offered; the website should accept.[203] With

---

201   This careful drafting avoids the older problem of deciding where a contract was concluded. All that must be determined is where the consumer carried out all the steps necessary on his part to complete the contact. It will therefore make no difference whether the website is so constructed as to accept offers or make them. It is also submitted that the effect of the Electronic Commerce Directive's 'acknowledgement' is also irrelevant here. The relevant country will be identical.

202   OJ 1980, C282/10 at C282/24.

203   See 'Website acceptance and acknowledgement', at p 31.

this mechanism in place it becomes easy to ask consumers to complete details of where they are habitually resident or to where they want the goods, if relevant, shipped. The site can reject the offers from the unwanted jurisdiction. It can be seen that if the website made offers, even with conditional drafting as to habitual residence, it could be in breach of contract by refusing to supply to certain locations.

---

29. A website sells 'self-help' manuals. The website allows any consumer to fill in his details, including address and payment details. The contract chooses Swiss law. On clicking a button labelled 'Let me help myself' (an acceptance button), the manuals are sent to the consumer by mail. By fulfilling each order without checking the habitual residence of the consumer, the website may be leaving itself open to litigation or unexpected defences. It may be that the site should refuse to contract with consumers from certain jurisdictions.

These steps are also relevant, as explained above, to avoid the bite of art 15 of the Brussels Regulation. It remains relevant, therefore, to consider whether drafting differences between the Rome Convention, art 5 and Brussels Regulation, art 15, are commercially relevant. This author has always expressed the view that both the Brussels Convention, art 13 and Rome Convention, art 13 apply to protect most consumers accessing websites.[204] This author's view is therefore that the changes introduced by the Brussels Regulation were introduced not to *change* the law but to *clarify* it. The majority of the delegates of the contracting states certainly had the view that changes to the Brussels Convention were not needed.[205] Website operators should not, therefore, assume that the current Rome Convention is now exposed as not protecting consumers. The Rome Convention, but more so, the Brussels Regulation, protects consumers who contract using websites that make no attempt to exclude them.

2.5.3　Absence of choice

Although it has been advised that a contract should always have a statement as to the law that will apply, there will be situations where a contract has no such statement. To cover these situations, rather than endorse them, the following section considers how a court will establish the applicable law. As above for an express choice, the section later goes on to address the radical difference made by contracting with a consumer without an express choice of law.

Without a choice under art 3, the general rule is that the applicable law shall be that of the country with which the contract is most closely connected.[206] There is a presumption, however, which is of direct relevance to website contracts. Article 4(2) makes the presumption that the contract is most closely connected with the country in which the person is located who effects the characteristic

---

204　Gringras *The Laws of the Internet* (1st edn, 1997) pp 38 and 50.
205　European Commission Proposal, (1999) OJ C376/1.
206　Rome Convention, art 4(1).

performance. The following section breaks down this article into two discrete elements: characteristic performance and location.

2.5.3.1   Characteristic performance

For a unilateral contract made over the Internet, the performance which is characteristic will always be straightforward. For a bilateral contract, as is recommended for the Internet, the answer may be more involved.[207] The Giuliano and Lagarde report illustrates the complexity over what is performance in a bilateral contract.[208]

> 'It is the performance for which the payment is due, i.e. depending on the type of contract, the delivery of goods, the granting of the right to make use of an item of property, the provision of a service. . . which usually constitutes the centre of gravity and the socio-economic function of the contractual transaction.'

Where a viewer enters a website to download material or order its supply, the website owner will be the person effecting the characteristic performance. Providing money or digital cash is not, as seen, characteristic performance.[209] Where a business logs on to a business-to-business website to conduct electronic procurement or other corporate activity, again, it will be the website owner who effects the characteristic performance. For example, in a bidding contract, the provision of the bidder's professional services was considered to be the characteristic performance.[210] In a contract between a client and lawyer, the French court determined that the lawyer's provision of legal advice was the characteristic performance.[211] A distribution agreement, however, has a characteristic performance of supply to the distributor, not the supply to third parties by the distributor.[212] It can be said with some conviction that a website owner will usually be the contracting party making the characteristic performance.

2.5.3.2   Location

Once the characteristic performance of the contract is established, art 4(2) provides a separate test to determine the law that will apply to that Internet contract.

---

207   Art 4(5) explains that if the characteristic performance cannot be determined (not that *where* it is effected cannot be determined) the presumptions of arts 2, 3 and 4 will not apply and the court may choose the country with which the contract as a whole is more closely connected as the basis for the applicable law. This must be shown to the court by the party seeking to establish a country other than that determined by art 4(2). *Definitely Maybe (Touring) Ltd v Marek Lieberberg Kanzertagentur GmBH* [2001] 4 All ER 283.
208   OJ 1980, C282/10 at C282/20.
209   More involved transactions such as a contract for the provision of digital cash can result in strange results with this reasoning. It would appear that the location of the account determines the law of the contract rather than the bank's location: *Sierra Leonne Telecommunications Co Ltd v Barclays Bank plc* [1998] 2 All ER 821 at 827.
210   *HIB Ltd v Guardian Insurance Co* [1997] 1 Lloyd's Rep 412, QB.
211   *S v K D* 1983, J146, Tribunal de Grande Instance de Paris.
212   *Print Concept GmBH v GEW (EC) Ltd* [2001] ECC 36, CA.

It is vital not to make the wrong assumption that having determined the characteristic performance of a contract one has also found the law that will apply. The correct approach is to assess which party makes the characteristic performance and then to determine which law reflects this transaction. There are two possibilities: first, the contract has been entered into in the course of that party's trade or profession; second, the contract has been entered into otherwise.

2.5.3.2.1 Course of trade or profession

It is likely that those parties who own a website to make contracts will be considered to be acting within their trade or profession. In this situation, art 4(2) states that the law that shall apply is that of the country where the principal place of business is situated, with a proviso. If the terms of the contract specify that the performance is to be effected through a different place of business, the law of that place shall apply.

---

30. A Parisian clothes manufacturer sets up a website in Paris and allows retailers to place their orders over the web. There is no choice of law made on the online order form. The clothes being shipped will constitute the characteristic performance of the contract. The manufacturer effects this performance, so the law of the principal place of business, France, will apply to the contract. If the contract specifies that the clothes shall be shipped from a German warehouse, the law of Germany shall apply being a place of business other than the principal one.

2.5.3.2.2 Website's place of business

Contracts made over the Internet grant freedoms to both parties: neither needs to be located in the same country as the website that takes and completes an order. It is possible that an order to acquire a digitised picture is made from England, and that the order is placed with a German company, trading out of Germany, but that the server which digitally effects the performance is located in the US. It would be equally easy if the server is located in Vietnam, or anywhere else in the world with a telephone network. The obvious question is therefore, does a server that can effect performance constitute a place of business? It is submitted, in the absence of any direct authority, that a server *per se* cannot constitute a place of business. This conclusion is drawn from a number of factors.

The wording of art 4(2) indicates that effecting the characteristic performance through a place does not necessarily constitute a place of business. This can be reasoned from the wording of the article that performance must be effected through a place of business other than the principal place of business. It does not merely state that performance through another place will trump the principal place of business.[213]

The Giuliano and Lagarde report complements this point. It states that[214]:

---

213   It is admitted that such a literal analysis of a European Convention is, perhaps, inappropriate, and that a more purposive approach should be used. This follows.

214   OJ 1980, C282/10 at C282/20.

'[t]he law appropriate to the characteristic performance defines the connecting factor of the contract from the inside, and not from the outside by elements unrelated to the essence of the obligation such as the nationality of the contracting parties or the place where the contract was concluded.'

This interpretation suggests that it is naïve to look solely at where a server is plugged in. What the Convention requires is to look to the reality of the transaction; the characteristic performance must be linked to 'the social and economic environment of which it will form a part'.[215] Indeed, the Giuliano and Lagarde report endorses this holistic approach by later stating: '[t]he place where the act was done becomes unimportant... Seeking the place of performance or the different places of performance and classifying them becomes superfluous.'[216] A company needs to do far more than simply connect a server abroad to have established a place of business there.

What and where is 'a place of business' is a vexed question for the purposes of choice of law and there are differing definitions concerning taxation and the service of proceedings. But there is little doubt that the policy considerations when establishing jurisdiction over a defendant differ from those to establish from where performance was effected. It is inappropriate and an over-simplification of the relevant factors to attempt to utilise a court's views on 'place of business' from one area of the law, say jurisdiction, to another, choice of law.

---

31. An Italian publisher charges viewers to read its newspaper which it uploads daily on to its two websites, one in Italy and one based in New York for speed purposes. Its contract with viewers has no choice of law clause, but does stipulate that, when demand is high, the American server may supply the information. When a viewer accesses the newspaper, and unbeknown to him, receives this information through the American server, the law of the contract will not be that of New York. A server simply based in New York is an insufficient link to constitute a place of business. The law that will apply is that of the place of the principal place of business: Italy.

2.5.3.2.3   Outside trade or profession

Where a party is not acting within his trade or profession but uses a website to make a contract, a slightly different, but more certain, rule applies. In this situation, art 4(2) states that the law that shall apply is that of the country where, for an individual, he habitually resides at the time. For a corporate or unincorporated entity, the law that applies is that of the place of its central administration.

The commercial reaction to this academic debate is short: where possible specify a law for any e-commerce contract made over the Internet. There is some truth in the statement that not providing a choice of law gives slightly more opportunity for argument at an interim stage as to which law will apply to a contract. This opportunity comes at the cost of distinctive uncertainty.

---

215   OJ 1980, C282/10 at C282/20.
216   OJ 1980, C282/10 at C282/21.

2.5.3.3   *Modifications to applicable law*

2.5.3.3.1   Consumer contracts

What constitutes a consumer contract under art 5(2) has already been addressed in some detail.[217] It was found that a contract made over the web with a consumer will generally benefit from the protection afforded under the Convention.[218] Where the contract does not provide a choice of law, the effect of the transaction being a consumer contract is far more critical.

If no choice of law is made and art 5(2) is applicable, art 5(3) specifies that the law which governs the contract is that of the consumer's habitual residence.[219] This is in stark contrast to where a consumer contract does include a choice of law. In that situation, art 5(2) does not deprive the consumer of the protection afforded by the mandatory rules from his habitual residence.

---

32. A website sells 'self-help' manuals. The website allows any consumer to fill in his details, including address and payment details. On clicking a button labelled, 'Let me help myself' (an acceptance button), the manuals are sent to the consumer by mail. By fulfilling each order without checking the habitual residence of the consumer, the website will be forming contracts under many different laws all around the world. Its contracts may be unenforceable, or worse, they may be illegal. To avoid leaving itself open to these risks it must include a choice of law and refuse to contract with consumers from certain jurisdictions.

There is an elementary solution to the problem that any law could apply to a contract if any consumer is allowed to contract: choose a law for the contract. Then, to ameliorate the effect from the consumer's mandatory rules, apply the technical and legal precautions already described to 'block' certain jurisdictions.[220]

---

217   See 'Consumer contracts', at p 77.
218   See 'Websites and consumers', at p 77.
219   Subject to the two exceptions that the rule does not apply to a contract of carriage or a contract where the services are to be supplied to the consumer exclusively in a country other than that in which he has his habitual residence. See the Rome Convention, art 5(4).
220   See 'Avoiding certain consumers', at p 78.

CHAPTER THREE

Tort

'The difficulty and inconvenience of requiring operators to analyse either the message or the senders from either a factual or legal standpoint is manifest. The indispensability of the telegraph, on the other hand, is as unchallenged as the realisation that speed is the essence of its worth.'

William M Martin, 1940[1]

The open nature of the Internet and web allows users to connect both intentionally and unintentionally with more people than ever before. A website created by an individual can be seen by all other Internet users. A message sent to a bulletin board or website chatroom can be read across the planet, almost simultaneously, by millions. Unfortunately, this global communication has its disadvantages. A computer file harbouring a computer virus can, in a matter of hours, spread across continents, damaging data and programs without reprieve. A spammer can send tens of thousands of unsolicited emails simultaneously, clogging and slowing systems, and irritating recipients. A careless or vicious comment is immediately published and readable throughout the world.

The law of tort demands that, in certain circumstances, we are answerable for our actions and our inactions. Whether there is a contract between two individuals or not, the courts have the authority to make someone provide compensation for damage caused. Put simply, English law demands that users of the Internet operate with responsibility towards others.

This chapter considers these responsibilities in relation to four particular types of damage that can occur over the Internet. The opening section focuses on negligence and the liability of those who, even accidentally, exacerbate the spread of a computer virus by particular conduct and negligence as a potential action against spammers. The second and third sections look at the potential use of torts of trespass, interference with goods and other tortious actions, against senders of spam and malware. The fourth considers the possibility that, if a person relies to their detriment on information provided by another over the web, the provider of the information may, occasionally, be liable for the loss. The final tort that is then

---

1   'Telegraphs and Telephones – Qualified Privilege of Telegraph Company to Transmit Defamatory Message Where Sender is Not Privileged' 2 Wash & Lee L Rev 141 at 147 (1940).

examined from the perspective of the Internet is defamation. The openness of the Internet brings benefits to those who wish to publish information, but sometimes the courts will deem them responsible for the damaging words of another.

This chapter examines the following issues:

1. How may someone be liable for the damage caused from accidentally spreading a computer virus?

2. From a legal perspective, what type of damage occurs when digital data is altered?

3. Might not using an anti-viral program, or not backing-up important data, be viewed by the courts as contributory negligence?

4. Does a sender of spam or malware trespass against another's property?

5. When may information published over the web be the basis of litigation over a negligent misstatement?

6. Can contracts and disclaimers prevent victims of these torts from having a right of action?

7. What are the risks of website operators and of Internet service providers being sued for defamation?

8. Which country's courts have the jurisdiction to adjudicate on these cases?

9. Which law will apply to resolve such a dispute?

3.1   NEGLIGENCE

There has been a notable absence (in the UK at least), so far, of tortious actions in connection with the Internet. On one level this is surprising, since the media is so often filled with stories of the Internet being used to cause harm or distress: the malicious code which crashes systems and causes widespread damage, the forum user who is harassed or bullied, email inboxes inundated with adverts for libido enhancements. This appears to present a veritable feast for litigators, and yet tort as a basis of action has been marginalised.

In some cases this is to be expected. A tortious action will rarely be an appropriate or attractive starting point for the lawyer instructed by a company seeking redress for hundreds of thousands of pounds worth of damage to its data and systems caused by the hacking, spam or virus-spreading pleasures of a young cyber delinquent.[2] Criminal prosecution by the appropriate authorities or, in the case of spam, action pursuant to applicable data protection legislation,[3] will be the more likely route of action against the instigator, as discussed in Chapters 5 and 6. However, particularly in the case of computer viruses, the instigator is not

---

2   But see section 3.2 of this chapter in relation to potential trespass actions.
3   See Chapter 6 on Data Protection, including, in particular, the sections relating to the Privacy and Electronic Communications (EC Directive) Regulations 2003.

the only potential defendant and, because of the nature of Internet services and relationships, third parties (even the company itself, in this example) could be called to account to others for their actions or inactions. In such circumstances, tort will often be the only means available to seek redress.

This section considers what responsibilities may be owed to users and others. A claim in tort may not as yet have been brought in the English courts but, as this section shows, there is no clear reason why this should be so and, indeed, tort-based claims have already had success in the US.

To examine negligence, section 3.1 focuses on the limbs which must be made out in any negligence case. We will then apply these limbs to some possible Internet scenarios.

Although in the majority of cases it is the most useful approach, negligence is not the only basis of action; and sections 3.2 and 3.3 consider some alternative bases of tortious action in the context of hacking and spam, as well as virus activity including strict liability under the rule in *Rylands v Fletcher*, trespass and occupier's and product liability.

3.1.1 Constituent parts

A defendant will only be liable in negligence where he breached his duty of care to the claimant, resulting in a recoverable form of damage. This requires that each limb be considered in turn: duty of care; breach of duty; type of damage; and causation of damage, together with the defences which may be available.

3.1.1.1 Duty of care

The Internet, more than any other medium, permits one person to affect almost every other person connected to it. For example, viruses can spread widely and it is possible for one person to make a fundamental difference to this spread. One only needs to have regard to potential victims where these people are one's legal 'neighbours', however.

An appropriate starting point to determine who is your neighbour on the Internet is the two-part test expressed by Lord Wilberforce[4]:

> 'First one has to ask whether, as between the alleged wrongdoer and the person who has suffered damage there is a sufficient relationship of proximity or neighbourhood such that, in the reasonable contemplation of the former, carelessness on his part may be likely to cause damage to the latter, in which case a prima facie duty of care arises. Secondly, if the first question is answered affirmatively, it is necessary to consider whether there are any considerations which ought to negative, or to reduce or limit the scope of the duty or the class of person to whom it is owed or the damages to which a breach of it may give rise.'

The law is less ready to impose a duty of care where harm results from a failure to act, rather than by action of the defendant. In other words, the law does not gen-

---

4 *Anns v London Borough of Merton* [1977] 2 All ER 492 at 498.

erally impose a duty to save a potential victim, but only a duty not to harm that person.[5] Of course, it is semantically possible for a claimant, and the court, to frame a system operator's activities as actions, rather than failures to act. A train driver was liable for failing to shut off steam, so allowing his train to run into a dead-end.[6] The court described the driver's conduct in the active terms of negligently managing the train to allow it to 'come into contact with the dead-end'.[7]

---

1. A website controller is aware that one of the applets on its home page is capable of deleting data on computers that are using a particular browser. The site controller takes no precautions and then receives a claim form alleging damage as a result of his negligence. It is unlikely that a defence that he was not negligent, having performed no action, would succeed.

3.1.1.2   Breach of duty: standard of care

Negligence arises where a defendant owes a duty of care and then breaches that duty, causing harm as a result. Victims must prove that the defendant breached his duty; they must prove on the balance of probabilities that, say, a system operator was negligent in allowing a virus to be spread.[8]

To assess negligence the courts compare the actions and inactions of the defendant with those of a reasonable man 'guided upon those considerations which ordinarily regulate the conduct of human affairs'.[9] The most important point is that the courts will construe the level of duty by reference to industry practice. This is not to say that a court will simply assume that the latest notice of advice from the CERT[10] should be followed to avoid acting negligently.[11] The court may, however, draw an inference of negligence and reverse the burden of proof, forcing the system operator, in effect, to argue against the industry.[12] In the converse situation, if a system operator does keep up-to-date with industry practice, the victim will have this burden.[13]

---

5   Lord Diplock illustrates this by claiming that in the parable of the Good Samaritan, there would be no liability under English civil law for the conduct of the Levite and the priest who passed by the other side, 'an omission which was likely to have as its reasonable and probable consequence damage to the health of the victim of the thieves': *Home Office v Dorset Yacht Co Ltd* [1970] 2 All ER 294 at 326. This stated, this section takes a slightly less forgiving view of the liability which may fix to a system operator. In short, it is assumed that a 'pure omissions' argument will not save an operator from all liability.
6   *Kelly v Metropolitan Rly Co* [1895] 1 QB 944.
7   [1895] 1 QB 944 at 947 per Rigby LJ.
8   Sometimes the evidential burden on the claimant can be lessened by the court accepting an allegation of *res ipsa loquitur*.
9   *Blyth v Birmingham Waterworks Co* (1856) 11 Ex Ch 781 at 784 per Alderson B.
10 The Computer Emergency Response Team is an American publicly-funded establishment that tracks Internet security issues.
11 In *Thompson v Smiths Shiprepairers (North Shields) Ltd* [1984] 1 All ER 881, Mustill J held that an employer was not in breach of his duty when advice was contained in the Lancet; breach occurred 12 years later when the government released an advisory note.
12 Of course, occasionally the industry practice itself is below the standard required by the law. See *Edward Wong Finance Co Ltd v Johnson Stokes & Master* [1984] AC 296.
13 *Morris v West Hartlepool Steam Navigation Co Ltd* [1956] 1 All ER 385 at 402 per Lord Cohen.

System operators should not rely solely on official industry statements; they should also aspire to reach the generally understood standards of Internet security and responsibility.[14] The law does try to inject some proportionality into the standard that it expects from defendants. System operators will be judged not purely on the extent of risk, but balanced with the difficulty of taking precautions to avoid that risk. Lord Denning put this succinctly[15]:

> '[T]his is an obligation which keeps pace with the times. As the danger increases, so must the precautions increase.'

3.1.1.3   Damage

If it is proved that a defendant has breached a duty of care, the claimant must then prove that this breach caused the loss complained of. Losses include non-pecuniary losses for personal injury, loss of amenity and enjoyment. Damage may also include physical damage to property and consequential losses arising from this.

3.1.1.4   Causation

There are two tests of causation. The first test is factual: did the defendant actually cause the damage? After satisfying a court that a system operator's negligence actually caused the damage, the claimant has in addition to prove that the damage was not too remote. Remoteness is a judicial limit on liability. It is used by the courts to prevent a defendant being liable for 'all the consequences [of an act of negligence] however foreseeable and however grave'.[16]

The general statement of the law on remoteness is drawn from the *Wagon Mound* case.[17] In that case the defendants allowed oil to pour from their ship onto the claimant's dockyard. The claimant's manager was assured by a manager of an oil depot that there was no reason to stop welding work; oil on the sea is not inflammable. The welding recommenced and some sparks fell onto some floating debris, which in turn ignited the oil. The claimant's dockyard was burnt. Viscount Simonds was convinced, as the courts have been since, that[18]:

---

14   In *Aiken v Stewart Wrightson Members' Agency Ltd* [1995] 3 All ER 449 at 480, Potter J relied on the 'common ground' that in the US there was an escalation of asbestosis claims which would therefore increase the risk that the level of claims against Lloyd's would rise. Similarly, even without any industry guideline, it is 'common ground' that the move towards using executable code on web pages will escalate the amount of malicious code which can be transmitted. A system operator who seeks to avoid negligence actions should not wait for a reported 'Advisory' from CERT before employing precautions.

15   *Lloyds Bank Ltd v Railway Executive* [1952] 1 All ER 1248 at 1253.

16   *Overseas Tankship (UK) Ltd v Morts Dock and Engineering Co Ltd, The Wagon Mound (No 1)* [1961] 1 All ER 404 at 413 per Viscount Simonds.

17   *Overseas Tankship (UK) Ltd v Morts Dock and Engineering Co Ltd, The Wagon Mound (No 1)* [1961] 1 All ER 404. The case remains supported by the House of Lords: *Jolley v Sutton London Borough Council* [2000] 3 All ER 409, HL.

18   [1961] 1 All ER 404 at 413.

'a man must be considered to be responsible for the probable consequences of his act. To demand more of him is too harsh a rule, to demand less is to ignore that civilised order requires the observance of a minimum standard of behaviour.'

Cases following *Wagon Mound* have modified its effect on remoteness. Woolf J applied *Wagon Mound* together with these three important modifications:

3.1.1.4.1   Thin skulls

In *Dulieu v White*[19] Kennedy J formulated the rule of English negligence law that a defendant takes his victim as he finds him[20]:

'it is no answer [to a negligence claim] that he would have suffered less injury, or no injury at all, if he had not had an unusually thin skull or an unusually weak heart.'

In *Smith v Leech Brain*[21] the court was asked to discount this rule in the light of *Wagon Mound*; if a claimant suffers from a rare condition, the defendant should not be liable in relation to this condition, as it is not reasonably foreseeable. However the court was unconvinced by the defendant's argument, and ruled that the thin-skull rule applied along with the *Wagon Mound* test.

In the House of Lords case, *The Edison*,[22] Lord Wright stated that the thin-skull rule was concerned only with actual physical damage.[23] This would indicate that the thin-skull rule may not apply to the state in which a claimant leaves a computer. However, *The Edison*, although not overruled, has been heavily distinguished and is unlikely to be followed.[24] It may therefore be said, with some conviction, that a fault or vulnerability of the claimant's computer to infection will not make the damage suffered too remote. A claimant may be able to rely on the thin-skull rule: this does not, as will be discussed, prevent the defendant alleging contributory negligence for the claimant not having a working anti-viral program or firewall.[25]

3.1.1.4.2   Type, not kind, of damage

The second gloss on the *Wagon Mound* test distinguishes between the need for the type of damage to be foreseeable, rather than the need to foresee the precise extent and manner of infliction. Lord Denning put this as follows[26]:

---

19   [1901] 2 KB 669.
20   [1901] 2 KB 669 at 679.
21   [1962] 2 QB 405.
22   *Liesbosch, Dredger v Edison SS* [1933] All ER Rep 144, sub nom *The Edison*.
23   [1933] All ER Rep 144 at 159. See also *Bailey v Derby Corpn* [1965] 1 All ER 443 at 445 per Lord Denning.
24   In particular see the Court of Appeal's ingenious distinguishing of the case in *Dodd Properties (Kent) Ltd v Canterbury City Council* [1980] 1 All ER 928.
25   See 'Contributory negligence', at section 3.1.1.5.1 of this chapter.
26   *Stewart v West African Terminals Ltd* [1964] 2 Lloyd's Rep 371 at 375.

'It is not necessary that the precise concatenation of circumstances should be envisaged. If the consequence was one which was within the general range which any reasonable person might foresee (and was not of an entirely different kind which no one would anticipate) then it is within the rule that a person who has been guilty of negligence is liable for the consequences.'

3.1.1.4.3 Intervening acts

The final gloss, and one that may come into play when a claimant suffers secondary damage, is a general principle. The chain from breach of duty to damage can be broken by an intervening act by another person, including the claimant. Any intervening act by a third party in the chain of causation must reduce the probability that the defendant was responsible in fact for the damage suffered. Each new entrant into the chain of actions which finally results in the damage will decrease a judge's conviction that the defendant was liable for the harm. But when considering remoteness, the court is posing a different question: are the actions of others so significant as to exonerate the defendant?

This area is one of substantial academic debate. There are cases that indicate a retreat from *Wagon Mound*[27] or a realignment of its terms[28] together with those suggesting *Wagon Mound* 'repay[s] full rereading'.[29] Here, it will be assumed that *Wagon Mound* and its glosses will apply to the question of third party intervention. A relevant question is, therefore, whether the interventions or their consequences were reasonably foreseeable by a person such as the defendant at the time of the accident?

---

2. An Internet service provider admits negligence in allowing a virus to spread to its members' computers. One member refuses the ex gratia settlement offered by the Provider, and sues for the damage done not simply to the connected computer but to the entire network of which this computer forms a part. One aspect of the damages claim is for the emotional distress suffered by the Head of the IT Department. On remoteness, the ISP has two main arguments: first, it was unforeseeable that an entire network would be connected to an Internet computer without any firewall in place; second, it was unforeseeable that the virus would result in the emotional distress of the Head of IT. The first argument will probably fail, as the ISP must take the company as found. This will not, however, preclude a defence of contributory negligence. On the second argument, it is possible that a court would view the damage to data and physical property as within the type of foreseeable damage. The court would be less likely to view the emotional distress to the Head of IT as within the same type.

3.1.1.5 Defences

There are three defences which are likely to be relevant in Internet negligence cases. The first, and one that will most commonly be invoked, is contributory negligence. This is where the defendant admits that he caused to an extent the damage,

---

27   *Lamb v Camden London Borough Council* [1981] 2 All ER 408.
28   *Home Office v Dorset Yacht Co Ltd* [1970] 2 All ER 294.
29   *Delaware Mansions Ltd v Westminster City Council* [2002] 1 AC 321.

but that the claimant also caused some of the damage himself. The second defence is that of consent, or *volenti non fit injuria*. The third, relevant to all Internet cases, is the range of defences under the Electronic Commerce (EC) Regulations.

3.1.1.5.1   Contributory negligence

The Law Reform (Contributory Negligence) Act 1945 provides the partial[30] defence of contributory negligence. The scope of the defence is clear from s 1(1):

> 'Where any person suffers damage as a result partly of his own fault and partly of the fault of any other person or persons, a claim in respect of that damage shall not be defeated by the reason of the fault of the person suffering the damage, but the damages recoverable in respect thereof shall be reduced to such an extent as the court thinks just and equitable having regard to the claimant's share in the responsibility for the damage.'

3.1.1.5.2   Consent

Although a consent defence remains appropriate for intentional torts such as assault, there is now some doubt as to the extent of the defence for negligence.[31] Whether or not the defence applies to negligence, what is certain is that if it does, a high degree of complicity is required by the claimant. Asquith J compared the degree of consent needed for a defence of *volenti* to 'inter-meddling with an unexploded bomb or walking on the edge of an unfenced cliff'.[32] For example, the Court of Appeal judged that a claimant who watched a pilot drink the equivalent of 17 whiskies would have his claim for negligent flying defeated by the defence of *volenti*.[33] Fox LJ stated: 'Flying is intrinsically dangerous and flying with a drunken pilot is great folly.'[34]

---

3. A website acts as a depository of supposedly neutralised virus code. A claimant downloads one of the latest viruses with a view to writing an anti-viral code as an antidote. The code was not actually neutralised and the claimant's computer becomes infected, forcing him to lose one day's working time. On poor advice, he sues. Putting aside the inherent difficulties of establishing negligence, a court will probably allow the full defence of *volenti*: dealing with virus code is tantamount to dealing with unexploded bombs.

3.1.1.5.3   Electronic Commerce Regulations defence

There are several defences under the Electronic Commerce (EC) Directive Regulations which are likely to be relevant. These are considered in detail in relation to defamation claims in section 3.6.3.2 of this chapter.

---

30   See the Court of Appeal's decision in *Pitts v Hunt* [1990] 3 All ER 344.
31   See *Morris v Murray* [1990] 3 All ER 801 at 806 in which Fox LJ distinguishes between the dicta of Diplock LJ in *Wooldridge v Sumner* [1962] 2 All ER 978 at 988 and Asquith J's test in *Dann v Hamilton* [1939] 1 All ER 59 at 63.
32   [1939] 1 All ER 59 at 64. Applied by the Court of Appeal in *Morris v Murray* [1990] 3 All ER 801.
33   *Morris v Murray* [1990] 3 All ER 801.
34   [1990] 3 All ER 801 at 809.

3.1.2 Application to Internet cases

This section seeks to apply the tests for negligence to two key Internet scenarios, and with particular emphasis on the potential use for negligence in virus cases. The selection of these two should not be read as mutually exclusive. The principles of negligence could be applied in a variety of other Internet cases including, for example, the spread of spam.

3.1.2.1 Viruses

3.1.2.1.1 Duty of care

As a useful analogy for computer viruses, the courts have previously considered the duty that arises when storing biological viruses. Widgery J had little doubt that a defendant had a duty to those owners of cattle which would be affected by the spread of a virus.[35]

> 'In the present case, the defendants' duty to take care to avoid the escape of the virus was due to the foreseeable fact that the virus might infect cattle in the neighbourhood and cause them to die. The duty of care is accordingly owed to the owners of cattle in the neighbourhood...'

There appears little to suggest that, when a person is aware of a computer virus in his control, the operator may not owe a duty to potential victims; the Foot and Mouth Disease Research Institute owed a duty to all the farmers in the neighbourhood whose cattle were killed.

Like their biological counterparts, computer viruses will infect not only the direct recipients but also subsequent ones; this is well known. It may therefore be alleged that the controller of an infected system is in a sufficiently proximate relationship with the owner of any equipment which becomes infected by the virus emanating from his system. It is submitted that this is too wide. In the above case a duty of care was only owed to farmers 'in the neighbourhood', but a network riddled with a computer virus may spread this worldwide: can it be liable for all such possible infections? With the Internet, is the neighbourhood, and therefore are one's 'neighbours', in fact global? A system operator, like all tortious defendants, has a duty to a claimant not simply if the harm is foreseeable, but also where the whole concept of relationship demands it.[36] It is therefore impossible to speak generically of a 'system operator's duty to victims'; the law requires that the 'whole relationship' be taken into account. A significant factor is the distinction between primary damage and secondary damage which may be caused.

Primary damage

A person who is sent an email from an infected system is owed a duty by the sender if that sender knew the email was being sent and was infected. If an inter-

---

35   *Weller & Co v Foot and Mouth Disease Research Institute* [1965] 3 All ER 560 at 570.
36   See the 'widening' of Lord Wilberforce's first test by the Privy Council in *Yuen Kun Yeu v A-G of Hong Kong* [1988] AC 175.

nal network is infected, the system operator should block all emails from leaving the system until the suspected malicious code is treated. If it is technically difficult to block emails leaving, the system operator has a duty to external recipients to inform the employees not to send potentially infected material. It is worth noting that Californian law goes further, requiring state agencies to actually notify potential customers if a suspected security breach is found, a move which has gained support in the UK recently following several high-profile breaches of security by major financial institutions.[37]

In the case of websites, there are likely to be a large number of people who experience primary damage by being directly infected by malicious code on a site, in contrast to an email where probably only one person suffers primary damage.[38] The owner has a real problem, since they have nominal control over the person who left the virus (for example, a user posting a clip), and no control over those who become infected with it. They will be unable to rely solely on a disclaimer to avoid liability,[39] because the law tends to impose a duty to act to prevent harm where the defendant is in control of both the claimant and the injuring third party.[40] Technical solutions obviously include ensuring that no files can be uploaded without first passing through the site's anti-viral program. This will probably be sufficient to comply with the controller's duty to his visitors, although it would be legally safer if a contractual disclaimer were also provided.[41] Additionally it may be evidentially useful for the controller to maintain a log of which person leaves which file. If a claim is brought against the controller, it may be crucial that the claimant can add, as co-defendant, the person who deposited the virus initially. Defences are discussed later.

---

4. A software programmer distributes software from her website and is careful to include a disclaimer of liability in the licence downloaded with each item of software. Unless the programmer is sure that no damaging code can be distributed simply by viewing her site, say by executable code, a disclaimer should also be placed on the website.

Secondary damage

The greatest concern for a defendant is not in respect of the limited number of primary infections, but in respect of the unlimited numbers of secondary infections. Fortunately, the duty to prevent damage for secondary infections will be less onerous than for primary infections because the law tends to avoid opening up the 'floodgates' to too many similar claims. Also, the courts will only impose a duty where that is fair, just and reasonable. It is the nature of viruses that they

---

37   Amendment effective as of 1 July, 2003, to the Information Practices Act of 1977, codified in California Civil Code, §§1798.29 and 1798.82.
38   The Melissa virus primarily infected only 50 people.
39   See 'Contracts and disclaimers' at section 3.5.
40   *Ellis v Home Office* [1953] 2 All ER 149. See also *Cowden v Bear Country Inc* 382 F Supp 1321 (DSD 1974) in which it was held an operator of an animal park had to exercise a high responsibility to prevent damage to the zoo's visitors. Some may say that there is a higher duty where a site's visitors access it not to view viruses but to download safe code.
41   See 'Contracts and disclaimers' at section 3.5.

spread; it is not improbable and is not unreasonably foreseeable that a victim who is far removed from the source of the infection will be infected.[42] By Lord Wilberforce's test it may appear an easy matter for a victim of secondary damage to allege successfully that the system operator owed a duty of care. But, as mentioned, a duty is wider than mere foreseeability[43]:

'As Lord Wilberforce himself observed in *McLoughlin v O'Brian* [1982] 2 All ER 298 at 303, [1983] 1 AC 410 at 420, foreseeability of harm is a necessary ingredient of such a relationship, but it is not the only one. Otherwise there would be liability in negligence on the part of one who sees another about to walk over a cliff with his head in the air, and forbears to shout a warning.'

This statement makes it clear that a claimant, having suffered secondary digital damage, will have to show more than simply that the system operator knew this would be possible. Each claimant will have to prove a close and direct relationship with the system operator. This will depend greatly on the facts before the court, the balance of powers of the parties, and the potential to open the floodgates to similar claims.

---

5. A famous brewery provides on its website a free screensaver program which mimics its television advertisement. Viewers are free to download this software. Unbeknown to the brewery, the program is infected with a virus. The program is very popular, so, to ease the strain on its web server, the brewery encourages owners of the program to copy it for their friends, rather than direct them to the website. Some time after the promotion finishes, a virus infection breaks out on those computers which have the program. The brewery may owe a duty to those who downloaded the program from the website, and to those people who were directed to copy the program. Those claimants who became infected from the spread of the virus, rather than the program in which it incubated, are unlikely to be owed a duty; they do not have a sufficiently direct relationship with the brewery.

3.1.2.1.2 Breach of duty

The precautions that a system operator should take are unlikely to be expensive, but, as the aphorism prescribes, they must keep pace with the times.[44] System operators must ensure that the seriousness of virus control is understood by all users of a network. They should maintain equipment audits to check that the users of the network are not connecting modems; these may permit viruses to enter the system without passing an anti-viral program. The main precaution, of course, is to keep installed the latest anti-viral program, while watching the industry press for any other security issues, and not simply to do nothing.

---

42 Cf, the catalogue of unlikely events in, say, *Palsgraf v Long Island Railroad* 162 NE 99 (1928).
43 *Yuen Kun Yeu v A-G of Hong Kong* [1987] 2 All ER 705 at 710 per Lord Keith.
44 In *Tutton v AD Walter Ltd* [1986] QB 61 a landowner sprayed a chemical on his yellow rape field which killed a neighbouring beekeeper's bees. The court held that the precautions he could have taken would have prevented the bees from dying and cost little. Similarly, a recently updated anti-viral program will prevent most malicious code leaving or entering: prevention at little cost.

What security safeguards should be taken, and to what extent, is still unclear, and there have been no English cases on such issue at the time of writing. However, those taken in the US may provide a useful indicator of where virus actions have used negligence, and of how pertinent the practical advice set out above may prove. In 2003, Verizon sought to avoid payment to the Competitive Local Exchange Carriers for use of the system, on the basis that it had been forced to shut down its network in order to quarantine the virulent Slammer worm from spreading further. It claimed that this virus was outside of its control. The State of Maine Public Utilities Commission, however, argued that the worm attacks had been foreseeable and Verizon had been negligent in not taking all reasonable and prudent steps to avoid potential damages. Verizon's claims were damaged by the fact that it had not applied and tested a patch circulated by Microsoft with warnings three months earlier, as its competitors AT&T and Worldcom had.[45] Verizon was fined $62,000.

---

6. An owner of an old Apple computer traces the source of a viral infection to an email that was forwarded to him by a friend in an accountancy firm. It is discovered that this virus was present on all the computers in the firm as well. The reason that no symptoms were present on the firm's computers was that they are IBM-compatible computers, not Apples, and the virus was specific to the latter. The system operator will owe a duty of care to the owner of the infected computer, but it is unlikely that he breached this duty. It is a slim possibility that cross-infection can occur and one which involves an expensive precaution: to have every system together with its anti-viral programs merely to prevent this unlikely occurrence.

3.1.2.1.3   Damage

A claimant infected by a virus spread over the Internet may seek to claim for the cost of 'repairing' his computer.[46] In addition, claimants who rely on their computers for commerce will also seek to claim their wider losses such as loss of business and loss of profit. A discussion on some of the likely heads of damage is considered below.

Digital damage

The operating system of a computer is a complex program that digitally binds together the various aspects of a computer. For instance, it ensures that the central processing unit responds appropriately for each key pressed on the keyboard. It also allows the central processing unit to store data on the screen, the memory or on a storage device. Application programs, such as word processors and drawing packages, run 'on top' of an operating system: they rely on the operating system to run; the operating system relies on the hardware. Data files are the raw information that are used, or shown through an application program. A word processing document or a list of client names would be classed as data files.

---

45   *Re Verizon Related Reduction Claim*, 2003 Me. PUC Lexis 181 (State of Maine Public Utilities Commission, 30 April, 2003). Docket No. 2000-849.
46   Technically, this should read 'cost of cleaning of malicious code and the reinstallation of software and data'.

When any of these programs or data are 'damaged' the question arises as to exactly what has occurred. It will be recalled that computers work with and store only ones and zeros. Programs and data are stored as magnetic representations of zeros and ones, either in memory or on a device, usually a disk. To damage a program or data, therefore, is not to cause any physical damage, in the way in which it is normally considered: all that is occurring is that the magnetic particles are being altered. The memory or disk remains operative in a physical sense; but what it was storing has been altered.

This discussion suggests that a virus causes no property damage. It is more accurate to state that virus damage causes no physical damage: property is a wide term and encompasses more than 'that which can be touched'. In two cases the criminal courts[47] decided, for the purposes of the Criminal Damage Act 1971, that altering magnetic media can be classed as damage to property.[48] The Court of Appeal, based on previous authorities,[49] read widely the concept of damage.[50] Applying the reasoning that an impairment of the value or usefulness of a disk will constitute damage, it is clear that part of a damages claim could justifiably be for the price of the program or software which the disk held.

---

7. An accountancy firm distributes free tax assessment software from its website. An individual retrieves this software, which works well, only to discover that it had harboured a virus that crashed his word-processing application program which he had installed from CD-ROM. The firm admits its negligence, but disputes that its damages should include the cost of a new word-processing application. The firm is correct: there is no recoverable damage to the word-processing application; it can be easily reinstalled restoring the individual to the same position as he was in before the infection. The only new piece of software that the individual can claim damages for is the cost of an anti-viral program to clean his disk drive.

Economic loss

A claimant whose business is the quick design and production of leaflets may well lose trade as a result of his operating system being infected by a virus. But, strictly speaking, the virus has damaged the operating system and not the additional programs that the claimant uses for the design and printing. Whether the claimant can claim for this loss of business is partly a question of causation, but it is also one of economic loss. The relevant issue here is that the law will not permit the recovery of damages for pure economic loss. Recovery is permitted

---

47 It is accepted that one cannot simply transpose the judgment on a point of law in a criminal case to answer a point of law in a civil dispute. However, here the transposition is not of the ratio, rather merely the judicial reasoning: it is persuasive, not authoritative.

48 By the Criminal Damage Act 1971, s 1(1): 'A person who without lawful excuse... damages any property... intending to... damage any such property... shall be guilty of an offence'; by s 10(1): '... "property" means property of a tangible nature'. This chapter does not suggest that tortious damage to property is restricted to tangible property.

49 *Cox v Riley* (1986) 83 Cr App Rep 54; *Morphitis v Salmon* [1990] Crim LR 48.

50 *R v Whitely* (1991) 93 Cr App Rep 25 at 29 per Lord Lane CJ. Lord Lane distinguished between tangible property being damaged and the damage itself being tangible: 'Where... the interference with the disc amounts to an impairment of the value or usefulness of the disc to the owner, then the necessary damage is established.'

only where this economic loss is dependent on the negligently caused damage to property.

The question, then, is when are the damages claimed by a claimant for infection by damaging code 'dependent' on physical damage? Applying Lord Denning's analysis in *Spartan Stell & Alloys v Martin & Co (Contractors) Limited*,[51] it would appear that the loss of business profit while an operating system is being repaired or replaced is irrecoverable, either as being too remote, or as pure economic loss. What would be recoverable is any work that at the time of infection is damaged by the virus.

---

8. A data warehouse performs online data-processing operations on behalf of poll researchers for general elections. It is imperative that this processing is not delayed as such a delay would make the results irrelevant. Larger polls can take many hours to process. During the processing of one such poll, the entire system crashes as a result of a virus spread from a negligently operated Internet service provider. The warehouse will be able to claim damages in respect of the poll being processed, but probably not for the profit from the polls which it is unable to process during the disinfection. These damages will be pure economic loss.

If it is accepted that data being corrupted is damage to property it becomes easy to see that the economic loss, such as profits from the use of that data, will be recoverable. But it is vital to appreciate that this is the key to recovery: a claimant must hang any claim for economic loss on the corruption of the data being damage to property. Of course, a claimant must also be careful not to value the data twice: the 'value' of the data and business profits lost as a result of its damage can overlap in certain circumstances. It is this problem of calculation of which Lord Denning was wary[52]:

'It would be well-nigh impossible to check the claims. If there was economic loss on one day, did the applicant do his best to mitigate it by working harder next day?'

Ongoing damage

A program or data that is damaged by a malicious code will suffer repeated damage unless it is stopped by an anti-viral program which digitally cleans the infected computer. At law, without suitable settlement after initial damage, a claimant can bring numerous actions for each repeated damage caused by the defendant's negligence.[53] This, in theory, would suggest that a claimant infected by a virus spread through the negligence of another could bring a new claim each time the computer is prevented from working properly as a result of the ongoing infection. In practice, a claimant who became infected by a virus but attempted to continue working with that computer without cleaning it first would not have mitigated his damages. He probably would have made a voluntary assumption of risk so denying a cause of action.

51   [1972] 3 All ER 557.
52   [1972] 3 All ER 557 at 564.
53   See *Hudson v Nicholson* (1839) 5 M & W 437.

3.1.2.1.4 Causation

The claimant in a digital damage case must show that it was reasonably foreseeable that the negligence by the defendant, be they system operator or software manufacturer, would lead to the damage. Where the claimant claims only for damage to the actual data or program, it will be difficult for the defendant to rebut this claim with a statement that it was not reasonably foreseeable. For example, it is well known that if any executable files are sent over the Internet they can be hosts for malicious code. Not to screen for this malicious code before sending, or allowing the retrieval of this code, has the reasonably foreseeable consequence of damaging data or programs. Likewise, not to apply a software patch provided to guard against a particular worm or virus, has the reasonably foreseeable consequence that the underlying system will not be able to cope with the malicious code if it hits it.

Test of causation and remoteness are particularly significant for Internet virus cases because there is a chance that a person infected by a virus from one site was already infected by the same virus from another location.[54]

---

9. A website system operator is sued for negligence in allowing an animation file to be infected with a virus which damages a viewer's browser on the first of the month. During the disclosure stage of the litigation, the defendant is able to see that the viewer's computer had already been infected by this virus. While the website operator may well have owed a duty of care to check his site for viruses, the breach of that duty did not cause the damage; the claimant's software would have been damaged with or without the negligence.

Viruses are rife on the Internet and, like viruses of a biological variety, a strain cannot be eliminated completely without destroying every last active virus and carrier. One legal approach to whether the defendant factually caused the damage is to structure a question using the 'but-for' test. This is often employed by the courts. For example, but for the system operator's negligence would the user have suffered damage to data? Where the claimant can prove that the code which caused the damage was downloaded from a site under the control of the system operator the test will apply and the court will be able to decide that the operator actually caused the damage. It is common for a claimant to be infected more than once. A claimant may allege that but for the defendant's negligence her data would not have been damaged. The defendant could counter this by showing that the claimant was already infected from an unrelated site.[55]

---

54 This common occurrence on the Internet is a practical example of the three-house fire problem. This is where a house, sandwiched between two others, is burnt by a fire that has been started by the two separate negligent owners of each of the neighbouring houses. In the problem, each negligent owner may claim that, but for their actions, the middle house would still have burnt down.

55 It may be possible using 'time-stamps' on infected code to assess exactly which virus caused which damage. Cf in *Cook v Lewis* [1952] 1 DLR 1, two hunters negligently shot through some trees. As a result of one of those shots, the claimant is hit by a bullet. The court, unable to prove absolutely which hunter was responsible for the wounding shot must decide whether the claimant can recover, and if so, whether from both or just one.

10. A new word processor that integrates with online translation services on the Internet becomes the target of many virus writers. Three particularly vicious viruses attach to the program and scramble or delete any documents at the point of saving them. A firm's internal network, with a 'safe' connection to its main supplier, becomes infected with one variety of the virus. They sue their supplier for damages resulting from negligence. It is then discovered that the claimant's internal network is also infected with the other two strains. Because of poor retention of the evidence, the claimant is unable to show that the infection from the defendant is the actual cause of the damage complained of. But, the claimant does adduce that the defendant's negligence added to their risk of damage. They have not proved in fact that the defendant's negligence increased the risk of damage from the offending code.

Because most viruses do not become more damaging in numbers and act absolutely, a defendant may simply be able to allege that because of a prior infection, the claimant was destined to be damaged anyway. Such an approach has been successful in medical negligence cases such as *Barnett v Chelsea and Kensington Hospital Management Committee*,[56] in which a patient was admitted to hospital with arsenic poisoning. The doctor was negligent in taking so long to see the patient, but the court stated that even without this negligence, the patient had no reasonable prospect of living.

11. An unfortunate software programmer downloads the latest version of a programming tool from a supplier, only to realise that, on running the program, her hard disk is corrupted. The hard disk cannot be repaired and prevents the programmer retrieving any of her data. She sues the supplier, who discovers that her hard disk was old and would have been prone to corruption at some point in the future. The court must take expert evidence as to the probability not merely of 'natural' corruption, but of data-caused corruption of the drive. If this is less likely to have caused the corruption at that point in time than the presence of the virus, the court must deem that the supplier is the factual cause of the damage.

3.1.2.1.5   Defences

Contributory negligence

Anti-viral programs are fortunately more effective than medical anti-viral treatments: they work absolutely, either preventing an infection or allowing an infection to take place. Without an appropriate anti-viral program the computer will be infected; there are no proportions of damage. Similarly there are road traffic accidents where the victim's damage could have been completely prevented by the victim wearing a seat belt. Before moving to the law's treatment of this, it should be understood that a direct comparison between data damage and personal injury is not entirely appropriate. Clearly, whether the policy is stated or underlies a court's decision, a claimant with severe personal injuries will be looked upon more favourably than a computer user with corrupted data. This

---

56   [1969] 1 QB 428.

said, the comparison does reveal that a negligent defendant will not be able to avoid all damages merely by casting the aspersion that the claimant should have used an anti-viral program.

In *Froom v Butcher*,[57] Lord Denning's analysis was given unanimous approval by the other members of the Court of Appeal. He said[58]:

'[T]he cause of the accident is one thing. The cause of the damage is another. The accident is caused by bad driving. The damage is caused in part by the bad driving of the defendant, and in part by the failure of the claimant to wear a seat belt.'

This distinction drawn between accident and damage allowed Lord Denning to ensure that[59]:

'It should not lie in [the defendant's] mouth to say: "You ought to have been wearing a seat belt."'

This has parallels with negligence resulting in data damage. It too consists of an accident that would not have resulted in damage if the claimant had taken precautions. While it may be wise to use an anti-viral program, not to do so does not eliminate the defendant's duty not to cause an accident through negligence.

The aspect of Lord Denning's judgment that cannot be so readily extrapolated is the level of 25 per cent as the appropriate reduction in damages. At the time of *Froom v Butcher* it was well known that one should wear a seat belt and the government encouraged it.[60] The use and regular updating of anti-viral programs by users is, arguably, not yet at a similar level of awareness (at least for private users) to wearing a seat belt or crash helmet or stopping smoking,[61] but it is increasing. It would be interesting to see the percentage reduction in damages a court would deem appropriate to apply therefore.

---

12. A corporation's network is infected by a virus and it claims over a million pounds in damages from its law firm which allowed the virus to pass through their 'safe' connection. The law firm is both shocked at the claim and at the fact that the infected corporation does not use a virus checker which would have prevented all the damage. The firm is advised to focus their attention on proving that they had no duty of care, as it is foreseeable that a commercial organisation would have no anti-viral program. This is sensible because it is unlikely that even a successful defence of contributory negligence would reduce the damages by more than 50 per cent.

Where the damage caused by malicious code is purely loss of data, there is a factual, and possibly legal, argument that if the claimant had backed up the data, far

---

57　[1975] 3 All ER 520.
58　[1975] 3 All ER 520 at 525.
59　[1975] 3 All ER 520 at 525.
60　Between 1972 and 1974 the government had spent millions of pounds on advertising to encourage people to wear seat belts.
61　In the recent case of *Badger v MoD*, QB, [2006] 3 All ER 173, a man's refusal to stop smoking despite repeated healh warnings, contributed to his lung cancer brought on through exposure to asbestos fibres.

less damage would have occurred.[62] A legal basis for this argument could be based on contributory negligence, but it has less force than an argument that the victim should have used an anti-viral program. As to other arguments, the defendant could allege that the victim may have mitigated his damages by making a backup before the damage. It is submitted that such a claim is better pleaded as a remoteness issue: mitigation is usually a post facto issue.

Consent

As for contributory negligence, it is difficult to extrapolate from a personal injury defence to one for data damage. If lessons can be learnt, clearly any defendant, who by negligence has caused data damage, will have a struggle to convince a court that the claimant was entering a dangerous area.

Electronic Commerce Regulations defences

There are several defences under the Electronic Commerce (EC) Directive Regulations which are likely to be relevant. These are considered in detail in relation to defamation claims in section 3.6.3.2 of this chapter.

3.1.2.2   Harm to website user

With the increasing popularity of website forums and social networking sites, the potential for users to be physically or mentally harmed by other users or by the content contained on a site itself increases. There have been no cases in the UK to date, but it is possible to see the potential for such claims. Take, for example, the case of Internet 'grooming' where a child may have met another user through a website, who then goes on to sexually assault or otherwise harm them, or a user who is otherwise harassed through a site or exposed to pictures or content which causes them distress and mental harm.

In all such cases there is likely to be an obvious direct cause of action against the perpetrator, but what about the website owner or other Internet Service Provider who provided the forum in which such crime occurred? Can they be held liable in negligence for failing to protect such a user and prevent such harm?

3.1.2.2.1   Duty of care

It is easy to see how a duty of care could be made out in such cases, particularly where the user is a registered member of the site. The victim will be directly impacted and therefore the issues of secondary damage and remoteness which are so relevant in virus cases will be irrelevant here. The duty owed will change fundamentally, however, depending on the type of site. A networking site set up specifically for children is likely to be expected to owe a different duty of care to a forum directed at sharing of adult content and which only allows those who can prove they are over 18 to view any content.

---

62   Some damage would have occurred owing to the time taken to restore the data from the backup and the loss of unrecoverable data having been created after the last backup.

3.1.2.2.2 Breach of duty: standard of care

Industry practice will again be relevant here. A court is likely to consider the use of appropriate age restrictions, the placement of appropriate warnings, including links to help services and recommendations for prudent behaviour, as well as the availability of complaints mechanisms. Was the user made aware of the content of the site, or guarded against giving personal details out to strangers?

3.1.2.2.3 Damage

Damage here will almost certainly be non-pecuniary.

3.1.2.2.4 Causation

Causation will need to be considered on a case-by-case basis, depending on the harm actually caused. It may well be foreseeable that a young user would be distressed by a seriously violent image, but not necessarily that a responsible adult would fail to heed any warnings on a dating site and meet up with another user without precautions, and be abducted and assaulted.

3.1.2.2.5 Defences

The defences available will be absolutely essential in such cases and be likely to make many such actions by a claimant unsuccessful.

Where physical harm is caused to a user, it will almost certainly have required that they take independent actions and decisions to meet with another user in person or to access an area of a site to communicate with others or view content they select. The basis for contribution or consent on the part of the user in such cases is clear.

The Electronic Commerce Regulations defences will also be significant where the service provider was not aware of the contents of the site, or third party postings which lead to the harm. Although there have been no relevant cases in the UK, a recent US case[63] tried in Texas provides a useful example where the defence relied successfully on the US Communications Decency Act, which contains similar exemptions to liability for third party intermediaries in respect of third party content. On this basis the court dismissed claims of negligence and gross negligence brought against MySpace for failing to institute safety measures to protect minors. The case concerned the use of the site by a minor (although she had lied about her age on joining) who was sexually assaulted by a 19-year-old she arranged to meet up with through the site. The judge held that MySpace had no duty to protect minors and could rely on the third party content defence (similar to that under the Regulations).

Under the Regulations, relevant issues are likely to be whether the site owner could be said to have any control or authority over the perpetrator. Of course, often a service provider will have a contract with its members or customers. Will this constitute 'authority' or 'control'? This author and the DTI believe it will not. The DTI states in its unbinding note on the Regulations that the concept of

---

63 *Doe v MySpace, Inc.*, No. A-06-CA983-SS (W.D. Tex. 2/13/2007).

control or authority will be akin to 'effective control' under the Defamation Act 1996.[64] In other words, a mere contract to provide services to the third party will not be sufficient to bring the third party under the service provider's 'control' or 'authority'.

An open question remains relating to whether or not the ability to control the third party will constitute control for the purposes of the first prong of the defence. After all, most, if not all service providers have the ability to remove material that is damaging. Again, US authority on a similar question is convincing that, were such an interpretation to be applied, it would be contrary to the spirit of the legislation itself. It would, in effect, state that those who are able to comply with the onus to remove material once notified must be able to remove the material and so are deemed to control it[65]:

> 'First, the "right and ability to control" the infringing activity, as the concept is used in the [Digital Millennium Copyright Act ("DMCA")], cannot simply mean the ability of a service provider to remove or block access to materials posted on its website or stored in its system. To hold otherwise would defeat the purpose of the DMCA and render the statute internally inconsistent. The DMCA specifically requires a service provider to remove or block access to materials posted on its system when it receives notice of claimed infringement. See 17 U.S.C. §§ 512(c)(1)(C). The DMCA also provides that the limitations on liability only apply to a service provider that has "adopted and reasonably implemented ... a policy that provides for the termination in appropriate circumstances of [users] of the service provider's system or network who are repeat infringers". See 17 U.S.C. §§ 512(i)(1)(A). Congress could not have intended for courts to hold that a service provider loses immunity under the safe harbor provision of the DMCA because it engages in acts that are specifically required by the DMCA.'

Another important consideration is whether or not the provider had 'actual knowledge' or 'awareness'. The concept of 'awareness' is a wide one. However, the Electronic Commerce Regulations implement the Electronic Commerce Directive. Article 15(1) states that:

> 'Member States shall not impose a general obligation on providers, when providing the services covered by [the] Articles [concerning mere conduit, caching and hosting], to monitor information which they transmit or store, nor a general obligation actively to seek facts or circumstances indicating illegal activity.'

This Article is not explicitly implemented in the Regulations. The reason for this must be that Parliament believed that nothing in the Regulations did impose a general obligation to monitor such facts and circumstances. It follows that the Regulations do not, in effect, force service providers to watch websites, to be able to benefit from the defence.

---

64   *A Guide for Business to the Electronic Commerce (EC Directive) Regulations 2002*, para 6.7(c).

65   *Hendrickson v Ebay, Inc* 2001 WL 1078981, CD Cal, 4 September 2001.

3.2 TRESPASS/WRONGFUL INTERFERENCE WITH GOODS

The law protecting against interference with chattels is a complex area involving various potentially overlapping rights of action. The Torts (Interference with Goods) Act 1977 brings conversion (which concerns actual denial of the possessor's title to the goods), trespass and negligence and other torts resulting in damage to goods under an umbrella of 'wrongful interference with goods', although such torts retain some unique characteristics. In this section we focus on trespass, which is most likely to be relevant in Internet cases.

Torts of trespass include tortious liability for trespass to land, trespass to the person and trespass to goods (including conversion). The first of these immediately presents the same problems as are discussed below in section 3.3.3 in the context of *Rylands v Fletcher* as regards the narrow confinement to land. The second requires actual physical harm to the person along the lines of statutory battery offences. The last of these, however, may present a useful tool against a whole range of different Internet actions. Such an action is most likely to find a place (alongside other pleadings) for those seeking redress against a spammer or distributor of adware, spyware or other malware and, indeed, has been used in recent years both before the English courts and overseas. Although trespass has not been used to date in connection with virus claims (either against the instigator or other intermediaries), it should not be discounted.

3.2.1 Physical interference with goods

Trespass to goods is a wrongful, direct physical interference with such goods. Directly accessing a computer, hard disk or physical software clearly falls within the ambit of such interference, but what about the sending of an email, or a hundred emails? What about accessing of data with or without its permanent alteration?

These are difficult questions, which have not yet been tested before the English courts. Although trespass was included on the anti-spam claim forms in *Microsoft Corporation v Paul Fox* and *Virgin Net v Adrian Paris* (along with breach of contract and unlawful interference with economic interests), both were settled before the courts could properly analyse the claims. It should also be noted that the *Virgin Net* claim was brought before the introduction in the UK of the Privacy and Electronic Communications (EC Directive) Regulations 2003. These Regulations are likely now to be the basis for an action in relation to spam, although there is no reason why both could not be pleaded. See Chapter 6 on data and data protection for an analysis of these Regulations.

A claimant is likely to refer to the Criminal Damage Act 1971 based action of *R v Whitely,* discussed at section 3.1.2.1.3, to offer some support in overcoming objections that the physical access and damage has not been caused. They will also find encouragement in the number of successful actions there have been in digital trespass actions in the US to date (see below), which this author believes present some prudent decisions that could usefully be followed here. Interestingly, in such US actions, the main obstacle was showing that damage had occurred (potentially easier to make out under UK law, as discussed below), rather than demonstrating physical interference.

3.2.2   Possession

Although at first glance a seemingly obvious point, it is generally believed that a claimant should own and be in possession of the relevant goods at the time of the alleged trespass, for an action to be made out.[66] In the context of an action concerning the Internet, problems immediately present themselves, however. For example, websites subjected to an attack may be hosted on third party servers, or hosted off-site. Further, if the claimant's affected servers are located in another jurisdiction, such as the US (as is commonly the case with Internet service providers), it is not certain that the English tort of trespass would be deemed to protect them. Whilst it may seem perverse to deny a claim on any such grounds, given that the claimant still possesses such chattels in terms of ownership and control, this is a classic example of English laws based on physical notions which a judge may find too far a stretch to expand to protect Internet interests.

3.2.3   Damage

An action for trespass to goods is actionable without needing the removal of the goods from the claimant's possession. Indeed, it is generally now believed that mere touching (as long as it is intentional) may be sufficient for a trespass to arise, although some have argued that there must be some proof of damage.[67]

3.2.3.1   Trespass actions in the US: some examples

Intel Corporation v Kourosh Kenneth Hamidi[68]

Intel sought an injunction to prevent former employee Hamidi from sending further emails to Intel employees. The Supreme Court reversed the decision of the Californian Court of Appeal, and held that the tort of trespass to chattels did not encompass the defendant's email communications. It held there was no actual damage and 'a mere momentary or theoretical deprivation of use is not sufficient unless there is a dispossession.' Although the contents of the emails may have been annoying to the claimant, the sending of them had not actually impaired the functioning of its systems. In this respect, the Court distinguished the rulings in *Compuserver Inc v Cyber Promotions, Inc*, *America Online, Inc v IMS* and *eBay, Inc v Bidder's Edge, Inc*. The defendant, they said:

---

66   There are a few limited exceptions in respect of trusts, franchises and administrators. See *Winfield & Jacovich on Tort* (ibid) for an analysis.
67   See for example *Slater v Swann* (1730) 2 Stra. 872.
68   Supreme Court of California No. S103781 June 30, 2003.

'no more invaded Intel's property than does a protester holding a sign or shout-
ing through a bullhorn outside corporate headquarters, posting a letter through
the mail or telephoning to complain of a corporate practice.'

Compuserve Inc v Cyber Promotions, Inc[69]

ISP Compuserve claimed that mass unsolicited mailings, especially from non-
existent addresses such as the defendant's, had placed 'a tremendous burden' on
its systems, using up disk space and draining processing power, which made
such resources unavailable to it to provide to subscribers. Its claim of trespass
was upheld.

eBay, Inc v Bidder's Edge, Inc[70]

In this case (another claim for an injunction to prevent further actions, rather than
a claim for damages) the claimant's website was accessed around 10,000 times
per day by the defendant which was an auction site aggregator. The court upheld
the claim finding sufficient proof of threatened harm in the potential for other's
to imitate the defendant's activity and accordingly that, if the actions were left
unchecked, eBay would suffer irreparable harm from reduced system unavail-
ability or data losses.

America Online, Inc v IMS[71]

In a ruling following *Compuserve*, the court held in summary judgment in favour
of the claimant that the defendant's sending of bulk email was a trespass to chattels costing money, time and placing a burden on equipment.

Register.com, Inc v Verio, Inc[72]

This trespass case, interestingly, did not concern spam but a claim against a web
hosting site which robotically searched the claimant's site to obtain information
from its database of newly registered domain names, without permission, in
order to obtain potential business. Although no physical damage was claimed,
the court held that there was sufficient evidence of threatened harm to the system
and that, as with eBay, it could set a precedent to other users causing more harm
to the claimant. The court therefore found that Register.com had a legitimate
concern which required action in order to prevent its servers being flooded with
similar search code.

3.3 OTHER TORTIOUS ACTIONS

Section 3.2 has dealt almost exclusively with using the law of negligence to
claim for damage from a viral infection. Section 3.3 considers some other

69   Above, 962 F. Supp. 1015, 1021-1023.
70   *eBay, Inc v Bidder's Edge, Inc.* (N.D.Cal. 2000) 100 F. Supp.2d 1058, 1060-1061.
71   *America Online, Inc v IMS*, above, 24 F.Supp. 2d.
72   *Register.com, Inc v Verio, Inc.* above, 126 F. Supp.2d.

tortious actions which may be available in Internet cases but which, crucially, may prove more difficult.

To understand the Internet, metaphors are often employed. A presence on the Internet is called a website. People using the Internet are said to 'browse' it. Even the 'information superhighway' implies a tangible presence, like a road, the websites being like shops and billboards along the way. Such comparisons are useful to conceptualise the Internet, but they may not be reliable for legal analysis.

A website which may be stored on a server in one jurisdiction, operated in another and accessed and enjoyed in countless others, is not the same as premises or land which enjoy many traditional protections (but indeed also certain obligations). Further, when one's data is harmed by a computer virus caught from browsing a company's website, nothing physical occurs. The site is no more than a collection of digital information, and browsing is simply the transferral of information in the form of ones and zeros from one computer's memory to another's. Damage occurs, not because of faulty wiring or fire, but because of inappropriate vetting of the digital information stored on the accessed computer. Laws, both statutory and common, that relate to occupiers' liability, product liability and nuisance may therefore be a stretch too far to apply.

3.3.1   Occupiers' liability

The Occupiers' Liability Acts 1957 and 1984 replace common law rules on occupiers' liability with a statutory equivalent. A website controller is liable only as an occupier of premises, which is any fixed or movable structure.[73] A website may be notional premises, but the reality is that a person who browses a website has no physical presence there. The Act will not apply between website controllers and those who gain access to websites.

3.3.2   Product liability

The Consumer Protection Act 1987 provides that almost anyone connected with the sale of a defective product may be liable for harm caused by the product.[74] The Act is unlikely to be applicable to digital materials transmitted over the Internet, but it will still apply to physical products conventionally sent and it is recognised that software can be an intrinsic part of a product (the Department for Trade & Industry cites the example of an airline navigation system or production line robots which may cause personal injury or property damage[75]). This is because the Act applies to defective products, and does not explicitly include information: incorrect information on a website is unlikely to be classed as a product, and even defective software, unless incorporated into a machine,[76] is

---

73   Occupiers' Liability Act 1957, s 1(3).
74   Consumer Protection Act 1987, s 2.
75   Page 5, Guide to the Consumer Protection Act 1987, produced by the Department of Trade and Industy.
76   Consumer Protection Act 1987, s 3(2).

arguably not a product. In addition, there is a defence for new technologies which may be applicable to exclude liability where the state of knowledge at the time was not such that a producer of the products might have been expected to discover the defect.[77] Arguably, using the latest anti-viral program, firewall or spam filter is enough to be able to rely on this defence, although a flaw in the program which prevented it from performing correctly may not.

3.3.3 Rylands v Fletcher

Comparisons seem reasonable between a reservoir owner allowing water to damage another's property and a website owner allowing code to damage another's property. However, in *Rylands v Fletcher*, in which the reservoir owner was liable for damage done owing to the escape of water, the House of Lords was careful to stress that the ruling applied only to escapes from land.[78] This was affirmed by the House of Lords in *Cambridge Water Co Ltd v Eastern Counties Leather plc*,[79] in which Lord Goff considered an earlier case,[80] stating[81]:

'there can be no liability under the rule except in circumstances where the injury has been caused by an escape from land under the control of the defendant.'

It seems, therefore, that the ruling in *Rylands v Fletcher* (which imposes strict liability) is narrowly focused on escapes from land, and often to other land. It seems improbable that the courts will stretch its application to the Internet, particularly as the Law Commission has expressed misgivings about any generalised test for 'especially dangerous' activities.[82]

Further problems may be presented in an action against the spreader of spam or viruses even if this hurdle is overcome, since the rule in *Rylands v Fletcher* will only apply if the use of the land is 'non-natural', as distinguished from 'any purpose for which it might in the ordinary course of the enjoyment of land be used'.[83] It may therefore be difficult for a claimant to show that a website or system owner who allows emails or viruses to be brought onto and spread from its network is thereby allowing special use of its land. The material may be dangerous but it is still digital code or communication distributed via a network designed for digital communication. Could this really be said to be equivalent to noxious gases or the construction of a reservoir that goes beyond the usual type of use of the place where it is kept that one would expect? This author's view is that it is not.

---

77   Consumer Protection Act 1987, s 4(1)(e).
78   (1868) LR 3 HL 330; affg *Fletcher v Rylands* (1866) LR 1 Ex 265.
79   [1994] 1 All ER 53.
80   *Read v J Lyons & Co Ltd* [1946] 2 All ER 471.
81   [1994] 1 All ER 53 at 76.
82   Civil Liability for Dangerous Things and Activities (Law Com no 32) 1970 in paras 14–16. Lord Goff stated, 'If the Law Commission is unwilling to consider statutory reform on this basis, it must follow that judges should if anything be even more reluctant to proceed down that path' [1994] 1 All ER 53 at 76.
83   Lord Cain, in *Rylands v Fletcher* ibid.

Nevertheless, there does appear to be a judicial movement, albeit glacially slow, to make nuisance indistinguishable from negligence.[84]

3.3.4   Economic torts

No chapter on torts would be complete without reference to the less than popular melting pot of economic torts. Comprising actions for procurement of breach of contract, intimidation, unlawful interference with economic interests and conspiracy, it is easy to see why a claimant may see some benefit in including such a claim along with other actions against a defendant whose actions have caused a disruption to its businesses.

To cover with due regard the potentials and pitfalls of such an action would be a dissertation in itself, and it suffices to say here that, although economic torts should not be ignored, a claim based solely on any of these is likely to be fearfully complex and not just a little bit speculative.

3.4   NEGLIGENT MISSTATEMENT

The Internet allows wide, unfocused dissemination of information, and also concentrated, targeted distribution. For commerce this is special. The website that acts as a brochure for a mortgage adviser can also act as the e-commerce site to provide the quotes to be given to a customer. A stockbroker can host a web page that lists the current prices of stocks, allows customers to buy shares and provides, at an additional cost, tips on which shares to buy.

This ability easily to provide information, advice, and help to any person, anywhere in the world has massive potential. But this potential should be balanced with the law on negligent misstatement. In appropriate circumstances, a website controller or emailer may be found liable for the damage resulting from the information he provides. This section considers the scope of this doctrine in relation to the Internet.

3.4.1   Hedley Byrne v Heller

Much has been written on negligent misstatement, and this will not be repeated here.[85] What this section undertakes to do is to assess a stylised test for negligent misstatement considering the Internet. This section will only discuss the law where the peculiarities of the Internet affect the application of the test.

The ruling on negligent misstatements can be derived from *Hedley Bryne & Co Ltd v Heller & Partners Ltd*,[86] but Lord Oliver in a later case summarised the

---

84   See *Marcic v Thames Water Utilities Ltd* [2002] 2 All ER 55 at 70, para 55.
85   For the 'classic' professional advice issue, see *Law Society v KPMG Peat Marwick* [2000] 1 All ER 515.
86   [1963] 2 All ER 575.

position well.[87] He suggested that there are four factors that indicate a necessary relationship exists between the maker of the statement and the recipient who acts in reliance on the advice:

1.   The advice is required for a purpose, whether particularly specified or generally described, which is made known, either actually or inferentially, to the adviser at the time when the advice is given.

2.   The adviser knows, either actually or inferentially, that his advice will be communicated to the advisee, either specifically or as a member of an ascertainable class, in order that it should be used by the advisee for that purpose.

3.   It is known, either actually or inferentially, that the advice so communicated is likely to be acted on by the advisee for that purpose without further independent inquiry.

4.   The advisee acts upon the advice to his detriment.

3.4.1.1   Identity

There is a famous *New York Times* cartoon that depicts one dog, sitting at a computer, talking to another dog sitting on the floor. The dog at the computer is saying, 'On the Internet, nobody knows you're a dog'. There is some truth in this. Without the use of encryption authentication, the Internet makes it difficult to establish who (or what) has sent an email and similarly, who controls a website. This difficulty of identification does have legal ramifications.

The rules on negligent misstatement do not apply between all individuals. It has been said that the ruling applies only to those who are possessed of some special skill or expertise.[88] But this is not limited to particular categories of persons or situations. A dictum has been followed[89] which states[90]:

> 'when an enquirer consults a businessman in the course of his business and makes it plain to him that he is seeking considered advice and intends to act on it in a particular way, any reasonable businessman would realise that, if he chooses to give advice without any warning or qualification, he is putting himself under a moral obligation to take some care . . . [T]he principles established by the *Hedley Byrne* case . . . translate his moral obligation into a legal obligation.'

This wider statement suggests that the courts will not allow an adviser to discount his duty by stating that he was not actually qualified to provide such advice. If a website or an email gives the impression, without limitation or disclaimer, that advice or information is considered advice, a claimant may rely on

---

87   In *Caparo Industries plc v Dickman* [1990] 1 All ER 568 at 589.
88   See [1963] 2 All ER 575 at 594, per Lord Morris.
89   *Esso Petroleum Co Ltd v Mardon* [1975] 1 All ER 203 at 219.
90   *Mutual Life and Citizens Assurance Co Ltd v Evatt* [1971] 1 All ER 150 at 163.

that to establish a duty. It will be remembered that the claimant needs only to show that the defendant could have inferred that the advice was to be relied upon.

---

13. An individual establishes a home page with the domain name 'www.mpg.com'. This website, which is entitled 'Official Petroleum Institute', lists a number of supposed methods of improving the fuel consumption of a car. Poor proofreading allowed one piece of advice to be published without specifying that the method applies only to vehicles using unleaded petrol. A claimant with a damaged engine sues. The defendant will not benefit from proving to the court that he was not qualified to provide the advice. The court will assess how the website appeared to the claimant.

3.4.1.2   Reasonable reliance on the Internet

The courts need to establish that the reliance made by the claimant was reasonable. There are two aspects to this. First, is it reasonable to rely on the Internet at all for particular advice? Lord Denning interpreted the term 'considered advice' as excluding informal situations such as a casual conversation in the street, or in a railway carriage, or an impromptu opinion given offhand, or 'off the cuff' on the telephone.[91] There are analogies for the Internet.

3.4.1.2.1   'Instant messaging'

'Instant messaging' such as MSN Messenger and Sykpe are methods by which two or more users connected to the Internet can type messages to each other, these messages appearing as they are typed. It is like a telephone conversation but using text rather than voice. This would appear to accord with the kinds of casual circumstances that Lord Denning envisaged. Other means of communication over the Internet are harder to pigeon-hole.

---

14. A tenant worried about being evicted from her flat logs on to an instant messaging group. She locates an individual who purports to know her rights in this situation. He informs her that she can change the locks of the flat if she is worried about her landlady entering. The adviser's email address is rogerg@gbgb.com. The tenant changes the locks and is given notice for having breached her contract. The tenant is unlikely to have a right of action against rogerg@gbgb.com; it will be difficult to show that the advice was 'considered' and that it was reasonable to rely on it in the circumstances.

3.4.1.2.2   Bulletin boards, forums and networking sites

Certain websites allow members to 'deposit' content for all other members to read. These members are then free to reply by leaving another message, and so on. This is called a conversation thread.

---

91   *Howard Marine and Dredging Co Ltd v A Ogden & Sons (Excavations) Ltd* [1978] 2 All ER 1134 at 1141.

Some may consider that these conversation threads are as casual as instant messaging. This may not be the case. First, any such forum or site is likely to have a name. A name such as the Cancer Forum or alt.advice.cancer gives a far stronger impression that the material being discussed and advised upon is serious and in no way casual. The courts should take account of these surrounding circumstances. The second factor that distinguishes a forum from the informal situation is that the advice provided, unlike instant messaging, does not have to be given immediately. Users of forums are free to read questions, research and then provide an answer in due course. It does not need to be 'off the cuff' at all. Some messages remain unanswered for numbers of days. This may influence a court into thinking that the advice was considered.

---

15. An individual accesses a website called AIDSAdvice. He is worried that he may have contracted HIV the previous night and seeks advice on how to assure himself that he hasn't. He leaves an appropriate question on the bulletin board and checks for a reply the next day. As he wanted, his question had been replied to. The reply advises him to carry on as normal for the next three months as it takes this long for the virus to incubate; he will place no one at risk during this 'window'. On checking the source of the reply, the personal details reveals a doctor's name and surgery. These circumstances should influence a court into thinking that the advice was not off the cuff, despite being incorrect.

3.4.1.2.3   The Web

The name 'home page' for a portion of a website is quite an accurate description. The electronic documents stored on the web are like pieces of paper. The authority of the information written on paper depends not on the fact that paper is used, but rather on the printing and the general impression given by the information. Similarly, a website may contain official and considered advice from professional sources, or it may be no more than a collection of ramblings from an idiotic individual. This spectrum of information, from high quality to no quality at all, often presents a problem for users of the web. If a site has a relevant domain name and looks official, is it reasonable to rely on the advice it provides? This is a question that can only be answered with the fullest understanding of the surrounding circumstances. Nevertheless, that the information was provided over the web, without more, is inconclusive that it was reasonable to rely on the advice. Unlike Lord Denning's conversations in the street, the web hosts a plethora of information; those who supply this information should be cautious of providing this information without appropriate warnings.

3.4.1.3   Reasonable reliance on information

The Internet, like any means of communication, can carry information of any quality; therefore, the medium itself is not conclusive as to whether it was reasonable to rely on that advice. As for any negligent misstatement, the courts should look to whether in the actual circumstances it was reasonable for the claimant to rely on the advice. This issue depends on the facts, but some issues specific to the Internet can be mentioned.

Those who publish on the web may believe that no liability will attach to them if the words on their home page are not advisory but are merely informative or are stated as opinions. Certainly, one could arrive at such a belief by taking a superficial glance at Lord Denning's speech in *Candler v Crane Christmas & Co*[92]:

> '[A] scientist or expert . . . is not liable to his readers for careless statements in his published works. He publishes his work simply to give information, and not with any transaction in mind.'

However, this aspect of Lord Denning's much-approved dissenting judgment does not classify what types of words are actionable, but rather, what types of transactions. It is perfectly possible for a scientist's published statement on the web to be relied upon, with his knowledge, and to be the basis of a negligent misstatement suit. Lord Denning was attempting to provide an indication of to whom an adviser owes a duty, not over what he may owe a duty. Indeed, the court in a later case indicated that the operation of negligent misstatement is not restricted to a statement of fact or opinion, or even advice. It also applies where a notice should have been given but is not. The key is to establish whether a duty exists; if it does, it does not matter 'whether the breach takes the form of malfeasance or nonfeasance'.[93]

3.4.1.3.1   Tailored websites

To create such a duty over the web, at first, appears difficult. The web can be seen as no more than a collection of documents aimed at nobody in particular, and of such a generic nature as to prevent a duty arising. But many sites are quite the opposite. Their supporting business plans clearly define a market. Their advertising and material focuses on specific clients. Many tailor the experience. For example, an investor inputs their stock portfolio and the site not only allows the investor to trade in stocks but also advises the investor of suitable stocks to add in order to balance the portfolio. It is likely that a duty to provide non-negligent advice will arise in this situation. The more 'focused' a website, the more it uses software and specific content to make the site attractive for an audience, the more individuals will be owed duties of care by the controllers of the sites.

3.4.1.3.2   Finding or requesting

Advice provided from a tailored website raises a further issue that the courts have previously managed to avoid. In *Caparo Industries plc v Dickman* the claimant was considering making a takeover bid for a company.[94] To assess a good price it consulted the company accounts, prepared by auditors. Relying on the accounts, the claimant made its bid that was accepted, only to discover that the accounts were misleading. The claimant sued the defendant auditors, but eventually lost in the House of Lords. One justification for the Lords taking this

---

92   [1951] 1 All ER 426 at 435.
93   *Midland Bank Trust Co Ltd v Hett, Stubbs & Kemp* [1978] 3 All ER 571 at 595.
94   [1990] 1 All ER 568.

restrictive view of negligent misstatement was that the defendant should not be liable for information which the claimant, in effect, finds rather than requests.

When a user of the Internet requires to view information that is stored on a website, is this person 'finding' the document, or are they requesting it from the controller? Certainly, where the site has no entry terms it may be analogous to picking up some company accounts from the foyer of a company: hardly the proximity required by the House of Lords. But where the viewer is required to enter some details as to who he is, where he heard about the information and why he requires it,[95] the situation approaches one where the defendant will be unable to deny the necessary inferential knowledge.

---

16. Sites on the web often host a collection of commonly asked questions and answers on a particular subject; they are called Frequently Asked Questions, or FAQ as an acronym. A website with the URL 'www.authors.co.uk' hosts an extensive FAQ on how authors can have their work published. It also contains a number of questions and incorrect answers on how to protect a work. If an author relies on these to her detriment, it will be difficult for the controller of the site to avoid having a duty to the author.

The Internet is an open source of information and material: if companies and individuals wish to avoid creating a duty with third parties, they have two choices. First, they do not have to use the Internet for all types of material. Like any means of communication, the Internet is inappropriate for certain types of information. A more conservative attitude to the Internet will eradicate most of the glaring problems with negligent misstatements. The site could simply provide a summary and details of how to contact the provider for specific, tailored advice. The second choice is to publish the information, but with a suitable contract and disclaimers, as considered below.

3.5   CONTRACTS AND DISCLAIMERS

Unlike a brochure or paper leaflet, well-designed websites allow themselves to be 'tailored' by their readers. This is achieved by using 'cookies' and other identifiers which allow a site to 'know' who is reading it. These features, and the lack of an 'order' to have to view web pages, alter the conception that a website is like a book. It may have many 'front covers', but individuals are no longer bound to view the pages in any particular order. Indeed, most websites allow an individual to jump straight to any one of the pages of a site, rather than passing through the home page.[96] The utilisation of frames that can be scrolled separately also adds to this fluidity. This creates a problem for legal advisers: to be effective, exclusions of liability are generally required before damage can occur; they should be the first text seen, but this hardly embraces the usual vogues in website design.

---

95   These type of questions are often asked, no doubt generally for marketing rather than legal reasons.

96   This is particularly influenced by search engines that will locate any given text in a website and permit the user to move straight to that page.

3.5.1   Exclusions

3.5.1.1   Digital damage

The safest way of excluding damage from malicious code is to incorporate appropriate terms in a contract, rather than to rely simply on an exclusion notice. Details of how best to form a contract with a viewer of a website are described in Chapter 2.

A site should attempt to exclude any warranty as to the quality of any software downloaded on request or automatically by executable code and exclude its fitness for purpose.[97] In addition a disclaimer should be clear that the website controller is not liable for any damage caused by the software or code attaching to the software; this covers viruses and worms. The drafting for such a disclaimer must be carefully worded and with a prudent eye to the different types of limitations and exclusions that will be appropriate for consumer as opposed to business users. For example, one will want to be sure that such a disclaimer refers to indirect and consequential losses as well as specifically excluding damages from loss of data, profit revenue and contracts of business, although with consumers, care must be taken to ensure that plain English is used to clarify what is meant, and the effect on the consumer (see section 3.5.2.2.2 below and Chapter 2 on contract for more details on important considerations which need to be taken into account when dealing with consumers). It is all too easy simply to draft general sweeping exclusions that have the advantage of being concise, but have the distinct disadvantage of being ineffective and potentially unenforceable.

If a viewer is permitted to download an executable file he should be warned before he can download the code that, although the code has been checked, he is at risk from digital damage and its consequences unless he first checks the code himself for viruses.

3.5.1.2   Negligent misstatement

To disclaim responsibility for damages from a misstatement, a term or notice should state that the website or forum posting is for general consumption and does not indicate any assumption of responsibility to the viewer or reader (the aim being, generally, to seek to provide support to rebut any claim that a duty of care is owed). The term or notice should ideally then address each element of the four-part test derived by Lord Oliver.[98] It should be stated that the wording and graphics on the site or posting are not provided for any specific or generally described purpose. To try to stop a third party seeing and relying on the advice[99]

---

97   It is a moot point whether the Sale and Supply of Goods Act 1994 would include software as goods, or whether, in strict legal terms what is occurring is that the owner of the website is making a licence with a viewer over goods. Sir Iain Glidewell in *St Alban's City and District Council v International Computers Ltd* [1996] 4 All ER 481 at 493 states that 'the program is not "goods" within the statutory definition [of the Sale of Goods Act 1979]. Thus a transfer of the program [where it was transferred onto the computer by a third party] does not, in my view, constitute a transfer of goods'.

98   See '*Hedley Byrne v Heller*' at section 3.4.1.

99   It is very common on forums for statements to be copied from one forum, or section, to another.

n notice of terms should insist that third parties are alerted to the same conditions. The last main disclaimer is that because the advice is not provided for any particular purpose it is assumed that no reliance will be made on the site or forum without having first taken specialised professional advice. Although strictly of no legal effect, for the avoidance of doubt, some sites and forums include a statement that the provider of information will not be liable for any loss caused as a result of doing or refraining from doing anything as a result of the wording, links or graphics.

3.5.1.3 Negligent links

Often a site on the web will feature links to other sites that may be of interest to its viewers; such is the nature of the web. In response to concerns that these links may increase liability, certain website owners use notices to viewers that, upon their leaving a website, the owners are not responsible for content outside their website. To some extent, such a practice addresses a risk that is almost non-existent.

There are two situations where such a notice is used: first, where the linked site is a 'subsidiary' of the main site; second, where the linked site is not associated with the first. Clearly, for the first situation, if the site is within the overall control of the website owner, say where a set of websites are collected together under the same domain, the controller will have some responsibility to viewers of the other sites. In the second situation, however, it is difficult to see how a duty would arise from providing a link to another's site.

The right of action against the first website owner who provides the link will, most probably, be based on negligent misstatement.[100] The claimant will have to claim that by relying on the advice to follow that link the claimant suffered damage (probably as a result of further relying on advice on that linked page). Putting aside the rather stretched notion of causation that the court would have to accept, the fundamental question must be answered: was there a duty to the viewer concerning the link?

The four rules stated by Lord Oliver must apply. First, the links would have to be rather specifically referred to for a particular purpose. Advice required for a purpose known by the website controller would not be satisfied by listing some links under the heading 'Other sites of interest'.[101] The site would have to use a special heading like 'Sites to consult for advice on swollen ankles'. The site owner would also have to know, either actually or inferentially, that as a result of the heading and the link that the viewer would not only follow the link but would take advice from the linked page without independent inquiry. It is submitted that it would be difficult for a claimant to convince a court that his reliance on the link

---

100   It is admitted that a case of negligent construction of a website could be brought, but it would appear easier for a claimant to satisfy the court as to the four rules of a negligent misstatement than to prove that a duty existed and that the website designer fell below the standard reasonably expected of website designers!

101   In the same vein, the footnotes in this book referring to other sources do not amount to a statement as to the reliability of the information contained in those sources.

could constitute reasonable reliance on the information contained in the linked site. In addition, there is the question of causation. It should be remembered that the advice is to follow the link; once at the linked page, the viewer will further have to act to be damaged. The courts will more readily break the chain of causation when the resulting damage depended on the claimant taking yet more negligent advice.

In short, although it is prudent to use markers such as 'You are now leaving our site' followed by a group of disclaimers as to the information on linked sites, it is submitted that it addresses a slim risk. A cleaner approach is merely to use a heading for the linked sites, 'Other sites of interest'. This simple statement distances the website owner from the other content and should be general enough not to form considered advice.

3.5.2   Effectiveness of exclusions

There are two factors that may limit the effectiveness of an exclusion or notice: incorporation and legal enforceability. The first is a factor which will have greatest impact on the web.

3.5.2.1   Incorporation of exclusion

Unless an exclusion is within the terms of a contract accepted by a user and therefore binding, it must be otherwise incorporated to have binding contractual effect. On the web such notices are often produced just before a viewer decides to download some executable code: 'If you proceed you agree that the file you are downloading may contain viruses and other damaging code which may damage your data and programs'. For general website content, common practice is to include a notice via a permanent link at the bottom of each page. The controller of a website does not need to show a court that a viewer understood such a notice, or even that it was read; the controller must, however, show that he took reasonable steps to bring it to the claimant's notice. This does not require having the actual wording of the exclusion shown but its wording should be made available by a simple and prominent link.

---

17. A viewer uses a search engine to search for the websites that are supplying a free game. The search engine lists one particular page on a website. The viewer downloads the software advertised on the website's page by clicking a button labelled 'Download'. He sees no disclaimer because the website has only one link to its disclaimer notices, and this is on the home page that was bypassed by the search engine. The site will be unable to rely on the disclaimer as they did not take reasonable steps to alert each person who downloads software of the disclaimer.

Owners of websites must be careful not to assume that every viewer will read the pages on the site in a particular order or know where to find an important disclaimer. The very essence of the web is that it is constructed with hypertext and that a portion of a site (unless blocked) can be 'framed' by another site thereby obscuring the disclaimer. A viewer is free to browse around a site or many sites in any order. The terms may need to be incorporated repeatedly throughout the site with a simple link called 'Disclaimer'.

Those who advise website designers should be conscious that drafting a contract or disclaimer may not be enough: they should also have an input into exactly where on the website the disclaimer and links are placed; the approach taken may vary, depending on the potential risks presented by the content in question. What is certain is that if the notice is intended to be incorporated into the web contract to exclude negligence, the viewer must have been able to view the notice or disclaimer before the web contract is made.[102]

---

18. A software manufacturer decides to distribute its software utilities from its website. Before each utility is downloaded a notice is shown which excludes liability for negligently caused damage. After downloading some software from the site, a viewer's computer begins to slow down. It is discovered that some executable code that was on the website is retarding the computer. The notices provided before downloading the software will be inoperative: first, they relate to the downloaded software not the website's software; second, the poorly written executable code will have been downloaded to the viewer's computer before he had a chance to view the notice.

3.5.2.2 Limitations on exclusions

It is vital to pay due regard to the Unfair Contract Terms Act 1977 and its successors and the Unfair Terms in Consumer Contracts Regulations 1999.

3.5.2.2.1 The Unfair Contract Terms Act 1977

Despite the title of the Act, the Unfair Contract Terms Act 1977 applies to simple notices which are not incorporated into a contract in addition to contractual terms. In the main, this Act makes ineffective the exemption clauses in contracts in relation to a 'business liability',[103] and with a person 'dealing as a consumer'[104]. However, as the web contains many amateur sites that are not operated in the course of a business it is worthwhile checking whether the Unfair Contract Terms Act 1977 will apply. A term that seeks to exclude liability for damage resulting from negligence will operate only where it is reasonable.[105]

It has been discussed that a term of a contract must be properly incorporated to be effective. A simple notice, in contrast, can be made at any point about the information being provided. The safest option, however, is to disclaim responsibility before a viewer has a chance to rely on any advice.

For a website, a viewer should be confronted with a page or frame of disclaimers or at the least a prominent notice that the viewer should follow the link

---

102   See *Olley v Marlborough Court* [1949] 1 All ER 127, approved by the Court of Appeal in *Hollier v Rambler Motors (AMC) Ltd* [1972] 1 All ER 399 at 407.
103   Unfair Contract Terms Act 1977, s 1(3).
104   Unfair Contract Terms Act 1977, s 12(1)(a) and (b).
105   Unfair Contract Terms Act 1977, s 2(2). For guidance on what is reasonable, consult the Unfair Contract Terms Act 1977, s 11. This includes where the provider of information attempts to construct a notice as stating he has no duty at all. Section 13 prevents the exclusion or restriction of the duty itself unless it is reasonable.

to the disclaimers page of the site.[106] For the Unfair Contract Terms Act 1977, what is relevant is not the precise wording of a disclaimer but more its reasonableness regarding all the circumstances.[107] An adviser should not simply draft a form of wording and allow the client to place the words on the site. The adviser should check that the format and construction of the site or forum makes it reasonably clear to all viewers that the controller is disclaiming responsibility. Position on a site and clarity may be as legally relevant as wording.

3.5.2.2.2   Unfair Terms in Consumer Contracts Regulations 1999

These Regulations strike at a more limited set of exclusions than those under the Unfair Contract Terms Act 1977. First, the Regulations apply only to contracts and only those contractual terms that have not been individually negotiated.[108] This will cover most contracts made over the web. The second requirement is that the contract must be between a consumer and a supplier of goods or services.[109] The contract does not need to be for the supply of goods or services so it seems probable that the Regulations will apply to a licence over software. If applicable, the Regulations will exclude any term that is 'unfair'.[110] There is very little peculiar about the Internet which means that certain terms will be more or less fair. This said, terms must be incorporated before contracting with the consumer. The Regulations provide that a term may be regarded as unfair if it has the object or effect of 'irrevocably binding the consumer to terms with which he had no opportunity of becoming acquainted with before the conclusion of the contract'.[111] This may occur on the Internet where terms are flashed up on a consumer's screen without him actually having an opportunity to review or even repudiate their content. Useful guidance on disclaimers and other contractual exclusions which may contravene the Regulations is available from the Office of Fair Trading's website. Those drafting such terms are urged to consider such guidance if their terms are to be effective and to avoid complaints from Trading Standards or the Office of Fair Trading which investigations may result in public censure.

3.6   DEFAMATION

A high proportion of Internet cases concern defamation. Part of the reason for this is that the Internet provides the man on the street with a unique opportunity to have his thoughts published instantaneously throughout the world. Moreover,

---

106   See 'Incorporation of exclusion' at section 3.5.2.1.
107   This general approach was affirmed by the Court of Appeal in *Smith v Eric S Bush* [1988] QB 743.
108   See Unfair Terms in Consumer Contracts Regulations 1999, reg 3(3).
109   See Unfair Terms in Consumer Contracts Regulations 1999, reg 2(1). Unlike the Unfair Contract Terms Act 1977, a consumer must be a natural person.
110   For detailed advice, readers should consult specialist texts and the House of Lords judgment in *Director General of Fair Trading v First National Bank plc* [2002] 1 All ER 97.
111   Unfair Terms in Consumer Contracts Regulations 1999, Sch 3, para 1(i).

the Internet, particularly in its early years, encouraged a spirit of unrestrained comment or discussion.

There is nothing special about the law as it relates to a person sending defamatory statements over the Internet. What is, is that to 'publish' on the Internet, one generally must submit the material in an electronic form to a third party (be that a website or an ISP transmitting an email); it is this third party that, in effect, publishes the material. The key legal question in this section is therefore when will liability fix also to these intermediaries?

Before September 1996, the answer was the subject of much speculation based on old English common law and analogies from abroad. The Defamation Act 1996 now provides for when a third party Internet 'publisher' will have no liability and when the party will have to rely on one of the limited defences. Unfortunately, the application of the Act, particularly when combined with the Electronic Commerce (EC Directive) 2002, can be confusing.

Before considering the legal issues, it is useful to appreciate the technical aspects of the Internet that may impinge on any defamatory statement made over it and which make Internet cases unique.

3.6.1 Technicalities

3.6.1.1 Third party

Information over the Internet cannot be sent single-handedly. In contrast to a poster that can be drawn and pinned to a wall without third party help, to publish on the Internet necessarily involves others. Chatrooms or networking sites that hold written conversation threads or user-generated clips and postings are stored in a digital form on a server computer. The same is true for electronic mail: it is not generally sent directly to the recipient's computer; it is sent to a 'digital pigeon-hole' from which the recipient downloads new messages. This reliance on a third party to publish the material has a significant impact on the analysis of a defamation action. In defamation, it is not only the writer or creator of the statement or content who may be liable, but also those who are involved in its publication and distribution.

3.6.1.2 Identity of first defendant

Often it will be difficult to discover the identity of the person who typed the defamatory statement. It is easy and common to use a pseudonym when an email is sent, or a posting to a website made. It is also possible to 'blind' an electronic message, making it impossible to tell even the source of the statement. This is achieved by sending an email to what is called an 'anonymous remailer' which is a computer program that automatically strips any message of any identifiers.[112] This difficulty of identification makes it attractive to litigate the third party who actually distributed the message; this legal individual will

---

112 See *Takenaka (UK) limited v David Frankl*, unreported 11 October 2000.

be necessarily identifiable as the statement will be stored on this equipment or published on their website. In addition, the third party may be a substantial commercial organisation with deep pockets and more able to pay libel damages than the possibly impecunious real authors. This also makes them attractive targets for libel actions.

3.6.1.3   Extent of publications

To bring a defamation action, the statement concerned must have been published to at least one other person. The extent of publication is also a factor in the assessment of damages for a claimant. For a statement published on the Internet, this distribution has the potential to be global and numerous.

With a statement available on the Internet, there is no rebuttable presumption[113] that the statement has been read by a third party.[114] However, if publication is in dispute, providers may be required to disclose all logs showing accesses to the page in question. A wise claimant will notify the provider at the beginning of the action that if the fact and/or the extent of publication is likely to be in dispute, he will require this material to be disclosed and demand that it be retained.

3.6.2   The Defamation Act 1996

The Act does not alter what constitutes a defamatory statement; it addresses who should be liable for this defamatory statement.[115] For the sake of completeness, however, the following is a short summary of what constitutes a defamatory statement[116] and procedures for claims. Below is a summary of some key considerations in the context of defamatory statements .[117]

3.6.2.1   Defamatory statements

Material is defamatory if it tends to 'lower the claimant in the estimation of right-thinking people generally', or if the material causes people to 'shun or avoid' the claimant or, more narrowly, hold the claimant up to 'ridicule, hatred or con-

---

113   This contrasts with the position with publications in newspapers where there is such a presumption.

114   Ruling of Gray J in *Loutchansky v Times Newspapers Ltd (No 2)* [2001] EMLR 876.

115   Of particular relevance to Internet defamation are the new procedures of: Offer to make amends (ss 2–4); reduction of limitation period to one year from the date on which the cause of action accrued (ss 5–6); and Summary disposal of claim (ss 8–11).

116   There are two kinds of defamation: libel and slander. The importance of this distinction is that in a limited class of slander cases the claimant must prove 'special damage'; in libel the claimant does not need to prove any loss to succeed. Slander is where the defamation is in transitory form. It appears, therefore, that with the possible exception of Internet telephony, any defamatory material on the Internet will be a libel.

117   Specialist texts should be consulted in relation to what exactly can constitute a defamatory statement. The information provided here is the general position with application to some Internet specific issues.

tempt'.[110] These tests are not entirely objective; part of the court's deliberations (usually before judge and jury) will be directed to the attitudes and likely response of the people who actually read the statement.

3.6.2.2 Similar interests

On Internet forums the individuals involved often have similar interests and an understanding of the frivolity of the messages or content posted. This may be a factor that a court should take into account. This author was surprised for example recently to find that some of her father's ex-students had created an appreciation society in his name on a well-known networking site, through which reminiscences were exchanged of his lessons and apparently 'memorable' teaching style. With this example, like many others (fortunately not defamatory, as far as this author is aware to date!), only a small set of individuals would be interested in reading and responding with their jokes, or even know who the subject was.

A defendant should be prepared to emphasise the readership or likely readership of a forum either to demonstrate that the posting in question would not have been taken seriously or, even if taken seriously, it would not have lowered the person in the minds of its readers.

3.6.2.3 Types of defamatory material

It is not unique to the Internet that a person can be defamed by more than simply words. A defamatory statement means 'words, pictures, visual images, gestures or any other method of signifying meaning'.[119] Under this definition, it is possible that a computer-manipulated image posted on the Internet that shows a person performing a degrading act may be considered as defamatory. It is this wide scope of what is defamatory that makes it so difficult to operate automatic screening of potentially defamatory material.

3.6.2.4 Publication

A person who merely unwittingly contributes to the dissemination of a defamatory statement by providing an Internet service may claim that it is not publishing the statement at all. The cause of action in libel arises on publication rather than the writing of the defamatory material. The crucial questions for those who provide and store material on the Internet are therefore, can they be liable and, if so, what defences are available to them.

It is also important to note in terms of publication that each hit on a website constitutes a separate publication, each actionable and each with its own limitation period.[120]

---

118 Respectively: *Sim v Stretch* [1936] 2 All ER 1237 at 1240; *Youssoupoff v Metro-Goldwyn-Mayer Pictures Ltd* (1934) 50 TLR 581 at 587; *Thorley v Lord Kerry* (1812) 4 Taunt 355 at 364.

119 Defamation Act 1996, s 17(1).

120 *Louchansky v Times Newspapers Limited* [2001] EWCA Civ 1805. Publication was not when the article first appeared but arose each time it was accessed.

3.6.2.5   Mere conduit

It has never been determined in English common law whether a telephone company or Royal Mail could be held liable for communications they convey.[121] The Electronic Commerce (EC Directive) Regulations 2002, however, almost put this beyond doubt. A telecoms company usually acts as a true 'mere conduit' in that it does not initiate transmissions nor choose the final recipient of a transmission. It is the digital equivalent of a 'middle man'.

The Regulations provide that such mere conduits shall not be liable in damages for defamatory material sent over their 'pipes' (nor any other material) on three conditions: first, as discussed above, they must act as a true 'middle man' and neither initiate nor, second, determine the recipient of the transmission.[122] The third condition is that they must not select or modify the information contained in the transmission.

Of course, for very small periods of time, a telecoms company or other 'mere conduit' will be storing the material being transmitted. This short-term storage will still be classified as 'transmission' where it is necessary and quick. More particularly, this sort of storage must be 'automatic, immediate and transient' for no longer than is reasonably necessary and must take place for the sole purpose of the transmission.[123]

However, where a company is providing an Internet hosting service which contains defamatory material, it will be deemed to be publishing the material if it fails to remove it once notified of the defamatory nature of the material.[124]

3.6.2.6   Storage providers

Since the implementation of the Electronic Commerce Regulations, service providers have two possible defences to a defamation claim: first, under the Regulations, reg 19 and then, if appropriate, under s 1 of the Defamation Act 1996.

The reason for the potential of these 'two bites at the cherry' is that the Defamation Act 1996 provides, it can be argued, a wider defence than the Regulations. The Regulations do not repeal the Defamation Act, but rather provide the 'minimum' protection for service providers. And, of course, the Regulations only benefit those service providers that are established in a member state (including EEA states),[125] whereas the Act applies to all English defamation cases, whether or not the service provider is established outside the EU.

---

121   In the US, it has been held that a telephone company does not publish a message spoken down its lines – *Anderson v New York Telephone Co* 361 NYS 2d 913 (NYCA 1974).
122   Reg 17(1).
123   Reg 17(2).
124   *Godfrey v Demon Internet Ltd* [2001] QB 201. In his judgment, Morland J referred to the words of Greene LJ in *Byrne v Deane* [1937] 1KB 818 (a case which related to the failure of a golf club to remove a defamatory statement from a notice board under its control) as follows: 'The test it appears to me is this: having regard to all the facts of the case is the proper inference that by not removing the defamatory matter the defendant really made himself responsible for its continued presence in the place where it had been put?'
125   Electronic Commerce Directive, recital 19; Electronic Commerce Regulations, reg 2(1).

3.6.3   Defences

Before considering the defences under the Defamation Act and Electronic Commerce Regulations separately, it is worthwhile giving a short précis of their potential differences.

1.   The Defamation Act, s 1 defence applies only to secondary publishers being those who are not authors, editors or publishers of the defamatory material; the Regulations are wider and apply to any service provider storing the third party material.

2.   The Defamation Act, s 1 defence applies only where the secondary publisher such as a service provider took 'reasonable care' in relation to the publication in question; the Regulations do not require a duty of care, they essentially require that the service provider 'unwittingly' published the statement, without knowledge or awareness.

3.   The Defamation Act, s 1 defence will cease to apply where the service provider does not remove the material on notice, probably within a reasonable time period; the Regulations require that the service provider must act 'expeditiously' to remove or disable the material once notified.

3.6.3.1   The Defamation Act 1996, s 1 defence

If the provider of an Internet service is held to have published a defamatory statement, it may seek to avail itself of the defence contained in s 1 of the Act. To succeed, the third party provider:

(a)   must not be the author, editor or publisher of the material. Only if they are not considered to be one of these persons may they then rely on the defence;

(b)   must take reasonable care in relation to the publication in question; and

(c)   must not know or have no reason to believe that which it did caused or contributed to the publication of a defamatory statement.[126]

3.6.3.1.1   Not authors, editors or publishers

The Act defines these individuals along with providing presumptions. If the third party's activities fall within one of the presumptions listed below, they may then seek to rely on the defence. If they do not fall squarely within the presumption, they will have to prove that their activities are not those of an author, editor or the publisher as defined. If they do not fall within these definitions, i.e. they are not an author, editor or publisher, they may seek to rely on the defence.

---

126   In *Godfrey v Demon Internet Ltd* [2001] QB 201, the fact that a posting remained available on the defendant's servers some 10 days after the notification proved fatal for the defence. It is submitted that the courts will interpret 'expeditiously', a new import from the Electronic Commerce Regulations, to mean the defence is not lost where the material continues to be available an instant after notification. However, service providers should always err on the side of caution and remove the defamatory material as soon as possible after notification.

3.6.3.1.2   Definitions

If a third party has been unable to convince a court that it falls within one of the presumptions or an analogous situation, it has one last chance of pleading that, in the alternative, it is not an author, editor or publisher within the definitions of the Act.[127]

> '"author" means the originator of the statement, but does not include a person who did not intend that his statement be published at all;
>
> "editor" means a person having editorial or equivalent responsibility for the content of the statement or the decision to publish it; and
>
> "publisher" means a commercial publisher, that is, a person whose business is issuing material to the public, or a section of the public, who issues material containing the statement in the course of that business.'

It is clear from the definition of 'publisher' that the Act does not contemplate a person being a publisher where publishing is merely incidental to their business.[128] For example, many firms have internal networks or intranets on which various pieces of information are posted. Should defamatory material be posted on this internal network, by an employee, the employer is unlikely to be viewed as a publisher for the purposes of the Act. Their business is not the issuing of material to the public and they are not a commercial publisher; their business does not depend on the issuance of material on the intranet.

3.6.3.1.3   Presumptions

The relevant presumptions for the Internet are that a person shall not be considered the author, editor or the publisher of a statement if he is only involved[129]:

> '(c)   in processing, making copies of, distributing or selling any electronic medium in or on which the statement is recorded, or in operating or providing any equipment, system or service by means of which the statement is retrieved, copied, distributed or made available in electronic form;
>
> . . .
>
> (e)   as the operator of or provider of access to a communications system by means of which the statement is transmitted, or made available, by a person over whom he has no effective control.'

The key to interpreting these sections is that the party must 'only' be involved in these activities. If a third party does no more than that described in s 1(3)(c) or (e) they may be able to rely on the defences described below. To illustrate the scope of these presumptions, this chapter applies them to the following issues:

---

127   Defamation Act 1996, s 1(2).
128   It should be noted that, although the words 'publication' and 'publish' retain their common law meanings, the word 'publisher' is specially defined for the purposes of s 1: Defamation Act 1996, s 17(1).
129   Defamation Act 1996, s 1(3)(c), (e).

sending and forwarding emails; hosting a website; hosting a mirror site; designing websites; providing access to newsgroups; and providing forums.

Sending and forwarding emails and allowing uploading of content

One safe example of an activity that falls within s 1(3)(c) is the facilities of a provider to send and forward emails. When an email is sent to another individual, or a group of individuals, there are two third parties who are additionally often involved. The first is the defendant's service provider. The email is sent out onto the Internet from this provider's server computers. There will also be a second third party, the provider or providers to which the defamatory email is sent. These providers will pass on the email to their respective intended recipients.

The providers to the defendant and recipients will not be viewed as editors or publishers under the presumption. They will only have provided a service by means of which the defamatory email statement is distributed (for the defendant) and retrieved (for the recipients).[130] Each of the controllers of the intermediary computers on the Internet that automatically shunted the email nearer and nearer its destination will also fall within the presumption that they are not an editor or publisher. A server linked to the Internet has packets of zeros and ones 'passing through' every second. These packets originated as messages and data created and sent by other servers over which they have no control. What is more, the nature of the Internet is such that it may be impossible even to know who was the original sender of a message.[131]

The High Court has also held that internet service providers whose services are used to upload statements to a website (but which the ISP did not host) are not liable but merely act as facilitators providing a means of transmitting communications without participating in that process. The case[132] concerned alleged defamatory statements posted by several individuals on a website. The claimant brought actions against the indivduals and their service providers for allowing their services to be used for such purposes. The court struck out the claims on the basis that the ISPs had played only a passive role.

Hosting a website

Another safe example of an activity falling squarely within one of the presumptions is where a provider rents out space on a web server to individuals to use as home pages. For example, many Internet service providers, by way of subscription, will provide a person with a website address at which he can leave material to be viewed by others. Again, such a provider has no hand in the actual content of the site and would be viewed as providing a service by means of which the

---

130 Defamation Act 1996, s 1(3)(c).
131 There is also the technical argument that the email is not even published by these intermediaries. Any email is broken into packets which are in a human unreadable form, and some of the packets will not pass through the same computer. It would be a momentous task to prove that one of the intermediary computers actually transmitted all of the packets in relation to one particular email, all in order.
132 *John Blunt v (1) David Tilley (2) Paul Hancox (3) Christopher Stephens (4) AOL UK Limited (5) Tiscali UK Limited (6) British Telecommunications Plc* [2006] EWCH 407 (QB).

material on the defamatory website is made available.[133] The provider would be able to rely on the defences, as would the provider used by the viewer of the website.[134]

Hosting a mirror site

A server that stores a website or ftp site must be able to cope with all the requests, sometimes simultaneously, from viewers' computers. Occasionally the most popular sites become so inundated with digital requests that they begin to slow. To solve this problem, a controller of a website will set up or rent space on a mirror site. As the name suggests, this site is an identical copy of the original site; it simply allows another route into the website, so reducing the strain on the original. The controller of the mirror site appears not to be presumed to be an author, editor or publisher as he is only providing equipment by means of which the statement is retrieved, copied, distributed or made available in electronic form.[135] He would be able to rely on the defences.

Designing websites

The above examples should not be taken to indicate that all those involved in the website will not be viewed as authors, editors or publishers. There are many companies who design websites for other individuals, companies and advertising firms. These designers are involved in more than only making the statement available in an electronic form and have effective control over their contractor. Indeed, often these companies will amend text and include graphics to best represent the client's activities on the website. It is rare that a client will approach such a designer with the code ready to be used for the website. For website designers, therefore, it is important that they acquire an indemnity from their client over any defamation actions.

Providing access to newsgroups

Newsgroups, like forums, are collections of written conversations and files that are left for everyone to reply to or purely retrieve. Many of these forums have fairly specialised and often sexual subject matters; these run a great risk of holding defamatory material. To access these newsgroups, a viewer will generally have only to access his provider's servers. This is because service providers store copies of the newsgroups on their local machines. Because of this, they may re-publish defamatory material so they should be careful to fall within one of the presumptions.

There is, however, a problem with attempting to persuade a court that, in relation to the newsgroups, the provider is only providing a service by means of which a statement is copied or made available in an electronic form. This problem occurs because a provider will rarely carry all the many thousands of news-

133   Defamation Act 1996, s 1(3)(c).
134   Defamation Act 1996, s 1(3)(e).
135   Defamation Act 1996, s 1(3)(c).

groups; they are selective. For example, many providers avoid the overtly porno-graphic groups. In doing so, it could be alleged that the provider is doing more than only electronically distributing the material: they are censoring, for what-ever reasons, certain of the newsgroups. In doing this, it is arguable that they are acting as an editor. That is they are assuming responsibility for the decision to publish a statement.[136]

It is submitted that this reasoning relies on an excessively constrained view of the presumptions. The decision to exclude certain newsgroups without having seen their content should not be translated into having editorial responsibility for the content of the others: the provider is still only making the copies of the news-groups available in an electronic form.[137] Merely because there was certain mate-rial that the provider chose not to make available should not indicate that the provider has assumed some responsibility over the distributed newsgroups. It is when a provider begins to edit or delete the actual text of the individual state-ments within a newsgroup that the provider approaches the position of editor.

Providing forums

Many service providers and websites provide forums for their members. These are collections of conversations/files and clips that can be accessed by any mem-ber of the forum. The providers of these forums face the greatest problem of lia-bility. Rather than simply allowing anyone to post up anything on a forum, the providers will often moderate the text and messages before or soon after they are posted. They do this, presumably, to protect the other members of the forum from vulgarities and irrelevancies. Of course, in doing this, just like a newspaper edi-tor edits a reader's letter, they are, in effect, acting as an editor. The provider is no longer only making the copies of the statements available in an electronic form; the provider is editing the statement.

This would appear to indicate that the prudent provider who attempts to screen out defamatory comments may not be able to benefit from the defence. In con-trast, the provider who turns a blind eye to defamatory comments and does not edit the messages will be able to rely on the defence.[138] There are two justifica-tions for this seemingly counter-intuitive conclusion.

136   From the definition of an 'editor' in the Defamation Act 1996, s 1(2).
137   The nature of the 'flooding algorithm' through which the newsgroups are distributed amongst providers also gives the provider little effective control over material.
138   An example of this is provided by the American case, *Cubby Inc v Compuserve Inc* 776 F Supp 135 (SDNY 1991). Compuserve carried a forum, 'Rumorville', that was managed by a company unrelated to Compuserve. A defamatory statement was published on this forum and Compuserve was sued. The court compared Compuserve to an 'electronic, for-profit library' (at 140) and stated that summary judgment should be given in favour of Compuserve. This was primarily because the claimants did not set forth any specific facts showing a genuine issue of Compuserve knowing or having reason to know of the forum's contents. (Cf Defamation Act 1996, s 1(1)(b) and (c).) Although this judgment and Compuserve's argu-ments were heavily steeped in the First Amendment, the case can be used to illustrate that the more distance a provider puts between itself and the forum, the more likely it will be able to rely on the defence. Conversely, this imposes a burden on the claimant to adduce evidence that the provider, by making this distance, was not taking reasonable care and should have known the risk of defamation. A forum name like 'Rumorville' must surely place the provider on notice.

Stratton v Prodigy

The first is a commercial justification that is provided by the court in one of the first Internet defamation cases from America: *Stratton Oakmont Inc v Prodigy Services Co.*[139] Prodigy is a large Internet service provider; one of its services was a bulletin board called 'Money Talk'. An unknown individual posted a defamatory remark that the claimant company was guilty of fraud. The claimant sought partial summary judgment against Prodigy on two issues, namely: whether Prodigy may be considered 'publisher' of the statements[140]; and whether the Board Leader for the bulletin board on which the statements were posted was Prodigy's 'agent' for the purpose of the claims.

Prodigy prided itself on exercising editorial control over the content of messages posted on its computer bulletin boards, differentiating itself from its competition and expressly likening itself to a newspaper. In the case, Prodigy is quoted as stating:

> 'We make no apology for pursuing a value system that reflects the culture of the millions of American families we aspire to serve. Certainly no responsible newspaper does less when it carries the type of advertising it publishes, the letters it prints, the degree of nudity and unsupported gossip its editors tolerate.'

It was precisely this editing, both manual and automatic, that the court reasoned brought the defendant within the realms of a publisher, or more widely, made the defendant responsible for the content. The court was content to rule that, despite Prodigy's aim to protect its members, it should be liable when this protection fails. To the proposition that this decision will simply force Providers not to edit postings, so avoiding liability, the court drew on a 'market forces' argument.

> 'For the record, the fear that this court's finding of publisher status for Prodigy will compel all computer networks to abdicate control of their bulletin boards, incorrectly presumes that the market will refuse to compensate a network for its increased control and the resulting increased exposure... Presumably Prodigy's decision to regulate the content of its bulletin boards was in part influenced by its desire to attract a market it perceived to exist consisting of users seeking a "family-oriented" computer service. This decision simply required that to the extent computer networks provide such services, they must also accept the concomitant legal consequences.'

Looking strictly at law, the Prodigy case provides little authority for an English court. Under English law the Defamation Act 1996 is quite clear that editorial decisions, like those made by Prodigy, will bring the Provider into the realms of an editor or publisher. This is particularly true where, like certain Providers, members are charged an extra rate to access certain 'moderated' forums. In this situation, the Provider appears to be within the definition of a 'publisher' under the Act.[141]

---

139 NYS 2d Index No 31063/94, 1995 WL 323710.
140 In the case Prodigy were seeking to prove themselves as 'distributors' and thus able to rely on a defence of innocent dissemination.
141 Defamation Act 1996, s 1(2).

'"publisher" means a commercial publisher, that is, a person whose business is issuing material to the public, or a section of the public, who issues material containing the statement in the course of that business.'

What the case does illustrate is one justification for a court imposing a ruling that a prudent provider should be liable whereas a reckless provider has an opportunity to rely on a defence. This justification is that individuals will pay for quality and editing; too much of the Internet is of very dubious quality. This increase in income gained by being able to charge more to a discerning member has a concomitant legal risk.

There is a second explanation for the seemingly unjust rule that 'the prudent Provider is punished'. This is described below.

3.6.3.1.4 Strength of defences

In much of the discussion about the Defamation Act 1996 there seems to be an assumption that, if a provider is reckless as to content, the provider has an easy task to plead a defence. This is not so. As will be considered below, a provider who turns a blind eye to defamatory material will have difficulties in meeting the test of reasonable care. But there is also a commercial advantage in being a prudent provider: you may be sued less often and may increase the confidence of target users. Would a parent be keen for their child to use an unmonitored site? A prudent provider screening as much content as is feasible may eliminate many potential defamation and, indeed, other actions. In contrast, a reckless provider may find itself defending many lawsuits having to hope that they will be able to satisfy the defences. These two situations will obviously affect the level of insurance premiums payable by the two types of provider.

This lengthy discussion on the liability for providing forums indicates that what at first appears as counterproductive legislation is explicable, even if not palatable, to those in the online industry.

The s 1(1) defence requires two hurdles to be cleared by the defendant. First, he must show that he took reasonable care in relation to the statement's publication. In addition, he must show that he did not know, and had no reason to believe, that what he did caused or contributed to the publication of a defamatory statement.[142]

To determine what is reasonable and what should be known, the Act provides three considerations to which the court shall have regard. The first consideration is the extent of the responsibility for the content of the statement or decision to publish.[143] This provides little guidance for a service provider. The second and third considerations are more helpful. Regard shall be had to the nature or circumstances of the publication and the previous conduct or character of the author, editor or publisher.[144]

---

142 For some interesting submissions as to what 'reasonable care' may constitute in the case of an ISP, for example, through the inclusion of warnings to users in terms and conditions, see *John Blunt*, ibid.

143 Defamation Act 1996, s 1(5)(a).

144 Defamation Act 1996, s 1(5)(b) and (c).

These last two considerations indicate that to take reasonable care one must first judge the care which is required in a given scenario. It will not be reasonable care simply to republish an entire newsgroup that has a reputation for being scurrilous and defamatory. It is no defence for the provider to state that it did not know that a particular posting was defamatory. This is because the court is required to judge that the provider did not know and had no reason to believe that the material would be defamatory.[145] Service providers are advised not to turn a blind eye to the nature of the material that they publish. If a forum is known to carry postings of dubious veracity, a provider is taking a risk to publish its material without vetting.

The prospect of vetting the contents of a site or forum raises two problems: one commercial, the other legal. The commercial problem is how can a provider feasibly vet the thousands of postings that are posted each day? It is no surprise that an industry of monitoring and moderating services has grown, using a combination of technical (word and 'flesh' searching) and human (employees who screen content round the clock) to give comfort to some. For many providers, this will be simply impossible. However, the Act does not impose an absolute requirement that postings are vetted; it is more rational than that: reasonable care must be taken.

This does not mean vetting every posting, but it also does not mean blindly republishing dubious newsgroups and entertaining the postings made by known defamers. During the passage of the Bill through the House of Commons, Mr Streeter explained[146]:

'We must put distributors, printers, wholesalers and retailers on notice that they should have regard to the nature of a publication if they seek to rely on that defence.'

A commercial balance must be struck. Providers may choose to vet one hour of postings on a particular forum every day. Providers may also choose to allow members to alert them, by priority email, of a defamatory comment.

The legal problem that has been raised about vetting material is that it produces a circular argument. This goes as follows. To take reasonable care (under the Act) a provider must occasionally edit some material. By editing some material the provider cannot now be only involved with one of the five presumptive activities. This conclusion strips the presumption from the provider that it is not an author, editor or publisher.

This legal problem is not as confusing as it appears. As this section has shown, a provider can rely on a presumption that it is not an author, editor or publisher, but failing that, the provider is not necessarily an author, editor or publisher. The

---

145 Defamation Act 1996, s 1(1)(c).
146 Parliamentary Secretary, Lord Chancellor's Department (promoter of the Bill), 280 HC Official Report (6th Series) col 119, 24 June 1996. This is added as an indication of the intention of Parliament; it is not mentioned as a statement upon which a court could rely under the strict criteria laid down in *Pepper (Inspector of Taxes) v Hart* [1993] 1 All ER 42 and *Melluish (Inspector of Taxes) v BMI (No 3) Ltd* [1996] AC 454. Although perhaps prejudicial to Internet Service Providers, it is this author's submission that the Bill does not meet the criteria of being ambiguous or obscure or its literal meaning leading to an absurdity.

provider remains able to plead that it does not fall within the definitions of author, editor or publisher. So, by editing material the provider is not prevented from relying on the defence, it is simply prevented from relying on the presumption. The court remains able to hear evidence that the provider is not a publisher or editor under the definitions. And if convinced, the court can still allow the provider to rely on the defence of reasonable care.

Of course, the ramifications of this analysis are that the Defamation Act 1996 has impaled many service providers on the horns of a dilemma. If they turn a blind eye to all content, they may be able to rely on the presumption that they are not a publisher. They will, however, be unlikely to convince a court that by doing nothing they took all reasonable care and so must rely on the Electronic Commerce Regulations only. Conversely, if they are prudent and edit out potentially defamatory material, they will not be able to rely on the presumption as they are now only involved in non-editorial activities. They will be left with convincing a court that they are not a publisher, which under the Act, as a person whose business is issuing material to the public, they probably are.

In this 'lose-lose' predicament a service provider should be aware of four practical issues. First, if the provider does edit its content effectively, it will be sued less frequently as it will republish defamatory statements less often. Ignoring content will increasingly lead one to a position of being unable to ignore litigation. The second issue is that insurance is available to service providers, but premiums may be significantly lower if the provider takes some responsibility. The third issue is one of identification. If a provider ensures that each of its members provides a full name and address before entering a forum, it makes it more likely that a claimant may consider suing only the author of the statement. In *Prodigy* the offending posting was made by an unknown person.[147] The final issue is one of legal procedure. A court will often pay attention to whether the parties have 'clean hands'. In this respect, a court will not look favourably on a provider who has deliberately avoided reading material to allow a technical plea of one of the presumptions.

3.6.3.1.5 Evidence

It is critical that Internet service providers appreciate the burden they are under, evidentially, to prove that they fall within the defence. It is the provider, rather than the claimant, who must prove that it is not an author, editor or publisher. It is also the provider that must meet the two tests to prove the defence.[148] It is therefore sensible for a service provider to maintain complete records of all its automatic or manual dealings with third party material. In particular, a service provider should be able to provide a court with evidence to satisfy the three issues to which the court will have regard to judge the level of care and knowledge of the provider.[149] It is also worthwhile noting that the term 'reasonable

---

147   This advice is applicable only to internal forums. Clearly, if a Provider republishes a Usenet newsgroup, many of the postings will be made from outside the control of the Provider.
148   This is in contrast, say, to secondary infringement under the Copyright, Designs and Patents Act 1988, s 23.
149   Defamation Act 1996, s 1(1)(b) and (c) and s 1(5)(a), (b) and (c).

care' introduces a relative test: providers may find it useful to adduce expert evidence as to the reasonableness of their care in relation to industry practice.

3.6.3.2 Electronic Commerce Regulations hosting defence

It was discussed earlier that the Electronic Commerce Regulations might provide an additional defence for service providers faced with a defamation claim. The reasoning is that the Regulations simply provide another defence; they do not repeal or amend existing legislation.

A service provider defending a claim of defamation may be able to rely on two possible defences under the Electronic Commerce Regulations 2002, reg 19 ('hosting defence') or on the 'mere conduit' and 'caching' defences under regulations 17 and 18, depending on the circumstances. These are considered below.

3.6.3.2.1 Hosting defences

(a) No actual knowledge, no awareness, no control

The first defence is essentially that the service provider must be unwittingly publishing the defamatory material.[150] This is in three parts. First, the host must not have 'actual knowledge' that the publication of the statement or material was in breach of any law, here defamation law. The second part is that the host must *also* 'not be aware of facts or circumstances' from which it would have been apparent that the activity or information was unlawful. Third, and considered below, the provider must have no authority or control over the defamer.

No actual knowledge of breach of law
This first part of the defence is akin to the Defamation Act 1996, s 1(1)(c). It should be taken to mean that the hosting company has not been provided with 'notice' about the defamatory material. This notice need not, however, be in writing and it certainly need not originate from a court. The court must, however, have regard to the extent to which the notice identifies its sender, the location of the material and the defamation. The court shall also factor in where the notice was sent.

In *Godfrey v Demon Internet Ltd,*[151] on 17 January 1997 the defendant service provider's managing director was sent a fax from the claimant complaining about a posting on a Usenet news server hosted by them. This was enough for the court, under the Defamation Act 1996, to indicate that, at full trial, the defendant would be deemed to be 'on notice'; they had actual knowledge after 17 January 1997.

No awareness of facts or circumstances
If the service provider has no actual knowledge, they must then demonstrate that they have no awareness of relevant facts or circumstances which would lead them to believe the statement is unlawful. If they can do this, they will still need

---

150   Reg 19(a)(i).
151   [2001] QB 201.

to prove that the defamer was outside their authority or control, described below.

The courts may interpret this in a similar manner as the requirements in the Defamation Act 1996, s 1(1)(b) and (c). The nub of this part of the defence is that service providers who simply turn a 'blind eye' to a defamatory statement being on its service, cannot benefit from this aspect of the defence. Indeed, this warning rings clear in the obiter judgment of the High Court in *John Blunt v David Tilley and Others*, the first English case considering the Regulations (although its focus was the mere conduit and caching defences, discussed below):

> 'It is clear that the state of a defendant's knowledge can be an important factor. If a person knowingly permits another to communicate information which is defamatory, when there would be an opportunity to prevent the publication, there would seem to be no reason in principle why liability should not accrue.'[152]

The court clarified that, although it is possible for editors or publishers to be fixed with responsibility notwithstanding lack of knowledge, for persons to be involved: 'there must be knowing involvement in the process of publication … It is not enough that a person merely plays a passive role in the process.'

(B)   No authority or control and expeditious action

The second hosting defence concerns the actions of the service provider once they have knowledge or awareness. They will have the benefit of the defence if they meet two conditions. They must not be in control and they must have no authority over the person who defamed. The second condition, as for the first defence, is that they must act expeditiously to remove or disable access to it as soon as they know about it[153].

No authority or control

The first condition to meet is for the service provider not to have 'authority' or 'control' over the third party who originally published the defamatory statement on its service.[154] Of course, often a service provider will have a contract with its members or customers. If they defame, will this constitute 'authority' or 'control'? This author and the DTI believe it will not.

The DTI states in its unbinding note on the Regulations that the concept of control or authority will be akin to 'effective control' under the Defamation Act 1996.[155] In other words, a mere contract to provide services to the third party will not be sufficient to bring the third party under the service provider's 'control' or 'authority'. The Regulations require a closer relationship such as between an employee, the third party, and an employer, the service provider.

An open question remains relating to whether or not the ability to control the third party will constitute control for the purposes of the first prong of the

---

152   *John Blunt*, ibid.
153   Reg 19(a)(ii) and (b).
154   Reg 19(a)(ii).
155   *A Guide for Business to the Electronic Commerce (EC Directive) Regulations 2002*, para 6.7(c).

defence. After all, most, if not all service providers have the ability to remove material that is defamatory. Indeed, in a worst-case scenario, a service provider can always simply disable all publication of the statement; will that be 'control'?

US authority on a similar question is convincing that, were such an interpretation to be applied, it would be contrary to the spirit of the legislation itself. It would, in effect, state that those who are able to comply with the onus to remove material once notified must be able to remove the material and so are deemed to control it[156]:

> 'First, the "right and ability to control" the infringing activity, as the concept is used in the [Digital Millennium Copyright Act ("DMCA")], cannot simply mean the ability of a service provider to remove or block access to materials posted on its website or stored in its system. To hold otherwise would defeat the purpose of the DMCA and render the statute internally inconsistent. The DMCA specifically requires a service provider to remove or block access to materials posted on its system when it receives notice of claimed infringement. *See* 17 U.S.C. §§ 512(c)(1)(C). The DMCA also provides that the limitations on liability *only* apply to a service provider that has "adopted and reasonably implemented... a policy that provides for the termination in appropriate circumstances of [users] of the service provider's system or network who are repeat infringers." *See* 17 U.S.C. §§ 512(i)(1)(A). Congress could not have intended for courts to hold that a service provider loses immunity under the safe harbor provision of the DMCA because it engages in acts that are specifically required by the DMCA.'

Remove or disable expeditiously

The second condition is essentially that the service provider must act to stop any further harm as soon as they know about it. The Regulations state that 'upon obtaining such knowledge or awareness the service provider [must act] expeditiously to remove or to disable access to the information'.[157]

So, how fast is 'expeditiously'? There is little doubt that this is quicker than 'reasonably quickly' but nevertheless will be assessed with reference to the facts and circumstances of the situation. It can be said with some certainty that a service provider who is sent a specific notice about defamatory material on 17 January will need to act well before the 27th to do so expeditiously.[158]

3.6.3.2.2   Mere conduit and caching defences

Where a service provider does not host websites or content containing defamatory statements, they may still have access to a defence where they act as a mere conduit or are only involved through the caching of such content. Both defences were relied upon with success, along with the defence available in s 1 of the Defamation Act, in the case of *John Blunt v David Tilley & Others*.

---

156   *Hendrickson v Ebay Inc* 2001 WL 1078981, CD Cal, 4 September 2001.
157   Reg 19(a)(ii).
158   In *Godfrey v Demon Internet Ltd*, this was the timing of the fax from the claimant to the eventual removal of the statement from the servers.

Mere Conduit

A service provider will not be liable provided they:

(1)   did not initiate the transmission;

(2)   did not select the receiver of the transmission; and

(3)   did not select or modify the information contained in the transmission.[159]

Caching

Regulation 18 states that a service provider will not be liable where:

> 'The information is subject of automatic, intermediate and temporary storage where that storage is for the sole purpose of making more efficient onward transmission of the information to other recipients of the service upon their request.'

This will only be available provided the defendant has not modified the information and (as for hosting), acts expeditiously to remove or disable access to the information.

---

19.   KoolistKidzKlub is an online club through which children can enter competitions, get information on their favourite childrens' TV programmes and exchange comments and clips with other club members. The website owners will have to make a judgment, on the one hand, to pre-vet and even amend user postings to prevent offensive behaviour or any defamatory or other content which is unsuitable for children from being posted, and thus lose its defences under the Defamation Act and Electronic Commerce Regulations. On the other hand they could monitor and ensure that users and their parents have confidence in the site and its integrity. KoolistKidzKlub could consider speaking to professional moderator companies to obtain quotes for a third party to conduct such checking for them.

3.6.4   Damages

3.6.4.1   Presumption of damage

Publication of a defamatory article carries with it a presumption that the person defamed has suffered damage under English law but this does not mean that damage is immediately made out and that any publication can result in an actionable case.

Readers may wonder how such a potentially wide presumption fits against rights publishers may have of freedom of expression. This question has been resolved in a recent Court of Appeal case.[160] The case concerned the publication by the *Wall Street Journal* of articles concerning individuals allegedly funding Al Qaeda. A list of potential donors including the claimant's name were published

---

159   S 17(1) Electronic Commerce Regulations.
160   *Jameel v Dow Jones & Co Inc* [2005] EWCA Civ 75, 3 February 2005.

and he issued proceedings in the English courts for defamation. The court dismissed the publisher's assertion that the presumption of damage to the claimant was incompatible with Art 10 of the Human Rights Act.

However, despite this, the court agreed that the publication of the article and name had had minimal impact and done no significant damage to the claimant's reputation. On this basis it did not amount to a real and actionable tort. The court therefore dismissed the case as an abuse of process.

3.6.4.2 Extent of publication

The damages for defamation are based on a number of factors, although the extent of publication is very relevant: 'a libel published to millions has a greater potential to cause damage than a libel published to a handful of people'[161]. This statement leads some to presume that the damages for an Internet libel will be huge because so many people have access to it. This is false. That the Internet has potentially millions of people accessing it bears no relationship to the number of people accessing the defamatory piece. The jury should not be allowed to infer that the extent of publication must be great because the material is available over the Internet. What the claimant should adduce is the actual extent of the publication of the defamatory piece. On the Internet, it is far easier to estimate how many people actually viewed a particular piece than it is to prove how many people had access to a newspaper[162]. Figures should be able to be provided with quite a high degree of accuracy. The case considered in section 3.6.4.1 above demonstrates this clearly. In that case, the action was dismissed since, although the article appeared in the well-known and distributed *Wall Street Journal On-line*, the claimant's name was only listed in a hyperlink from such article and it was demonstrated that only five UK subscribers had actually followed this. The Court of Appeal in this case emphasised that defamation claims may not be used solely for vindication.

---

20. An Internet service provider defames an individual on a much used forum called 'GossipsVille'. Liability is not in issue. The individual claims that GossipsVille is the most popular forum on the Internet and hosts over 500,000 readers every day. Counsel for the Provider should attempt to provide evidence of the exact number of individuals who actually read the statement. It is very likely this will be significantly less than the 500,000 average so acting to reduce the award.

3.6.4.3 Reductions and recommendations

The general level of defamation damages is declining. Since the Courts and Legal Services Act 1990, the Court of Appeal has been able to reduce the dam-

---

161 *John v MGN Ltd* [1996] 2 All ER 35 at 48.
162 It can be said, in contrast with this, that it is difficult to tell the number of times a particular piece was copied and redistributed to other servers. This, it is submitted, is as far as one could go: it is difficult. It is not impossible and it is the claimant's burden to adduce the best evidence of circulation.

ages on appeal.[163] The most spectacular example was when the singer Elton John saw his £350,000 damages reduced by the Court of Appeal to £75,000.[164] Clearly, for Mr John, this was a significant reduction. What is of greater significance to all claimants is what the Court of Appeal said about future defamation cases. The first, almost revolutionary, point of law made was[165]:

> '[t]he time has in our view come when judges, and counsel, should be free to draw the attention of juries to these comparisons [between the awards for personal injury and awards for injury to reputation].'

The court called it 'offensive to public opinion' that the damages for injury to reputation may be greater than if the claimant had been rendered a 'helpless cripple or an insensate vegetable'.[166] To guide the jury from such offensive awards the court also added that the judge should be free to give indications to the jury as to the realistic bracket for the damages.[167]

This judgment may have a chilling effect on claimants who seek to gain vast damages from providers. In negotiation of settlement, defendants should be aware that awards in the hundreds of thousands of pounds will become increasingly rare.

3.6.5 Strategy

The area of defamation is problematic for service providers because the law appears to place them under a huge burden even after the Electronic Commerce Regulations. This section describes some strategies that may be of assistance in reducing their exposure to risk.

3.6.5.1 Withdraw quickly

Service providers should have a quick response policy for dealing with defamation allegations. They have the advantage over the paper publishers that they can withdraw the statement from circulation in a matter of seconds. This reduces their damages liability and can also increase the chance of settling the matter more quickly.

163 Courts and Legal Services Act 1990, s 8.
164 *John v MGN Ltd* [1996] 2 All ER 35. To avoid misleading the reader, the majority of the reduction is accounted for by the court's substitution of £50,000 for the awarded £275,000 for exemplary damages. This was justified by the statement of the law that exemplary damages are awarded where the publisher had no genuine belief in the truth of what he published, suspected that the words were untrue, yet deliberately refrained from taking the obvious steps to turn 'suspicion into certainty' (at 57–58). For Internet defamation, an exemplary damages award will only be appropriate where the Provider is not considered the author, editor or publisher of the statement. In these cases, the Provider would have had no real opportunity to read, let alone consider and investigate, the statements. The ruling on exemplary damages, therefore, will be applicable only where the Internet Service Provider is unable to field a defence because of being an author, editor or publisher.
165 [1996] 2 All ER 35 at 54 per Sir Thomas Bingham MR delivering judgment for the court.
166 [1996] 2 All ER 35 at 54.
167 [1996] 2 All ER 35 at 55.

3.6.5.2   *Grievance channel*

The provider must have a channel available to receive complaints. If a postal address is the only point of communication provided, the statement may have been published hundreds of thousands of times before the provider is made aware. A special, not just the general, email address should be employed. Complainants should be requested to send a digital copy of the allegedly defamatory statement to the special email address for consideration.

3.6.5.3   *Indemnity and identity*

Two further strategies relate to the relationship between the provider and the author of the alleged defamatory statement. There will be times where the defamatory material is authored by a person who has no relationship with the provider. This is generally the case with providers who host Usenet newsgroups: any person may have access to the groups from any provider in the world. There will be other times where the provider already has a contract with the author of the statement. It may be that the author is renting space on the provider's server for a website, or that the author is a registered member of a particular forum hosted by the provider.

In these contractual situations it is advisable to include a term in the contract that the member will indemnify the provider against costs and damages as a result of any defamatory statement made by the author, published by the provider (subject of course to careful drafting to comply with consumer laws, for which see Chapter 2). Of course, the problem with such a term is that it is worthless if the indemnifier is a man-of-straw. It may, however, provide some financial support in the wake of an action.

The second strategy is for the provider to maintain records of the actual identity of a member. This can be used if there is litigation to provide, on request of the claimant, the identity of the actual author of the statement.[168] Although there is a likelihood that a claimant will prefer to pursue a wealthy Provider than an individual, the claimant will have no choice unless the provider can supply the identity of the first defendant. For example, in the *Prodigy* case, Prodigy was unable to identify the individual who made the defamatory remark. This duty to provide litigants with the details of a defamer should be alerted to each member. They should be reassured that their details will be only provided in the light of a bona fide dispute.[169]

---

168   The House of Lords in *Norwich Pharmacal Co v Customs and Excise Comrs* [1974] AC 133 provided that where a person had facilitated or become mixed up in the wrongdoing by another, that person is under an enforceable duty to disclose to a party harmed by the wrongdoing the identity of the wrongdoer in order to enable the party to sue the wrongdoer. This was followed in *Totalise plc v Motley Fool Ltd* [2002] 1 WLR 1233 where the service provider was required to disclose the identity of a defamer on a web chat site to the claimant. As with most *Norwich Pharmacal* applications, Aldous LJ stated that, in general, the innocent intermediary should have its costs met.

169   Providers should be careful not to provide personal details without first consulting their data protection notification and their terms of confidentiality with each member.

3.6.5.4 *Outsource moderation*

Content moderation companies have sprung up in recent years as the popularity of user-generated content sites has increased. Using technical and human screening techniques, content can either be pre-vetted or monitored after posting. A robust policy can hugely reduce potentially damaging content and customers may be able to (at least contractually and through indemnities) push some of the risks of failing to spot or remove content onto such service provider.

3.7 JURISDICTION

The Internet allows digital material to be downloaded or seen simultaneously by individuals in every country in the world and, as we have seen, it allows harmful code to spread fast through networks, regardless of geographical boundaries. If a person is damaged or aggrieved by the material or code, his claim will not necessarily fit neatly into a purely English legal dispute. The international growth of the Internet and its disregard for borders will probably introduce a number of non-English legal factors into the person's claim. More than any other means of communication, the Internet will produce truly transnational disputes. Users of the Internet and their advisers must therefore be fully conversant with the English court's rules on jurisdiction and choice of law and the impact of the country of origin rule in the Electronic Commerce Regulations. A deep understanding of private international law combined with the Internet's global dissemination can arm a litigator with additional causes of action and defence. It is crucial that advisers pay due regard to the conflict of laws that may be present in an Internet dispute before wading into an assessment of the substantive law. It is also important that advisers act quickly and appraise themselves fully of the differences in local remedies that may be available, as forum-shopping may be possible.

This first section deals with jurisdiction: English courts' authority to judge disputes.

The Brussels Regulation on Jurisdiction and the Enforcement of Judgments in Civil and Commercial Matters is, as with contractual claims, the starting place for any tort committed over the Internet with a foreign element[170]. First, one must assess whether the Brussels Regulation (or the similar Lugano Convention) apply, i.e. is the defendant domiciled in a state which contracts to these (and if so, which one), or whether jurisdiction is transferred to the English common law.

Section 3.8 focuses on choice of law issues which determine what law will govern an action since, as with contractual claims (see Chapter 2), this must be considered separately from where the action may be brought.

---

170   This entered into force, replacing the Brussels Convention, on 1 March 2002 (2001 OJ L012, 16/01/2001).

3.7.1   Brussels Regulation and Lugano Convention

The analysis required to establish whether or not either the Brussels Regulation (to which all European member states are contracted (Denmark as of 1 July 2007)) or similar Lugano Convention (for European Free Trade Association (EFTA) countries (with the exception of Liechtenstein)) applies, is the same as that required for contractual disputes and is considered in detail in Chapter 2.

For the purposes of this section, our analysis is of the Brussels Regulation and therefore all references to a 'contracting state' are references to countries contracted to that Regulation.

> 21. An English academic who teaches in an English University defames a Dutch academic by posting a message to a forum. This forum is stored on a server in America and the Dutch academic has a substantial reputation only in Holland. The English courts will have jurisdiction over the dispute as the defendant is domiciled in England. The location of the server and the reputation are of little relevance for jurisdiction over the academic in the English courts.

3.7.2   Brussels Regulation jurisdiction over torts

Having established that the defendant to an action is domiciled in a contracting state it can be said with certainty that the Brussels Regulation rules on jurisdiction apply. For matters relating to tort there are rules that supplement the main rule under art 2, that the defendant can be sued in the courts of his domicile. The tort rules provide a claimant with additional jurisdictions in which the defendant can be rightly sued. For example, a German individual may have defamed an English individual by posting a message on a Spanish Provider's bulletin board. Without more than the art 2 rule, the English claimant would have to sue in either Spain or Germany: a practice that may be expensive and complicated. The rules under the Regulation broaden the jurisdiction for tortious claims and specify[171]:

> 'A person domiciled in a Member State may, in another Member State, be sued:... in matters relating to tort, delict or quasi-delict, in the courts for the place where the harmful event occurred or may occur.'

> 22. An estate agent company is incorporated and operates from France. It provides advice to wealthy Australians who are considering buying property in the South of France. Its server is physically based in Perth and the domain address has the suffix 'co.au' which indicates an Australian firm. An Australian arrives at a newly bought property to discover that the company's advice was negligent. Now having a base in France, the Australian decides that it will be cheaper to conduct the litigation from France. He will be able to do this as long as the French courts consider that the estate agent company has its seat within France.

171   Art 5(3).

3.7.2.1 What is a tort?

The heading above, 'What is a tort?' may surprise those who are unfamiliar with jurisdiction issues. The reason it is included is that the terms 'tort, delict or quasi-delict' in art 5(3) must be given an autonomous Community meaning; one cannot simply check whether the dispute would be included in an English textbook on torts. The European Court puts it like this[172]:

'[T]he term "matters relating to tort, delict or quasi-delict" within the meaning of Article 5(3) of the Convention [meaning here the Brussels Convention, the precursor to the Brussels Regulation] must be regarded as an independent concept covering all actions which seek to establish the liability of a defendant and which are not related to a "contract" within the meaning of Article 5(1).'

This approach has been endorsed by the House of Lords in *Kleinwort Benson Ltd v Glasgow City Council*.[173] For the purposes of this section, therefore, art 5(3) will apply in relation to digital damage, defamation and negligent advice.[174]

3.7.2.2 Location of harmful events

A defendant domiciled in a contracting state who commits a tort may be sued in the court of the defendant's domicile or in the court where the harmful event occurred or may occur under art 5(3).[175] Having examined above what constitutes a tort, it is now crucial to consider where a tort occurs (as opposed to where it is suffered, considered in more detail below)

The first European case to deal with this concerned a claimant who carried on the business of nursery gardening in the Netherlands and used water to irrigate the seed beds mainly from the Rhine.[176] The defendant mined in France and was alleged to have increased the salt content in the irrigating water by discharging from Alsace large quantities of residuary salts into the Rhine. On a reference from the national court the European Court held that the phrase 'the place where the harmful event occurred' could refer to two jurisdictions.[177]

'[T]he claimant has an option to commence proceedings either at the place where the damage occurred or the place of the event giving rise to it.'

---

172   *Kalfelis v Schroder, Munchmayer* [1988] ECR 5565 at 5585 [18].
173   [1999] 1 AC 153 and *Agnew v Länsförsakringsbolagens AB* [2000] 1 Lloyd's Rep IR 317.
174   It is useful to note that Rix J correctly states in *Trade Indemnity v Försäkrings AB Njord* [1995] 1 All ER 796 at 820 that an action for misrepresentation or non-disclosures in making a contract is not covered by art 5(1) which relates to contracts. One is therefore bound by *Kalfelis* (see fn 172 above) to conclude that art 5(3) will apply to misrepresentations. A misrepresentation made on a website may be therefore sued upon not only in the defendant's domicile but also in any state in which the claimant acted upon the representation on the web pages; an exclusive jurisdiction clause in the contract will, for this claim, be to no avail.
175   It should be clarified that the option to sue where the harmful event occurred does not remove the fact that the defendant must be domiciled in a contracting state for this to be possible: it just means that you don't have to bring the action in the place of domicile.
176   *Handelskwekerij G J Bier BV v Mines de Potasse d'Alsace SA* [1978] QB 708.
177   [1976] ECR 1735 at 1745–1747 [19].

For an Internet tort, particularly one made over the web, this ruling has a significant effect. Defendants who are domiciled in a contracting state may face claims from any jurisdiction which is signatory to the Regulation. This is because it is technically difficult to prevent a server from being accessed from a particular place in the world. In illustration, malicious code on a website can infect any person accessing that from anywhere in the world; negligent misstatements made on a website or forum may be relied upon by any person anywhere in the world; and defamatory statements on a website or forum may be read by any person anywhere in the world. Likewise, it is not always clear to what jurisdiction an email may be sent or received.

The commercial effects of this are substantial. Companies and individuals domiciled in a contracting state who use the Internet to provide information, services or products risk being sued in any jurisdiction party to the Regulation. Some more specific points are made below.

3.7.2.2.1   Digital damage

There are striking similarities between allowing a computer virus into the Internet and allowing pollutants into a water supply. Both cross borders. Both originate from a fixed source yet can spread in many directions, affecting many claimants. In one way computer viruses have more impact because they have a longer life owing to their perfect replication. These comparisons make it probable that, where the Brussels Regulation applies, a court will follow the European Court's ruling in *Bier*. Under art 2 the claimant will be permitted to sue the defendant in a court of the defendant's place of domicile. In addition, by art 5(3), the claimant can sue the defendant in the place of digital damage: the claimant's 'home' and also in the court of the place of the source of the virus.

---

23. A Spanish architect sent some unsolicited plans to an English property agent. The plans contained a computer virus which corrupted some entries on the agent's database. Were the agent to sue the architect for damage caused by negligence, the agent would have the jurisdiction of the English courts, because the damage occurred there.

3.7.2.2.2   Secondary damage

It has been discussed that viruses and other malicious code will damage not only those directly in contact with the contaminated computer, but also those in contact with an already infected computer. This is coined 'secondary damage'. Such 'ricochet' damage has been criticised as a basis for ousting the right that any defendant has to be sued in the courts of his domicile.

In *Dumez France v Hessische Landesbank (Helaba)*[178] two French parent companies sued in France two German banks. The claim was for compensation for damage arising out of the winding up of their two German subsidiaries. The subsidiaries, it was claimed, had to be wound up because the German banks had withdrawn credit facilities to one of the subsidiary's customers. The European

---

178   [1990] ECR 49.

Court was asked whether the 'place where the harmful event occurred'[179] can be interpreted as including damage claimed by a claimant that is the consequence of harm suffered by other persons who were direct victims.[180] An affirmative answer would have allowed the French companies to sue the German banks in France, as that was the place where they claimed the harmful event occurred.

The court accepted the approach made by the Advocate General that a victim 'by ricochet' cannot bring an action in the courts of the place of that damage. The court is looking not for where damage is suffered, but rather where it occurs. As seems to be obvious, this ruling may often be applicable for digital damage by viral infection. The application is more difficult for economic loss that may occur as a result of viral damage or negligent misstatement.

---

24. A company based in Holland, through the negligence of a supplier also based in Holland, becomes infected by a logic bomb which damages important data. Before the logic bomb is triggered, the infected company sent an infected file to a customer in England. The customer's computer was damaged and there was no indication that the Dutch company was negligent in sending the file. The English customer's action must be solely against the Dutch supplier but the jurisdiction of the English courts will not be supported by art 5(3). The English customer's damage was the consequence of harm suffered by direct victims.

3.7.2.2.3 Negligent Misstatement

An individual or company domiciled in a contracting state providing negligent advice on a website risks being sued in a court within any contracting state. This is because application of the judgment in *Bier* establishes that a claimant can sue the defendant in a state of his domicile, or, where the server was situated, or where the damage occurs. The damage will usually occur where the claimant accesses the negligent advice.

---

25. A luxury boat mortgage company is incorporated in and operates from Italy. It provides mortgages and advice to wealthy Italian-Americans who are considering buying a boat moored in Italy. The company rents web space on a server that happens to be based in Ireland; its domain name 'moorings.com' clearly gives little indication of its base. An American mortgages a boat through the site that turns out to be far from seaworthy and sinks off the coast of Spain. The Spanish courts will not have jurisdiction over the tort; the damage from the negligent advice occurred in Italy where the mortgage report was relied upon; that the actual damage was suffered in Spain is not relevant for art 5(3).

Often negligent advice results in economic loss as one of the heads of damage. Apart from the domestic question of whether such loss is recoverable, there is the issue of where economic loss occurs. If a claimant's bank account is in England but the claimant accesses and relies upon information on a website from

179   See [1976] ECR 1735.
180   [1996] All ER (EC) 84 at 94[8].

Germany, will the English courts have jurisdiction purely because the bank account was situated there?

A similar question was answered by the European Court in *Marinari v Lloyds Bank plc (Zubaidi Trading Co intervening)*.[181] Mr Marinari, domiciled in Italy, sued Lloyds Bank plc, whose registered office is in England. His claim was that he had deposited promissory notes with a value of $750 million with a Manchester branch of the bank. The bank staff suspected that the notes were bogus, kept them and advised the police who arrested Mr Marinari. He sued in Italy for compensation for the payment of the notes, damage to reputation and loss of contracts. Lloyds Bank objected to the jurisdiction of the Italian courts arguing that the damage occurred in England.

The court derived from *Mines de Potasse d'Alsace* and *Bier* that the choice generally afforded to a tort claimant could provide a significant connecting factor from the point of view of jurisdiction. But, the choice must not be extended, so negating the general principle in Art 2, to encompass any place where the adverse consequences of an event that has already caused actual damage has occurred.[182] In short, it affirmed that one must look for where damage occurs (and now, where it may occur), not where it is suffered.

Whatever the flaws in the court's solution, it does have the quality of certainty for torts committed over the Internet. By focusing on the tangible and fixed aspects of damage the court is able to ensure that the court with jurisdiction is appropriate to determine the legal dispute. The court was particularly wary of the fluidity of damaged assets and therefore the possibilities of 'entirely inappropriate' courts having to take the relevant evidence. It is submitted that this is correct. Although the Internet does allow intellectual property, advice and funds to be moved and accessed from any jurisdiction in the world, it is not necessarily in the interests of justice that any court in Europe could govern the relevant dispute. The rules on jurisdiction attempt to delineate which cases are appropriate to be heard and decided by which courts; it is naive to suggest because the Internet has no technical boundaries to the flow of digital material that the law should drop its boundaries also.

---

26. A Russian entrepreneur owned a number of shares in an English company, held by an English bank. From Russia he logged on to a French investor's web page, and on the basis of information there, sold the shares in the English company. The information was provided negligently. Under the Brussels Regulation, the Russian will be able to sue only in France under art 2: the damage occurred in Russia, which is not a contracting state, and where the damage was suffered is irrelevant under art 5(3).

3.7.2.2.4   Defamation

The Internet and associated technologies allow the whole world to have access to information about one individual; it is now possible to have a truly global reputation. For the same technical reasons it is possible for a defamatory statement to

181   [1996] All ER (EC) 84.
182   [1996] All ER (EC) 84 at 95 [10–15].

be read from anywhere in the world; it is possible to defame someone on a global scale. These two conclusions present the law with an issue as to a court's jurisdiction over defamation. If a celebrity is defamed on a worldwide forum, which court is appropriate to hear the dispute between the claimant and defendant?[183] There are a number of options. Two main ones are: first, only ever in one jurisdiction, the so-called 'single publication' rule; second, in multiple jurisdictions, wherever the claimant has a cause of action. We shall see, both at common law and under the Brussels Regulation, that the highest courts in Europe agree that there is no such 'single publication' rule in European jurisprudence.[184]

The answer for defamation claims falling under the Brussels Regulation is provided by the European Court in *Shevill v Presse Alliance SA*.[185]

Presse Alliance SA, a French company, published its daily newspaper with an article that mentioned the claimant's name in relation to a drug trafficking network that was raided by the drugs squad. The claimant was in England at the time of the raid, having only been in France for three months. 237,000 copies of the newspaper containing the defamatory article were sold in France; 230 were sold in England. The claimant asserted that the English courts had jurisdiction over the dispute by virtue of art 5(3); the defendants objected, eventually appealing to the House of Lords. The Lords then referred seven preliminary questions to the European Court.

The important answer provided by the Court was that the claimant in a defamation action may sue in the courts of the defendant's domicile, under art 2, and under art 5(3) may sue in the courts of the place from where the libel was issued and circulated. And any one of these courts have jurisdiction to hear the action for damages for all the harm caused by the unlawful act. Alternatively, the claimant may sue in the courts of any contracting state in which the defamatory publication was distributed and in which the victim claims to have suffered injury to reputation. These courts have jurisdiction only to rule on the injury caused to the victim's reputation in that state. The 'single publication' rule, which would force a claimant to choose, is not therefore European law.

Again, this answer takes due account of justice to the parties: the courts best suited to consider damages must include those which are territorially the best placed to assess the libel committed in the state and determine the corresponding level of damages. That the claimant has the option of suing once for all the damages in the court of the defendant's domicile accords with the basic rule of the Brussels regime: 'defendants should be sued at home'.

Of course for the Internet such a decision has a great impact. Without careful deployment of certain technologies, a website or a forum will be available throughout the world. A victim defamed on one of these globally accessible sites

---

183   It is not assumed that the defendant is necessarily an individual and may well be the host of the website, discussion board or forum itself. If the host is not domiciled within a contracting state it may still be brought within the regime of the Defamation Act 1996 where the actual defamer is domiciled in England. In this situation the claimant would be relying on art 6(1) of the Regulation.

184   This is in sharp contrast to the long-standing US rule preventing such a multiplicity of suits. See *Ogden v Association of the United States Army (a corpn)* 177 F Supp 498 at 502, (1959).

185   [1995] All ER (EC) 289.

needs only to find a very limited number of 'hits' from a particular contracting state to be able to litigate there.[186] In most cases of Internet defamation the claimant will be able to sue in the courts of their domicile; a scenario that was to be avoided under the Brussels Regulation. It is a scenario, however, which makes legal sense.

There are advantages and disadvantages with every form of communication. The Internet's advantages include that there is little increase in marginal cost to distribute information throughout the world. If it is useful information, the global reputation of the provider will increase; if it is defamatory information, the global reputation of the victim will decrease. That this is somehow 'unfair' or 'prejudices the Internet', does not take into account that one cannot expect to reap the rewards from cheap global distribution without bearing its risks.

---

27. A UK resident soap star is defamed on a French bulletin board by an Australian co-actor who had since left the programme. The bulletin board operator included the Australian's comments in a highlighted section of the bulletin board called 'Celebrity Clangers'. The victim can sue the French bulletin board in England as long as it can be proved that the board was accessed from England. This will be sufficient to establish that damage occurred in England giving the English courts jurisdiction under art 5(3).

3.7.3   Common law jurisdiction over torts

If the defendant to an Internet tort is not domiciled within a contracting state,[187] the court must apply its domestic laws to determine jurisdiction.[188] The main method of service abroad with leave is examined below.

3.7.3.1   Service out

There are two separate and distinct aspects to serving out of the jurisdiction.[189] The first aspect is jurisdiction: does the claimant's claim fall within one of the sub-rules of CPR r 6.20(8)(a) or (b). These are where the tortious damage was sustained within the jurisdiction, or, the damage sustained resulted from an act committed within the jurisdiction. Although not yet deeply analysed by the courts, it is likely that this test does not need to be satisfied to any high degree of proof: a good arguable case that the claim is covered by one of the sub-rules is probably sufficient.[190] The second aspect, which will not be covered here in great

186   In *Shevill* less than 0.1% of the distribution was in England. There presumably must be some *de minimis* amount although the court did not appear to take notice that less than a thousandth of the distribution occurred in England. This said, the amount of distribution in absolute terms may reduce the possible damages which may be awarded.

187   See Chapter 2 and section 3.7.1 of this chapter.

188   Art 4.

189   See *Seaconsar v Bank Merkazi Jomhouri Islami Iran* [1994] 1 AC 438, which applied, and it is suggested remains applicable, under the old Rules of the Supreme Court, Ord 11.

190   See *Attock Cement Co Ltd v Romanian Bank for Foreign Trade* [1989] 1 All ER 1189, which applied, and it is suggested remains still applicable, under the old Rules of the Supreme Court, Ord 11.

detail, is one of discretion: no permission to serve a claim out of the jurisdiction will be given unless the court is satisfied that England and Wales is the proper place in which to bring the claim. This is specified by CPR r 6.21(2A).

3.7.3.1.1 Jurisdiction under tort sub-rule

The head that will apply for most torts committed over the Internet is CPR r 6.20(8)(a) or (b)[191]:

> 'the claim is made in tort where the damage was sustained within the jurisdiction, or the damage sustained resulted from an act committed within the jurisdiction.'

Until 1987 the provision used to relate only to a claim 'founded on a tort committed within the jurisdiction'. This was amended in the light of the *Bier* case[192] and the amendment carried through from the Rules of the Supreme Court to the Court Procedure Rules. A claimant is now required to satisfy two requirements. First, the claim must be made in tort. Second, the damage must be sustained in the jurisdiction or have resulted from an act committed in the jurisdiction. The second question has been discussed in relation to the Brussels Regulation and it would appear that the reasoning given there is equally applicable.[193] What must be considered here, in contrast, relates to the first question: simply put, what is a tort?[194]

The answer to this question can be found by considering the main precedent in this area: *Metall und Rohstoff AG v Donaldson, Lufkin & Jenrette Inc.*[195] In this case the defendants whilst in New York had sent to English persons inducements to break contracts which subsisted with other English persons. The tortious claim was for inducing breach of contract in which the damage was sustained in England. The court permitted service abroad, but not before making an analysis of this complex area. It is submitted that this remains good law.

Choice of law under jurisdiction

The court decided that to determine whether a 'tort' has been committed,[196] one had to consider the choice of law rule in *Boys v Chaplin* to ascertain whether the

---

191 Of course, CPR r 6.20(2) may be more appropriate in some circumstances.

192 See 'Location of harmful events', at section 3.7.2.2.

193 See 'Location of harmful events', at section 3.7.2.2. This said, the English courts appear keener to look for a 'substantial act' rather than merely any tortious act. See *Metall and Rohstoff AG v Donaldson, Lufkin & Jenrette Inc* [1989] 3 All ER 14 at 25; *Schapira v Ahronson* [1999] EMLR 735.

194 This was discussed in relation to the Brussels Regulation but it is clear that the autonomous meaning under the Brussels Convention (which the Regulation replaces) is inapplicable for an English court to adopt in these circumstances. See 'What is a tort?', at section 3.7.2.2.

195 [1989] 3 All ER 14. Readers should note that the overruling of this decision in *Lourho plc v Fayed* [1992] 1 AC 448 was on other aspects.

196 It should be noted that the sub-rule 6.20(8) head refers not to a 'wrong' but to a claim made in 'tort'; this is therefore a legal question that is distinct from the question of where, in substance, a wrong is committed.

relevant events would have given rise to liability in tort under English law.[197] The court expresses this ruling as[198]:

> 'if [the court] find that the tort was in substance committed in some foreign country, they should apply the [*Chaplin v Boys*] rule and impose liability in tort under English law, only if both (a) the relevant events would have given rise to liability in tort in English law if they had taken place in England, and (b) the alleged tort would be actionable in the country where it was committed.'

In short, the court must consult the choice of law rules first to check that the 'wrong' is actionable here as a tort; it must be a claim capable of being pleaded as a tort. But, as the following section explains, the choice of law rule for torts other than defamation, is no longer that expounded in *Chaplin v Boys*. It is contained in the Private International Law (Miscellaneous Provisions) Act 1995 (which excludes defamation from its scope); s 10 of the Act abolishes the common law rules in *Chaplin v Boys* replacing them with the rules in ss 11 to 13.[199] Where a potential defendant is not domiciled in a contracting state, the English courts have granted permission for claimants to issue proceedings here without direct reference to *Chaplin v Boys*. In the case of *King v Lewis and Others*, boxing promoter Don King, living in Florida, was granted the right to serve a claim for libel against champion boxer Lennox Lewis and his promotions company, living and based in the US. The Court of Appeal held that England did have *forum conveniens* for the conduct and trial or the proceedings because it was undisputed that the claimant had been libelled in England, since the alleged libellous statements had been downloaded from a website here and, further, Don King had a substantial reputation in England.[200] This represented an important success for the claimant, who was then able to pursue proceedings in a court with more amenable defamation laws than the US, where he may have encountered more difficulties in the context of constitutional freedom of expression rights.

Proving jurisdiction under tort head

For a 'wrong' committed over the Internet, it would appear that the convoluted scheme for determining whether one can serve out is as follows:

197　[1971] AC 356. Apologies are made to those who are unfamiliar with the conflict of laws. It is correct but confusing that in *Metall und Rohstoff* the court conflated the usually distinct considerations of jurisdiction and choice of law. If a reader is unfamiliar with choice of law in tort it is advised, at this point, to read this chapter's following section on these rules. Normally one can consider jurisdiction separately from choice of law. For service out on a tortious claim, however, one must decide whether the 'wrong' is a tort in the first place and this is only achievable with recourse to English choice of law rules. The circularity of this section is regretted but unavoidable.

198　[1989] 3 All ER 14 at 32.

199　Readers unfamiliar with the operation of the new Act are advised to read this chapter's following section on choice of law. Issues arising in relation to defamation are still governed by the common law.

200　*King v Lewis and Others* EWCA Civ 1329.

1. Check whether damage was sustained within the jurisdiction or whether the damage resulted from an act committed within the jurisdiction.[201] If neither apply, the claimant will be unable to serve out under CPR r 6.20(8).

2. Check whether, under English law, the claim relates to issues arising in any defamation claim, including claims for slander of title, goods or other malicious falsehood.[202]

3. Looking back over the series of events establish where in substance the cause of action arose.[203]

4. If the cause of action arose in England, the claimant will have established jurisdiction under CPR r 6.20(8).

5. If the cause of action arose outside England and Wales, the claimant will have to prove that the 'wrong' is actionable in England as a tort:

   5.1. If the claim relates to a defamation claim (see 2) the claimant will have to apply the old common law test in *Boys v Chaplin* or otherwise satisfy the court that both the relevant events would have given rise to liability in tort in English law if occurring in England, and that the alleged tort is actionable in the country where it is committed (see also the 2004 case of *King v Lewis* as discussed above).[204]

   5.2. If the claim does not relate to a defamation claim (see 2) the claimant will have to apply the Private International Law (Miscellaneous Provisions) Act 1995 satisfying the court that the 'wrong' is actionable under the law of the country where the tort occurs,[205] or if more than one country is involved, the law of the country in which the most significant element of the events occurred.[206]

6. If points 1 and 4, or points 1 and 5, are satisfied, the claim falls within CPR r 6.20(8).

---

28. Revealing pictures of a British film director and his mistress are released onto the Internet by an American journalist. Under English law, the director has no legal redress against the journalist, but under American law a law of confidence would protect him.

---

201 As confirmed by *Metall and Rohstoft AG v Donaldson, Lufkin & Jenrette* [1989] 3 All ER 14.
202 Private International Law (Miscellaneous Provisions) Act 1995, s 13.
203 See *Distillers Co (Biochemicals) Ltd v Thompson* [1971] All ER 694 at 699 per Lord Pearson with refinement in *Castree v ER Squibb & Sons Ltd* [1980] 2 All ER 589; and also *Schapira v Ahranson* [1999] EMLR 735.
204 It is admitted, but ignored for the sake of simplicity, that the flexible exception in *Red Sea Insurance Co Ltd v Bouygues SA* [1995] 1 AC 190 may be invoked allowing a defamation-type claim which is not actionable in England to be actionable here. This said, in the light of Parliament's intention to prevent the Act applying to defamation claims, a strong case would have to be put to invoke the *Red Sea* exception.
205 Private International Law (Miscellaneous Provisions) Act 1995, s 11(1). This country will probably be the same as that decided for point 3.
206 Private International Law (Miscellaneous Provisions) Act 1995, s 11(1). This country will probably be the same as that decided for point 3.

> The director has a good arguable case that the dispute falls within CPR r 6.20(8). Damage to the director's reputation has occurred in England, and the cause of action arose in America where the 'wrong' is actionable as a tort. The director may have the jurisdiction of the English courts to serve out to the journalist suing him under American law.

3.7.3.1.2   Discretion under service out

It is not sufficient simply to satisfy a court of a good arguable case under sub-rule (8) under CPR r 6.20. The claim must also be a proper case for service out under CPR r 6.21(1A). The discretion to serve out includes as a main factor, an assessment, perhaps not overtly, of whether England is the *forum conveniens*, the most suitable forum in which to hear the dispute. This will be considered briefly in the following section on staying actions.[207] This discretionary factor should not be overlooked by legal advisers: for a tort committed over the Internet it may be difficult to persuade a court to serve out. If the defendant, in contrast, is domiciled in a member state, the court has far less discretion over jurisdiction.[208]

3.7.3.2   *Staying actions*

It is always open to a putative defendant to apply to stay the common law jurisdiction of the English courts by pleading that it is not the most suitable forum in which to resolve the dispute.[209] Whether a court stays an action is decided with recourse to the principle of *forum non conveniens*. This principle is impressively explained and stated in the House of Lords decision in *Spiliada Maritime Corpn v Cansulex Ltd*.[210] In a later case Lord Goff explains *forum non conveniens* as 'a self-denying ordinance under which the court will stay (or dismiss) proceedings in favour of another clearly more appropriate forum'.[211] A full discussion of this case is beyond the scope of this chapter, but an appreciation of its implications is worthwhile. Until courts approach wrongs committed over the Internet and Internet disputes with the familiarity and understanding that they approach, say the telephone and newspapers, litigators must be prepared to argue that despite the transnational nature of the Internet, some forums are more suitable than others.

Lord Goff provided the leading judgment given in *Spiliada*. He set out a number of guidelines[212] that may guide a court as to whether England is a suitable and appropriate forum: the court must, in effect, balance the suitability of England against that of another forum. This forum must be clearly and distinctly more

---

207   The court's assessment is the same, although for service out, the plaintiff must ask the court to exercise discretion; for staying service as of right, the defendant must persuade the court to stay the action.

208   See the Court of Appeal's interpretation of the Civil Jurisdiction and Judgments Act 1982, s 49 in *Re Harrods (Buenos Aires) Ltd* [1992] Ch 72.

209   CPR, Pt 11 provides the necessary procedure.

210   [1986] 3 All ER 843.

211   *Airbus Industrie GIE v Patel* [1999] 1 AC 119 at 132C.

212   The necessary details of these guidelines can be found in specialist texts but readers are also directed to the very full judgments in *Lubbe v Cape plc* [2000] 4 All ER 268, HL.

appropriate: one 'with which the action [has] the most real and substantial con-nection'.[213] At this point, 'the court may nevertheless decline to grant a stay if persuaded by the claimant, on whom the burden of proof then lies, that justice requires that a stay should not be granted'.[214]

This discretion, unlikely to be disturbed on appeal,[215] may be of paramount importance in an Internet dispute. In contrast to most other means of communi-cation, the Internet can make it appear that a defendant has little connection with any country. A server may be in a country far away from the defendant's domi-cile. A defendant may have mirror servers, identical websites, scattered through-out the world. The information or product that is the root of the dispute may have passed through as many as one hundred countries. Worse still, it is a question of technical semantics to resolve whether the digital information moved from the server to the claimant or whether the claimant 'collected' the digital information from the server.

These issues, and many more like them, may cloud the answer as to which is the *forum conveniens* for the dispute. Of course, one may take the more prag-matic approach and look at the dispute trying to ignore the Internet complexities. To describe computer virus damage, one may state that, say, an individual's property in England was damaged as a result of the negligence of an individual, whose property was in America. While this may appear a precis of the dispute, it does not address the question before the courts: which is the suitable forum in the interests of all the parties and the ends of justice?

To answer this question involves examining the mechanics of hearing the dis-pute as well as its geographical basis. In illustration, often it is important to know where the relevant evidence is held and where the relevant witnesses live.[216] For many Internet disputes, however, such factors may not be weighty enough to dis-turb the jurisdiction of the court. Computer files will often be the main evidence and often the claimant in England will be the sole human witness to the tort itself. So for an Internet dispute, the jurisdiction of the English court may be less easily upset. As a further illustration, the issue of convenience, often a factor for the court, may be less convincing when all of the actual evidence is in a digital for-mat. Such evidence can be sent to England, over the Internet, cheaply, quickly and accurately. Again, the actual nature of the Internet may lead to the conclusion that little is lost by hearing the dispute in England.

A court will also consider the residence of the defendant. The claimant, no doubt, will attempt to persuade the court that the Internet allows persons to have no residence as such. In this sense, those who use the Internet have no claim over one country any more than another. The defendant's argument may take a more common-sense view: the Internet is a means of communication that operates from one fixed point to another. In addition, the defendant who would be forced into the English courts has a fixed residence; that the defendant is alleged to have

---

213   *The Abidin Daver* [1984] 1 All ER 470 at 478 per Lord Keith.
214   *Conelly v RT2 Corpn plc* [1998] AC 854 at 872A, per Lord Goff for the House of Lords restating the second stage of the *Spiliada* test.
215   [1986] 3 All ER 843 at 846 to 847 per Lord Templeman.
216   See [1986] 3 All ER 843 at 856.

committed a tort over the Internet which is difficult to locate may not be relevant as to where is the most appropriate place to litigate the dispute.

For the purposes of jurisdiction, the defendant's argument is the more realistic. If a tort committed over the Internet seems to have no geographical locus then, presumably, any court is equally suitable to gather evidence on the Internet aspects of the dispute. What will tip this finely balanced situation is the fact that the court is judging which is the natural forum: which is the forum with the closest and most real connection to the dispute. This is a relative not absolute requirement: the forum need not be close, but simply the closest out of many; the forum need not have a real connection, but simply the most real out of the other connections. The court is seeking, at times, the 'best out of a bad bunch'. The court must consider all the relevant factors, such as where the defendant and claimant are and which law will apply to this dispute.

Under the Private International Law (Miscellaneous Provisions) Act 1995, except for defamation issues, the law that generally will apply to a tort dispute is the law of where the tort occurred. And Lord Goff in *Spiliada* notes that the law of the dispute will often be a relevant factor.[217] What can be concluded from all this is that presence of the Internet in a dispute will never create the situation where no court is appropriate to hear the case. All the Internet may complicate is the question of where the tort occurs; there are numerous other factors that will, despite this complication, prove that England is, or is not, the natural forum.

---

29. A publisher resident in Calcutta publishes an online newspaper. In one edition an Indian domiciled in England is gravely defamed. He seeks to serve a writ out of the jurisdiction against the Indian publisher. Evidence is adduced that the newspaper has 73,000 subscribers in India but only 15 in England. The court in deciding whether England, or Calcutta, is the appropriate forum may consider that the courts of the place where the publisher is resident, publishes and has the greatest distribution, is the place with the most real connection with the dispute.

3.7.3.3   Extent of circulation

The last scenario is included for a number of reasons. First, it relates to a real case involving not online newspapers, but paper newspapers.[218] Second, the result is supported by the House of Lords in a similar precedent in *Berezovsky v Michaels*[219] in which 780,000 copies of a *Forbes* magazine were circulated containing a defamatory article about a Russian businessman. However, only 6,000 readers were in the jurisdiction of the English courts. The third reason is that it

---

217   With reference to *Crédit Chimique v James Scott Engineering Group Ltd* 1982 SLT 131. In this Scottish case, Lord Jauncey goes further and asks that a court look not simply at the fact that foreign law will be applied, but to look deeper at the nature of the foreign law. It may be that it is trivial for an English court to turn its mind to the foreign law, but it also may be that the law is so alien that the most appropriate court to consider the legal issues is a court which regularly deals with them.
218   *Pillai v Sarkar* (1994) Times, 21 July.
219   [2000] 2 All ER 986.

acts as a nice comparison with *Shevill* and other defamation claims heard under the Brussels Regulation.[220]

What is clear from these cases, and others[221] is that the extent of circulation is in no way conclusive as to where an action may commence. In both *Shevill* and *Berezovsky*,[222] one under Brussels Regulation rules and the other under common law rules, the concept of a 'global tort' or a 'single publication rule' is rejected. Since the *Duke of Brunswick v Harmer*[223] in the late 1800s, each communication is a separate libel. This applies across borders (for the purposes of jurisdiction assessment) as in *Berezovsky* and *Shevill* and at any time in the future (for purposes of limitation periods and damages).

Under the Brussels Regulation, in fact, circulation seems not to be a factor at all. At common law, circulation figures and 'hits' on websites are merely one of the factors relevant for the *Spiliada* test.

This section has shown that, if a defendant of an Internet tort is domiciled within a member state, a claimant will have little difficulty in suing in the English courts. In contrast, if the defendant is not domiciled in a member state, a claimant will have to concentrate on convincing the court of their substantial connection with England; the number of 'hits' or downloads may not influence the court either way.

3.8 CHOICE OF LAW

Establishing that the English courts have jurisdiction over an Internet tort dispute does not determine which law they must apply to resolve the dispute. This is a separate issue decided by reference to English law's choice of law rules for foreign torts. It may be a complex issue because the court must determine where the tort occurs before deciding which law will apply. Over the Internet, such geographical issues may be difficult to resolve, but, it is submitted, of no increased difficulty over other transborder torts. What the Internet will increase is the frequency with which courts are pressed on these issues of choice of law.

3.8.1 Common law choice of law

The Private International Law (Miscellaneous Provisions) Act 1995 leaves in place the old common law rules to determine the law to apply to the determination of issues arising in any defamation claim.[224] Defamation claims include not

---

220 See 'Defamation', at section 3.6.
221 See *Kroch v Rossell* [1937] 1 All ER 725; *Schapira v Ahranson* [1999] EMLR 735 at 745; *Chadha & Discom Technologies Inc v Dow Jones & Co Inc* [1999] EMLR 724; and the judgment pending in the Australian case *Gutnick v Dow Jones & Co Inc* [2001] VSC 305 (28 August 2001).
222 See Lord Hoffman at [2002] 2 All ER 986 at 1005.
223 (1849) 14 QB 185.
224 Private International Law (Miscellaneous Provisions) Act 1995, s 13(1). See *Lukowiak v Unidad Editorial SA* [2001] EMLR 1043.

only libel and slander but also slander of title, slander of goods or other malicious falsehood and their equivalents.[225]

3.8.1.1   Double-actionability test

The common law rules are well covered in specialist texts so what follows is a short introduction to their vestigial application to an Internet defamation claim. The basic rule is that the claimant must have a cause of action under English domestic law[226] and under the law of the place where the tort occurred.[227] Without this 'double-actionability' the claim cannot be brought unless it falls within the exception. This is that, in the interests of justice, single-actionability may suffice. In *Boys v Chaplin* the exception was 'created' and invoked by the House of Lords to permit a claimant to recover in England that which he could not recover under the foreign law.[228] In *Red Sea Insurance Co Ltd v Bouygues SA* the Privy Council invoked the exception to allow the claimant to recover under the foreign law for a claim not actionable under English law.[229]

---

30. An Internet service provider in Spain publishes a web page for a known libellous sports commentator. As could be expected, this individual uses the web page to defame an English football player. The player seeks to sue in England the individual and the provider. The player has the jurisdiction of the court under art 5(3) of the Brussels Regulation. Under English law, the Internet provider may be liable not having taken reasonable care considering the author's previous conduct. Under Spanish law, however, the provider may be liable for defamation only where the publisher knew that the material was defamatory. Unless a court becomes convinced of the need to invoke the exception, the player will have no right of action against the provider in the English courts.

3.8.2   Statutory choice of law

3.8.2.1   Applicable law: general rule

The Private International Law (Miscellaneous Provisions) Act 1995 introduces a regime for choice of tort law. It abolishes the common law test of double-action-ability[230] and instead looks primarily to the law of the place where the events constituting the tort occurred.[231] To aid the courts in assessing where this place is when events occurred in different countries,[232] the Act provides two rules of

---

225   Private International Law (Miscellaneous Provisions) Act 1995, s 13(2).
226   See *The Halley* (1868) LR 2 PC 193.
227   See *Phillips v Eyre* (1870) LR 6 QB 1.
228   [1969] 2 All ER 1085.
229   [1994] 3 All ER 749. See approval of rule by House of Lords in *Kuwait Airways Corpn v Iraqi Airways Co* (No 3) [2002] UKHL 19, [2002] 3 All ER 209.
230   Other than for defamation claims as discussed, Private International Law (Miscellaneous Provisions) Act 1995, s 13(1).
231   Private International Law (Miscellaneous Provisions) Act 1995, s 11(1).
232   Private International Law (Miscellaneous Provisions) Act 1995, s 11(2).

relevance to the Internet.[233] The first is that the applicable law for a cause of action in respect of damage to property is the law of the country where the property was when it was damaged.[234] The second is that in any other case, the applicable law is the law of the country in which the most significant element or elements of the events occurred.[235] The European Commission is currently consulting on a European-wide statute of similar effect: a European Council Regulation on the law applicable to non-contractual obligations. This author believes that one of the reasons for the UK's refusal to be bound by the Regulation[236] is that there is no demonstrated requirement for the new Regulation.

---

31. A controller of an American website knowingly and maliciously allows virus code to be transmitted to its viewers' computers. One English corporation suffers huge data damage and sues the American controller in the English courts. The American seeks to prove that the law of the State of New York should apply as it is from there that the virus spread. This is incorrect. The property that is damaged is in England; English law will apply. There is no real conflict of laws.

---

32. A controller of an English website provides dubious financial advice on which reliance is placed by a Canadian company with offices around the world. The company suffers loss and decides to sue the controller in England. The applicable law for resolving the dispute will not be English law. The significant elements of the tort occurred in Canada. It is there that the company received, acted upon and was damaged by the negligent advice. Canadian law will be the applicable law. That the dispute is brought in the English courts is of no consequence to which law applies.

3.8.2.2 Applicable law: displacement of general rule

A court is not entirely bound by the rules in s 11; it can displace the general rule where it appears from a number of factors that there is a substantially more appropriate law for determining the issues.[237] Section 12 contains three factors to consider which are persuasive, not definitive, as to when it is appropriate to dis-

---

233 The Act provides three rules in total; the other rule is excluded from this discussion as it relates to personal injury (s 11(2)(a)). It is assumed, at least for now, that a rule relating to personal injury is generally irrelevant to the Internet. This said, the Act does specifically define 'personal injury' to include 'any impairment of physical or mental condition' (s 11(3)). Therefore, the recovery for nervous shock as a result of seeing or hearing about a tragedy provides a possibility that the Internet will be the messenger of such bad news and that claims will be brought blaming the Provider or creator. Cf *Alcock v Chief Constable of South Yorkshire* [1991] 4 All ER 907 at 921 per Ackner LJ: 'I agree, however, with Nolan LJ that simultaneous broadcasts of a disaster cannot in all cases be ruled out as providing the equivalent of the actual sight or hearing of the event or its immediate aftermath'.

234 Private International Law (Miscellaneous Provisions) Act 1995, s 11(2)(b).

235 Private International Law (Miscellaneous Provisions) Act 1995, s 11(2)(c).

236 Art 1(3).

237 Private International Law (Miscellaneous Provisions) Act 1995, s 12.

place the general rule. This is not meant to be invoked regularly, it is an exception and should be treated as such. Litigants should be conscious of the fact that the general rule in s 11 is 'not to be dislodged easily'. The word 'substantially' is meant as a high hurdle for those seeking to displace s 11.[238]

238   *Roerig v Valiant Trawlers Ltd* [2002] 1 All ER 961 at 968, per Waller LS for the Court of Appeal.

CHAPTER FOUR

Intellectual property

'[T]he Internet is the world's biggest copying machine.'

Marybeth Peters, Register of Copyrights, 1995[1]

The material stored and transmitted through the Internet is intangible and much of it will be protected by intellectual property rights. These rights can protect the intangible but substantial assets of companies and creative products of the mind from damage and unauthorised use. This chapter focuses on two of these rights: trade marks and copyright.

A trade mark or a brand name is forever important to businesses and consumers. For businesses the goodwill built up through sales under a brand can be extremely valuable. For consumers, a trade mark indicates the source of a product and so indicates its quality. It is therefore crucial that where ecommerce takes to the Internet, where it is easy to fake an identity, the law protects trade mark owners and consumers from imposters. This is crucial in the area of domain names.

Copyright protects almost all the material used and transferred over the Internet and the World Wide Web. This right can protect emails, websites and the programs and content shipped across the Internet. It is therefore relevant for users and Internet service providers to understand the ambit of these rights and what activities will lead to their infringement.

This chapter examines the following issues:

1. What is the relationship between trade marks and domain names?

2. What are the legal remedies against those who use another's trade mark as a domain name?

3. What is the best way to protect a domain name?

4. What are the legal issues involved in using trade marks on a website and as metatags?

1   US News and World Report, 23 January 1995, p 59.

5. What are the legal issues involved in search engines using trade marks?

6. What is the reach of the English court's jurisdiction over trade mark infringers?

7. Where must an Internet work be created to be protected by copyright?

8. What is the nature of copyright protection over emails, conversation threads, file collections, and websites?

9. How do moral rights protect material published on the Internet?

10. How may those who store and cache Internet material be liable?

11. What are, and what are the legal ramifications of, peer-to-peer networks?

12. What are the legal restrictions over the use of frames, deeplinks and spiders?

13. What is the English courts' jurisdiction over those who deal with copyright works from abroad?

4.1   TRADE MARKS, DOMAIN NAMES AND PASSING OFF

A webpage provides a business with both a method of advertising and a method of selling to customers. The difference between any other advert and one on a website is that the nature of the Internet means that the advertisement can be viewed anywhere by anyone.[2] This provides incredible commercial benefits to a business, as it no longer has to have any local physical presence to sell to customers. But in both the real world and the virtual world, trade marks and branding are essential. The potentially global reach of the Internet, however, makes issues about trade marks far more complicated than was ever previously the case. This first part of the chapter will look at trade marks, in particular how domain names can be used as trade marks. It then moves on to consider passing off and its application to domain names through the instrument of fraud doctrine. It then considers the special arbitration rules which apply to domain names before looking at jurisdictional matters in relation to trade marks on the Internet.

4.1.1   Technical rights v legal rights

As early as 1994, domain name disputes were starting to appear in courtrooms. In *MTV Networks v Adam Curry*,[3] Adam Curry had beaten the famous Music Television Network to a domain name. Before August 1993 he had registered

---

2   Geo-blocking technologies are becoming increasingly effective, and courts are starting to require website providers to institute location-sensitive access.
3   867 F Supp 202 (SDNY 1994).

and operated a website with the domain name 'www.mtv.com'. This site provided information about the music business, and dovetailed with the television business of MTV. On 19 January 1994 MTV sought to reacquire the domain name. By spring 1994 millions of Internet users had accessed the 'www.mtv.com' site. This is a common scenario in domain name clashes. The only right which Adam Curry had over the site was a technical one: he was the owner of the domain name alias: he was not the owner of any legal rights to use the name (or trade mark) MTV.

This problem is also affected by the fact that although there can be only one '.com', there has always been the risk that there may be many variations of the domain name with different suffixes. For example, in November 1993, Merritt Technologies Inc was granted the domain name 'mit.com'. From 30 December 1993 Merritt used the domain to provide free Internet access to the handicapped, disabled and elderly. On 6 May 1996, Merritt received a letter from the Massachusetts Institute of Technology asking Merritt to select an alternative domain name. Their rights to insist upon this were based on their use of the MIT trade mark since 1861, having a worldwide reputation and five registered trade marks in classes unrelated to Merritt's use of the mark. The Institute already owned the domain names 'mit.org' and 'mit.edu'. There was no crossover in fields of activity: the Institute was simply worried that its trade mark was being used at all. This is a scenario that is occurring more and more frequently. This is because the naming committees both here and elsewhere are expanding, and will continue to expand, the numbers of suffixes available; but as the late Jon Postel of the Internet Assigned Name Authority wrote[4]:

> '[T]he trade mark issue is just a mess. McDonalds is going to want to have mcdonalds.com, mcdonalds.biz, and other domain names involving McDonalds.'

This chapter looks at the conflict between legal rights in cyberspace, where in most cases little has really changed, and the conflict between technical rights (in domain names) and legal rights (in trade marks). When the first edition of this book was published in 1997 the best that could be done was to speculate how the courts would answer some of the questions posed by the Internet. Indeed, even the basics of trade mark law in the United Kingdom (and the Community) were more or less unknown as the Trade Marks Directive had only recently been implemented.[5] By the second edition some of the answers were starting to appear on the horizon. Now, however, the understanding of the Internet and the application of legal concepts to it means that it is now much easier to advise on many of these matters.

---

4   Information Law Alert, 02/09/96, 'Antidilution trade mark law gets first court case'.
5   Directive 89/104 to approximate the laws of the member states relating to trade marks.

4.1.2 The nature of trade mark protection

Trade marks are, like all intellectual property rights, territorial by nature. This means that a person who registers a trade mark at the UK Intellectual Property Office is entitled to protection for that trade mark only within the United Kingdom and the Isle of Man. He is only entitled to protection in other countries if he specifically makes a separate application in those countries. This means that a trade mark can be owned by two entirely separate and unrelated entities in two different countries; for example, one business could own the mark 'DOG' for clothing in the United States, and another could own and use 'DOG' on clothing in the United Kingdom. The territorial nature of trade marks means that, in the real world at least, there is no overlap of rights as each trade mark owner can operate only within the geographic territory where they have rights.

In addition, a trade mark only grants protection in relation to the goods and services in respect of which it is registered. This means that two traders can use the same mark for different goods in the same marketplace (e.g. 'Green' used in respect of musical instruments by one trader and in respect of footwear by another) without infringing each other's rights. In such cases, therefore, there is no conflict of rights. It is also possible for two traders to agree between themselves that they can both use the same mark in respect of the same goods in the same (or part of the same) marketplace (co-existence agreements).

Trade marks are not unique. It is possible, therefore, to have conflicts between trade mark rights where two trade mark owners (one from the US, one from the UK) both use the mark on the Internet at the same time. The nature of the Internet also means that problems may arise in relation to genuine goods which are sold under the trade mark, but which have yet to be put on the market inside the Community (i.e. parallel imports). This can cause problems when consumers see products (e.g. jeans) on sale on a United States website for less than they are sold in the United Kingdom, and then seek to buy from abroad. The basic questions of trade mark law which these businesses face, however, is little different from real world activities. The nature of the Internet raises different matters only in some areas. It is these areas which this chapter concentrates on, but a general introduction to trade mark law is included although those wanting answers to more technical questions should consult a specialist text.

4.1.3 Domain names

Every computer on the Internet has an IP (Internet Protocol) address. These addresses are made up of a series of numbers, which have the form 123.45.678.910.[6] The numbers can be assigned permanently or temporarily (floating), for example most home users of the Internet have a new IP address allocated by their Internet service provider every time they log onto the Internet.

---

6   This is an IP version 4 address of the type used by virtually all networks.

In contrast, businesses often have a permanent IP address for the server; although users of the business's network might have a temporary address.

The problem with IP addresses is that they are not very easy to remember.[7] To remedy this problem a sort of phone directory was set up which assigned a name to every IP address. This meant that instead of typing up to a 12 digit number, users could type a domain name ending with one of the so-called generic top level domains (.com, .org, .net, .biz, .tv) (gTLD) or one of the country code top-level domains (.uk, .fr) (ccTLD). Where a domain name has a ccTLD[8] (e.g. olswang.co.uk) it does not necessarily mean that the user of that domain name is in the United Kingdom or that the server where the material is stored is in the UK. A postal address necessarily changes whenever one moves from one town to another, but a domain name may remain the same wherever one moves. The only way to locate the owner of a domain name is to geographically locate the Internet Protocol Address.[9]

Domain names, like company names, are not simply taken; they are registered. They are also unique (so www.flower.com is different from www.flowers.com) and so no two people can separately own the same domain name. Most registration companies do not check that an applicant has the right to use a particular name as a domain name and so the registrars allocate them on a first-come, first-served basis. In the United Kingdom, this approach was been approved of (or at least accepted) by the Vice-Chancellor in relation to the domain name 'pitman.co.uk'.[10] He concluded that because the claimant, Pitman Training Ltd had no rights to proceed for passing off or any other tort, Nominet (responsible for 'co.uk' domain names) was entitled to register domain names as and when they are requested by an applicant and did not have to investigate entitlement in advance.

4.1.4 Trade marks v domain names

The unique nature of each domain name means that unlike trade marks there is no way to exercise rights independently of each other. There can only be one

---

7 Because the domain name which humans remember and type merely 'refers' to a unique number, it is possible to expand the quantity of IP addresses without having to alert consumers to the change. This is clearly different from telephone numbers where, if extra numbers are required to allow for growth, every existing number must change. At present most IP addresses still use version 4 (which uses 32-bit binary numbers). It is possible for a network to change to using IP addresses using version 6, which is a 128-bit hexadecimal number. Although this format is not widely used, when it is adopted it will not change domain names and most users will be totally unaware of the change.

8 There are also a number of quasi-ccTLDs, such as '.uk.com'. These are not actually ccTLD, but are privately owned sub-domains in the gTLD '.com'. Accordingly, 'uk.com' is registered as a domain name and if there were '7newsquare.uk.com' then if the 'uk.com' domain name is not renewed all those relying on sub-domains would lapse at the same time.

9 There are a number of geo-locating websites, which can provide details of where a particular site was accessed from.

10 *Pitman Training Ltd v Nominet UK* [1997] FSR 797.

apple.com despite both Apple and Apple Records both wanting to use the name and despite, until the launch of *iTunes*, there being only limited overlap between the businesses. In contrast, Apple can own the trade mark in relation to some goods and services whereas Apple Records can own in relation to others without there necessarily being any conflict of the rights.[11] John Gilmore of the Electronic Frontier Foundation sums up the issue well[12]:

> 'Trade marks are registered in a system that permits many companies to share a name legitimately without interfering with each other, such as Sun Photo, Sun Oil and Sun Microsystems. Domain names only permit one user of a name; there is only one sun.com, which Sun Microsystems registered first. Neither lawyers nor governments can make ten pounds of names fit into a one-pound bag.'

The different nature of domain names and trade marks can lead to commercial, technical and legal problems relating to conflicts between trade marks. If a business owns a trade mark in the United Kingdom can it stop a US company using it as a domain name? This question, and others, will be explored below.

4.2   REGISTRATION OF TRADE MARKS

In the United Kingdom there are three types of registered trade marks, as well as certain protection for unregistered marks and certain well-known[13] marks.[14] First, it is possible to register a mark under the Trade Marks Act 1994, which grants a trade mark only in the United Kingdom; secondly, it is possible to register a Community trade mark under the Community Trade Mark Regulation (No. 40/94) (the CTM Regulation), which grants uniform protection across all 27 members of the European Community; and finally, it is possible to obtain protection under the Protocol Relating to the Madrid Agreement Concerning the International Registration of Marks (the Madrid Protocol). The last of these options enables a single application to be made which grants protection in up to 72 countries by way of 72 separate registrations from a single application.[15]

11   Nevertheless, there has been a long-running dispute between the two companies over the right in the name, which was settled in February 2007: see http://news.bbc.co.uk/1/hi/entertainment/6332319.stm [accessed 27 November 2007].
12   *The Economist*, Letters, 13 July 1996.
13   Protection under Art 6*bis* of the Paris Convention (s 56 of the Trade Marks Act 1994).
14   Special protection also exists for other symbols and signs both within and outside the trade mark system. International organisations and states have special protection for their emblems under Art 6*ter* of the Paris Convention (which is given effect by ss 57 to 59 of the Trade Marks Act 1994), the Olympic and Paralympic symbols are also given special protection under the Olympic Symbols etc (Protection) Act 1995 (also see the London Olympic Games and Paralympics Games Act 2006).
15   In the UK this is given effect by the Trade Marks (International Registration) Order 1996 (SI 1996/714).

Whether a mark is registered under the 1994 Act, the CTM Regulation or in accordance with the Madrid Protocol the protection that is granted is the same in scope within the United Kingdom and the requirements that the mark must satisfy to be registered are more or less the same.

4.2.1 Signs that can be registered as trade marks

It is possible for any sign which is capable of graphical representation to be registered as a trade mark[16] provided that the representation is clear, precise, self-contained, easily accessible, intelligible, durable, unequivocal and objective.[17] These requirements will always be met in relation to a word mark such as a domain name as it can be written in straight text. Most traditional trade marks can also be represented to this standard, it is only where a mark is unusual (such as smell or sound) that problems arise; however, these unusual marks will not be examined here.[18]

4.2.2 Absolute grounds of refusal

In addition to the basic requirement that a sign is capable of being graphically represented, there are several other so-called absolute grounds of refusal that lead to an application to register a trade mark being refused. These are, in summary, that the mark is devoid of distinctive character, that it is descriptive, that it has become generic, that it is functional or that it is deceptive or otherwise contrary to public policy.[19] These various grounds will not be examined generally here. Instead this section will look only at the registration of domain names as trade marks.

4.2.2.1 Descriptive domain names

In some industries, it is often better to be listed under one's services than under one's name. For example, it may be more profitable for a chemist to be listed under 'pharmacies' than under his name. It may appear that the same is true for the Internet: the domain name, 'flowers.com' may appear to be far more valuable than 'lindasflorist.com'. However, the advantages of such a registration can be greatly overestimated. Most Internet users will search the Internet using a search engine (such as Google) and searching under 'florist' would bring up both 'flowers.com' and 'lindasflorist.com'.[20] Indeed, there is probably significantly more

---

16   Trade Marks Act 1994, s 1(1); CTM Regulation, art 4.
17   Case C-273/00 *Sieckmann* [2003] EMTR 37 at para 46.
18   See D. Kitchin *et al*, *Kerly's Law of Trade Marks and Trade Names* (14th edn, Sweet and Maxwell, 2005).
19   TMA 1994, s 3; CTM Regulation, art 7.
20   In fact, a simple Google search using 'florist' generates 21,500,000 hits (27 November 2007).

commercial benefits in being a sponsored link (and so being highlighted at the top of the page) than there is from having a generic web address.

Nevertheless, there is always a benefit from Internet users knowing what a website provides without having to access it and so these generic names do provide some commercial benefit. This commercial benefit, however, may not be possible to protect under trade mark law as flowers.com is descriptive of the goods it provides (flowers) and descriptive marks only become registrable where they have become distinctive through use. In other words, it is necessary to show that the mark, although at first blush descriptive, has now become associated in consumers minds with the relevant business. In contrast, marks like 'lindasflowers.com' are more likely to be distinctive and so could be registered without waiting for it to acquire so called secondary meaning.

This means that those individuals who are considering acquiring a domain name are advised to use a distinctive name: this has few disadvantages on the web, particularly now search engines are well developed and utilised, but has the obvious advantage of being registrable at the outset.

4.2.2.2   Registration of 'www' and '.com' etc

The prevalence of the Internet means that many brands exist which only have an online presence. Such businesses want to register their full domain name as a trade mark to stop others using similar marks (or domain names). In general, at both the UK Intellectual Property Office and OHIM, it is possible to register trade marks which include the prefix 'www' or with the suffix '.com'/'.co.uk'. However, both this prefix and such suffixes are normally not thought to have any trade mark significance. This has two important implications.

First, a mark which is not distinctive or descriptive in itself (e.g. 'flowers' for flowers) does not cease to be descriptive simply by the addition of 'www' or '.com'.[21] Accordingly, just as 'book' is descriptive for books so www.books.com for books will also be descriptive.[22] Secondly, when considering infringement or the relative grounds of refusal 'www' or '.com' might be ignored as having no independent significance.[23] This means that 'www.flowers.com' will usually be considered to be identical to 'flowers' or 'flowers.com'.

Nevertheless, some businesses may wish to register as trade marks their actual domain name, prefix, suffix and all. For example, in America, MovieFone Inc registered as a trade mark the domain name 'moviefone.com' as well as 'movielink.com'.[24] From a pragmatic perspective, there seems little reason to register as a trade mark a domain name including the suffix, rather than purely

---

21   UK IPO, Trade Mark Practice, Chapter 3, para 28 (domain names and s 3(1)); OHIM Draft Guidelines, Examination, Part B, para 8.5.4.

22   Example of OHIM, ibid.

23   E.g. *Reed Executive v Reed Business Information* [2004] EWCA Civ 159, [2004] RPC 40, para 36; also see *Compass Publishing BV v Compass Logistics* [2004] EWHC 520, [2004] RPC 41.

24   4 November 1994: applications 74/595, 293 and 74/595, 294.

the name element of the domain name as these will give less rather than more protection. This is because registering as a trade mark the name element of the domain name will also protect the name's use within a domain name.

---

1. David Peters Ltd is a one-man company that specialises in repairing old hi-fi equipment. As the company grows in experience, its owner realises that there is a market in repairing old computer equipment for a pre-determined quotation. The company sets up a website on which restored equipment is offered for sale and on which viewers may enter details of their ailing equipment to receive an emailed repair quotation. The domain name for the site is 'www.compair.com'. To provide added protection for this sign, David Peters Ltd may seek a trade mark registration over the word 'compair' in the appropriate classes. Such a registration is normally sufficient to prevent uses by third parties of the mark www.compair.com as well.

4.2.3 Registering in relation to goods and services

A trade mark is registered in relation to goods and services and trade mark applicants must indicate on their applications which goods and services in respect of which protection is sought. Accordingly, a trade mark ('flower') which is registered in respect of milk (Class 29) cannot be used to prevent that mark being used by another trader in relation to laundry detergent (Class 3).[25] This means that trade marks are quite different from domain names. A domain name is necessarily unique and so the one person who owns a particular domain name automatically precludes anyone else from using the domain name for whatever goods that second person sells.

---

2. A data recovery company registers the domain name 'data-recovery.co.uk.' It is the only owner of this domain name; it is unique among not only all data recovery companies, but also all domain name owners. This does not mean that the name is capable of distinguishing the services of its owner from any other company. Without more the company will be unable to register a trade mark over the name.

4.2.4 Classification

To assist with both the application for, and searching of, trade marks goods and services are classified in accordance with the Nice Classification.[26] This system is used both by the United Kingdom Intellectual Property Office[27] and the

---

25 Unless the mark has a sufficient reputation to be protected under s 10(3) of the Trade Marks Act 1994 or Art 9(1)(c) of the CTM Regulation.
26 The Nice Agreement Concerning the International Classification of Goods and Services for the Purposes of the Registration of Marks.
27 Trade Marks Rules 2000 (SI 2000/136), r 7 (note the significant amendment made by SI 2006/3039).

Community Trade Mark Office (OHIM).[28] It has 45 different classes and each class includes a detailed list of goods and services. Practically, there will be few occasions when a registered trade mark proprietor will need to broaden the scope of his trade mark registration when using the name as a domain name. It is wrong to think that because the medium of exploitation is the Internet that the trade mark registration needs to be expanded into the other classes as well.

---

3. Artsake Ltd is a manufacturer of artists' materials within the UK. It has a trade mark registration in Class 16 to reflect the use of its name Artsake in relation to paper, cardboard goods and other artists' materials. It now wishes to expand its business by setting up a website through which customers can place orders. It chooses the domain name 'artsake.co.uk' and is concerned that it will require additional trade mark protection for the domain. It does not; its existing registration will equally protect its domain name in respect of artists' materials sold over the Internet.

There may be times where an individual already has a trade mark registration but is providing new goods or services through a website. In this circumstance there may be a reason to broaden the number of classes or specification for which a trade mark is registered. Some websites are, in trade mark terms, still little more than a digital billboard or leaflet. In contrast, true ecommerce solutions which allow the site to obtain information about the viewer and take payment from a user may lead to an increase in the activities provided through a website. An illustration is where the proprietor of a small local newspaper starts to allow and charge for sophisticated searching of its archives from its website. A change in the nature of the business may be taking place. This proprietor should not simply rely on a registration for paper products, but should widen the specification to include the use of computers to search and access data.

---

4. A car manufacturer that uses its trade mark as a domain name decides to make its website more than merely a digital version of its paper brochures. To do this the dealer includes on its website a JAVA program that acts as a route finder: individuals may type in where they are and where they wish to go and the program generates a map of the quickest route. The map also includes the miles per gallon that the dealer's car would use on the same route, so promoting the fuel economy of the car. The business now involves not only the sale of cars but also the provision of a route-finding service. It would be prudent to broaden the trade mark protection to cover these new goods accordingly.

Similarly there will be times where the trade mark owner continues to use the trade mark in a slightly different market of goods or services. For example, a travel agent may well have a trade mark registered in classes including class 39 for travel services. If, however, the agent expands its business to include taking

---

28   Commission Regulation 2868/95, r 2.

bookings over its website, it may want to consider carefully its existing specification on the trade marks register. In this situation it may be wise to ensure its registration covers the provision of travel services by means of a global network.

It is tempting for Internet-related firms to apply for a mark in relation to class 38 which relates to, amongst other things, telecommunication of information. But in fact, registration in this class is only appropriate for infrastructure providers for the Internet[29] and those providing the core activities of Internet service providers, such as search engines, hosting chat-rooms, email services and so forth.[30]

Some of the more complex services provided on the Internet might, however, be better classified as computer programs (in class 9) and any computer programs which are intended for download should be registered in class 9. But as the court indicated in *Mercury Communications Ltd v Mercury Interactive (UK) Ltd*[31]:

> '[T]he defining characteristic of a piece of computer software is not the medium on which it is recorded, nor the fact that it controls a computer, nor the trade channels through which it passes but the function it performs.'

4.2.4.1   Computer software and electronic communications specifications

In general, however, broad specifications or vague terms like 'multi-media services', 'Internet services' and 'online services' are unacceptable as they are too vague.[32] Once an applicant has decided the classes for which a trade mark registration should be obtained, an appropriate specification within that class must be provided. Applicants should be aware that the specification needs to be drafted sufficiently clearly so that each good or service is only classified in one class.[33] Further, they should be aware that if the specification is overly broad then, in the UK at least, the application might be treated as having been made in bad faith,[34] which is a basis for an application to be refused.

In particular, specifications that include the generic term 'computer programs' are likely to be viewed as too wide. 'Electronic communication apparatus' may be appropriate.[35] In *Mercury Communications,* a specification for the trade mark *Mercury* was drafted to include both 'computers' and 'computer programs'. The claimant alleged that the defendant was infringing the trade mark when it sold analysis and bug-tested computer software. However, Laddie J held that the term 'computer software' or 'computer programs' is normally far too wide as a specification because it would cover any set of digitally recorded instructions used to

---

29   IPO, Trade Marks Practice Manual, para 5.2.29, under class 38.
30   Ibid.
31   [1995] FSR 850 at 865.
32   IPO, Trade Marks Practice Manual, para 5.2.29.
33   CTM, r 2(2); TMR, r 8(2)(b).
34   Manual of Trade Mark Practice, Ch 2, paras 4.1.10 and 5.1.14.
35   In *Second Sight Ltd v Novell Inc and Novell UK Ltd* [1995] RPC 423 an overly wide specification in class 9 for 'computer software' was the cause of a clash between two rights-holders in different fields both asserting rights over the same trade name.

control any type of computer. It would include software in the medical diagnos-
tic field, software for controlling the computers on the London Underground and
software for designing genealogicial tables.[36] Such a wide registration is unacceptable as it provides excessively broad protection over goods and services
which are unconnected with the true trading interests of the trade mark proprietor. It was Laddie J's opinion that such a registration is ripe for having its registration removed entirely on the grounds of non-use,[37] or at the least, having the
specification of the goods dramatically pruned during rectification proceedings.

In *Avnet Incorporated v Isoact Ltd*[38] Jacobs J was required to assess, in trade
mark terms, the services offered by Internet service providers to those subscribers who use their websites as a means of advertising their businesses. Avnet
was the registered proprietor of the 'Avnet' trade mark under class 35 (advertising and promotional services etc, all included within class 35). The defendant
was an ISP using 'Avnet' in the course of business as a domain name and trading
name. This mark was used to promote its usual ISP services of: providing email
addresses and providing server space to customers on which they could host their
own websites.

Jacob J found that ISP services did not fall within 'advertising and promotional services' within class 35, even where the ISP allowed its subscribers to use
its services for this purpose. This decision, of course, defeated the claim, but it
also indicates that ISPs must draft their trade mark specifications with care.
Jacob J warned:

'... specifications for services should be scrutinised carefully and they should
not be given a wide construction covering a vast range of activities. They should
be confined to the substance, as it were, the core of the possible meanings attributable to the rather general phrase.'[39]

4.2.5   Opposition and registration

Once an application has been examined on absolute grounds, assuming it is not
found to be wanting, it will be published.[40] Once an application has been published it is possible for the application to be opposed by the proprietor of any earlier trade mark or right, who may oppose the registration on what are called
relative grounds of refusal. Essentially, these arise where the mark applied for
would infringe the earlier mark or right if it was used in the course of trade.
Accordingly, the relative grounds of refusal can be considered along with
infringement below.

---

36   Examples provided by Laddie J in his judgment: [1995] FSR 850 at 864.
37   See TMA, s 46; CTM art 50.
38   [1997] ETMR 562; for different reasons, Avnet was denied a transfer of 'avnet.net' by the
     WIPO Arbitration and Mediation Centre: *Avnet Inc v Aviation Network Inc Case* (WIPO
     D2000–0046).
39   Ibid, 565.
40   TMA, s 38(1); CTM, art 40.

Once the three-month opposition period is over, or if all opposition proceedings have been withdrawn or decided in favour of the applicant, the mark will be registered.[41] The protection afforded by a trade mark begins at registration, although this is backdated to the date the application was filed.[42]

4.3 REGISTRATION OF DOMAIN NAMES

The usual way to register a domain name is to use a registrar, which is either an Internet service provider or a registration agent; direct registration is possible but requires some technical knowledge. When an online registrar is used the process is incredibly straightforward. A domain name is selected and paid for. There is little more to it.

There are, however, some things that registrants should take into account. As mentioned previously, domain names are unique. If you want a domain name that is owned by someone else, you have only three choices. First, wait for the domain name to become available if the owner chooses not to renew it;[43] secondly, buy it from the owner; or finally, litigate for it. With domain names registered for a year or two at a time, still changing hands for vast sums, such as $7.5 million paid for 'Business.com' on 30 November 1999 beaten by the sale of the same domain name and business in late 2007 for $345 million, it is hardly surprising that so many turn to litigation or dispute resolution under one of the arbitration schemes. These will both be considered below.

4.3.1 Trying to identify the domain name owner

The technical nature of domain names is such that, presently, one may not know who owns a domain name. Even if one knows the owner, pinpointing them on the planet to issue and serve proceedings can be complex. The domain name registrars do not necessarily require, and certainly do not check, whether the name and address of the registrant is correct; although the 'wilful' provision of inaccurate ownership data can be used to trigger domain name cancellation (or transfer).[44] Where, for whatever reason, one cannot locate the defendant, how can one prevent the infringement from occurring?

If the domain name is 'pointed' at a website, there is a good argument that, once on notice, the host of the website may be jointly liable. If the domain name is not yet pointed to a website, the claimant may want to pursue the domain name itself 'in rem'. In England it is not presently possible to file proceedings against a domain name as an action *in rem*. The English courts have adopted a very

---

41   TMA, s 40; CTM, art 45.
42   TMS ss 9(3) and 40(3). Different rules apply to the Community trade mark.
43   This can happen deliberately or accidently; for example, in 1999 Microsoft did not renew 'hotmail.com', fortunately somebody external to the company did it on their behalf.
44   *T-nova.com* (NAF FA 94646).

narrow interpretation of when such jurisdiction is available.[45] But in the United States it is possible to bring an action against a domain name under the Anti-Cybersquatting Statute.[46] Accordingly, claimants may wish, in some circumstances, to consider filing a claim relating to .com's, .net's etc. in the United States, rather than in the UK.

4.4   TRADE MARK INFRINGEMENT

Once a trade mark is registered, within the territories it has effect, it grants the proprietor certain exclusive rights. These rights do, however, vary between jurisdictions, and just because a particular use of a trade mark would infringe in the United States does not mean that equivalent use in the United Kingdom would also infringe, and vice versa. The territorial nature of a trade mark also means that it is possible to both have clashes between two legitimate right holders; for example, a trade mark may be owned by different people in Australia and in the United Kingdom. Indeed, such clashes could potentially involve a number of different traders, all of whom have rights in relation to identical or similar marks. The US Court of Appeals for the Ninth Circuit warned of the particular problems which occur on the Internet:

> 'We now reiterate that the Web, as a marketing channel, is particularly susceptible to a likelihood of confusion since, as it did in this case, it allows for competing marks to be encountered at the same time, on the same screen.'[47]

These clashes of rights have led to an attempt to provide a uniform solution to the problem,[48] but as there has been no international consensus to follow such an approach the rules remain country specific.

The basic act of infringement in the United Kingdom is set out in s 10 of the Trade Marks Act 1994 (similar rights are granted in relation to a Community trade mark by art 10 of the CTM Regulation). This reads as follows:

> '(1) A person infringes a registered trade mark if he uses in the course of trade a sign which is identical with the trade mark in relation to goods or services which are identical with those for which it is registered.
>
> (2) A person infringes a registered trade mark if he uses in the course of trade a sign where because—

---

45   In one case, despite the provision in the Administration of Justice Act 1956 (now replaced by the Supreme Court Act 1981) covering 'aircraft' in three paragraphs this was not enough to cover a 'glider'; the Glider Standard Austria SH 1964, *Schenipp-Hirth Kommandit-Gesellschaft (owners of The Glider Standard Austria SH 1964) v Persons Having Possession of The Glider Standard Austria SH 1964* [1965] 2 All ER 1022.

46   Lanham Act, s 43(d)(2)(A).

47   *GOTO.com v Disney*, 202 F. 3d 1199, 1207 (9th Cir 2000).

48   See WIPO Joint Recommendation Concerning the Protection of Marks, and Other Industrial Property Rights in Signs on the Internet (WIPO Publication 845) (2001).

(a) the sign is identical with the trade mark and is used in relation to goods or services similar to those for which the trade mark is registered, or

(b) the sign is similar to the trade mark and is used in relation to goods or services identical with or similar to those for which the trade mark is registered, there exists a likelihood of confusion on the part of the public, which includes the likelihood of association with the trade mark.

(3) A person infringes a registered trade mark if he uses in the course of trade, in relation to goods or services, a sign which—

(a) is identical with or similar to the trade mark,

where the trade mark has a reputation in the United Kingdom and the use of the sign, being without due cause, takes unfair advantage of, or is detrimental to, the distinctive character or the repute of the trade mark.'

There are, therefore, three classes of infringement: identity, similarity and what might loosely be called dilution. Each of these classes will be looked at in turn, but there are some things which must be shown in respect of each. The first of these was that it was the use of a sign in the course of trade.

4.4.1   Use of a sign in the course of trade

The two concepts to examine are the simple question of what is 'use' of a sign and then, the more complex concept of what is 'use' of a sign in the course of trade. A person uses a sign in particular when he:

'(a) affixes it to goods or the packaging thereof;

(b) offers or exposes goods for sale, puts them on the market or stocks them for those purposes under the sign, or offers or supplies services under the sign;

(c) imports or exports goods under the sign; or

(d) uses the sign on business papers or in advertising.'[49]

In relation to a sign being used on the Internet the most relevant uses are (b) and (d). The European Court of Justice in *Arsenal v Reed*[50] explained that in the course of trade means that the use of the mark is in the context of a commercial activity with a view to economic advantage, and not as a private matter.[51] A person using a trade mark on a website for non-commercial purposes, for example a fan site for the Rolling Stones,[52] where the words the 'Rolling Stones' are used in relation to music (class 9) would not be trade mark infringement because the use

---

49   Trade Marks Act 1994, s 10(4).
50   C-206/01 *Arsenal v Reed* [2003] ETMR 19, para 40; followed C-48/05 *Adam Opel* [2007] ETMR 33, para 18.
51   C-206/01 *Arsenal v Reed* [2003] ETMR 19, para 40; C-48/05 *Adam Opel* [2007] ETMR 33, para 18.
52   CTM No. 169680.

was not in the course of trade. However, if someone was selling Rolling Stones CDs online or even simply for download, this would be use in the course of trade.[53] Furthermore, where, a trade mark is used on a website which is run for a commercial purpose, for example, to generate advertising revenues, this would be use in the course of trade.

---

5. A website lists various programs for sale under the Microsoft logo and uses the Microsoft logo on the small icons that represent each program itself. The name of each program begins 'Microsoft' or 'MS'. Microsoft is not the developer of any of these programs. It is of little legal consequence that this is on a website: this is use of a sign by exposing and offering goods for sale under a registered trade mark.

4.4.1.1   When is use on the Internet use in the United Kingdom?

A question of paramount importance in the global marketplace is whether a person is using a trade mark in the United Kingdom (or in the case of a Community trade mark, outside the Community) when they run a website outside that jurisdiction to sell within it. This problem arises because the 'very language of the Internet conveys the idea of the user *going* to the site – 'visit' is the word'[54] the question is, therefore, when does the availability of the site mean that a business is touting for trade from within the United Kingdom?

In *1-800 Flowers*[55] the Court of Appeal, following Jacob J's reasoning in the High Court, rejected the suggestion that a website merely being accessible ('a tentacle' on the user's screen) was enough to constitute use,[56] stating:

> 'There is something inherently unrealistic in saying that A "uses" his mark in the United Kingdom when all he does is place the mark on the Internet, from a location outside the UK, and simply wait in the hope that someone from the UK will download it and thereby create use on the part of A ... the very idea of "use" within a certain area would seem to require some active steps in that area on the part of the user that goes beyond providing facilities that enable others to bring the mark into the area.'[57]

Accordingly, the fact that an Internet search will produce a lot of foreign results and enable users to view foreign sites should not, in itself, mean that the use of any trade mark on one of those sites should be construed as use in the course of trade.[58] Instead, as Jacob J held in *Euromarket Designs v Peters*,[59] it is necessary

---

53   If the CDs had previously been put on the market within the EEA then the rights might be exhausted: TMA, s 12; CTM Regulation art 13.
54   *Euromarket Designs v Peters Crate & Barrel* [2001] FSR 20, para 24.
55   [2002] FSR 12.
56   It also seems apparent that the scant facts of trade being conducted within the UK did not help the applicant. The Court of Appeal mentioned on more than one occasion that there was no evidence as to the extent to which the website had even been 'accessed' from the UK, let alone traded in the UK.
57   [2002] FSR 191, paras 137 and 138, per Buxton LJ.
58   *Euromarket Designs v Peters and Crate & Barrel* [2000] ETMR 1025, paras 23 and 24.
59   [2000] ETMR 1025.

to examine the purpose and effect of the advertisement incorporating the mark. If the purpose is to solicit customers abroad (and not within the UK) then this should not make the use of the mark infringing. Therefore, when assessing the question, the court should look at whether, on visiting the website with an intelligent and discriminating attitude and on a fair reading, the information contained on the site would convey to a reasonable person (or an average consumer)[60] an offer to sell within the UK (or the Community).[61] The Court of Session, in *Bonnier Media v Smith*,[62] adopted a similar rationale:

'The person who sets up a website can be regarded as potentially committing a delict in any country where the website can be seen, in other words in any country in the world. It does not follow that he actually commits a delict in every country in the world, however. It is obvious that the overwhelming majority of websites will be of no interest whatsoever in more than a single country or a small group of countries. In my opinion a website should not be regarded as having delictual consequences in any country where it is unlikely to be of significant interest. That result can readily be achieved by a vigourous application of the maxim de minimus non curat praetor; if the impact of a website in a particular country is properly regarded as insignificant, no delict has been committed there. In determining whether the impact of a website is insignificant, it is appropriate in my opinion to look both at the content of the website itself and at the commercial or other context in which the website operates.'[63]

The Scots threshold, that anything more than insignificant use is sufficient to infringe, is more generous to right holders than that adopted south of the border. Accordingly, when the evidence is not very strong it may be in a right holder's interest to start proceedings in Scotland rather than England. However, it is doubtful that these differences will be significant enough for this to be advisable in many cases, and even in those marginal cases, right holders may well lose out when the Scottish courts consider the matter further. The German courts, in *MARITIM TM*, found no infringement where the defendant's services were only available abroad.[64] Importantly, the German court did not think that use of the German language would create a sufficient connection with Germany. This reasoning is sound. However, it does not mean that the converse should not also be true. If a site is in German then, it is suggested, this is relevant evidence that it is not directed at a market which is predominately English-speaking (such as the UK).

The latitude given to website providers around the world should not be abused. If, as in *V&S Vin & Sprit Aktiebolag v Absolut Beach*,[65] a business was

---

60 In *Euromarket Designs*, Jacob J suggests that the objective test should be the 'reasonable trader', whereas in *Dearlove* (para 25) Kitchin J suggests it should be the average consumer. It appears the latter is better in accord with general principles of trade mark law.
61 *Sony v Pacific Game Technology* (2006) EWHC 2509 (Ch), para 23.
62 [2002] ETMR 86.
63 Ibid., 19.
64 [2003] IL Pr 17; this approach has been criticised by some German commentators see: T. Dreier 'Reconciling National Copyright Traditions: Conflict of Laws Rules – the German Example' in *Mélanges Victor Nabhan* (EYB 2004) pp 123, 126-127.
65 [2002] IP & T 203.

willing to accept an order from a customer located in a particular country then it is quite reasonable that liability should arise if that business uses somebody else's trade mark to obtain that business. It is suggested that a foreign website owner's activities will be lawful as long as they are not a connivance to avoid intellectual property rights by hosting and maintaining a website outside the UK (or the Community) to sell to customers within that area.[66]

This approach does not assist where a website has no real regional controls and is used for promotional purposes rather than direct sales. Such use is becoming increasingly important to the entertainment industry (and to artists striving to enter that industry). At present this use is dominated by sites such as *MySpace* or *YouTube*, but the speed the industry is developing means that it is quite possible these sites will be superseded by new models at some point in the future. The problems these sites present were aptly demonstrated in *Dearlove v Combs*,[67] where Sean Combs's use of 'P.Diddy' was challenged as infringing by Ian Dearlove (known as Diddy). The case revolved around material that Combs had included on *MySpace* and *YouTube* as well as www.badboyonline.com. The content of those sites included buttons saying 'DIDDY PRESS PLAY' ('Press Play' was the name of his latest Album) and 'DIDDY TV', which linked to other material and websites. Kitchin J concluded that Combs's use of DIDDY in this was directed at the UK (as part of an 'international' campaign). He reached this conclusion on the basis that Combs's album was on sale in the UK and *MySpace* and *YouTube* were the primary method of the album being advertised and promoted. In addition, Combs had a substantial business in the UK evidenced by his then imminent UK tour. Indeed, the fact that there were alternative links for the UK (where DIDDY was owned by Dearlove) and the US (where it was not) did not stop the use being conducted with the United Kingdom.[68] Unfortunately, as these links were either inactive or difficult to find, the court did not move on to consider whether they could be an effective way of 'staying out' of the jurisdiction.

4.4.1.2   Factors to determine if use is in the course of trade in the United Kingdom

The Internet permits access from any country in the world. This does not, without more, mean that every use of a trade mark on the Internet is an infringement in every country where rights subsist. This section will briefly set out the considerations that should be taken into account to determine if there is infringement in the United Kingdom (based on the English, rather than the Scottish, approach).

The extreme position that a 'passive provider' is liable for infringement has been rejected. The courts must look to the nature of the website: if its content is aimed at UK customers there may be infringement. In *800 Flowers* particular attention was paid to the commercial audience of the website. A site which 'faces' the UK and possibly trades with UK consumers is more likely to find

66   *Sony v Pacfic Game Technology* (2006) EWHC 2509 (Ch), para 27.
67   [2007] EWHC 375 (Ch).
68   Ibid., para 35.

itself infringing a UK trade mark than one which both is clearly not directed at a UK audience and which does not permit trading with UK consumers.

The second point to bear in mind is that non-Internet based advertising in the UK is likely to influence the decision that there is use within the jurisdiction. In *Mecklermedia*, *Euromarket* and *V&S* the courts took into account the nature, if any, of advertising within the UK. Such activities within the jurisdiction go to the intention of the defendant to trade with consumers in the UK.

The final consideration is blocking. Simply because the Internet technically permits worldwide distribution does not necessarily mean that this limitless dissemination must be utilised in every case. It is possible to block use in a particular country by technical measures, by not accepting emails from certain ccTLD (e.g. to block out the UK, all email address with a '.uk' are ignored). Those customers who pass through these precautions can be warned to go no further if they are from a particular country. Finally, if services or goods are provided over the Internet, consumers from certain jurisdictions can be screened out at the contractual stage. So if goods or a download are ordered from a particular country (as designated from credit card or other details) then the sale could be aborted.

Where defendants do not take these preventive steps they must bear the consequences, as Jacob J stated in *Mecklermedia* 'when an enterprise wants to use a mark or word throughout the world... it must take into account that in some places, if not others, there may be confusion'[69] which can result in passing off or trade mark infringement.

4.4.1.3 The use of domain names in the course of trade

In *BT v One-in-a-million*[70] the High Court considered when a domain name is used in the course of trade:

> 'The first and most obvious [use] is that it may be sold to the enterprise whose name or trade mark has been used, which may be prepared to pay a high price to avoid the inconvenience of there being a domain name comprising its own name or trade mark which is not under its control. Secondly, it may be sold to a third party unconnected with the name, so that he may do or attempt to do the same thing or to use it for the purposes of deception. Thirdly it may be sold to someone with a distinct interest of his own in the name, for example a solicitor by the name of John Sainsbury or the Government of the British Virgin Islands, with a view to its use by him. Fourth it may be retained by the dealer unused and unsold, in which case it serves only to block the use of that name as a registered domain name by others, including those whose name or trade mark it comprises.'[71]

It is clear that the first three of these 'uses' could be construed as being 'use of a sign in the course of trade in relation to goods or services'. The fourth 'use' is, however, misconceived and was recognised as such by the Court of Appeal. The

---

69 *Mecklermedia v DC Congress* [1997] 627, 640.
70 [1999] 1 WLR 903 CA, [1998] FSR 265 HC.
71 [1998] FSR 265, 268.

registration of a domain name does not actually block the brand owner from exploiting its brand name as a domain name. All the claimants had lost was a single domain name which reflected their brand names; they simply wanted to prevent any other confusingly similar domain names from existing. The Court of Appeal puts this as follows:

> 'The registration [of a domain name] only blocks the identical domain name and therefore does not act as a block to registration of a domain name that can be used by the owner of the goodwill in the name.'[72]

It would therefore appear that a domain name could be registered but not 'used' for the purposes of trade mark infringement if it is retained unsold and unconnected to an IP address. Nevertheless it will be difficult to persuade a court that one does not intend to 'use' the domain name having registered it. Despite the prejudicial evidence adduced as to 'One in a Million's previous conduct'[73] their approaches to the claimants in the action had all been careful to pre-empt any suggestion of illegal use of the domain names. To J Sainsbury plc, one defendant wrote: 'We are not trading under the name Sainsbury nor do we intend to trade under the name Sainsbury. We have merely purchased the Internet domain names j-sainsbury.com, sainsbury.com and sainsburys.com as part of our personal collection.'[74] This raises the question of when possession of a domain name becomes its use in the course of trade.

For example, the putative claimant can write to the domain name owner asking for his undertaking that he will either sell the domain name to the claimant for the amount of money it cost him to register the domain name or undertake not to sell or transfer it at all. If the domain name owner does not confirm this, or offers to sell it for more than the mere registration cost he is, arguably, threatening to use the domain name in the course of trade. In *Tropical Resorts Management Ltd v Morgan*[75] Mr Morgan did just this. He registered a domain name incorporating the claimant's trade mark 'Banyan Tree'. When approached about the domain name, he tried to bargain for a higher price than the claimants would pay. And when they refused to pay, he threatened to auction the domain name. This case was brought in passing off, but there is no reason to suppose that if the domain name includes a trade mark that this would be used in the course of trade. In *Britannia Building Society v Prangley*,[76] Mr Prangley, having registered the domain name 'britanniabuildingsociety.com' (apparently for the purposes of

---

72   [1999] 1 WLR 903, CA.
73   In September 1996, one of the defendants wrote to Burger King: 'Further to our telephone conversation earlier this evening, I confirm that I own the domain name burgerking.co.uk. I would be willing to sell the domain name for the sum of £25,000 plus VAT. In answer to your question regarding as to what we would do with the domain name should you decide not to purchase it – the domain name would be available for sale to any other interested party.' The threat to sell the inherently deceptive name possibly to a person passing off the trade mark is explicit. It should not be forgotten that Burger King was not a plaintiff in the action (ibid., 922-3).
74   Ibid., 923.
75   [2001] All ER (D) 38 (Jul).
76   Ch.D, June 12, 2000 (unreported).

u new business providing services to British builders in Iran) refused to sell it to the claimants. He did not threaten to sell it to anyone else. In these circumstances, Rattee J was concerned that there was no use of a sign at all, let alone use of a sign in the course of trade.

---

6. RRZ Ltd is a well-known stockbroker with a registered trade mark over the mark 'RRZ' in the appropriate classes. It wishes to register the domain name 'RRZ.co.uk' and instructs a domain name agent accordingly. The agent reports back that RRZ.co.uk is already registered as a domain name but that no website is 'pointed' to the domain name. Without some indication of trade from the domain name owner, RRZ Ltd will have a difficult task to sue the owner for trade mark infringement as the domain name (the sign) does not appear to be being used in the course of trade.

4.4.2 Use as a trade mark

The courts have struggled[77] with the question of whether a mark has to be used as a trade mark to infringe. In other words, does the use of a trade mark have to be used to indicate the origin of the goods for such use to be infringing? The Court of Justice has finally answered this question positively, in other words the use of a mark which is not for the purposes of guaranteeing origin is not infringing.[78] This initially appeared to provide an answer to the question, namely that uses which were for purposes other than indicating origin are permitted. However, the Court of Appeal correctly pointed out in *L'Oreal SA v Bellure NV*[79] this does not conclude whether trade mark use includes uses related to other functions of a trade mark.[80] A question was referred to the Court of Justice as to what uses in relation to the other functions of a trade mark (i.e. other than indicating origin) would be infringing.[81]

If this final point is put to one side, the basic question is are consumers likely to interpret the sign as designating or tending to designate the undertaking from which the goods originate?[82] If the relevant public does not perceive the use of the sign to be an indication of origin there is no infringement.[83]

---

77 In the UK, under the Trade Marks Act 1938 the answer was relatively clear, see *Unidoor v Marks and Spencer Plc* [1988] RPC 275 at 280; *KODAK Trade Mark* (No.2) [1990] FSR 49.
78 C-206/01 *Arsenal v Reed* [2003] ETMR 19 at [52]; Case C-245/02 *Anheuser-Busch Inc v Budejovicky Budvar Narodni Podnik* [2005] ETMR 27 at [59]; also see Case C-17/06 *Celine Sarl v Celine SA* [2007] ETMR 80, at [16].
79 [2007] EWCA Civ 968, [2008] ETMR 1.
80 *Parfums Christian Dior SA v Evora BV* (C-337/95) [1998] ETMR 26 (the advertising function).
81 *L'Oreal* [2007] EWCA Civ 968, [2008] ETMR 1, para 48.
82 C-245/02 *Anheuser Busch v Budejovicky* [2005] ETMR 27 at [60]; C-17/06 *Celine*, [2007] ETMR 80, at [27] (which was suggested to be the effect of C-206/01 *Arsenal v Reed* [2003] ETMR 19 at [56] and [57]).
83 This means that the decision of the Court of Appeal in *Arsenal v Reed* [2003] EWCA Civ 696, [2003] ETMR 73, does not correctly represent the law, but that of the House of Lords in *R v Johnstone* [2003] UKHL 28 better reflects the position.

4.4.3   In relation to goods or services

The sign purportedly infringing the trade mark must be used in relation to goods or services.[84] This question is sometimes mixed up with trade mark use, but it is distinct.[85] In most cases this hurdle is very low, as use is in relation to goods if it concerns the affixing of a sign to the trade mark onto goods and subsequently offering for sale, or stocking, those goods.[86] It is also use in relation to goods or services where a trader uses the sign in such a way that a link is established between the sign which constitutes the business name and the goods marketed or services provided by that trader.[87]

Most websites appear to be purely providing information but usually they also have banners or links to other pages that advertise or provide goods or services. In such cases, the use of the mark would be in relation to goods or services. Few commercial sites are no more than an electronic poster. If the site is used to interact with customers then the domain name would appear to be used in relation to goods or services. There is no other route to access the website than by using the domain name.[88] There must, therefore be a greater question as to whether the domain name is being used in 'relation' to anything.

4.4.4   Identical sign to registered trade mark

The most straightforward type of infringement arises where a sign identical to the trade mark is used on identical goods or services in respect of which the mark is registered. In determining whether a sign is identical to the mark it should be considered whether the sign reproduces, without modification or addition, all the elements constituting the mark or where, viewed as a whole, it contains differences so insignificant they may go unnoticed by the average consumer.[89] Nevertheless, certain parts of the mark which have no trade mark significance can be ignored.[90]

---

84 See C-245/02 *Anheuser Busch v Budejovicky* [2005] ETMR 27, para 62.
85 As may have happened in *Bravado Merchandising Services v Mainsteam Publishing* [1996] FSR 205; see *British Sugar v James Robertson* [1997] ETMR 118, 124.
86 C-48/05 *Adam Opel* [2007] ETMR 33, para 20; C-17/06 *Céline* [2007] ETMR 80, para 22; this premise is derived from somewhat more opaque wording in C- 206/01 *Arsenal v Reed* [2003] ETMR 19, para 40 and 41.
87 C-17/06 *Céline* (11 September 2007), para 23.
88 Of course, off the Internet, the domain name may be used not in relation to registered goods or services. For instance, a designer of the Harrods website may set up his own website to advertise his previous commissions, including Harrods'. The presence on his website of the domain name 'www.harrods.co.uk' would not be the use of the trade mark in relation to goods or services for which Harrods had a trade mark. See *Harrods v Schwartz-Sackin* [1986] FSR 490. In contrast, Harrods were granted an injunction against defendants who registered the domain name 'harrods.com' when Harrods had already registered 'harrods.co.uk' (unreported, Mr Justice Lightman, 9 December 1996).
89 C-291/00 *LTJ Diffusion SA v Sadas Vertbaudet SA* [2003] E.C.R. I-2799; [2003] E.T.M.R. 83, at [54].
90 'Compass Logistics' not identical to 'Compass': *Compass Publishing BV v Compass Logistics Ltd* [2004] EWHC 520; [2004] R.P.C. 41.

Many uses of signs on the Internet will be simple straightforward trade mark infringement. A business which sells goods online is no different from any other act of infringement. A website selling books to United Kingdom consumers under the name Penguin is little different to selling those books from a shop in Birmingham. It is for this reason that the discussion will concentrate on domain names and the peculiar rules that may apply to them.

It has already been explained in relation to domain names that when registering a mark the prefix 'www' or the suffix '.com' does not make a mark distinctive if it was not otherwise so. Similarly, as neither the prefix nor the suffix have any trade mark significance, they can be ignored when considering infringement. By extension this may also mean that where a person has 'www.company.co.uk' registered as a trade mark this will be considered to be identical to 'www.company.com', the differences between the two marks being only technical.

---

7. SOUK Ltd have registered the mark SOUK. Southern Orphanages UK ltd registers the domain name www.souk.co.uk and starts trading from the site. The domain name used is identical to the registered mark and so might be infringing.

4.4.4.1   Identical goods

The court will take on the mantle of the relevant customer to assess whether the goods or services in respect of which the mark is being used are identical to those for which it is registered. The views of an expert in the field, on the other hand, are of little relevance because they cannot provide assistance on whether that consumer would consider the goods to be the same or not.[91]

4.4.5   Similar or identical sign with similar or identical goods or services

Similarity type infringement is the most common before courts and tribunals. The central question is: does the person's use of the sign lead the average consumer to be confused as to the origin of the goods,[92] so that they believe the goods and services sold under the sign come from the same undertaking or one economically linked to it.[93] It is therefore important to know if there is a risk of mistaking the origin of the goods, not whether consumers actually *do* mistake the origin of the goods or services.[94]

---

91   *Beautimatic v Mitchell* [1999] E.T.M.R. 912. The construction of specifications relating to services may be construed more narrowly than those for goods: *Reed Executive v Reed Business Information* [2004] EWCA Civ 159; [2004] ETMR 56 at [43].
92   C-251/95 *Sabel v Puma* [1998] ETMR 1, para 23.
93   C-342/97 *Lloyd Schufabrick Mayer v Kliysen Handel* [1999] ETMR 690, para 17; C-39/97 *Canon v MGM* [1999] ETMR 1, para 29-30.
94   *Thomson Holidays v Norweigan Crusie Lines* [2003] RPC 32, para 26.

The mark has to be appreciated globally, taking into account all the relevant factors of the case.[95] In particular, the global appreciation of the visual, aural and conceptual similarity of the marks in question must be based on the overall impression given by the marks, bearing in mind their respective distinctive and dominant components.[96] But it must be remembered that the average consumer perceives a mark as a whole and does not break it down into its various details.[97] A more detailed discussion of judging similarity is outside the scope of the book.

4.4.5.1   Distinctiveness

A mark which has become very distinctive is entitled to enhanced protection. Before it is possible to rely on additional distinctiveness it is necessary to provide sufficient evidence that a mark has become that distinctive. This broader protection can be particularly useful for well-known marks as they will be more distinctive and, accordingly, easier to infringe.

4.4.5.2   Similarity of goods

The issue of confusion is not merely concerned with a comparison of the two marks. The similarity of the goods or services in relation to which the sign is used by the parties is also important. Indeed, the greater the similarity between the goods the less similarity there needs to be between the marks (and visa versa).[98] Notwithstanding, there still needs to be some similarity of goods or services for infringement. If there is no such similarity then the claim should be made on the basis of dilution. The factors that should be taken into account when assessing the similarity of the goods or services include their nature, their end users and the methods of use and whether they are in competition with, or complement, each other.[99] The nature of the Internet is not going to affect this basic determination as it is in most cases only a method of selling.

4.4.5.3   The average consumer

The characteristics of average consumers, the centre of any comparison, are that they are reasonably well-informed and reasonably observant and circumspect. Such consumers rarely directly compare the two marks and so they will have an imperfect recollection of a mark. They will give more attention to some purchasing decisions than to others[100] (high-volume low-cost goods, for example, would have less attention than other types of goods). But the confusion of the careless and stupid is never enough to make out infringement.[101] As the use made of a

95   C-251/95 *Sabel v Puma* [1998] ETMR 1, para 23.
96   Ibid.
97   Ibid.
98   C-39/97 *Canon v MGM* [1999] ETMR 1, para 18.
99   Ibid., para 23.
100   C-342/97 *Lloyd Schufabrick Mayer v Kliysen Handel* [1999] ETMR 690, para 26.
101   *Reed Executive v Reed Business Information* (2004) RPC 40, para 82.

trade mark on the Internet could be for a wide range of goods and services, the average consumer will vary accordingly.

4.4.6 Dilution protection

When the new law was first adopted protection was given for the first time to prevent uses of certain marks on dissimilar goods. However, in *Davidoff v Goffkid*[102] the Court of Justice held that the protection extended to uses of those marks on both similar and dissimilar goods where the use of the mark, without due cause, took unfair advantage of, or was detrimental to, the distinctive character or repute of the trade mark.[103] This protection only applies to marks which have sufficient reputation. The test that the mark must satisfy is that the mark is known by a significant part of the public concerned with the goods or services in relation to which it is registered[104] and this knowledge must exist in a substantial part of the territory.[105] The greater the mark's[106] reputation, the easier it is to establish that detriment is caused.[107] In assessing whether the mark has a reputation the following should be taken into account: the market share held by the trade mark, the intensity, geographical extent and duration of its use, and the size of the investment made by the undertaking in promoting it.[108] Once it has been established that the mark has sufficient reputation it is necessary to prove lack of any due cause to use the mark.

4.4.6.1 Due cause

If a user wants to argue that they had *due cause* to use the mark it is for them to prove it. This requires proof that there was both due cause to use the mark and to take unfair advantage of, or to cause detriment to, it.[109] It is not enough for the user to show merely that a trader adopted the famous mark innocently.[110] It is more likely that the user will have to show that he had a reasonable justification for using the mark.[111]

In a domain name dispute, this phrase may become pivotal. If for example, the owner of a domain name owns a trade mark representing the text of a trade mark

---

102 C-292/00 *Davidoff v Goffkid* [2003] ETMR 42; this was confirmed in C-408/01 *Adidas v Fitnessworld* [2004] ETMR 10.
103 The law in the UK was changed by the Trade Marks (Proof of Use, etc) Regulation 2004 (SI 2004/946); the CTM Regulation has not been amended but the law is now clear.
104 C-375/97 *General Motors v Yplon* [1999] ETMR 950, paras 24 and 26.
105 Ibid, paras 28-29.
106 The reputation must be in the mark relied upon and not another related mark: *CDW Graphic Design TM App* [2003] RPC 30, para 17 et seq.
107 *Premier Brands v Typhoon* [2000] ETMR 1071, 1095 per Neuberger J.
108 C-375/97 *General Motors v Yplon* [1999] ETMR 950, para 27.
109 *Premier Brands v Typhoon* [2000] ETMR 1071, 1097.
110 Ibid., 1097.
111 The same approach as was previously adopted by the Benelux court: see *Lucas BAS* [1976] IIC 420 at 425.

in one class, but the more famous mark is used in relation to a different class the using the famous mark might be with due cause. In the MIT case mentioned above (see section 4.1.1) this was more or less what happened. Merritt Technologies, the owner of the 'mit.com' domain name, was legitimately using the mark and the Massachusetts Institute of Technology was trying to extend its influence beyond its trading sphere on the grounds that any use of MIT was objectionable. Use for this reason may be both with due cause and justifiable. Accordingly, it does not appear to be without due cause to use one's trade mark as a domain name.[112]

4.4.6.2   *Unfair advantage or detriment*

To prove infringement on the broad dilution based protection requires more than merely using a mark which reminds the consumer of the famous mark, it is necessary to show real, not just a theoretical risk, of unfair advantage or detriment.[113] This would cover any use of a mark which is clearly exploiting or free-riding on the famous mark or trying to trade on its reputation.[114]

4.4.6.2.1   Unfair advantage

Accordingly, using another mark's renown as a domain name to try and get users to take an interest in the site is likely to be considered to be taking unfair advantage; it is unfair because the benefits from creating and maintaining a mark's reputation belong to the person who made the investment in that mark.[115] The advantage taken, however, must be significant.[116]

To defeat this in a domain name dispute, a business is expected to be able to 'distance' its sign from the trade mark. In many cases, where there is a good reason for selecting the domain name address, it will be difficult to see how an unfair advantage is achieved. The very nature of the web is that there are a number of documents which are interlinked. Using a site as a thoroughfare to another is no more taking unfair advantage of the destination site as is walking into one shop on the high street while on the way to another. Clearly, any use of a domain name must not be a sham; the courts will look for any ulterior motives in choosing the domain name. This said, the domain name owner should nevertheless do all possible not to take unfair advantage of their domain name. They should make it clear to their site's viewers that they may be at the wrong site owing to a contingency of the domain name system, rather than any motive of the site controller. It will be a sign of good faith to include on the home page a link to the 'other' site.

---

112   As noted by Neuberger J in *Premier Brands v Typhoon* [2000] ETMR 1071 at 1091, in the Uniform Benelux Trade marks Law 1971, art 132, 'due cause' has been construed narrowly, and even that Art embraces the idea of prior rights in the sign.

113   E.g. *Inter Corp v Sihra* [2004] ETMR 44, para 23; and *Intel v CPM UK* [2007] ETMR 59.

114   See Advocate-General in C-408/01 *Adidas v Fitnessworld* [2003] ETMR 91, para 39.

115   R-308/2003-1 *Mango Sports v Diknah* [2005] ETMR 5 (BoA).

116   *Oasis Stores's TM* [1999] ETMR 531, 541 (Regy); *DaimlerChrysler v Alavi* [2001] ETMR 98, para 89.

In general, it is unlikely that a disclaimer would allow a person to avoid liability for dilution type infringement as confusion is not an element of the infringement. But it may also be possible to argue that the presence of a disclaimer may negate any unfair advantage taken of the mark.

4.4.6.2.2 Detriment

Businesses could also be pursued if their use of the mark was detrimental to the mark's distinctive character. The purpose of this type of protection is to prevent the whittling away of the unique nature of very famous marks.[117] If everything is branded with a particular mark, it loses all its exclusivity and singularity:[118] this is called blurring. Alternatively, an unpleasant mental association between the use of the mark and the goods of a third party can be detrimental to the earlier mark.[119] This is called tarnishment.

In *One in a Million* it was shown that, in relation to domain names, 'detriment' is not a high hurdle. The High Court suggests 'It seems to me to be equally clear [that the trade mark Marks & Spencer has a reputation in the UK] that the Defendant's use of it is detrimental to the trade mark, if only by damaging the Plaintiff's exclusivity.'[120] The Court of Appeal takes this further:

'[The] domain names were registered to take advantage of the distinctive character and reputation of the marks. That is unfair and detrimental.'

These statements rely on the court's perception that the defendants were fraudulent and so should release the domain names, other than on the strict legal analysis of what constitutes 'unfair advantage' and 'detrimental' use of a domain name.

This sort of reasoning may be contrasted with *Avery Dennison v Jerry Sumpton*,[121] a decision of the US Court of Appeals for the Ninth Circuit which, like Marks & Spencer, is a distinctive brand name constructed from common-use surnames. The defendant, Mr Sumpton, 'rented' vanity email addresses to individuals. In illustration, say, Phillip Jacobs may be able to rent for $19.95 the email address Phillip@Jacobs.com for the period of one year. Two of the surnames available for rent were 'Avery' and 'Dennison'. This offering led to Avery Dennison, the office supplier, challenging Mr Sumpton's registration. The court considered the 'motivation' of the defendant was to 'capitalise on the surname status of "Avery" and "Dennison"'[122] and not to take advantage of Avery Dennison's brand so Sumpton's conduct was found to be lawful.

Although not of direct relevance to English law, this decision demonstrates how courts on both sides of the Atlantic look to the 'intention' of a domain name

---

117   This originates from F. Schechter 'The Rational Basis of Trade mark Protection' (1927) 40 Harv LR 813, 825.
118   See comments in *Taittinger v Allbev* [1993] FSR 641, 678 per Bingham MR.
119   R-1004/2000 *Ferreo v Kindercare* [2005] ETMR 6 (BoA), para 30.
120   *BT v One in a million* [1998] FSR 265, 272.
121   189 F3d 868 (9th Cir 1999).
122   Ibid., 880.

registrant, rather than merely basing their decisions on typographical compar-isons between trade marks and domain names. Indeed, both in *One in a Million* and *Avery Dennison* the courts' conclusions were based on other registrations as well as those at issue. This means that even if a defendant can construct a plausi-ble argument in relation to one domain name, if there are other registrations these can be used to undermine what might otherwise be a good case.

4.4.7   Metatags

Websites include information which cannot normally be seen by the user, some of this information is deliberately concealed, but there is also information which is contained on a website to assist the workings of search engines. This informa-tion stored in this 'meta' section of a website is called metatags. These tags are divided into 'keywords' and a 'description' of the website. These mean that a site can be included in web search despite having no obvious connection. This code will be invisible to most visitors to the website[123] and so they will have no indi-cation of why the site has been listed in the search results. For example, the fol-lowing could be included in the HTML code making up a law firm's website: <META name='keywords' content='law, legal, lawyer, litigation'>. The law firm includes this code to ensure that, even if the words 'law', 'legal', 'lawyer' and 'litigation' are not actually used within any articles on the website, someone entering 'lawyer' into a search engine may still be directed to the firm's website. This issue was observed by Jacob J in *Avnet v Isoact*:[124]

> 'It is a general problem of the Internet that it works on words and not words in relation to goods or services. So, whenever anyone searches for that word, even if the searcher is looking for the word in one context, he will, or may, find Web pages or data in a wholly different context ... Of course, users of the Internet also know that that is a feature of the Internet and their search may produce an altogether wrong Web page or the like. This may be an important matter for the courts to take into account in considering trade mark and like problems.'[125]

4.4.7.1   Metatags and trade marks

The first question is whether using a trade mark in a metatag is use of a trade mark at all.[126] It was originally accepted by the English courts that invisible use (such as metatags) could amount to trade mark infringement[127] as it was by the Benelux,[128] French,[129] German[130] and Italian[131] courts. However, Jacob LJ in *Reed*

123   Some, of course, will use the 'View Source' command from their browser to see this, and other, hidden code.
124   [1998] FSR 16.
125   Ibid., 18.
126   Jacob LJ, *Reed Executive v Reed Business Information* [2004] EWCA 159, [2004] RPC 40.
127   See *Road Tech Computer Systems v Mandata* [2000] ETMR 970.
128   *VNU Business Publications v Monster Board* [2002] ETMR 111.
129   *Viaticum v Google France* [2004] ETMR 63.
130   *Estée Lauder v Fragrance Counter* [2002] RTMR 843.
131   *Trieste e Venezia Assicurzzioni Genertel v Crowe Italia* [2001] ETMR 66.

Executive v Reed Business[132] questioned, without deciding the point, whether using a trade mark in metatags could be use of a trade mark at all.[133] The problem he identified was that the ordinary user of the Internet would only be aware of the defendant's use of the mark as a metatag to the extent that it had been used as part of the search criteria. Furthermore, the trade mark will only be visible in the input box at the top of the search results and, possibly, in the listing for the competitor's site, but it will not be visible in the defendant's entry.

Even if the use of a trade mark in a metatag amounts to trade mark use, in relation to infringement on the grounds of similarity (or passing off) it is necessary to show confusion (or misrepresentation). The nature of the Internet is such that users are accustomed to be given what appear to be totally irrelevant 'hits' amongst those with more relevance. Indeed, even experienced users will not know, without some investigation, why a particular website came up on a search; whether because it was a metatag, the word is included for some innocent reason or in a different context (in relation to REED, it might include hits relating to a newspaper or a book on wind instruments). This means the confusion is rarely going to be evident at the time of the search and even if one of the sites is viewed, the metatags without more would not be visible and there is nothing to cause confusion.

It is likely, therefore, that the risk of trade mark infringement by using metatags is not particularly high. Indeed, the approach of the English courts avoids the problems identified by the US Court of Appeals for the Ninth Circuit in *Playboy Enterprises v Terri Welles*[134]

'Forcing Welles and others to use absurd turns of phrase in their metatags, such as those necessary to identify Welles, would be particularly damaging in the Internet search context. Searchers would have a much more difficult time locating relevant websites if they could do so only by correctly guessing the long phrases necessary to substitute for trade marks. We can hardly expect someone searching for Welles' site to imagine the same phrase proposed by the district court to describe Welles without referring to Playboy – "the nude model selected by Mr. Hefner's organization . . ." Yet if someone could not remember her name, that is what they would have to do. Similarly, someone searching for critiques of Playboy on the Internet would have a difficult time if Internet sites could not list the object of their critique in their metatags.'[135]

Nevertheless, if metatags' use is not restricted, it does mean that there may be some departure from commercial reality. Websites will pay substantially to be ranked on the first page, and at the top of the first page, of any search listings. Some search engines make a virtue out of being 'even-handed' and not permitting the purchase of higher rankings. It follows that damage may well be caused by being relegated below a certain position on the listings page. On the one hand, if the use of a metatag will simply ensure that the defendant's site is listed in the

132   [2004] RPC 40.
133   Ibid., para 140 and 149(a).
134   279 F3d 796 (9th Cir 2002).
135   Ibid., 803-804.

search results together with the claimant's site, there may be no damage at all. The metatag will not exclude the claimant's site. But the more rogue the entries, such as from those with infringing metatags, the greater the risk of the genuine site being displaced.

4.4.7.2   'Keywords'

Search engines rank the results for any given search in one or both of two ways: objectively or subjectively. The objective method strictly utilises an algorithm or program to rank the results in some decreasing order of relevance. Depending on the particular interests of the user, the most relevant results should be shown at the top of the listing. The relevance of a page can be determined by hundreds of different factors. Google's PageRank system uses factors such as popularity, position and size of the search terms and the proximity of the search terms. Other search engines use slightly different systems. But most include some form of 'sponsored' link, where a particular web page has purchased a 'keyword' from the search engine. In such a situation, the search engine will bestow the purchasing website with a greater prominence than it otherwise may have had. As with metatags, complaints will occur when a search engine sells keywords that are trade marks owned by entities other than the purchaser.

It follows that when a user searches for a brand name, an 'accurate' search engine will display the brand owner's website together with the other highly ranked search results. In fact, users performing search queries for a company's trade names and marks are clearly relying on the goodwill inherent in the name or mark, and are probably searching for the source of the goods corresponding to those names or marks. Conversely, a search engine may highly promote results of sites that have purchased the searched-for brand name. This is sometimes called 'paid placement' or 'bid for location'. In this situation, the search engine may be accused of trade mark infringement, or passing off. In the United States, this issue has been widely litigated but there is still no certainty as to whether the sale of keywords is use of a mark in commerce and so trade mark infringement.[136]

The mixed reception to such arguments in the United States does not mean that there would be a similar reception in English courts. In the last edition, it was suggested that key words are discussed, negotiated and form the subject of a contract between the search engine and a purchaser. Such use it was suggested was use as a sign and in the course of trade. Since the last edition, however, the law relating to trade mark use has moved on as discussed above. It is now clear that use which is not for the purposes of indicating origin of the goods does not fall within a trade mark's function.[137] The initial sale of the key word is not using

---

136   *GEICO v Google*, 300 F.Supp 2d 700 (ED Va. 2004); *800-JR Cigars v GoTO*, 437 F.Supp 2d 273 (DNJ 2006) (both use in commerce); *Merck v Mediplan Health*, 425 F. Supp 2d 402 (SDNY 2006); *1-800 Contacts v WhenU.com*, 414 F.3d 400 (2d Cir 2005) (not use in commerce).

137   It is possible that there might be use in relation to the other functions of a trade mark. This question has recently been referred by the Court of Appeal to the ECJ: see *L'Oreal SA v Bullure NV* [2007] EWCA Civ 968, [2008] ETMR 1.

them as trade marks. Once a keyword has been sold the purchaser is in much the same position as had he used a metatag. This means the results are likely to be the same. If the person using the keyword is not liable for infringement, it is difficult to see how a search engine would be liable either for selling the keyword, as a mere technical connivance, or as joint tortfeasor for it being used.

4.4.8 Defences

If an action for trade mark infringement exists, the alleged infringer may still come within one of the defences. This section will briefly examine some of those defences and, in particular, look at where they might apply to the Internet.

4.4.8.1 Consent and acquiescence

The most straightforward defence to trade mark infringement is consent; in fact the absence of consent is not strictly a defence but a missing element of the cause of action (accordingly the burden of proving there was no consent falls on the proprietor of the mark). The nature of consent[138] is such that it can be express or implied and, unlike a licence, does not need to be in writing. It is also a defence to show that the proprietor has granted a licence to use the mark. Of course, if licensees operate outside the scope of their licences they will infringe (and probably also be in breach of contract).

4.4.8.2 Registered mark and own name

Section 11 of the Trade Marks Act 1994[139] sets out numerous defences; of those, the defences in subss (1) and (2) are worth setting out in full:

'(1) A registered trade mark is not infringed by the use of another registered trade mark in relation to goods or services for which the latter is registered (but see s 47(6) (effect of declaration of invalidity of registration)).

(2) A registered trade mark is not infringed by—

(a) the use by a person of his own name or address,

(b) the use of indications concerning the kind, quality, quantity, intended purpose, value, geographical origin, the time of production of goods or of rendering of services, or other characteristics of goods or services, or

(c) the use of the trade mark where it is necessary to indicate the intended purpose of a product or service (in particular, as accessories or spare parts),

provided the use is in accordance with honest practices in industrial or commercial matters.'

---

138   Consent can also be given during the registration process: see TMA, s 5(5).
139   S 11(2) is replicated in relation to Community trade marks in art 12.

Section 11(1) makes it clear that it is not an infringement of a registered trade mark to use it[140] in relation to goods and services for which it is registered.[141] The defence requires that the mark is used as registered (and without some variation) and solely in relation to those goods for which it is registered. This would provide a defence where a trade mark is owned by different traders for different goods and only one of those traders is able to use it as a domain name.

There is also a defence available to traders who trade using their own name[142] (meaning the name by which they are usually known[143]). This clearly applies to individuals but it also applies, in principle, to trade names[144] and company names.[145] This defence may be particularly important in relation to domain names. If a Mr Paul Smith owned and runs a website at www.paulsmith.net then provided his use is in accordance with honest practices in industrial and commercial matters this defence will be available. But it goes further than that; the defence might cover all sorts of companies and traders using domain names which follow their own names.

The other defences under s 11(2) will not be discussed here as they will have little relevance to the Internet and where they apply in other cases there is little difference that the conduct is taking place online or in the real world. In any event, the own name defence (and the other defences in s 11(2)) are only available where use is in accordance with honest practices in industrial and commercial matters.[146] This is an objective test[147] and the court must undertake an overall assessment of all the circumstances, and, in particular, assess whether the other trader might be regarded as competing unfairly with the proprietor of the mark.[148]

The purpose of the proviso[149] is to ensure a trader using another's mark acts fairly in relation to the legitimate interests of the trade mark owner,[150] rather than preventing any possible confusion about trade origin that might arise.[151] The English courts have formulated the question as follows: would reasonable members of the trade concerned say, upon knowing all the relevant facts that the

---

140   Although a Community trade mark is not encapsulated within the meaning of registered trade mark (TMA, s 2) and so it appears that it does not fall within this defence there is some authority suggesting that CTMs are covered (see *Daimler Chrysler AG v Alavi* [2001] RPC 42, para 2).

141   This provision has no equivalent in the TMD or CTMR.

142   TMA, s 11(2)(a); TMD Art 6(1)(a); CTMR Art 12(a).

143   See *Mercury Communications v Mercury Interactive* [1995] FSR 850, 860-1; *Reed Executive v Reed Business Information* [2004] RPC 40, para 115.

144   C-245/02 *Anheuser Busch v Budejovicky* [2005] ETMR 27, para 81.

145   C-17/06 *Céline* [2007] ETMR 80, para 36.

146   This is based on Paris Convention Art 10*bis*(2).

147   *Reed Executive v Reed Business Information* (2004) RPC 40, paras 131-132.

148   C-100/02 *Gerolsteiner Brunnen* [2004] RPC 39, paras 23-26; C-63/97 *BMW v Deenik* [1999] ETMR 339, para 61.

149   It is not clear whether as a restriction on a proviso it should be interpreted narrowly or not: but it appears that it probably should be: see the comments of the Advocate General in C-48/05 *Adam Opel* [2007] EMTR 33, para AG 50.

150   C-63/97 *BMW v Deenik* [1999] ETMR 339.

151   To this effect see C-100/02 *Gerolsteiner Brunnen* [2004] ETMR 40, para 25 (likelihood of confusion is not enough to make use not in accordance with honest practices).

trader knew, that the use complained of is honest?[152] The courts have also indicated that where the use might deceive the ultimate consumer (but not an intermediary) such use may not be honest.[153] The Court of Justice, on the other hand, has given some indicators of the factors which should be considered when assessing whether a particular use is honest:[154]

- is the mark used in a manner as to give the impression that there is a commercial connection between the other trader and the trade mark;

- does the use affect the value of that trade mark by taking unfair advantage of its distinctive character or repute;

- does the use entail the discrediting or denigrating of the mark;

- what is the overall presentation of the goods marketed by the other trader, in particular the circumstance in which the mark of which that person is not the owner displayed in that presentation;

- what efforts have been made by the other trader to ensure that customers distinguish its goods from those which are licensed by the trade mark owner.

The effect of this proviso is that any attempt to use a mark in a domain name which is not in accordance with honest practices will remain infringing, even if it is using a trader's own name.

4.4.9 Trade mark infringement remedies

Some of the remedies for trade mark infringement in the real world are rarely as important in the virtual world. But as with all cases of infringement, it is necessary to examine what remedies should be sought at a very early stage. The usual remedies for trade mark infringement are damages, an injunction, an account of profits, delivery up or erasure.[155]

Usually, the claimant wants more than simply stopping the other party using the domain name, or any similar, but also to take over the domain name.[156] For this reason, in addition to any claim for damages and injunction, claimants should seek delivery up of the infringing materials.[157] These materials are essentially the domain name registration; the actual content of the site may, or may not, be infringing material. Section 17(4) of the Trade Marks Act 1994 defines

152   *Volvo v Heritage* [2000] FSR 253, 259.
153   *L'Oreal v Bellure* [2007] EWCA Civ 968, para 51.
154   C-228/03 *Gillette v LA Laboratories* [2005] ETMR 67, para 40 to 49; C-17/06 *Céline* [2007] ETMR 80, para 34.
155   Trade Marks Act 1994, ss 14 to 20; Community Trade Mark Regulation 2006 (SI 2006/1027) reg. 5.
156   The right to an interlocutory injunction under the Trade Marks Act 1994, s 14(2).
157   Trade Marks Act 1994, s 16(1).

'infringing material' to include material bearing a sign identical or similar to the infringed mark which either is used for advertising goods or services in such a way as to infringe the registered mark, or is intended to be so used and such use would infringe the registered trade mark.

Under this definition it appears possible that a domain name registration could be delivered up. Nevertheless, a domain name does not fit comfortably into 'infringing materials'. The High Court in *One in a Million* accepted this is not an 'unjust' remedy[158] but, should a court take the view that a domain name cannot constitute 'infringing materials', the claimant should seek an order that the defendant 'takes all steps as lie within its power to release or facilitate the release or transfer or facilitate the transfer to the claimant of the domain name' and appeal to the court's general discretion to grant 'all such relief' to the claimant. It may be also relevant to the court that the High Court in *One in a Million* accepted that 'assigning the domain name' is the equivalent, in this particular context, of the delivery up of infringing goods.[159]

4.5   PASSING OFF

Where a sign is not registered as a trade mark this precludes an action for trade mark infringement, but it does not mean that the sign owner (or more technically the owner of the goodwill in the sign) has no remedies available. It is possible to bring an action for passing off. Indeed, a passing off claim can, and often should, be brought in conjunction with an action for trade mark infringement. A claim of passing off requires three basic elements to be established: goodwill in the get-up of goods or services; a misrepresentation leading the public to believe the goods supplied by the defendant are those of the claimant; and damage caused by reason of the erroneous belief.[160]

4.5.1   Goodwill of plaintiff

The concept of 'goodwill' was succinctly defined by Lord MacNaghten in *IRC v Muller & Co's Margarine Ltd*:

> 'It is the benefit and advantage of a good name, reputation and connection of a business. It is the attractive force which brings in custom.'[161]

If a company has customers who would think of using its name, or the name of a product, as a domain name, there appears little to suggest that the company does not have goodwill in the domain name. And as businesses have pervaded the

158   *BT v One in a million* [1999] 1 WLR 903, 924.
159   Ibid.
160   *Reckitt & Coleman v Borden* ('Jiff Lemon') [1990] RPC 341, 499; also see the five elements identified by Lord Diplock in *Erven Warnink v Townend* ('Advocaat') [1979] AC 731, 742.
161   [1901] AC 217 at 223–224.

World Wide Web they advertise and provide goods and services to their customers using the Internet. This, in turn, increases the chances of a company extending its goodwill from merely its name to the domain name of the company. To demonstrate the existence of this goodwill the claimant would need to provide evidence of sales, advertising expenditure or direct evidence from customers indicating that they believed that goods sold with a particular get-up must come from the claimant, rather than any other person.

4.5.2 Misrepresentation by defendant

The term 'misrepresentation' does not imply any malice or intention; it is more a statement of the perception of the public.[162] It is actionable to misrepresent that one's business or trade is that of another person or is connected with that person in any way likely to cause damage.[163] The misrepresentation must be made to customers of the other's goods or services (i.e. web users)[164] and it should be judged against how the relevant goodwill was acquired in trade. This means customer confusion is central to the action for passing off.[165] The trading practices of the person making the representation are also relevant and so, for example, where a sign or badge is not used as a 'trade mark' it is unlikely to amount to passing off.[166]

4.5.2.1 Misrepresentations involving domain name

Using a domain name may by passing off as is the use of certain telephone numbers:

> 'The defendants are right that a misrepresentation must be established, but are wrong in believing that it requires an express statement. A person who adopts the mantle of another can by his silence misrepresent that he is that other. Thus a person who selects a confusingly similar telephone number or a similar name may well represent that he is that other by either saying so or by failing to take steps when telephoned or called to disabuse the person who is making the telephone call.' [167]

---

162 Innocence does not provide a defence to an injunction. The court will simply assess whether on an objective basis injury was a reasonably foreseeable consequence of the misrepresentation. See *Taittinger v Allbev Ltd* [1993] 2 CMLR 741 at 751 [21]–752 [25].

163 *Ewing v Buttercup Margarine* [1917] 2 Ch 1, 11-13; *Clock v Clock House Hotel* (1936) 53 RPC 269, 275 per Romer LJ; *British Telecommunications v Nextcall Telecom* [2000] FSR 679 (where the defendant sold phone services allowing customers to believe that defendant was part of British Telecom found to be actionable).

164 *Erven Warnink v Townend* [1979] AC 731.

165 But confusion per se is not sufficient to found such an action: see *My Kinda Town v Soll* [1983] RPC 407, 418.

166 *Arsenal v Reed* [2001] ETMR 77 (this aspect of the case was not appealed, but doubt was still expressed by Aldous LJ, para 70-71: [2003] ETMR 73).

167 *Law Society of England and Wales v Griffiths* [1995] RPC 16 at 21.

This can be applied to domain names. If instead of Adam Curry setting up the copycat MTV website (see section 4.1.1), Martin Trevor Vantram had established the site with his initials as a domain name it may be easier to argue that it was a misrepresentation.[168] Indeed in *MBNA America Bank NA v Stephen Freeman*[169] the court was not convinced either way that the abbreviated domain name 'mbna.co.uk' for Mr Freeman's new business 'Marketing Banners for Net Advertising' was a misrepresentation by Mr Freeman of the MBNA America Bank's mark, MBNA.

The Court of Appeal in *One in a Million* goes so far as to rule that: 'The placing on a register of a distinctive name such as www.marksandspencer.com makes a representation to persons who consult the register [a WHOIS search] that the registrant is connected or associated with the name registered and thus the owner of the goodwill in the name.'[170] So, unlike mere registration as a trade mark, mere registration of a domain name, for passing off purposes, makes a representation which is false.

4.5.2.2   Disclaimer

This raises the question as to whether anything could be done to disabuse the public of this misrepresentation. Certainly the defendant, in the knowledge that its domain name is confusingly similar to another's name, may seek to distinguish its site from the potential claimants. It may be thought that, by using the words, 'Unofficial MTV Site' the misrepresentation is stopped. In certain circumstances this may be true. After the domain name has been entered into a browser and the site is seen through the web, information on the site may make clear the true nature of the site, but this may be too late to defeat the misrepresentation element of passing off in relation to that domain name.[171] What is key to a passing-off case is the influence of the defendant's representations at or prior to the point of sale not later.[172] The court will consider whether the 'public is moved in any degree to buy the article because of its source'.[173] This may present some interesting issues in relation to some websites as no trade may exist until after the site has been viewed. This will, of course, depend on the circumstances in each case. It may be of no relevance that after entering the site the viewer is instructed that it is not the one expected.

---

168   That this may be a misrepresentation does not mean there is passing off. Indeed, it has been said, 'a man must be allowed to trade in his own name and, if some confusion results, that is a lesser evil than that a man should be deprived of what would appear to be a natural and inherent right': *Marengo v Daily Sketch* (1948) 65 RPC 242 at 251 per Lord Simonds.

169   [2001] EBLR 13.

170   *BT v One in a Million* [1999] 1 WLR 903,924.

171   Its effect may be to defeat the element of consequent damage, or at the least reduce the damages awarded if the claimant is successful at trial.

172   See *Bostik v Sellotape GB Ltd* [1994] RPC 556.

173   *Crescent Tool v Kilborn & Bishop*, 247 F 299 (1917), per Judge Learned Hand. Cited with approval by Jacob J in *Hodgkinson and Corby Ltd v Wards Mobility Ltd* [1995] FSR 169 at 178.

Because domain names and their owners are put on a publicly accessible register held on the web by the registration companies, avoiding litigation may be difficult. A defendant may seek to introduce 'true' distance between its site and that of the claimant by using disclaimers. Associations could be avoided, but even so, the domain name and representation is at large on the public register. This said, if concerned, a defendant might be able to persuade the domain name registrar who controls the register to include a disclaimer on the record itself. Of course, there will always be some individuals who will remain confused as to the source of a website because of the domain name, but as Gibson LJ stated bluntly:[174]

'It is not right to base any test on whether a moron in a hurry would be confused, but it is proper to take into account the ignorant and unwary.'

4.5.3 Damage

The third aspect of passing off is that the claimant must show that he has suffered, or is likely to suffer, damage to the goodwill because of the misrepresentation. This requirement to show damage, however, is not onerous in quality or quantity.

If the infringing website is selling goods or services, the test will be easy to satisfy. But the World Wide Web contains many sites that serve not as shops but as shop fronts. A website under the domain name 'mtv.com' may not provide products and services for payment; it may merely provide useful information such as the latest releases and Top 20 sales. The damage therefore cannot be equated to lost sales but to a 'dilution' in the distinctiveness of the name MTV or harm to the reputation attaching to it. This will have the likely consequence that the goodwill in the name MTV will be reduced. Aldous LJ in *One in a Million* in relation to the famous mark 'Marks & Spencer' held that: '[R]egistration of the domain name including the words Marks & Spencer is an erosion of the exclusive goodwill in the name which damages or is likely to damage Marks & Spencer plc.'[175]

The level of damage need not be high. In fact, the level required is expressed in terms of a presumption that there will be damage unless proved to be below a *de minimis*.[176]

'The question is whether the relevant activities of the defendants are on such a small scale leading to such a small injury that it can be ignored.'

---

174 *Taittinger v Allbev Ltd* [1993] 2 CMLR 741 [20]. See *Singer Manufacturing Co v Loog* (1882) 8 App Cas 15 at 18, per Lord Selborne LC.
175 Ibid.
176 *Taittinger v Allbev Ltd* [1993] 2 CMLR 741 at 753 [27] per Gibson LJ.

4.5.4   Instrument of fraud claim

The problems associated with cyber-squatting are occasions where an individual with no legal rights over a name acquires a domain name incorporating that name and then offers to sell the domain name to a more bona fide owner. It first came to prominence in relation to the McDonald's domain name when Josh Quittner registered mcdonalds.com and wrote about it[177] much to McDonald's disgust. Quittner also reported how fourteen percent of US Fortune 500 companies had their names registered by others. This practice can work where the policy of the domain name registration company permits such arbitrage. Such a practice is common for company names[178] and the Court of Appeal confirms that precedents from that area may be applicable for domain names.

4.5.4.1   BT v One in a Million

The defendant in *BT v One in a Million*[179] had registered a number of domain names, which included 'bt.org', 'ladbrokes.com', 'markandspencer.com', 'virgin.com' and others. The domain names were not active and were not being used (except one, which was accidently activated). The claimants were some of the owners of the trade marks which were incorporated into the domain names. They alleged trade mark infringement and passing off. In its analysis, the Court of Appeal looked at two classes of mark: those where the name is 'unique' and those where it is not. In relation to each of these classes the Court of Appeal found infringement both on the grounds of traditional passing off and as an instrument of fraud.

Where a sign denotes one business and nobody else (e.g. Marks and Spencer), then when a domain name incorporating that sign is registered, it is passing off. The misrepresentation arises because a substantial number of persons who conduct a WHOIS search will think the name of the registrant is connected with the first business. The Court of Appeal held that such a registration erodes the goodwill in the mark and so amounts to straightforward passing off.[180] It also suggested that the conduct of the defendants had amounted to an express or implied threat to trade using the domain name or to transfer it to another to so trade. This, the court held, was a threat to pass off. The Court went further and argued that in such cases the domain name was an instrument of fraud because any realistic use whatsoever would constitute passing off.[181]

Where a sign denotes more than one business (e.g. Virgin or Ladbrokes) then use of it as a domain name is not inherently deceptive. Nevertheless, the court

177   Wired, October 1994 (www.wired.com/wired/archieve/2.10/mcdonalds.html).
178   See *Habib Bank Ltd v Habib Bank AG Zurich* [1981] 2 All ER 650; *Exxon Corpn v Exxon Insurance Consultants International Ltd* [1982] Ch 119; *Fletcher Challenge Ltd v Fletcher Challenge Pty Ltd* [1982] FSR 1; *Direct Line Group Ltd v Direct Line Estate Agency Ltd* [1997] FSR 374; *Glaxo plc v Glaxo Wellcome Ltd, Cullen, and McDonald* [1996] FSR 388.
179   [1998] FSR 265 HC; [1999] 1 WLR 903 CA.
180   Ibid., 924-925.
181   Ibid.

still concluded that passing off or threatened passing off had been made out on the same basis as before and also on the basis of it being an instrument of fraud[182]:

'The trade names were well-known "household names" denoting in ordinary usage the respective respondent. The appellants registered them without any distinguishing word because of the goodwill attaching to those names. It was the value of that goodwill, not the fact that they could perhaps be used in some way by a third party without deception, which caused them to register the names. The motive of the appellants was to use that goodwill and threaten to sell it to another who might use it for passing off to obtain money from the respondents. The value of the names lay in the threat that they would be used in a fraudulent way. The registrations were made with the purpose of appropriating the respondents' property, their goodwill, and with an intention of threatening dishonest use by them or another. The registrations were instruments of fraud and injunctive relief was appropriate just as much as it was in those cases where persons registered company names for a similar purpose.'[183]

It is clear that what was important to the court was the motivation for registering the domain name and not the use to which the domain name would be put. The 'value' of the domain name in such cases, the court opinioned, comes from the fact the mark might be used in a fraudulent way. It is clear, therefore, that where a domain name is registered for the purposes of selling it on to trade mark owner this will inevitably lead to a finding of passing off by using it as an instrument of fraud.

A word of warning before discussing this in more detail: each case turns on its facts. In *One in a Million* the court was clear the defendants were dishonest. For occasions where the case is not simply one of obvious extortion, the courts may be more conservative.[184]

4.5.4.2 Later cases

In *Britannia Building Society v Prangley*[185] the defendant registered the domain name britanniabuildingsociety.com, but had not yet used the domain. The Building Society brought a claim for passing off and was awarded summary judgment. The defendant claimed that he intended to provide the services of British builders to Iranians, but this was rejected by the court. The court found the defendant to be aware of the commercial value of the domain name and concluded:

'I regard the evidence as wholly incredible, and I have no doubt that the defendant registered the [domain] name that he did having regard to the fact that it represented the name of the claimant, a very well-known British trading organ-

---

182   Ibid.
183   Ibid., 24.
184   See *Ben & Jerry's Homemade Inc v Ben & Jerry's Ice Cream Ltd* (unreported, 19 January 1995).
185   (Unreported, 12 June 2000).

isation, and the fact that the first defendant regarded such a domain name as being a commercially usable instrument is apparent from ... his particulars of defence ...'

In *Global Projects Management v Citigroup*[186] the claimant registered citi-group.co.uk and, upon receipt of a letter threatening trade mark infringement, sued for making unjustified threats.[187] The defendant counterclaimed for passing off and infringement. The decision was interesting as there was no evidence of any use of the domain name in business or any attempt to sell the mark or anything else and the defendant denied 'cybersquatting'. Nevertheless, the judge concluded that the defendant had no credible reason for holding the domain name and so found it to be an instrument of fraud. Most recently,[188] in *Phones4U v Phone4u.co.uk*[189] the defendant registered the domain name phone4u.co.uk (amongst others). At the time the domain name was registered he was not aware of John Caudwell's company Phones4U. After the registration of the domain name, goodwill developed in Caudwell's business and by the time the action was commenced it was found by the Court of Appeal that there was no realistic use of the name which would not cause deception.[190] Finally, in common with *One in a Million* the defendants tried to sell the domain name. This final point meant there was no material difference between the two cases as in both the domain name was an instrument of fraud.

The nature of the action means that there is little authority going the other way. The best example of such a case is *MBNA America Bank v Freeman*, which was an application for an interim injunction.[191] The defendant had registered 'mbna.co.uk', which he claims he did for the purpose of running a 'banner exchange' business (Marketing Banners for Net Advertising). He also produced evidence of use of another web address as a 'banner exchange' covering a period of 18 months. The judge concluded that there was an arguable case that the domain name was registered for an improper purpose and so he granted an injunction pending trial. However, the injunction extended to preventing transfer or dealing in the domain name, but not its use.

4.5.4.3   The approach in context

These cases illustrate certain things which should be taken into account. The first is whether or not by reason of the similarity between the domain name and the brand name, there will inherently be passing off. The more famous and distinctive the brand name, therefore, the greater the likelihood that a similar domain name will lead to passing off.

---

186   [2005] EWHC 2663 (Ch), [2006] FSR 39, Park J.
187   Under TMA 1994, s 21.
188   There are a handful of other cases, including *Metalrax Group v Vanci* [2002] EWHC 167; *Easygroup IP Licensing v Sermbezis* [2003] All ER (D) 25 (Nov); *Tesco Stores v Elogicom* [2006] EWHC 403 (Ch), [2007] FSR 4.
189   [2006] EWCA Civ 244, [2007] RPC 5.
190   Ibid, para 35.
191   (Unreported, 17 July 2000), Nicholas Strauss QC.

The Court of Appeal's reasoning in *One in a Million* could be taken further and in an undesirable direction. The court seemed to distinguish between signs which could never be used other than as an instrument of fraud (e.g. Marks and Spencer) and marks which in some cases could be so used. In the former situation, the Court did not seem to be concerned about the defendant's intention or purpose for registration; but in the latter it was the deciding factor. This raises the question of what happens where a person registers a domain name for purposes other than cybersquatting. For example, if the defendant had registered the mark-sandspencer.com domain name to run a 'sucks' site (where the company is lampooned or criticised) anyone searching on WHOIS will still lead confusion (at least according to the Court of Appeal) as to the connection. But any person accessing the site will know straight away that the site is unconnected to Marks and Spencer; unless a conventional passing off or trade mark infringement case is made out.[192]

The Court of Appeal was clearly concerned about the use and abuse of domain name registration. This concern led to the grant of incredibly broad protection to trade mark owners to resist cybersquatters. The problem is, however, that it might have gone too far if the comments of the Court are used to suggest that where a mark is only used by one business ('it is unique') the intention of the registrant is irrelevant. There is previous authority suggesting that where something could be used as an instrument of fraud it is necessary to look at the context of use or expected use.[193] But this wide, liberal, approach to preventing cybersquatting has been followed by the later cases.

The second consideration arises if the domain name does not inherently lead to passing off. In this situation the court may look at the 'wider' issues such as the intention of the defendant, the type of trade and all the surrounding circumstances. Claimants should therefore investigate the past conduct of the defendants. In *One in a Million*, the fact that the defendants had previously offered to sell domain names to Burger King, although not parties to the action, was used to illustrate the defendants' intention to use the domain names for cyber-squatting purposes. Advisors should therefore check to see what other domain names have been registered by the defendants.

4.5.5 Passing off remedies

Like the remedies for trade mark infringement, the key remedy that the claimant should seek is to restrain the defendant from providing or describing any website, email access or other Internet access under or by reference[194] to the relevant domain name or any other domain name which is confusingly similar. The injunction is unlikely to be awarded in a form wide enough to prevent the use of the material on the website itself, as long as, subject to the main restraint, it does

---

192   Indeed, this is a reason to distinguish between company names and domain names.
193   On this point see the case of *Singer v Loog* [1882] 8 LR App Cas 15.
194   This will include the use of the domain name in a page of links on which viewers click rather than retype into their browser.

not use the domain name. This is, of course, unless it too passes off the claimant's reputation. Whether the court would order the domain name to be transferred to the claimant is a matter of debate. It is not necessary to restrain the passing off. The situation therefore may theoretically result in no one being able to use the domain name; the court may refuse to grant mandatory relief on motion.[195]

4.6   PROTECTIVE DOMAIN NAME MEASURES

There are a series of steps which should be considered by someone considering registering a domain name. As has been discussed, registering a domain name which is protected by another's registered trade mark can lead to problems. Conversely, registering a domain name and then protecting that domain name with a registered trade mark can provide additional security over the domain name. Potential applicants for domain names should therefore first perform some clearance exercise over the name they wish to register as a domain name. Having registered a domain name they may then seek to protect it from third parties and the registration authorities.

4.6.1   Check availability of domain name

Domain names are not simply taken: they are registered. Over 100 registrars have registered tens of million of domains ending in '.com'. For domains ending 'co.uk', 'ltd.uk', 'net.uk', Nominet UK is the provider. All these companies charge a small fee to register a domain name and generally sell the domain names through agents. The difficulty arises because the registrars do not have the resources to check that an applicant has the right to use a particular name and so allocates them on a first-come, first-served basis. Because of this policy, many names are already registered. The first step is therefore to use online searches to check whether the intended name has been registered. Companies should try to consider variations of their names and attempt to register these also. This can be done using a WHOIS search.[196]

4.6.2   Register domain name

Increasingly, domain names which are desirable have been registered. This is as a result of the first-come, first-served system. But it is also as a result of the huge increase in domain names being registered each second. This does not lend itself to careful selection and 'mulling over' of a number of possible brands before 'plumping' for the best. Having searched and found that a number of domain

---

195   In such a case, after a given time, the registration authority would reclaim the name at which the 'truer' owner could register it.

196   E.g. www.whois.net.

names are free, any delay in registering one of them could lead to disappointment if the desired domain name is registered in the meantime.

To be safe, therefore, each possible domain name should be registered (up to a commercially sensible number). Once these 'possibles' are secured, each should then be 'cleared' to reduce the risk of trade mark infringement. It should be understood that even the registration of a domain name can give rise to a claim for passing off. This is a risk that, unfortunately, must be taken to avoid seeing a 'cleared' brand registered as the domain name during the clearing process. Registrants may therefore like to register the domain name, pre-clearance, in a shelf company and then assign the domain out of the limited liability shell when the clearance is positive. This has two advantages. First, thoughtful naming and corporate structuring of the shelf company should ensure that nobody else gets wind of a new product launch or branding strategy before time. Second, if the mere registration does infringe a trade mark, the liability arising from this is restricted.

It is admitted that it is not ideal for a company to spend hundreds, if not thousands, of pounds registering domain names it may not use because of later rejection at the 'clearance' stage. When hundreds of thousands of domain names are being registered during the 24 hours of each day across the planet, however, registering pre-emptively may be the safest option.

4.6.3   Clear use of domain name

Registering a domain name does not provide any legal rights over the domain, only technical rights. A company that seeks a particular domain name should search to see whether or not a third party is using the intended domain name as a trade mark. As far as practicable and economically justifiable, this search should be performed on an international basis to take account of the transnational nature of the Internet, and so the multinational nature of any rights claims.[197]

4.6.4   Protect domain name with trade mark registration

As described earlier, an applicant's domain name may already be protected under its existing trade mark registrations. If this is not the case, the domain name owner should seriously consider obtaining a trade mark registration in respect of the trade mark within the domain name. It has been illustrated that a trade mark registration provides significant rights against a user of a commercially-impinging domain name. Even without a registration, the use of a domain name may build up trade mark rights in the name. To signify this to the 'world' the domain name can be followed with the ™ symbol on the website content.[198]

197   See *JackSpade.com* (WIPO D2001–1384) para 6.9.
198   One should pay particular attention to the fact that it is a criminal offence to use in relation to an unregistered trade mark any word, symbol or express or implied reference that the trade mark is so registered. Use of ® should be carefully monitored – it is not akin to misuse of © or ™, for which there is no criminal sanction: Trade Marks Act 1994, s 95.

4.6.5   Consider domain name dispute rules

Domain names are bought from a commercial third party. The majority of these purchase contracts (certainly those relating to .com, .net, .org) incorporate the Uniform Domain Name Dispute Resolution Policy.[199] The policy is limited to deliberate, bad-faith, abusive registrations. Any other dispute is a matter for the court and will not be considered by an arbitration panel. This limited scope of adjudications means that where there are complex legal issues over varying rights the matter is left to the court. The discussion will now turn to that policy.

4.7   UNIFORM RESOLUTION DISPUTE POLICY

The Dispute Resolution Policy regulates how, without resorting to the courts, an applicant may defend the use and ownership of their domain name or trade mark. The main arbitration provider is WIPO where on average 1,800 to 2,000 cases are heard a year.[200] In 2007 about 85.34 per cent of cases resulted in the domain name being transferred[201] and over the life of the system the figure is 83.71 per cent (and 0.91 per cent cancelled).[202] The system is, therefore, a very effective tool for trade mark owners to reclaim domain names from squatters. It is based on a contractual provision which is incorporated into the agreement between a domain name registry and a registrant. The term typically reads:

> 'The registrant agrees to be bound by ICANN's Uniform Domain Name Dispute Resolution Policy ("UDRP"). Any disputes regarding the right to use your Domain Name will be subject to the UDRP.'

It is recommended to weigh up the costs and benefits of this grievance procedure with those of the courts. The logistics and timing of the Resolution Policy are as follows:

1.   An individual or corporation may complain about the ownership of a domain name by submitting a complaint to a nominated Provider[203] in hard copy and electronic form.

2.   The complaint must address three types of issue; first, formal issues; second, factual issues; third, legalistic issues.[204]

---

199   Can be seen with explanatory notes at www.icann.org. This has been in force since 1 January 2000.
200   www.wipo.int/amc/en/domains/statistics/cases.jsp.
201   www.wipo.int/amc/en/domains/statistics/decision_rate.jsp?year=2007.
202   www.wipo.int/amc/en/domains/statistics/decision_rate.jsp?year=.
203   Rules for Uniform Domain Name Dispute Resolution Policy, para 3(a) and (b).
204   Para 3.

4.7.1 Formal issues

The complaint must[205]:

1. request that the complaint is to be submitted for a decision in accordance with ICANN'S Policy and Rules;

2. provide the hard copy and email contact details of the complainant and representatives;

3. specify with whom and on what medium the provider should conduct the Dispute Policy; elect for either a single member, dispute panel or select the three members for a three-member panel;

4. state that the copy of the complaint and copies of Rules have been sent to the domain name holder;

5. state that the complainant will submit to the jurisdiction of the domain name holder's local court or the registrar's local court to resolve any challenges to the application of the Rules. Complainants should note that this does not prevent either party suing in any other court of competent jurisdiction;

6. state verbatim the waiver of all claims against the dispute resolution panelists, registrar, ICANN and their representatives and officers; and

7. state that the complaint has been made in good faith and is complete and accurate etc.

4.7.2 Factual issues

The complaint must[206]:

1. specify domain names subject to the complaint;

2. specify the Registrar with whom the domain names are registered;

3. specify, with supporting evidence, the trade mark or service mark upon which the complaint is based;

4. specify the goods or services with which the mark is used or is intended to be used;

5. identify any other legal proceedings that have been commenced or terminated in connection with the domain names.

---

205   Paras 3(b)(i), 3(b)(ii), 3(b)(iii), 3(b)(v), 3(b)(xii), 3(b)(xiii), and 3(b)(xiv).
206   Rules for Uniform Domain Name Dispute Resolution Policy, paras 3(b)(vi), 3(b)(vii), 3(b)(viii), 3(b)(xv), and 3(b)(xi).

4.7.3   Legal issues

The complaint must describe the three grounds on which the complaint is made, in particular:

(a)   The manner in which the domain name is identical or confusingly similar to a trade mark or service mark in which the complainant has rights;[207]

(b)   that the domain name holder has no rights or legitimate interests (other than technical ownership) in the domain name;[208] or

(c)   the domain name has been registered in bad faith and is being used in bad faith.[209]

4.7.3.1   Trade mark or service mark

First, one must address what is encompassed by a 'trade mark or service mark'.[210] Having established this, one can consider when a domain name is 'identical' and when it is merely 'confusingly similar'. The cases on the ambit of a 'trade mark or service mark' show that the panellists view the term generously. Certainly a registered trade mark falls within its scope, even where the trade mark is registered in one jurisdiction but the respondent was in another.[211] Beyond registered trade marks, the panellists have also accepted unregistered rights under common law,[212] but generally not trade mark applications.[213] The rights in a trade mark or service mark can be exercised either by the proprietor of the mark or a licensee.[214]

Difficulties have arisen where celebrities have been concerned that their names have been used as a domain name. Here, it would appear, the more uncommon the name, the more likely it is for the panellists to deem the name is a trade mark or service mark. So, for example, Julia Roberts,[215] Jimi Hendrix[216] and Jeanette Winterson[217] (or their estates) were able to assert their common law rights in their names. The pop singer Sting, however, was not able to assert his common law rights because his name 'is in common usage in the English

---

207   Paras 3(b)(ix)(1).
208   Para 3(b)(ix)(2).
209   Para 3(b)(ix)(2).
210   In the United Kingdom there is no longer a distinction between a trade mark and a service mark.
211   *thetimesofindia.com* (WIPO D2000–0015); also see *microinfospace.com* (WIPO D2002-0074).
212   *48hours.com* (WIPO D2000–0379).
213   *usdocuments.com* (WIPO D2003-0538); see some earlier conflicting cases e.g. *seek-amerika.com* (WIPO D2000-0131).
214   *sizeunlimited.com* (WIPO D2000-0013).
215   *juliaroberts.com* (WIPO D2000–0210).
216   *jimihendrix.com* (WIPO D2000-0364).
217   *jeanettewinterson.com* (WIPO D2000–0235).

language, with a number of meanings'.[218] It is also necessary to show that a person exploits their name commercially; fame is not enough.[219]

4.7.3.2 Is the domain name identical or confusingly similar to the mark?

Once a trade mark or service mark has been established, it must be determined whether the domain name is identical or confusingly similar to it. The basic test is confusion as to commercial origin between the mark, the domain name and the relevant goods and services.[220] The exact application of this test depends on the legal background of the panellists. Those from a US law background have often relied heavily on the decision of the Court of Appeals for the Ninth Circuit in *AMF v Sleekraft Boats*[221] with its list of eight factors to be taken into account:

1. strength of the mark;

2. the proximity of the goods;

3. similarity of the marks;

4. evidence of actual confusion;

5. marketing channels;

6. types of goods and the degree of care likely to be exercised by the purchaser;

7. defendant's intent in selecting the mark; and

8. likelihood of expansion of the product lines.

The application of this test has led some panels to consider some matters which it is suggested are not relevant. The first, and most obvious, of these are considerations of the goods and services sold under the mark/domain name.[222] A domain name, in contrast to a trade mark, can only be used once. This means that simply because a domain name is used for different goods does not mean that it is not cybersquatting. The relevance of whether the goods are the same or different, it is submitted, should only come into play when considering whether the holder of the domain name has any legitimate interest in the mark. If the holder has a pre-existing trade under the domain name (or something similar) then it is relevant that this is conducted lawfully (i.e. not infringing any trade mark) or if the domain name has developed a sufficient business to make the use of the domain name legitimate then the fact that they are similar goods might be relevant, but in neither case is it relevant to confusion.

---

218 *sting.com* (WIPO D2000–0596) at para 6.6; also see *scorpions.com* (WIPO D2001-0539).
219 *Tedturner.com* (WIPO 2002-0251); *leonardasper.com* (WIPO D2001-0539); cf *Irvine v Talksport* [2002] FSR 60; [2003] FSR 35, CA (for passing off need to be in the business of endorsements).
220 *Guiness-sucks.com* (WIPO D2000-0996); *walmartcandasucks.com* (WIPO D2000-0477).
221 599 F 2d 341 (9ᵗʰ Cir 1979).
222 *Efitnesswarehouse.com* (WIPO D2000-0127); *soundchoice.net* (NAF FA 93631).

Similarly, consideration of marketing channels misses the point. The channel for both businesses will be the Internet and the territorial nature of real world marketing channels does not work when considered in the context of the global reach of the Internet. Only where the domain name holder has taken steps to exclude the domain name's use from a particular jurisdiction (such as geo-blocks), blocking orders etc, should marketing channels have any impact on an arbitration decision as to confusion.

It is therefore submitted that the comparison should only be of the trade mark and the domain name alone. This sort of approach has now been adopted by the majority of panels, but the minority still follow the old approach.[223] Despite this many panels struggle as they still tend to follow the trade mark law they are most familiar with and where that law includes consideration of the goods it makes real world precedents more difficult to apply.

4.7.3.2.1 Initial confusion and disclaimers

The application of real world concepts to domain name disputes has led to some decisions finding on the basis of 'initial confusion', this is where there is confusion when the domain name is typed in, but once the site is accessed no confusion remains.[224] Where this sort of approach is adopted it means that disclaimers[225] and the content of the website[226] are irrelevant to confusion. Such matters do however relate to whether or not registrations are in good faith or not.

4.7.3.2.2 Irrelevant changes

The panelists accept that the '.com' or suffix should be disregarded when comparing the domain name with the trade mark.[227] Similarly, 'typo-piracy' (where the deliberate misspelling to a domain name is used to attract those with spelling or typing deficiencies) means that minor typographical differences are usually ignored.[228] Similarly, in *Draw-Tite Inc v Plattsburgh Spring* the panel held that the addition or deletion of a hyphen or a space does not necessarily affect the confusing nature of the domain name and mark.[229] Where, however, the domain name and trade mark are not alphanumerically identical but are phonetically similar under a particular language, the panel will doubtlessly seek to rely on trade mark law of the relevant jurisdiction. This view is supported by the fact that the panel is able to decide a complaint using any rules and principles of law that it deems appropriate.[230] Descriptive terms are also widely ignored when consider-

---

223   E.g. *sydneymarkets.com* (WIPO D2001-0932); *Motorola v New Gate Internet* (WIPO D2000-079).

224   *Holidayinnhotelreservations.com* (WIPO D2003-022).

225   *Carsands.com* (WIPO D2001-1157); *insideeneworleans.net* (WIPO D2001-0449).

226   *Guiness.com* (WIPO 2000-1698).

227   See *kcts.com* (WIPO D2001–0154).

228   *luisvuitton.com* (WIPO D2000-0430); *guinses.com* (WIPO D2000-0541).

229   *drawTite.com* (WIPO D2000–0017).

230   Rules for Uniform Domain Name Dispute Resolution Policy, para 15(a). See *AmericanVintage.com* (WIPO D00–0004) and *MusicWeb.com* (WIPO D00–0001).

ing similarly, but only where those terms lack trade mark significance. Complainants and their advisors are therefore well-advised to support all their legal arguments with court decisions from, it would appear, any relevant jurisdiction to regulation confusion.

4.7.3.3 Domain name holder has no rights or legitimate interests in the domain name

The complaint must prove that the domain name owner has no rights or legitimate interests in the domain name.[231] The difficulty of proving that someone has no interests in a site is mitigated by the guidance provided on how to demonstrate one's rights to and legitimate interest in the domain name. There are three non-exhaustive issues that should be discussed and they must be proved by the complainant. The following discussion will explain how such interests can be established, of course, someone challenging a domain name will need to prove that they are not shown.

First, prior to the dispute, the domain name holder should have used or made preparations of use of the domain name in connection with a bona fide offering of goods or services.[232] The use of a name on a product (even if not used as a trade mark) may be adequate to grant rights, and legitimate interests, in a name).[233] Only in rare circumstances will offering to sell the domain name to the complainant be considered a bone fide use of the domain name.[234] In the main, unless the domain name is particularly descriptive or generic, offering to sell the domain will not get the respondent off the hook.

Second, the domain name holder must prove to be commonly-known by the domain name.[235] This can apply to any individual's name, for example, Anand Ramnath Mani registered the domain name 'armani.com'. This matched his business cards which, since 1982, displayed the name A. R. Mani. The owners of the Armani fashion brand complained to the WIPO panel and lost.[236] The panel stated: 'This is therefore not a case of the type sometimes encountered, where an opportunistic registrant adopts a name which is intended to give a spurious air of legitimacy to an otherwise questionable registration.' It also apply to a person's nickname,[237] provided they have evidence they are known by the name.[238] Having unregistered rights, even as against a complainant's registered rights may constitute 'rights' under this section.[239]

---

231 Rules for Uniform Domain Name Dispute Resolution Policy, para 4(a)(ii).
232 Para 4(c)(i); rights acquired after knowledge of the dispute are disregarded: see *euro2000.com* (WIPO D2000-0230).
233 *Cellcontrol.org* (WIPO D2000-1257) (use as title of software product); *avnet.net* (E-Res No AF-0160) (use as business name); *scientologie.org* (WIPO D2000-0410) (use as title of book).
234 See the oft-cited, rarely followed decision in *Allocation.com* (WIPO D2001–0537).
235 Rules for Uniform Domain Name Dispute Resolution Policy, para 4(c)(ii).
236 *Armani.com* (WIPO D2001–0537).
237 *Penguin.org* (WIPO 2000-0204).
238 *Redbull.org* (WIPO 2000-0766).
239 *SixNet.com* (WIPO D2000–0008).

Third, the domain name holder has an interest where the use made of the domain name is a legitimate non-commercial or fair use.[240] This third issue is often relied upon by those who register domain names with the trade mark followed by the word 'sucks' to criticise the company or product. It may come as no surprise that 'natwestsucks.com' and 'dixonssucks.com' were domain names registered, apparently, to condemn those companies.[241] These sorts of cases attract a mixed response from the panels as they raise questions of freedom of expression. Any attempt to commercialise the site (by trying to sell it to the trade mark owner) or failure to actually run a critique of the trade mark owner is likely to mean that the use is legitimate. Furthermore, non-commercial users should be aware that the inclusion of banner ads or other ways of funding a website can be used as evidence that the site is commercial.[242]

4.7.3.4   Registration in bad faith[243]

The final requirement is that the complainant demonstrates that the registration was in bad faith. There are a number of examples of what amounts to bad faith registrations:

(i)   registration in circumstances indicating the registration was primarily for the purposes of selling, renting or otherwise transferring the domain name to the owner of a trade mark or service mark over the name or their competitor for a sum greater than the out-of-pocket expenses to acquire it;

(ii)   registration in order to prevent the owner of a trade mark or service mark from reflecting the mark in a corresponding domain name, having engaged in a pattern of such conduct;

(iii)   registration in order to disrupt the business of a competitor;

(iv)   use of the domain name intentionally to attempt to create a likelihood of confusion as to the sponsorship, affiliation or endorsement of the website or location or product or service on the website or location.

The first ground makes clear that any offers to sell the domain name at greater than cost will automatically lead to an inference of bad faith.[244] Domain name registrants are therefore advised to be careful when negotiating the sale of a domain name. Even though they may have registered it in good faith, a high offer to sell it will indicate bad faith. Nevertheless, it will be particularly difficult to prove bad faith if there was a long period of honest use by the domain name

240   Rules for Uniform Domain Name Dispute Resolution Policy, para 4(c).
241   *natwestsucks.com* (WIPO D2000–0636) and *dixonssucks.com* (WIPO D2000–0584).
242   *Mediaenforcer.com* (NAF FA 95345).
243   Rules for Uniform Domain Name Dispute Resolution Policy, para 4(a)(b)(i)–(iii).
244   Of course, where a domain name owner has legitimate rights to a domain name, offering to sell it for more than out-of-pocket expenses may, nevertheless, be acting in good faith: *avnet.net* (WIPO D2000–046).

owner before the offer to sell was made.[245] Without prejudice communications should therefore be used at all times during negotiation.[246] Conversely, a complainant should try to draw out from the registrant an open offer to sell the domain at a high cost.[247]

The second ground is particularly wide and can be used with great effect when a trade mark is well known or famous.[248] This is important because it is necessary to show that the domain name holder knew of the trade mark.[249] This ground and the third ground do not warrant individual examination.

---

8. Arrgh Inc is the owner of a registered trade mark, 'Arrgh', which it licenses to its European-based group of pain therapists. It also owns the domain name 'Arrgh.com'. Since registering the trade mark a competitive anaesthetist has registered the domain name, 'Arrh.com', and publishes at that website distressing stories of why pain therapy can be damaging. Arrgh.com have a right to dispute the ownership of 'Arrh.com'. Trade mark holders and their advisors should note that disruption of business is not merely concerned with disruption of business but disruption by a competitor of that business.

---

9. Ladybird Ltd runs an extremely successful children's book-publishing business and catches on, perhaps a little late, that it could use its reputation and warehouse for an ecommerce website. It has a registered trade mark which covers its activities and attempts to register the domain name. It discovers that Ladybird.com, Lady-bird.com, LadyBird.com and many other such variants have been registered by a pornographic website. Despite the perception of the damage caused by children accessing 'Ladybird.com', Ladybird Ltd will have difficulty in proving the bad faith requirement, particularly as it does not compete with Ladybird.com.

The fourth ground is where the domain name is used in an intentional attempt to attract, for commercial gain, Internet users to the website or another online location, by creating a likelihood of confusion with the complainant's trade mark as to the source, sponsorship, affiliation or endorsement of the website or locating or of a product or service on the website or location. This is a significant requirement: the domain name must not merely be registered but also used (passive use is not enough[250]). An intention to use a domain name for such a purpose is also

---

245 *Theone.com* (WIPO D2004-0528); similarly with generic names: *eshow.com* (NAF FA 94659).

246 No guidance has been given as to whether 'without prejudice' communications may be relied upon in such proceedings but it is expected that this is likely to be the case, particularly if the panelists come from a jurisdiction which include the rules of privilege.

247 There is a suggestion by the panel that an offer to sell a domain name for a six-figure amount 'was clearly' bad faith: *Easyjet.net* (WIPO D2000–0024).

248 *Thecaravanclub.com* (NAF FA 95314).

249 Some panels, where both parties are located in the same jurisdiction, have used a trade mark registration as constructive knowledge of its use: *barneysnewyork.com* (WIPO D2000-0059).

250 *Jupitercasion.com* (WIPO D2000-0574).

sufficient,[251] but clearly much more difficult to prove. Offering to sell the domain name (ie 'offline' use of it) constitutes 'use' of the domain name where this offer to sell is at a price in excess of the out-of-pocket expenses. A good example of this is where a domain name is 'posted' on a domain name auction site such as in *Ellenbogen v Pearson*.[252]

> 10. 2L8.com is a company which registers the '.com' domain names of newly merged companies. Websites are not established for each domain name. 2L8.com lists all the domain names it has for sale and conducts auctions as soon as each corporate merger is officially announced. Even though the domain names are not pointed to operating web-sites, this is use of the domain names and use in bad faith.

It should be obvious, therefore, that the requirement of 'use' is easily met. Interestingly, there are now precedents that the registration and use of a domain name by a legitimate re-seller of a particular product under that name does not necessarily constitute bad faith. In *Draw-Tite Inc v Plattsburgh Spring*, Plattsburgh Spring was a legitimate promoter and seller of Draw-Tite trailer accessories. This was enough to allow it to be seen as using the domain name 'Draw-Tite.com' in good faith despite being registered as a trade mark by Draw-Tite.[253]

Other indicators of where a registration is in bad faith include, providing incorrect or false details in the registration agreement;[254] registering another domain name as the holder of a domain name to keep the true identity secret;[255] failure to carry out a trade mark search;[256] and stockpiling of domain names.[257]

4.7.3.5 Other matters that need to be included in a complaint

Once the legal basis for the complaint has been spelt out, the remedies sought must be stated.[258] These are either cancellation of a domain name or transfer of the domain name to the complainant.[259] It is difficult to conceive of a complainant who does not wish for the transfer of the domain name but who would rather cancel it. This is because cancelling a registration leaves open the chance that another usurper will register the name.

Finally, the complainant must specify any legal proceedings connected with the domain name.[260] Where there are existing legal proceedings, the panel may in

---

251   *Tourplan.com* (E-Res AF-96).
252   WIPO D00–0001.
253   WIPO D2000–0017. But see *heelquick.com* (NAF 92527).
254   *T-nova.com* (NAF FA 94646).
255   *Tonsil.com* (WIPO D2000-0376).
256   *Jackspade.com* (WIPO D-2001-1384).
257   *Redeglobo.net* (WIPO D2000-0351).
258   Rules for Uniform Domain Name Dispute Resolution Policy, para 3(b)(x).
259   Para 3(b)(i).
260   Para 3(b)(xi).

its absolute discretion decide not to proceed to its decision or suspend or terminate its proceedings.[261] Clearly, it is in the interests of any domain name holder to initiate declaratory legal proceedings prior to a trade mark holder starting a complaint under the Rules. This may dissuade or delay the panel from adjudicating over the domain name.

4.7.4 Timing of the arbitration

The arbitration will follow a standard timetable. This begins with the provider reviewing the complaint and then either:

(i) within three calendar days, forwarding the complaint to the respondent ('commencement date');[262] or

(ii) informing the complainant and respondent that the complaint is administratively deficient, allowing the complainant five calendar days to correct the deficiencies.[263]

The timeline after this decision is as follows:

(a) within 20 days of the commencement date, the respondent must submit a response akin in all requirements to the complaint;[264]

(b) within 15 further days (35 days post commencement date) the constitution of the panel is decided;[265]

(c) within 14 days of its appointment (49 days post commencement date) the panel will decide the dispute and inform the provider;[266]

(d) within three days of the provider receiving the decision (52 days post commencement date) the provider informs the parties of the decision.[267]

Once the parties have been informed of the decision, assuming the complainant wins and the domain name is to be cancelled or transferred, the domain name holder has ten business days (at least 62 days post commencement date) to start legal proceedings so to stop the implementation of the decision.[268] In summary, it would appear that a domain name holder has little to lose by using the approximate two months to prepare legal proceedings to retain the domain name.

261 Para 18(a).
262 Para 4(a).
263 Para 4(b).
264 Para 5.
265 Para 6(b)–(f).
266 Para 15(b).
267 Para 16(a).
268 Rules for Uniform Domain Name Dispute Resolution Policy, para 4(k). See *Jay D Sallen v Corinthians Licenciamentos* 273 F 3d 14 (1st Cir, 2001).

4.7.5   Domain names and registration companies

All registration companies would prefer to remove themselves from any disputes as quickly as possible. Indeed the ICANN policy states that it:

> 'will not participate in any way in any dispute between you and any party other than us regarding the registration and use of [the] domain name.'[269]

This policy, and concerns regarding liability, have led some domain name owners finding that these 'middle men' are a little too willing to transfer, cancel or 'hold' a domain name where there is any indication of a dispute. This may assist one party to the dispute, but it can be extremely inconvenient if unwarranted. It has also led to domain name owners attempting to restrain registration companies from suspending or transferring the domain name until the outcome of any parallel trade mark dispute is settled.

4.8   JURISDICTION OVER INFRINGEMENT

Conflict of laws and intellectual property law has an uneasy coexistence. The mismatch became more pronounced as the Internet developed. The first question when it comes to conflict of laws is whether or not a court has jurisdiction (or competence) to hear a particular claim. The second is what law that court should apply to the dispute. These difficulties are compounded by the fact that there are a number of issues which are often conflated into one. A court which has jurisdiction over a defendant will not necessarily apply its own law to a dispute.

4.8.1   Jurisdiction

There are two sets of rules determining whether a person can be brought before the English courts. The first set of rules applies where the defendant is domiciled in an EC member state, the second set of rules applies in any other case. Even when an English court has jurisdiction over a matter, it does not mean that it must apply English law. Indeed, once the Rome II Regulation[270] comes into force, English courts will have to apply the law of the country from which protection is sought. Thus, an English person being sued for infringing a German trade mark (in Germany) would have German trade mark law applied by the English High Court (albeit this is 'harmonised' within the Community).

---

269   ICANN Uniform Domain Name Dispute Resolution Policy, para 6.
270   Reg 864/2007 on the law applicable to non-contractual obligation.

4.8.2 Jurisdiction and EC domiciles

The rules of jurisdiction are, in relation to those domiciled in the EC,[271] governed by the Brussels Regulation (No. 44/2001). The purpose of this harmonised regime, was according to Laddie J in *Coin Control Ltd v Suzo International (UK)*[272] 'to replace the differing domestic rules, at least in relation to forum, by a simple set of rigid provisions forcing litigation into the courts of one country and out of the courts of others.'[273]

4.8.2.1 E-Commerce Directive

The rules of jurisdiction should not lead to the conclusion that the Electronic Commerce Directive, and its implementing Electronic Commerce (EC Directive) Regulations 2002, addresses questions of private international law.[274] These rules only apply to those service providers which are established within the EU. Second, the Regulations certainly do not determine which country's courts will decide a particular dispute and certainly not which country's law will apply in a given situation. They merely prevent, in particular circumstances, a service provider established in a member state outside the UK being restricted from conducting activities inside the UK which would have been legal in their member state.[275] In any event, these particular rules do not extend to intellectual property issues.[276] The Electronic Commerce Directive and Regulations therefore have absolutely no influence over the jurisdiction and applicable law rules applied to intellectual property disputes.

4.8.2.2 Basic rules of jurisdiction

The Brussels Regulation provides simple rules on where a party can sue when 'choosing' between the member states. Article 2 sets out the primary rule: defendants must be sued in the courts of their domicile unless another article derogates from this rule. In the words of Laddie J, 'ie the plaintiff must play away'.[277] Article 5 provides a list of particular types of proceedings that may be brought in additional courts. Article 5(3) states that in matters relating to tort, one may sue

---

271 The Danish are not subject to the Regulation under Community law, but they have agreed to be bound: see Council Decision 2005/790/EC on the signing, on behalf of the Community, of the Agreement between the European Community and the Kingdom of Denmark on jurisdiction and the recognition and enforcement of judgments in civil and commercial matters. This Regulation replaces the Brussels Convention.
272 [1997] FSR 660.
273 Ibid., 671.
274 However, as the Department of Trade and Industry point out 'the Directive as a whole does not make clear whether the role of private international law is retained or superseded': DTI 'A Guide for Business to the Electronic Commerce (EC Directive) Regulations 2002 (SI 2002/2013)' (DTI, 31 July 2002), [4.8].
275 Reg 7.
276 Reg 4(4)(1) and art 3(3), Annex, first indent.
277 *Fort Dodge Animal Health Ltd v Akzo Nobel* [1998] FSR 222.

in the courts of the place where the harmful event occurred or may occur. It is clear from the Regulation, and clarified by the courts' consideration of the provision, that intellectual property infringements fall within this article.[278] The most important question, when considering Article 5(3), is determining where 'the harmful event occurred'. The Court of Justice, in *Bier BV v Mines de Potasse D'Alsace*,[279] made it clear that this covers both the place where the event giving rise to the damage occurred and the place where the damage itself occurred, so giving the claimant a choice between the two forums.

Article 2 appears to provide the foundation for jurisdiction over a foreign intellectual property infringement, indeed a multiplicity of infringements, to be brought before the UK courts. However, in *Shevill v Presse Alliance*[280] the court held that where jurisdiction is based on damage within the jurisdiction, the court could only hear those parts of the matter that relate to that damage.[281] Thus, a claimant has two choices, they can rely on Article 5(3) and sue in each member state where damage was suffered, or they can sue in the defendant's domicile and recover for all the damage caused by the tort. Unfortunately, this matter is confused by the rules on exclusive jurisdiction.

4.8.2.3   Exclusive jurisdiction

Article 22(4) of the Regulation states that proceedings concerning the validity of patents and other registered rights must be determined in the country of registration; accordingly, a determination of the validity of a UK trade mark must take place before the UK courts even if the defendant is domiciled abroad. This restriction applies whether the claim was started as an infringement claim (and there was a counterclaim for invalidity) or the claim began as one of invalidity.[282] Therefore, where a claim of UK trade market infringement was started on the basis of jurisdiction under Article 2 in France, if invalidity becomes an issue then the case must be stayed and transferred back to the United Kingdom courts for the issue to be decided.

This distinction is extremely important for trade mark infringements committed over the Internet because, as will be seen, infringement of registered trade marks may be treated differently to infringement of unregistered trade marks, such as passing off actions.

4.8.2.4   Infringement of unregistered rights across Europe

Mecklermedia Corporation was a Delaware corporation whose subsidiary, Mecklermedia Limited, had been involved in the organisation of trade shows in

---

278   In the UK: *Molnlycke v Procter & Gamble (No. 4)* (1992) 1 WLR 1112 at 1117; *Pearce v Ove Arup Partnership* (1997) Ch 293 (reversed on different grounds (2000) Ch 403) and *Fort Dodge v Akzo Nobel,* above; in France: *Wegmann v Elsevier Science* (1997) ILPr 760; in Germany: *Re Jurisdiction in Tort and Contract* (1988) ECC 415.
279   (1976) ECR 1735 (Case 21/76).
280   (1995) 2 AC 18 (Case C-68/93).
281   Ibid. at 62. Also see *Wegmann v Elsevier Science* (1999) ILPr 379.
282   *GAT v Luk* (2006) (Case C-4/03), [2006] FSR 45.

the UK. These shows used the name 'Internet World' and were organised in conjunction with a licensee. The shows were widely advertised and well attended. DC Congress was a German company which organised trade shows also called 'Internet World', but in Germany. To promote these shows, DC prepared a letter and brochure in English which were sent out to prospective attendees, including in the UK. They also established a website to promote their show at www.Internetworld.de.

Mecklermedia alleged that DC committed the English tort of passing off and sought relief in relation to the tortious activities of DC originating from Germany. DC Congress applied inter alia for an order setting aside the writ on the grounds that the court does not have jurisdiction over it under the, then in force, Brussels Convention and thereby forcing Mecklermedia to litigate the UK issues in Germany.[283] Jacob J considered the general rule in Article 2 that '[I]n footballing terms the plaintiff must play away', but Article 5(3) permitted derogation from this in matters relating to tort where a defendant is sued in the courts of the place where the harmful event occurred. This left the question: where did the harmful event occur?

Jacob J stated that, for English passing off, the harm is to the goodwill in England and to the effect of the reputation in England; the direct effect is of harm to the plaintiff's English property. He was confirmed in this view by extensively referring to the European Court of Justice's decision in *Dumez France v Hessiche Landesbank*[284] and *obiter dicta* by Knox J in relation to a hypothetical supposition in *Modus Vivendi v British Products Sanmex Co Ltd*.[285]

So, where unregistered intellectual property rights are in issue, such as passing off or copyright, a claimant within the EU may sue where those rights subsist. But as Laddie J noted 'The fact that registered and unregistered rights (eg passing off and registered trade mark proceedings) may be subject to different regimes could well produce a proliferation of litigation rather than the opposite.'[286]

4.8.3 Jurisdiction and non-EC domiciles

The English traditional rules of jurisdiction, which apply where a defendant is not domiciled in the Community, permit jurisdiction over a defendant where they are served with process within the jurisdiction.[287] Where a person cannot legally be served, a court has no jurisdiction over them.[288] In certain circumstances, the English courts also permit process to be served outside the jurisdiction,[289] which

---

283 *Mecklermedia v DC Congress* [1997] FSR 627.
284 Case C–220/88 [1990] ECR 49.
285 [1996] FSR 790 at 802.
286 [1999] Ch 33 at 53.
287 A claim is started by the issue of a claim form (CPR, r 7.2) which must be served within four months (CPR, r 7.4).
288 Although English courts now allow what is called substituted service at an address for service: see CPR, r 6.5; Companies Act 1985, s 725.
289 These grounds are set out in CPR, r 6.20.

is equivalent to granting additional special grounds of jurisdiction. Such service is permitted in particular where the tort is committed, or damage is sustained, within the jurisdiction.[290]

The English courts are also willing to accept jurisdiction over a dispute where the parties have agreed that the court should have exclusive jurisdiction. Further flexibility is provided by the possibility of parties submitting to the jurisdiction.[291] The courts have recently made it clear that this willingness extends to intellectual property litigation.[292] Despite having personal jurisdiction over a case the traditional rules include some subject-matter restrictions.

In *Tyburn Productions v Conan Doyle*[293] Vinelott J ruled that infringement of foreign intellectual property rights cannot be adjudicated before the English courts. The Court of Appeal in *Pearce v Ove Arup Partnership*[294] suggested that the ruling in *Tyburn* should be confined to the facts of that case; although, the Court found it unnecessary to determine whether the particular action was justiciable in the English courts. However, the ruling in *Tyburn* was criticised by Peter Prescott QC, sitting as a deputy High Court Judge, in *Griggs and Others v Evans and Others*,[295] when he stated that the English court's traditional rules of jurisdiction should be similar to those under the Brussels Regulation.[296] Therefore, only where validity is at issue should the English courts decline jurisdiction; otherwise it should be free to determine matters of foreign infringement.

4.8.4 Applicable law

In English law,[297] the law applicable to tort (such as trade mark infringement)[298] is determined according to the rules set out in Part 3 of the Private International Law (Miscellaneous Provisions) Act 1995,[299] s 9(1) of which states that the provisions apply 'for choosing the law… to be used for determining issues relating to tort…'. The general rule, once a matter is tortious, is that:

---

290 CPR, r 6.20(8); this provision is intended to mirror that in the Brussels Regulation.

291 This can be achieved by contesting the case on the merits (see *Marc Rich v Societa Italiana (No.2)* (1992) 1 Lloyd's Rep 624) or instructing a solicitor within the jurisdiction to accept service (see *Manta Line v Sofianites* (1984) 1 Lloyd's Rep 14).

292 *Celltech R&D Ltd v Medimmune* (2005) FSR 21.

293 (1991) Ch 75; this extended to trade marks by *LA Gear v Gerald Whelan & Sons* (1991) FSR 671.

294 (2000) Ch 403 at 439-440.

295 (2004) FSR 48. This decision was appealed, however, this aspect of the appeal was not pursued: *Griggs v Evans and Others* (2005) FSR 31 at 708.

296 Although he discussed it in terms of the Convention.

297 Until the Rome II Regulation (No. 867/2007) comes into effect, on 11 January 2009 (see Art 32).

298 Intellectual property infringement is clearly a matter related to tort: see J. Fawcett and P. Torremans, *Private International Law and Intellectual Property Law* (Oxford 1998), p 615.

299 The provisions of this Act only apply to a tort which occurred after its commencement on 1 May 1996: s 14(1). Due to the six-year limitation period, no new actions can be commenced on the basis of the old common law rules. Therefore, the old rules will not be considered here.

'the applicable law is the law of the country in which the events constituting the tort…in question occur'.[300]

Thus, the law of the place where the tort was committed applies. The rule does not allow issues to be split. Accordingly, if a trade mark was infringed in the Netherlands, Dutch law will apply to the entirety of the dispute by virtue of this rule.[301] However, where a tort involves more than one country then the special rules apply:

> 'Where elements of those events occur in different countries, the applicable law under the general rule is to be taken as being … the law of the country in which the most significant element or elements of those events occurred.'[302]

It was suggested by the draftsman of the Bill that this special rule would not apply to infringement.[303] Nevertheless, it is clear that where a UK trade mark is infringed then UK law will apply to the dispute and where a US trade mark is infringed US law will apply to the dispute.

4.9   COPYRIGHT

Most material on the Internet is protected by copyright. It protects emails sent from one person to another and protects all the elements of an intricate website including all its mini-programs or executable code. Copyright can also protect the underlying material beneath that which appears on a screen: it protects say the original drawings which were converted into a digital animation on a home page. This width and depth of protection means that everyone using the Internet should be aware of their rights as creators of copyright works and their obligations as users of others' works. In addition, the Copyright, Designs and Patents Act 1988 grants not only a 'right to copy and not be copied' but also certain 'moral rights'.

This section considers the exact extent of copyright protection of material on the Internet. It examines the copyright in emails and postings to websites including user-generated content, and the copyright that protects websites. This examination of websites reveals that, although copyright protects the whole website, its constituent elements are also protected: a separate copyright attaches to the text, the graphics, and more active elements such as animations and sounds. Copyright even protects the complex executable programs embedded within a website.

Having discussed that copyright protects most material on the Internet, this section goes on to show that most material on the Internet is copied on a regular basis. This width of copying results in a simple conclusion. Copyright disputes

---

300   S 11(1).
301   *Pearce v Ove Arup Partnership* (2000) Ch 405 at 444.
302   S 11(2), para (c).
303   Special Public Bill Committee, Parliamentary Counsel, 61.

involving the Internet will rarely turn on the existence of copyright or if copying took place: the key will be whether or not the copier was explicitly or implicitly permitted to copy the work and whether the Electronic Commerce Regulations provide them with a suitable defence. This is particularly important when considering peer-to-peer copying groups which have culminated in some significant litigation overseas.

The Internet works by copying. Emails are not actually sent and web pages are not purely viewed: they are both broken into packets and copied from one computer to another. Emails therefore are copied at least once – the original exists on the sender's computer and the recipient holds a copy. Web pages are also necessarily copied – the server computer hosts the original and each client computer stores another copy. Internet service providers who host chat rooms do not simply store people's original postings: like emails, the Internet service provider stores a copy of the posting. Even the executable code that livens most web pages is automatically copied from its host to a client computer. Although this indicates that all those involved in the Internet copy copyright material, they do not all infringe those copyrights. Much of the copying that takes place on the Internet is impliedly authorised by those who hold the copyright: the law implies a licence. This section focuses on the types of copying that regularly occur on the Internet and attempts to partition that which is legitimate or defensible copying from that which is infringement of copyright or moral rights.

The final section on copyright considers the force of English law on a telecommunications medium which facilitates infringements around the world. It is as easy to copy an English copyright work on the Internet from Brazil as it is from England. This section therefore concludes by examining the conflict of copyright laws that exist on the Internet. It then summarises the disputes that will be actionable in the English courts and those which may have to be litigated elsewhere.

This book considers only when English law will grant copyright and moral right protection. This section also only deals with the law as it applies to works created after 1 August 1989. The section is concerned with the rights afforded to copyright works created *for* the Internet, rather than the wider rights afforded to copyright works that can be *used* on the Internet.

4.9.1 Copyright protection

There are two important questions that must be answered at the outset. First, is the work itself protected by copyright at all? Second, who owns the copyright? This is a query that is always relevant to a copyright issue, but particularly relevant for the Internet. More than any other medium, the Internet allows many individuals to interact to produce a copyright work. Taking the most simple of examples: a website company selling books hosts a 'Review and Rant' board on its website to which customers may post reviews, about which other customers may comment. This is repeated over many days creating a 'thread' that is shown on the website and stored on its Internet service provider's server. What rights have the individual customers who have posted up their reviews and comments? What rights has the website owner in relation to the entire thread, and the individual postings? These questions, and many more like them, will be examined but first there must be some analysis of what works are protected by copyright.

4.9.2 Protected works

4.9.2.1 Types of work

The Copyright, Designs and Patents Act 1988, s 1(1) states eight different types of work that can qualify for protection as a copyright work. These are:

'(a) original literary, dramatic, musical or artistic works,

(b) sound recordings, films or broadcasts, and

(c) the typographical arrangement of published editions.'

In addition, certain performances can qualify for protection under performers' rights.[304] These performers' rights will not be examined separately in this part. Before moving to discuss which categories of work encompass which aspects of the Internet (see section 4.9.5), an important point should be noted. The work which appears on the screen of someone viewing a website is not simply one copyright work, it is a collection of works, some side-by-side and some underlying the work shown on screen. For example, a home page consisting of graphics, text and which plays a recorded tune has at least four discrete copyright works that are evident and others underlying those. Separate copyrights will attach to the text on the page, the graphics and the sound recording. In addition, the copyright that protects computer programs may protect the entire home page. However, deeper than this is the protection that may attach to the musical score that was composed to play the recorded tune. Controllers of websites in particular must therefore understand that their servers are not holding simply one copyright work, but a montage of works. They should ensure that they have the right to use all the works and understand that a visually small aspect of a website may represent an entire copyright work.

4.9.2.2 Fixation

A requirement for most copyright works distributed over the Internet is that they are fixed in a material form; if a work is not fixed, even indirectly, then it is no more than an idea or concept. The Copyright, Designs and Patents Act 1988, s 3(2) provides a specific endorsement of this principle in relation to authorial works:

'Copyright does not subsist in a literary, dramatic or musical work unless and until it is recorded, in writing or otherwise[.]'

304 See s 180 of the Copyright, Designs and Patents Act 1988.

Copyright does not protect ideas; it protects the skill, labour and judgment exercised in converting an idea into something tangible. Merely recording an idea, however, does not provide protection over that idea.

---

11. Four individuals use a special instant messaging service which allows them to type messages to each other in real time; they can see one another's typing on their own screen as each letter key is pressed. The controller of the website realises that one of the individuals is a famous actor and keeps a copy of everything typed by the actor with a view to publishing it. Without a licence or assignment, the controller does not have the copyright to do this; the actor's typing is a copyright work that was formed when he converted his ideas into expressions through his keyboard.

This requirement has proved particularly tricky in the area of computer programs underlying Internet sites and services. *Navitaire v Easyjet Airline Company and BulletProof Technologies Inc*[305] provides a useful example. The claimant, Navitaire, accused Easyjet of copyright infringement of various works comprised in its ticketless airline booking software, despite the fact that it was not disputed that the defendant had had no access to, and therefore had not copied, the source code in any part of the site. One set of works the claimant argued was infringed was the commands entered by a user to achieve specific results (for example, an agent typing in a request for a particular date and destination which acts as a command to format certain results of available flights and times). The court found that these did not qualify for copyright protection. Although, technically, it was possible to analyse the source code to see whether the machine, in following such command, recognised the commands, the command codes themselves were not recorded and therefore were not an identifiable literary work: they did not meet the requirement of fixation.

This case also provides a significant (and much criticised) precedent on the distinction between ideas, which are not protected, and fixed expressions which are. In this case, the defendant's overall system was clearly similar to that of the claimant and, indeed, Easyjet did not attempt to argue that it was not. In a subsequent case of *Nova Productions Ltd v Mazooma Games Ltd and ORS*[306] a defendant's arcade game Pocket Money was also very similar to the claimant's game. But, in both these cases, where source code or plans had not directly been copied, the courts held that copyright did not extend to the ideas or instructions behind the source code. Such ideas and instructions were not 'fixed' and therefore could not be copied. We will return to consider other elements of this judgment later in this chapter.

Every copyright work has an author.[307] The person who is the author is the person who creates it. Generally, the first owner of a copyright work is its author[308].

---

305   *Navitaire Inc v Easyjet Airline Co Bulletproof Technologies Inc* [2004] EWHC 1725 (Ch), [2006] RPC 111.
306   [2007] EWCA Civ 219.
307   Copyright, Designs and Patents Act 1988, s 9.
308   Copyright, Designs and Patents Act 1988, s 11(1).

This is, however, a general statement and those who work for others in creating websites and online graphics should be aware that works made in the course of employment are first owned by their employer, subject to any prior arrangement[309]. Particular care is needed however where contractors or third party developers are used to create websites or content. Without addressing the assignment of copyright in such works to the customer, the supplier will be the author and owner. Nevertheless, in some circumstances a commissioning contract may include by implication an equitable assignment to the commissioner or alternatively some form of licence.[310]

---

12. A designer is employed by a bank for general design work and is asked to create a website for the bank: the site looks like the inside of a bank with graphics of cashiers counting money, help-desks and other features. Some months later the designer resigns from his post and starts working as a freelancer. He is asked to design a similar website for a building society. He reuses the graphics of the cashiers and help-desks. Unless this is provided for in his contract, he does not own the copyright in those graphics. He may be the *author* of the works, but having created them during his employment, the bank is the copyright *owner*.

4.9.2.3 Original works

Most copyright works must be original to be protected. The term 'original' does not mean novel or new; it refers to the fact that the work must *originate* from its author. It will therefore not be original if it is purely copied from another work and no independent skill, labour or judgment was used to produce the copy.[311]

This requirement that the work originates with the author has a second effect: because a work need not be novel or unique to acquire protection it is possible that two identical works are both protected by copyright and owned by different authors. In most areas identical works are rare and are the result of copying; on the Internet, there are instances of works being identical without copying. The most common example of this is the use of search engines. These are programs that can search for a given word or phrase amongst many websites with the engine producing a list of every occurrence of the searched term. Two different search engines both searching for the same term may well both produce identical lists. That these lists are identical does not mean that the works are not original; it is simply a quirk of digital precision and both may attract a separate and equally valid copyright[312].

---

309   Copyright, Designs and Patents Act 1988, s 11(2).
310   See *Ray v Classic FM* [1998] FSR 622; followed in *Griggs v Evans and Others* (2005) EWCA Civ 11.
311   *Interlego v Tyco Industries* [1989] AC 217, 261.
312   It is, however, unlikely.

---

13. A budding journalist 'cuts' an article he finds on a website (by pressing two keys) and 'pastes' it into an email. He sends this email to an editor of a newspaper claiming to have written the article. The editor publishes the article without paying the journalist. The journalist, however, may not be entitled to payment: he had no copyright in the email sent to the editor as it did not originate with him.

4.9.2.4   Skill, labour or judgment

Until 1990 the aphorism, 'what is worth copying is worth protecting' was much in vogue. It originated from Peterson J's statement in a 1916 case, _University of London Press v University Tutorial Press._[313] It seems to suggest that if a person seeks to copy a work, then the law will ensure that the work has sufficient protection to prevent that copying. This _post facto_ attribution of rights has been doubted; the House of Lords in _Re Smith Kline & French Laboratories_ said it was 'not the law'.[314] Jacob J also stated that the aphorism 'proves too much' and 'if taken literally [it] would mean that all a plaintiff ever had to do was to prove copying'.[315]

The second element of originality required by English law is that some skill, labour or judgment must have been utilised to convert the idea into the fixed expression. The level of skill and labour needed to qualify is low.[316] Unlike the US, which looks more for creativity than mere labour, the fact that an author expends 'sweat of the brow' is generally enough to be granted copyright's protection over that work.[317]

This has the legal result that most works that originate with the author in the copyright sense will also have the minimal level of skill and labour required to enjoy protection. This becomes important where individuals on the World Wide Web have generated lists of useful sites for others to view. Under American jurisprudence there may be an argument that the list does not possess the 'minimal degree of creativity'.[318] Under English law, in contrast, copyright may be granted over such a list without the courts having significant recourse to the effort, or creativity of its author.[319] Additionally, a list may qualify as a 'database' protected by the database right as considered in section 4.9.7.

4.9.3   Scope of copyright protection

Copyright provides copyright owners with protection in the form of economic rights. These differ slightly for each particular category of copyright work but

---

313   [1916] 2 Ch 601 at 610.
314   [1990] 1 A C 64 at 106.
315   _Ibcos Computers Ltd v Barclays Mercantile Highland Finance Ltd_ [1994] FSR 275 at 289.
316   _Autospin (oil Seals) Ltd v Beeline Spinning (a firm)_ [1995] RPC 683 at 694 (1991).
317   See _Feist Publications Inc v Rural Telephone Service Co_ 499 US 330 at 345 (1991).
318   Ibid., 330 at 345.
319   Cf _CCC Information Services Inc v Maclean Hunter Market Reports Inc_, 44 F 3d 61 (2nd Cir 1994).

can be broadly summarised as follows: the owner of the copyright in a work has the exclusive right to copy it, issue it to the public in any form (therefore including issuing copies, lending and renting and performing or showing or playing the work in public), communicate the work to the public and adapt the work. In addition the authors of certain types of copyright work enjoy moral rights which protect the integrity of the work and the right to be identified as the work's author. The implication of these rights on the Internet will be discussed in the context of key aspects of the Internet below.

4.9.4 Qualification requirements

There are three alternative routes for a work to qualify as protected under the Copyright, Designs and Patents Act 1988:

1.   in relation to its country of first publication;

2.   by reference to its author;

3.   where applicable, by reference to the place from where it was broadcast.[320]

If any one of the routes is satisfied, the work benefits from protection.

4.9.4.1   Place of publication

The question of where the work (other than broadcasts) is first published[321] is complicated in an Internet environment. It is made available simultaneously throughout the world but where is it published? To address this question it is initially important to understand the stages in creating and 'publishing' a website.

When people speak of 'designing a website' they are technically creating a computer program. Either the designer creates the program by typing commands or uses another program visually to design the site and then allows that program to generate the appropriate commands. These programs that represent websites are written in special computer languages called HTML, Java, Flash and XML. For copyright purposes, these languages describe to a computer what a particular web page should look like and how it should operate. The program is then 'run' through a viewer's browser (maybe thousands of miles away) which interprets the commands and converts these back into a visual layout for the website. Similarly, any executable code embedded in the code is written on the designer's computer and then interpreted by the viewer's. For example, a designer may create some executable code in the form of a Java applet. This is stored on the designer's computer in and interpreted on the viewer's computer.

The 'publication' of a website occurs only when a viewer's computer is provided with a copy of the code from the server computer and the viewer's browser program converts this into a visual representation.

---

320   Copyright, Designs and Patents Act 1998, s 153.
321   Copyright, Designs and Patents Act 1998, s 153(1)(b).

So a website is not published as such; it is made available on a server for the public to access over the Internet. It is published by means of an electronic retrieval system rather than an electronic distribution system. The Act construes this as being 'publication'[322]. But this still leaves open the issue of where that publication takes place. It is submitted that the old principles apply and that publication takes place not in the place of receipt[323] of a copy but where the publisher invites the public to view the copies. Were this not the case, 'a periodical which is offered to the public by postal subscription and has 10,000 subscribers would have 10,000 places of publication'[324]. Applying this to the web, the relevant place is from where the site material is made available.[325] If this is located in the UK or in another country to which the section applies,[326] UK copyright will protect the site. This important question of place of publication for a website is therefore answered by where the server is located as this is where the information is made available for the public. This will be the physical location of the web server which may be located by reference to its Internet Protocol Address (the unique number which has a domain name as its alias).

---

14. A non-British individual establishes a website, stored on a server based in his own country, to publish anti-English propaganda aimed at his own countrymen living in England. This propaganda is printed, verbatim, in a scathing newspaper article in an English newspaper. It will not be deemed to have been first published in England, even if the only accesses to the website are from England. England is the place of receipt; the individual's homeland is the place of first publication under English law.

In view of the conclusion that the place of the server is the place of publication it is vital to address how this rule works for a website on more than one server. These are called 'mirror sites' and are server computers holding identical copies of the website code so allowing more people to access the code at once. Website designers who wish to benefit from the English copyright regime must ensure that their porting of website code to such servers will not constitute first publication outside the requisite countries.

Simultaneous publication, for the purposes of the Act, appears reserved for when two separate distribution channels exist in separate countries. This will be the situation for two or more mirror sites. The rule that applies to this situation is simple: as long as material on one server inside a requisite country was made

322   Copyright, Designs and Patents Act 1998, s 175(1).
323   See the Canadian cases, *Grossman v Canada Cycle* [1901-4] Mac CC 36.
324   *British Northrop Ltd v Texteam Blackburn Ltd* [1974] RPC 57 at 66.
325   See *McFarlane v Hulton* [1899] 1 Ch 884; and *British Northrop Ltd v Texteam Blackburn Ltd* [1974] RPC 57 as applied in *Television Broadcasts Ltd v Mandarin Video Holdings* [1984] FSR 111. This also accords with the definition that both 'publication' and 'commercial publication' refer to the issuing of the work to the public: Copyright, Designs and Patents Act 1988, s 175(1)(a) and (2)(a).
326   Copyright, Designs and Patents Act 1988, ss 155 and 157. The Act extends to countries where the Act becomes the law of that Country (until recently, this was the case in Gibraltar). The Act applies to works or authors from foreign countries (e.g. France).

available within 30 days of the site's publication on another server, the site will qualify for copyright protection.[327]

---

15. An individual establishes a website based on a server outside the qualifying countries. After a couple of months the popularity of his site has grown so much as to warrant renting space on a server based in London. Unfortunately, one week after establishing this mirror site, a copycat site springs up also in London. The individual has missed by one month having his work qualify for protection.

The lesson of this is obvious: it makes little practical difference where a website is hosted. The server can physically be based anywhere in the world. Those web designers outside the requisite countries can therefore be advised to publish simultaneously their site material on two servers, one within a requisite country. It is hard enough preventing worldwide infringement, but it is easier if rights over the work are gained in as many countries as possible.

4.9.4.2   Author qualification

There is another method to fall within the Copyright, Designs and Patents Act 1988 for copyright protection: if at the time the work was created its author was a 'qualifying person'.[328] A wide spread of people qualify, including:

> 'a British citizen, a British overseas territories citizen, a British National (overseas), a British Overseas citizen, a British subject, a British protected person within the meaning of the British Nationality Act 1981, an individual domiciled or resident in the United Kingdom or a British dependency, a body incorporated under the law of a part of the United Kingdom or a British dependency.'[329]

This is in addition to those citizens and subjects of the extra countries will qualify by means of the Copyright and Performances (Application to Other Countries) Order 2007.[330]

---

16. An American web designer does not get a chance to publish her work before it is copied onto a London-based server. The copyright work in question, the Macromedia Shockwave animation, has not been published but the author is resident and domiciled inside one of the qualifying countries. The work is, therefore, protected in the UK.

---

327   Copyright, Designs and Patents Act 1988, s 155(3).
328   Copyright, Designs and Patents Act 1988, s 154.
329   A paraphrasing of the Copyright, Designs and Patents Act 1988, s 154(1) and (2).
330   SI 2007/273.

4.9.4.3   Broadcasts

A broadcast will qualify if it is made or sent from the UK or another country to which the Act has applied.[331] The concept of broadcasts in the Act was substantially amended by the Copyright and Related Rights Regulations 2003.[332] The main change is the removal of a distinction between broadcasts and cable programme services; the latter now removed from the Act. Section 6 now defines broadcasts in wide terms encompassing any:

'electronic transmission of visual images or other information which –

(a)   is transmitted for simultaneous reception by members of the public and is capable of being lawfully received by them, or

(b)   is transmitted at a time determined solely by the person making the transmission for presentation to members of the public.'

There is a specific carve out of an Internet transmission being deemed a broadcast unless it is:

'(a)   a transmission taking place simultaneously on the Internet and by other means,

(b)   a concurrent transmission of a live event, or

(c)   a transmission of recorded moving images or sounds forming part of a programme service offered by the person responsible for making the transmission, being a service in which programmes are transmitted at scheduled times determined by that person.'

This means that transmissions over the Internet will only constitute broadcasts where they, in effect, replicate more traditional television broadcasts. Live or other streaming of programming delivered at scheduled times will therefore constitute a broadcast. An 'on-demand' or other 'e-interactive' service will not however because the user is able to determine the time of receiving the service and need not necessarily have a simultaneous experience to other users.

4.9.5   Term of protection

The term of copyright varies for different works and when they were made[333]. Websites contain a variety of different works (music, film, text) which need to be considered in terms of their constituent parts. For works produced on or after 1 August 1989, the key provisions relevant to the Internet are:

(i)   Literary, dramatic, musical or artistic works: 70 years from the end of the year in which the author dies.

---

331   Copyright, Designs and Patents Act 1988, s 156.
332   SI 2003/2498.
333   Copyright, Designs and Patents Act 1988, ss 12-15.

(ii) Broadcasts: 50 years from the end of the calendar year in which the broadcast was made.

(iii) Sound recordings: 50 years from the end of the year in which the work was made or first released or communicated to the public.

For works which pre-date this, it may be necessary to consider the complex transitional provisions contained in the legislation.

4.9.6 Internet examples

This section takes the principles of copyright legislation considered in sections 2.1 to 2.4 above and applies them to the most common Internet scenarios.

4.9.6.1 Emails

Electronic mail will be protected as a literary work if it meets the threshold of not being copied and of using the requisite skill, labour and judgment in its creation. The Act defines, rather widely, a literary work as any work, other than a dramatic or musical work, which is written, spoken or sung.[334] Emails are not generally spoken or sung,[335] they are typed. Typing, in any language, even using symbols, appears to fall within the Act's definition of 'writing' that includes any form of notation or code. And this may be by hand or otherwise regardless of the fixing medium. This presumably includes the use of 'emoticons' which are little pictures made from the characters of the email viewed from the side.[336] It will also encompass an email which is not written but dictated to a voice recognition or dictation system. If the author is an employee creating the email in the course of employment, the first owner will be deemed to be the employer. Unless there are agreements to the contrary, sending an email to someone does not alter its copyright owner or its owner's rights over that copyright. So, for most emails sent to other individuals, the ownership and exclusive rights remain with the sender of the email. Receivers of emails, therefore, unless they are aware of an implied licence or have an express one, should not forward the email to others. By forwarding an email one is not simply performing the equivalent of putting a letter in another envelope (which would not constitute a breach of copyright, but perhaps only one of confidence). By forwarding an email one is involved in copying and therefore may infringe its copyright. This, and the issue of moral rights, is covered below.

334 Copyright, Designs and Patents Act 1988, s 3(1).
335 The emailing of digital recordings of messages is more appropriately protected as a sound recording under s 1(1)(b).
336 For example, ;-) is a smiling, winking man when turned sideways.

4.9.6.2   Forums

A 'forum' is the term used by this chapter to encompass newsgroups, commercial bulletin boards controlled by Internet service providers and website-based chat rooms and social-networking services. Forums contain a variety of digital information. Some contain only postings and replies from members (here we will refer to this as a conversation thread) whereas others allow users to post digital sound, picture and video files (user-generated content, or 'UGC'). These two types of posting will be considered separately.

4.9.6.2.1   Conversation threads

A conversation thread is a collection of postings by individuals collected together as a written conversation. An individual, instead of sending an email to another person, sends the email to the forum and a particular thread. Anyone else who also accesses the particular thread may then read this email. These readers can either reply to the public email or can simply read the emails and their replies. Over time, sometimes minutes, a conversation thread emerges in which questions are asked and answered and those answers prompt other questions.

The controller of the thread maintains this collection of emails in one of two ways. First, the conversation thread may be 'moderated'. This means that the controller, or his agent, takes an active part in the management of the thread: certain parts of messages or whole messages may be deleted and certain conversations may be 'steered' in their content. The controller acts as an editor. The second way is where the controller does not manage or oversee the content of the thread in any way. The controller, in such a system, is simply providing a storage system for a group of individual's emails. A collection of emails sent to a forum is a compilation. Such compilations of emails may themselves be entitled to copy protection as literary works.[337] However, it will be recalled that copyright does not protect 'literary works' but 'original literal works' for the creation of which the author expended skill, labour or judgment.[338] This raises the issue of whether a conversation thread is original and whether it has the requisite level of skill, labour or judgment.

It may be thought that a conversation thread falls at the first hurdle of originality; after all, the thread is simply a copy of others' emails. In fact, the subject of protection is not the individual emails but *their collection*. In addition there is copyright in a database extending to the collecting, the arrangement and the selection of the emails[339] (see section 4.9.7.1). For an unmoderated conversation thread, however, it is unlikely that there will be sufficient skill, labour or judgment to warrant copyright protection.

It is admitted that the tests for skill, labour and judgment are not particularly onerous,[340] but it is nevertheless submitted that a thread that is created without

---

337   Copyright, Designs and Patents Act 1988, s 3(1)(a).
338   See 'Original works', and 'Skill, labour or judgment', above.
339   Copyright, Designs and Patents Act 1988, s 3A(1).
340   See *University of London Press Ltd v University Tutorial Press Ltd* [1916] 2 Ch 601 at 609.

any human interaction cannot possibly be a copyright work. Of course, those who would wish to claim copyright in a conversation thread may seek to allude to their skill, labour and judgment in setting up the conversation thread[341] or in writing the computer program which allows the individuals to post their email messages. Again, it is submitted that such underlying skill, labour and judgment are not sufficient to create a copyright work.[342]

This should be contrasted with the situation where a moderator has a hand in editing and guiding the stored conversations. In this situation, the moderator does add that element of human skill, labour and judgment. Moderated conversation threads therefore probably do have protection as literary works.

What is true for either type of thread is that, without an agreement to the contrary, the controller does not own the copyright in the individual postings, but only in the compilation of the postings. It will be examined below what rights the controller does have in the individual postings.[343]

---

17. A bulletin board is unmoderated and is published through many different Internet service providers. One Internet service provider objects to a particular competing Internet service provider also publishing the newsgroup. One aspect to the provider's objection is breach of copyright. This is groundless. The provider has no rights in the newsgroup. Simply storing the postings is not enough to warrant copyright or database right protection.

4.9.6.2.2 UGC forums

In the same way as some controllers simply store emails, others store and publish the files of members. These may be sound recordings or movies in a compressed format such as MP3 or DivX that a member wishes to share with others, clips or comments. In some cases the files themselves are infringements of copyright. In addition to the question of what liability the controller may have over such postings (which is considered in section 4.12.4.4 below), another concern is what copyright a controller has over the collection of postings. The fundamental question is whether the collection of files could constitute a copyright work at all. Compilations, to be protected by copyright, must constitute literary works in

---

341 Another option is for the controller to claim that the conversation thread is a computer-generated work under the Copyright, Designs and Patents Act 1988, s 9(3).

342 An Internet service provider may allude to the protection afforded to the journalist in *Walter v Lane* [1900] AC 539, whom the court decided had copyright in his verbatim transcript of Lord Rosebery's speech: (still good law, see *Express Newspapers v News* (UK) [1990] FSR 359). Of course a written transcript is very different in character to the transcribed oral speech and also takes judgment and skill. An Internet service provider who does not moderate a forum or newsgroup simply republishes the text typed by others, formatted by others. The Internet service provider does not even select the order to republish the various postings; the poster decides whether to 'follow' a thread or create a new one. There is little that the Internet service provider adds to alter the quality and character of the raw material (see *Macmillan & Co Ltd v Cooper* (1923) 40 TLR 186 at 188 per Lord Atkinson).

343 See 'Forums' above.

their own right. Case law indicates that the concept of a literary work, however, is wide enough to embrace collections of sound recordings or pictures in certain contexts[344]. The widest point in this reading of a literary work came in *Anacon Corpn Ltd v Environmental Research Technology Ltd*[345]. The question facing Jacob J was whether a circuit diagram could constitute a literary work under the Copyright, Designs and Patents Act 1988. Like most people's initial reaction to such a question, Jacob J said[346]: 'My first thought was that it would be absurd to regard a circuit diagram as a literary work'. He went on to state that on further thought it becomes apparent that the Act's use of the expression 'writing' encompasses almost anything:

> 'provided it is all written down and contains information which can be read by somebody, as opposed to appreciated simply with the eye'.[347]

This may well serve as a protection for a collection of meaningful symbols that are grouped together, or a series of instructions in the form of diagrams. It does not serve as any indication that the group of sorted pictures, sound recordings, animations and messages found on bulletin boards benefit from protection as literary works. These files are simply to be appreciated with the eye or ear.

It is certainly arguable, therefore, that controllers of collections of assorted files do not hold any copyright over the unsorted collection as such. If they wish to prevent others copying the collection they must rely upon establishing a contract with their viewers that prevents this copying or create something worthy of database right protection. Such a contract, as all, suffers from the limitation on privity: it may serve to restrict contractually primary copiers, but those who duplicate the copy will not be bound by the contract. They, and the controller, may also be restricted by the copyright vested in the individual files themselves.

So far this section has discussed the copyright that subsists in postings as compilations. It is also important to highlight the issue of who owns the copyright in the individual item. As this section has stated, without prior agreement, the copyright to a posting is vested in its author. Most forums ensure that members accept a contract which grants a wide licence to the website or provider over any postings made to the site. Often such licences permit these providers to 're-post' on other forums or even further afield. Members of these forums should be careful to read the licence agreement if they are concerned that their postings may be read or used outside the forum.

4.9.6.3   Websites

Websites are the most legally complicated of all works on the Internet. Websites consist of many overlapping and adjacent copyright works each of which may have protection separate from the whole and each of which may have a different

344   *Geographia Ltd v Penguin Books* [1985] FSR 208.
345   [1994] FSR 659.
346   [1994] FSR 659 at 663.
347   [1994] FSR 659 at 663.

owner. To appreciate these many copyright works it is perhaps useful to outline how one creates a website.

4.9.6.3.1 Creation of a website

To most website designers what is important is how the site looks, how it interacts and how quickly it can be displayed.[348] The first stage is usually to create a scheme that shows how each of the different pages of a site fit together. For example, the first page, or home page, will generally link to many pages, rather like a contents page of a book. Each one of these connections will be drawn either on paper or on a computer screen. Eventually the designer will have built up a skeleton for all the various pages of the site. For the most complex sites, it is at this stage that a designer concocts some animations and may draw in some frames within each one of the pages. Animations may be used. Frames allow some information to remain on the screen even though the viewer chooses a new page. Candidates for frames are contents sections and legal disclaimers; these then remain on the screen for any page of the website.

The second phase of the site's design is the preparation of the individual pages. A designer must be aware of where every element of a page will be placed. This is because the language used to store the site eventually is a layout language, and like all computer programming languages demands certainty.

Designers do this 'storyboarding' either on paper (converting it subsequently by eye into programming commands), or on a computer screen using a special program that performs the conversion.

A page may consist of many discrete, individually designed elements. The most basic of these is the text: this is the line of characters from the first letter to the last, rather than the layout that is concerned with how the characters are portrayed, in which typeface[349] and in which format. The other common element is graphics. These are digitally stored pictures but it is crucial to realise that their digital nature refers only to the method of storage. A picture on a website could just as easily have been an oil painting on canvas as a digitally created picture made using a computer-painting software package. Each graphic is stored on the website and 'anchored' into the page at the correct place. Unlike a newspaper, the graphics are stored and are accessible separately from the main page. All the page holds is a link to the graphic.

Certain websites use a particular script or include an executable program which allows interaction with the viewer of the site. At its simplest, viewers can enter their name and other details to receive information. More involved scripts allow certain areas of the screen to become 'hotspots' which respond to a viewer's clicks on those parts.

The most complex element to websites is executable code. These 'applets' and 'objects' are, in short, whole computer programs that are automatically run

---

348   This section refers extensively to web designers in the sense of a person or company, who creates the code to put on a server. The legal conclusions reached, however, are equally applicable to anyone who designs a website whether for themselves or their company.

349   Also known as 'font'.

whenever a website is viewed or an event is triggered. Some executable code may perform a simple task such as playing a three-note tune. Other code is more intricate and displays animations and allows viewers to play games. For instance, some websites will allow their viewers to draw pictures, others to write letters. Many ensure that an entered credit card is both valid and subsequently debited. Of course the effort which goes into coding one applet may be extensive involving the work of many people including designers and programmers.

Having explained this factual background it is now possible to examine the copyright that will, inevitably, protect not only the whole website, but also its constituent parts.

4.9.6.3.2   Preparatory material

Most websites start life as a few sketches on paper or computer. The Copyright, Designs and Patents Act 1988 protects the preparatory design materials for a computer program as a literary work.[350] In addition, the Act protects the original artistic works being[351] any painting, drawing, diagram, map, chart or plan, engraving, etching, lithograph, woodcut or similar work, and photograph, sculpture or collage, irrespective of artistic quality. So, the visual chart of how the website fits together, even though not on computer, if fixed and originating from its author, will be protected by copyright as an original artistic work. Each of the individual graphics, even as rough sketches, are protected as original artistic works.

This underlying protection cannot be ignored: if the designer is not the owner or the licensee of the underlying protected works, he will probably infringe their copyright by incorporating them into a website. This is dealt with below. What should be noted is that those who design websites cannot simply scan, say, a photograph[352] from a magazine and legally use it on their website without being the owner or licensee of the copyright in the photo[353]. Web designers cannot hide their work, as a website is available for viewing by anyone who wants to type the corresponding URL. Designers must be wary of using infringing works as they can easily be spotted.

---

18.   Many websites use a backdrop that gives each page a patterned background. One designer decides that the patterned wallpaper on his office walls would be appropriate for a particular background. He uses a digitised version as the backdrop. Although he may have incorporated the graphic and designed the other portions of the site, he is not entitled to use the textured background to the site. The wallpaper can be protected as an original artistic work and he may face infringement proceedings for copying it.

---

350   Copyright, Designs and Patents Act 1988, s 3(1)(c),
351   Copyright, Designs and Patents Act 1988, s 4(1)(a) interwoven with s 4(2)(a) and (b).
352   See *Bauman v Fussell* [1978] RPC 485.
353   In July 2000, Rodney Fitch & Co Ltd was sued for designing an antiques website that had infringed the copyright in photographs from a well-known antiques encyclopaedia, [2001] FSR 345. The defendant used small copies of the photographs to form icons and other graphics. The claimant was entitled to summary judgment on the basis that there was copyright in the photographs which had been infringed by the claimant.

4.9.6.3.3 Text

The text that is used on a website is clearly a literary work and as such will probably be protected by copyright. The web designer, by simply retyping the text, gains no copyright over it unless a contract specifies this.

---

19. A web designer is employed to create a site for a law firm. As to be expected, the firm supplies a page of carefully drafted disclaimers to put on the site in a frame. Months later the designer is approached to design a site for an accountancy firm and offers them a site, 'including web-specific disclaimers'. If the designer uses the same disclaimers on the accountant's site, without permission from the lawyers, he is copying a literary work protected by copyright. He may be sued for doing so.

4.9.6.3.4 Graphics

Web designers are often approached by companies and firms who already have graphics to put on their site. These may include logos and photographs already used on the commissioner's paper literature. Sometimes the designer will have to go to considerable trouble to convert these paper graphics into a suitable format for viewing on a website. For example, a website may use just 256 colours, whereas a supplied photograph may be full-colour.[354] The labour and judgment expended by the designer in creating a new, 256-colour artistic work could possibly lead to the designer having a new copyright over the digital version of the photograph. But this right should not be confused with the right to copy the original photograph: the designer's right is in the fixed conversion not in the underlying photograph. The designer should therefore seek explicit permission if he seeks to reuse the digitised photograph on another website.

---

20. A well-known petrol company commissions a web designer to produce a website for it. It supplies the designer with its logo which is a small yellow fish. The designer sets about writing a Java applet that will appear to rotate this fish in three-dimensions on the screen. Some time later the designer is approached by a high-class seafood restaurant which also wants a website. The designer, rather than 'reinventing the wheel' colours the fish grey and uses the same Java applet on the restaurant's site. If copyright subsists in the fish logo, the designer can be prevented from displaying the copy even though his skill, labour and judgment went into the production of the animating applet.

4.9.6.3.5 Music and sounds

Websites often play or 'stream' music. They allow a sound recording to be played. But the technical conversion from a musical score to a recording or MIDI file should not be confused with any legal rights over that underlying musical score. If original in the copyright sense, a musical score is protected as an

---

354   See 'A substantial part', below.

original musical work.[355] That does not translate into having a legal right to reproduce the tune of a musical score on a website. Again, therefore, a web designer must look to the owners of the rights in the underlying works for permission before reproducing them in another form on a website.

It is more common on websites to hear sounds and recordings than music, however. For example, a site advertising a new film set in space may open with the sound of laser fire. The 'sound' is recorded in a digital format called a 'sample'. This sample is sent from the website server to the client computer. The browser program on that computer then interprets the sample's series of binary codes as pitch and amplitude variations and will play the sound back in perfect quality.

This sample will be a sound recording in a copyright sense. A sound recording means either a recording of sounds from which the sounds may be reproduced, or a recording of the whole or any part of a literary, dramatic or musical work from which sounds reproducing the work or part may be produced. This *is regardless of the medium on which the recording is made or the method by which the sounds are reproduced or produced.*[356] This definition is wide enough to protect both digital recordings on a computer, stored in a digital format, and a MIDI file, storing the music in a special musical notation that allows the computer to 'play' the music directly. No rights subsist in a sound recording that is a copy of another.[357] This sample may also be an infringement of the copyright in the copied recording.

---

21. The owner of a news website decides to use a sound recording of Big Ben chiming one o'clock. The owner digitally records BBC Radio's use of the same chime on its one o'clock news programme. The website owner not only may have infringed the copyright in the BBC's own recording, but also, the owner has no copyright in his own recording. If the owner had stood beside Big Ben and digitally taped the chiming himself, he would have a copyright in the sound recording.

4.9.6.3.6   Commercial point

This discussion of the individual elements of a website serves two purposes. First, it shows that those who design websites should be careful to form explicit arrangements with their commissioners. They should ensure that they are indemnified from any copyright infringement by virtue of using material supplied to them by those who commissioned them. They should, conversely, be sure to indicate what rights are to pass back to the commissioner and what is to remain vested in the designer.

There are a number of cases,[358] albeit not concerned directly with the Internet, which indicate the necessity of explicitly specifying which party owns what

---

355   Copyright, Designs and Patents Act 1988, s 1(1)(a).
356   Copyright, Designs and Patents Act 1988, s 5(10).
357   Copyright, Designs and Patents Act 1988, s 5(2).
358   *Pierce v Promco SA* [1999] ITCLR 233; *Fylde Microsystems Ltd v Key Radio Systems Ltd* [1998] FSR 449.

works and what each party is entitled to do with the works. The most scathing comment is rightly given by Mr Justice Lightman in relation to the rights over a database created by a consultant:

'This litigation springs from the failure of the parties (and more particularly the advisors who were then acting for them) at the time that the parties entered into the Consultancy Agreement to consider, or provide for, the intellectual property rights that would arise in the course of the engagement of the [claimant]. This expensive lesson of this litigation is the vital necessity for provision for these rights in such agreements.'[359]

Another, more recent, High Court example[360] concerned certain computer program interfaces written by a programmer, Mr Landamore, for a car manufacturer business run by a Mr Wrenn. After relations deteriorated between the parties, Mr Landamore demanded payment for his interfaces. Mr Wrenn argued that he should have access to the source code in the programs. Seeking to resolve the problems, the two entered into an agreement under which the rights in the software were owned by a new company in which both parties became directors and 50 per cent shareholders although no effective assignment was entered into. The parties were subsequently unable to agree what this meant in practice. The court held that the software was vested in the new company to be jointly owned by the two parties. It was not necessary to imply an assignment in order to make the arrangement commercially workable but that an exclusive licence could be implied which included access to the source code. Advisors and users are best placed not to make the same mistake or to rely on perpetual licences being inferred.

The second purpose of looking at the copyright that subsists in the elements of a website is that it is trivial for infringers to copy only those elements. It is better to show a court that one owns the copyright in a graphic that is copied than to have to demonstrate that the graphic copied constitutes a substantial part of the whole website so is an infringement.[361]

4.9.6.3.7 Websites as computer programs

Although a website is built up from a number of smaller elements, the whole site is the code which is stored on the server computer. This is the website absolute. This section explains the assumption that a website is a computer program within the Copyright, Designs and Patents Act 1988, s 3(1)(b) and accordingly a literary work states that computer programs should be considered as literary works. The same requirements of not being copied and skill, labour and judgment apply, and it will be assumed that they are met for most websites that are created independently.

---

359   *Ray v Classic FM plc* [1998] FSR 622.
360   *Laurence John Wrenn and Integrated Multi-Media Solutions Limited v Stephen Landamore* [2007] EWHC 1833 (Ch), 23 July 2007.
361   See the Copyright, Designs and Patents Act 1988, s 16(3)(a). This will be addressed in greater detail in terms of infringement below.

Computer program, for this section of the Act, is wisely left undefined by the draftsman; there are too many examples of legislation serving only a bygone technology. So, the term should be given its reasonable meaning. There would be few programmers or lawyers who would disagree that a program is a set of instructions that can be interpreted by a computer into a set of functions. So is HTML or XML code a program? It is a set of instructions which when read by a browser program produces functional, visual and/or audible changes in the operation of the computer.[362]

In *Ibcos Computers Ltd v Barclays Mercantile Highland Finance Ltd*, Jacob J considered the extent to which copyright protects programs[363]. There are two critical aspects to his lucid judgment: first, the American case of *Computer Associates v Altai*[364] relied on by a previous judgment,[365] is not 'particularly helpful' and its main concept 'merely complicates the matter so far as our law is concerned'.[366] The second aspect of the judgment of direct relevance is that copyright may protect not simply the whole program but also the sub-programs which make up the complete program.

Copyright protects the program at two levels: one, the actual words, symbols and numerals of the code[367] and two, the compilation of the various smaller programs or elements within the whole. These are both literary works. It has already been shown in section 4.9.2.2, that commands themselves, do not constitute a copyright work. For a website this is no mean protection. The entire coding from the first instruction to the last is protected as a pure literary work. In addition, the individual programming elements are also protected as smaller literary works. This becomes particularly important for websites that use a considerable amount of executable code. If a person copied one small applet without licence there is an argument that, in relation to the whole HTML or XML listing, the applet is

---

362   It will be rare for sites also to have protection for their typographical arrangement under the Copyright, Designs and Patents Act 1988, ss 1(1)(c) and 8. The reason that only few sites will benefit from this protection is that most web pages allow the area in which they are viewed to be resized and allow the viewer's browser to realign and reset the information to fit inside this resized area. For these cases, it would be difficult for the coder of such resizable websites to assert that the layout has been fixed and so is capable of copyright protection. For sites that do not allow such reformatting, their term of copyright protection over the layout is 25 years from the end of the calendar year of first publication on the World Wide Web: Copyright, Designs and Patents Act 1988, s 15. See *Newspaper Licensing Agency Ltd v Marks & Spencer plc* [2001] 3 All ER 977 for a discussion of the strict nature of typographical arrangement copyright protection.

363   [1994] FSR 275.

364   982 F 2d 693 (2nd Cir 1992).

365   *John Richardson Computers v Flanders* [1993] FSR 497 at 526.

366   [1994] FSR 275 at 302. This author is in full agreement with this assessment: the US Copyright Code 102(b) actively excludes from copyright protection any 'process, system, method of operation'. This is partly the reason why the court in Altai developed the 'filtration' of such aspects from protection, eventually to reduce the work to a 'core of protectable material'. The Copyright, Designs and Patents Act 1988 does not exclude these aspects of a work.

367   Some might use the word 'source code' to refer to this listing. This is perhaps not strictly accurate as the distinction between source and object code for HTML and XML code is not as pronounced as for compiled computer languages.

insubstantial so its copying is not infringement.[368] If the programmer of the code can claim that the copyright work is not the whole website but is the copied applet only, an argument of insubstantiality will fail. The whole work is copied.

---

22. An insurance company establishes a website over which it conducts business. One aspect of the site is a form to fill in one's personal details. The website has over 200 graphic-rich pages of information taking up 20 Mbytes of storage space; the form takes up half a page and less than one Mbyte. The form is copied, no doubt for its neatness and compactness. If the company claims copyright only in the whole site, the taking of the form may be viewed as not substantial. The company can, however, also claim a separate literary copyright in the code for the form for which the 'defence' of insubstantiality will surely fail.

4.9.6.3.8 'Look and feel' of website or computer program

Where there has been no actual access to the underlying computer program or code contained in a website, the concepts, ideas or even the make-up of a website or system may still seemingly be duplicated. Completely different computer code can nevertheless produce identical results in the software.

The appearance of a website is often referred to as its 'look and feel'. The limits in copyright protection over this were demolished in *Navitaire v Easyjet*.[369] As discussed above, this case was brought against Easyjet (who had previously had a licence of the claimant's ticketless booking service software). Easyjet had created its own system which bore such similarities to the claimant's that Navitaire argued it must have involved some form of copying even though there had been no access to the underlying software code but had created its own in order to achieve the same form of system.

Since claims for copying of certain commands, screens and the structure of a database (used to deliver the results of a search) failed, a central issue concerned whether there was 'something else' which was capable of copyright protection. For what is an incredibly technical and complex case, readers will welcome the consideration by Pumphrey J of two basic analogies: books and puddings. Navitaire claimed that the copying by Easyjet, although not word for word, was akin to the copying of a book's plot, relying on the judgment in *Designers' Guild Ltd v Russell Williams Textiles Ltd*.[370] Pumphrey J rejected this as inappropriate to computer programs – they did not have characters or storylines but were more of an instruction manual. The creator of a computer program was not the author of a book but more like a chef inventing a new pudding, he said:

'After a lot of work he gets a satisfactory result and thereafter his puddings are always made using his written recipe. Along comes a competitor who likes the pudding and resolves to make it himself. Ultimately after much culinary labour he succeeds in emulating the earlier result and he records his recipe. Is the later

---

368   Copyright, Designs and Patents Act 1988, s 16(3)(a).
369   *Navitaire Inc v Easyjet Airline Co Bulletproof Technologies Inc* [2004] EWHC 1725 (Ch), [2006] RPC 111.
370   [2001] 1 All ER 700, [2000] 1 WLR 2416, [2001] FSR 113.

recipe an infringement of the earlier, as the end result, the plot and purpose of both (the pudding) is the same? I believe the answer is no.'

Whether this analogy is appropriate or not, there are significant policy justifications behind this decision which are unlikely to be easily overturned. The 1991 EU Software Directive[371] specifically seeks to exclude both computer languages and underlying ideas of interfaces from protection. On this basis, Pumphrey J felt unable to make such an 'unjustifiable extension of copyright protection into a field where I am far from satisfied that it is appropriate'. From all this talk of plots and puddings, one clear lesson for developers and users emerges: for the time being it is the code, not the functionality or user interfaces, which is protected.

4.9.6.3.9   Joint authorship of website

The Act is of little guidance in this area, demanding only that joint authorship requires both collaboration and contributions that are indistinct.[372] Fortunately, the case law provides some useful guidance on the requirements for joint authorship[373].

In *Cala Homes (South) Ltd v Alfred McAlpine Homes East Ltd* the requirements for joint ownership were examined[374]. Employers of Crawley Hodgson were the sole draftsmen of some architectural drawings. However, Mr Date, a designer who worked for the client often provided the ideas for the drawings, even to very small details. The draftsmen of Crawley Hodgson worked to Mr Date's brief but, for the drawings in question, he did not 'move the pen on the paper'[375]. This should not detract from the fact that most of the design features of the drawings came from and were insisted to be included by Mr Date. The question before Laddie J was whether Mr Date could be viewed as the joint author of these drawings. He was sure that he could:

> 'In my view, to have regard merely to who pushed the pen is too narrow a view of authorship. What is protected by copyright in a drawing or a literary work is more than just the skill of making marks on paper or some other medium. It is both the words or lines and the skill or effort involved in creating, selecting or gathering together the detailed concepts, data or emotions which those words or lines have fixed in some tangible form which is protected. It is wrong to think that only the person who carries out the mechanical act of fixation is an author.'[376]

This conclusion in *Cala Homes* has been applied in the context of computer programs and their creations. In *Fylde Microsystems Ltd v Key Radio Systems Ltd*[377]

---

371   Directive 91/250.
372   Copyright, Designs and Patents Act 1988, s 10(1).
373   Previously, the cases have been indicative but not guiding: *Murray v King* (1983) 2 IPR 99; *Prior v Lansdowne Press Pty Ltd* [1977] RPC 511.
374   [1995] FSR 818 at 834–836.
375   [1995] FSR 818 at 833.
376   [1995] FSR 818 at 835.
377   [1998] FSR 449.

Mr Justice Laddie suggested that the court must check that a claimant has the 'right kind of skill and labour' and then that the contribution is 'big enough'.[378]

Clearly it is not simple to decide whether a web designer or in-house designer contributed to the 'right kind of skill and labour' to the creation of a detailed idea. This, therefore, highlights the need for both parties in a website design agreement to make explicit who owns what and what can be done with the works one owns.

4.9.6.4 Web links

Before the amendments made to the Copyright, Designs and Patents Act 1998 in 2003, the Scottish *Shetland Times* case indicated that there was copyright in a link to a site.[379] The *Shetland News* was a website, like many others, which provides its readers with access to web pages on other sites by including links to those pages. These included links to CNN's website and other major newspapers. At no time did the *Shetland News* provide its readers with copies of the articles themselves. The links are simply listed on the website as a series of headlines from the other websites.

The *Shetland News* had included among the links on its home page a number of headlines appearing in issues of the *Shetland Times'* website. The headlines on the *Shetland Times'* website were identical to those on the *Shetland Times'* list of links. If a viewer were to select one of these headlines from the list, the user's brower would then connect the viewer to the *Shetland Times'* website at the point of the headline. The *Shetland News* did not copy nor provide the copy of the relevant article. The *Shetland Times* sought declarator that the *Shetland News'* actions constituted an infringement of copyright in the headlines.

On 24 October 1996 Lord Hamilton granted the *Shetland Times* an interim interdict (the Scottish equivalent of an interim injunction) for copyright infringement. Without being referred to any authority on the point, Lord Hamilton rejected the defendant's submissions that a headline was not an original copyright work. His opinion was that there was copyright in the newspaper headline and that it is an infringement to copy it in an electronic form or to incorporate it in a cable programme. What is important here is to assess whether copyright vests in the headline and then assess the relevance of this.

The amendments to the Act which removes the concept of cable programmes go some way towards resolution of this issue.

There are a number of cases which indicate that it will be rare for there to be copyright in a headline, or indeed any other single line of text.[380] This, perhaps, does not reflect the position accurately. A page of text on a website may well be protected by copyright as a literary work. To infringe the copyright in the work one must copy the whole or a substantial part of the work.[381] One line of text, or

---

378   [1998] FSR 449 at para 25.

379   *Shetland Times Ltd v Dr Jonathan Wills* [1997] FSR 604.

380   *Dicks v Brooks* (1880) 15 Ch D 22; *Francis, Day and Hunter Ltd v Twentieth Century Fox Corpn Ltd* [1940] AC 112.

381   Copyright, Designs and Patents Act 1988, s 16(3)(a). See 'A substantial part', below.

one link, is clearly not a 'whole' copyright work. The question then is, is the line or link a substantial part of the copyright work of which it makes up a part? The House of Lords has addressed this question:

> 'No doubt [headlines] will not as a rule be protected, since alone they would not be regarded as a sufficiently substantial part of the book or other copyright document to justify the preventing of copying by others.'[382]

For the web a distinction should be made between including the text from another's website in your own and including a link to that website. A link is no more than a reference to other material, rather like the footnotes on this page. The typical codes in HTML include 'HREF' and 'IMG' followed by the URL reference to the linked material. HREF generally refers the user to text and does not usually 'incorporate' this text within the referencing website. IMG, in contrast, tends to be used to display an image 'inline' so that the referencing website actually incorporates the referenced image within its 'four corners' creating a digital patchwork quilt of images from other's. It is submitted that there is either no copyright in such a link by virtue of it not taking skill, labour and judgment to create, or that by itself it cannot form a substantial part of its embodying copyright work.[383] Including the text from another's site is subject to all the usual checks and balances in copyright law. If a substantial part of that site is included on one's site, without defence, the copyright in the work is infringed.[384]

4.9.7   Databases

Database rights were introduced into UK law by the Copyright and Rights in Databases Regulations 1997,[385] which implemented Directive 96/9/EC. There are two separate types of protection for databases. First, copyright protection as a new category of literary work in the Copyright, Designs and Patents Act 1988 (separate from compilations which may also be relevant in some cases). Second, a separate database right which is contained in the Regulations themselves.

This section considers each in turn.

---

382   *Ladbroke (Football) Ltd v William Hill (Football) Ltd* [1964] 1 WLR 273 at 286 per Lord Hodson.

383   In addition, there may be a fair dealing defence that the justification for including a link to another's website must have been for the purposes of the viewer reviewing that website: Copyright, Designs and Patents Act 1988, s 30(1).

384   One can presumably imply a licence from the commissioner to make the adaptation (Copyright, Designs and Patents Act, 1998, s 16(1)(e)) although the web designer should ensure that the commissioner has the right to grant this licence. The photographer may hold the copyright and have granted a limited licence to the commissioner that does not extend to its use on a website.

385   SI 1997/3032.

4.9.1.1 Databases as literary works

Under the Act, a database is defined as a collection of independent works, data or other materials which are arranged in a systematic or methodical way, and are individually accessible by electronic or other means.[386] It is submitted that most websites, or at least most websites worth framing, deep linking or spidering, store a high degree of data in a systematic or methodical way. Indeed, most large websites use content management systems or other applications to arrange the content from their site into a database (in the computer sense). It is also relevant that a database may be more than merely text or digits. It may also encompass sounds, images, and other data.[387]

To qualify for copyright protection as a literary work, a database must also fulfill the criteria for originality as considered in section 4.9.2.3. In relation to databases, s 3A(2) of the Act clarifies that, in order to be 'original', the selection or arrangement of the contents of the database must constitute the author's own intellectual creation. This additional hurdle may prove relevant in several Internet scenarios. In particular, it is not clear whether a purely automatic, software generated database will qualify. A more obvious category which may not qualify consists of databases based on simple organisation, for example a list of customer contact details or postings structured in alphabetical order. Here neither the contents themselves (which are simply names and addresses and postings given by customers themselves), nor their arrangement, can be said to be the website owner's own intellectual creation.

4.9.7.2 Database rights

4.9.7.2.1 Scope of the database right

A database is protected by a database right (regardless of whether it also qualifies for copyright protection as a literary work) if there has been a substantial investment in obtaining, verifying or presenting the contents of the database.[388]

It is vital here to appreciate that the maker of a database takes the initiative and risk of investing in the *database* but not necessarily its contents. A database is a collection of *other* works and data. The maker of the database may have had no hand in the creation of these underlying elements. To be a maker of a database one needs only to have taken the initiative and risk of obtaining, verifying or presenting the underlying data. Databases are therefore more about 'contents pages' and 'indexes' than chapters and sentences.

The concept of investment is wider than mere financial investment. It also includes human or technical resources.[389] Many complex websites utilise the skills of database architects and other computer programmers to ensure that the

---

386   Copyright, Designs and Patents Act 1988, s 3A(1).
387   Recital 17.
388   Reg 13(1).
389   Reg 12.

database supporting a website functions correctly. This is an ongoing and expensive task; most websites, in particular ecommerce websites, have a continually changing structure and appearance to keep both stock and the look of the website fresh.

Although this may suggest that many websites may find protection in the form of database rights, a key case indicates that the scope of such right is far narrower than at first sight. The key case is that of *British Horseracing Board v William Hill*[390]. In this case, the British Horseracing Board (BHB) complained that their database of details relating to horseracing and horses was infringed by William Hill, the bookmakers. The claimants spent in the region of four million pounds each year to obtain, verify and present the contents of its database. Each year would see 800,000 new records or changes made to the database. The claimant provides the data from this database to many participating elements of the racing industry, including bookmakers. The defendant had and paid for a licence to use this data in its licensed betting shops, on television's Ceefax service and for telephone betting. It did not have a licence to publish the data on its website and yet each day, it repurposed its existing non-Internet data feed to republish pertinent data on its website. BHB's case centred on the premise that William Hill's continued daily use if its information constituted an extraction or reutilisation of a substantial part of its database. The court referred several questions to the European Court of Justice and their judgment came as a shock to many.

The ECJ held that the BHB had no valid database right in its collection of pre-race data: it had not made a sufficient substantial investment in creating the database over and above that invested in the creation of its constituent parts. The ECJ drew an important distinction between creation of the data and the actual database. This decision was reached on several counts:

> First in relation to 'obtaining', the ECJ stated that 'investment' must refer to investment in the creation of the database itself. Resources used to seek out existing independent materials and collect them in a database were relevant but not resources used to create materials or data.

> Second, *'investment in verifying the contents'*, referred to the resources used to ensure the reliability of the information, or to monitor the accuracy of the materials collected when the database was created and during its operation. Resources used for verification during the stage of creation of the data (which were subsequently collected in a database) could not be taken into account to assess whether there was substantial investment.

The ECJ opined that the fact that the maker of a database was also the generator of the data did not preclude protection of the database right. To be protected, however, resources must be expended to arrange the data systematically, independent of those used to obtain or verify the data at the stage it was created.

On the facts, the ECJ concluded that BHB's activities and investment related to the creation of racing data and not the database. The selection of the horses admitted to race did not constitute investment in obtaining the contents of the database. Further, the checks conducted as to the identity of the person making the entry, the classification of the horse, its owner and its jockey took place when the data was created, and were not conducted to monitor the accuracy of the database at a later stage. As a result they did not constitute an investment in the verification of the contents of the database.

The Court of Appeal subsequently dismissed BHB's argument that the ECJ had exceeded its jurisdiction. It was entitled to rule on the legal consequences of given primary facts. Lord Justice Jacob explained the logic behind the finding that BHB is creating the list of runners and riders, rather than collecting together existing information provided by owners. Only BHB can provide an official list of runners and riders. He said:

> 'The database contains unique information - the official list of runners and riders. The nature of the information changes with the stamp of official approval. It becomes something different from a mere database of existing material.'

In a wider ecommerce context this ruling has mixed implications. For businesses compiling databases, the extent of protection has been narrowed – particularly if the database is a spin-off from its primary activities. Further, the effect of the ECJ's ruling is to raise the bar for finding that the right has been infringed, this could in turn affect the value of databases. Copyright may offer an alternative route for protecting the databases itself and the material contained in it, but only where the requisite element of originality is present.

4.9.7.2.2   Term of protection

The database right protects the database for 15 years from the end of the calendar year in which the making of the database was completed or, if earlier, 15 years from the end of the calendar year in which the database was first made available to the public. In addition, a new 15-year period will commence if there are any substantial changes made to the contents of a database, including a substantial change resulting from the accumulation of successive additions, deletions or alterations, which would result in the database being considered to be a substantial new investment[391].

4.10   MORAL RIGHTS AND THE INTERNET

The Copyright, Designs and Patents Act 1988 does not purely provide economic rights to copyright owners. It also provides certain 'moral' rights to the authors[392] of copyright works.[393] These rights include the right to be attributed as author of

---

391   Reg 17.
392   Performers also get moral rights, in relation to performances given since February 2006, see Part 2 of the Copyright, Designs and Patents Act 1988.
393   The rights do not apply where the work was created by an employee in the course of employment: Copyright, Designs and Patents Act 1988, ss 11(2), 79(3), 82(1)(a).

a copyright work, the right to object to derogatory treatment of a copyright work and the right not to be falsely attributed as the author of a copyright work. This section considers the first two of these rights: the so-called rights of 'paternity' and of 'integrity'.

The two rights do not apply to computer programs or computer-generated works, so much of the work on the Internet is excluded from protection. The rights attach only to literary, artistic, musical and film works. This does not mean that a site on the World Wide Web cannot *infringe* a work's moral rights. What this means is that those who construct web pages, and those that control forums, should be wary of infringing the moral rights in one of the works they are using.

4.10.1   Paternity

The author of a literary work has the right to be identified as the author of that work whenever it is published commercially, performed in public, communicated to the public or included in copies of a film or sound recording which are issued to the public.[394] The author of an artistic work has the right to be identified as the author of that work whenever the work is published commercially, exhibited in public or communicated to the public[395]. It has been discussed that making a work available on a website will constitute commercial publication; money does not need to change hands.[396]

To rely on the right, an author needs first to assert it.[397] This is achieved in relation to general or specific acts on an assignment of copyright or by an instrument in writing signed by the author.[398] A relevant question for those who see their works commercially published on the Internet is, therefore, whether this right can be asserted *over* the Internet.

The term 'writing' is widely defined as including any form of notation or code, whether by hand or otherwise and regardless of the method by which, or the medium on, in or on which, it is recorded[399]. No specific amendment has been made to the Copyright, Designs and Patents Act 1988 under the Electronic Communications Act 2000 to expressly clarify that signatures made in electronic form will be valid. As discussed in Chapter 2, in the absence of specific requirements for paper copies or hand signatures, there is no such specific restriction and even an email clearly sent by an individual may potentially prove sufficient provided it can be considered to have been 'signed'. Given the importance of

---

394   Copyright, Designs and Patents Act 1988, s 77(1) and (2)(a).
395   Copyright, Designs and Patents Act 1988, s 77(4)(a).
396   See 'Place of publication', above.
397   Copyright, Designs and Patents Act 1988, s 78(1). See *Christoffer v Poseidon Film Distributors* [2000] ECDR 487 per Park J.
398   Copyright, Designs and Patents Act 1988, s 78(2).
399   Copyright, Designs and Patents Act 1988, s 178. Cf Law of Property Act 1925, s 40 which is silent on what may constitute 'writing' forcing a court to rely, therefore, on the Interpretation Act 1978, Sch 1. This provides that '[w]riting includes typing, printing, lithography, photography and other modes of representing or reproducing words in a visible form ...'

evidence in relation to copyright, whether that be assertion, waivers or assignments, many may be reluctant to take the risks of relying on anything other than traditional paper signatures.

---

23. An individual posts a poem to a forum and ends the email with the words 'This author asserts his right to be identified as the author of this work under the Copyright, Designs and Patents Act 1988'. This is problematic as a valid assertion since, although in writing, it is not clearly signed and could be open to challenge. Subject to copyright infringement, the forum and others using the forum may reproduce his email without reference to his authorship.

Artistic works may have their paternity right asserted simply by being identified on the original or copy of the work in relation to a public exhibition.[400] For this method of assertion it appears likely that the assertion may be made over the Internet. Most websites that show artistic works may be considered as public exhibitions and it is easy to include on a digital copy of a work a typed or 'signed' name.

---

24. A website serves as an advertising medium for young artists. One artist posts up on the site a computer-generated graphic that he designed. He includes on the graphic his name and is perturbed when he sees his work republished on a website without payment and without acknowledgment. He may well have a strong case of copyright infringement. He would have a similarly strong case of infringement of his moral rights but there are no moral rights over computer-generated artistic works. A hand-generated work digitised and posted on the Internet, in contrast, could be protected by a paternity right.

The right of paternity applies to the whole or any substantial part of the work.[401] This right is infringed where the work is commercially published or exhibited without the author's identity being brought to the notice of a viewing person.[402]

4.10.2   Integrity

In appropriate circumstances, the author of any literary or musical work has the right not to have the work subjected to derogatory treatment[403]. Similarly, in appropriate circumstances, the author of any artistic work has the right to object to any derogatory treatment of a copyright artistic work in a commercial publication or public exhibition.[404] In comparison to the right of paternity, the right of

---

400   Copyright, Designs and Patents Act 1988, s 78(3)(a).
401   Copyright, Designs and Patents Act 1988, s 89(1).
402   Copyright, Designs and Patents Act 1988, s 77(7)(c).
403   Copyright, Designs and Patents Act 1988, s 80(1).
404   Copyright, Designs and Patents Act 1988. s 80(4)(a).

integrity is far more powerful: it does not need to be asserted, it applies to any part of the work not merely substantial parts[405] and it has far wider scope for infringement.

A 'treatment' of a work means any addition to, deletion from or alteration to or adaptation of the work. It does not include a translation of a literary work or a transcription of a musical work involving no more than a change of key or register.[406] As should be apparent, this is a very wide definition. It may include the re-colouring of an artistic image to look appropriate on a website with a limited palette.[407] It will also include the reduction in size of an artistic work, or cropping of an artistic work to fit in a particular space on a website. More technically, an artistic work will also be 'treated' where it is converted into a digital format with a lower resolution so that the picture appears more grainy or 'pixelated'. Literary works may be treated by over-zealous editing or 'snipping' as it is termed in conversation threads. Obviously, literary works are also 'treated' when they are blatantly altered.

A treatment is derogatory if it amounts to distortion or mutilation of the work or is otherwise prejudicial to the honour or reputation of the author.[408] This has not been tested at full trial, so it is difficult to guess how favourably the courts will interpret the phrase. Some indication can be provided by a summary judgment given by Rattee J. In *Tidy v Trustees of the Natural History Museum*,[409] Bill Tidy, a well-known cartoon artist, objected to a 16 per cent reduction in size of his cartoons when displayed. The claimant claimed that this reduction constituted derogatory treatment as a distortion of the work or by being prejudicial to his honour or reputation.

Rattee J decided that it would be difficult to decide that a treatment was prejudicial to an author's honour and reputation without recourse to evidence from the public as to how the reduction affected the claimant's standing in their eyes.[410]

If anything can be drawn from this summary judgment it is that the opinion of the author, while sometimes persuasive, is not the final arbiter of whether treatment is derogatory. What can outweigh the author's opinion, when reasonably arrived at, is the reaction of the public. On the Internet, therefore, the public may be aware that a computer screen does not always faithfully represent the artistic works it portrays. Often this lack of quality is as a result of the quality of the viewer's screen or computer specifications; something for which the owner of a server or website cannot be legally responsible.

For literary works, the result is less than clear. Those who edit conversation threads should therefore be careful to treat with respect the postings made by others.

---

405   Copyright, Designs and Patents Act 1988, s 89(2).
406   Copyright, Designs and Patents Act 1988, s 80(2)(a).
407   See the analogous French judgment of *Angelica Houston v Turner Entertainment* [1992] ECC 334.
408   Copyright, Designs and Patents Act 1988, s 80(2)(b).
409   (1995) 39 IPR 501.
410   Rattee J was not clear that the opinion of the author was essential to decide the point, so doubting the application of the Canadian decision *Snow v Eaton Centre Ltd* (1982) 70 CPR (2d) 105.

4.10.3 Waiver of rights

The uncertainty and scope of moral rights should make every user of another's copyright on the Internet think carefully about obtaining a waiver from each contributing author. It is not an infringement of the moral rights if the author waives those rights.[411] Unlike assertions, a waiver does not have to meet any formal requirements and can be in relation to any works for any purposes.[412] The waiver can also be made unconditional.[413]

Web designers would therefore be wise to obtain such a waiver in respect of any work that they use for a site and Internet service providers can also be advised to obtain a waiver on all works submitted by their members. Finally, the terms and conditions for any site should include an express wavier in relation to any posting.

4.10.4 Copyright and database right infringement

A copyright infringement occurs where one of the acts reserved for the right of the property owner are carried out or authorised by a person without a licence or defence for doing so in relation to the whole or a substantial part of a copyright work.

Therefore, if one has the licence to copy a copyright work, one does not infringe it. If one copies only an insubstantial part of a copyright work, one does not infringe the copyright in the work. These two non-infringing methods of copying are particularly relevant. This is because the only way to use the Internet involves copying. It is not only unlicensed substantial copying that infringes a copyright; visually presenting a work in public may also infringe the copyright in the work.[414] One also infringes copyright by authorising anyone to perform an act restricted by copyright.[415] In addition the law provides for secondary infringements where one deals in a restricted way with an infringing copy of a work.[416]

4.11 COPYRIGHT PROHIBITED ACTS

The acts reserved for copyright owners are set out in s 16(1) of the Act as follows:

'(a) to copy the work;

(b) to issue copies of the work to the public;

(ba) to rent or lend the work to the public;

---

411   Copyright, Designs and Patents Act 1988, s 87(1).
412   Copyright, Designs and Patents Act 1988, s 87(3)(1).
413   Copyright, Designs and Patents Act 1988, s 87(3)(b).
414   Copyright, Designs and Patents Act 1988, s 19(2)(b).
415   Copyright, Designs and Patents Act 1988, s 16(2).
416   Copyright, Designs and Patents Act 1988, ss 22–26.

(c) to perform, show or play the work in public;

(d) to communicate the work to the public;

(e) to make an adaptation of the work or do any of the above in relation to an adaptation.'

All may be relevant in the context of the Internet, and the examples in section 4.13 illustrate some common scenarios.

4.11.1   Copying

4.11.1.1   Technical copying

Technically, a copy is made each time one views a website, or accesses a forum, or even forwards an email. This is because, unlike the postal system, any material of any form that is sent over the Internet or viewed over it is copied. What occurs is that the viewer's computer transmits a request to the server computer to forward a duplicate of some particular material it is storing. This duplicate material is not passed directly to the viewer's computer. It is broken into packets, each with a delivery address, and sent across the Internet. It is passed from one computer on the Internet to another until all the packets are eventually received at the viewer's computer. In reality, each of these intermediary computers has made a copy of the packet that it received and forwarded.

When the material is finally received by the viewer's computer it is stored in the computer's memory – another copy. This transfer does not physically alter the information held by the server, rather it reproduces in the memory of the viewer's computer the material held by the server. The material on the server remains unchanged. The material now held in the viewer computer's memory is then 'interpreted'[417] or 'executed'.[418] This will allow the viewer to experience the website. But this is the result of another copy. The computer's main memory translates the material received from the server into graphic images and sound and these are sent to the screen memory – further copies.

4.11.1.2   Legal copying

From a legal perspective, the Act defines copying widely. A copy is made by reproducing the whole, or any substantial part, of the work in any material form. This includes storing the work in a medium by electronic means.[419] As has been examined, all material on the Internet and World Wide Web is, or had underlying it, a work protectable by copyright. The Act goes further and makes explicit that any reproduction will be deemed to be copying. This is even where the copying

---

417   For pure HTML or XML.
418   For executable code.
419   Copyright, Designs and Patents Act 1988, s 17(2).

is indirect,[420] and even where it is transient or incidental to some other use of the work.[421]

This wide ambit of what is copying can be translated into one simple truth: using the Internet creates copies. Sometimes, the retention, and further copying or distribution is coined 'caching'. When a website is viewed, all the server computers on the Internet that pass on the packets will be deemed to have copied the site. Their copying is transient and incidental to another's use, but this still remains copying under the Act. The computer that finally receives the copies will also be deemed to have copied the site. The computer's copy may not be on paper, but storage by electronic means is sufficient to constitute copying under the Act. When emails are sent, received, even viewed, copies are made in a similar way as described above.

As almost all use of the Internet involves copying, the main legal issue in copyright actions will be whether the copying constitutes infringement.[422]

4.11.2 Issuing copies to the public

This act, as further defined in s 18 of the Act, has an obvious application to the publication of works within the EEA and the reference to 'putting into circulation' in that section enforces such an interpretation. Whilst there is no specific carve out for intangible copies of a work, which we have discussed above commonly arise in the context of the Internet, in most circumstances reliance on an act of communication to the public will be simpler and clearer.

4.11.3 Renting or lending to the public

This right, as set out in s 18A exists in relation to literary, dramatic, musical and artistic works. Given that the definitions of rental and lending refer to the potential for return of the work, this act is less likely to be of relevance in the context of Internet infringements. For example, where music or other infringing copies are made available, even where there are conditions on, say, the amount of time for which it may be viewed, there will not be an expectation of a return of the file, it will simply be deleted and duplicate copies used elsewhere.

4.11.4 Performing, showing or playing in public

As set out in s 19 of the Act, this right applies to literary, dramatic or musical works only but encompasses any mode of visual or acoustic presentation of such a work (including broadcasts or sound recordings). In addition, the section

---

420   Copyright, Designs and Patents Act 1988, s 16(3)(b).
421   Copyright, Designs and Patents Act 1988, s 17(6).
422   Of course, there may be many factual disputes as to whether the defendant actually did copy the work.

makes the showing or playing of a broadcast, film or sound recording a separate act of infringement.

In this way, a transmission of a work via the Internet or playing of a sound recording across the Internet, seemingly constitute a public performance or the playing or showing of such a work. However, s 19(4) states that:

> 'Where copyright in a work is infringed by its being performed, played or shown in public by means of apparatus for receiving visual images or sounds conveyed by electronic means, the person by whom the visual images or sounds are sent, and in the case of performance the performers, shall not be regarded as responsible for the infringement.'

The effect of this is to provide welcome protection for broadcasters and ISPs against liability where the showing is on a monitor. Broadcasts are separately covered by the act of communication to the public. A further qualification is also significant for Internet performances: it must be 'in public'. This means that a screening in, say, a bar or workplace would be before an audience and therefore qualify. However, an individual watching on their computer at home will not be public for the purposes of such performance.

4.11.5   Communication to the public

This addition to the Act is specifically targeted at information society services and does provide much needed clarity in the context of Internet activities.

Applying in s 20 of the Act to literary, dramatic, musical and artistic works and to sound recordings in a film or broadcasts, a communication to the public comprises any broadcast or 'making available of the work by electronic transmission in such a way that members of the public may access it from a place and at a time individually chosen by them.'

Such an act therefore covers the placement of material on a website or Internet webcasts. Exclusions in the context of broadcasts are considered in section 4.9.4.3.

4.11.6   Making or acts in relation to an adaptation

Contained in s 21, this right applies to literary, dramatic and musical works only. In relation to computer programs, an adaptation includes an arrangement or altered version of the program or a translation of it and its translation a conversion into or out of computer language or code into a different computer language or code.[423]

---

423   S 50C of the Act prevents standard, lawful use of software being an automatic infringement as considered in section 4.12.4.1; there is also a defence in relation to decompilation: s 50B.

4.12 DATABASE INFRINGEMENT

A person infringes a database right if, without the consent of the owner of the right, he extracts or re-utilises all or a substantial part of the contents of the database.[424] The term 'extracts' means the permanent or temporary transfer of those contents to another medium by any means or in any form.[425] It does not therefore necessarily entail the contents being made visible to the public nor does it mean that the copied database remains permanently. It may serve a short-term purpose, be deleted, and yet still have been extracted. Extracted can therefore be contrasted with 're-utilises' which means making the database contents available to the public by any means.[426] It is critical to understand that a 'substantial part' need not be extracted or re-utilised all at once: repeated and systematic extraction or re-utilisation of insubstantial parts of the contents of a database may amount to the extraction or re-utilisation of a substantial part of those contents.[427] And substantial may mean in terms of quantity or quality or a combination of both.[428]

Finally, a lawful user of a database which has been made available to the public in any manner is entitled to extract or re-utilise insubstantial parts of the contents of the database for any purpose.[429]

4.12.1 A substantial part

To infringe a copyright work by copying it one must not only have no licence to copy the work, but also the copy must be of a substantial part of the claimant's work.[430] There is no statutory definition of what constitutes a 'substantial part'. This absence is complicated further by the two senses of the word 'substantial'. The *Concise Oxford Dictionary* defines the word both qualitatively as 'of real importance or value' and quantitatively as 'of considerable amount'. The courts have indicated that the test is more one of quality than one of quantity but it appears that even aspects of a claimant's work that are quantitatively small may

---

424 Reg 16(1).
425 Reg 12.
426 Reg 12.
427 Reg 16.
428 Reg 12.
429 Reg 19(1).
430 Copyright, Designs and Patents Act 1988, s 16(3)(a). 'The question is whether the defendants' [work] reproduces a substantial part of the [plaintiff's work], not whether the reproduced part of the [plaintiff's work] forms a substantial part of the defendant's [work]': *Warwick Film Productions v Eisinger* [1967] 3 All ER 367 at 385 per Plowman J. Approved by the House of Lords in *Designer Guild Ltd v Russell Williams (Textiles) Ltd* [2001] 1 All ER 700.

still constitute a substantial part.[431] What constitutes a substantial part of a conversation thread may be a familiar issue for a court to assess; what constitutes a
substantial part of website may be more difficult.

A website may consist of 200 individual instructions to the computer and a
copier may copy 100. But whether this quantitatively substantial taking is substantial in a copyright sense may depend on how the 100 lines appear on interpretation. If the lines are part of some executable code that merely animates a
small graphic on a many-page website, this may not be substantial. This said, the
courts must not forget that copyright protects not the expression itself but the
skill, labour and judgment that was expended in creating that expression. So, if
the animation of the graphic was a very complex and time-consuming piece of
programming it may be a substantial part of the whole copyright work.[432]

Assessing substantiality is a question that will always rest on the facts of a
case.[433] The last word on its determination is left for Jacob J in *Ibcos Computers
Ltd v Barclays Mercantile Highland Finance Ltd*:

> 'Even in the case of technical drawings it is possible to examine the parties'
> drawings to see whether a substantial part of the [claimant's] work is to be
> found in the defendant's. In a computer program case, however, the court can-
> not so readily assess the question of substantial part unaided by expert evidence.
> I believe I should therefore be largely guided by such evidence.'[434]

In illustration, a large parcel delivery company sets up a website. It consists of
information about the company, parcel-tracking facilities and lists of all its services. It amounts to over 30 pages of web pages and just under 1,000 lines of
code. It features animations, sound jingles and forms to be filled in where appropriate. One such form was copied from a newspaper's site on the Internet. The
form takes up one-third of one page and the coding is about 30 lines. The company admits unlicensed copying but deny that it is a substantial part when the
form amounts to only 3 per cent of the code on their page and 1 per cent of the
visual reproduction of their site. This is focusing on the wrong work and the
wrong concept. The question should be how much of the newspaper's site has

---

431   '[T]hough it may be that it was not very prolonged in its reproduction, it is clearly in my
      view, a substantial, a vital, and an essential part which is there reproduced': *Hawkes & Son v
      Paramount Film Service* [1934] Ch 593 at 606, per Slesser LJ; '[I]t is quite clear that the
      question of substantiality is not determined solely by any process of arithmetic': *Joy Music v
      Sunday Pictorial* [1960] 2 QB 60 at 68, per McNail J; '[T]he question whether he has taken
      a substantial part depends much more on the quality than on the quantity of what he has
      taken. It will, therefore, depend not merely on the physical amount of the reproduction but on
      the substantial significance of that which is taken': *Ladbroke (Football) Ltd v William Hill
      (Football) Ltd* [1964] 1 All ER 465 at 469, per Lord Reid, and at 473 per Lord Evershed.

432   In such a case, the claimant should not overlook the issue that the website, although a com-
      puter program, is also a compilation. He may therefore be advised also to plead infringement
      of the Java applet by itself. This then eliminates the question of whether the taking is a sub-
      stantial part of the website. This can be compared to the approach used in Ibcos.

433   See the Court of Appeal in relation to substantiality in drawings: *Biotrading & Financing OY
      v Biohit Ltd* [1998] FSR 109 at 122, per Aldous J.

434   [1994] FSR 275 at 301.

been lifted (even this question should not be answered with percentages); the significance of the form in programming terms should determine its substantiality. Merely because the code creating this form, if removed, would prevent the whole newspaper's site from functioning does not prove that it is a substantial part. Indeed, most computer programs are created using many modules and without any one module, the program would not operate. This is not, by itself, enough to prove the module or element is substantial.[435]

4.12.2 Secondary infringement

Reproducing without licence a substantial part of a copyright work is a copyright infringement. Sections 22 to 26 of the Act also provide circumstances where other dealings with a copyright work with a 'guilty mind' will constitute secondary infringements of copyright.[436] These dealings include the possession in the course of business of an article which is an infringing copy of a copyright work; a dealing that may be satisfied by a hosting company storing a copy of an infringing work. The requisite guilty mind is where the defendant knows or has reason to believe that the article is an infringing copy. These two aspects to a secondary infringement are discussed below with specific reference to those service providers, usually Internet service providers or web hosting companies, who store and transmit digital material on behalf of others.

4.12.3 Dealings

Sections 22 to 26 of the Copyright, Designs and Patents Act 1988 provide the types of dealings in a copyright work that, together with a guilty mind, will constitute a secondary infringement. This section illustrates those dealings by examining them with reference to a website hosted for an individual.

Section 23 provides four situations where, with the requisite guilty mind and without licence of the copyright owner, a person will infringe the copyright in a work, as follows:

1. in the course of business he possesses an article which is an infringing copy of the work;

2. if he sells or lets for hire, or offers or exposes for sale or hire an article which is an infringing copy of the work;

3. in the course of a business he exhibits in public or distributes an article which is an infringing copy of the work; or

---

435   *Cantor Fitzgerald International v Tradition (UK) Ltd* [2000] RPC 95.
436   It is not dealt with here, but it also should be considered that there can be secondary infringement.

4.   otherwise than in the course of a business, he distributes an article which is
      an infringing copy of the work to such an extent as to affect prejudicially
      the owner of the copyright.

4.12.3.2   Infringing copy

An article is an infringing copy if its making constituted an infringement of the
work in question.[437] It is presumed that an article was made at the time that copyright subsisted in the work if it is shown that the article is a copy of the work and
that copyright subsists, or has subsisted, in the work at any time.[438]

4.12.3.3   Course of business

A business is defined by the Act to include a trade or profession.[439] A question
arises as to the circumstances under which a person 'dealing' with an infringing
copy will not be seen as doing so in the course of business. The cases which have
considered the meaning of 'course of business' all point to the conclusion that an
Internet service provider hosting a website or even a newsgroup will do so in the
course of business.[440] It has been stated that 'transactions which are only incidental to a business may not be possessed in the course of that business'.[441] It is clear
that the Internet service providers that provide web space for its customers to
host their sites do so very much as part of their business. It costs the Internet service provider in terms of support and, albeit marginally, in terms of storage costs.
Storing third party data and material is not incidental to the business of any
Internet service provider and some websites: attracting customers to pay rental
charges or to bolster advertising is integral to its business.

It is less likely that an individual who hosts a blog or forum purely as an amateur does so in the course of business; of course, even if he does not, he may still
be caught under s 23(d) where his distribution is to such an extent as to affect
prejudicially the owner of the copyright.

4.12.3.4   Exhibit, distribute and possess

The four subsections of s 23 use the words 'exhibits', 'distributes' and 'possesses' in relation to infringing articles. There appears to be little doubt that the
word 'possesses' carries a wide connotation; the presence on a hard disk drive or
memory of a computer would seem to constitute possession. It is for this reason
that even if an Internet service provider is able to show that no person viewed a

437   Copyright, Designs and Patents Act 1988, s 27(2).
438   Copyright, Designs and Patents Act 1988, s 27(4).
439   Copyright, Designs and Patents Act 1988, s 178.
440   *LA Gear Inc v Hi-Tec Sports plc* [1992] FSR 121 (re copyright); *Davies v Sumner* [1984] 3
       All ER 831 (re trade descriptions); *R & B Customs Brokers Ltd v United Dominions Trust Ltd*
       [1988] 1 WLR 321 (re Unfair Contract Terms Act 1977).
441   *Pensher Security Doors Ltd v Sunderland City Council* [1999] EWCA Civ 1223, [2000] RPC
       249 per Aldous J.

website or downloaded a particular file, so that there was no distribution, there may still be secondary infringement by virtue of its storage of the file. Of course, with no distribution any damages will probably be minimal, s 23(a) will therefore probably be appropriate for any infringement in the course of Internet business[442].

4.12.3.5 Knowledge or reason to believe

This is the most important aspect of secondary infringement and is relevant for the hosting defence: the claimant must prove that the defendant knew or had reason to believe that the article is an infringing copy of the work in question. The proof, for the purposes of this chapter, can be rephrased as: did the controller of the digital depository know or have reason to believe the file was an infringing copy of the copyright work?

Clearly, in most cases, a claimant will be seeking only to show 'reason to believe'; proving knowledge is more onerous than proving a reason to believe. In *LA Gear Inc v Hi-Tec Sports plc* Morritt J decided that 'reason to believe':

> 'must involve the concept of knowledge of facts from which a reasonable man would arrive at the relevant belief. Facts from which a reasonable man might suspect the relevant conclusion cannot be enough. Moreover, as it seems to me, the phrase does connote the allowance of a period of time to enable the reasonable man to evaluate those facts so as to convert the facts into a reasonable belief.'[443]

On appeal the court upheld this decision for, in Nourse LJ's words, substantially the same reasons as those given by Morritt J. The principle has again been applied by the Court of Appeal in *ZYX Music GmbH v Chris King*.[444] The test would be applied as follows: the claimant should prove that the facts known by or brought to the attention of the controller would have made the reasonable *controller of such a server* believe that the file or element of the site perhaps is infringing. This need not be immediate; a period of time may elapse during which the reasonable controller may come to the belief. If this is satisfied, the actual controller may rebut the allegation by proving that facts in his knowledge made him believe that the article was not infringing.

4.12.3.6 Reasonable belief on the Internet

The application of this test to the Internet is vexed. On the one hand, Internet service providers are fully aware that pirated software and copyright-infringing images, sound recordings and movies are posted on their servers. In some situations, this will be enough to indicate that a posting is an infringing article. On the other hand, this general knowledge may not be enough to prove a reasonable

---

442 It is perhaps an anomaly of the digital world that it is impossible to distribute a digital file without first possessing it.
443 [1992] FSR 121 at 129.
444 [1997] 2 All ER 129, CA.

belief: the very 'work in question' must have been reasonably thought to be infringing.[445] Also, knowing that many files on a server are infringing does not translate into a reasonable knowledge that a *particular* file is an infringement.[446]

4.12.4   Licences and defences

It will be recalled that it is not an infringement to copy the whole or a substantial part of a copyright work with licence from the copyright owner.[447] A licence does not need to take any particular form. Licences can be implied from statute[448] and by the courts from the circumstances in which the copyright work or part of it is transferred.[449] What will be at issue in most Internet cases is the existence, scope and duration of these implied licences. It should also be kept in mind that the Electronic Commerce Directive also provides a defence for those who make temporary copies on behalf of others. This defence is examined in some detail below. Some licences can be readily implied for dealings over the Internet. For example, the intermediary computers involved with an Internet dealing would seem to be impliedly licensed to copy the packets being passed to the end user. This can be inferred from the fact that the copyright owner made the information available over the Internet, so, surely a licence must be implied for business efficacy. If the owner of every server computer on the Internet infringed any packet that passed through it, the Internet would collapse because no one would want to connect to it. It seems also fair between the parties that the licence is implied only to the extent that the intermediary can pass on the packets. It would be outside the scope of the implied licence to retain copies of the packets after they are confirmed to have been accurately sent.

4.12.4.1   Temporary 'licence'

Section 28A of the Act converted this 'licence' in a copyright exception allowing temporary copies to be made:

> 'Copyright…in a work . . . is not infringed by the making of a temporary copy which is transient or incidental, which is an integral and essential part of a technological process and the sole purpose of which is to enable –
>
> (a)   a transmission of the work in a network between third parties by an intermediary; or

---

445   Copyright, Designs and Patents Act 1988, s 27(3)(b).
446   See *Columbia Picture Industries v Robinson* [1986] FSR 367.
447   Copyright, Designs and Patents Act 1988, s 16(2).
448   Copyright, Designs and Patents Act 1988, ss 50A–50C.
449   *Springfield v Thame* (1903) 89 LT 242; *Hall-Brown v Iliffe & Sons Ltd* (1928–35) Macq Cop Cas 88; *Blair v Osbourne & Tomkins* [1971] 2 QB 78; *Solar Thomson Engineering Co Ltd v Barton* [1977] RPC 537 at 560–561; *Roberts v Candiware* [1980] FSR 352; *Anvil Jewellery Ltd v Riva Ridge Holdings Ltd* (1985–87) 8 IPR 161.

(b)   a lawful use of the work;

and which has no independent economic significance.'

Consequently, following the implementation of this section, the technologically necessary copies of works made every second across the Internet will no longer be possible infringements. Of course, where an intermediary temporarily copies a work for the purposes of generating advertising revenues, or direct revenues, that intermediary may then infringe the work. One should also note that this exception also does not apply to computer programs nor to databases. Does this mean that the necessary temporary copying of a website purely for transmission of the work is possibly an infringement? Here, s 50 of the Act assists.

The Copyright, Designs and Patents Act 1988, s 50C provides that it is not an infringement of copyright for a lawful user of a copy of a computer program to copy it provided that it is necessary for his lawful use and is not prohibited by contract. As a website is a computer program and the only way to 'use' the website is to copy it, it is implied that a lawful viewer of a website and the intermediaries working on behalf of the website owner are entitled to copy it. It will be examined below whether a user or server may also store a copy on a disk and for how long this copy may be stored.

4.12.4.2   Creative Commons licences

Not a specific defence under the Act, Creative Commons is a project which provides a novel form of licensing structure of particular interest and application on the Internet. The aim of the project is to build a layer of reasonable, flexible copyright licensing to exist alongside more restrictive copyright laws and traditional licensing models.

Taking inspiration from the Free Software Foundation's GNU Public Licence, Creative Commons has developed a web application that purports to allow people to dedicate their work to the public domain or retain their copyright while licensing the work for certain uses, encouraging the practice of 'remixing' which involves artists using the past works to create new works.

Like Open Source software, Creative Commons does not mean the removal of intellectual property rights. Both involve the use of carefully crafted licences which still set contractual parameters on the permitted uses of the applicable code or works. Creative Commons provides a set of 6 key licences which allow the use and distribution of works providing the user abides by certain conditions chosen by the author, with different levels of restriction:

4.12.4.2.1   Attribution non-commercial, no derivatives

Permit others to copy, distribute, display, and perform the work and derivative works based upon it only if they credit the author and the work can not be changed in any way or used commercially.

4.12.4.2.2   Attribution non-commercial share alike

Similar to above but remixing and changes to the work are permitted providing there is a credit to the author and the new work is licensed on identical terms.

4.12.4.2.3   Attribution non-commercial

The same as Attribution Non-commercial Share Alike but without the restriction requiring licensing on identical terms.

4.12.4.2.4   Attribution no derivatives

Permit others to copy, distribute, display and perform only verbatim copies of the work, not derivative works based upon it.

4.12.4.2.5   Attribution share alike

Permit others to distribute and create derivative works only under a licence identical to the licence that governs the work.

4.12.4.2.6   Attribution

Allows others to distribute and create derivative works as long as the author is credited.

The licences are expressed in three ways:

1.   'Human readable commons deed';

2.   'Lawyer readable legal code';

3.   Machine-readable metadata that can be used to associate creative works with their public domain or licence status so that it is searchable and so that a link can be used to link from the website containing the work to the licence.

Stepping outside the boundaries of such a licence constitutes a potential copyright infringement in the normal way.

4.12.4.3   The caching defence

A web cache is a computer with vast storage capacity which holds copies of the most popular pages on the World Wide Web. If this cache is located on the local network, users can be saved the delay of gaining access to the over-burdened site. It also means that the network can restrict access to the Internet, thus reducing the risk from hacking and viruses.

Commercially, a web cache may be unwelcome for a website owner, few companies publish on the web out of charity; they wish to advertise, to sell to and to find the demographics of those who visit their site. A web cache may hide this information from companies. Companies whose sites are cached may be unable to establish exactly how many people are 'hitting' their site, and also they cannot find out who makes up their audience. These statistics are an attractive aspect of the Internet.

Caching can also adversely affect companies whose income comes from selling advertising space on their pages. To increase this income, these companies often show a different advertisement each time the site is viewed; they 'roll' a number of adverts. This multiplies each page's earnings. Unfortunately, the caching computer stores just one copy of the popular pages. So there may be just one advertiser who is getting their money's worth. Clearly then, these companies have a commercial objection to caching.

The EC Directive on Certain Legal Aspects of Electronic Commerce in the Internal Market introduced a defence for intermediaries who make temporary copies of material under six conditions[450]. The Electronic Commerce (EC) Regulations 2002 implement this defence at regulation 18. The defence is absolute and the intermediary is not liable for damages or for any other pecuniary remedy or for any criminal sanction as a result of the storage and subsequent transmission. It remains, however, possible for a person to get an injunction even where a person acts within the exception. In addition, s 97A of the Act gives the power to the courts to grant an injunction to remove infringing material.

4.12.4.3.1 Automatic, intermediate and temporary

This defence applies where the copyright work in question is both the subject of automatic, intermediate and temporary storage and where that storage is for the sole purpose of making more efficient onward transmission of the work to other recipients of the service upon their request.[451] In essence, therefore, the storage of the copyright work must not be an end in itself; the work must be stored automatically to transmit it to others.

---

25. ForeverThere.com spots a gap in market for search engines. It realises that other search engines' index of websites become inaccurate in a matter of weeks because websites continually update the web addresses on which they store pages. This leads to 'broken links' where an individual is unable to relocate the page indexed by the search engine. As a strategy, ForeverThere.com takes full copies of websites as it indexes them to allow its users to locate the information requested, even if the website moves the page in question. This may be automatic and intermediate but it is not temporary; ForeverThere.com may not be able to rely upon the caching defence.

4.12.4.3.2 No modification

This second condition is that the intermediary must not modify the 'information', here a copyright work, to benefit from the defence.[452] This is self-explanatory.

4.12.4.3.3 No technical interference

The following three conditions are similar.[453] Each addresses the manner in which the information, or copyright work, is to be treated by the intermediary web cache. First, the intermediary must comply with conditions on access to the information. An example of this is where a password is required to access the

---

450   Art 13.
451   Reg 18(a).
452   Reg 18(b)(i).
453   Reg 18(b)(ii)–(iv).

copyright work and the web cache stores a copy of the pages *beyond* the password point. As a result this website would allow those without passwords to access the copyright work. Such a tactic would bring the intermediary outside the scope of the defence.

Second, the intermediary temporary copier must comply with any rules regarding the updating of the information, specified in a manner widely recognised and used by industry. Some websites include 'objects' which cannot be cached as they are defined as 'PRAGMA:No Cache' or must be dynamically retrieved each time they are accessed, say, from a database. If a web cache were to circumvent these well-known strategies, it would, again, lose the benefit of the defence.

Third, the intermediary must not interfere with the lawful use of technology, widely recognised and used by industry, to obtain data on the use of the information. Again, certain websites are concerned with the number of visits that they receive. There are certain ways of allowing the majority of one's website to be cached but ensure that a small element is required to be accessed from the original site. This allows the website to be cached but still to be able to know how many visits there have been to the site. Interference with this important data will be enough to prevent the cacher from relying on the defence.

4.12.4.3.4   Act expeditiously on obtaining actual knowledge

The final condition to permit legal temporary copying is that the intermediary must act expeditiously to remove or to disable access to the copyright work he has stored upon obtaining actual knowledge of the fact that the information at the initial source of the transmission has been removed from the network, or access to it has been disabled, or that a court or an administrative authority has ordered such removal or disablement.

In the main, this part of the defence will be taken to mean that the caching company has not been provided with 'notice' about the ordered or actual removal or disablement. This notice need not, however, be in writing and notice of actual removal or disablement certainly need not originate from a court. The court shall, however, take into account whether the cacher received the notice through its published email address, and whether the notice contains its sender's name, address, details and location of the unlawful information. The web cache need not, however, monitor those websites it caches from to check whether material has been removed.

Article 15(1) from the Electronic Commerce Directive states that:

> 'Member States shall not impose a general obligation on providers, when providing the services covered by [the] Articles [concerning mere conduit, caching and hosting], to monitor information which they transmit or store, nor a general obligation actively to seek facts or circumstances indicating illegal activity.'[454]

This Article is not explicitly implemented in the Regulations. The reason for this must be that Parliament believed that nothing in the Regulations did impose a

---

454   See *C-275/06 Promusicae* (18 July 2007), AG Opinion.

general obligation to monitor such facts and circumstances. It follows that the Regulations do not, in effect, force those who cache or take temporary copies for other justifiable reasons to monitor for changes on the websites they copy from, to be able to benefit from the defence.

This leaves the issue of how fast is 'expeditiously'. There is little doubt that this is quicker than 'reasonably quickly' but nevertheless will be assessed with reference to the facts and circumstances of the situation.

4.12.4.4   Hosting defence

It should be obvious from the discussion above that an Internet-specific defence will be very welcome to those intermediaries who find themselves unwittingly storing and distributing others' infringing material. These intermediary hosts of such material may be able to rely on two possible defences under the Electronic Commerce (EC Directive) Regulations 2002, regulation 19. These 'hosting' defences ensure that ISPs and other such service providers are not liable in any manner for storing the material and have been considered in detail in other chapters of this book and the same principles apply here and readers are urged to also refer to those sections for further details. This section outlines some further considerations in the context of copyright infringing material.

4.12.4.4.1   No authority or control

The common element for both defences is that the third party who originally provided the infringing material for storage is not to be acting under the service provider's 'authority' or 'control'[455]. Of course, often a service provider or website will have a contract with its members or customers. Will this constitute 'authority' or 'control'? This author and the DTI believe it will not.

The DTI states in its guidance on the Regulations that the concept of control or authority will be akin to 'effective control' under the Defamation Act 1996[456]. In other words, a mere contract to provide services to the third party will not be sufficient to bring the third party under the service provider's 'control' or 'authority'. The Regulations require a closer relationship such as between an employee, the third party, and an employer, the service provider.

An open question remains relating to whether or not the *ability* to control the third party will constitute control for the purposes of the first prong of the defence. After all, most, if not all service providers have the *ability* to remove material that is infringing. Indeed, in a worst-case scenario, a service provider can always simply 'pull the plug' and prevent *all* communication with the outside world; will that be 'control'?

US authority on a similar question is suggested that were such an interpretation to be applied, it would be contrary to the spirit of the equivalent legislation itself. It would, in effect, state that those who are able to comply with the onus to

---

455   Reg 19(b).
456   A Guide for Business to the Electronic Commerce (EC Directive) Regulations 2002, para 6.7(c).

remove material once notified must be able to remove the material and so are deemed to control it:

> 'First, the "right and ability to control" the infringing activity, as the concept is used in the [Digital Millennium Copyright Act ('DMCA')], cannot simply mean the ability of a service provider to remove or block access to materials posted on its website or stored in its system. To hold otherwise would defeat the purpose of the DMCA and render the statute internally inconsistent. The DMCA specifically requires a service provider to remove or block access to materials posted on its system when it receives notice of claimed infringement. See 17 U.S.C. §§ 512(c)(1)(C). The DMCA also provides that the limitations on liability only apply to a service provider that has "adopted and reasonably implemented ... a policy that provides for the termination in appropriate circumstances of [users] of the service provider's system or network who are repeat infringers." See 17 U.S.C. §§ 512(i)(1)(A). Congress could not have intended for courts to hold that a service provider loses immunity under the safe harbor provision of the DMCA because it engages in acts that are specifically required by the DMCA.'[457]

Having determined that the person storing the infringing material was not so acting under the authority or control of the service provider, one can look to the key elements of the two hosting defences.

4.12.4.4.2   No actual knowledge and no awareness

The first defence is essentially that the service provider must be unwittingly hosting the infringing material[458]. This is expressed in two parts. First, the service provider hosting the material must not have 'actual knowledge' that the storage was in breach of any law. The second part is that the host must *also* 'not be aware of facts or circumstances' from which it would have been apparent that the activity or information was unlawful.

4.12.4.4.3   No actual knowledge of breach of law

In the main, this part of the defence will be taken to mean that the hosting company or person has not been provided with 'notice' about the infringing material. This notice need not, however, be in writing and it certainly need not originate from a court. Indeed, an email to a published email address about the damaging code, or even a telephone warning, is likely to be enough to put the provider 'on notice' and so be fixed with actual knowledge. There is therefore no particular form which will provide the requisite 'actual' knowledge; it is a question of fact for the court. This said, a court will, however, have particular regard to whether a service provider received the notice through an email address published on the provider's website. The court will also have regard to the extent to which the notice includes the sender's full name and address, details of the location of the

---

457   *Hendrickson v Ebay Inc* 165 F.Supp.2d 1082 (CD Cal 2001).
458   Reg 19(a).

dubious material and the details of the unlawful nature of the activity or information in question[459].

In the well-publicised US summary judgment *Religious Technology Center v Netcom Online Communications Services Inc*, a member of the Centre left the religion and then published the centre's materials through a Netcom Internet connection on a Usenet newsgroup: alt.religion.scientology[460]. The Centre sued Netcom for both direct and contributory infringement of copyright. While the court was sure that there was no direct infringement, it was clear that the claimants[461]:

'raised a genuine issue of fact regarding whether Netcom should have known that Erlich [the former member] was infringing their copyright after receiving a letter [fixing them with notice] from [claimants], whether Netcom substantially participated in the infringement, and whether Netcom has a valid fair use defense. *Accordingly, Netcom is not entitled to summary judgment on [claimants'] claim of contributory copyright infringement.*' [462]

In this case, therefore, the letter from the claimants was the means by which the service provider was put on notice. This is relevant. Even though the Regulations state that a court shall take into account whether or not email was used to serve the notice, the Regulations do not prescribe that email must be used. Indeed, service providers and other intermediaries should ensure that all their 'official' addresses, in particular registered office addresses, are staffed with individuals who can spot, and act upon, such notices.

4.12.4.4.4 No awareness of facts or circumstances

Even if the service provider has no actual knowledge, to act as a defence to claims to damages, they must still be able to demonstrate that they have no awareness of relevant facts or circumstances which would lead them to believe the material was unlawful. If they cannot do this, they will need to rely on the second defence to escape liability.

For much infringing material stored with service providers, this will be very difficult to prove. Most sound recordings are still not available in a digital format which can be stored on a website; CDs remain the main form of their distribution. Consequently, the storage of a well-known sound recording on a website is very likely to be infringing and also likely to be within the awareness of the service provider once alerted. Admittedly, certain material is encrypted or given coded titles; here it is more difficult to prove awareness. In most situations, however, a service provider will therefore be unable to demonstrate the necessary level of unawareness to 'pass' this second test. As a consequence, they will also not benefit from the first hosting defence.

---

459   Reg 22.
460   907 F. Supp. 1361 (N.D. Cal. 1995).
461   Emphasis added.
462   The action was entirely settled on 22 August 1996.

4.12.4.4.5   Expeditious action on notice

The second hosting defence, again as a prerequisite requires the infringer not to be acting under the authority or control of the intermediary. Once this is satisfied, the service provider will have the benefit of the defence if they act expeditiously to remove or disable access to it as soon as they know about it.[463]

4.12.4.4.6   Remove or disable expeditiously

This requirement is essentially that the service provider must act to stop any further harm as soon as they know about it. The Regulations state that 'upon obtaining such knowledge or awareness [the service provider must act] expeditiously to remove or to disable access to the information.'[464]

The concept of 'actual knowledge' and the requisite 'awareness' is discussed above but 'awareness' in this context deserves more attention. The concept of 'awareness' is a wide one; it seems to encompass the service provider having a general 'sense' of the state of the technical and legal standards for unlawful material. Does this mean that a service provider unwittingly hosting infringing material will be liable because a well-respected website publishes details of the infringement of the copyright work? The answer is 'no' for two good reasons.

First, the Electronic Commerce Regulations implement the Electronic Commerce Directive. Article 15(1) states that:

> 'Member States shall not impose a general obligation on providers, when providing the services covered by [the] Articles [concerning mere conduit, caching and hosting], to monitor information which they transmit or store, nor a general obligation actively to seek facts or circumstances indicating illegal activity.'

This Article is not explicitly implemented in the Regulations. The reason for this must be that Parliament believed that nothing in the Regulations did impose a general obligation to monitor such facts and circumstances. It follows that the Regulations do not, in effect, force service providers to watch the press and websites for details of possible infringements to be able to benefit from the defence.

The second justification for the unwitting service provider not being liable is that, on awareness or knowledge, they are required to remove or disable access to the infringing material. Of course, if all they know is that the material is being copied 'somewhere', how are they to remove or disable access to it? They would need actively to search for it on their network. As explained above, a general obligation to seek or search for such information, is not envisaged within scope the legislation.

Of course, where the service provider acts to *facilitate* the infringement, they will be deemed to have the requisite knowledge but not to have acted quickly enough. In the US case *Playboy Enterprises Inc v George Frena*, Frena operated a bulletin board on a subscription basis.[465] The board stored copies of Playboy's

---

463   Reg 19(a)(ii).
464   S 19(a)(ii).
465   839 F Supp 1552 (MD Fla 1993).

pictures but these were not posted there without Frena's knowledge or awareness: he actually removed from the photographs Playboy's own text and substituted his own name and contact details! Under the Electronic Commerce Regulations, any operator who did such an activity would then certainly have (or be deemed to have) the requisite awareness that the uploaded images infringed Playboy's copyright. They will then need to remove or disable access to them expeditiously.

This then leaves the issue of how fast is 'expeditiously'. There is little doubt that this is quicker than 'reasonably quickly' but nevertheless will be assessed with reference to the facts and circumstances of the situation. It can be said with some certainty that a service provider who is sent a specific notice about an infringing movie file on a Thursday evening will need to act well before the weekend to do so expeditiously.

---

26. A software developer uses some executable code on his website to make the viewer's mouse cursor appear to shine a beam of light on the current web page like a torch. A manufacturer of high-durability torches copies the code and uses it on its site. It docs not credit nor pay for its use of the code. Some time later a small retailer copies the majority of the manufacturer's site substituting its details on the contact page. This retailer is sued for infringement of copyright and passing off. It should not rely on a defence that the manufacturer has also copied a copyright work; as long as the manufacturer has notified the software developer and undertakes to account for the developer's proportion of the damages, the claimant has a valid claim of copyright infringement.

4.13 COPYRIGHT INFRINGEMENT AND THE INTERNET: EXAMPLES

In this section we consider some specific infringement scenarios in the context of the Internet.

4.13.1 Email

4.13.1.1 Infringement by recipient

This section considers what might constitute infringement of the copyright in someone's email. It is assumed that there is copyright in the email. When an email is received, it has already been copied; it is copied into the memory and probably the hard disk drive of the receiver's machine. That much copying will certainly be implied by the common law and statute not to be infringement: it is necessary for business efficacy and can be implied by sending it over the Internet rather than, say, by post. What is not implied is for an individual (rather than a server because that is likely to be an essential part of a technological process)[466]

---

466 See the discussion above relating to the Directive on Harmonisation of Certain Aspects of Copyright and Related Rights in the Information Society, art 5.1.

to forward the message without either an express or implied licence to do so. A good example of this is any email that is headed 'Private & Confidential'.

> 27. Paul sends an email to Robbie. It ends, 'Actually, you should tell Charlotte about this.' Robbie forwards the email to Charlotte who then replies to Paul. Paul is upset that Charlotte read the email, but he has no legal redress in copyright. His endnote was an implied licence that Robbie would not infringe the copyright by copying the whole message to Charlotte. Charlotte also does not infringe Paul's copyright; her licence is implied by the common law.

4.13.1.2   Infringement by Internet service provider

It has been described that an Internet service provider may legally hold a copy of all its member's emails until they are collected by the member. But there are times, say for backup or security purposes, that the emails are retained for longer. Internet service providers are advised to alert members to this additional copying by including such a statement in their terms and conditions with each member. The legal difficulty is that, while a member can provide a licence to their Internet service provider in respect of emails authored by them, the member cannot provide a licence on behalf of others for emails sent to them. Of course here, the Internet service provider can rely on its hosting defence in reg 19 of the Electronic Commerce Regulations 2002 as discussed above.

4.13.1.3   Infringement by forums

There are two discrete issues concerned with controllers of bulletin boards and storage website infringing copyright. The first is the issue of what the controller can do with copyright material owned and posted by its members. This will be discussed presently. The second issue is the liability a controller of a forum has in respect of copyright material *not* owned by its members but nevertheless posted on the forum. This issue of infringing material is discussed in the section below.

Every email posted by its author to a forum, bulletin board or conversation thread carries with it an implied licence, from common law. In addition, the Electronic Commerce Regulation's hosting defence provides a defence for the host in respect of any unwitting infringement. This licence and defence permit the copying of the email or message on the server itself and also onto any other viewer's computer that is legitimately permitted *by the controller* to access the email. What is uncertain is the extent to which the controller may repost or authorise reposting to other forums.

> 28. Mr Smith is a contributor to alt.female.erotica and ends all his postings with 'Not for reposting or redistribution on any other newsgroup.' Ms Jones reposts his messages to a forum dealing with women's exploitation. That reposting constitutes an unlicensed copy of the whole of a copyright work; it is an infringement of Mr Smith's copyright.

4.13.1.3.1   Human 'requests' to infringe

When a message is posted to a forum, it enters the forum at the 'request' of a human. So, Ms Jones will have used her connection to the Internet to provide Mr Smith's message, in digital form, to an Internet service provider which hosts the forum. Because this message is, or contains a large part, of a copyright work without licence from Mr Smith (the owner), Ms Jones will infringe copyright in the work.

4.13.1.3.2   Server 'response' to infringe

As soon as Ms Jones clicked the 'send' or 'OK' icon to post Mr Smith's message, this message was sent to the forum automatically. Many computers were involved in the request. These include: the first Internet service provider; possibly a second Internet service provider hosting a copy of the Usenet forum; all the other Internet service providers hosting a copy of the forum and the intermediary servers acting as conduits between the previous three 'families' of server.

We have seen that the posted message infringes Mr Smith's copyright. It can also be said with reasonable certainty that each of these computers has copied a substantial part of the work without licence from Mr Smith. However, the Electronic Commerce Regulation's hosting defence will provide a defence for the host in respect of any unwitting infringement until they receive a possible complaint from Mr Smith or are otherwise put 'on notice'.

4.13.1.3.3   Commercial forums

A controller of a commercial forum may attempt to assert copyright in the compilation that constitutes each conversation thread, and generally by express agreement, a licence over any individual's postings. As a result of such an express agreement it is likely that there will be terms that prevent any repostings by individuals of others' emails. An individual is unlikely to be contractually restricted from posting his own message elsewhere[467].

To republish an entire conversation thread to another forum may be an infringement of the copyright over the compilation where that compilation is protected by copyright.

---

29. A member of the Mechanics Forum is also a member of the Engineers Forum. These are operated by two rival service providers. The member reposts from the Mechanics Forum to the Engineers Forum a conversation between him and another mechanic. This lasts about 15 lines out of a thread that is made up from over 200 lines from 40 different contributors. The controller of the Mechanics Forum threatens the mechanic with an action for copyright infringement. The controller has three significant legal hurdles. First, it must be proved that there is a copyright in the compilation; second, that it, rather than all the 40 contributors jointly, own the compilation; and third, that the taking is a substantial part of the copyrighted conversation thread.

---

467   Or rather, such a contractual term would have to be drawn to the attention of a new member to be enforceable as it would be unusual.

Even if the conversation thread is not protected by copyright, for want of skill, labour or judgment, it is possibly protected as a database. Even if not, the service provider may still be able to assert its contractual rights. This is achieved by ensuring that every person who is allowed to access a conversation thread enters a contract which stipulates that no material, other than the member's own, will be reposted elsewhere. A person who does repost the material will be in breach of the contract. Reposting a thread from a commercial forum to a Usenet newsgroup will almost always be a clear copyright infringement of any compilation right and of the rights held by the individual author of the posted messages.

4.13.1.4   Infringement using peer-to-peer networks

This chapter has already considered the manner in which a central repository of files may be liable if these files infringe copyright. However, there is more than one way to store a group of digital files for access across the Internet. Another way is to *distribute* the storage and spread the files out across more than one computer. This method has spawned a huge number of programs and websites, singularly created, to facilitate the storage and distribution of infringing sound recordings, pictures, programs and even movies. The English law relating to these systems is described below; first, the technology.

4.13.1.4.1   Peer-to-peer storage systems

Suppose we wanted to store two files, 1 and 2. We could, as mentioned, put them both on a central server. A person could access the central server, search for one of the files, and with permission, download it. The alternative distribution method could work as follows. We could use two servers, A & B, each storing one of the files only but *both* holding details of where the files are stored. Let us say that server A stores file 1 and server B stores file 2. Each server will also store an 'index' which indicates that file 1 is found on server A and file 2 on server B. If one now wanted to download one of the files one could contact *either* server and it would either supply the download itself or use its index to direct you to its neighbour.

Now imagine that there are hundreds of thousands of servers and many millions of files spread amongst them. Now add to that network a more sophisticated index. Instead of each of the servers holding an index of the files held across the network, they each hold an index of their own files *and the locations of their neighbours* in the network. Now search for a file, say, 231. The first server you contact, say AAA, will search for the file on its hard drive. If it is there, you may download it. If not, server AAA will ask the same request of each of its neighbours, say, BBB, ABC, and FGH. Again, if they hold file 231, they will allow you to download it. If they too do not store the file they will ask their few neighbours the same request. Within seconds the search for file 231 will propagate across the network until it is found or all the servers have failed to find it.

Finally, instead of thinking of these servers as being special computers such as those used by Internet service providers, think of them as any old PC hooked up the Internet used by a regular individual. Suddenly you will be imagining a huge network of individuals distributing files, or even parts of files, amongst themselves without any central body either 'regulating' them or knowing the complete scope of the files stored. Try to picture about 62 million people currently. And, unfortunately for copyright owners, think of the files as software, movies, and sound recordings. Suddenly you are thinking of the proliferation of a peer-to-peer network just like Napster (now a legitimate service provider)[468] and its replacements.

4.13.1.4.2 User infringement

Users of such peer-to-peer systems generally conduct two activities. They copy their own material and store it on their own hard drive. They also download material from others' hard drives to their own and play it. Without a defence close at hand, these two activities would constitute infringement of the works. When one loads material onto one's hard drive, say a sound recording, the recording is copied and this copy is substantial. This therefore amounts, without more, to an infringement of the copyright in the sound recording (and any works included in it). There is no appropriate defence to this despite it being such a widespread activity.

Of course, users of a peer-to-peer network not only copy such works, they also title them and position them on their computer in such a way as to allow other members of the network to copy the works.

The Copyright, Designs and Patents Act 1988, s 16(2) states:

'[c]opyright in a work is infringed by a person whom without the licence of the copyright owner does, *or authorises another to do*, any of the acts restricted by copyright.'

In a peer-to-peer network, the restricted act that would be complained of is the copying and issue of copies of the work to the public[469]. An authorisation has been defined as[470]: 'a grant or purported grant, which may be expressed or implied, of the right to do the act complained of.' Indeed, users, with great care, specifically include some files within one 'folder' allowing others to copy them ensuring, presumably, that their personal and private files are kept well away from this published folder. It follows that the users are purporting to confer on all the other users of the network the right to copy the infringing works.

There are difficulties in suing individuals. Not only is the process expensive and fragmented but its impact as an effective deterrent is uncertain and some actions have resulted in negative publicity for the claimant. This does not mean

---

468 Napster was ultimately a victim of its own success. Its massive index of users' infringing sound recordings drew the attention of the record industry and its lawyers. After numerous cases it was eventually forced by the US courts to select out infringing material from its central index of stored files. In March 2001 the record industry duly supplied Napster with a list of 135,000 songs to be removed from its service. Napster was not able to comply and after an abortive acquisition by Bertelsmann, moved into a bankruptcy liquidation in September 2002. See *A&M Records v Napster Inc* 239 F 3d 1004 (9th Cir 2001).

469 Copyright, Designs and Patents Act 1988, s 16(1).

470 *CBS Songs Ltd v Amstrad Consumer Electronics plc* [1988] AC 1013 at 1054 per Lord Templeman, HL.

that claims against infringers are not made however. In the UK the British Phonographic Industry has brought many successful claims against illegal file sharers resulting in payments of up to £4,000 each in compensation.

4.13.1.4.3   Other infringement

Apart from the innocent Internet service providers and telecommunications companies who pass these infringing works to and fro (only storing them for a short period), and benefit from the Electronic Commerce Regulations, regs 17 and 18, who else is involved in these peer-to-peer networks? The programmers of the peer-to-peer software and those who distribute it, of course.

Such persons are the prime target for action but even these claims are without their difficulties and we have yet to see an action brought in the UK. The providers of P2P services are highly skilled at structuring their networks and systems both technically and geographically in order to minimise the risks to which they are exposed. Not only is it often difficult to even find the culprits and overcome the jurisdictional issues associated with bringing an action but there are then the legal hurdles of demonstrating a clear chain of liability between their service and the actions of and materials provided, not by them, but the users themselves.

In the UK, the leading case is *CBS v Amstrad*. In that case the defendant manufactured and sold music systems including a double cassette deck for copying tapes. There was little doubt in the minds of the House of Lords that a number of members of the public used them for copying pre-recorded tapes, so infringing the copyright in the works recorded on the copied tape. The House of Lords nevertheless held that the defendant had not *authorised* the infringements which would be committed by the public.

Lord Templeman gave the leading speech, stating:

> '… an authorisation means a grant or purported grant, which may be express or implied, of the right to do the act complained of. Amstrad conferred on the purchaser the power to copy but did not grant or purport to grant the right to copy.'[471]

The same can be said of peer-to-peer software and its sellers. It is well known that the software can be used to copy copyright works. What cannot be proved is that the software is purporting to grant rights to copy *a particular* file. And without this specificity all the software confers is the 'power to copy' but no purported right to copy.

Successful actions have, however, been brought in other jurisdictions. In particular, the *Grokster* case[472] in the US, which turned on different interpretations of *Sony Corp. v Universal City Studios, Inc*[473] (the 'Sony rule'). In *Sony* the Supreme Court held that the sale and distribution of video recorders could not, of

---

471   *CBS Songs Ltd v Amstrad Consumer Electronics plc* [1988] AC 1013 at 1054 per Lord Templeman, HL.
472   *Metro Goldwyn Mayer Studios Inc. v Grokster Ltd* 545 US 913, 125 SCt 2764 (2005).
473   464 US 417 (1984).

itself, give rise to contributory copyright infringement liability even though the defendant knew the machines were being used to commit infringement. Essentially, the Sony rule means that, under US law, if the product at issue is *not* capable of substantial or commercially significant non-infringing uses, then the copyright owner need only show that the defendant had constructive knowledge of the infringement. On the other hand, if the product at issue *is* capable of substantial or commercially significant non-infringing uses, then the copyright owner must demonstrate that the defendant had reasonable knowledge of specific infringing activity and failed to act on that knowledge to prevent infringement.

The parallels with *Amstrad* are particularly relevant from a UK perspective because the US Supreme Court eventually held that the P2P software and services offered by Grokster were distinguishable from *Sony*. Although it is not binding on the UK courts, the court's analysis of the role Grokster played in contrast to Sony is worth considering. In the *Grokster* case the Supreme Court analysed the Sony rule in detail but concluded that the case could be decided on alternative grounds, namely active inducement. It held that:

> 'One who distributes a device with the object of promoting its use to infringe copyright, as shown by clear expression or other affirmative steps taken to foster infringement, going beyond mere distribution with knowledge of third-party action, is liable for the resulting acts of infringement by third parties using the device, regardless of the device's lawful uses.'

The Supreme Court found 'a powerful argument for imposing indirect liability' given the scale of infringing downloads using the respondents' software. It contrasted the facts of *Grokster* from those of *Sony*. In the *Grokster* case 'evidence of active steps taken to encourage direct infringement, such as advertising an infringing use or instructing how to engage in an infringing use, shows an affirmative intent that the product be used to infringe.' This was distinguished from a *Sony*-type scenario in which 'a defendant merely sells a commercial product suitable for some lawful use.'

On the evidence, the respondents' unlawful objective was 'unmistakable'. Three key features of the evidence of intent were identified:

> the respondents marketed their services to former Napster users, and this indicated 'a principal, if not exclusive, intent to bring about infringement';

The respondents made no attempt to develop filtering tools or other mechanisms to combat the infringing activity. In contrast to the Ninth Circuit, which had treated that failure as irrelevant because it had found that the respondents lacked an independent duty to monitor their users' activity, the Supreme Court took this as evidence pointing to 'intentional facilitation of their users' infringement'; and the commercial model used by Grokster and StreamCast was also significant. The business was funded by the sale of advertising space and the targeting of ads to users' screens. This meant that the commercial success of the software depended on high-volume use, which in turn relied on the lucrative infringing rather than non-infringing uses. This evidence alone would not justify an inference of unlawful intent, said the Court, but was significant in the overall context.

By distinguishing the facts of *Grokster*, the Supreme Court has reached the outcome sought by the entertainment industry without displacing the Sony rule. The Court resisted calls by content providers and creators to elaborate further on the Sony rule to 'add a more quantified description of the point of balance between protection and commerce when liability rests solely on distribution with knowledge that unlawful use will occur', preferring instead to 'leave further consideration of the Sony rule for a day when that may be required.'

The *Grokster* ruling will certainly make it more difficult for technology providers to hide, disingenuously, from secondary liability behind the Sony rule where they are complicit in copyright infringement. The more difficult question is whether the latest ruling provides enough protection for providers whose legitimate technologies become hijacked for unlawful uses and whether the UK courts would follow the same line of argument.

4.14   SEARCH ENGINES AND WEB LINKS

Search engines operate by providing hyperlinks to websites matching the user's search. Hyperlinks to other websites or content such as third party files can also be found on other types of websites. The content linked to is not created or controlled by the search engine or website, but can it still have any liability for providing the access to it?

Some cases have suggested that liability may be established. In the Dutch case *BREIN v Techno Design 'Internet Programming' BV*,[474] concerning the website ZoeKMP3.NL, the Court of Appeal found the website operators liable for providing links to infringing MP3 files. Similarly, in *Cooper v Universal Music Australia Pty Ltd*[475] the Australian Full Federal Court found that the operator and host of the website 'mp3s4free' which provided links to illegal MP3 files are liable for authorising copyright infringements. The website which was owned and operated by Stephen Cooper and, although it did not itself contain any music files, it contained links to remote websites on which MP3 digital music files – the majority of them infringing – were stored. By clicking on these links users could download the MP3 files direct from these remote sites. The remote websites on which the recordings were stored were not owned or operated by the defendants. The action was brought by the major record labels and other rights holders. Cooper's appeal focussed on the meaning of the term 'authorisation'. He challenged the finding of the primary judge that simply by providing the hyperlinks to the MP3 files he had authorised the making of infringing copies or authorised the communication to the public of infringing copies by the uploaders.

Significantly, from a UK perspective, Cooper tried to rely on the observations of the House of Lords in *CBS v Amstrad,* and the later Australian case of *Nationwide News v Copyright Agency*,[476] that 'a person does not authorise an

---

474   [2006] ECDR 21.
475   [2006] FCAFC 187.
476   (1996) 136 ALR 273.

infringement merely because he or she knows that another person might infringe the copyright and take no steps to prevent the infringement'. However Branson J took the view that Cooper had 'engaged in additional relevant conduct' which took him outside the scope of this observation. She concluded that:

'a person's power to prevent the doing of an act comprised in a copyright includes the person's power not to facilitate the doing of that act by, for example, making available to the public a technical capacity calculated to lead to the doing of that act'.

It was Cooper's deliberate choice to establish and maintain his website in a form which did not give him the power immediately to prevent, or immediately to restrict, Internet users from using links on his website to access remote websites for the purpose of copying sound recordings in which copyright subsisted. Cooper was therefore liable for having authorised the infringements carried out by the uploaders and downloaders of the files.

Some commentators have warned that the decision creates legal uncertainty for more general search engines such as Google, and for web hosts. Cases involving authorisation of copyright infringements by others involve judgements over degree and will therefore always turn on their own facts, which makes it difficult to draw general conclusions. The risk is debatable, because of the particular facts of this case and the availability a search engine would have of the defences pursuant to the Electronic Commerce Regulations as discussed in sections 4.12.4.3 and 4.12.4.4 above.

Cooper himself tried to rely on an analogy between his website's facilities and those of Google, citing a US decision *Perfect 10 Inc v Google Inc*.[477] This was rejected as 'unhelpful' by the court firstly because the US authority turned on 'fair use' which was not relevant here and secondly because Google is a general purpose search engine rather than a website designed specifically to facilitate the downloading of music files. The *Cooper* decision turned on the fact that the primary purpose of the site was to provide links to music files the 'overwhelming majority' of which were infringing. The court did not consider where the line should be drawn – but a case involving a more multi-purpose search engine would be far less clear-cut.

4.15 WEBSITES

This section now looks to the other side of the coin and considers how the copyright in a website may be infringed. This is an issue often overlooked by those who deal with the World Wide Web; merely because a site is available for all to view does not mean that all the images and applets and text can be used at will. It is all too often said that, because a website is in the 'public domain' (whatever

---

477   416 F Supp 2d 828 (CD Cal 2006); but this decision was reversed in part by the US Court of Appeals for the Ninth Circuit.

that term legally means) that the website can be freely copied. This is a classic misunderstanding of the nature of copyright: merely because a copyright owner chooses to publish his work in a particular way does not entitle the rest of the world to copy the work without permission.

Framing, linking and searching are integral aspects of the World Wide Web. For this reason, many have sought to deny the application of the law to prevent it. Of course, there are many circumstances when the activities may be illegal. A prior contract, maybe even one at the 'entry' to the site, may be breached. The use of a frame or particular link may infringe the claimant's trade marks leaving viewers confused into whose text they are reading. After examining backup copies of websites, this section considers the way in which copyright and database rights may be utilised to prevent such framing and repeated searching.

4.15.1   Backup copies

Some users believe that a website comes complete with an implied licence to take a backup copy, on disk rather than the normal memory only.[478] Indeed, the 'offline viewing' facility standard with Microsoft's Internet Explorer makes it trivial to create these copies. There are also useful websites that allow one to make a perfect copy of a website and to hold that copy on its servers. This is unlikely to be implied by either the courts or the law. It has been discussed that a website is a program for the purposes of copyright. Under the Copyright, Designs and Patents Act 1988, s 50A(1) lawful users of a computer program do not infringe copyright by making a backup copy of it *which it is necessary for him to have for the purposes of his lawful use*. It will rarely be necessary to take a backup copy of a website. The material that is being backed up is already available 24 hours a day on the website that originally supplied it. It may be *convenient* not to have to re-access a website but is seldom *necessary*. And as more owners of websites compete for advertising income they are increasingly aware of the need to have viewers re-accessing their pages to have 'sticky' content. The more 'hits' on a page each hour, the more one may be able to charge advertisers for space.

Increasingly, however, websites have explicit restrictions on copying in certain situations. Viewers and users of websites should be cautious of these restrictions which may be found in the context of a positive licence. Some prevent viewers from even making a printed copy of a site. Other sites prevent the use of their graphics[479]. These explicit licences are not added on sites as rhetoric. If contravened they will have the result that the viewer has infringed copyright. If this infringement is then 'advertised' by, say, posting a copied graphic on one's own website, the copyright owner may well take action.

478   A website viewed but not saved will not be available for re-viewing after the computer is switched off and then on again. A website saved to disk will be re-viewable even after the computer has been switched off.

479   The popular browsers allow users to copy a graphic to be used as the computer screen's backdrop; even this may be infringement by the viewer.

30. An online newspaper has a classified adverts section which allows a user to search for a particular item for sale. Where this item is not currently advertised, the newspaper automatically searches its competitors' online classifieds and provides a link to suitable items for sale on their sites. No doubt many sites linked-to will be happy to benefit from this seemingly altruistic link. They are receiving additional traffic to their site. However, if their terms and conditions bar such 'deep-linking' the online newspaper will be infringing the database right which subsists in the collection of adverts by utilising the database as an unlawful user.

4.15.2   Framing

The World Wide Web was created to link together documents in a seamless fashion. Like a 'live' footnote, a link on one document can be clicked upon and the linked document is then retrieved. The browser replaces the linking document with a freshly retrieved document; this new document may have been stored on a different web server. A browser can also be instructed to display on one screen a collage of images and text all from different web servers at the same time. This appears to the viewer as one document from one source; in fact and at law there are a number of different owners of the copyright in these images and some of them may see this selective copying as an infringement of copyright.

The commercial concern at this framing is evident from the US case *Washington Post Co v Total News Inc.*[480] Total News operated a website deriving its revenue from selling advertising on the site. To attract advertising, the site provided its audience with news articles published by the claimants. Each article enclosed had been within a 'frame' around which was the totalnews.com logo and advertising. There is one commercial issue which needs to be highlighted before discussing the legal aspects of the case. Each of the claimants also sold advertising on their site next to their articles. The defendant, therefore, was competing for this advertising revenue but was not troubled with first having to write the content; it merely had to gather the stories together.

The claimant's complaint included allegations of trade mark infringement but also copyright infringement of the text of the articles. The case was settled and the defendant agreed not to republish material from the claimant's sites as long as it was entitled to link to this material without passing off or infringing the claimant's trade marks. Paragraph 4(d) of the Settlement Order provides:

'[Claimants] agree that Defendants may link from Totalnews.com website or any other website to any [claimant's] website, provided that: … (d) each [claimant's] agreement to permit linking by Defendants remains revocable, an IS business day's notice in accordance with [manner of providing notice] at each [claimant's] sole discretion. Revocation by any [claimant] shall not affect any other terms and conditions set forth herein.'

---

480   97 Civ 190 (PKL) (SDNY complaint filed 20 February 1997).

This clause indicates that the claimants believed that at law they were entitled to prevent a mere link being made to their sites. It is submitted, as has been discussed, that a link of itself does not infringe the copyright in the title, or headline of the article because it is likely not to qualify for protection. Further, it is submitted that there is also no work qualifying for protection in a single URL which points to the content-bearing site and article. It is therefore conceivable that only trade mark issues would entitle the blocking of a link to one's site as has been discussed earlier. No doubt for these and other reasons, the Settlement Order continues:

'If Defendant refuse [*sic*] to cease linking upon notice, and any [claimant] brings an action to enforce its rights under this subparagraph, it shall be an affirmative defense that Defendant's conduct does not otherwise infringe or violate [claimant's] rights under any theory of any intellectual property, unfair competition or other law.'

4.15.3   Making an unlicensed article

The copyright owner of a computer graphic used within a website has the right to license, or choose not to license, almost any use of the image and material. What is questionable is whether it is an infringement, not to copy another's graphics or text, but instead to include a command that instructs the *viewer's* computer to copy those graphics. Although this is untested in the UK courts, it is submitted that, inclusion without permission of the owner of these in-line graphics or other frames may infringe their copyright. There is certainly copying; no website can be viewed without there being copying. The question that arises is who is doing the copying? From a technical perspective the copying is actually being conducted by the viewer *with the instruction* from the framer's website.

Section 24(1)(a) of the Act provides that it is a secondary infringement to make an unlicensed article specifically designed or adapted for making copies of the copyright work when the maker knows or has reason to believe that it is to be used to make infringing copies. It is submitted that a line of code can be an article and that as the URL refers to a specific graphic or element on a specific website this article is specifically designed for making copies of a work.[481] The final requirement is a guilty mind that the article would be used to make infringing copies. This also is satisfied. Unless the viewer turns off the automatic loading of images, the framer's programmer knows that a copy will be made of the material. As the programmer is the person who has electronically contacted the material's true site, this person will know that the copy will infringe. It will be outside the bounds of most implied or explicit licences on websites. It is clearly arguable that using in-line links or frames without a licence is secondary copyright infringement.

481   Unlike a tape recorder that makes copies per se rather than makes copies of specific CDs.

4.15.4   Deep links and spiders

Occasionally, a website finds its links being systematically 'searched' by another website. This is often conducted so that the searching website can keep abreast of, say, the prices on the harvested website. This may allow the harvesting website to conduct 'comparison' shopping across many similar websites. It is often called 'spidering'. Further, a series of links from the harvested site may then appear on the other site, so-called 'deep links'.

In *Ticketmaster Corpn v Microsoft Corpn*, Ticketmaster, the world's largest provider of computerised ticket services, complained that Microsoft, the world's largest software company, was operating a website which contained various links to Ticketmaster's website[482]. Many of these links were created automatically by Microsoft repeatedly searching the Ticketmaster site for particular items of interest.

One could imagine that Ticketmaster would be flattered and would benefit financially from this link. Instead, Ticketmaster suggested that Microsoft was 'feathering its own nest at Ticketmaster's expense'. Microsoft, however, merely 'referenced' Ticketmaster's site; it did not include on its site any of Ticketmaster's content, only its brand. As a consequence, Microsoft was not infringing the significant copyright held by Ticketmaster. Ticketmaster's complaint therefore focused only on trade mark issues.

Under English law, this case and others like it, may well involve an application of database rights to the facts.

4.15.4.1   Deep links, spiders and database rights

It is argued above that many websites will be supported by databases. And because of the investment in these databases, they will be protected by database rights. What remains to be answered is how these database rights may be infringed by taking deep links from them and spiders over them.

Often those who deep link to websites do so both automatically and often. As in the *Ticketmaster* case these individuals and companies are trying to 'fill' their website with links from others. Where this is prevented by terms and conditions applicable to the website, these individuals will not be lawful users. They are therefore re-utilising (and probably have extracted) the various links that they sport on their site. These links form part of the database that is protected by the database right. All that remains for factual analysis is whether or not the parts re-utilised and extracted form a substantial part of the database. One will recall that the concept of 'substantial' here is defined by the legislation (unlike for copyright) as being qualitative or quantitative or both. Where the links copied, time and time again, are those most pertinent or most important, there will be a good basis to plead that the links form a substantial part of the whole database.

---

482   CV 97–3055 RAP (CD Cal filed 28 April 1997).

31. A meteorological website is funded by advertising and features seven-day fore-casts for about 50 popular holiday destinations. One can search the site with reference to a city name, a country and even a desired temperature. A travel website creates a program that automatically 'grabs' ten relevant links from the weather website and inserts them next to its descriptions of its package holidays. The weather site uses a database to drive its sophisticated search engine. The travel website is not only extract-ing from the database but also re-utilising it by publishing the links on its own site. Bearing in mind the travel website systematically and repeatedly copies ten links, it is likely to be a substantial extraction from the database.

4.16   JURISDICTION OVER INFRINGEMENT

This section considers the type of situation where a UK copyright work on the Internet is dealt with abroad in a way that would be an infringement here. The sort of situation considered is where a web developer in the US uses a UK copy-right graphic on his website that is maintained in Holland but accessed through-out the world. In this situation do the English courts have any jurisdiction to hear complaints of an infringement from the UK copyright owner?

4.16.1   Infringement of UK copyright abroad

The English courts' approach to foreign infringement of English intellectual property has already been considered in relation to trade marks. Some of the con-clusions reached there will be equally applicable here. Infringement is a legal term in relation to a legal right granted within a territory. One cannot infringe a UK copyright abroad because 'abroad' is outside the width of the monopoly granted by the UK legislation:

> 'The owner of the copyright in a work has, in accordance with the following provisions of this Chapter, the exclusive right to do the following acts *in the United Kingdom* ...'[483]

Copyright is, in essence, a territorial right. One can perform actions in relation to a UK copyright work that are the descriptive equivalent of infringement but those actions will not be infringement unless within the UK territory. Courts have been restraining the rights of copyright holders in this way for many years.

> 'It is therefore clear that copyright under the English Act is strictly defined in terms of territory. The intangible right which is copyright is merely a right to do certain acts exclusively in the United Kingdom: only acts done in the United Kingdom constitute infringement either direct or indirect of that right.'[484]

---

483   Copyright, Designs and Patents Act 1988, s 16(1). Emphasis added.
484   *Def Lepp Music v Stuart-Brown* [1986] RPC 273 at 275.

This means that establishing where an act of infringement is committed is essential. an activity carried on *outside* the UK that is purported to be an infringement *inside* the UK is problematic. The courts are attempting to resolve the conflict of laws where the intellectual property right is dealt with in a territory other than the one that granted the right initially. To illustrate, to copy in the US a UK literary work is clearly outside the jurisdiction of the English courts: the action that constitutes the infringement occurs outside the UK. But these are not the only types of infringement. There are situations where the *action* takes place outside the UK, but the action may still be litigated in the UK, because the Brussels Regulation permits the trial of the nevertheless *foreign* infringement in the UK's courts. There are other situations (as opposed to 'rights to sue') where the action takes place outside the UK, but the infringement occurs within the territory.[485]In *ABKCO Music and Records Inc v Music Collection International Ltd* the Court of Appeal was faced with an authorisation to infringe made from abroad.[486] ABKCO claimed a British copyright over certain sound recordings made by Sam Cooke. The second defendant was a Danish company that carried on no business in the UK but granted a licence to the first defendant to manufacture and sell copies of the sound recordings in the UK.

ABKCO sued under the Copyright, Designs and Patents Act 1988, s 16(2) of which states:

> '[c]opyright in a work is infringed by a person who without the licence of the copyright owner does, *or authorises another to do*, any of the acts restricted by the copyright.'[487]

The restricted act complained of being authorised was the copying and issue of copies of the work to the public.[488] The Court of Appeal had to consider two discrete legal issues: could an authorisation made abroad be litigated within the jurisdiction of the English courts? The second issue was the substantive one: was the granting of a licence an authorisation under the Act?

Hoffmann LJ was clear, even in the fact of the general authority, that for authorisations of infringement the Copyright, Designs and Patents Act 1988 did apply to foreigners:

> 'It does not matter that the acts which preceded that consequence [of infringement] all took place abroad. It is I think sufficient that the definition of a tort requires an act and that that act is performed within the United Kingdom, however it may be linked to the preliminary act performed abroad.'[489]

As a final indication of the common sense of this approach Lord Justice Hoffmann added,

---

485   It is also possible that, because of the Brussels Regulation arts 2 and 6(1), an infringer is sued in a contracting state other than the state which vested the copyright in the claimant.
486   [1995] RPC 657.
487   Emphasis added.
488   Copyright, Designs and Patents Act 1988, s 16(1).
489   [1995] RPC 657 at 660. Agreed to by Neill LJ.

'I think that a territorial limitation on the act of authorising would lead to anomalies. Anyone contemplating the grant of a licence to do an act restricted by copyright would be able to avoid liability simply by having the document executed abroad.'[490]

This case teaches that for authorisation the place of communication is irrelevant so long as the authority is to do an infringing act within the jurisdiction. This reasoning can be applied to the Internet, specifically, the World Wide Web[491]. An authorisation has been defined as[492] 'a grant or purported grant, which may be expressed or implied, of the right to do the act complained of.' This raises an interesting issue which can best be illustrated with the following scenario.

---

32. A programmer in Brazil copies an entire applet from an English website. As the copying takes place outside the UK, the UK copyright is not infringed. The Brazilian then places the applet onto his own website which can be accessed around the world. An individual accesses the website from the UK. Necessarily the applet is copied onto the individual's own computer. This will constitute a copy under the Copyright, Designs and Patents Act 1988. As the applet's copyright owner has not provided a licence to copy this work the Brazilian is actually providing an authorisation to infringe a UK copyright. This is an infringement within the United Kingdom.

This scenario indicates that one who copies a UK copyright work from elsewhere but then specifically allows it to be retrieved over the Internet will be providing authority to infringe the copyright. The reason for this is that the Internet does not transport copyright works; it allows them to be copied. So specifically to put an infringing work on the Internet should always be viewed as an authorisation to copy the work, infringing it once more. To counter this, a foreign defendant would have to prove that the work was not copied within the UK.[493] This may appear to some as being a conclusion that strikes at the heart of the Internet itself. To intellectual property owners, on the other hand, it is serious and worrying if a work can be copied without permission outside the UK but then freely distributed within the UK without fear of litigation. The law will apply to the individual abroad where that individual seeks to erode, using the transnational scope of the Internet, the rights that an owner has over a work within the territory. The law will certainly apply to those domiciled in contracting states who seek to infringe UK copyright works.

490   [1995] RPC 657 at 660–661.
491   There is a risk that infringement actions based on the Copyright, Designs and Patents Act 1988, ss 17, 18, or 19 will be viewed by the courts as 'occurring' outside the jurisdiction.
492   *CBS Songs Ltd v Amstrad Consumer Electronics* plc [1988] AC 1013 at 1054 per Lord Templeman, HL. The mere existence of the infringing work on a website that can be accessed from the UK should be enough on which to base a quia timet action unless the site can be blocked from access from the UK.
493   See n 483 above.

The reasoning used in relation to authorisations may also apply to other types of primary infringement. A claimant may allege that the issuing of copies occurs where the copies are received. By this reasoning, a website holding material infringing a UK copyright can be construed as issuing the copies within the UK, so within our courts' jurisdiction.[494] This author doubts the strength of such a pleading[495]. The location of the activity of issuing copies is more likely to be construed as being the place from where copies are issued, rather than where they are received.[496]

4.16.2 Enforcement of copyright abroad

To sue the authoriser of the infringement over the Internet is simply a case of viewing the authorisation as a tort and proceeding on the basis of a tort committed within the jurisdiction. The defendant will have to be served with the proceedings outside the jurisdiction.

---

33. A Dutch architect opens a sophisticated ecommerce website which permits, for a fee, any of its plans to be downloaded and utilised as the basis of a building. The server hosting this site is based in Holland. A Dutch builder pays the fee, downloads a plan, builds an office to the specification and is promptly approached by a UK company wishing to open an office in Holland. Contrary to the terms of the site he passes the plans, for a fee, to the UK company who build their office in Amsterdam. Knowing that the builder has few funds to pay damages, the Dutch architect sues the builder and UK company in England.

The Brussels Regulation permits actions to be commenced in England even though the dispute relates to activities which occurred abroad. Despite the Regulation there has been considerable uncertainty[497] that an English court could nevertheless adjudicate on matters of foreign copyrights being infringed abroad. The two issues raising this uncertainty[498] are now issues of historical legal interest following a robust judgment given by the Court of Appeal in *Pearce v Ove Arup Partnership*.[499] The Court of Appeal makes clear that the English court will

---

494 Copyright, Designs and Patents Act 1988, s 18(2).
495 It is submitted that it is also a weak allegation that a visual or acoustic presentation, a primary infringement, occurs where it is seen or heard: Copyright, Designs and Patents Act 1988, s 19(2)(b).
496 Cf the concept of 'distributes' in *Playboy Enterprises Inc v Chuckleberry Publishing Inc*, 939 F Supp 1032 (SDNY 1996). The reasoning in this case would be applicable to a secondary infringer under the Copyright, Designs and Patents Act 1988, s 23(c) or (d).
497 *Pearce v Ove Arup Partnership* [1997] 3 All ER 31 at 34; *Mother Bertha Music Ltd v Bourne Music Ltd* [1997] EMLR 457.
498 First, is an action under a foreign copyright law actionable in the English court; second, is such an action justiciable?
499 [2000] Ch 403.

hear an action for infringement of copyright where the work is protected under a signatory country's copyright law and is infringed in that signatory country.

For Internet users and abusers, this is significant. Infringers may not avoid the English courts merely because their activities take place abroad. If they are domiciled in the UK[500] or a co-defendant is[501] they may find themselves facing claims under a foreign law but in the English courts.

The Private International Law (Miscellaneous Provisions) Act 1995, s 11(1) provides that the general rule is that the applicable law is the law of the country in which the events constituting the tort in question occur. As the work is protected by one country's copyright law and the acts complained of occurred in that country, it will be that country's law which will apply. Further reasoning is given by relying upon s 11(2)(b) which provides that the applicable law for a course of action in respect of damage to property is the law of the country where the property was when it was damaged. Because copyright is a territorial property right (it cannot cross borders) it must be 'damaged' in the country in which it is infringed. Where advisors seek to base an action on this possibility, they must clearly plead the foreign law or laws on which they rely. There is strong authority that the English courts will not entertain the fiction that English law also applies in other countries. Mr Justice Ferris states 'it is simply not realistic to suppose that the [claimants] intend to go to trial on the basis that the copyright of every Convention country is the same as the law of England.'[502]

500   Brussels Regulation, art 2.
501   Brussels Regulation, art 6.
502   *Mother Bertha Music Ltd v Bourne Music Ltd* [1997] EMLR 457.

CHAPTER FIVE

Crime

> 'It is easy to run a secure computer system. You merely have to disconnect all dial-up connections and permit only direct-wired terminals, put the machine and its terminals in a shielded room, and post a guard at the door.'
>
> Grampp FT and Morris RH, AT&T Bell Laboratories Technical Journal[1]

From the press coverage, one imagines the Internet as a breeding ground for international crime and new ominous sounding 'cybercrimes' which threaten to steal our identities, assets and childrens' confidence. In August 2007 a report from the House of Lords Science and Technology Select Committee warned that the Internet has become a 'criminals' playground'. The Report criticised the government for exposing the public to the risks and security threats of a 'wild west' Internet.[2] This all suggests that the Internet is inherently insecure and that new and special technical crimes are being perpetrated on a regular basis. In fact, the overwhelming number of crimes committed via the Internet are traditional crimes. They are now simply being facilitiated through another medium. This is not to diminish the impact Internet crimes may have, however. Figures published by the campaign awareness group Get Safe Online (a government-sponsored initiative) in March 2007 indicated that 12 per cent of UK Internet users (around 3.5 million people) were victims of online fraud in the previous year. Each attack, they stated, costs an average of £875, totalling more than £3 billion. However, as a 2006 House of Lords report[3] reveals, the fact is that 'figures on the scale of the problem are hard to come by' and so the exact scale of the problem remains unknown.

What is clear is that a reference to Internet crime or cybercrime oversimplifies the legal wrongs and potential remedies. To understand the nature of crime over the Internet and the rules which seek to circumscribe and define it, it is useful to distinguish the different types of criminal activity and offence.

---

1   UNIX operating system security. AT&T Bell Laboratories Technical Journal, 63 (8, Part 2): 1649–1672, October 1984.
2   BBC news (www.news.bbc.co.uk), Friday 10 August 2007.
3   House of Lords Science and Technology Committee, 5th report of session 2006–2007 'Personal Internet Security', published on 10 August 2007.

One set of crimes comprises those in which Internet and computer networks provide an essential tool for seemingly new crimes. Examples include email spamming and copyright piracy, many of which have only become possible with technological advances in broadband speeds and the utilisation of peer-to-peer networks. The traditional legislative frameworks have been required to adapt: the data protection regime to deal with unsolicited marketing via electronic communications services; the Copyright Designs and Patents Act 1988 to deal with the circumvention of digital rights management systems and the Regulation of Investigatory Powers Act 2000 to extend phone tapping prohibitions to offences, of interception of communications via any 'electronic communications network'. These type of crimes are considered separately in Chapters 6 (Data and Data Protection) and 4 (Intellectual Property).

A second set of offences, which forms the statistical majority, are pre-existing crimes which are simply facilitated through the use of computers, networks and the Internet. Examples include identity theft and fraud (such as the infamous 'Nigerian 419' scam), online money laundering, the exchange of paedophilic materials, and harassment (known also by its more fear-inducing name, 'cyber stalking'). As with the first category, these crimes do not have special and separate Internet-specific laws dedicated to them. However, they do require that lawyers navigate various pre-existing and occasionally non-technically focused statutes. Some steps have been made to update these laws, and sections 5.2 to 5.5 of this chapter consider some of the most common crimes and their statutory basis.

A third set consists of crimes which actually target computers and computer networks themselves. These computer misuse offences do require specific and focused legislation, and are the subject of section 5.1 of this chapter.

Even if many of the crimes are not in themselves new, crimes perpetrated over the Internet or against computer networks do raise some unique issues which are often the real cause for concern. First, because the Internet knows no territorial boundaries, the co-ordination of an approach to such crimes is problematic. UK legislation to counter electronic fraud may be robust, but if a UK user is targeted from a jurisdiction where there are lesser or even no controls, then such user may rightly feel exposed and the enforcement authorities may be powerless. Second, prosecution even within the UK is hampered through the ability of an offender to remain invisible or take on a fake persona and hide the traces of their crime. Internet crime therefore demands new techniques for gathering and preserving evidence, ensuring its integrity and tracing perpetrators.

Legislation for dealing with these problems has developed. Changes over the last few years draw upon attempts towards greater harmonisation internationally. The EU Framework Decision on Attacks against Information Systems[4] and the

---

4   The Council of the European Union Framework decision on attacks against information systems, 17 January 2005.

Council of Europe Convention on Cybercrime[5] are Europe-wide responses to the increasing severity of the threat from viruses, Internet-based fraud and other computer-based crime. The UK is a signatory to both and is obliged to implement the EU Framework Decision through domestic law by March 2007. It has not, at the time of publication, ratified the Convention. Both Decision and Convention have, however, had an impact on shaping the changes to the Computer Misuse Act 1990 and extradition arrangements in general in order to fulfil the UK's obligations.

These crimes, and the evidence needed to support their prosecution, are examined as follows.

1. When does one commit the computer misuse crime of unauthorised access using the Internet?

2. How does the more serious computer misuse offence of unauthorised access with ulterior motive address the wrongful interception of credit card numbers or digital cash?

3. What are the laws, and how do they control the electronic spread of viruses, logic bombs and other malicious code?

4. For crimes committed over the Internet, what is the special significance and difficulty of adducing computer-generated evidence?

5. Those who gain unauthorised access to computers often follow the same pattern; what are the key legal issues involved in their techniques?

6. What is the English courts' jurisdiction over criminals who use the Internet, and how may they be extradited?

7. What are the criminal laws that apply to obscene digital articles, and more serious indecent photographs?

5.1 COMPUTER MISUSE

5.1.1 Introduction

There are currently three main statutory types of computer misuse, although a fourth is subject to implementation expected in 2008. First, there is unauthorised access, or 'hacking'. This is where a person without authority physically or electronically penetrates a computer system. This may be compared with breaking and entering, where no further offence is intended or then committed. The second type of digital crime is the more serious form of unauthorised access. This is where a person without authority accesses a computer with the intention to commit a further offence such as theft. Distinct from unauthorised access is the third

---

5   European Convention on Cybercrime, Budapest, 23 November 2001.

type of digital crime, where a person does any unauthorised act in relation to a computer, intending the computer to be impaired or access to it prevented (and once implemented, is reckless as to the impact). A common example of this is a computer virus which may prevent a computer from working.[6] A new, fourth offence (yet to formally come into force) concerns the making, supplying or obtaining of articles for use in any of the other offences. Aimed at capturing those who knowingly facilitate computer misuses, this last offence has given cause for concern to many IT professionals who believe it could capture dual-use tools used for highlighting or testing security flaws.

The unique legal question in relation to all these crimes is who or what is actually the victim? Everything which exists in a computer is represented as zeros and ones. These binary digits, or bits, are generally stored using a magnetic medium. So, to destroy a computer file a person may only have to change the state of, say, 100 bits from one, on, to zero, off. Previously, courts were forced to wrestle with older statutes which concerned physical property to fit the misuse of new technology before them.[7] Even where this was successful, there was an obvious need for legislation to take account of computers. Prosecutions were troublesome.[8]

To counter the distrust of computers which was emerging, stemming from the ineffectiveness of the criminal law to deal with computer viruses and hacking, Parliament introduced the Computer Misuse Act 1990; an Act[9] 'to safeguard the integrity – what I call the trustworthiness – of computers.'

The Act introduced three new criminal offences.[10] With computer crime on the increase but convictions under the Act remaining in single figures annually, the Act came under scrutiny. It was accused of containing dangerous loopholes, and insufficient teeth to act as an effective deterrent or to appropriately punish offenders. As a consequence the Act was amended under the Police and Justice Act 2006. This reworked the third offence to give it wider application, introduced a new offence of making, supplying or obtaining articles for use in computer misuse offences, and doubled the maximum sentence for hacking. However, with work in Parliament currently underway in respect of a new Serious Crime Bill (which at the time of writing is before the House of Lords and seeks to introduce new procedures, abolish common law offences of incitement and in its place

6   An action under the Computer Misuse Act may not always be the most appropriate recourse for access or damage caused by viruses. Chapter 3 considers the bases in tort which may be relevant.
7   For example, Forgery and Counterfeiting Act 1981 in *R v Gold and Shifreen* [1988] 2 All ER 186.
8   In an obvious signal to Parliament, Brandon LJ in *R v Gold and Shifreen* said, 'there is no reason to regret the failure of what [Lord Lane CJ] aptly described as the Procrustean attempt to force the facts of the present case into the language of an Act not designed to fit them' [1988] 2 WLR 984 at 991.
9   Michael Colvin MP, *Hansard* 166 HC col 1134. Despite statements in April 2001 by the then Home Secretary, Jack Straw, to consider 'whether [the Act] needs to be reviewed, the Computer Misuse Act 1990 remains the United Kingdom's key statute addressing general hacking and malicious code'.
10   Computer Misuse Act 1990, ss 1, 2 and 3.

create new offences in respect of the encouragement or assistance of crime), the Secretary of State has delayed bringing these amendments into force as required pursuant to s 53 of the Police and Justice Act. It is necessary then, to consider both existing and pending legislation. We analyse each section in turn, below.

5.1.2   Section 1: unauthorised access

The following discussion of hacking over the Internet focuses on the Computer Misuse Act 1990. Prosecutions presently remain in the single figures yearly with only five proceedings brought (by way of a criminal offence) under this section in each of 2004 and 2005.[11]

Despite these low figures, it is generally easy to prove the conduct aspect of the offence, the *actus reus*. The structure of the Act is such that, where the Internet is involved, it is almost impossible for a defendant to interact in any way with a victim computer without satisfying the physical requirements of the section of 'causing the performance of a function'. The tough burden on the prosecution however lies elsewhere. It is proving the necessary intention and satisfying the rules to admit computer-generated evidence. Before considering these burdens it is necessary to appreciate the ambit of the activity required to satisfy the conduct aspect of the offence.

5.1.2.1   Conduct or actus reus

Section 1 creates the summary offence. The details of the *actus reus* are set out in full in s 1(1) of the Computer Misuse Act 1990 as follows (with square bracketed sections indicating the provisions still pending implementation by the Police and Justice Act 2006 as discussed above):

'1. (1) A person is guilty of an offence if –

(a)   he causes a computer to perform any function with intent to secure access to any program or data held in any computer [or to enable such access to be secured];

(b)   the access he intends to secure [or to enable to be secured] is unauthorised; and

(c)   he knows at the time when he causes the computer to perform the function that that is the case.'

There are three main questions which must be addressed in relation to this section. First, what is meant by a computer, program or data? Second, what is required to cause a computer to perform a function? Third, what is entailed in securing access to (or enabling access to be secured to) any program or data?

---

11   Figures from RDS Office for Criminal Justice Reform as reported in House of Commons *Hansard* Written Answers for 20 April 2007: Column 830W.

5.1.2.1.1   Computers, programs and data on the Internet

The conduct element of a s 1 offence is causing a computer to perform any function with intent to secure access to any program or data held in any computer. At an early stage it should be noted that the words 'program', 'data' and 'computer' are not defined by the Act.[12]

Computer

The Computer Misuse Act 1990 does not define 'computer'. This was intentional on the part of Parliament, following recommendations of the Law Commission to ensure that the legislation would not become restricted in the face of technological advances.[13] The absence of the definition has not caused any difficulties for proving unauthorised access over the Internet to date and the All Party Internet Group's review of the Act which helped frame the provisions of the Police and Justice Act 2006 recommended that no further clarification would be necessary or helpful.[14] For a machine to be a victim or conduit of hacking over the Internet, that machine must be a computer within any reasonable definition. The very nature of the Internet is that it joins together networks of computers.[15] For the purposes of this chapter, therefore, where the hacking is conducted over the Internet, the functioning 'machine' and accessed 'machine', as well as the network to which they provide access, will both be considered as computers within the ambit of s 1.

Some considered that digitial rights management systems should be specifically included within the definition of computer. This would have strengthened the protection for copyright works. This call was resisted but rightsholders can now find specific protection through the amendments to the Copyright Designs and Patents Act 1988.

Program, data

The terms 'program' and 'data' within s 1 are also left undefined by the Act for the same reason. That said, it remains crucial for a computer misuse prosecution that the conduct element of the offence, the *actus reus*, is proved and, therefore, that the two terms are understood in a reasonable context.

The main difficulty with these terms is in appreciating what, other than 'a program' or 'data', can be accessed in a computer. The answer is that the two terms

---

12   Mr Harry Cohen MP did attempt to amend the Act at the Committee Stage with a definition of the word 'computer'. This was unsuccessful. Cf Law Commission No 186 on Computer Misuse at para 3.39: 'it would be unnecessary and indeed might be foolish, to attempt to define computer ... We cannot think that there will ever be serious grounds for arguments based on the ordinary meaning of the term "computer".'

13   Interestingly, the European Convention on Cybercrime refers to a 'computer system' and defines a computer as a device that uses a 'program' to run 'data' but does not go on to define these other terms.

14   Revision of the Computer Misuse Act: Report of an Inquiry by the All Party Internet Group, June 2004.

15   It is not doubted that the future of ecommerce is away from the conception of simply linking computers as such but more towards connecting together 'intelligent appliances' such as personal digital appliances and wireless devices, and even household appliances such as fridges!

encapsulate all that can be accessed digitally in a computer. But if the terms were absent from the section, one could commit a s 1 offence by turning off a computer before prising open the casing. Turning off the computer causes it to perform a function, and opening its metal casing would be accessing the computer in the physical sense.

In summary, the absence of definitions should not concern a court where the accused has used the Internet to gain access to information which resides in a digital form. In this form, the information will constitute data or a program within the ambit of the relevant section.

---

1. A company runs a mobile phone and WAP-enabled website which tracks business news stories on particular companies. Users pay a subscription fee and, in return, are given a password to grant them access to the site. A hacker attempts to use a password which he has not paid for in order to enter the site to read the stories. The home page is mainly constructed using a computer language called Java, and much of the site's content is data. The hacker is intending to secure access to a program and its associated data without authority.

Held in any computer

Before examining the remainder of s 1 and its application to the Internet, this section analyses the notion of data or programs being 'held in a computer'. A computer can be reasonably thought to include the processing unit, its memory and storage devices. Computers are simple machines; they are so simple that they can purely store and work with two numbers: a zero and a one. But that sentence illustrates one division which exists within a computer: it *stores* and it *works*; it executes instructions on those numbers. The central processing unit of a computer is able to store very few of these numbers at one time but is able to process them very quickly: it is where all the real work is performed. However, certain other physical parts of the computer cannot process or work with these numbers: they can only store them. Examples of these are the computer's hard disk drive and its memory. These are purely components of a computer that can store vast quantities of digital information.

Section 17(6) clarifies the phrase 'held in a computer' by providing that it includes references to data or programs held in any removable storage medium which is in the computer for the time being. This particular inclusion refers to the possibility of obtaining access to the data or program which is stored on a floppy disk: these allow the storage of small quantities of data, but are physically small and portable. A CD-ROM is a further example of a removable storage medium. Section 17(6) does not define the term and seeks only to clarify the phrase 'held in a computer' with one example, one inclusion. 'Held in a computer' may therefore also be reasonably read to include data or programs which are stored away from the processing unit of a computer, but accessible by it.

---

2. A hacker uses an authorised person's password to log in to a UK insurance company's computer. The hacker is hoping to gain access to the company's customer details. The computer to which he logs in stores these details in a huge data storage unit

> which is located elsewhere. The data itself is stored on a magnetic tape. The processing unit of the computer retrieves this information through fibre-optic cables. The computer would be thought to include the magnetic tape, and so the data would still be considered as being 'held in a computer'.

5.1.2.1.2   Performing any function

If it is concluded that any machine which is connected to the Internet will fall into the category of 'computer' in s 1(1), it is then necessary to establish how one causes that computer to perform a function. The word 'function' is also undefined within the Act, but the interpretation section of the Act provides some indication of the wide scope of the term. It appears that there is no activity which one can perform in relation to a computer that does not cause a function to be performed. Even typing on a computer's keyboard or using an input device, such as a mouse, will alter the state of the computer's processor. This alteration has been effected by the person causing the computer to perform a function.

Function on any computer

The computer performing the function does not need to be the same computer on which the data or programs are stored. So, a client computer, being made to perform a function, which is intended to secure access *to the server computer*, falls within the ambit of s 1(1). Section 1(1) also encompasses the use of a home computer to log in to an Internet service provider's server from which the user intends to penetrate another computer. The home computer is caused to perform a function, and so is the Internet service provider's computer.

Where a hacker uses the Internet to attempt to gain access to a victim computer, signals may pass through many computers, as described in this book's introduction, before reaching the victim. Indeed, when Yahoo.com, one of the busiest sites on the Internet, was brought down in February 2000, it was attacked from a vast number of other computers. Each had been made to act in concert, having been themselves infected with a 'daemon' program. Each of these infected computers was then under the control of a 'master' program (generally without the computer owners' knowledge). In the case of Yahoo!'s attack, the 'master' program probably instructed its 'daemons' to simultaneously bombard Yahoo!'s servers with a flood of requests to be sent data or web pages: a 'SYN flood'. This was probably combined with a set of other attack procedures variously called 'spoofing', 'smurfing' and 'fraggle'. In short, a vast range of computers, all compromised in the same way, were made to focus their attentions on one victim computer, this time Yahoo.com. This so-called 'denial of service' attack illustrates the way in which the computers made to perform the function are often not the same computers on which the data or programs being attacked are stored.

What is important to the prosecution, though, is that each of these intermediary computers is caused to perform a function. And the cause of the performance of this function is the instructions which the hacker has provided to the first computer in the chain. This allows the prosecution to rely on the functioning of any computer in the chain to establish this aspect of the *actus reus*. What is difficult for the prosecution to prove is that the *accused* was the cause of the performance of this function. This difficulty is considered in greater depth below.[16]

---

3. A hacker uses a set of software tools called a 'root kit' to break into an insecure computer on the Internet. A 'master program' is installed onto this computer with a view to controlling a large number of 'daemon' programs installed on other computers. Using a program called 'Tribal Flood Network' the hacker remotely calls on all the 'daemon' computers to launch a distributed attack on a well-known sports site. For a s 1 offence, the prosecution does not need to prove that the hacker's own computer was made to function: all the computers involved, 'daemons' and 'masters' will suffice. The prosecution may have a problem in proving that it was the accused who caused these functions.

Unsuccessful attempts

The broad drafting of s 1 has the effect that even unsuccessful hackers can be guilty of the offence. Usually, to gain unauthorised access a person must enter a login procedure and masquerade as another, or attempt to bypass the login procedure altogether. In the first instance, if the victim computer rejects the unauthorised login, the person has caused at least two computers to function: his own, and the victim computer. The victim computer has performed a function: it rejected the hacker. Where the hacker attempts to log in with the requisite intention, a guilty mind, despite being unsuccessful, the hacker may have committed the offence.

Of course, the difficulty for the prosecution in such a situation is proving that the victim computer did foil the attempt, and proving that the attempt was made by the accused. This will be hard unless the victim computer maintains a log of all unsuccessful logins as well as successful ones.[17] It is more technically complex to prove the source of an unsuccessful login, weakening further a prosecution.

If the person is somehow able to bypass the standard login procedure, this bypassing itself will constitute the function. If the standard procedure for the victim computer is to ask for login details from each person wishing to gain access, by avoiding this the person must be causing the computer to perform a function.

---

4. A hacker oversees a password being entered by someone logging-in to a remote computer. The login prompt specifies that you must be authorised to access the computer. Later, the hacker then attempts to use the password himself. Because the remote computer only allows one login each day, the unauthorised login attempt is rejected by the computer. This would still constitute a s 1 offence: the rejection constitutes a function and this function was caused by the hacker using a password at the wrong time.

Automatic causation of a function

Many hackers will automate part of the process of unauthorised access. Denial of service attacks rely on automatic co-ordination between computers. As another

16   See 'Evidence', at section 5.6.
17   Evidence used to convict one hacker consisted of a log which his computer maintained of all functions!

example, a home page may require two items of information from each of its users to allow them to enter the site. The first may be the person's name, followed by the second, their password, which is say a number seven digits long. To penetrate this site digitally a hacker may write an automatic login program. Its first task is to enter a common name, 'John Smith'. The hacker's program then tries to enter the password. First the password 0000001 is tried. If the victim computer rejects this as being incorrect, the login program will simply move the password number to 0000002. Often after a number of unsuccessful attempts, the victim computer will reject the attempting client.

As automation usually plays some part in hacking, it is necessary to address whether this may constitute a s 1 offence.[18] The key question is whether a computer has been caused to perform a function. The running of the hacker's program would constitute the conduct element of the offence. It is at the point of executing that code that a computer is caused to perform a function, so the physical element of the offence can be made out. Establishing the intention for this automated hacking is less straightforward.

5.1.2.1.3   Securing access

The Computer Misuse Act 1990 prescribes that securing access to a program or data is established where the defendant, by causing a computer to perform a function[19]:

'(a) alters or erases the program or data;

(b) copies or moves it to any storage medium other than that in which it is held or to a different location in the storage medium in which it is held;

(c) uses it; or

(d) has it output from the computer in which it is held (whether by having it displayed or in any other manner).'

The purpose of considering this aspect of s 1 is to establish the *intention* of the defendant to secure access to any program or data held in any computer.[20] That the defendant actually *did* secure such access, a question of fact, may bolster the case that the defendant has the requisite intention; it is not a prerequisite of proving this intention. The amendments in the Police and Justice Act 2006 will expand this to incorporate enabling the access. In so doing it will no longer be

---

18   A similar program can be used to search automatically for the vulnerable hosts on the Internet, which, once discovered, may be probed further. See Cheswick WR and Bellovin SM, *Firewalls and Internet Security* (Addison-Wesley Publishing Company, Wokingham, 1995) at p 145. Similar programs were used to scan a range of telephone numbers to test whether they were connected to a modem, and were thus potential targets. Such a program is described in the now deleted book, *The Hacker's Handbook* by Hugo Cornwall (Century Communications, London, 1985).

19   Computer Misuse Act 1990, s 17(2).

20   The author submits that no emphasis should be placed on the Act's use of the word 'secure'. It is the author's understanding that this verb is introduced because, while using the word 'access' as a verb is grammatically dubious, it also makes the word ambiguous.

necessary to show actual access or that any of the items under (a) to (d) has been or was intended or attempted to be done by the defendant. A defendant will still be acting unlawfully where the function which they cause the computer to perform allows a third party actually to obtain the access. In this way hackers who only undertake the first steps, leaving the door open for others (or themselves at a later date) to obtain access, are still caught.

Which computer?

It is helpful to consider to which computer s 1(1)(a) refers. Section 1(1)(a) states 'to secure access to any program or data held on *any* computer (or, once it is implemented, to enable any such access to be secured)'. Following a judgment of the Court of Appeal in June 2006, it is clear that the access does not need to be directed at a different computer to the one on which the defendant caused performance of the function, but can be programs or data accessed either directly from a computer or indirectly via another computer.[21] It will now be illustrated that the Computer Misuse Act 1990 leaves very little scope for interacting with a computer over the Internet without that interaction being classified as securing access or enabling such access to be secured.

---

5. A hacker uses a Telnet connection to attempt to gain unauthorised access to a company's Intranet. Three main computers are used to attempt the access: the hacker's own computer and the computer to which he connected to by Telnet. This 'distance' alone will not prevent a successful hacking prosecution. There are two computers caused to function: the hacker's own and the Telnet computer. That the hacker sought to secure access to data held on a third computer is not a bar to a conviction: it is still 'any computer'.

Copying or moving programs and data

Section 17(2)(b) defines securing access as a person copying or moving data or programs to any storage medium other than that in which it is held or to a different location in the storage medium in which it is held. The word which widens this section dramatically is 'copies'. Computer data and programs cannot even be viewed on a screen without there being copying. To show characters on a screen, the characters making up the program or data are copied from the storage unit, be that memory or a hard-disk drive, to the video memory of the computer. The same is true of a hacker who uses the Internet to view the content of programs or data which are held on a victim's computer. By being able to view their content, a part of those data must have been copied into the memory of the hacker's computer. It therefore appears that viewing files which are held on any computer will constitute securing access to those files and, even if the defendant does not themselves view the files, enabling this will be sufficient.

21 *Attorney General's Reference (No 1 of 1991)* [1992] 3 All ER 897. This concerned a case in which the defendant keyed instructions into a wholesaler's computer without authority in order to obtain a 70% discount on his purchases. In the initial action, the judge held that, in order to prove the offence, the defendant would have had to use one computer in order to secure unauthorised access to another. This was rejected.

> 6. A hacker makes a connection to a secured part of a server. Once within this portion of the server the hacker views the contents of a password data file. To avoid drawing attention to the breach in security, the hacker does not make a digital copy of the data file. Nevertheless the hacker has secured access to the file by having read it: to view the file it must have been copied from the storage unit on the server to the memory of the hacker's computer.

Using a program

Section 17(2)(c) states that one secures access to a program if one 'uses it'. The Act elaborates on the meaning and context of this word 'use'. Section 17(3)(a) explains, first, that one uses a computer program if the program is executed. This is, pragmatically, covered by subsection (2)(b). Section 17(3) explains that running a program indicates the gaining of access to that program. This will therefore cover programs executed on a client computer, having been copied there, or programs executed on the server computer.

> 7. An employee uses her firm's intranet to attempt to read the online diary of her supervisor. She is unable to read the diary because the program requests her to enter a password which she does not know. That the diary program is able to reject her attempt shows it had, at the least, been executed. The employee did intend to access the diary program.

In *Ellis v DPP*,[22] John Ellis, a graduate of the University of Newcastle appealed to the Divisional Court against three convictions under s 1. He had used computers left logged on by others to access certain websites. The evidence was that he used already-running Internet browsers on the computer and that he accessed already-'activated' sites. Nevertheless, and technically correct, the Divisional Court unanimously judged that he did 'use' the computers knowing that use to be unauthorised.

Output of programs or data

Section 17(1)(d) expands the term 'access' by not only including executing a computer program, but also *reading* a computer program. A computer program is made up from a list of instructions. Each instruction tells the computer to perform a function. Some functions are imperceptible, such as moving a byte from one storage area to another. Others make a perceptive difference, for example clearing the screen. Section 17(1)(d) defines securing access as including 'ha[ving the program or data] output from the computer in which it is held. . .'. Section 17(4)(a) refines this section by further defining 'output' as including the instructions of the program being output. So, executing a program over the Internet is deemed to be securing access to it. This therefore compromises the 'classic' thin-client where the server executes the program but outputs the *results* to the client computer. This was explained above.[23] In addition, merely looking at the instructions which make up the program will also be securing access.

---

22   [2001] EWHC Admin 362, [2001] All ER (D) 190 (May).
23   See 'Using a program'.

It is crucial that a court appreciates the mischief at which this section is aimed. It is concerned with the 'integrity'[24] of programs and data. It is not directed at subsequent use, or utility, of the digital information compromised. For this reason, s 17(4)(b) clearly expresses that the form of output, whether executable or otherwise, is immaterial. This expression applies also to data: it is of no concern that, say, the data is unusable. The fact that it has been output *per se* is sufficient to constitute securing access.

---

8. A company, worried about data security, encrypts all data held on its network. Each individual who is permitted to gain access to the data is provided, on disk, with a de-encrypting key. The network security is breached and a hacker prints out some of the encrypted data. The hacker has still gained access to that data despite the issue that the output is unreadable. In addition, the data will be deemed to have been copied onto the hacker's computer for printing; this also denotes securing access.

Erasure or alteration

Subsection (a) of s 17(2) illustrates the final type of access to programs or data: alteration or erasure of programs or data. This would constitute a 'classic' hack: data are deleted and programs are altered. Complex issues of proving the program has been altered, where the program itself is the source of that proof (an activity-logging program for example), are covered below.[25]

5.1.2.2 Intention *or* mens rea

The prosecution must prove the two limbs of the intention aspects of the offence. The first, that the defendant intended to secure access to any program or data held in any computer (or, once this section is implemented by the Secretary of State, to 'enable such access to be secured'), has been considerably examined above.[26] Nevertheless, a few additional points are mentioned below. The second limb is that at the time of causing the computer to perform the function the defendant knew that the access intended to secure (or enable to be secured) was unauthorised. This can be a difficult intention to prove where the defendant had limited authority, but is accused of operating outside this authority. A common example of this is where the defendant is an employee of a company and is accused of using the company's intranet or other systems outside their authority.

The prosecution need only make out these two limbs and any consideration of the motivations and reasons for securing or enabling such unauthorised access is irrelevant. The case of Dan Cuthbert,[27] a system penetration tester, provides a useful example. On making a £30 charitable donation following the 2004 Asian tsunami via a website run by the Disasters Emergency Committee, Mr Cuthbert was concerned by the slowness of the system in processing his payment. Having

---

24   See n 9 above.
25   See section 5.6.
26   See 'Securing access', at 5.1.2.1.3.
27   *R v Cuthbert* (unreported, Horseferry Magistrates' Court, 7 October 2005).

read about alleged 'phishing' attempts, he decided to use his skills to check whether the site was in fact vulnerable to security breaches. He tried to breach the system and it did not seem to be weak, and so he thought no more about it. Unfortunately for Mr Cuthbert, his tests triggered an alarm and he found himself facing prosecution under s 1 of the Computer Misuse Act for unauthorised access. His defence centred on the fact that Mr Cuthbert's motivations for the access were innocent, and indeed considered his own and other users' welfare. However, the court found the intention to be irrelevant; he had clearly known that the action was unauthorised and the fact that no damage had been caused was irrelevant in the context of a s 1 offence. 'With regret' the court fined him £400.

5.1.2.2.1   Intention to secure access

Much has been explained about what constitutes securing access; a little needs now to be added to what is an *intention* to secure access (or, once this amendment is implemented, to enable such access to be secured). First, it should be reiterated that this intention can be directed at *any* computer. The defendant does not need to have been aware of exactly which computer he was attacking, and nor will he have to make such access himself once the pending amendments are finally brought into force.[28] This suits the Internet: often it is complicated to prove that a person intended to log in to a specific computer. This is particularly true where the defendant used a program to check automatically the security, or otherwise, of a computer. The intention to secure access also does not need to be directed at any particular, or particular kind of, program or data. It is enough that an individual intends to secure access to programs and data *per se*. The section encompasses the hacker who intends to access a computer with no clear perception of what data or programs will be held on the computer.

5.1.2.2.2   Unauthorised

The second limb of intention is focused on the authority of the defendant to secure access. Section 1(1)(b) prescribes that the access the defendant intends to secure (or, once this amendment is implemented, enable) be unauthorised. Section 1(1)(c) makes it clear that the person must have the relevant knowledge that the access is unauthorised at the time the computer is forced to perform a function.

5.1.2.2.3   Outsiders

The question of authority is generally not difficult to prove when an 'outsider' to a system uses the Internet to attempt to secure access to any programs or data on the system. Where a person must resort to using 'techniques' to gain access to programs or data, it can be readily inferred that it is an insecure defence to claim

---

28   The amendments under the Police and Justice Act 2006 currently pending formal implementation after the Serious Crime Bill is adopted and implemented, as discussed above.

he did not know he was unauthorised. The concept of authority is elaborated, but thinly, by s 17(5). This section states that access is unauthorised if the person is not entitled to control access of the kind in question, and the person does not have the consent of the person who does control access.

A person must *know* that he is unauthorised in this sense. The question of fact as to whether the individual knew the limits of his authority will often be a finely balanced one.

---

9. An art gallery uses a website to advertise forthcoming displays. On its home page it states that the graphics which follow on subsequent pages may not be downloaded to a storage medium. A person saves one of the graphics to his hard disk. The person has authorised access to copy the file to memory, but not to his hard disk. Access was unauthorised; the issue would be whether the evidence would be strong enough to prove that he did not see the limitation to disprove he had the necessary intention.

This raises an issue of relevance for advisers to server operators. Where a server seeks to provide limited authority, say with an extranet site, the boundaries of this authority must be clearly stated.[29] If not, it will be doubtful an offence has been committed. If publicly available but subject to a limitation, a court will be unenthusiastic to hold that an offence has been committed. What is more, because the intention must have been formed at the time of causing the function, the stipulations of any limitations should be obvious at all times. An ftp site appears to a user as a catalogue of the files and directories on the particular computer. Unless security is in place, a user can secure access to any file without having to pass through any limitations statement. Similarly, if poorly constructed, it is possible that a person may select a single page of the website to view, missing the opening page altogether.[30] A viewer may not have seen a limitation statement.

5.1.2.2.4 Insiders

The ubiquity of intranets and extranets within organisations creates a potential arena for insiders to secure unauthorised access to programs and data. Disgruntled employees, temporary staff and even happily employed staff may all attempt to read information which is actually out of their authority to view. This is possible where there are various strata within a system each for different users of the network. For example, personnel files may be uploaded to the intranet but

---

29 A website may state the following on its terms and conditions page: 'Permission to use, copy and distribute documents and related graphics available from this server ("Server") is granted, provided that . . . (2) use of the graphics available from this Server is for non-commercial purposes . . . (4) no graphics available from this Server are used, copied or distributed separate from accompanying copyright notices.' Accessing the site with the intention to use the graphics in a commercial brochure would therefore constitute a s 1 offence, if these disclaimers were known at the time of downloading the graphic.

30 This is a very common occurrence where a person uses a search engine to search for a particular term.

only made available to the personnel department. Before considering the problems of an insider's unauthorised access it is necessary to mention how an insider may access the files.

An insider can secure access to unauthorised information held on an intranet through a connected computer, or through the actual server on which the information is held. In the early case of *R v Cropp*,[31] Sean Cropp, without authority, entered a discount into a computerised till to obtain key-cutting equipment at 30 per cent of cost. This is a straightforward example of unauthorised access.

Aglionby J, after consulting the statute, held that there was no case to answer. Section 1(1)(a) refers to:

> 'causing a computer to perform any function with intent to secure access to any program or data held in any computer.'

He construed this wording did not apply where only one computer is used; he felt the word 'any' referred to any *other* computer. To confirm this interpretation, Judge Aglionby considered s 17 of the Act. Here, a s 3 offence is described as only addressing[32]:

> 'the computer concerned or *any other* computer . . . It seems to me to be straining language to say that only one computer is necessary.'

Concern at this decision was so widespread that an opinion on a point of law was sought from the Court of Appeal.[33] The question was asked if, to commit an offence under s 1(1), does the computer caused to perform a function have to be a different computer to the one in which unauthorised access is intended? The Court of Appeal set the Act back on course[34]:

> 'In our judgment there are no grounds whatsoever for implying, or importing the word "other" between "any" and "computer". . .'

This leaves no doubt that, all things being equal, insiders who gain access to unauthorised files through the computer on which they are stored can commit the offence.

For an insider to be convicted, the prosecution has two hurdles to prove intention. The first is that the person intended to secure access to any program or data (or, once this amendment is implemented, to enable such access to be secured). This may not be disputed. What will often be disputed is the second, higher

---

31   *R v Cropp*, unreported, although see [1991] 7 Computer Law and Practice 270.
32   Per Aligonby J in *R v Cropp*, transcript of shorthand notes, p 9F. Emphasis added.
33   *AG's Reference (No 1 of 1991)* [1993] QB 94 under s 36 of the Criminal Justice Act 1972. While explaining s 1 offences, in the House of Commons, Michael Colvin MP added: '[The section] is also aimed at insiders who try to get into parts of the system where they know that they should not be'. *Hansard* 166 HC col 1138. Parliament's intention is confirmed by the unanimous opposition to and later withdrawal of Harry Cohen's amendment proposing that 'any computer' be replaced with 'another computer'.
34   [1992] 3 WLR 432 at 437.

hurdle, that the insider knew that he was unauthorised to secure (or enable) this access at the time of causing the computer to perform a function.[35]

In a perfect organisation, the boundaries of each employee's actions are clear and known. In practice, an employee's role changes over time. This is especially the situation for a temporary worker, who may work for many different sectors of an organisation within a short period. It will therefore often be important for the prosecution to show clear guidelines which were made known to the employee at the time of causing the computer to perform the function.

On this point the Law Commission has provided the following guidance[36]:

> 'We think there is some importance in requiring the court, in a case where there is a dispute about authorisation, to identify, and to be clear about the status of, the person alleged to have authority to control the access which is in issue.'

Unclear company guidelines, or none at all, in relation to the use of the intranet can only weaken the prosecution's case that a person knew they were acting outside of their authority. Conflicting authorisations will also weaken any case.

---

10. An employee secures access to the personnel section of her company's intranet. She copies her personnel file using a stolen password. Clearly the employee does not have authority to enter the personnel section of the intranet, but her intention was to gain access to her own personnel file. The relevant knowledge and intent may be inferred from her stolen password.

Without a clear indication of boundaries, the defence is at liberty to question whether the defendant actually knew of these limits.[37]

This discussion highlights the theoretical applicability of the Computer Misuse Act 1990 to insider access, but also the practical difficulty of satisfying the criminal standard of proof in such a case.

The most complex situation concerning insiders is where they are carrying out their duties with 'technical authority' but without 'actual authority'. The *Bignell* case illustrates this concept.

---

35 A 'bootstraps' approach to this question is to assess whether the ultimate purpose of the access was unlawful. As unlawful, it must, necessarily, have been unauthorised by the controller of the programs or data. That this was known by the defendant remains a question of fact, but an unlawful purpose will indicate such knowledge.

36 Law Commission No 186, para 3.37.

37 This said, the defence should be wary that 'it is always open to the tribunal of fact, when knowledge on the part of a defendant is required to be proved, to base a finding of knowledge on evidence that the defendant deliberately shut his eyes to the obvious or refrained from inquiry because he suspected the truth but did not want to have his suspicion confirmed'. Per Lord Bridge, *Westminster City Council v Croyalgrange Ltd* [1986] 2 All ER 353 at 359. This 'wilful blindness' approaches a subjective recklessness threshold of intention. It is the author's opinion that this lower level of intention was not intended by Parliament. Emma Nicholson's Bill, proposed but rejected, included recklessness; the Computer Misuse Act 1990 does not. Further, the proponent of the Act explained, '[Section 1] is also aimed at insiders who try to get into parts of the system where they know that they should not be'. *Hansard* 166 HC col 1138.

Paul and Victoria Bignell were police officers and lived together. A dispute arose in relation to two cars owned by the new partner of Mr Bignell's former wife. On six occasions between December 1994 and May 1995 the Bignells instructed police computer operators to extract from the Police National Computer details of the two cars. Such instructions would have been perfectly legal were the Bignells discharging genuine police duties. However, they were not.

On 28 June 1996, the respondents were convicted by a stipendiary magistrate and fined under the Computer Misuse Act 1990, s 1.[38] They each appealed against these convictions to the Crown Court. The appeals were heard on 19 September 1996 and the Crown Court upheld their submission that, even if their use of the police computer was for private purposes, it was not within the definition of 'unauthorised access' under s 17(5) of the Act because the *access* was with authority, even though the authority was used for an unauthorised purpose.

The DPP appealed, its main question to Pill LJ and Astill J being whether or not it was correct in law to conclude that a police officer does not commit an offence contrary to s 1 of the Computer Misuse Act 1990 if he intends to secure access to the Police National Computer for purposes other than policing.[39]

Mr Justice Astill gave judgment for the court in a systematic manner. Access is unauthorised if it meets the conditions in s 17(5): one is not entitled to control access of any kind in question, and, one does not have consent to access from any person so entitled. Section 17(2)(a) to (d) sets out four ways in which a person secures access, including altering data, copying data, using it, or outputting it. Section 17(5), however, is drafted in terms of access 'of the kind in question'. This, the court judged, referred to the four kinds of access set out in s 17(2)(c) and (d) at least. The court felt this indicated that as the respondents were authorised to secure access by s 17(2)(c) and (d), they had not committed the s 1 offence. In short the respondents had authority to access even though they did not do so for an authorised purpose.

The effects of this ruling would have been devastating. It would suggest that, because all employees have authority to touch the keys connected to a computer, any employee may use the computer to gain unauthorised access to material in the computer without criminal sanction.

The Bignells had instructed that a false 'reason code' be typed into the Police National Computer.[40] Why? They wanted the computer to perform this function to allow them to gain access to data which was 'not necessary for the efficient

---

38   In a remarkably similar case, the CPS prosecuted a police officer, David Keyte, of conspiring to commit 'misconduct in a public office'. The officer was found guilty and jailed for two years. See *Computing*, 10 July 1997.

39   *DPP v Bignell* [1998] 1 Cr App Rep 1.

40   A question remains whether when a third party touches the computer this is sufficient for the offence. Certainly, precedent suggests it is: *R v Pearce, Farquharson* (unreported, Croydon Magistrates' Court, 9 December 1993). Mr Farquharson was convicted under s 2 for instructing Ms Pearce to access her employer's computer system to obtain details of numbers and electronic codes which would have facilitated the cloning of mobile phones. Mr Farquharson did not touch the computer.

discharge of genuine police duties'.[41] In other words, they were not authorised *in those circumstances* to secure access to the data. The offence should have been made out. The reason that the court did not come to this conclusion was because they did not restrict their analysis of the facts to the precise wording of the statute. The Act is drafted in terms of 'causing a computer to perform a function', together with the intention to 'secure unauthorised access to any program or data'. It is therefore an error in law for the court to have provided a judgment littered with references to 'accessing a computer'. The Act does not sanction those who access computers, it sanctions those who use computers to secure access to data and programs.

Unfortunately, this ruling was relied upon by Kennedy, LJ and Blofeld, J in *R v Governor of Brixton Prison ex p Adeniyi Momudu Allison*.[42] Allison was accused by the US government of conspiring when in England with an employee of American Express (then in Florida) to defraud the credit card company. The committal had sought that Allison, within the jurisdiction of the US, conspired with this US employee to secure unauthorised access to the American Express computers with intent to commit theft, forgery and to modify their computers' contents. The employee had access to accounts of American Express cardholders and relayed the secret information about these accounts to Allison. This permitted them to forge credit cards and obtain substantial sums of money.

The court relied upon the ruling in *Bignell*. It decided that the US employee was, under more usual circumstances, entitled to access the data about the American Express accounts. Consequentially, the court determined that the access was not 'authorised' access within the Computer Misuse Act 1990, s 17(5).

The case was appealed from the Divisional Court to the House of Lords.[43] Lord Hobhouse delivered judgment for all five Lords and was clear that the Divisional Court fell into error by relying on the *Bignell* judgment. Indeed, the House of Lords ruled that the *Bignell* case wrongly elided 'kinds of access' and 'kinds of data'. The Act is not concerned with authority to access kinds of data. It is concerned with authority to access the *actual* data involved. The 'level' of security that an individual has is therefore largely irrelevant; the question is whether, given the circumstances, the individual had authority to access the data.

In short, Allison's accomplices, although no doubt trusted employees of American Express at the time, were not authorised to provide data to third parties to allow frauds to be committed. Similarly, by disapproving of the decision made in *Bignell*, the House of Lords was also impliedly stating that the police officers in that case had accessed data without authority.

---

11. Cleerdz.com operates a credit card clearance system for other websites. It allows a website to offer credit card payment facilities to customers without having the capability themselves. Cleerdz.com is entitled to debit from the entered card where the card's 'fraud score' is below an agreed maximum. An operator at Cleerdz.com re-enters old

---

41 Directions on the use of the Police National Computer, para 3.8.
42 [1999] QB 847.
43 [2000] 2 AC 216.

> customer details to pay for a holiday for himself. Even though his usual job and usual
> level of authority would have permitted him to enter card details, he was not authorised
> to do so in those particular circumstances. He accessed a computer and data without
> authority.

5.1.2.3   Sentencing

Criticised for a long time for being too lenient, the amendments to the Computer
Misuse Act 1990 effected through the Police and Justice Act 2006 will, once formally brought into force by the Secretary of State, make the punishments stricter
(although lobbyists have been disappointed that the potential sentence was not
increased to sit in line with ss 2 and 3).

Once the amendments are implemented, a person guilty of an offence under
s 1 will become liable on summary conviction to imprisonment for a term not
exceeding 12 months (six months for Scotland) or a fine not exceeding the statutory minimum and, on conviction on indictment, to imprisonment for a term not
exceeding two years or to a fine or both.[44] This increase, allowing the offence to
be indictable, means it is now possible to prosecute for criminal attempt.

For the time being, however, liability on summary conviction is to imprisonment for up to six months or to a fine not exceeding level 5 on the standard scale
or both.

5.1.3   Section 2: hacking to offend further

The s 2 offence applies to someone seeking to access a computer for a further
criminal purpose. That is, where a s 1 offence has been committed with the further intent to commit a serious criminal offence.[45]

It will be discussed below that this section applies to interception of digital
cash and credit card numbers. It also applies to the interception of goods or services which are delivered over the Internet, for example software.[46]

5.1.3.1   Further offence

If a s 1 offence is made out, the s 2 offence may be proved by establishing that
the defendant committed that offence with the intention to commit a further
offence. This type of further offence is defined as one punishable by at least five

---

44   Computer Misuse Act 1990, s 1(3).
45   No exhaustive list of these further offences is provided by the Computer Misuse Act 1990. The
     offence must carry either a fixed sentence penalty, such as murder, or be punishable with
     imprisonment of five years or more. This appears to cover the majority of serious offences.
46   The application of the Computer Misuse Act 1990 to such a mischief, however, may not
     always be possible. In that scenario, the Law Commission has concluded that if a service (not
     product) were obtained deceitfully, no offence would be committed because no human mind
     would be deceived: Law Commission Report on Fraud and Deception, May 1999.

years' imprisonment. This covers theft and fraud, and most other dishonesty offences.[47] Importantly, it now covers an offence of dishonestly obtaining a money transfer by deception.[48]

---

12. A hacker gains unauthorised access to a computer and takes a copy of an encryption key used for Internet-safe e-commerce transactions. The hacker then uses the key to pay for services without the permission of the account owner. The hacker may be convicted of the s 2 offence because the s 1 requirements are met and the defendant intended to commit the further offence of obtaining a money transfer by deception.

5.1.3.2 Intention

The hacker is not required actually to commit the further offence. Simply committing a s 1 offence with the intention of committing the further offence is sufficient. Where the hacker is accessing encryption keys to digital cash accounts, it seems probable that the secondary intention will be inferred. Gaining access to another's email account though, with no other evidence of intent, would not appear to provide sufficient evidence to make out a conviction.

Towards the end of 1999, an individual accessed without authority a database of 300,000 accounts held by CD Universe, a leading online music retailer. The individual demanded $100,000 in ransom from the company. CD Universe refused and the individual threatened to post 25,000 credit card account details on the Internet. This is a classic example of a s 2 type offence.[49]

If a hacker is found not guilty under s 2, the jury may still find the defendant guilty under s 1.[50]

5.1.3.3 Future intention

Section 2(3) states:

'It is immaterial for the purposes of this section whether the further offence is to be committed on the same occasion as the unauthorised access offence or on any future occasion.'

This eliminates difficult issues for the prosecution of whether the subsequent offence was sufficiently connected in time with the s 1 offence. It also creates a wider frame of culpability for the defendant: the intention may be to use the data at some time in the future.

---

47 In illustration, although Cropp was acquitted for other reasons, Aglionby J stated: 'There is no doubt that false accounting contrary to s 17(1)(a) of the Theft Act 1968 falls within the statutory definition of 'further offence.' *R v Cropp* Transcript of Shorthand Notes, p 7G.
48 Theft Act 1968, s 15A as inserted by the Theft (Amendment) Act 1996.
49 For details, see *The Observer*, 12 February 2000.
50 Computer Misuse Act 1990, s 12(1)(a).

5.1.3.4   Impossible further offence

Similar to the House of Lords' ruling in *R v Shivpuri*[51] in relation to the Criminal Attempts Act 1981, 'objective innocence' does not save a hacker who attempts a factually impossible crime. A hacker may be guilty of an offence under s 2 even though the facts are such that the commission of the further offence is impossible.[52] But the Computer Misuse Act 1990 is wider than the existing provisions under the Criminal Attempts Act 1981 and, say, the Theft Act 1968. This is because, even under the wider reading of the Criminal Attempts Act 1981 in *Shivpuri*, the defendant must still have done 'an act which is more than merely preparatory to the commission of the offence'.[53] In contrast, under the Computer Misuse Act 1990, an act less than merely preparatory may suffice as evidence of the additional intention needed for a s 2 offence.

---

13. A hacker uses a computer to obtain another person's encryption key with which he intends to access the owner's online bank account. The hacker does not know that the bank will only allow access through its own dial-up connection and not over the web. The hacker's attempt would fail. Despite this, the hacker may have committed a s 2 offence, although he would probably not have made sufficient preparation for a statutory attempt.

5.1.3.5   Sentencing

A person guilty of an offence under s 2 is currently liable, on summary conviction, to imprisonment for a term not exceeding six months or to a fine not exceeding the statutory maximum or both and, on conviction on indictment, to imprisonment for a term not exceeding five years or to a fine or both. Once the amendments of the Police and Justice Bill 2006 are formally brought into force by the Secretary of State, the potential term of imprisonment will be increased to 12 months (six months in Scotland) on summary conviction and up to five years on indictment.[54]

5.1.4   Section 3: unauthorised acts to impair or to prevent or hinder access

In 1865 Mr Fisher was convicted of damaging a steam engine by plugging up the feed-pipe and displacing other parts to render the engine useless.[55] There was no removal of any part, no cutting and no breaking. Pollock CB upheld the conviction, stating[56]:

---

51   [1987] AC 1, especially at 21.
52   Computer Misuse Act 1990, s 2(4).
53   See Lord Bridge, [1987] AC 1 at 21; cf *Anderton v Ryan* [1985] AC 560 at 582–583.
54   Computer Misuse Act 1990, s 2(5).
55   (1865) LR 1 CCR 7.
56   (1865) LR 1 CCR 7 at 9.

'It is like the case of spiking a gun, where there is no actual damage to the gun, although it is rendered useless ... Surely the displacement of the parts was a damage ... if done with intent to render the machine useless.'

Malicious computer code is similar to Mr Fisher's feed-pipe plug. Often the victim computer program remains intact, as does the data it generates or uses; what alters is the computer's 'usefulness'. Before the Computer Misuse Act 1990, courts were forced to rely on the Criminal Damage Act 1971 to reason that the value of a computer's storage medium was impaired by altering the storing magnetic particles.[57]

Prosecutions are more straightforward under s 3 of the Computer Misuse Act 1990. However, since its adoption, this section had come under increasing criticism for perceived problems in failing to address denial of service attacks and interference by authorised users of systems (insiders). This author writes 'perceived problems', since, in fact the previous drafting of s 3 was wide enough to capture these offences. Indeed, in 2006, the first prosecution for a denial of service attack was successfully brought, whilst the amendments to s 3 were still being debated in Parliament.[58] The amendments were nonetheless enacted through the Police and Criminal Justice Act 2006, making the offence even broader, although these amendments are still subject to formal introduction into force by the Secretary of State (expected to be delayed until 2008 to coincide with the intended introduction of the Serious Crime Bill, as explained above).

The current wording of s 3 provides that:

'3. (1) A person is guilty of an offence if:

(a) he does any act which causes unauthorised modification of the contents of any computer; and

(b) at the time when he does the act he has the requisite intent and the requisite knowledge.

(2) For the purposes of subsection (1)(b) above the requisite intent is an intent to cause modification of the contents of any computer and by so doing:

(a) to impair the operation of any computer;

(b) to prevent or hinder access to any program or data held in any computer; or

(c) to impair the operation of any such program or the reliability of any such data.'

As amended, s 3 will read:

'3. (1) A person is guilty of an offence if:

(a) he does any unauthorised act in relation to a computer; and

---

57   See *Cox v Riley* (1986) 83 Cr App Rep 54; also *R v Whiteley* (1991) 93 Cr App Rep 25. The Criminal Damage Act 1971 is no longer applicable owing to the Computer Misuse Act 1990, s 3(6).

58   *Director of Public Prosecution v David Lennon* [2006] EWCH 1201, 11 May 2006.

(b)   at the time when he does the act he knows that it is unauthorised; and

(c)   either subsection (2) or subsection (3) applies.

(2) This subsection applies if the person intends by doing the act -

(a)   to impair the operation of any computer;

(b)   to prevent or hinder access to any program or data held in any computer;

(c)   to impair the operation of any such program or the reliability of any such data; or

(d)   to enable any of the things mentioned in paragraphs (a) to (c) above to be done.

(3) This subsection applies if the person is reckless as to whether the act will do any of the things mentioned in paragraphs (a) to (d) of subsection (2) above.'

5.1.4.1   Conduct or actus reus

5.1.4.1.1   Unauthorised act or modification

Modification

Currently, any act which causes an unauthorised modification of the contents of a computer can be the necessary conduct for a s 3 conviction.[59] Modification is exhaustively defined as taking place where, by the operation of any function, any program or data held in a computer is altered or erased or is added to.[60] The concept is widened by the clarification that 'any act which *contributes* towards causing such a modification shall be regarded as causing it'.[61]

---

14. A programmer is commissioned to write a Java applet which will show an animation on a home page. Without authority he also includes a logic bomb which downloads to each client computer and wishes them 'Happy Christmas' on 25 December. The logic bomb will not directly alter any program or data as it does not attach to other code stored on the computer. On the set date, however, the program will alter the contents of data held in the computer. The applet causes a modification.

Defence counsel should be alive to the fact that it is not unlawful to possess malicious code. Further, it is not prohibited to write it.[62] The hard task for the prosecution is therefore to prove that the defendant distributed or contributed to the release of malicious code. This is the case for two reasons.

First, malicious code is often spread by people other than those who wrote them initially. It can therefore be difficult to prove to the high burden of criminal

---

59   Computer Misuse Act 1990, s 3(1)(a).
60   Computer Misuse Act 1990, s 17(7)(a) and (b).
61   Computer Misuse Act 1990, s 17(7). Emphasis added.
62   Sadly, there are countless examples of 'macro virus construction kits' for large programs such as Microsoft Office. Use of inchoate offences to prosecute such virus writers, while possible, has never been tested in the UK's courts.

proof that the source of the infection on the victim computer was the defendant's action. The existence of the virus on other systems prior to the alleged infection can weaken the prosecution's case by suggesting someone other than the defendant caused or contributed to the modification. The second difficulty for the prosecution is that, at present, there is no equivalent of a DNA fingerprint test for computer code. It will often be impossible to state categorically the source of an infection other than by extrapolating the code's dissemination. Occasionally, though, the prosecution will be able to rely on evidence gained from the defendant's own computer. In *R v Pile* the defendant surreptitiously stored programs on his computer which he used to write and distribute the viruses.[63] The FBI was helped by 'globally unique identifiers' (such as the embedding of Ethernet adaptor addresses in Microsoft Office 97 documents) to capture David L Smith, the Melissa virus writer.

Act

The amended s 3 offence, once in force, will capture any 'unauthorised act in relation to a computer' and therefore creates an even wider *actus reus*. There is no longer any need to demonstrate that the act 'causes an unauthorised modification of the contents of a computer' which will be a welcome amendment for prosecutors given that many forms of malicious code do not actually cause any alteration but just have an impact such as slowing down, jamming or simply making systems behave in a different way.

It has already been shown that 'computer' has a very wide meaning.[64] In addition, 'act', like 'function' in s 1, is not defined, although s 3(5) clarifies that this will encompass not just a single act but also a series of acts and that it also includes 'causing an act to be done'.[65]

Unauthorised

For both existing and pending provisions, the concept of 'authority' is central. As for ss 1 and 2, demonstrating that the defendant's act was unauthorised is rarely difficult to prove when the malicious code is spread from outside an organisation. Sometimes within an organisation the act is so obvious that the defence can raise no serious questions of authority. Two real case examples should suffice. A male nurse pleaded guilty to two charges under s 3. He had altered prescriptions and treatment of various patients in his hospital.[66] In *R v Spielman* the defendant, a former employee of an online financial news agency, tampered with and deleted employee emails.[67]

---

63 Unreported, Plymouth Crown Court, May 1995. See *The Guardian*, 16 November 1995.
64 See the discussion in the context of the s 1 offence at section 5.1.2.1.1 of this chapter.
65 Computer Misuse Act 1990, s 3(5)(a) and (b).
66 *R v Rymer* (unreported, Liverpool Crown Court, December 1993). See *The Guardian*, 21 December 1993.
67 Unreported, Bow Street Magistrates' Court, March 1995. See *Computer Weekly*, 2 February 1995.

A third case indicates the widening of the court's approach to acts which are deemed to be 'unauthorised'. Teenager David Lennon was fired from his position at Domestic and General after only three months in the job. As an act of revenge, Lennon used a mail bomb program to send up to five million emails to the company, the majority using the human resources manager's email address. A classic, 'denial of service' attack, the program operated by sending email upon email, copying to the employees within the company and increasing the email traffic so as to slow down systems and cause annoyance. The device was set up to keep going until manually stopped by Lennon. The Wimbledon youth court initially held that s 3 did not apply because the sending of emails was authorised. The whole purpose of the recipient's server was to receive email. The quantity was just 'unwelcome rather than unauthorised'. Lord Keen and Mr Justice Jack sitting in the High Court disagreed, concluding that implied consent had limits and the email bombing had to be considered as a whole and not on an email-by-email basis. On this basis, the emails were not sent for the purpose of communication (which was authorised), but to disrupt the systems (which was not).[68]

As stated previously, the more vague the internal guidelines on authority, the more difficult it may be to prosecute an insider who is regarded to have acted outside such authority.[69] Of course, employers may not resort to calling the police when an existing employee can be dealt with internally for gross misconduct.[70]

5.1.4.2   Intention or mens rea

The prosecution have several limbs to prove the *mens rea* elements of the offence.

Currently, there are two limbs of a 'guilty mind' for s 3: the defendant must have the 'requisite intent' and the 'requisite knowledge'.[71] Simply put by the Act, the 'requisite knowledge' under s 3(1)(b) is that any modification intended to be caused is unauthorised. The examination under s 1 of the degree of 'knowledge' is equally relevant for this section.[72] In terms of intention, the defendant must not only have intended to modify the contents of a computer, but also this modification should have at least one of four results set out below.[73] This does not mean that the defendant must have intended one particular kind of modification: an intention to modify is sufficient.[74] These results are considered below with

---

68   *Director of Public Prosecution v David Lennon* [2006] EWCH 1201, 11 May 2006. The defendant subsequently pleaded guilty and was sentenced to a two-month curfew and electronic tagging.

69   See section 5.1.2.2.3.

70   In *Denco v Joinson* an employee's unauthorised access was stated by the Employment Appeal Tribunal to be gross misconduct [1992] 1 All ER 463.

71   Computer Misuse Act 1990, s 3(1)(b).

72   See the dicta of Lord Bridge, *Westminster City Council v Croyalgrange Ltd* [1986] 2 All ER 353.

73   Computer Misuse Act 1990, s 3(2).

74   Computer Misuse Act 1990, s 3(3)(c).

specific reference to potential rogue code which may be spread over the Internet. It is not a defence that the results were intended to be merely temporary.[75]

Under the new s 3 there will still be a two-step test. First, the defendant must have known at the time he did the act that it was unauthorised. This issue of authority has been considered at some length above in relation to the s 1 offence, and so is not considered further here. Second, the prosecution must show that the defendant's intention in doing such act was to do one of five things (since a new addition has been made). Alternatively, the prosecution can now prove that the defendant was reckless as to whether the act would do any of these things. Each of these components and options is considered below.

5.1.4.2.1 Intent to impair or prevent or hinder access

In s 3 the motive and intention are tied up together. With s 1, it is enough that a defendant intends to secure unauthorised access; it is irrelevant why or what they then intend to do or permit. With s 3, the unauthorised modification or act must be intended to have some sort of impact namely, to do one of the following[76]:

3(2)(a) To impair the operation of any computer
To impair the operation of a computer itself, without impairing the operation of any program, would suggest that this subsection caters for a worm. A worm is a program which replicates and grows in size.[77] This reproduction and expansion can cause a computer storage system to run more slowly and can also cause the computer itself to slow down. Legally it is important to note that it does not attach itself to the operating system of the computer, to a program or data it infects; it does not *directly* impair the workings of a computer. The most infamous example of such a program is Robert Morris's worm. This was released on 2 November 1988 and within a couple of days had almost crashed the entire Internet which existed at the time, including NASA and the US Defense Department. Morris was convicted of violating the Computer Fraud and Abuse Act.[78]

Another example of impairment can be seen in the case of university student Joseph McElroy, who used hacking tools to gain access to vulnerable systems so as to use their storage facility for uploading music, games and software for his own use and by his friends. Unfortunately, the vulnerable system he thought was an academic site, turned out to be owned by the US Department of Energy which is, amongst other things, responsible for America's nuclear weapons (although in fact the breach was found to be restricted to several unclassified computers). The storage caused the Department's systems to slow down, thereby impairing its operation. The systems needed to be repaired, costing tens of thousands of pounds.[79] McElroy (only 18) was convicted, but sentenced to just 200 hours of community service.

---

75 Computer Misuse Act 1990, s 3(5).
76 Although, as the cases and examples considered below indicate, the intention does not need to extend to the actual full impact of the act.
77 Not to be confused with the acronym WORM.
78 *United States v Morris* 928 F 2d 504 (2nd Cir) (1991). For additional details see Hafner K and Markoff J, *Cyberpunk* (Corgi, London, 1993).
79 *R v Joseph McElroy* (unreported, Southwark Crown Court, 3 February 2005).

3(2)(b)   To prevent or hinder access to any program or data held in any computer
A worm will hinder access to a program or data, indirectly, but there are three
other types of code which will cause this. A virus which obstructs the use of a
computer will certainly fall within this section. One of Christopher Pile's viruses,
Pathogen, after infecting a computer 32 times, would at a particular time on a
Monday evening show a message, 'Smoke me a kipper, I'll be back for breakfast.
Unfortunately some of your data won't.'[80] This virus certainly hinders the access
to the program being used at the time.

This type of result is also satisfied where a programmer seeks to use a logic
bomb to 'lock out' an individual from accessing a program or data. Again, disgruntled employees appear to be the main culprits. Mr Hardy, an IT manager,
added a program to his company's system which encrypted stored data, and de-
encrypted it on retrieval. One month after he left the firm the program stopped
unscrambling the data. This left his former company hindered from accessing its
stored information. He pleaded guilty.[81]

---

15. As a joke, a person attaches a virus to a word processing document which he forwards to a friend at work. The virus was intended simply to play a rude sound when the
machine was next switched on. Owing to a special sound device attached to the friend's
machine, the computer, and then the entire network, crashed. The more limited result
intended by the joker is not relevant to the issue of culpability under the old s 3 wording; it may be relevant for sentencing or under the amended wording of s 3 however.

**3(2)(c)   To impair the operation of any such program or the reliability of any such
data**
This subsection focuses on how a program executes when some code has run.
The 'operation' can be taken to mean how the program should function without
the malicious code. It should not be read narrowly to mean the use that the victim
makes of the program. The Melissa virus would automatically 'send itself' to the
first 50 addresses listed in the address book of the Microsoft Outlook program.
The operation of Microsoft Outlook was impaired on the infected computer.

'Impairing the reliability of data' should be viewed by defence counsel as an
objective notion of reliability. It is not enough for an infected computer owner to
claim that he now cannot rely on the data because he feels it may be unreliable.
The prosecution must prove the alteration or reduction in quality of the data on
an objective basis.[82] This approach is supported in a case mainly concerning the

---

80   See *The Guardian*, 16 November 1995. See also fn 65 at p 307.
81   *R v Hardy* (unreported, Old Bailey, November 1992).
82   This approach is confirmed in *A-G's Reference (No 1 of 1991)* [1993] QB 94. Lord Taylor
      stated obiter that it is questionable whether it is correct to 'giv[e] the word "reliability" the
      meaning of achieving the result in the printout which was intended by the owner of the com-
      puter. It may not necessarily impair the reliability of data in the computer that you feed in
      something which will produce a result more favourable . . . than the [owner] intended'. [1992]
      3 WLR 432 at 438.

extradition of two Kazakh hackers.[83] The facts of the case concerned the hacking of the Bloomberg financial computer system, so allowing the appellants to send messages that appeared to come from someone else; they were, in effect, forging the messages. The Divisional Court was asked whether or not *adding new* data to a computer system would fall within the section. Mr Justice Wright's terse judgment pointed out that s 17(7) of the Act provides that any addition of data to the contents of a computer amounts to a modification of the contents.

3(2)(d)   To enable any of the things mentioned in paragraphs (a) to (c) above to be done

This provision is added under the Police and Justice Act 2006 and not yet in force at the time of publication. It widens and clarifies the acts which will be caught, meaning that the defendant need not themselves have actually caused the impairment or hindrance. It is sufficient that he intended that this would be enabled (whether by someone else, or by a user simply triggering the harm, for example by opening an attachment).

---

16.   A website has a virus which is downloaded secretly and automatically to any computer which accesses the site. This virus reduces the security of any credit card transactions which the user makes using their browser. It is of no importance that the only victims of the virus do not actually use their browser for such a purpose. The operation of the browser, as it was originally designed, has been impaired by the unauthorised modification.

Any computer, program or data

The intention to modify does not need to be directed at any particular computer, or particular program, data or kind of program or data.[84] The drafting of s 3(4) in this way is essential to encompass fully the mischief which it addresses. Computer viruses and other malicious codes are disseminated in a random manner. The initial release of the code then results in it being passed to, and perhaps replicated by, any number of computers anywhere on the Internet. The prosecution would not be able to show a defendant had the intent to infect each victim of his code.[85]

Temporarily

The pending (at the time of writing) amendment to s 3 at sub-s (5)(c) clarifies that 'a reference to impairing, preventing or hindering something includes a reference to doing so temporarily.'

---

83   *Zezev and Yarimaka v Governor of HM Prison Brixton and Government of the United States of America* [2002] EWHC 589 (Admin) [2002] 2 Cr App Rep 515.
84   Computer Misuse Act 1990, s 3(3)(a) and (b).
85   This is confirmed by the conviction in *R v Pile* (unreported, Plymouth Crown Court, May 1995). Mr Pile's viruses were placed on bulletin boards and then spread by other people. See *The Guardian*, 16 November 1995.

5.1.4.2.2   Recklessness as to act

The Police and Justice Act 2006 introduces a new sub-s 3 to the s 3 offence which means that a defendant need not have intention but can still be found guilty if they were 'reckless as to whether the act will do any of the things mentioned in paragraphs (a) to (d) of subsection (2)'.

This reintroduces the recklessness element which exists in criminal damage cases, the main basis for action prior to the Computer Misuse Act. The recklessness requirement is objective.

5.1.4.3   *Sentencing*

Currently, a person guilty of an offence under s 3 is liable, on summary conviction, to imprisonment for a term not exceeding six months or to a fine not exceeding the statutory maximum or to both and, on indictment, to imprisonment for a term not exceeding five years or to a fine or to both.

Once implemented, the amendments brought in through the Police and Justice Act 2006 will increase the potential term of imprisonment to up to 12 months (six months for Scotland) on summary conviction and up to 10 years on indictment.

5.1.5   Section 3A: making, supplying or obtaining articles for use in computer misuse

The most controversial of the amendments to the Computer Misuse Act which found its way into the Police and Justice Act 2006 is the inclusion of a new offence of making, supplying or obtaining articles for use in computer misuse. As with the other amendments to the Act, at the time of writing, this section had not yet been formally brought into force, but was expected to be in 2008. It is still useful to outline its provisions here.

One of the main drivers behind this new provision is Art 6 of the Council of Europe Convention on Cybercrime, which requires the criminalisation of the distribution or making of a computer password through which a computer system is capable of being accessed with intent to commit a crime. The Convention was opened for signature at a signing in ceremony in Budapest on 23 November 2001, when 30 countries signed. The terms of the Convention require that it enters into force only once it has been ratified by five countries. The UK has signed but is yet to ratify the Convention, despite considerable pressure to do so. Nonetheless, it is clear from the amendments to the Computer Misuse Act, together with other changes in e-crime legislation (including the current discussions on the draft Serious Crime Bill) that the government has taken its provisions and motivations into consideration.

Section 3A reads:

> '(1) A person is guilty of an offence if he makes, adapts, supplies or offers to supply any article intending it to be used to commit, or to assist in the commission of, an offence under section 1 or 3.

(2)   A person is guilty of an offence if he supplies or offers to supply any article believing that it is likely to be used to commit, or to assist in the commission of, an offence under section 1 or 3.

(3)   A person is guilty of an offence if he obtains any article with a view to its
being supplied for use to commit, or to assist in the commission of, an
offence under section 1 or 3.'

In this way, three separate offences are created. This section considers the *actus
reus* and *mens rea* of each in turn.

5.1.5.1   Making, adapting, supplying or offering to supply article for commission
of an offence

This offence captures the manufacture, supply, adaptation of or offering (for
example advertising) of any equipment for the use in connection with the commission of an offence under s 1 or 3 of the Act. 'Article' is defined in sub-s (4) as
including any program or data held in electronic form and we have already seen
above, how wide program and data can be construed.

Although perhaps the simplest of the offences, this section has come under
recent criticism for failing to address the real problem of botnets, which are a
vehicle typically used for the delivery of spam or denial of service attacks. The
House of Lords' 2007 report on Personal Internet Security calls for a gap to be
filled in order to cover those persons who purchase or hire botnets and those who
sell them regardless of the purpose. The reasoning here is that a botnet is inherently designed for criminal use and 'can only exist by virtue of the criminal acts
by those who recruited it'.[86]

5.1.5.2   Supply of an article to commit or assist in commission of an offence

This offence only captures the sale or offering of an article but where the defendant believed that it is likely to be used to commit or to assist in the commission
of an offence under the Act. The most debated of the changes, particular concerns
have been raised over the problem this presents for suppliers of tools which
(unlike the issue with botnets) may be used for legitimate as well as illegal purposes. The IT and testing industry have been very alarmed by this development
since it means that a risk hangs over them that the sale or offer of code which
may be designed or intended for use in penetration testing or the permitted sending of email or distribution of code, could result in prosecution.

The main problem is the inclusion of the words 'believing it is likely to be
used'. Programmers and developers are generally all too well aware of the capabilities of their creations or how a password tool could be used if in the wrong
hands, say, of a hacker. Although discussed, no definition of what may constitute
'likely' has been included in the Act and attempts to replace this with 'primarily'

---

86   House of Lords Science and Technology Committee, 5th report of session 2006–2007
'Personal Internet Security', published on 10 August 2007, para 7.12.

resisted. Hansard discussions reveal that Ministers intended this to be a high test in practice, with the prosecution needing to prove beyond reasonable doubt that the person supplying the tool knew it would be used for unlawful purposes in most instances. This provides little comfort when the actual wording is around likely belief, rather than knowledge, however.

As the Earl of Erroll stated: 'One is trying to criminalise people who advertise on the Internet saying, "Great hacker tool available, derived from such and such, best thing ever, why don't you buy it for X?"'[87] Without clarification in the legislation itself, it is left open to the courts to give its own interpretation to these words in due course.

5.1.5.3   Obtaining an article for supply or assistance in commission of an offence

This new offence catches the defendant who has obtained but not yet put to use an article which may be used for the commission of an offence under the Act. In this way it usefully opens the door to preventative action by the authorities. The difficulty, as ever in such possession cases, is in proving the intention where no acts have yet taken place.

5.1.5.4   Sentencing

A person guilty of an offence under s 3A is liable, on summary conviction, to imprisonment for a term not exceeding 12 months (six months for Scotland), or to a fine not exceeding the statutory maximum or to both or, on indictment, to imprisonment for a term not exceeding two years or to a fine or to both.[88]

5.1.6   Jurisdiction and extradition

Jurisdiction and extradition can be fundamental to an Internet-based case. The Computer Misuse Act 1990 operates within tight jurisdictional confines. Computer misusers do not. It has been discussed that a hacker will often log in to computers across the globe in a bid to disguise his true location and identity. Malicious code, such as viruses, can spread across the whole Internet, and are therefore capable of modifying any data or program in any jurisdiction.

The physical location of the hacker or other misuser is not an indication of where the crime is committed. And what may not be legal here, may well be caught by the laws of another jurisdiction. These other laws are not considered in this chapter, but the rules on extradition to those countries are.

---

87   Lords *Hansard* 11 July 2006: Column 581.
88   Computer Misuse Act 1990, s 3(A)(5).

5.1.6.1 Jurisdiction

The Computer Misuse Act 1990 provides its rules on jurisdiction in ss 4 to 7.[89] They are complex and apply differently to each of the offences. If the English court does not have jurisdiction over the offence the offender may still face charges from abroad.

5.1.6.1.1 Section 1 jurisdiction

The court will have jurisdiction over a computer misuse offender under s 1 where the offence has at least one 'significant link' with England and Wales.[90] For a s 1 offence, a significant link can be either[91]:

'1. that the accused was in England at the time when he did the act which caused the computer to perform the function; or

2. that the computer containing any program or data to which the accused secured or intended to secure unauthorised access by doing that act was in England at that time.'[92]

The second situation has been replaced by the amendments of the Police and Justice Act 2006 (yet to be formally brought into force as considered above, but expected in 2008) with:

'2. that any computer containing any program or data to which the accused by doing that act secured or intended to secure unauthorised access, or enabled or intended to enable unauthorised access to be secured, was in England or Wales concerned at that time.'

These changes are natural consequences of the amendments to the s 1 offence and do not represent a substantial change.

Location of accused

This is a simple test. Neil Woods and Karl Strickland were convicted and sentenced to six months' imprisonment under s 1. They had used UK computers, mostly academic, to break into databases in 15 countries outside the UK.[93]

---

89 Readers unfamiliar with rules as to jurisdiction are warned not to conflate the assessment of jurisdiction with assessment of culpability under the offence itself. The rules described below are necessarily wider than the rules for a conviction. It is perfectly possible that the courts have jurisdiction over a person, who at trial, is found not to be guilty of the offence itself. Nevertheless, the defence should be prepared to fight on jurisdiction, without which there will be no trial in England at all.

90 Computer Misuse Act 1990, s 4(2).

91 Computer Misuse Act 1990, s 5(2).

92 A 16-year-old pleaded guilty to 12 s 1 offences. All the unauthorised accesses were performed from his north London home. The victim computers were top security military computers based in the US. The Senate said that 'he had caused more damage than the KGB': *R v Pryce* (unreported, Bow Street Magistrates' Court, 21 March 1997).

93 Unreported, Southwark Crown Court, 21 May 1993.

17. A French postgraduate student at university in England logs in to his former university computer in France. From this computer he runs an automated hacking program which fails to gain access to a further computer in America. The English court has jurisdiction, even though the computer caused to function was outside England, as was the victim computer. The act causing the function was made while the postgraduate was in England.

Location of victim computer

The nub of this subsection is that the misuser secured access or intended to secure access to *any* computer situated in England. It is of no consequence that the hacker was only using an English computer as a 'stop' on the way to a victim computer outside the jurisdiction. Jurisdiction can result from the victim computer or any computer through which the hacker journeys being within England.

18. A programmer based in America has for some time been plotting to hack into an English oil company's computer. He is caught by American police, having secured access to an American computer which has a secure line to the English computer. The English court, perhaps not alone, has jurisdiction over the American. It is sufficient that his intentions were directed to an English computer.

19. A hacker based in a country with no extradition treaties gains unauthorised access into a computer with weak security in Bolivia. She uses this computer to plant daemon programs in countless other computers across the globe. Finally, she uses a program called Tribal Flood Network to launch attacks at a UK newspaper's websites. It is brought down by the attack in seconds. The English court has jurisdiction over the hacker as her intention was to impair a UK computer.

5.1.6.1.2   Section 2 jurisdiction

The jurisdiction over s 2 offences is wider than that for s 1. Either or both of two rules give the court jurisdiction:

1. subject to 'double criminality' below if the accused intended to do or facilitate anything outside England which would be a s 2 offence if it took place in England *and* the offence has a significant link to England for a s 1 offence[94];

2. if the accused gained unauthorised access to a computer abroad with the intent to commit the further offence in England.

Not only the English courts must view the conduct as falling within the ambit of the offence. The relevant country abroad must also view the conduct as criminal, although the offences here and abroad need not be the same.[95] The further offence

94   Computer Misuse Act 1990, s 4(4).
95   Computer Misuse Act 1990, s 8(4).

must involve the commission of an offence under the law in force where the whole or any part of the further offence was intended to take place.[96]

Defence counsel must note that the onus is on them to serve a notice on the prosecution stating that the double-criminality is not satisfied. Full facts and grounds for that opinion must be included in the notice.[97]

---

20. An American bank protects its records by storing them with an English data warehouse, fully encrypted. From a mobile device, a hacker, at the time in Switzerland, gains access to this data warehouse and appropriates a number of confidential files, still encrypted. After cracking the encryption, the hacker intends to steal electronically from the American bank. The English court has jurisdiction over the hacker, having both a significant link with England, constituting an offence if in England and being punishable in the US.

5.1.6.1.3   Section 3 jurisdiction

The court will have jurisdiction over s 3 misuse where the offence has at least one 'significant link' with England.[98] For a s 3 offence, a significant link can be either[99]:

1.   that the accused was in England at the time when he did the act which caused the unauthorised modification; or

2.   that the unauthorised modification took place in England.

Again, minor amendments will be implemented to this to reflect the changes to the s 3 offence pursuant to the Police and Justice Act 2006.

It has been mentioned on numerous occasions that a virus may spread throughout the entire Internet. It is possible to affect computers in multiple jurisdictions. An effect of the 'significant link' is to allow the English courts to prosecute a person who disseminates malicious code from England, even if no computer in England is modified. Also, the significant link contemplates a computer modifier from anywhere in the world being prosecuted for a computer in England being affected.

Location of accused

---

21. An English public schoolboy uses his school computer to post on a French Internet bulletin board a logic bomb which corrupts an important part of any computer it infects. It is of no consequence that the logic bomb is 'defused' before it reaches a computer in England. The act constituting the offence was committed within the jurisdiction.

---

96   Computer Misuse Act 1990, s 8(1).
97   Computer Misuse Act 1990, s 8(5) and (9).
98   Computer Misuse Act 1990, s 4(2).
99   Computer Misuse Act 1990, s 5(3).

As previously stated, executable code which is on a website may cause an unauthorised modification or impairment. The act of uploading this code to the website will constitute the relevant act for the purposes of jurisdiction.

Location of victim computer

The jurisdiction of the court is triggered by any computer situated in England affected by the unauthorised modification or act. It does not matter that the modifier had no intention to infect an English computer.

5.1.6.2   Extradition

The law concerning extradition is complex and it is considered more appropriate that readers consult a specialist text in the field before providing or acting on any advice. The following is a brief indication of the aspects of digital crime over the Internet which should be factored into any extradition evaluation.

The rules of extradition are largely governed by way of international treaties and agreements between states.

In the UK, statutory rules (implementing certain of these arrangements) are set out in the Extradition Act 2003 (repealing the Extradition Act 1989). This Act separates out the procedures for extradition to 'category 1 territories', which are part of the European Arrest Warrant Scheme, namely European member states, and 'category 2 territories', which are designated territories which are not. The Act also incorporates controversial arrangements of an extradition treaty with the US, against which alleged hacker Gary McKinnon was fighting, at the time of writing. Mr McKinnon gained access to various US government computers specifically out of curiosity, he maintains, as to evidence of UFO attacks, rather than with any terrorist intention. At the time of publication a hearing by the House of Lords was still pending, having been granted appeal on 31 July 2007.

For category 1 territories, the process is now expedited allowing, essentially, for the mutual recognition of warrants issued in one member state in the courts of another. In relation to crimes, of which computer crime is punishable by up to three years' imprisonment, extradition within such territories is therefore intended to be automatic and it is not necessary to consider whether such an offence would be an offence in both relevant territories. In other cases, such dual criminality assessments may still apply. Both ss 2 and 3 of the Computer Misuse Act therefore fall within this automatic category. (Remember of course that extradition is a different matter to the making out of an offence in the UK in the first place for the purposes of s 2, which is considered above, so although seemingly at odds and complex, these are different things.)

For category 2 territories, the 'double criminality test' applies (therefore an offence must be made out in each of the relevant territories although not necessarily the same offence). An order from the Secretary of State is required.

The following discussion of an actual extradition case illustrates the way a hacker from abroad may be extradited to a place where his actions were illegal.

In *R v Governor of Brixton Prison, ex p Levin*, the US government sought the extradition of a Russian expert computer programmer who had gained access to

Citibank's computer in New Jersey, America.[100] Levin, using his skill as a computer programmer, was able to monitor the transactions of substantial customers and insert unauthorised instructions to make payments from their accounts into those of a Russian accomplice. If the scheme had been successful, sums in excess of $10 million would have been obtained. Levin was detained on 3 March 1995 in execution of a warrant under s 1(3) of the Extradition Act 1989 at the request of the US government. He was accused of having committed in the US offences of wire fraud and bank fraud and of conspiring to commit those offences. No single criminal offence under the law of England and Wales equates to the offence of wire fraud or bank fraud.

The prosecuting authority gave details of acts and conduct which translated into 66 offences under the criminal law of England and Wales, including unauthorised access to a computer with intent to commit or facilitate further offences, conspiracy to commit offences under the Computer Misuse Act 1990 and unauthorised modification of computer material.

The applicant challenged his committal on the main grounds that the computer print-out records could not be admitted under s 69 of the Police and Criminal Evidence Act 1984 since that section did not apply to extradition proceedings, because they were not criminal proceedings within s 72 of the Act.

The Divisional Court and House of Lords held that as the extradition crimes involved conduct punishable under the criminal law, they were criminal proceedings for the purposes of the Police and Criminal Evidence Act 1984. Evidence of the computer print-outs in extradition hearings should be, and rightly in this case, was admitted in evidence under s 69 of the Act.

One of the other grounds was that as the appropriation took place in Russia, where the computer keyboard was situated, the English courts had no jurisdiction. For the purposes of the Theft Act 1968, the Divisional Court had to decide where the actions of Mr Levin took place. They said[101]:

> '[T]he operation of the keyboard by a computer operator produces a virtually instantaneous result on the magnetic disk of the computer even though it may be 10,000 miles away. It seems to us artificial to regard the act as having been done in one rather than the other place. [T]he fact that the applicant was physically in St Petersburg is of far less significance than the fact that he was looking at and operating on magnetic disks located in [America]. The essence of what he was doing was done there.'[102]

Mr Levin's extradition to the US took place in September 1997. In January 1998 Federal prosecutors announced that they had reached a plea agreement with Mr Levin: three years in prison together with $240,000 payable in restitution.

---

100   [1997] QB 65; affd [1997] 3 All ER 289, HL.
101   [1996] 3 WLR 657 at 671.
102   In *Zezev and Yarimaka v Governor of HM Prison Brixton and Government of the United States of America* [2002] EWHC 589 (Admin) [2002] 2 Cr App Rep 515 the Divisional Court also judged that the UK court could extradite two hackers who committed computer misuse from Kazakstan against Bloomberg LP in New York.

5.2   INTERNET FRAUD

Internet fraud is not a new crime, it just takes traditional scams and schemes and uses new technical means to trap its victims. As the Law Commission had revealed in a comprehensive 2002 report,[103] the previous offences contained in the Theft Act 1968 and 1978 (governing goods and services respectively) were outdated and overly complex and therefore unable to deal with this new development. In particular, the legislation contained a loophole which meant that it was not possible to deceive a machine. This had the natural consequence that a whole raft of computer and Internet-based frauds were not in fact criminal, for example the giving of fake credit card details in order to purchase goods fraudulently. As the Law Commission pointed out, the fraud should be the offence, and the means by which it is effected should be immaterial.

The Fraud Act 2006, implemented in line with the Commission's recommendations, creates a general offence of fraud, with three ways of committing it: by false representation; by failing to disclose information; and by abuse of position. The new offence of 'fraud by false representation' carries a maximum sentence of 10 years' imprisonment and is drafted broadly so as to encompass fraudulent Internet and other online activities such as 'phishing'. Government resisted calls for a specific anti-phishing offence, preferring a broader approach which would capture this and future forms of fraudulent activity.

The Act also requires that the person must make the representation with the intention of making a gain or causing loss or risk of loss to another, regardless of whether the gain or loss actually takes place. A representation is defined as false if it is untrue or misleading and the person making it knows that it is, or might be, untrue or misleading. A representation means any representation as to fact or law, including a representation as to a person's state of mind. It can be stated in words or communicated by conduct. There is no limitation on the way in which the words must be expressed: they could be written, spoken or posted on a website.

In respect of the gain, there is no limitation in the Act, which means that this need not be limited to goods or services. This is good news for those increasingly concerned with the appropriation of credit card or identity details across the Internet. Confirmation is provided in the Explanatory Notes to the Act, which expressly give Internet-based examples. One such example includes that of 'a person who disseminates an email to large groups of people falsely representing that the email has been sent by a legitimate financial institution. The email prompts the reader to provide information such as credit card and bank account numbers so that the "phisher" can gain access to others' assets.' Although a very welcome development, problems still arise in terms of public confidence and the manner of investigation and reporting of Internet fraud. The House of Lords has condemned in particular[104] the approach taken by the government, which seeks to discourage the reporting of these sorts of crimes to the police, instead asking

---

103   Law Commission Report on Fraud (Law Com No. 276, Cm 5560, 2002).
104   House of Lords Science and Technology Committee, 5th report of session 2006–2007 'Personal Internet Security', published on 10 August 2007.

those affected to report it to APACS (the UK trade association for payments services and institutions).

5.3 OBSCENE AND INDECENT MATERIAL

It has always been possible to acquire by mail order obscene and paedophilic material from within England or from abroad which is illegal in England. The Internet has made this process easier, it may have also made this activity more prevalent; it has not, however, altered the legal ramifications of the activity.[105] The Obscene Publications Act 1959, as amended by the Criminal Justice and Public Order Act 1994, covers material which has the effect of depraving and corrupting. Additionally the Sexual Offences Act 2003, which came into force on 1 May 2004, amends parts of the Protection of Children Act 1978 to extend protection in relation to indecent photographs of children of 16 and 17. It also introduces a new offence under s 15, intended to target those who may use the Internet for sexual grooming.

This section considers the different liabilities which may arise where a person either publishes indecent or obscene material over the Internet, or takes, downloads, distributes or possesses indecent photographs. We then consider the position as regards liability of intermediaries for such content.

5.3.1 Publication over the Internet

An offence is committed under the Obscene Publications Act if a person publishes an obscene article: merely possessing an article is not an offence.[106] Possessing an obscene article for publication for gain is an offence.[107] Often, those who use the Internet for these purposes do not pay money for obscene articles; rather, they exchange them for other articles. This too will be seen as 'for gain'.[108] It is for the possessor of the article to prove that it was not for gain.

An amendment to the Act introduced the concept that it is publication to transmit electronically stored data which is obscene on resolution into a viewable form.[109]

---

22. A person sends an email attached to which is an encrypted graphics file depicting an obscene activity. Only the recipient has the unlocking key. The person will have transmitted the obscene material: it does not matter that the data is encrypted; when de-encrypted it will be obscene.

---

105   See also Telecommunications Act 1984, s 43 and Indecent Displays (Control) Act 1981.
106   Obscene Publications Act 1959, s 2.
107   Obscene Publications Act 1959, s 2.
108   Obscene Publications Act 1959, s 1(5). See *R v Fellows; R v Arnold* (unreported, CA, 27 September 1996).
109   Obscene Publications Act 1959, s 1(3), as amended by Criminal Justice and Public Order Act 1994, s 168 and Sch 9.

5.3.1.1   *Transmission or retrieval*

Often, obscene material is not transmitted to an individual. It is uploaded to a website or an ftp site. Interested parties download this material by instructing their computer to issue a command to the holding site. It is clearly an important question whether this constitutes transmission, and thereby constitutes publication.

This question was addressed by the Court of Appeal in *R v Fellows*; *R v Arnold*.[110] The appellants argued that publication within s 1(3) requires some form of active conduct, and that providing the *means* of access to a website or ftp site is passive only. In short, putting obscene pictures on a website, although no doubt allowing them to be *seen* by many people, is not publication of those pictures; technically it is each viewer who retrieves the picture.

The Court of Appeal was prepared to accept that some form of activity is required for publication. In this case they thought that there was ample evidence of such conduct. The first appellant:

> 'took whatever steps were necessary not merely to store the data on his computer but also to make it available world-wide to other computers via the Internet. He corresponded by e-mail with those who sought to have access to it and he imposed certain conditions before they were permitted to do so.'

This 'activity' prior to the actual offence appears to have satisfied the court that the storage of the material alone would be distribution.[111]

5.3.1.2   *Publication abroad*

It has been stated that possessing an obscene article is not an offence. However, where a person possesses an article and then transmits this *abroad,* where it is there published, a question arises as to whether this is an offence.

In *R v Waddon* the Crown Court[112] and Court of Appeal[113] were asked whether a UK resident creating obscene articles in the UK and uploading them to non-UK websites was 'publishing' for the purposes of the Obscene Publications Act. The courts reasoned that 'publishing' an article includes 'transmitting' that data.[114] Transmitting, the Crown Court held, means to send on from one place or person to another. Consequently, the transmission by the defendant to his UK Internet service provider took place within the jurisdiction. The Court of Appeal added that there was not one publication, but rather 'further publication when the images are downloaded elsewhere'. The fact that the appellant would not have been directly responsible for any downloads into the UK, so therefore could not have been prosecuted for them, is ignored by the Court of Appeal. This author prefers the arguments of the Crown Court as being a more robust application of the law to the known facts.

---

110   [1997] 2 All ER 548.
111   See also *R v Pecciarich* (1995) 22 OR (3d) 748 at 765.
112   (Unreported, Southwark Crown Court, 30 June 1999).
113   (Unreported, 6 April 2000).
114   Obscene Publications Act 1959, s 1(3)(b), as amended.

In a similar case, *R v Perrin*,[115] the Court of Appeal was asked to consider an appeal to a conviction of publishing an obscene article. The article in question was a sexually obscene web page, able to be viewed by anyone, and a further much larger set of sexually obscene material only viewable by subscribing with a credit card. The site was, in part, managed from outside the UK. The appellant appealed the conviction on a number of grounds. One was that it was necessary for the Crown to show where the major steps in relation to publication were taken. The Court of Appeal rejected this as being a necessary precursor to any prosecution. Instead, they deemed it enough to rely on a strict application of *Waddon*: there was 'transmission' within the jurisdiction.

These cases illustrate the rather parochial (and maybe morally justified) application of the Obscene Publications Act to published material on the Internet. Perhaps not unreasonably, in *Perrin*, the appellants sought to convince the Court of Appeal of the legal consequence of 'the sites [being] legal where they were managed'. In effect, the appellants unsuccessfully tried to appeal to the Court's commercial sense: 'Community standards as to what tends to deprave and corrupt are not Europe-wide, and the court should look at the problem from the point of view of a publisher who is prepared to comply with the law.' Of course these arguments are neither novel nor unique to English Internet jurisprudence. In the US, the Court of Appeal (Third Circuit) has (reluctantly) judged that only where the 'major' steps in relation to publication take place in the jurisdiction should the court take jurisdiction over a prosecution.[116] The US court in that case noted that 'web publishers cannot restrict access to their site based on the geographic locale of the Internet user visiting their site'.[117]

It is clear from these cases that the UK criminal courts' jurisdiction in cases of this kind will not be upset by the careful placing abroad of servers or 'management'.[118]

---

23. A woman living in Manchester establishes a Dutch company which operates a series of servers in Holland. The servers host a website which, after a credit card is entered, shows a number of obscene pictures involving sexual acts with animals. These obscene articles are uploaded to the Dutch servers from her home in Manchester. By transmitting the obscene articles from within the UK she is publishing obscene articles in the UK. She will not be able to avoid the jurisdiction of the UK courts by pointing to the 'major' steps being taken outside the UK.

---

115 [2002] EWCA Crim 747, [2002] All ER (D) 359 (Mar). It should be noted that the Court of Appeal also rejected the various pleas that the European Convention on Human Rights, arts 7 and 10, were sufficient to overturn the conviction.

116 *ACLU v Reno (No 3)* [2000] F 3d 162. The case concerned the preliminary injunction against the Attorney-General to prevent the enforcement of the Child Protection Act.

117 *ACLU v Reno (No 3)* [2000] F 3d 162, at 176. Cf *Groppera Radio AG v Switzerland* (1990) 12 EHRR 321.

118 In *Gold Star Publications Ltd v DPP* [1981] 2 All ER 257, the House of Lords was asked to consider whether thousands of hard-core pornographic magazines due for export from the UK would fall within the jurisdiction of the courts. Only Lord Simon dissented, taking the narrow view that the Obscene Publications Act 1959 should not be interpreted to grant UK courts powers to prevent activities abroad.

5.3.2   Indecent material

Section 1(1) of the Protection of Children Act 1978,[119] as amended by the Criminal Justice and Public Order Act 1994 and Sexual Offences Act 2003 (specifically to raise the age of a person considered to be a child from 16 to 18), makes it an offence:

'(a)   to take, or permit to be taken, an indecent photograph of a child (meaning in this Act a person under the age of 18); or

(b)   to distribute or show such indecent photographs or pseudo-photographs; or

(c)   to have in his possession such indecent photographs or pseudo-photographs with a view to their being distributed or shown by himself or others. . .'

Although the circumstances will be rare, there may be occasions where an individual possesses such items without knowledge of them. This is possible because most Internet browsers automatically store a copy of every graphic file viewed, called a 'cached' copy. In *Atkins v DPP*[120] the defendant was not convicted of the offence where he was not aware that his computer's cache held copies of the illegal photographs he had once viewed. This can easily be contrasted with 'making' by downloading and or printing indecent material, which does constitute an offence.[121] Downloading and printing are intentional acts and so may constitute 'making'. Even the deliberate copying of such material in the process of deleting it, may constitute the offence.[122]

5.3.2.1   *Photographs and pseudo-photographs*

The changes brought by the Criminal Justice and Public Order Act 1994 have been implemented to address the use that paedophiles make of computers. The term 'photographs' includes data stored on a computer disk or by other electronic means which is capable of conversion into a photograph.[123] This includes digital graphic images. The court will take a 'purposive approach': if the data can be converted into an indecent image, the data will be classed as a photograph.[124] A

---

119   This legislation remains unaffected by the coming into force of the Human Rights Act 1998, and therefore the European Convention of Human Rights, arts 8 and 10. In *R v Smelhurst*, the Court of Appeal were clear that the exception in art 10(2) covers the Act and it does not contravene the provisions of the Convention.
120   [2000] 2 All ER 425.
121   *R v Jonathan Bowden* [2001] QB 88.
122   *R v Mould* (unreported, CA, 6 November 2000).
123   Protection of Children Act 1978, s 7(4)(b), as amended.
124   See the US Court of Appeals for the Sixth Circuit, *United States v Thomas* 74 F 3d 701 (1996).

'pseudo photograph' is an image, whether made by a computer graphic or otherwise, which appears to be a photograph.[125] This inclusion, apparently, reflects the practice of paedophiles who use pornographic images of adults and then digitally alter them to look like indecent photographs of children. In *G v DPP*, two paper photographs taped together were not held to be a pseudo-photograph as they did not 'appear' to be a single photograph.[126] This can surely be contrasted with two digital graphic images which, when aligned, do appear as one.

5.3.3   Transmission, retrieval and downloading

As in the case for obscene material, *R v Fellows* indicated that it will be distribution simply to allow indecent images to be transmitted.

In addition, in considering s 7(2) of the 1978 Act, the court held that a computer file containing data that represented the original photograph in another form was 'a copy of a photograph' for the purposes of that section. Therefore, the downloading of an indecent photograph from the Internet constituted the 'making a copy of an indecent photograph', since a copy of that photograph had been caused to exist on the computer to which it had been downloaded.

This decision was taken further in *R v Jayson*,[127] in which the defendant was found to hold child abuse images in the temporary cache created by his Internet browser. Although the image was not stored for subsequent retrieval (i.e. the defendant had just been viewing the images on the Internet), the Court of Appeal ruled that 'the act of voluntarily downloading an indecent image from a web page on to a computer screen is an act of making a photograph or pseudo-photograph'. The period of time for which it was held and whether it could be retrieved was judged irrelevant.

'Making' may therefore arise through the copying of an image to removable storage media, where a 'hard copy' is printed out or simply where indecent content is voluntarily viewed on the Internet.

Of course the natural consequence of it being an offence to download or copy indecent images from the Internet or computer files means that law enforcement and network operators were also potentially liable for copying the contents of suspects files for evidence purposes. This issue has been resolved by amendments to include a statutory defence where the making is necessary for the purposes of the prevention, detection or investigation of crime or for the purpose of criminal proceedings, through the Sexual Offences Act.

125   Protection of Children Act 1978, s 7(7), as amended.
126   *R v DPP* (unreported, Divisional Court, 8 March 2000).
127   [2002] EWCA Crim 683, CA.

5.3.4   Liability of Internet service providers

As a starting point, because publication can be 'passive', an Internet service provider who facilitates, by storing, the transmission of an obscene file may be culpable as the publisher of obscene material. Similarly, under the Protection of Children Act 1978, mere possession on a server may be an offence under s 1(1)(c).

5.3.4.1   Internet Watch Foundation

The high risk of liability where 'blind eyes are turned', together with an interest in the 'common good', led Internet service providers to concoct a remarkably impressive system of self-regulation and authority co-operation. The Internet Watch Foundation (IWF) was formed in October 1996. It is an independent self-regulatory body funded by the EU and the online industry and aims (and succeeds) in restricting the availability of criminal content on the Internet. It operates a hotline and a 'notice and take down' procedure for Internet service providers which has resulted in less than 1 per cent of potentially illegal content being hosted in the UK since 2003, down from 18 per cent in 1997.[128] The IWF works closely with relevant authorities, forwarding child or adult pornography details on UK servers to relevant British police forces. Child pornography on foreign servers is forwarded to the Child Exploitation and Online Protection Centre, disseminated by Interpol.

Demonstrating the effectiveness of this 'hotline' together with 'notice and takedown' and 'authority notification' is the case of Leslie Bollingbroke. The IWF discovered that an individual using the pseudonym 'Sammy' was posting illegal images of children on the Internet and discussing them on newsgroups. The IWF forwarded the information to the Metropolitan Police. 'Sammy' was discovered to be one Leslie Bollingbroke, who was subsequently jailed for four years.

A second reason for the effectiveness of this 'self-regulation' is the interaction between the Internet Service Providers Association (ISPA) and the IWF. Both are independent bodies, but the ISPA acts, among other objectives, to represent and lobby for ISPs before government and the public. Consequently, most ISPs are ISPA members. However, their Code of Practice[129] obliges members to register with the IWF and receive and act upon 'take down' notices in accordance with the IWF's own Code of Practice. On 15 February 2002 the IWF strengthened its role yet further by recommending to all UK ISPs that they do not carry newsgroups which IWF identifies as regularly hosting child pornography and which have names that appear to advertise or advocate paedophile content or activity.[130]

---

128   IWF published statistics.
129   Adopted 25 January 1999.
130   This approach has echoes of the approach taken by New Scotland Yard in 1995 when they, in effect, put all Internet service providers 'on notice' of the newsgroups which mainly carry illegal material: *The Independent*, 20 December 1995.

A lull IWF member who fails to comply with the Code may be reported to the IWF Executive Committee, receive a formal warning and a report may be filed with the relevant law enforcement authority. Serious breaches may result in suspension.

5.3.4.2 Electronic Commerce (EC Directive) Regulations 2002

The Electronic Commerce (EC Directive) Regulations 2002[131] now provide Internet service providers with a 'global' defence to their liability under the Obscene Publications Act 1959 and the Protection of Children Act 1978 together with other criminal statutes.[132] Four conditions must be met: ISP has no actual knowledge; ISP is not aware of unlawful nature; ISP acts expeditiously to remove or disable on knowledge; ISP has no control.[133]

The first condition is that the Internet service provider must not have actual knowledge that an activity or information was in breach of any law.[134] This 'actual knowledge' is likely to involve the Internet service provider knowing, with some precision, about the activity or information. This precision, particularly relating to the location of the offending material, is essential because the defence envisages the Internet service provider needing to 'remove or disable' the information.[135] If the ISP is not able to locate the material, it does not have sufficient knowledge.

---

24. A very popular UK-based Internet service provider has over 500,000 users, most of whom have a website which the ISP hosts. It provides a freephone answerphone for any complaint about the material on these websites. A young girl leaves a message on the answerphone that there are 'horrid pictures of me on a website', bursts into tears and then puts down the phone. While the Internet service provider may well have very serious concerns about this complaint, it does not have 'actual knowledge' of any breach of law. It neither knows the nature of the breach nor the identity or location of the complained-of material.

The second condition, wider than the first, is that the ISP is also not aware of facts or circumstances from which it would have been apparent to the service provider that the activity or information was unlawful.[136] The IWF's notification

---

131 Implementing the Directive 2000/31/EC of the European Parliament and of the Council of 8 June 2000 on certain legal aspects of information society services, in particular electronic commerce, in the Internal Market (Directive on electronic commerce) (OJ L178, 17.7.2000, p 1).

132 As discussed elsewhere in this book, such defences only apply in respect of statutes which were in force prior to the adoption of the Regulations or to those enacted after such date where the government has so provided on a case-by-case basis.

133 Regs 19 and 22.

134 Reg 19(a)(i).

135 See below, reg 19(a)(i).

136 Reg 19(a)(i). Cf 'Once it is or should be appreciated that the material is indecent then its continued retention or distribution is indecent then its continued retention or distribution is subject to the risk of prosecution': *R v Land* [1998] 1 All ER 403 at 407, CA.

to ISPs of suspicious newsgroups will doubtlessly move ISPs into being in the position of being 'aware of facts or circumstances', from which it will be apparent that information on those newsgroups is unlawful.

The third condition is that upon obtaining such knowledge or awareness, the service provider acts expeditiously to remove or to disable access to the information.[137] There are two issues that arise from this. First, how quickly must an ISP act to ensure that they are removing or disabling 'expeditiously'? Neither the Regulations nor the originating Directive provide a definition. The courts will initially rely on the dictionary definition, if pressed to judge an ISP's 'reaction time'. The dictionary talks of the concept of 'speedily'. The ISP must (despite discussions in respect of a two working day rule, considered in section 5.4 of this chapter in the context of the Terrorism Act 2006) therefore treat the knowledge or awareness with some urgency and not merely as some 'housekeeping' that can wait.

A second issue arising from the obligation to remove or disable access to the material is the ISP's risk of doing so. What if the 'notice' to the ISP was malicious or plain wrong but, in good faith, the ISP removes the material anyway? The Regulations are silent on this very real possibility. In contrast, this exact situation is considered by the US Digital Millenium Copyright Act. In that Act the ISP has a 'good samaritan' defence to such an act.[138] UK ISPs are therefore advised to state in their contracts with users that they reserve the right to remove or disable access to material in these circumstances. In addition, ISPs must ensure that their contracts exclude any of their liability for so removing or disabling access to such material.

The final condition of the defence, obviously, is that the person responsible for the storage or transmission of the illegal material must not have been acting under the 'authority or the control' of the Internet service provider.[139] It is submitted that for an ISP to have 'authority or control' over someone, they would need to have gone further than merely having a usual member contract with the individual. In this sense the concept of 'authority or control' is akin to the concept of 'effective control' in the Defamation Act 1996, discussed in detail in Chapter 3.[140]

5.4   ANTI–TERRORISM AND TERRORIST MATERIALS

The Terrorism Act 2000, which came into force on 19 February 2001 and is amended by the Anti-terrorism, Crime and Security Act 2001 and the Terrorism Act 2006 bolster the Computer Misuse Act 1990 and Fraud Act 2006 for the most serious of computer attacks. As can be seen below, however, the two separate Acts have rather different effects for Internet service providers and website owners.

---

137   Reg 19(a)(ii).
138   47 USC §§ 230(c)(2)(A).
139   Reg 19(b).
140   S 1(3)(e).

5.4.1 Threat to electronic systems

The Terrorism Act 2000 addresses, inter alia, the use or threat of an '[action] designed seriously to interfere with, or seriously to disrupt an electric system'[141] where two other conditions are met. First, the use or threat of the action must be 'designed to influence [any] government or to intimidate the public or a section of the public [including public of a country other than the United Kingdom]'.[142] The second precondition which must be met is that the use or threat must be made for the 'purpose of advancing a political, religious or ideological cause'.[143]

---

25. A British-based cult from the UK threatens to disrupt the computer systems and power supplies in every US hospital that carries out abortions. It threatens to do so in accordance with its governing religious doctrine, that 'all life is sacred'. This serious threat, despite being targeted at a non-UK, non-governmental section of society, will fall within the provisions of the Terrorism Act 2000.

5.4.2 Liability for terrorist material

5.4.2.1 Publication of terrorist statements

The Terrorism Act 2006 introduces, inter alia, criminal liability for the encouragement of terrorism. A party is liable if:

'2(a) he publishes a statement to which this section applies or causes another to publish such a statement; and

(b) at the time he publishes it or causes it to be published, he—

(i) intends members of the public to be directly or indirectly encouraged or otherwise induced by the statement to commit, prepare or instigate acts of terrorism or Convention offences; or

(ii) is reckless as to whether members of the public will be directly or indirectly encouraged or otherwise induced by the statement to commit, prepare or instigate such acts or offences.'

A prohibited statement is defined under s 1 of Part 1 of the Act as one which 'is likely to be understood by some or all of the members of the public to whom it is published as a direct or indirect encouragement or other inducement to them to the commission, preparation or instigation of acts of terrorism or Convention offences'.

Publication can be in any form, with the effect that website providers or Internet service providers may (subject to a defence being available as discussed below) potentially find themselves liable for such statements which appear on their site.

---

141 Terrorism Act 2000, s 1(2)(e).
142 Terrorism Act 2000, ss 1(1)(b) and (4)(c).
143 Terrorism Act 2000, s 1(1)(c).

5.4.2.2   *Dissemination of terrorist publications*

Section 2 of the Act introduces a further offence which is relevant to those providing Internet services. Section 2(2) sets out the *actus reus* or conduct element of the offence:

'For the purposes of this section a person engages in conduct falling within this subsection if he—

(a)   distributes or circulates a terrorist publication;

(b)   gives, sells or lends such a publication;

(c)   offers such a publication for sale or loan;

(d)   provides a service to others that enables them to obtain, read, listen to or look at such a publication, or to acquire it by means of a gift, sale or loan;

(e)   transmits the contents of such a publication electronically; or

(f)   has such a publication in his possession with a view to its becoming the subject of conduct falling within any of paragraphs (a) to (e).'

The *mens rea* for the offence is set out in s 2(1) and provides that the offence is committed if:

'(a)   he intends an effect of his conduct to be a direct or indirect encouragement or other inducement to the commission, preparation or instigation of acts of terrorism;

(b)   he intends an effect of his conduct to be the provision of assistance in the commission or preparation of such acts; or

(c)   he is reckless as to whether his conduct has an effect mentioned in paragraph (a) or (b).'

Again, as with s 1, the fact that the wording is technology-neutral means that a website or network provider may be liable if they themselves (or if they permit others to) disseminate terrorist content on their site or via their network. Care must therefore be taken by those who allow advertising or discussions to be conducted on their site. Without the defences which are available as are discussed below, this offence would present a significant threat for intermediaries who, unwittingly have such material posted or sent by third parties.

5.4.2.3   *Defences*

5.4.2.3.1   Statutory take down regime

Some comfort is found in respect of both the s 1 and s 2 offences under ss 3 and 4 which provide a form of take down notice procedure. The Act provides that a constable may issue a notice to an Internet service provider or hoster, requiring the removal or amendment of a statement, article or record which such constable believes to be 'unlawfully terrorist related'.[144]

---

144   Terrorism Act 2006, s 3(7).

On receipt of such a notice, a provider must remove or amend any offending postings from the Internet within two working days. Although non-compliance with a notice is not in itself an offence, a failure gives rise to liability under ss 1 or 2 for endorsing or disseminating such statements or material. This would result in the Internet service provider being unable to take advantage of the defences which might otherwise be available for such offences under ss 1(6) and 2(9). These sections apply if it can be shown that the statement or publication did not express the defendant's views nor had his endorsement and this was clear in the circumstances.

There is a further risk of liability under s 3(4) in respect of repeat postings of the same material which continue to appear after receipt of the take down notice and the initial removal or amendment of the offending statements. This species of liability may arise unless the defendant is able to show that they have 'taken every step he reasonably could to prevent a repeat statement from becoming available to the public and to ascertain whether it does'.[145] This indicates a heavy burden indeed, appearing to impose an obligation on providers to pro-actively check their sites and systems in order to ensure that no repeat publications appear. This de facto monitoring obligation runs contrary to the provisions of the Electronic Commerce Directive, which prevents member states from imposing a general obligation on intermediary service providers to monitor the information which they transmit or store.[146] Government recognised this as a genuine concern during the passage of the Act through Parliament, promising secondary legislation to address the interrelationship of the Act with the provisions of the Directive. This is considered below.

5.4.2.3.2 E-commerce defence

Acting on its promise made during the legislative path of the Terrorism Bill, the Government brought into force in June 2007 the Electronic Commerce Directive (Terrorism Act 2006) Regulations 2007. As has been explained elsewhere in this book, the Directive, as implemented through the provisions of the Electronic Commerce (EC Directive) Regulations 2002, only has application in respect of legislation passed *before* it came into force, with the effect that any legislation brought into force *after* 2002 must either incorporate or be amended to incorporate the provisions of the Directive on a case-by-case basis.[147]

The 2007 Regulations do several things. First, they respect the country of origin approach of the Directive, meaning that a service provider established in the UK and doing anything in the course of providing information society services in an EEA state other than the United Kingdom which would, if done in a part of

---

145   Terrorism Act 2006, s 3(5)(a).
146   Art 15, Directive 2000/31/EC.
147   Another example is the Electronic Commerce Directive (Racial and Religious Hatred Act 2006) Regulations 2007.

the United Kingdom constitute a relevant offence, is liable in the UK for such offence.[148]

Second, and most significant for Internet service providers (who, as discussed above, may otherwise have found themselves liable for the dissemination of publication of third party terrorist materials or statements, specifically in respect of repeat postings), the Regulations mirror the mere conduit and hosting defences available under the general 2002 Regulations for the Terrorism Act offences. There are several interesting points to note in respect of the way in which this defence now fits alongside those under the Act itself.

The Regulations essentially copy out the relevant provisions of the 2002 Regulations. This therefore provides a defence, for hosters, where such a person 'does not have actual knowledge of unlawful activity [and] … upon obtaining such knowledge or awareness, acts expeditiously to remove or to disable access to the information.' Since there is currently no guidance either in the Regulations or the Directive as to what constitutes 'expeditiously', it is not clear how this tallies with the specific two working days' notice requirement in the Act. This author's view is that it certainly would not be taken to give a longer period of time in order to act, but whether it naturally leads to a two-day period is uncertain. Some suggestions have been made that the Terrorism Act approach provides a strong argument that any action required under either the 2007 Regulations or the more general 2002 Regulations (therefore extending to defamatory or copyright-infringing postings) will be permitted, provided it is done in two working days. This author suggests that such an assumption is dangerous. Even if terrorist material is acknowledged as lying on the more serious side of any scale of offending content, a proscribed statutory take down notice from an authorised officer is a deliberately different process. Particularly in the case of repeat postings, it is arguable that a shorter period in which to act is appropriate. Internet service providers would therefore be well advised not to assume that they always have a two working day window for all unlawful content, and to act as soon as possible in the circumstances.

The other issue to note is that the defence under the Regulations relates to 'actual knowledge' and does not specifically refer to the provision of an official notice. Whilst it is clear that the giving of notice by a constable under the Act would give rise to actual knowledge, it is still possible that other forms of warning or tip-off are sufficient for a provider to acquire knowledge of the material and be required to act under the Regulations. Members of the Internet Service Providers Association lobbied during the drafting of the Regulations for a clarification that 'actual knowledge' would only be deemed to have been acquired where the host or conduit has been given notice of the terrorism-related material by those responsible for giving notices under s 3 of the Terrorism Act, and not where it is given by any other person. The Association's move was resisted by the Home Office on the grounds that it both goes beyond the requirements of the

148   The Electronic Commerce Directive (Terrorism Act 2006) Regulations 2007, reg 3(1).

Directive and would unduly limit the effect of ss 1 to 4 of the Act. Service providers will therefore need to act in accordance with their usual procedures for upholding their defence under the Directive's implementing legislation, although with a view to the high penalties and risks presented under the Terrorism Act 2006 in the event of any failure – which is no small detail.

5.5 CYBERSTALKING/HARASSMENT

Stalking is acknowledged to be an increasing phenomenon, with reports in the UK of up to one woman in 10 experiencing it in the last 10 years, and one in five expected to at some point during their lifetime.[149]

The Internet presents another medium via which victims can be found and tracked and targeted. Threatening or abusive messages can be posted anonymously, to an individual alone or in front of a wide audience in a manner which is intended to both offend them and to harm their reputation amongst others. Specific concerns have been raised as to the increasing use of social networking sites and forums for bullying and harassing behaviour, and it is clear that the Internet presents unprecedented new and imaginative avenues for harassment. Take, for example, Ms Debnath, who was imprisoned and given a restraining order after a long campaign of 'revenge' against an ex-colleague with whom she had had a one night stand. The defendant employed hackers to infiltrate the claimant's emails and inbox, signed him up to positivesingles.com and to a gay American prisoner exchange, set up a spoof 'A is gay.com' website, and sent countless offensive emails to the claimant and his fiancée.[150]

The legal framework to deal with such crimes encompasses both the general, in the form of the Protection from Harassment Act 1997, and the specific, in the form of the Malicious Communications Act 1988 and Communications Act 2003, which provide separate offences related to the sending of abusive communications via electronic networks. These are considered below.

Another important form of redress which should not be overlooked is the ability for a service provider to enforce its terms and conditions against a member who engages in such behaviour. In this way, if the owner of a website forum receives complaints of bullying or harassment via the site, if it has crafted its terms of membership correctly, it should be able to exercise rights of termination or other action directly against the errant member itself. Further steps may well need to be taken with the most persistent offenders, however, unless the site owner is able to effectively block such person from creating new membership accounts (a difficult task with the age of the anonymous Internet café). Issues surrounding contract are considered in Chapter 2.

---

149 Survey by Leicester University and the Network for Surviving Stalking, as reported by Theresa May, MP on BBC News, *Panorama*, 12 March 2007.
150 *R v Debnath* [2005] EWCA Crim 3472.

5.5.1   The Protection From Harassment Act

The Protection From Harassment Act 1997 introduced welcome new protections. Although aimed at tackling stalking, it is drafted widely and covers a range of different forms of harassing and threatening behaviour. There are two specific prohibitions, each of which is considered below.

5.5.1.1   Harassment

The first form of prohibited behaviour is the pursuit of a course of conduct which '(a) amounts to harassment of another, and (b) which he knows or ought to know amounts to harassment of the other'.[151] Knowledge is based on that of a reasonable person in possession of the same information thinking that the course of conduct amounted to harassment.[152]

Action may be taken either by way of criminal proceedings or civil proceedings. Section 2 of the Act makes it a summary offence. Section 3, allows a victim to take civil action for damages for (among other things) any anxiety caused by the harassment and any financial loss resulting from the harassment.

Most importantly, injunctions and restraining orders are available, breach of which is also a criminal offence.[153] This often makes the use of this Act, a more attractive option than the Malicious Communications Act or Communications Act, considered below, which do not provide such tools.

In June 2007, Felicity Lowde was convicted of harassment resulting in her imprisonment as well as a restraining order and a five-year anti-social behaviour order. Lowde had launched a vicious campaign against Rachel North, a victim of the July 7 bombings, accusing her, amongst other things, of using her experience for financial gain. Lowde used her own blog as well as email and postings to Rachel's site and blog between May 2006 and January 2007, when she was finally caught at an Internet café in Brick Lane. The prosecution centred on a harassment claim under the Act, but also relied on computer misuse acts, given the modification to email systems which she employed.[154]

5.5.1.2   Causing fear of violence

Section 4 of the Act creates an offence where 'a person whose course of conduct causes another to fear, on at least two occasions, that violence will be used against him is guilty of an offence if he knows or ought to know that his course of conduct will cause the other so to fear on each of those occasions'.[155]

Again, knowledge is judged in the basis of the reasonable person in possession of the same information, and injunctions and restraining orders are also available.

---

151   The Protection From Harassment Act 1997, s 1(1).
152   The Protection From Harassment Act 1997, s 1(2).
153   The Protection From Harassment Act 1997, s 5.
154   See section 5.1 of this chapter for a discussion on computer misuse offences.
155   The Protection From Harassment Act 1997, s 4(1).

A person found guilty of an offence is liable (a) on conviction on indictment, to imprisonment for a term not exceeding five years, or a fine, or both, or (b) on summary conviction, to imprisonment for a term not exceeding six months, or a fine not exceeding the statutory maximum, or both.

---

26. Hugo joins an alumni networking site run by the university he attended. An ex holding a grudge starts responding with nasty comments every time he makes a posting, saying he has sexual perversions and a criminal record. This escalates, until Hugo is receiving scores of abusive emails from her daily, together with postings appearing on the site. Hugo should contact the site administrator to see if her membership can be terminated. Hugo may also wish to report her to the authorities for action to be taken under the Malicious Communications Act, the Protection from Harassment Act or Communications Act, or may also take civil proceedings himself. In relation to the public statements, Hugo may also want to take advice concerning his rights under defamation laws.

5.5.2 Malicious Communications Act

The Malicious Communications Act 1988 has been amended by s 43 of the Criminal Justice and Police Act 2001 to extend offences of sending offensive letters to cover the sending of any indecent or offensive article with intent to cause distress or anxiety. The Act now covers writing of all descriptions, electronic communications (therefore including email or postings to websites), photographs and other images in a material form, tape recordings, films and video recordings. Section 1 reads:

'1. Any person who sends to another person

(a) a letter, electronic communication or article of any description which conveys

    (i) a message which is indecent or grossly offensive

    (ii) a threat or

    (iii) information which is false and known or believed to be false by the sender or

(b) any article or electronic communication which is, in whole or part, of an indecent or grossly offensive nature,

is guilty of an offence if his purpose, or one of his purposes, in sending it is that it should, so far as falling within paragraph (a) or (b) above, cause distress or anxiety to the recipient or to any other person to whom he intends that it or its contents or nature should be communicated.'

Given that the offence relates to the sending of the article, it is irrelevant whether it actually reaches the recipient intended. However, what is significant is that the sender must have intended it to cause distress or anxiety to the recipient. Applying this reasoning to the examples contained in the case of Ms Debnath, discussed in the introduction to this section, general postings about the claimant on adult sites he was not a member of, would not be likely to fall under this offence, although the emails to him would.

Following the House of Lords' judgment in *Director of Public Prosecutions v Collins*,[156] it is clear that this crime can be distinguished from an offence under s 127 where, as Lord Brown stated, 'the very act of sending [a] message over ... public communications network ... constitutes the offence even it if was being communicated to someone who the sender knew would not be in any way offended or distressed by it.'[157]

Restraining orders are not available.

5.5.3   Section 127 Communications Act

The history of this offence can be traced back to the Post Office (Amendment) Act 1935 which created an offence of sending messages by telephone which are grossly offensive or of an indecent, obscene or menacing character. Similar provisions later appeared in the Telecommunications Act 1984, culminating in s 127(1)(a) of the Communications Act 2003, which reads:

'(1) A person is guilty of an offence if he—

(a)   sends by means of a public electronic communications network a message or other matter that is grossly offensive or of an indecent, obscene or menacing character; or

(b)   causes any such message or matter to be so sent.'

There is a separate offence under s 127(2):

'(2) A person is guilty of an offence if, for the purpose of causing annoyance, inconvenience or needless anxiety to another, he—

(a)   sends by means of a public electronic communications network, a message that he knows to be false,

(b)   causes such a message to be sent; or

(c)   persistently makes use of a public electronic communications network.

(3) A person guilty of an offence under this section shall be liable, on summary conviction, to imprisonment for a term not exceeding six months or to a fine not exceeding level 5 on the standard scale, or to both.'

This captures messages sent via the Internet or telephone. The case of *DPP v Collins* considered s 1(a) in detail. The court held that for the offence to be made out, it must be proved that the defendant intended the message or other matter to be offensive to those to whom they related or be aware that they be taken to be so. It is irrelevant whether the message is in fact received or whether those who

156   [2006] UKHL 40, [2006] 4 All ER 602.
157   *Director of Public Prosecutions v Collins* [2006] UKHL 40.

read or listen to it are themselves offended. What *is* key is whether reasonable persons in society would find it grossly offensive or not. On this basis, the Lords overturned the ruling of the lower court which had held that racially abusive language used in voicemails left with an MP were not grossly offensive because the MP had not found them so and the intention of the defendant was not to grossly offend him.

5.6 EVIDENCE

Chapter 6 (Data and Data Retention) describes the provisions of the Regulation of Investigatory Powers Act 2000 in relation to the retention of and access to certain computer evidence and records.[158] Other ways in which computer evidence can be obtained include the Police and Criminal Evidence Act 1984, together with specific investigatory powers contained in individual legislation such as the Terrorism Act and Data Protection Act 1998. The process for disclosure is governed under English law predominantly by the Criminal Procedure and Investigations Act 1996 (as amended).

This section focuses instead on the nature of computer evidence, how it can be adduced and relied on in court, and the problems of reliance on and seeking to locate it. Evidence is of course crucial in Internet-based criminal prosecutions and defences, and yet it holds some inherent weaknesses which impose unique burdens.

5.6.1 Common law presumption

Prior to the repeal of s 69 of the Police and Criminal Evidence Act 1984 (under the Youth Justice and Criminal Evidence Act 1999) it was necessary to prove through provision of a certificate that a computer was operating correctly and was not used improperly before the computer could be admitted as evidence. This had caused some practical problems and unnecessary administrative hurdles in requiring the examining and certification of all the technical operations of a computer and resulted in some surprising decisions. There was also a risk that a defendant would be prevented from using evidence which could demonstrate his innocence simply on the basis that he was not able to certify the computer on which it was held.

Following recommendations of the Law Commission, this was repealed and not replaced. Consequently, the admissability of computer records is governed by a common law presumption that the computer was operating properly in the absence of evidence to the contrary (as is the case in other jurisdictions such as Scotland and the US). If however evidence is produced that the computer was not operating correctly, then the party seeking to rely on this evidence is still required to prove its reliability.

158   Ibid.

5.6.2   The evidential burden

There are two main issues prevalent in an Internet crime case that may create an evidential burden on the prosecution. First, there must be continuity of evidence from the first computer used by a defendant to access content or a second computer, second, defendants rarely use their own names and addresses when perpetrating such crimes. This section analyses some of these problems.

5.6.2.1   Continuity of access evidence

To prove beyond reasonable doubt that the defendant was responsible for, say, the unauthorised access of the victim's computer or the dissemination of paedophilic material, the prosecution can be forced to prove continuity of evidence. That is, the prosecution should be able to 'follow' a line of access from the defendant's own computer to the victim's or the other subject of the crime. Any discontinuity may raise the court's reasonable doubt that the defendant in the court was not the person responsible for the action. With hacking, only the most simple cases will feature two computers and an identifiable abuser. More regularly a hacker's commands to his computer will pass through many different computers spread across the Internet. It is also usual that a hacker will attempt to disguise his true identity: he is unlikely to attempt unauthorised access using an electronic signifier which can identify him. This poses an evidential difficulty for the prosecution. Similarly, external events or actions may muddy the waters and obscure any clear link between the defendant and his crime. In 2003, charges against Karl Schofield of possessing indecent images of children were dropped because experts showed that a trojan horse infection on his PC could have caused the harm without his knowledge. In another case later that year, *R v Caffrey*[159] a similar defence to a s 3 charge was used successfully.

5.6.2.1.1   Fragmentation of Internet hacking

It has been explained that messages and commands sent over the Internet do not pass directly between the sender and receiver computer. Instead the message is broken into small packets, each with a destination address. Each packet is shunted from one computer on the Internet to another, and from that computer to the next; gradually moving the packet towards its destination. Eventually, all the packets arrive at their final resting computer in a matter of seconds.

Hackers' messages and commands are no different. Each message will be broken into packets and shunted through many different computers. The prosecution will have to establish that a hacker's message did travel to an unauthorised computer.

In addition, hackers rarely attempt to gain access to their victim computer directly. Their preferred method is to log in to one computer on the Internet and from there to log in to another. This process is repeated many times; it is the

159   (Unreported, Southwark Crown Court, 17 October 2003).

digital equivalent of speeding around many corners to shake off a chasing police car. And each new login made by the hacker presents another piece of evidence which the prosecution may have to prove to establish continuity from the first to the final unauthorised access.[160]

These computers can be contrasted with the thousands of computers which shunt data from the victim computer to the hacker's computer. In a sense, there are many computers involved with any hacking which merely act as 'conduits' – they do not 'process' the data passed between them. This must be contrasted with computers which carry out functions or process the data involved in a hacking prosecution.

In *R v Waddon* both the Crown Court[161] and Court of Appeal[162] were clear that the many computers involved in the downloading of obscene images by one individual from one website did not necessitate having s 69 certificates for each one. Hardy J referred to the numerous computers in the chain as 'mere post boxes'. The Court of Appeal, giving unanimous judgment through the Vice President, Lord Justice Rose, drew a distinction between the computers that 'produce' the evidence and those that 'transmit' the evidence. Only the former are addressed by the Act.

5.6.2.1.2 False identification – spoofing

The situation for the prosecution may be more complex. A hacker logging in to a computer on the way to his victim will often log in under a different identity. This is called 'spoofing'. The hacker is able to do this by having previously obtained actual passwords, or having created a new identity by fooling the computer into thinking he is the system's operator. Whatever the technical method, the legal result remains the same. The prosecution must establish that the hacker at his own computer was the person who has logged in to countless other computers.

---

160   *R v Cochrane* [1993] Crim LR 48 illustrates the utility of focusing on one computer in a chain to 'break' the continuity. This must be contrasted with more than one computer 'transmitting' the same evidence but only one computer 'producing' the evidence (*R v Waddon*, unreported, CA, 6 April 2000). In such a case, only the computer 'producing' the evidence is subject to the hurdles of s 69.
161   His Honour Judge Hardy (unreported, 30 June 1999).
162   (Unreported, 6 April 2000).

CHAPTER SIX

Data and data protection

'And while serious – very serious – the privacy issues we're dealing with today are trivial compared to what's ahead. What are the implications for individual privacy in a world where millions of people are driving Internet-enabled cars that have their movements monitored at all times? What happens to privacy for millions of people with Internet-enabled pacemakers?'

Lou Gerstner, Chairman & CEO of IBM[1]

Businesses demand that their digital presences, including websites, collect and analyse personal data. They collect it, not only to ensure that simple things are performed correctly, such as delivering goods to the right address and managing subscriptions. They also collect to predict their customers' needs. The more sophisticated collect personal data to sell or rent to *other* businesses to help *them* predict *their* customers' needs. In short, businesses view personal data as a critical asset.

For the customers and other individuals whose information comprises this asset, there is an increasing expectation that businesses will use their data responsibly; that they can retain some control over how it is used and not, for example, have their email inboxes inundated with unwanted marketing communications or their personal details sold or disclosed indiscriminately. In the UK, the Information Commissioner and data protection regime are positioned to ensure that businesses respect the individuals whose data is being harvested, and uphold their rights.

But in an industry where the valuable data of individuals may be traded and exchanged outside of the UK in an instant, and spam sent from anonymous sources located in other jurisdictions, such protections have immediately apparent limitations.

From another angle, personal information is valuable not only to the businesses who collect and trade in it, but is also an essential source of evidence for law enforcement and other agencies wishing to build up profiles and details of a suspect's communications, tastes, movements, behaviour and transactions. Any Internet business which may collect or have access to such data therefore

---

becomes a significant law enforcement and investigation resource, and may expect requests for disclosure of information. How do these businesses know how to balance their obligations to the data subjects against requests from other regulatory or enforcement bodies?

As criminals become ever more technically savvy, but also dependent on Internet communications, and concerns grow about international terrorism and crime, it is clear that the importance and value of such data, and therefore the number of disclosure requests, will only increase. In the UK and throughout Europe, legislation has been developed to put in place a procedural framework for handling and responding to such requests, safeguarding fundamental rights and clarifying when disclosures may be made without fear of legal action. In addition, steps have also been made to require that Internet service providers retain minimum communications data precisely so that it can be available for law enforcement purposes.

This chapter deals with the following issues concerning data, data protection and the Internet:

1.   What different legislation impacts on data collection and usage?

2.   What types of data and data activity over the Internet are regulated?

3.   Are Internet service providers, and users of websites classed as data controllers or data processors?

4.   What are the obligations of notification for Internet data controllers and processors both in the UK and abroad?

5.   What are the principles for processing personal data and data security over the Internet?

6.   Given that the Internet is global, to where in the world may personal data from the UK be transferred?

7.   What are the requirements for sending marketing messages over the Internet and how can this be enforced?

8.   What data does a service provider have to retain and make available for law enforcement purposes?

9.   How should a service provider respond to requests for disclosure of data from different bodies?

6.1   THE LEGISLATIVE LANDSCAPE

UK legislation on data breaks down into three interrelated areas. First, the basic data regime which upholds individuals' rights in respect of the processing of their data by imposing obligations on those who control it. A second imposes specific obligations on how data may be used for electronic marketing and other value added purposes. The third sets the parameters in which data may be made available for law enforcement purposes. All of these have been introduced to enact European Directives.

6.1.1   The Data Protection Act 1998

The Data Protection Act 1998 replaces the Data Protection Act 1984. The new legislation was brought into force following a review of data protection across Europe by means of the Second European Convention on Data Protection and new Directive. The new regime introduced new rights and powers of enforcement, prohibitions on transfers of data outside of the EEA to countries with 'inadequate' data protection regimes, and a strengthening of security obligations.

The Act is the starting point for consideration of an Internet or website provider's obligations in respect of their customers' and users' personal data. Since its introduction the Information Commissioner's Office (which enforces the data protection and freedom of information regimes in the UK) has also published various guidance and codes of practice clarifying the scope of the Act's obligations on those with control over the processing of personal data. Although enforcement action has tended to remain at an informal level, the last few years have revealed that individuals are becoming more alert to their rights. The press is also more ready to publicise stories of security breaches and mismanagement of data, as concerns about fraud and identity theft have grown. In parallel, there are now indications that more robust and proactive enforcement may follow.

6.1.2   The Privacy and Electronic Communications (EC Directive) Regulations 2003

Although the Data Protection Act 1998 contains basic rights and protections for data subjects, European Directives have developed more detailed rules in respect of the sending of unsolicited direct marketing messages using publicly available telecommunications services (e.g. mobile or fixed telephone, fax and email). In the UK, this legislation was first implemented in March 2000 by way of the Telecommunications (Data Protection and Privacy) Regulations 1999 implementing European Telecoms Directive 97/66/EC. The Directive was implemented differently across Europe, however, resulting in uncertainties as to key definitions and potential bars to harmonisation. A new Directive 2002/58/EC on privacy and electronic communications followed and has been implemented in the UK in the guise of the Privacy and Electronic Communications (EC Directive) Regulations 2003.

These Regulations contain clearer rules concerning direct marketing via electronic means, specifically as relates to email or 'spam' marketing, but also regarding the use of website cookies and other tracking devices such as web beacons to harvest users' personal data; and the extent to which users' traffic and billing data may be used after a communication has ended.

6.1.3   The Regulation of Investigatory Powers Act 2000

The Regulation of Investigatory Powers Act 2000 (best known by its acronym 'RIPA') received Royal Assent on 28 July 2000. Very lengthy and technical in nature, RIPA covers five specific areas. First, it contains prohibitions on the interception of communications in the course of their transmission and defines the circumstances in which this may be authorised and subscriber data may be made available for law enforcement purposes. Second, it contains rules relating to surveillance, proscribing techniques that may be used with a view to safeguarding the public from unnecessary invasions of their privacy. These two parts will be of most interest to those providers or Internet networks and services. The latter parts of RIPA cover encryption of data, judicial oversight and the establishment of a tribunal providing redress against those exceeding their powers under RIPA.

Under RIPA sits various secondary legislation. The Regulation of Investigatory Powers (Maintenance of Interception Capability) Order 2002 provides for obligations which the Secretary or State may impose on service providers to establish and maintain system capability for interception in the event that this is required under RIPA. The Order only applies to providers of public telecommunications services offered to more than 10,000 persons in the UK.

The other key secondary legislation is the Telecommunications (Lawful Business Practice) (Interception of Communications) Regulations 2000 which authorises specified interceptions carried out by persons in the course of their business for the purposes relevant to that business (such as monitoring staff email and general running of the system) and using that business's telecommunication system which would otherwise be unlawful under RIPA.

6.1.4   Anti-Terrorism, Crime and Security Act 2001

The Anti-Terrorism, Crime and Security Act 2001, introduced following the 9/11 terrorist attacks in the US, provides government with further powers to counter threats to the UK. The provisions of the Act of specific interest to Internet providers concern the rights granted to government departments and agencies to require the disclosure of data for national security purposes. The Act itself contains little detail, but Part 11 allows for the development of a voluntary statutory code for retention and contains reserve powers to enable further powers to be brought in if needed.

A Code of Practice for voluntary retention of communications data was drawn up and came into force on 5 December 2003, despite reservations from the Internet service provider community. It seeks to encourage service providers to retain types of data which they already hold (as opposed to requiring the restructuring of systems to enable retention of new types of data) for specified periods ranging from four days to 12 months depending on the type of data.

6.1.5   Directive 2006/24/EC on data retention

Directive 2006/24/EC on the retention of data generated or processed in connection with the provision of publicly available electronic communications services or of public communications networks is the final key statute. This requires member states to implement measures to require the retention of certain data so that it can be made available to law enforcement authorities and government agencies for the investigation and detection of crime. This is an inevitable step forward from the voluntary Code of Practice under the Anti-Terrorism Act discussed above, to provide a compulsory and harmonised minimum level of data that must be retained by communications providers. Member states must bring in implementing legislation by 15 September 2007, although they are permitted (as the UK Government has done) to make a declaration to postpone the implementation of provisions relating to retention of Internet access, Internet telephony and email data until 15 March 2009.

At the time of writing, the Home Office was consulting on draft regulations for retention of fixed and mobile data which are not subject to the permitted delay.

6.2 DATA PROTECTION

Before investigating the application of the Data Protection Act 1998 to the Internet, it is vital to set out the main aspects to the legislation. It is unfortunate that the Act is particularly definition-based: to appreciate the responsibilities of a data user one must appreciate a great number of separate concepts: data, personal data, relevant filing system, processing of data, data subject and recipient. For ease of understanding, therefore, this section attempts to simplify the legislation by referring to these issues. This section describes each of these issues with specific Internet examples; the following sections consider the application of these issues to commonplace e-commerce transactions and activities on the Internet.

6.2.1 Personal data

6.2.1.1 Data

The Act applies only to personal data and those dealing with it. Assessing whether information is personal data is the starting point for all data protection questions. The word, 'data', is circularly defined with reference to further defined terms which themselves refer to 'data.'[2]

This wide definition is:

'information which:

(a) is being processed by means of equipment operating automatically in response given for that purpose;

(b) is recorded with the intention that it should be processed by means of such equipment;

(c) is recorded as part of a relevant filing system or with the intention that it should form part of a relevant filing system; or

---

2   Data Protection Act 1998, s 1(1). This definition is not drawn from the body of the Directive but rather its preamble.

(d)   does not fall within paragraph (a), (b) or (c) but forms part of an accessible
record as defined by s 68 [including health records, education records and
accessible public records].'

In this way 'data' encapsulates information processed by equipment, either automatically or that is intended to later be processed by equipment. One example
would therefore be information collected from individuals by way of physical
paper forms which are to be later transferred into computer files. 'Equipment' is
not defined in the Act and is deliberately technology-neutral. A computer would
be an obvious example of equipment caught by both (a) and (b) above (others
would include cameras, dictaphones, PDAs etc). Therefore any website or
Internet server is unlikely to be caught by section (a).

Although unlikely to be relevant to the Internet, the definition also captures
non digitally processed data which remains in manual files, but only if these form
a part of a 'relevant filing system'. 'Relevant filing system' is defined by s 1(1)
as:

'any set of information relating to individuals to the extent that although the
information is not processed by means of equipment generating automatically
in response to instructions given for that purpose, the set is structured as by reference to individuals or by reference to criteria relating to individuals, in such a
way that specific information relating to a particular individual is readily accessible.'

This is an important qualification, highlighted in the high-profile case of *Durant
v Financial Services Authority*.[3] This means that unsophisticated records such as
those which are structured purely by date rather than by name, for example, are
unlikely to be caught. Unfortunately for Internet providers, although relevant filing system is not stated as applying solely to manual records, the fact that computer records and Internet files will be caught by limb (a) of the definition of data
means that this caveat is not available. Although a digital record may be difficult
to search against an individual, a controller will not clearly be able to rely on this
in the same way as the Financial Services Authority did in relation to Mr
Durant's paper files.

---

1. RemCom gathers salary data from recruitment agents to allow prospective employees to gauge their potential remuneration package in a given job. When an employee
gains employment they are encouraged to feed back into RemCom their new salary and
benefits package. Even though some of this information is taken from the happy
employees by telephone operators, before it is inputted into RemCom's database, it will
be classified as data.

6.2.1.2   Personal data

The word 'personal' refers to the data[4]:

'which relate to a living individual who can be identified:

---

3   [2003] EWCA Civ 1746.
4   Data Protection Act 1998, s 1(1).

(a) from those data; or

(b) from those data and other information which is in the possession of, or is likely to come into the possession of, the data controller and includes any expression of opinion about the individual and any indication of the intentions of the data controller or any other person in respect of the individual.'

While this definition is fundamental to whether or not one has data protection obligations, personal data may not be fundamental to a successful Internet or e-commerce initiative.

---

2. An individual repeatedly visits a website and always downloads from it the latest screensaver of a particularly attractive tennis star. Because the individual has entered data into an on-screen form, the website 'knows' four items of data about the individual. The individual is male, between 25 and 35 years of age, earns over £45,000 a year and likes tennis. Each time the individual visits the site, the site confirms it is him by placing on his computer a small file containing a unique identifier. The site, therefore, 'knows' what he looks at, what he downloads, how often he visits etc. All this data is useful and helps the site target the individual with new relevant screensavers when he visits. Without more, however, the site holds no personal data. The Act is not applicable therefore but the Privacy and Electronic Communications (EC Directive) Regulations 2003, are.

This technique of using 'non-personal' data has led e-commerce businesses to explore whether or not they can avoid entirely the obligations of the Act.[5] To consider this avoidance of the Act, one first needs to appreciate the scope, and purposive interpretation, of the definition. Key elements are as follows.

6.2.1.2.1 Relate to an individual

Previously it was thought that the Act concerns the data rather than the individual to whom it relates. This view is rebutted by the Court of Appeal's ruling in *Durant v Financial Services Authority*.[6] The court in this case focused on when data can be said to 'relate to an individual'. The court held that data could only be said to be 'personal' if it 'is information that affects [a person's] privacy, whether in his personal, or family life, business or professional capacity'. It went on to give two ways in which this might be determined. The first was whether or not the information is 'biographical in a significant sense', meaning that it goes beyond just mere recording of data to require some kind of personal connotation. The second appears to go further still, being that the data should have the individual as its focus rather than some other individual.

The Information Commissioner has clarified this interpretation as meaning that the simple fact that 'an individual is referred to in data does not make the information personal data about that individual unless it affects their privacy'.[7]

---

5 Of course, companies still need to ensure they comply with the Act in relation to their other personal data: personnel, suppliers, contacts etc.
6 [2003] EWCA Civ 1746.
7 'The "Durant" case and its impact on the interpretation of the Data Protection Act 1998', guidance note of the Information Commissioner issued in February 2006.

Even if the decision in relation to relevant filing systems does not help those holding Internet or other computer records (see section 6.2.1.1 above), this part of the judgment does. Indeed the court specifically stated that 'not all information retrieved from a computer search against an individual's name or unique identifier, constitutes personal data'.[8] Obvious examples would include an email which a person is simply cc'd in on. However, a record which shows what a person bought, their payment records or address would do. Most website transaction records and even log records which show what pages and services an individual was using are still likely to be caught therefore. The *Durant* ruling forces one to analyse what personal data is and is thereby caught by the Act. Rather than assuming that any data which *can* be related back to an individual is, one must assess whether the data does actually relate to and affect an individual.

A common scenario concerns an email address. Most email addresses incorporate the actual name of an individual and therefore relate to that individual, but this does not mean that it is automatically personal data. If I am simply cc'd in on a chain of emails discussing someone else, then it is unlikely that my email in that context or the email itself constitutes personal data. One can see from just this example that the analysis required varies on a case-by-case basis and demands some thought. In most cases controllers will want and need to err on the side of caution in discharging many of their obligations, treating emails with care. However, when it comes to data subject to access requests (as discussed later), controllers may wish to consider this more closely, rather than simply handing over and redacting quantities of information and material.

The *Durant* ruling has subsequently been followed in the case of *Ezsias v Welsh Ministers*,[9] concerning information to be provided pursuant to a data subject access request. The High Court held that only information relating to Mr Ezsias, as opposed to that relating to, say, his complaints, had to be provided. Further, to use the provisions of the Act to seek disclosure of documents generated as the result of the applicant's own complaint, in order to further a legal claim of the applicant against a third party is a legal abuse.

6.2.1.2.2   Living individual

As long as the individual is living and is not a body corporate, the Act can apply. This includes all individuals, whether resident abroad or of foreign nationality.

---

3. A foreign national enters his personal details into an online form required to access a UK newspaper's website. The individual is now concerned that these personal data are being misused. All things being equal, he has rights under the Act to prevent this misuse because he is a living individual and the data held are personal. The individual's nationality is largely irrelevant to the newspaper's obligations.

The definitions of personal data in both the Act and Directive refer to 'person' and 'individual' and not 'people' and 'individuals'. A question therefore arises whether or not the Act applies to processed data about 'joint' individuals.

---

8   Ibid.
9   [2007] All ER(D) 65.

Certainly, joint bank account holders are likely to be considered each as an individual under the Act, as are joint tenants of property.

> 4. A well-known department store establishes an online wedding site for couples to create a 'micro-site' before their happy day. As well as displaying directions to the venue and a ceremony of service, the micro-site also provides the chance for guests to make purchases from the couple's gift list. Together with their address and wedding day, the department store does possess data relating to an individual.

6.2.1.2.3 Possession of other information

The definition of 'personal' data refers to identification in conjunction with other information in possession or likely to come into the possession of the data controller.[10] The Directive's recital 26 illustrates the likely width of 'possession'. It states:

> 'To determine whether a person is identifiable, account should be taken of all the means likely reasonably to be used either by the controller or by any other person.'

It follows that it is still possible to have 'possession' of data permitting identification for the purposes of the Act, even if one does not actually have physical possession of it. When assessing whether or not one is processing personal data, one must therefore examine data which is publicly available (which would 'confirm' the identity of the individual) and data available from a third party under contract or other relationship. This ties in closely with scenarios in which a company may believe that its data is not caught because it is anonymous. Since the key to decrypt or encode the data may be available, the data is still caught.

Another common example concerns IP addresses. An IP in itself appears as a number. This identifies a computer or log on point, rather than an individual. However, if a controller holds account details for an individual including their IP address and uses an IP address to collect further information (for example, tracking which pages are read on a website), the information so collected becomes personal data since it can be related back to the individual and says something about them. This is the case even if the IP collected information and the account data is held in separate files. The fact that it could be linked causes the problem.

> 5. SecuriFirst and Last is a security firm which generates digital 'safes' for people who wish to store digital data off their own hard drives. To do so, one must provide one's first name, date and place of birth to SecuriFirst and Last. One pays for the safe through a third party which takes one's full name and residential address. This third party then provides a password to enable 'unlocking' of the safe. The third party clearly can identify each customer using information in its possession; SecuriFirst and Last also is likely to come into possession of this information because of its relationship with the third party.

---

10 Data Protection Act 1998, s 1(3).

6.2.1.2.4   Opinions on individuals

The final test to establish whether data is personal data is to ascertain the nature of the data: if the data is an expression of opinion or indication of intention about the individual, then the data can be personal.

The definition also includes an intention being expressed by a third party. For this reason, repeating the intention of another with respect to a living individual will still fall within the definition; the data may still be personal.

6.2.1.3   Anonymous data

The Directive explicitly states that: 'the principles of protection shall not apply to data rendered anonymous'.[11] In addition, the Act refers only to living individuals who can be identified from the data processed. This has led many website operators and e-commerce businesses to seek to force (technically or legally) their data into being anonymous and so avoid the regulation of the Act. This is easier said than done.

When businesses talk of 'anonymised', 'aggregated', 'generic', or even 'neutered' data, they may be referring to a number of situations. What follows are the common explanations of anonymous data.

1.   'My business cannot identify living individuals from information we have in our possession. If we wanted to obtain extra information to do so, we could.' This business only possesses anonymised information. It will still be classified as personal data because reasonable enquiries would enable them to turn the anonymised data into identifying data.

2.   'My business cannot identify living individuals from information we have in our possession. We have come to an arrangement with a third party; they hold the personal data, we merely hold a unique identification number which allows them to resolve the identities.' This business only possesses anonymised information. Unless their contract with the third party is unambiguous, it is likely that their relationship will allow them to resolve the identification number into identifying a living individual. It is likely that the business will be classified as possessing personal data.[12]

3.   'My business can no longer identify living individuals from information we have in our possession. We have stripped out any information from our data which would allow us directly or indirectly to identify any living individual. Even other data sources would not assist us to identify particular individuals.' If the business truly has destroyed the identifiable features of its data, and even with reasonable enquiries, could not identify individuals,

---

11   Recital 26.
12   On 11 November 2000, *The Economist* wrote: 'Unlike DoubleClick's data, which is entirely anonymous, Abacus had 88m real names and addresses. Mr O'Connor [the chairman and founder of DoubleClick] realised that, by marrying the two, he could identify individual web users and not only track, but also predict their behaviour – making online advertising even more science than art. . .'. Had this integration of anonymised and identifiable personal data occurred, DoubleClick would have had personal data. Similar issues have faced Google, which has made an offer to acquire DoubleClick. Google, like Abacus, has personal data which it could link to DoubleClick's anonymous data.

then it is no longer able to be classified as processing personal data. The key words, however, are 'no longer'. The Act and Directive do not apply to anonymised data but the process *of* anonymising the formerly identifiable data would have been considered to be processing it under the Act. All the usual preconditions would have applied to such processing. One such precondition may well be 'consent' by the individuals *to* allow their personal data to be anonymised.[13]

> 6. A survey firm makes sure it removes all names and addresses from the survey results it collects. It does this on the understanding that this means it will not be classed as a data controller processing personal data. This is not correct. It should not collect any personal data in the first place if it wants this to be the case. The initial collection and the anonymising activity will themselves constitute processing of personal data.

In *R v Department of Health, ex p Source Informatics*, Source Informatics alleged that it was entitled to anonymise patient prescription data gained from general practitioners to sell to pharmacists. No supplied data could identify patients. Latham J in the Queen's Bench Division considered, inter alia, the Data Protection Act 1998 and suggested Source's use of the anonymised data was contrary to the Act.[14] On appeal, Simon Brown LJ, for a unanimous Court of Appeal, disagreed. He stated that the Directive does not apply to anonymised data.[15]

'My business does not even collect identifiable data from individuals; our systems even ensure that the collected data is insufficient to permit us to combine the data with other data to identify any individual.' This challengeable statement means that the Act does not apply to this particular dataset; the Act will apply to other datasets such as credit card processing, order or service fulfilment.[16]

It is also important to remember that the actual act of rendering data anonymous will itself constitute an act of processing personal data since something needs to be done to it in order to make it that way.

6.2.2 Processing

It will be recalled that the Act only impinges on certain activities in relation to data with a particular quality: it must be personal. Having defined personal data, any processing of that data which is undertaken is caught by the Act.

The Act defines processing as performing one of a defined set of operations on personal data. Section 1(1) defines processing as:

13 A consent of this type should be included in privacy policies to ensure such anonymisation is permitted.
14 [1999] 4 All ER 185 at 192.
15 [2000] 1 All ER 786 at 198–199.
16 Google openly admitted that its new toolbar application permitted Google to monitor the sites frequented by its toolbar users. It stated 'By using the Advanced Features version of the Google toolbar, you may be sending information about the sites you visit to Google.' Google spokesman David Krane said: 'We're looking at data en masse, not going record by record' (ZDNet News, 11 December 2000). Google's revised general 2005 privacy policy does not, however, contain this wording.

'in relation to information or data, means obtaining, recording or holding the information or data carrying out any operation or set of operations on the information or data, including:

(a)   organisation, adaptation or alteration of the information or data;

(b)   retrieval, consultation or use of the information or data;

(c)   disclosure of the information or data by transmission, dissemination or otherwise making available; or

(d)   alignment, combination, blocking, erasure or destruction of the information or data.'

The above list of what constitutes processing is non-exhaustive. The Directive's definition uses the magic words 'such as' and the UK's definition the similarly widening word 'including'. It is therefore difficult to imagine what operations or activities in relation to personal data would not constitute processing it.

However, one important 'gap' has been identified. In 2007 in *Johnson v Medical Defence Union*[17] the Court of Appeal considered whether the basis for a decision to terminate Mr Johnson's membership and professional indemnity services provided by his union constituted unfair processing of his personal data. The decision to terminate the membership had been made in accordance with the union's policy, which involved the review of Johnson's cases which were held in manual and computer records by a risk assessor who then summarised each case and produced a score sheet. This score sheet was then itself recorded using a computer. The Court of Appeal reversed the High Court ruling which had held that the risk assessor's selection of material and inputting of the report constituted 'processing'. The majority decision in the Court of Appeal was that the extent of the broad definition of processing has to be limited in scope by the definition of data. This means that processing is limited to either processing wholly or partly by automatic means or processing of data in relation to a relevant filing system. To this extent, the selection by the risk assessor of the computer records and the choice as to which information to put into an automatic system involved neither. It was an exercise of judgment which was not automatic at all, but a matter of human judgment.

This is a significant qualification, which demands that practitioners consider the interplay between these definitions and the place of any human intervention in any processing activities which may prevent them from being 'automatic'. It also narrows the previously notorious case of *Campbell v MGN Ltd*[18] which had given a very wide interpretation to the meaning of processing. That case concerned the publication of information and photographs which were alleged to infringe the privacy of Ms Campbell; processing was held to encompass any set of operations including obtaining and using information. Although each operation in itself was not necessarily an activity which could amount to processing, overall the set constituted an activity linked to automated processing at the insti-

17   [2007] EWCA Civ 262.
18   [2003] QB 633.

gation of the data controller. The Court of Appeal in *Johnson*, distinguished this case. The Appeals Court held that *Campbell* concerned publication of data which had *already been* processed automatically and was concerned with privacy as the prime interest of the Act and Directive. The court there had not considered 'pre-processing' stages where information had not previously been processed automatically as in the case it was considering.

In the context of the Internet, one of the key activities which is clearly encompassed by the concept of processing, is disclosure. The Internet, especially the World Wide Web and email, is heralded for the ease with which information can be disclosed to others. The novel legal issue for the Internet is whether there is disclosure and therefore automatic processing when information is not actively distributed but is merely 'left' on a server for collection.

Disclosure of data occurs where the data or information from the data is divulged to another person or recipient.[19]

---

7. An Internet Service Provider maintains a log of its members' log-in times. The Provider allocates each member a unique number and stores log-in times in conjunction with this number; in another database, the Service Provider stores a list of the unique numbers for each member. The Service Provider seeks to use this log to inform the local telephone networks of the most popular access times. It will be a disclosure for the Service Provider to supply only the log to the network, even when the members' numbers database remains unseen. The ISP is disclosing the information gleaned from the personal data.

One of the keys to the commercial success of the Internet is that it is very cheap to 'distribute' information to many recipients. There are two main ways: first, using a mailserver to emailshot a list of email addresses; the second way is to 'leave' information in a readily accessible area of the Internet, be that as an upload on an ftp site or published on a website. The commercial difference is that in the second scenario, it is the receiver of the information who acts to retrieve that information; the provider remains passive. Receivers may pay the online or connection charges to locate and download the posted information. By contrast, when emailing the provider takes the active role, by sending the information, the recipients cannot help but receive it, they remain passive.

It is now almost beyond doubt that disclosure is effected by publishing personal data on a web page or uploading it to an ftp site. In the case *R v Brown*, Lord Goff considered the concept of 'disclosure' under the 1984 Act, albeit then with reference to a definition to assist his interpretation. He said[20]:

> '[I]t may be readily inferred that the person effecting the transfer was inevitably therefore disclosing the data to another person or persons who, as he well knew, would retrieve the information from the second database and so have the information disclosed to him.'

---

19   Defined in s 70.
20   [1996] 1 All ER 545 at 549.

Although 'disclosure' is not defined in the 1998 Act, this is immaterial since it is encapsulated by the concept of processing. The European Court of Justice case of *Lindqvist*[21] confirms this. The case concerned a woman who was prosecuted in her home state for processing (as opposed specifically to disclosing) personal data by automatic means by composing a web page about some of her fellow parishioners on her computer and placing it on an Internet server. The ECJ held that the loading of the page on to the server meant that the process has been performed 'at least in part, automatically'. Although here the prior selection of such information on the parishioners was manual and involved some judgment (much akin to the case of *Johnson* considered above), this ruling is still consistent with the *Johnson* ruling, despite first appearances. *Johnson* concerned the actions which were taken *prior to* the assessor's report being placed on the computer (and whether this processing was unfair). In *Lindqvist*, the court was considering just the question as to whether the uploading of the page (i.e. the disclosure and publication) was itself processing. (In *Johnson*, it was not in dispute that the final report itself, when placed on computer was data able to be processed as disclosed.)

These cases and issues show that it is essential when considering whether or not an action involving the Internet or computers constitutes processing, that the different stages and any human involvement be analysed separately. Information held or transmitted via the Internet will inevitably involve data and processing. However consideration must still be had of any prior-actions undertaken where it is the alleged processing which is in dispute.

---

8. A UK firm of advisers to wealthy individuals seeks to advertise its work for clients. It chooses to use a website featuring lists of clients, each with a link to a further page describing the nature of the work undertaken for the person. Notwithstanding issues of professional conduct and confidentiality, the firm will be disclosing this personal data.

6.2.3   Processors and controllers

Even a company that processes personal data may not be subject to the provisions of the Act. This is because the key provisions of the Act only apply to those persons who are defined as 'data controllers'. Persons who are simply 'data processors' are not regulated (other than by virtue of certain separate criminal offences contained in the Act) but, because they are processing data, must be kept in check by the controller who instructs them. Understanding this distinction is therefore absolutely key, since a company that uses a third party processor cannot automatically rely on such processor's compliance with the provisions of the Act. They will therefore need to be responsible for the imposition of obligations (likely to be contractual) on their processor to safeguard the integrity of the data, the data subjects' rights and the controller's own risk of liability under the Act. It is also essential to appreciate that, even though a party may be described as a data processor, this is not conclusive and the actual actions that they undertake may make them a data controller even so. Both concepts are considered below.

21   *Bodil Lindqvist v Kammaraklagaren* (2003) (Case C 101/01), ECJ.

6.2.3.1 Data controller

A data controller is[22]:

> 'a person who (either alone or jointly or in common with other persons) determines the purposes for which and the manner in which any personal data are, or are to be processed.'

It is necessary to deconstruct two of the conditions listed above. First, determining the purposes and the manner of processing; second, alone or jointly.

6.2.3.1.1 Determines

The first of two conditions of being a data controller is that one determines the purposes and manner in which the personal data are or are to be processed. This determination may be joint or in common with others.

Determination of purposes and manner of processing

'Determining' can be distinct from processing. It is possible that one person compiles personal data, another formats and filters it and a third person then uses the data. This differentiation separates data controllers from data processors: data controllers (potentially with others) make the final decision as to the purpose of processing the personal data and how it is to be processed. Of course, where a data controller delegates any decisions to a third party, as is often the case with third party database architects, that third party becomes a data controller too. Because the statutory obligations are on data controllers it is important to understand what the Act means by 'determines'. If an Internet service provider is doing more than only processing personal data, and is actually deciding the ways in which it is processed, he may be committing a criminal offence by acting as an unnotified data controller. The relevant criterion therefore is not what a person or body does with the data or the means he uses, but their capacity to make decisions in relation to the purposes and means of the processing.

---

9. A UK bookseller maintains a website which allows customers to read rated reviews of selected books online and then place an order if desired. The bookseller seeks to establish whether there is any correlation between placing an order and reading a highly rated review. To establish this, the bookseller divulges all the data to a market researcher. The bookseller determines the purposes of the data and their use but is unlikely to know how the data will be correlated and analysed. The market researcher will, being the expert, determine the manner in which the customer data is processed. Both therefore have the relevant capacity to make decisions.

Key issues then concern the level of autonomy in deciding what actions are taken and any powers or management control that a person may have. There have been no UK cases on this issue. Nevertheless, the analysis of actions taken by SWIFT (a major co-operative providing a system for sending payment instructions

---

22 Data Protection Act 1998, s 1(1).

between banks) by the Article 29 Working Party (the EU data protection watchdog) provides a useful analysis of the activities various national data protection regulators deem may constitute those of a data controller. This analysis provides a persuasive indication of the view which may be considered by national courts in any future action. In such case, although SWIFT was an intermediary between banks and presented itself as a mere processor, it had in fact taken on responsibilities which went beyond the duties and instructions incumbent on a processor, and therefore did have liability under data protection legislation.[23]

Jointly or in common

The terms 'jointly' and 'in common' broaden the ambit of 'determine' not only by including data that are under the absolute control of the data controller, but also by including the data partially under the instruction of the data controller. Similarly, where many persons share one collection of data (for example a database of contact details), each person will be classed as determining the use of that collection in common. The inclusion of these terms is particularly relevant to the Internet because it is rare that only a single-entity will deal on the Internet with data: most organisations use one person to design a website, another to host it and perhaps even a third to provide access to the server.

---

10. A UK business rents space on a website to a number of retailers and service providers, rather like a shopping mall. The website collects personal data on each of the entrants to the mall. At the end of each day, the business provides to its 'tenants' a full list of each of the entrants to the mall. Each of the tenants uses the data at its discretion. The business and each of its tenants are data controllers in common.

Of course, use for a collection of data may vary with time. It is conceivable that a person who previously had no input over the content of data or processing of data, could begin determining issues as trust between the parties develops and expertise grows. The varying involvement of a web designer who takes an administrative role is one example. This variance of determination creates uncertainty: those individuals who consider that they only process data under instruction, without discretion, should maintain careful records of their activities to ensure that they can justify their position as a mere data processor.

---

11. An airline already using an online reservation system seeks to research the use of its system. To do this, it provides a list of its users' email addresses to a market researcher for the purposes of sending out a questionnaire. The market researcher reasons that geographical and age data will be useful to focus the questions. If the reasoning is accepted, the researcher has contributed to the content of the data and so may have determined the purposes of the data and manner of processing controlled and so used the data jointly with the airline.

---

23   Opinion 10/2006 on the processing of personal data for Worldwide Interbank Financial Telecommunication (SWIFT), adopted on 22 November 2006.

6.2.3.1.2 Actual or potential processed data

Where a data controller has a specific intention to reprocess the data (having processed it already), he will continue to process that data. This remains the case even if the data are converted into another format.

If the Information Commissioner were to class say, a web developer, as processing personal data but the developer is not notified as a data controller, the developer may be prosecuted. The scope of processing is therefore significant and should also not merely be considered once; a change in circumstances may change an activity into processing.

6.2.3.1.3 Jurisdictional scope

Section 5 contains details of those to whom the Act applies. It applies to data controllers both established and not established in the UK under different circumstances. First, therefore, one must determine whether or not a data controller is established in the UK. Depending on the place of establishment, one must then determine details relating to the processing taking place. These complex issues need to be examined in detail. There is a two-stage test to assess whether the Act applies in situations with a foreign element. First, where is the data controller established; second, what is the nature of the processing.

There are four specific situations where a data controller will be deemed established in the UK. In addition, it is submitted there is a general test of establishment which is wider in interpretation than the four specific situations amalgamated. The four specific situations are: an individual who is ordinarily resident in the UK; a body incorporated under the law of, or of any part of, the UK; a partnership or other unincorporated association formed under the law of any part of the United Kingdom, and, any person who does not fall within the previous three situations but maintains in the UK a regular practice or office, branch, agency through which he carries out any activity.

A partnership or other unincorporated association formed under the law of any part of the UK

While the first three concepts of 'residence', 'incorporation' and partnership or 'unincorporated association' are relatively straightforward legal constructs, the final concept needs investigation. For example, if a US company has no employees in the UK, and no equipment in the UK, but has a group of UK-established individuals who work on the company's behalf, does the US company come under the jurisdiction of the Act?

It is submitted that to answer this question one must refer to both art 4 and recital 19 of the Directive. These clarify that the concept of 'establishment' is not determined by legal 'personalities' but by 'effective and real exercise of activity through stable relationships'. It follows that the US company mentioned above is likely to be seen as being 'established' (for the purposes of this but maybe no other Act) in the UK.

Finally, it is possible for one data controller to be deemed established in more than one member state. In that situation (likely for multinationals), the controller must ensure that its establishment complies with the local national law.

12. A US corporation houses all its servers, bar one, in the United States. The non-US server sits in Telehouse in London, and processes the credit card transactions for the corporation. Its work is generated from the US and no UK company or individual has the right to access the data stored on the server. The US company is established in a non-EEA state but uses equipment in the UK to process its data. It must comply with the Data Protection Act 1998.

Established in the UK

If the previous test determines that the data controller is established in the UK, one further test is applied to determine whether the controller is fully within the jurisdiction of the Act. This second test is whether or not the data are processed in the context of that establishment. The word 'context' is not defined by the Act, nor by the Directive. Taking the ordinary meaning of 'context', it is difficult to conceive of processing being carried out by a UK establishment that would not be in the 'context' of that establishment. One interpretation is that 'context' means that the data and processing should relate to UK data subjects or related activities. For example, if a US company has US customers, but its UK subsidiary holds such data on its own servers in the UK, is such processing activity 'processed in the context of that establishment'? The position is by no means clear, and no guidance has been issued on this point. Caution should be exercised and data controllers established in the UK should generally consider that all of their activities could be caught.

Established outside UK and other EEA states

Where a data controller is deemed to be established outside the UK and other EEA states, they may still fall within the jurisdiction of the Act. These data controllers fall within the jurisdiction of the Act where they also meet a second 'equipment' test. This 'equipment' test is that the foreign controller must use equipment in the UK for processing data otherwise than for the purposes of transit through the UK. The first issue to address is that this 'equipment' may be automated and that would be enough to bring the foreign controller within the ambit of the Act. The second issue is that 'mere transmission' equipment (such as routers and switches) will not bring the controller under the auspices of the Act.

13. A US Internet service provider prides itself on allowing its members to access their accounts from anywhere in the world, on any computer they choose. For resilience and speed, the provider has a server in every major jurisdiction of the world, each with a complete set of data. One of the features of the system is that its members do not store their address book of email addresses on their computer, but on the provider's servers. This has the result that its members can process personal data using the provider's equipment. If one of the servers is in the UK, the provider will be resident here and will be governed by the Data Protection Act 1998.

6.2.3.2   Data processors

As discussed, the Data Protection Act 1998 applies to data controllers who process personal data. Those individuals who either allow users access to their equipment to process data, or perform the processing for them, are data processors and need not notify their activities to the Commissioner. More specifically, a person is a data processor if he:

1. not being an employee of the data controller;

2. processes data on behalf of the data controller.[24]

The following provides some Internet-specific examples of data processing and the demarcation between controlling and processing in practice.

6.2.3.2.1 Archives and data warehousing

A mere provider of equipment for backing-up a data controller's data will be a data processor. This is because it is usual that the data are stored and are also accessible by the data user if there is a breakdown or emergency. This access is likely to fall within the broad scope of processing; as such, the owner of a data warehouse (a company providing data storage services) is processing data on behalf of the data controller. It is rare that those persons will determine the nature of the data processing. In addition, the means of processing have arguably been determined by the data user in selecting that provider. Those who merely archive are therefore more likely to be data processors rather than controllers.

Another common scenario is that the owner of a data warehouse, on request, will perform actions on the data on the data controller's behalf. For example, where a data controller urgently requires a list of names and addresses from a particular database, the owner of the data warehouse will usually, on request, provide these data. In doing so, that person is taking on the role of data processor. The person is performing processing on behalf of the data controller but should take care not to go beyond the controller's instructions, and should refer back for further instructions or confirmation where necessary.

The short and important point is that when storing another's data, one should carefully assess whether one is acting as a data processor. The difficulty with such an assessment is that processing, as has been discussed, is a subjective term and who 'determines' is more a matter of opinion than fact.

---

14. An email provider holds emails for each of its members until the member logs in. At this point the member is informed that mail is being stored and is given a choice: either continue to store the mail, or, download the information. On choosing to download the mail, the mail is deleted from the provider's server. One copy only ever exists. Because the provider cannot determine the processing of the data, but requires its members' instructions, the provider will not be a data controller but merely a data processor.

6.2.3.2.2 Servers

Many online companies provide their customers with an area of storage space which could be used to store personal data. In itself, such storage makes these

---

24   Data Protection Act 1998, s 1(1).

companies data processors. The companies are likely also to hold personal data on those customers who use their service making them a data controller for this purpose.

6.2.3.2.3   Remote manipulation

Many companies provide facilities for remotely manipulating data. Clients may choose this because the remote computer is extremely powerful and is able to perform tasks far more quickly than the client computer. There are two ways in which this manipulation can be performed: one, where the client computer communicates directly with the remote computer, giving instructions over the Internet or using a direct line; the second way, owners of the remote computer are actually given instructions as to how to manipulate the data. It should be clear that the risk of a security breach is lower in the first way than the second. Where the owner of a computer does permit remote access and manipulation, it may fall within the ambit of a data processor.

---

15. Wonderlandweekend.com is a holiday company. It pays a commission to clients who send out mailings to their customers advertising Wonderlandweekend's luxury short breaks which generate sales. Clients give Wonderlandweekend their customer list to send out the mailings on their behalf. Wonderlandweekend does so acting solely on the client's instructions and can only use the data for the specified, one-off mailing purpose. It is likely that Wonderlandweekend is acting as a data processor when using such data. If a recipient then signs up with Wonderlandweekend to purchase a break, further processing of the customer's personal data will be undertaken by Wonderlandweekend in its own right, for its own purposes and at its discretion. Wonderlandweekend will be acting as a data controller in respect of this processing. Care should be taken in any contract between client and Wonderlandweekend to clarifiy the demarcation of responsibility and any relevant controls.

6.2.4   Data protection notification

The impact of the Data Protection Act on users of the Internet has been shown to be great. All information sent over the Internet will constitute data, and if personal, providing those data over the Internet will be viewed as processing. Data controllers are required to register with the Information Commissioner. If a person should notify but does not, this constitutes a criminal offence.[25]

Notifications must be submitted along with a fee (currently £35). The notification period is one year. Renewals do not occur automatically unless it has been arranged for the renewal fee to be paid by direct debit payment. Otherwise, the renewal notification and fee must be submitted prior to the expiry date of the entry. Although the Information Commissioner's office sends out reminder notices before the expiry date of a notification, it is essential to be alert to this

---

25   Data Protection Act 1998, ss 17(1) and 21(1).

date and to have arrangements in place to effect the necessary administration. Where a notification has passed its expiry date, notifications cannot be renewed and data controllers will be obliged to make a new notification.

Any changes to a notification must be notified within a period of 28 days from the date on which the entry becomes inaccurate or incomplete. Failure to do so is a criminal offence. Changes can be made free of charge by post using the specific form to add an additional purpose or a second form covering other amendments. These forms are available from the website, http://www.ico.gov.uk.

6.2.4.1 Notification exemptions

Certain data controllers are not required to notify, as they are exempt. Nevertheless, they may notify voluntarily[26] and in all cases are still bound by the other provisions of the Act.[27] The main exemptions extend to processing only for:

1. personal, family or household affairs[28];

2. maintaining a public register[29];

3. a non-profit organisation processing only for establishing or maintaining membership or providing or administering activities for individuals who are members of the organisation[30]; or staff administration, or, advertising, marketing and public relations, or, accounts and records but no other processing at all.[31]

6.2.4.2 Contents of a notification

A notification is a publicly available document explaining in standard terms the processing activities of a data controller. Notifications can be completed either by following a template available from the Information Commissioner's website at http://www.ico.gov.uk, or by creating a bespoke notification by selecting the relevant categories of information that apply.

Data controllers should pay attention to any partially completed template received from the Information Commissioner. This delineates the responsibilities of the data controller to its subjects. Data controllers should also ensure that their application includes 'free-text' references to the Internet, where appropriate. If this section does not accurately describe the ambit of a data controller's purpose for processing the data, that may expose the data controller to prosecution.

---

26 Data Protection Act 1998, s 18(1).
27 Voluntary notification is not available to the following exempt persons, being those who: hold personal data for personal, family or household affairs; hold personal data exempt under national security exemptions; hold personal data exempt under transitional provisions for payroll, unincorporated members' clubs and mailing list usage. Data Protection Act 1998, Part IV.
28 Data Protection Act 1998, s 36.
29 Data Protection Act 1998, ss 17(4) and 70.
30 Data Protection (Notification and Notification Fees) Regulations 2000, Sched, para 15.
31 Data Protection (Notification and Notification Fees) Regulations 2000, Sched, paras 1-4.

16. A UK company currently uses one free-standing computer to store and process the biographical details of its staff. Now that the company is expanding out of the UK, it wishes to port these data onto a website, to allow any member of the overseas operation to access the details. The company's notification should reflect this. For, say, the purpose of 'Maintaining and publishing biographical details of staff', the description should be expanded to stress this is 'over the Internet and World Wide Web'. An example of needing to amend the description of a purpose is where the Internet is integral to the purpose.

The notification breaks down information about data processing activities provided for each of the disclosed purposes the data controller processes personal data for. For each of these purposes, the data controller must then state: the data subjects of such data; the data classes (i.e. the types of data which are processed); data disclosees (the persons to whom data may be disclosed); and whether or not the data is to be transferred outside the EEA. The data controller is then required to sign a declaration and provide certain contact details and confirmation as to whether or not certain specific training and security requirements have been met (not compulsory).

Highlighting the importance of the seventh principle (discussed below), data controllers must also give a general description of the security measures to be taken to protect against unauthorised or unlawful processing of personal data and against accidental loss or destruction of, or damage to, personal data. Often this description will be very sensitive for the data controller and, as a consequence, is not published in the public register. Data controllers need to provide the necessary comfort regarding physical security, technical security and organisational security. Further details relating to security are discussed below in relation to the seventh principle.

17. An online UK car retailer has always sold its customer details to car insurance companies; appropriately, its registration notification included the purpose of trading in personal information. Previously, it provided its lists of personal data to the insurance company on disk. To keep the lists more up-to-date, it now has installed a server which acts as an ftp site for any person with the correct password. Despite this purpose remaining the same, the retailer should update the relevant description to reflect the change in provision.

6.2.5   Principles of data protection

All data controllers must abide by the eight principles of data protection which are set out in Sch 1 of the Act as follows:

1.   Personal data shall be processed fairly and lawfully and, in particular, shall not be processed unless:

   (a)   at least one of the conditions in Sch 2 is met, and

   (b)   in the case of sensitive personal data, at least one of the conditions in Sch 3 is also met.

2. Personal data shall be obtained only for one or more specified and lawful purposes, and shall not be further processed in any manner incompatible with that purpose or those purposes.

3. Personal data shall be adequate, relevant and not excessive in relation to the purpose or purposes for which they are processed.

4. Personal data shall be accurate and, where necessary, kept up-to-date.

5. Personal data processed for any purpose or purposes shall not be kept for longer than is necessary for that purpose or those purposes.

6. Personal data shall be processed in accordance with the rights of data subjects under this Act.

7. Appropriate technical and organisational measures shall be taken against unauthorised or unlawful processing of personal data and against accidental loss or destruction of, or damage to, personal data.

8. Personal data shall not be transferred to a country or territory outside the European Economic Area unless that country or territory ensures an adequate level of protection for the rights and freedoms of data subjects in relation to the processing of personal data.

6.2.5.1 First principle: processed fairly and lawfully and satisfies additional conditions

'The information to be contained in personal data shall be obtained, and personal data shall be processed, fairly and lawfully.'

This principle will be particularly relevant for those who use their websites or other digital activities to collect and then utilise personal data from visitors. In short, the principle attempts to ensure that those individuals who access a service or send information understand, and consent to, what will happen to their personal data. One must bear in mind that 'processing' encompasses the stages of first 'obtaining' data and then utilising it, by, say, organising, consulting or disclosing.[32] It is therefore important to consider, initially, whether a site is 'obtaining' data fairly and lawfully and then consider the method of fuller exploitation. The Act also specifies that 'In determining ... whether personal data are processed fairly, regard is to be had to the method by which they are obtained. . .'.[33]

6.2.5.1.1 Data obtained fairly

There is no one test to establish that a data user has fairly obtained information from personal data, but there are a number of factors that the Commissioner will take into account. One key factor prescribed by the Act is that the individual was

---

32 Data Protection Act 1998, s 1(1).
33 Data Protection Act 1998, Sch 1, Pt II, para 1(1).

not deceived or misled about the purpose for the data.[34] A data controller should try to indicate to the data subject the full potential use of that information. It is not enough to direct the subject to the notification or to assume that the subject knows the scope of a data controller's notification. To be safe, a data controller must make explicit the purpose to each potential data subject at the point of collection: a data user may breach this principle even where the data subject was misled unintentionally.[35] Unless it is obvious from the method to obtain the information, data controllers should inform their subjects of the potential disclosures and transfers of the information, and the purpose for processing that information.

A good, albeit US, example of the concept is the US Federal Trade Commission Complaint against Geocities.[36] Geocities operated a website consisting of 'virtual communities' of free and fee-based personal home pages. At the time of the complaint, it had more than 1.8 million members. Each member had the option to enter certain personal data with the various provisos that[37]:

> 'We will not share any information with anyone without your permission'
> '[W]e will NEVER give your information to anyone without your permission'
> 'We assure you that we will NEVER give your personal information to anyone without your permission'

Despite such assurances, Geocities did disclose the personal information to third parties. They, in turn, used the information to target Geocities members. In its consent order with the Federal Trade Commission (FTC), Geocities admitted these 'facts' as true. This blatant misrepresentation as to the use of personal data should amount to 'unfair' obtaining under the first principle. Under the US FTC codes, Geocities settled the complaint.

A UK example concerning unfair obtaining of personal data is the 2006 enforcement notice against B4U Business Media Limited; the first such enforcement action against a UK website. The site B4USearch.com provided online access to directory enquiries and electoral roll information. The Information Commissioner held that this was unfair processing. It was unfair for individuals to be compelled to provide information under statute (as part of the electoral roll) where that information was then available for resale without restriction. It was also unfair because B4U was deliberately using 2001 data, knowing that regulations had been brought in in 2002[38] to enable individuals to opt-out of having their data made available for other uses. B4U's use of the earlier data unfairly undermined the wishes of those who later chose to opt-out. This case also highlights the misconception of assuming that information obtained from a person with statutory authority to supply such information provides immunity. The processor must still comply with para 2, Part II of Sch 1 (i.e. information and data notices must still be provided).

34   Data Protection Act 1998, Sch 1, Pt II, para 1(1).
35   This was decided in the *Innovations (Mail Order) Ltd v Data Protection Registrar Data Protection Tribunal* case DA/92 31/49/1.
36   File No 9823015, 1998.
37   Respectively: New Member Application Form Privacy Statement, Geocites Free Member E-mail Program Privacy Statement, World Report Newsletter 1997.
38   The Representation of the People (England and Wales) (Amendment) Regulations 2002.

Identity of data user

Potential data subjects should be made aware of to whom they are providing their personal data. The seamless way that a viewer of a website can move between different websites may cause data protection problems. For example, many commercial sites outsource any payment mechanisms to a third party, who also operates a website. A viewer of the commercial site will be taken through the various stages of choosing a product to purchase. The final stage in this process is for the viewer to enter his personal details and payment particulars. To do this the viewer will often be instructed to click on a certain icon, perhaps labelled 'Payment'. At this point, unbeknown to the viewer, the viewer is connected with the payment website. The only way for the viewer to discover this, unless it is made clear, may be to watch the URL alter at the top of their browser. Where framing or imbedded applications are used, even the URL may not alter.

It is certainly unfair obtaining of data where the provider of that data is not alerted to the identity of the person obtaining the data. Controllers of websites that interact with others for the collection of personal data should make it clear to their viewers that this is the case. It is particularly important that data controllers at the very least make this information 'readily available' to the potential data subject.[39]

Non-obvious purposes

Often, a data controller will have more than one contemplated purpose for personal information. Where a purpose could not reasonably be expected, the data user must inform the subject prior to obtaining the data. Data controllers must give each individual the informed chance to refuse to become a data subject.[40]

Data controllers should assume that there is a need to inform the data subject of the intended use. Data controllers should alert their data subjects to any processing prior to obtaining. This is the case even where the data, once obtained, will be used solely by the data controller.

When and how to inform

A data controller's obligations are not to deceive or mislead the user about the likely processing of the data *prior* to processing the data or disclosure to a third party.[41] In practice this is likely to entail the data controller informing the potential subjects of all relevant information prior to obtaining the data. Otherwise, the data controller will be obliged to conduct the embarrassing and costly activity of re-contacting data subjects to ask their permission to exploit their data in a new undisclosed manner.

For commercial and legal reasons, therefore, data controllers are advised to inform their potential data subjects of all relevant information before the subject has opportunity to enter their data. A US import to achieve this is the 'privacy

---

39 Data Protection Act 1998, Sch 1, Pt II, para 2(1)(a).
40 This is specifically discussed below at 'Prior consent'.
41 Data Protection Act 1998, Sch 1, Pt II, para 2(2).

policy' which is often used to explain the 'who, why, what and where' of processed data. Despite the Information Commissioner stating that privacy policies are 'good practice'[42] they are not legally required. They are merely a now almost ubiquitous way of ensuring that *prior* to obtaining the data, the data controller has 'made available' to the subject all the relevant information.

The information that must be given is set out at para 2(3), Part II of Sch 1 to the Act. Those drafting these notices or a privacy policy should also be mindful of the information requirements under the Electronic Communications (EC Directive) Regulations 2003 and Electronic Commerce (EC Directive) Regulations 2002. The information in the notice or privacy policy should include a general description of all the purposes for which the data may be processed.

Where a data controller needs to do this, to broaden its purposes, silence should not be taken to be a data subject's consent. In *Midlands Electricity plc v Data Protection Registrar*[43] it was made clear to Midlands Electricity that:

> 'For the avoidance of doubt . . . consent shall not be inferred from the failure of any person to return any other documentation containing an opportunity to opt-out.'

This clarification is also repeated in the undertakings made by London Electricity plc[44] and Thames Water Utilities Ltd,[45] both given to avoid the Commissioner enforcing its sanctions. Data controllers would be prudent not to rely upon a data subject's silence.

---

18. An online pencil procurement website has fairly collected the email addresses and personal data of the stationery budget holders in the country's largest companies. Pressure from its venture capitalist investors leads it to expand into advertising conferences and jobs in the procurement field. It emails all its customers explaining this expansion and asking them to return the email if they have any objections to this new processing. Merely because no one returned an objection does not mean that the site's personal data is now fairly obtained for this new purpose.

Often a data controller will obtain personal data with one intention in mind, and then later decide to use the information for another purpose. Unless this new purpose is within the scope of the purpose reasonably contemplated or disclosed to the data subject, strictly speaking, the data user should seek new consent.

Prior consent

In the fiercely competitive e-commerce sector, it is important to keep open one's options for future business ventures. Unfortunately, it is not advisable to attempt

---

42   Internet: Protection of Privacy, Data Controllers, Version 4, January 2000. This document is published by the Office of the Information Commissioner.
43   Final form of the enforcement notice (as approved by the Data Protection Tribunal) 20 July 1999, at para 9.5.
44   London Electricity plc Undertaking, 1 January 2001.
45   Thames Water Utilities Ltd Undertaking, 1 January 2001.

to keep open one's options of dealing with personal data. A data controller can not try to get around this by making the initial description of the purposes vague in order to encompass future purposes for which they may later choose to use the data. Data controllers must make their intentions clear to potential data subjects before soliciting their personal data.

---

19. Fat?No!, a web-based health and fitness magazine informs its online subscribers that their personal data is held in order to 'send you details of competitions, events and articles that may be of interest to you and for any other related purposes'. The company is not generating enough income through advertising revenues on its site. It approaches a sponsor who requires that they directly send subscribers weekly promotions for its range of fat-free ice-cream. This is not within the scope of the original purposes stated, and even without this new purpose, the original notice is arguably unfair.

In *Innovations (Mail Order) Ltd v Data Protection Registrar*,[46] under the 1984 Act, the appellant collected individuals' names and addresses for completing order requests by them. After completing the order Innovations sent an acknowledgement on the back of which was a statement informing the customer that Innovations rents out its names and addresses. The company gave an address to its customers to write to if they objected to their data being used in this way. The Data Protection Tribunal held that this was too late: to be fair, data users must give their subjects the chance to consent to the use of personal information before it is taken. It upheld the enforcement notice served by the Registrar on 9 April 1992.

Surreptitious obtaining

One quality of the Internet is that a data controller may technically collect personal data without a data subject being aware. 'Cookies' can be deposited on a data subject's hard drive which, when combined with personal data knowingly entered by the subject, can create new personal data. If a site 'records' all the movements one makes within a site, and is able to link those movements to data identifying a living individual, it is obtaining personal data about *use* of its site. Controllers must only obtain such covert data, albeit valuable, where the data subject has been given clear information about the use and purpose of cookies. The Electronic Communications Directive (as implemented into UK legislation via the Privacy and Electronic Communications (EC Directive) Regulations 2003) addresses this issue. It prohibits the use of cookies or other similar devices, regardless of whether or not they actually involve the processing of personal data, unless data subjects are given 'access to clear and comprehensive information' about the cookies and other information[47] and provided with a means of disabling such device.

---

46   DA/92/31/49/1.
47   Art 5, para 3, also see recital 25. See Agreement between the Attorney General of the States of Arizona, California, Connecticut, Massachusetts, Michigan, New Jersey, New Mexico, New York, Vermont and Washington and Doubleclick Inc, 26 August 2002.

20. A successful version of browser software allows each site visited to store a small quantum of data about the visitor accessing the site. This data, or 'cookie', is stored on the visitor's hard disk and is used to compile data about each visitor when they revisit any site. If the visitor has no knowledge of this surreptitious method of obtaining information, be it stored at the client or server, it may be unfair obtaining of data. If the server then processes the information, again, without the client's tacit consent, this may also be a breach of the first data protection principle as unfair processing.

Disingenuous consent

It is likely to be unfair where a data subject has no choice but to provide consent to additional uses of his personal data. This is the situation where the data controller informs all potential subjects that their order or transaction will not be processed unless they agree to the secondary uses of the data. While the data subject does still have a nominal choice, to stop dealing with the data user, for certain dominant data controllers it will not be a genuine choice.

6.2.5.1.2   Information obtained lawfully

The first hurdle for the Information Commissioner to prove unlawful obtaining is to prove that the obtaining of the information was in breach of a law. Possible candidates for grounds for unlawful obtaining in the normal course of dealing with personal data are breach of confidence and breach of contract. In the Internet sphere the most likely law to be broken is not civil, but criminal: the Computer Misuse Act 1990.[48] Unauthorised access, an offence under the Computer Misuse Act 1990, may result in the obtaining of information unlawfully under the Data Protection Act 1998. Along with these more general laws by which data users must abide, certain data users are bound by rules specific to their industry. *British Gas Trading Ltd v Data Protection Registrar*[49] is a good illustration of this. In this case the Registrar (as then was) viewed the use of customer data to provide non-gas services was ultra vires. The Tribunal disagreed but concurred with the concept of an *ultra vires* act of a corporation being 'unlawful' under the first principle.

Whatever the unlawful activity alleged, it will always be open to the data subject or Information Commissioner to argue that, in the alternative, even if the obtaining was not unlawful, it was nevertheless unfair.[50] The protection for data subjects under the first principle of data protection is certainly broader when the accusation is unfair obtaining as compared with unlawful obtaining.

---

48   See Chapter 5 on Crime.
49   [1998] Info TLR 393.
50   There will be many situations where obtaining is both unfair and unlawful under the Unfair Terms in Consumer Contracts Regulations 1994/9 which make unenforceable against a consumer certain unfair contractual terms. A contracting party which by its unequal bargaining power is able to coerce a consumer into agreeing to supply personal data may be acting unfairly under the Regulations. The obtaining of those data may be outside the enforceable terms of the contract and classed as unlawful and, by virtue of the disparity in bargaining strength, unfair.

6.2.5.1.3   Data processed fairly

Fair processing is directed at protecting data subjects from treatment that may be described in a data controller's notification but is, nevertheless, prejudicial use of the personal data. The first question is necessarily to establish that processing itself has occurred. It will be recalled that 'processing' is a wide and far-ranging concept but that it is also important to consider the actual activity undertaken at the time of the alleged 'unfair' processing. This is because, as in the *Johnson* case considered above, where this concerns processing that is not automated or in respect of a relevant filing system, the question as to whether or not any action was unfair may become immaterial. As has also been discussed, the concept of 'fairly' is also very wide. Despite such a 'catch-all' provision, the Act further raises the hurdle for a data controller.

6.2.5.1.4   Additional conditions necessary for the first principle

The first principle stipulates both that data shall be processed fairly and lawfully 'and, in particular, shall not be processed unless. . . at least one of the conditions in Schedule 2 is met'. The additional conditions are discussed below in the context of Internet data controllers.

Data subject has given his consent to the processing

The consent condition under Sch 2 should not be confused with the specific requirement to obtain consent where data is being put to certain uses, as for example under the Privacy and Electronic Communications (EC Directive) Regulations 2003 in relation to direct marketing (see below). The factors in considering how this consent can be obtained over the Internet are the same, however.

On the Internet, just as in the offline world, one may consent in a number of ways. One may 'positively' consent by continuing to conduct oneself in a particular way. One may also actively consent by signing a particular document at a particular place.

On a website, data controllers and their web designers are faced with the difficulty of 'what is consent?'. Is it an opt-in box, pre-ticked? Is it an opt-out box[51] in a small font size and 'below the fold'?[52] There is no definition of 'consent' in the Act. In the House of Lords debate on the Act Lord Williams was adamant that there was no need to include a definition as existing law and the courts were enough.[53]

Further guidance can be drawn from the Act's spawning Directive at art 2(h). This states a person's consent is 'freely given, specific and informed indication of his wishes by which the data subject signifies his agreement to personal data relating to him being processed'. It is worthwhile considering the elements of this definition in the Internet context.

---

51   See discussion on the meaning of opt-in and opt-out consent below.
52   The hidden part of the current web page which is available for viewing by scrolling down the web page. This is, in part, a factor of the resolution of the viewer's screen.
53   Vol 586, No 108, col CWH 15, 23 Feb 1998.

Freely given

This will rarely be a difficult challenge for most data controllers. Even if a data subject must provide consent as an obligation under the contract with the data controller, the data subject does not need to enter into the contract. Consequently, it is acceptable to deduce the 'consent' was freely given. Difficulties can arise where, without acting in an anti-competitive or collusive way, a great number of organisations within a particular sector require consent to process certain data. In such a situation, a data subject may be unable to enter this type of contract with *any* supplier without giving 'consent'.[54]

> 21. A large group of airlines that fly from London to Paris each have websites and independently choose to allow bookings to be taken only over their respective websites. Each ticket sale contract includes a term to the effect of 'You agree that we may use your personal data to provide you with details of great hotel offers during your flight'. There is no opt-out box. Because it is impossible to fly directly to Paris without giving this 'consent' it may be deemed not to be freely given.

Specific

This aspect of 'consent' is the one which causes most clashes between the marketing team behind a site and its legal advisors. Specific means just that; general is not enough and reaching a form of statement next to a consent mechanism that is informative but also commercial and not unduly alarming can be a challenge. Explaining the temporary or permanent nature of the activity is also an integral aspect of being specific.

> 22. A fireplace installer establishes a website which allows customers to design and order their fireplaces. The 'fair collection' notice states: 'By ordering this fireplace you will also agree to allow one of our group of companies to contact you by email, yearly, to enquire only whether or not you require your chimney to be swept for your comfort and safety.' Such a notice is specific and leaves the data subject in no doubt as to the precise purpose of collecting their data.

Informed

Allied to 'specific' is the concept of 'informed': simply put, one cannot consent unless one knows what one is consenting to. For data protection purposes online, companies have taken to producing 'privacy policies'. These detail every possible activity that may be contemplated in relation to the data. Despite their almost viral, widespread usage across websites, there is a risk that they do not fulfil their intended effect. This is not down to their *content* wanting; it is because their *position* and *incorporation* is often so hidden that they are not immediately visible. Websites with unusual uses of personal data would be advised not merely to include details of the uses in their privacy policy. They must also bring the policy to a user's attention, not bury it at the bottom of a web page and/or in terms and conditions.

54   See Mr Lamidey's (Assistant Registrar under the 1984 Act) concern at high street bank practices: *Financial Times*, 2 February 1993.

> 23. An individual complains to the Information Commissioner that a certain website has used their personal data in a non-obvious manner. When approached, the website's owner directs the Commissioner to click on a tiny 'Terms of Use' link at the base of the home page followed by a further link on that page to the 'Privacy Policy'. The page on which personal data was collected has had no such links. Whatever the contents of the privacy policy, it is likely that its hidden position will mean no informed consent was given.

Indication and signifies

These two terms have been prised out of the Directive's definition to support the Information Commissioner's view that:

'Data controllers cannot infer consent from non-response to a communication, for example by a customer's failure to return or respond to a leaflet.'[55]

This approach to 'silence' is endorsed by the undertakings given by London Electricity plc and Thames Water Utilities Ltd[56] in relation to alleged breaches of the first principle. In both undertakings the statement is made:

'consent shall not be inferred from the failure of any person to return any leaflet or other document containing an opportunity to opt out.'[57]

Similarly, in the Final Form of the Enforcement Notice (as approved by the Data Protection Tribunal on 20 July 1999) against Midlands Electricity plc consent is stated to include where:

'[the individual customers] have returned a document to the [data] user or, by other means of communication received by the data user have indicated that they consented to, or by not filling in an opt-out box or other means have indicated that they do not object to such processing.'[58]

These cases do show that the Information Commissioner believes (and just as important, the Tribunal supports the view) that silence or acquiescence is unlikely to be an 'indication' of consent. The commercial lesson to draw from this is simple. Wherever possible, ensure that a data subject has to 'do' something having read the privacy policy or fair collection notice. The consent provisions of the Privacy and Electronic Communications (EC Directive) Regulations 2003 have provided further clarification on consent requirements in the context of marketing communications. See section 6.3.3.1 below for details.

Evidence of consent

If 'consent' is being relied upon to comply with Schedule 2, websites should ensure that they retain evidence of this consent. If a database contains only the

---

55 *The Data Protection Act 1998 – An Introduction*, Office of the Data Protection Registrar, October 1998, at p 10.
56 7 January 2001 and 11 January 2001.
57 Paras 1.5(iii) and 5(3) respectively.
58 Cl 9.2(ii)(bb).

email address of data subjects, how can this be used to prove that all their owners did consent, by say, ticking a box? If a privacy policy contains some unusual uses for data, how can its website owner prove that there was a specific, informed indication of the data subject's consent?

To answer these questions, the customer database needs to be constructed to record not merely the collected personal data but also the data relating to the consent itself. In addition, with websites under constant redesign flux, data users should maintain a secure, date-stamped copy of the main data protection aspects of the site to allow them to prove how the site was configured at the time that a data subject keyed in their details and consent.

Processing necessary for the performance of or entering into a contract[59]

At first glance, a data user could be forgiven for assuming that all that is needed to satisfy this paragraph is publishing an appropriate term in the data subject's contract. The correct focus, however, is on the word 'necessary'. An ancillary use of the data will not be necessary for the performance of the contract. The word necessary must be construed very narrowly and objectively.

---

24. NeuPub2 is a radical new type of online publisher: writers submit their manuscript and NeuPub2 distributes their work having edited the manuscript to include 'product placement' from well-known brand names. In return, NeuPub2 pays its writers a royalty on copies sold. For writers that do not sell well, NeuPub2 states: 'From time to time we will pass your details to experienced writing coaches who can help your next project be even more successful.' Processing the data for this ancillary purpose is not necessary for the performance of the contract.

Processing necessary for compliance with a data user's non-contractual legal obligation

This paragraph of Sch 2 relates to a statutory obligation on the data user to process the data in a particular manner. Owners of websites should take specific sectoral legal advice before relying only on this paragraph to satisfy their compliance with Sch 2.

Processing necessary for data subject's vital interests

It is clear both from the recitals to the Directive[60] and the Commissioner's guidance[61] that this condition is concerned with life and death situations for the data subject.

Processing necessary for public functions

This related to the administration of justice, functions of the Crown, minister, government department and related functions of a public nature exercised in the public interest. Again, this is narrowly construed because of the limiter 'neces-

---

59   Data Protection Act 1998, Sch 2, para 2.
60   Recital 31.
61   '[R]eliance on this condition may only be claimed where the processing is necessary for matters of life and death. . .'

ꜱꜱꜱy'. This condition should not concern private bodies and should not be confused with non-contractual obligations.

Processing necessary for a data controller's legitimate interests

This is an ambiguous condition. It requires the Information Commissioner, Tribunal and possibly the courts to balance the data user's legitimate interests with those legitimate interests of the data subject,[62] particularly his right to privacy[63] and other rights and freedoms provided for under the European Convention for the Protection of Human Rights and Fundamental Freedoms and the Human Rights Act 1998.

This author strongly believes that this condition does not allow in, through the back door, anything that a private body does for profit because 'profit making is a legitimate interest'. Legitimate interest in this context must mean those interests protected by the Treaty of Rome and other enabling provisions. It does not mean, in effect, any vires act a company chooses to conduct.

Even if such a wide interpretation were afforded to this condition, one must not forget why the condition needs to be met. To comply with the first principle, *first* the data must be processed fairly *and* then *also* it must satisfy one of the conditions.

Web businesses and their advisors are warned not to trust this condition as their way unfairly to process data and to avoid providing the data subject with the 'specific information' relating to the processing. In addition, all analysis and decision must be conducted on a case-by-case basis, which demands that the interests of one data subject are not assumed to apply for another.

---

25. SpamMethods Ltd is established as a company whose sole function is to harvest Director-level email addresses from corporate websites and then sell access to these email addresses to financial advisors. Such harvesting and processing, without the data subjects' knowledge, is obviously unfair. That the activity is the only reason SpamMethods was established does not make it a 'legitimate interest'. And, even if it were a 'legitimate interest', being 'unfair processing' it remains illegal.

---

26. A manufacturer creates a sophisticated home page that records the number of hits to its site and the email addresses of its members who view the site. This information is then analysed and certain addresses are targeted with 'follow-up' emails. Without a method for an individual to avoid being included in the emailshot, the processing, and obtaining, may be unfair, and therefore a breach of the first data protection principle.[64]

---

62   Data Protection Act 1998, Sch 2, para 6.
63   Directive 95/46/EC of the European Parliament and of the Council, arts 7(f) and 1(1).
64   It is a moot point, and discussed earlier, whether simply processing an email address can constitute processing under the Act as personal data must relate to a living individual. An email address may not actually relate to an individual and may not permit identification of the living individual. A similar point was raised by Equifax in a Data Protection Tribunal inquiry. Equifax processed purely in relation to an address. The Tribunal gave a purposive answer to the point saying that one should look to the purpose of the processing. Where that processing was to determine information in relation to the living individual, the processing will fall within the definition of the word in the Act.

6.2.5.1.5   Data processed lawfully

An obligation to process lawfully is narrower than fair processing and the fact that a data controller has satisfied at least one of the Sch 2 conditions does not, of itself, mean that the requirement for lawful processing is necessarily satisfied. If processing breaches another legal duty, including both criminal and civil duties, or would lead to such a breach, then it will also be a breach of the first data protection principle. The Registrar under the 1984 Act indicated three areas of law particularly relevant to breaches of the first principle of data protection.[65] It is submitted the same areas will be considered under the 1998 Act:

> 'Confidentiality, arising from the relationship of the data user with the individual;
>
> The ultra vires rule and the rule relating to the excess of delegated powers, under which the data user may only act within the limits of its legal powers;
>
> Legitimate expectation, that is the expectation of the individual as to how the data user will use the information relating to him.'

---

27. A data subject supplies to a data controller personal data encrypted using a public key. This encryption may be enough to give the subject the legitimate expectation that the personal data will be used by only the holder of the private key. Wider processing may be unlawful and constitute a breach of the first data protection principle.

6.2.5.2   Second principle: obtained for specified and lawful purposes

> 'Personal data shall be held only for one or more specified and lawful purposes.'

6.2.5.2.1   Obtained for specified purposes

To comply with this second principle is simply a matter of ensuring that all purposes for which a data controller obtains data are properly and accurately notified to the Commissioner,[66] and are properly specified to the data subject in accordance with the first principle.[67] Data controllers should be vigilant over their databases and appreciate that including an additional field against a set of personal data or using a database in a new way may constitute a new purpose which their notification to the Commissioner and specification to the data subject must reflect. A data controller must also be aware that obtaining is widely encompassing: newly received personal data may alter the capacity in which other data are being processed. And, the Interpretation Schedule of the Act states that 'regard' has to be had to the intended processing[68] when determining compatible obtaining. These other data may then become part of a collection of data which are intended to be processed. As such, these data will fall within the scope of data held.

---

65   Data Protection Guideline 4, para 1.18.
66   Data Protection Act 1998, Sch 1, Pt II, para 5(b).
67   Data Protection Act 1998, Sch 1, Pt II, para 5(a).
68   Data Protection Act 1998, Sch 1, Pt II, para 6.

28. A university has a list of academics who have applied for a new post. To gain more information on them, it enters each academic's name into a search engine that searches both the World Wide Web and Usenet. From these additional data, the university appends to its database two new entries: first, personal details gleaned form the search; second, opinions on the nature of each academic's postings on Usenet. To comply with the second data protection principle the university must check that their current notification and method of obtaining covers the newly held data.

6.2.5.2.2 Obtained for lawful purposes

As for the first data protection principle, the word 'lawful' relates both to criminal and civil laws. Depending on the intention for obtaining the data, it is feasible that an accurate notification is still in breach of the second data protection principle for being unlawful. It would, for example, be unlawful for an online travel agent to compile names and addresses of its customers to provide those details to criminals to burgle the customers' properties while they are on holiday.

6.2.5.2.3 Value of personal data database, including on insolvency

Increasingly, corporations are realising (in both senses of the word) the value of personal data. Personal data allows marketers to target more accurately products and services at individuals. The more a marketer 'knows' about an individual, the higher likelihood that the individual will be interested in the offering. This necessarily increases the return on (marketing) investment. Because of this real value, corporations are also beginning to understand the utility of *their* customers' personal data to *other* corporations.

It is this author's opinion that there are three main reasons why personal data is now viewed as a commodity. First, on the Internet, as the good joke tells 'no-one knows you are a dog'. In other words, unlike in the corner shop, the website cannot tell whether you are a regular customer, a new customer or even a troublesome schoolchild with no pocket money to spend. Consequently, websites have been forced into collecting information about a visitor to ensure they can greet them appropriately and even recommend purchases to them based upon previous interactions. The second main reason is that many websites have subsisted only on advertising revenues, not direct revenues. As detailed here, the more a marketer knows about an audience and its individuals, the higher price it will pay to access those 'eyeballs'. The third, and more recent, reason is the increasing demise of 'dot com' companies; investors, insolvency practitioners and creditors are needing to extract the greatest possible value from a company's assets. One such asset is the personal data database. And, for the first two reasons, this database has a value well worth paying for (or worth selling). Companies and their advisors or insolvency practitioners are, however, worried that the 'open market' value of the database may not be accurate; the company may be prevented by data protection law from selling the database at *any* price.

The second principle prevents a company from obtaining data and then, without having told the individual, processing it for the purposes of selling it to a third party. This absolute prohibition applies whether the selling company is on the verge of insolvency or not. The Toysmart bankruptcy is a good US illustration.

Since September 1999, Toysmart.com had posted a privacy policy stating 'When you register with Toysmart.com, you can rest assured that your information will never be shared with a third party'. By 19 May 2000, Toysmart had officially ceased operations having run into dire financial difficulties. It was prompted to sell its principal remaining asset, its customer information database. By 21 July 2000, the Federal Trade Commission had blocked the sale to 'any' buyer saying: 'Customer data collected under a privacy agreement should not be auctioned off to the highest bidder'. The FTC were only prepared to permit the entire website and data to be sold off to the 'highest bidder' who operates a 'family-orientated website'.

It is submitted that, under the UK's regime, the Commissioner would construe the word 'never' as just that. She would therefore determine that the Toysmart data, having been obtained for processing by Toysmart, could not merely, because of bankruptcy, be transferred to another entity. The second principle would have been breached. Indeed, the US FTC's Commissioner Swindle, in the minority, was of the strong opinion that:

> 'I do not think that the [Federal Trade] Commission should allow the sale [of Toysmart customer data]. If we really believe that customers attach great value to the privacy of their personal information and that consumers should be able to limit access to such information through private agreements with businesses, we should compel businesses to honor promises they make to customers to gain access to this information ... In my view, such a sale should not be permitted because "never" really means never.'

In a twist of fate, no appropriate buyers came forward for Toysmart. Eventually, by January 2001, a Walt Disney company subsidiary bought the company for $50,000 but was forced to destroy the customer records as the FTC had indicated.

Advisors and data controllers (and banks who believe they have security over customer databases) should be particularly guarded against use of phrases such as 'we will never' in collection notices and policies. It is this author's strong belief that once the word is uttered in a fair collection notice or privacy policy, no other processing changes may be introduced without clear data subject consent to the contrary. Each and every customer would have to be contacted for permission to 'purpose creep' and, on the basis of the principles of consent analysed above, their silence would *not* mean that they had consented. Very few privacy policies should not allow for the transfer of personal data to a third party who will operate under the same privacy policy and terms and conditions. This, at least, allows consensual transfer to a third party seeking to continue to operate the business of the data controller. The third lesson is for those who lend money to companies taking security over customer databases. Conduct detailed due diligence to ensure that this database *could* have a value to a third party.

6.2.5.3 Third principle: adequate, relevant, not excessive

> 'Personal data shall be adequate, relevant and not excessive in relation to the purpose or purposes for which they are processed.'

The Act does not define the limits of this principle and does not interpret it. In relation to the similar principle under the 1984 Act, the Registrar (as then titled) suggested that one method of determining the correct quota of data is to decide the absolute minimum amount of data needed to achieve the registered purposes. The Data Protection Tribunal has established that it will look closely at exactly what information is necessary for the specified purpose.[69] Information should not be held simply on the basis that it might come in useful one day with no clear idea how and when.

---

29. A sports website runs a competition to win two tickets to an important football game. The winner will be selected at random from the correct answers received to three simple questions. Email answers must be sent by contenders on the standard email form stating the dates on which they would be available for travel and the name of the individual who would accompany them if they win. This is excessive, since the company would only need this information from the winner.

6.2.5.3.1 Living individual focus

It is wrong to assume that the necessary quotum of data can be assessed purely in relation to the purpose. The principle applies to each living individual on which the data user holds personal data. What might be the minimum quantum of data for one individual may be excessive for another. To establish a breach, the Commissioner may well examine the data held on each individual for each purpose as specified. This assessment is conducted from an objective viewpoint; it is of little relevance to a breach whether a data controller had reasoned it was holding acceptable amounts.[70]

---

30. An online software supplier uses a standard online form for its customers to complete their order details. Owing to programming technicalities each field of the form must be filled in before the user can select the 'Okay' button to complete the order. This has the result that all users are required to include their home address, even users who will be sent the software by downloading it directly from the site. The supplier will be holding excessive data on all customers who wish their software to be delivered online: a breach of the third data protection principle.

6.2.5.3.2 P3P

The World Wide Web Consortium continues to promote the Platform for Privacy Preferences (P3P). This allows a user to set maximum criteria for the personal data his browser will share with any website. For example, this author may be happy to allow a website automatically to feed cookies onto their browser and automatically to store their name, but no more.

---

69 The Tribunal held that it was excessive for the Community Charge Registration Officers of the local authority of Rhondda to hold the date of birth of an individual. This seemingly innocuous piece of datum was sufficient to warrant the Tribunal deciding that the local authority had breached the relevant data protection principle: Case DA/90 25/49/2.
70 See Part A of 1984 Guidance Note 25.

This technology is a great advance in solving privacy problems; it is not, unfortunately, the data controller's way of avoiding obtaining excessive personal data. Whether data is excessive or not is an objective test and not subjective for either the data controller or data subject.

6.2.5.3.3   Future business models

The web lends itself to flexing and changing business models. This creates a tendency and a temptation to 'hedge one's bets' when collecting personal data and to collect personal data *in case* it may be useful at some point in the future. From a commercial prospective this makes sense: ask for all a person's personal data in one go; having collected the data, then decide how it can be utilised. Such a policy for obtaining personal data will be a breach of the third principle. One must have, at the time of obtaining, a view as to how the personal data will be used.

---

31. Office@Home sells high-quality home office furniture for home workers. Its Marketing Director observes that many of their purchasers are actually high-powered office executives who are buying office furniture for their studies at home. Office@Home changes its sign-up page to also collect details of the purchaser's work address, status and work type. Office@Home risks this additional data being viewed as excessive for the purposes of selling furniture for use at home.

6.2.5.4.   Fourth principle: accurate and up-to-date

'Personal data shall be accurate and, where necessary, kept up-to-date.'

6.2.5.4.1   Accurate personal data

The definition of 'accuracy' is:

'[D]ata are inaccurate for the purposes of this section if incorrect or misleading as to any matter of fact.'[71]

This definition excludes a mere opinion which does not include, or purport to be, a statement of fact. This may appear to be an onerous requirement for data users, especially using the Internet, where one search engine may provide links to reams of personal data, each of which would have to be checked independently. However, the interpretative schedule to this principle excludes the data obtained and accurately recorded from a third party, including the data subject, under two circumstances.[72] These are that the data controller has taken reasonable steps to ensure the accuracy (with regard for the purpose or purposes for which the data were obtained and further processed) and, if relevant, the data user records an appropriate indication of the data subject's notification of alleged inaccuracies. So, a data controller must be careful when trawling, say, the Internet for personal

---

71   Data Protection Act 1998, Sch 1, Pt II, para 7.
72   Data Protection Act 1998, Sch 1, Pt II, para 7.

data to buttress an existing data record. One should certainly record details of the source of the data.

Internet data sources and locations

Particularly on the World Wide Web, the location of data may be only one aspect of its source. For example, the data held on the home page at www.allserve.com/ourhome/coolhome are stored on the Allserve server in the coolhome directory that is within the parent directory, ourhome. This is its location. Its source, in contrast, will include the person who uploaded that data onto the home page. This will probably be the owner of the Allserve account, coolhome. This person's identity, together with the URL, will form the source of the information.

The reason for insisting on this distinction is twofold. First, the relevant section refers to receiving or obtaining data from the 'data subject or a third party.'[73] Both these terms refer to natural or legal persons. The source required under the section is therefore not the place where the data are stored, or from where they are retrieved, but the person who supplied the data to the data user. In illustration, if a data user obtains personal data from a particular book, it will not be enough to include as its source its location in a library; the publisher and author will be its source. By analogy, if personal data are obtained from a particular home page, it will not be enough to include as the source the URL on the Internet; the controller and creator of the home page will be the source.

The second justification for the source to be the person not the URL is that it is trivial to alter a URL. Indeed, the greatest difficulty for home pages on the web is that their links to other sites may become outdated. The person who created the site is therefore a more stable and certain source than the location of the data in question.

Notification of inaccuracy

If a data subject finds personal data inaccurate they may commence an action under s 14 for the court to order rectification, blocking, erasure or destruction of the data. The court may also order a verification enquiry, a supplementary statement and/or a communication order.

Database construction

This section of the book concentrates only on the final three remedies. What is relevant is the need with any of the section's orders to be able to identify all data relating to an individual from that individual's details. Databases, simple, relational, object-orientated or whatever type, must therefore be carefully constructed. It must be trivial for any of the data relating to an individual to be able to be:

(i)   rectified, i.e. corrected without necessarily deleting the previous data;

---

73   Data Protection Act 1998, Sch 1, Pt II, para 7(a).

(ii)   blocked, i.e. presented in the database structure but obscured from viewing or processing unless under certain restrictive conditions;

(iii) erased, i.e. erasure of reference to data and also erasure of data itself;

(iv)   verified, i.e. investigation of the source of the data being queried by the data subject; certainly contentious data must be recorded together with its source;

(v)   communicated to third party recipients, i.e., the data controller may be required to alert all subsequent recipients of the queried data as to the inaccuracy; this order, made under extreme circumstances, blocks the 'flow' of inaccurate data.

Reliability of Internet sources

One of the advantages of the Internet over other information sources is that it is quick and simple to retrieve vast quantities of data about almost any subject, including living individuals. There is no quality control, however, over this data. It is as easy for individuals to publish unsubstantiated personal data on the World Wide Web as it is for organisations who prudently vet their data. It is therefore unwise, and probably unreasonable, for a data controller to compile data about individuals using unsubstantiated material from the Internet. This reinforces the issue that the important details about data extracted from the Internet are the actual sources, which can be checked for the irreliability, potentially under a verification enquiry, not simply the URL of the material on the Internet.

6.2.5.4.2   Up-to-date, where necessary

The fourth data protection principle does not require that data users keep all their data up-to-date at all times; they must do this if it is *necessary*.

There will be circumstances where data held on an individual does need to be updated. Under the 1984 Act, the Registrar included data used to decide whether to grant credit or to confer or withhold some other benefit.[74] These are examples where what is required is a reflection of the data subject's current status or circumstances.

---

32. An online cinema-ticket agency establishes an account for each new customer. To set up an account a data subject must enter, among other details, his age in years and months on 1 January next. If the purpose of these data are to ensure that customers do not attend films under the required age, it must be updated each month to ensure that these data do not exclude individuals who have had a recent birthday.

6.2.5.5 Fifth principle: kept no longer than necessary

'Personal data processed for any purpose or purposes shall not be kept any longer than is necessary for that purpose or those purposes.'

---

74   Data Protection Guideline 4, para 5.3.

Data users should be diligent in deleting data when they have already served their purpose. Each set of data should have a lifespan. At the end of this time, the data should be reviewed and assessed against the specified purpose for holding that data. If the data no longer appear necessary to complete or continue the purpose, data users have one of two options. They can either delete the data, or they can obtain consent from the data subject and amend their notified purposes to reflect the reason for extending holding the data.

As detailed in section 6.4 of this chapter, a provider may in fact be required to hold certain data for specific periods under anti-terrorism or other legislation. Depending on the nature of the business, there may be other legal requirements to hold data which are relevant, for example financial service rules. It is essential that companies understand that these legal justifications are not blanket exemptions to the fifth principle. Real care must be taken to ensure that any justification is approached narrowly and with constant attention to the Act. For example, a requirement to hold data for, say six years, under separate legislation may in some circumstances still be complied with once the records have been anonymised or superfluous details removed.

6.2.5.5.1 Multiple purposes

There will be many occasions when one set of data is held for more than one purpose. Consequently, there will be occasions when, for one purpose, a data user should delete data, but for other purposes the data remain necessary and relevant. The principle's use of both the singular 'purpose' and the plural 'purposes' clearly envisages this situation. The solution is to attempt to segregate the use of the data into their various purposes and to ensure that all data which are not necessary for a purpose are deleted.

---

33. A firm publishes biographical data about its employees on its home page. One of these employees leaves the firm. The firm is able to hold on an internal database the necessary information about the former employee for many years for, say, legal claims. In contrast, it should, to comply with the fifth data protection principle, remove the personal data being held on the home page as soon as the employee leaves.

The ease with which data may be published and obtained on the World Wide Web acts also as a reason continually to check the relevance of data published on the World Wide Web. Data users should regularly check their website and other Internet sites to delete data which has served its purpose and is past its lifespan. It is therefore not simply good commercial practice to update one's website; it may be required under data protection, and possibly other, laws.

6.2.5.5.2 Holding historical data

Data users are at liberty to hold indefinitely data that they will purely use for historical, statistical or research purposes.[75]

---

75   Data Protection Act 1998, s 33(3).

6.2.5.5.3   No one or fixed rule

Too often, a general 'purge rule' is set for a personal data database. This cannot be correct unless all the data serves the same purpose and all the data subjects have an identical relationship with the data controller. Databases need to be constructed to allow deletion at particular times of particular types of data relating to particular types of data subject. No one or fixed rule can be adequate.

6.2.5.6   Sixth principle: process in accordance with data subject rights

'A person is to be regarded as contravening the sixth principle if, but only if:

(a)   he contravenes [a data subject's right to access personal data];

(b)   he contravenes [a data subject's justified right to prevent processing likely to cause damage or distress];

(c)   he contravenes [a data subject's right to prevent processing for the purposes of direct marketing];

(d)   he contravenes [a data subject's justified rights in relation to automated decision making].'

6.2.5.6.1   Data subject access

Validity of requests

If a subject access request is ignored or is incorrectly complied with within the usual 40-day period,[76] the Information Commissioner may make an access order forcing the data controller to reveal the data held on the subject. What is more serious, though, is that the Information Commissioner may also inspect the data held by the controller.

A valid subject access request must be made in writing[77] and to any valid address for the data controller. The request need not be in any particular form or style, and, data controllers may not impose a special format upon a data subject. The request is valid only when the appropriate fee is paid (being no more than £10.00, unless medical records are concerned).

---

34. A website is concerned that its staff may 'miss' a data subject access request being sent to them and so devise an online form, to allow requests to be made. Despite the form, an elderly gentleman sends a request (together with a £10 cheque) on paper to the website owner's registered office where it is ignored for two months. The website owner is at risk of an action, even though the gentleman utilised another medium to make his requests.

Data controllers need also only process a request where the data subject supplies him with the appropriate information both to satisfy himself as to the identity of the requesting person and the information being sought.[78]

---

76   Data Protection Act 1998, ss 7(8) and 7(10) subject to any variation by the Secretary of State under s 7(11).
77   Data Protection Act 1998, s 7(7).
78   Data Protection Act 1998, s 7(3).

35. An online secure spreadbetting site updates its 'credit risk' analysis on each of its members every 20 minutes. This allows it to extend the maximum line of credit to its customers at all times. Phillip makes a subject access request and within two days of making the request, he discovers that the site has now deemed his credit line to be zero. Bearing in mind the nature of the data, why the data is processed and the frequency of updating, it would be reasonable for Phillip to make a further request to discover what had changed.

When to provide data

Data controllers must supply to the data subject the relevant information under s 7 promptly, but at least within 40 days from receiving a request.[79]

Data users should pay respect to this sixth principle by ensuring that, on constructing and programming their database, there is a simple way of extracting all the data relating to one individual. It is important for data users to note that merely because a particular record has no reference to an individual's name does not mean that the information should not be provided to the subject. If the data user possesses sufficient information, wherever held or stored, to identify the individual, then the data can be classed as personal data, and so be requested by its subject. Where the data held on individuals are spread throughout many databases, throughout many buildings, it can be expensive and time-consuming to locate all the necessary data within the period set by the Act. This said, 40 days is the maximum period and so systems should be established early which allow a request to be processed rapidly.

Information disclosed on other individuals

A problem may arise where a data controller in complying with a subject access request would be disclosing information relating to an individual other than the individual making the request. The Act recognises this problem. In such circumstances a data controller is obliged to comply with the subject access request in only two situations. The first is where the other individual has consented to the disclosure of the information. The second situation is where it is reasonable in the circumstances to comply with the request without the consent of the other individual. Alternatively, of course, it may be necessary to redact any references to third parties.

36. Teenze FM, a website for teenage girls, runs a feature called 'nightmare date of the month'. It invites its members to send in photographs and stories of disastrous dates to be posted on the site. June's 'winner' is horrified to see his picture appear on the site together with a totally fictitious story. He submits a subject access request in order to find out who nominated him without his knowledge. The site would be breaching data protection rules if it disclosed the nomination email containing these details without the consent of the sender.

---

79 Data Protection Act 1998, s 7(8) and (10). This 40-day period begins on the first day on which the controller has both the fee and request.

What to provide

Data controllers cannot simply 'print out' their database entry for an individual. Indeed, doing merely this, complies with only one of seven requirements. These are listed and described below, but first it will be important to consider carefully whether the subject matter of the request does in fact concern 'data'. One should consider the decisions in *Durant* and *Ezsias*, as summarised at section 6.2.1.2.1 above, in particular as to whether information not held on computerised records which have been automatically processed, fall within the definition of a relevant filing system. If not, the data may not be discloseable and the following may not apply.

(i) Data controller to inform subject whether or not processing is being carried out in relation to data subject

In effect, the data controller must reply to a data subject whether or not they are holding or processing data. Because of potential difficulties involving misspelt or mistyped names, it may be safer for a data controller not merely to search on the precise details given by the subject, but also to use 'fuzzy logic' to search more widely.[80]

---

37. Jane Isaacs is worried that an auction site has retained her personal details. She sends an email from her home email address together with £10 to constitute a subject access request. The data protection officer at the company incorrectly searches for the name 'Jane Isaac' and for her home email address; both searches return a negative result. The auction site would have been better advised to reply to Jane, seeking, as they are entitled under s 7(3) the reasonable information they need to search for Jane's personal data.

(ii) Data controller to give subject description of personal data

This can be thought of as a requirement to 'put the data into context'. It is an obligation to explain what the data 'means' to the data controller.

(iii) Data controller to give subject description of purposes for which data is processed

'Processing' is described earlier in this chapter and readers may want to refresh their memories before responding to this element of a data subject access request. What is crucial is to describe not merely what the data is, but how it is being utilised and processed.

---

38. An online photo developing company allows anyone to store digital images and other files on their servers. Revenue to support this flows from advertising and printing. Its research suggests that men tend to use the storage facilities to store pornographic material. They therefore target 'relevant' advertising at those of its members who are male with many image files stored. To comply with a subject access by a male, the company must therefore include details of this processing and not merely report the member's sex and number of files held.

---

80   Data Protection Act 1998, s 7(1)(a).

(iv) Data controller to describe to subject recipients or classes of recipients of personal data

A recipient is defined as being any person, even an employee of the data controller, to whom data is disclosed in the course of processing the data. Data controllers do not need to disclose those recipients of data who receive it pursuant to a legal power, such as a police enquiry. Data controllers should be aware, therefore, that the suggested recipients of data in a fair collection notice or, privacy policy and notification can be confirmed by a data subject. Data controllers cannot hide their true processing of data.

---

39. TCI collects data from its membership and, for financial reasons, exports it for processing in Russia. A Russian company will therefore be a recipient of the data. This can consequently be discovered by any data subject. TCI will not be able to covertly send the data to Russia (potentially in breach of the eighth principle), without risk of it being discovered by any subject.

(v) Data controller to communicate to data subject in intelligible form the information constituting the personal data

The key aspect of this obligation is 'intelligible' form. Sending the data subject a series of zeros and ones may well provide the *data* to the subject; it does not provide the *information* underlying or surrounding the data. Data controllers must be prepared to disclose 'what the data means to them' not merely the data that has been recorded.

---

40. A business user of an online travel agency makes a valid subject access request. The agency provides a response detailing the user's name and address, the flights he has booked and a reference to 'cookie data' being 'AC8924EA29BBE'. To comply with the subject access request, the site should have resolved this cookie data into information making it clear what it means to the site.

(vi) Data controller to communicate to the data subject any available information on the sources of the data

Unlike under the 1984 Act, the sources of data do not need to be specified to the Commissioner in the data controller's notification (then registration). The information to be provided as to the sources of the data is only that which is available to the data controller. Clearly, a 'scorched earth' policy of destroying all source information would leave the controller unable to provide any information to the data subject.

Data controllers must be warned, however, that with no information about the source of personal data they may find it more difficult to defend an action brought under the first principle. Similarly, unless the source's information is retained, it will be difficult for the data controller to prove that they took reasonable steps to confirm the accuracy of the data, under the fourth principle.

(vii) Data controller to inform data subject as to any logic involved in automated significant decision-taking, subject to the information being a trade secret

This applies only where the decision being automatically taken is the sole basis of something which may significantly affect the data subject. It is therefore safe to opine that, automatic processing of a cookie to determine which adverts to show or which books to recommend, will not fall within the remit of this section. Conversely, decisions taken relating to a person's creditworthiness are more likely to be deemed to be significant.

---

41. A car manufacturer establishes a site at which prospective customers may enter their name, telephone number and postcode to receive a telephone call from their nearest dealer. In truth, they also utilise the postcode to decide the potential affluence of the customer and prioritise their enquiry appropriately. This automated decision-taking is unlikely to be significant enough to justify needing to inform the data subject.

6.2.5.6.2   Preventing direct marketing, including emails

In the context of the Internet, a significant right is to prevent processing for direct marketing, at any time. Even where the relevant 'tick' boxes have been 'ticked' (or 'unticked') an individual may change their mind and prevent further direct marketing at any time. Databases must be constructed to allow such processing to be stopped at any time.

Direct marketing is widely defined as:

'the communication (by whatever means) of advertising or marketing material which is directed to particular individulals.'[81]

This definition certainly will encompass emails and instant messages whether sent automatically or processed individually by a human.

---

42. Forex4X.com uses cookies to enable its site to show particular information based on previous uses by the particular member. It does not send out emails or faxes to its members. Nevertheless, its members are entitled to prevent Forex4X from processing their data for the purposes of customising the site they view.

The subject's right is framed in terms of ceasing processing for the purposes of direct marketing. It is therefore a substantially wider right than one which merely prevents direct mail being sent subject to certain requirements. The right, once activated, will prevent all data manipulation and mining activities, even where this processing does not result in material being sent.

Unlike many other provisions in the Act, data controllers cannot rely upon any exemptions. If they do not comply with a written request within a reasonable period,[82] the subject may request that the court orders that the notice is complied with.[83] Data-intensive companies must ensure that the architecture of their databases is sophisticated enough to block this type of processing.

---

81   Data Protection Act 1998, s 11(3).
82   Data Protection Act 1998, s 11(1).
83   Data Protection Act 1998, s 11(2).

---

43. E-masp is an Application Service Provider which facilitates companies in targeting and sending relevant emails to their customers. In the usual course of events, any individual who indicates that they do not consent to receive mailings is simply not included in the final, compiled, list. Their details are, in contrast, still analysed and processed. E-masp must refine its database to ensure it is able to exclude blocked individuals from even the first batch processing well prior to any mailing itself.

6.2.5.6.3 Preventing automated processing

There can be little doubt that computers are incredibly valuable when used to process personal data. Indeed, a whole sector of the IT industry, Customer Relationship Management, is fundamentally concerned with capturing, processing and better utilising personal data. These sophisticated 'back office' systems are increasingly utilised to process data on visitors to websites. They allow regulars to be greeted appropriately, orders to be tracked and requests pre-empted. In the broadest terms, they make automated decisions relating to personal data. Controllers of data need to consider whether this processing is 'solely' used to make decisions which 'significantly affect' an individual. If their systems do make such decisions, while no doubt very efficient, they are prone to subjects exercising their right under s 12 of the Act to prevent decisions being taken in that manner.

Significant effects

The Act and Directive provide a non-exhaustive list of significant issues. These include 'performance at work', 'creditworthiness', 'reliability' and 'conduct'.

Sole basis for decision

This aspect of the Act[84] and art 15 of the Directive is aimed at preventing computers making important decisions without humans being involved. Consequently, any human input into the decision, even where supported by volumes of automatically processed quantitative data, will bring the processing outside the ambit of s 12.

---

44. A busy recruitment department in a management consultancy builds a new online recruitment section to the firm's website. It requires that each candidate wanting to attend an open day enters their answers to a series of questions to create their VCV (Virtual Curriculum Vitae). To save reviewing certain applications by hand, the system automatically sends (a few hours later) a polite rejecting email to any candidate acknowledging less than a 2:2 in their first degree. Any candidate will be entitled to prevent the firm from taking such decisions in this way.

Exemptions

Automated decisions are exempt from the application of s 12 where they fall into one of a number of categories. These are where the effect of the decision is to grant the data subject a request relating to:

(a) considering whether to enter a contract with the subject;

84 Data Protection Act 1998, s 12(1).

(b)   with a view to entering such a contract;

(c)   in the course of performing such a contract.

Alternately, as long as the legitimate interests of the data subject are safeguarded, for example, permitted representations like an 'appeal', automated decisions can also be taken in relation to (1), (2) and (3) above.[85]

---

45. RideLiketheWind is a 'name your price' website for businesspeople who would prefer to travel by private jet rather than traditional airlines. Financing deals are available to allow one to travel today and pay off the cost over a subsequent number of months. An individual becomes convinced that his requests to obtain credit are automatically refused because of his home postcode. Even if such an automated decision is significant enough, the decision is exempt because the individual is making the request of the website with the view to entering into the contract to buy a seat on credit.

Procedure to prevent

A subject must write to a data controller asking them not to take such an automated decision.[86] As soon as reasonably practical, the controller must reply confirming (or not) that the decision was so taken.[87] Within 21 days, the individual may then demand that a new, non-solely automated decision is taken.[88] A further 21 days may lapse before the controller must explain how they now intend to reconsider the decision.[89] The court can force the data controller to comply with the individual's request.[90]

---

46. A data subject requests from a data user relevant information under the seventh principle and s 7. The data controller duly retrieves the pertinent data from the various relational databases and then realises that more data are held than has been notified or consented to by the data subject. If the data controller supplies all the data to the subject they are admitting processing data illegally. If the data user supplies the data only mentioned in the notification, they can be forced to comply with s 7(1)(a) which demands that all the data held by the controller must be supplied to the subject. The data controller must immediately contact the Commissioner and the data subject to rectify the data held and widen the notification if necessary for further processing.

6.2.5.7   Principle 7: kept secure

'Appropriate technical and organisational measures shall be taken against unauthorised or processing of personal data and against accidental loss or destruction of or damage to personal data.'

---

85   Data Protection Act 1998, s 12(6) and (7).
86   Data Protection Act 1998, s 12(1).
87   Data Protection Act 1998, s 12(2)(a).
88   Data Protection Act 1998, s 12(2)(b).
89   Data Protection Act 1998, s 12(3).
90   Data Protection Act 1998, s 12(8).

This seventh data protection principle demands lawyers understand, at the least, the basics of computer security. Complying with this part of the Act can be expensive. It is, however, essential that these controllers of personal data employ appropriate technological and supervisory methods to secure their subjects' data.

6.2.5.7.1 Security under the seventh principle

This principle tackles one of the most obvious tensions between the Internet and data protection. Back in the Data Protection Registrar's annual report of 1995, it is stated that:

> '[i]n connecting to the Internet [data users and computer bureau operators] are entering an open environment which exists to facilitate the exchange of and the publication of information. It is inherently insecure.'

This remains the case today. In contrast, data protection legislation attempts to ensure that personal data are not left in open environments but are stored in controlled, private environments. The seventh principle takes the idea of a controlled environment to its logical extreme by demanding that data are not simply secure from unauthorised or unlawful processing but also from alteration, destruction, damage and loss.

Appropriate

In the abstract it is difficult for a lawyer or security consultant to advise on the appropriate level of security for personal data. The Act's interpretation of this seventh principle highlights that one must have regard to 'state of technological development and cost of implementing the measures' appropriate to ensure a level of security taking into account the possible 'harm' and 'nature of data to be protected'.[91] The level of the security should be in proportion to the nature of the data and the harm which would ensue should there be a breach in security. For example, the Commissioner is likely to distinguish between personal data compiled from readily available sources, such as a list of names and addresses, and data which are sensitive[92] or are acquired in confidence.[93] On 18 January 2002, Eli Lilly, the pharmaceutical manufacturer of Prozac, settled a claim with the US FTC relating to sensitive data held on Prozac takers. It had established in March 2000 an email reminder service for those recovering from depression using Prozac. On 27 July 2001 it sought to tell all its subscribers by email that it was cancelling the service. Instead of sending each an individual email, or using the BCC field, an employee sent a group email to all the subscribers. Each was therefore able to see who else took Prozac. Not surprisingly, there were complaints about this disclosure of sensitive data and an investigation began in July 2001. The lesson for those needing to observe the seventh principle is simple. Even the

---

91   Data Protection Act 1998, Sch 1, Pt II, para 9(a), (b).
92   Personal data that may be seen as sensitive are defined in s 2(3). These include: racial origins; political opinions, or religious or other beliefs; membership of a trade union; physical or mental health or sexual life; and criminal convictions or alleged offences.
93   1984 Data Protection Guideline 4, para 8.3.1.

greatest security systems can be useless if those using them are inappropriately qualified and trained.

Data controllers and data processors must make their own decisions as to the adequacy of their data security, but they should consider their obligation to the data subjects and the possibility of a compensation claim by a data subject.

Appropriate outsourcing and ASPs

Data controllers do not shirk their responsibilities under this principle by shunting off their data to a third party processor such as an outsourcing company or Application Service Provider. In fact, the data controller must not only carry out due diligence to check the processor provides sufficient guarantees as to security but also take reasonable steps to ensure compliance with the technical and organisational measures.[94] Further, data controllers are obliged to enter into a written contract with the processor under which the processor will only act under instructions from the data controller and under which the data processor will comply with equivalent obligations to those of the data controller.[95]

---

47. ByteSyze is an office delivery fast-food outlet, well-utilised by London's IT community. Orders placed on their website are delivered within 64 minutes and the full range of 'geek food' (pizzas, high caffeine drinks etc) is offered. After a successful initial quarter, ByteSyze outsources their delivery to a squadron of motorcycle couriers. ByteSyze will be passing personal data to the courier companies and therefore must enquire and ensure that they take appropriate steps to protect the personal data.

Unauthorised

The seventh data protection principle stresses that security measures must be in place preventing unauthorised and unlawful processing of personal data. This does not refer solely to outsiders such as hackers; it is referring also to insiders who are acting outside the scope of their authority, potentially unlawfully. Controllers and processors should consider this authority from two angles: technical authority and social authority.

Technical authority

All equipment which stores, processes, transmits or discloses personal data must have passwords which only authorised people know. These passwords must not be the same for all aspects of data security within the organisation. Data controllers and data processors must treat distinctly those aspects of their equipment which they will use for activities relating to personal data.

To stop as early as is possible any security compromise it is advisable that each person granted the authority to access the personal data has an individual password. This, combined with an audit trail of all personal data, can permit a data controller or data processor to 'trace' the human source of compromised data, and so prevent its reoccurrence. It is essential that this technical authority is

---

94   Data Protection Act 1998, Sch 1, Pt II, para 11(a), 11(b).
95   Data Protection Act 1998, Sch 1, Pt II, para 12(a), 12(b).

granted by providing individuals each with a unique password, not by allocating one password for 'all personal data activities'. This latter method does not allow a data user to trace the source of a security leak as easily and results in one password being known by more people.

Social authority

Establishing a strict regime with passwords is not adequate unless there is also a strict regime over who has these passwords and how they are used. Data controllers and processors must give proper weight to the discretion and integrity of members of staff who are to have these passwords. They should be given adequate technical and data protection training; they should be made aware of the seriousness of their responsibilities. They should not process data outside of the appropriate consents and obligations of the data controller. If the unfortunate event occurs where a member of staff leaves the department, or is found to be unreliable, the data users must immediately 'lock out' that member from the system. There should be no 'old' or 'general' password for accessing personal data.

Processing

The obligation to take appropriate measures to prevent unauthorised and unlawful processing is obviously a wide obligation because of the all-encompassing definition of 'processing'. Some aspects of 'processing' are described below.

Organisation, adaptation or alteration

Certain data should be 'read-only': that is, the data cannot be altered or even deleted without appropriate authority. This authority is generally in the form of a password that allows the password-user to alter the 'read-write' properties of the data.

---

48. An Internet Service Provider allows its members to sign up to various services using an online form. As well as address and surname, one field of this form is the forename of the member. Unless it is clearly appropriate this particular field should retain a 'read-only' status. If it is freely able to be overwritten, it is feasible an accidental alteration will result in another member of the same family, at the same address, being treated as the data subject.

As is stated below, the safest solution is to have 'read-only' status both for data and the database structure along with regular, archival backups. If the backup is archival it will highlight any changes in data since the previous backup, so alerting a data user to a potential alteration. It will also allow the data user to regenerate an unaltered copy of the data, if necessary, from the previous backup. It is also recommended that only a limited set of reports and processes are available over a series of data.

Entitled deletion and backups

The fourth data protection principle entitles a data subject to delete data which it is inappropriate for a data user to continue holding. This required deletion will include both the personal data on the usual storage system and any backup copies of the data on whatever medium. Data users must therefore ensure that their archival backup system is sufficiently sophisticated to allow them to remove data fields without compromising the security of the remaining data which may breach the seventh data protection principle.

Destruction

The same security considerations apply to avoiding destruction, accidental or not, of data and avoiding alteration of data. Data users should classify as much data as possible as 'read-only' and maintain regular and frequent backups of the data. In this way, if data are destroyed on the main system, it is an easy task to regenerate those data. As above, data users should ensure that their backup facilities, while secure, do not prevent the deletion of personal data where this will be necessary to comply with a data subject's request.

6.2.5.7.2   Internet security issues

Connecting a computer to the Internet is easy and commonplace. But, with present levels of standard Internet security, going onto the Internet will result in the personal data held on the computer online becoming less secure. Data controllers and data processors must not rely on the inherent security on the Internet if they wish to avoid possible breaches of the seventh data protection principle. Some of the various ways that a data controller or data processors may tighten security are considered below.[96]

Automatic-answer modems

A modem connected to the Internet that is set to accept incoming calls will weaken security. The mere fact that an outsider can access a computer which is holding personal data reduces the security of that data. Data controller or data processors should take expert advice from the manufacturers of their automatic-answer software on how to partition securely certain aspects of their storage system from third parties. They should also investigate how to encrypt the personal data left on the connected system.[97]

Remote access

One of the advantages of the Internet and related networks is that it has made it possible for individuals easily to access computers from remote locations. This may be through a simple website, a Virtual Private Network (VPN), a bulletin board, an ftp site, a Telnet connection, or even a standard dial-up connection. All

---

96   Data controllers and data processors should take specialist advice; the comments on data security within this chapter are intended only to illustrate possible methods of improving security. The comments should not be implemented before checking with a security adviser that they are appropriate for the equipment and data in question.

97   The key to de-encrypt the data must not be stored on the computer storing the encrypted data.

these methods, without tight security measures, can as easily allow an individual to leave data on the remote computer as to copy data from the computer.

Security should therefore be in place which, unless it can be justified otherwise, does not permit remote users to access all the personal data on the system: a firewall. The passwords and logins used by remote users should be 'rolled' on a frequent basis. Remote users should not use an automated login procedure that stores the login details and password on their computer. With this set-up, if someone steals the computer the entire security of the personal data is at risk.

Email transactions

If a data controller or data processor uses the email system to send personal data he should be aware that a standard email system is not completely secure. He must not rely on the security of the Internet itself. Again, a good policy is to use encryption on all emails which contain personal data. It must also be remembered that any email is both a transferral and a disclosure of personal data or information. Data controllers should appropriately notify for such an activity.

Web servers

By definition a web server is connected to the Internet. As much as is possible, these computers should not be used for storing data collected from the World Wide Web. The use of an online form on a home page to collect personal data from, for example, customers, should generate data which is either encrypted on the server or is transmitted automatically to a further computer beyond a firewall. Users of the web to collect personal data must also enlist expert advice to ensure that while such an online form is being transmitted to the server from the customer-client, the most stringent safety measures are in place. The transferral of personal data between the subject and the data user is the most insecure time for the subject's personal data. Subjects must be informed of this risk before they transmit the data particularly to websites not utilising standard encryption methodology. Some sites 'pop up' a window allowing the subject to choose to transmit the data or to disconnect from the website.

Viruses

The Internet allows its users to 'view' documents on their screen, but it is also used to download material into the client computer. Sometimes this is with the knowledge of the user: he requests a file to download. At other times, the user may be unaware that the site on the Internet is accessing the user's computer and may be storing files and running programs on his computer. There is a real risk that with any file downloaded there will have been a computer virus in tow. Viruses generally attach to programs, but have been found incubating in word processing documents and even innocent looking pictures.[98]

---

98 '[Digital signatures] are clearly of great importance for executable code on the web': Tim Berners-Lee, W3C Director, viewed as the creator of the World Wide Web; 'Industry embraces Microsoft's Internet digital signature', Microsoft Press Release, PR1382/14 March 1996.

To take appropriate security measures, data processors and controllers must install virus scanning software set to screen regularly for viruses.

Network or intranet

All the above security issues are equally, if not more, relevant where an internal network or intranet is connected to the Internet. This may be through one computer connected to one modem or an established gateway, available to all users. The two scenarios pose risks to any personal data held on the network or intranet.

One computer to Internet

The ease with which one may connect a computer on an internal network to the Internet is almost inversely proportional to the risk involved with such a connection. That the connected computer does not hold or process personal data does not greatly reduce the threat to the personal data stored on the network. Because the computer is connected both to the Internet and the internal network it can act as a conduit for hacking attempts and the promulgation of viruses, network-wide. Data controllers and processors should therefore periodically check that no computer on an internal network is connected to the Internet without their knowledge. If one computer is to be connected, an appropriate technical and social security regime must exist.

Technically, the single computer should be appropriately firewalled from the main network; if it is not, it can form a very weak link in the data security of the network. The social security measures relate to the responsibility of those persons who will use the connected computer. Employers should give employees clear guidelines about whether they are permitted to download software; it is safer not to download. Employees should have clear instructions never to divulge any internal passwords to any other individual using email or any other means.

Network hacking

Hacking into the internal network from the Internet is always a great threat where any computer on the network is connected to the Internet. In this situation, a hacker can attach directly into the connected computer and, from there, may be able to penetrate the internal security of the network. Clearly this poses a substantial risk to any personal data on the network, previously treated as being secure. The risk from hacking is currently not as significant, however, as the threat from viruses and other rogue programs.

Network viruses

Every user who has access to the Internet will be tempted to download a file. In doing so, as described above,[99] the user risks introducing a virus to the client computer. But where this computer is connected to an internal network, the virus can spread throughout the network threatening the destruction and alteration of any personal data held within the network. Operators at a data controller and processor should install and update anti-virus programs throughout the network,

---

99   See the section relating to viruses in Chapter 3.

and where possible utilise virus antidote software to screen for viruses as software and emails are being downloaded from the Internet.

6.2.5.8 Eighth principle: prohibition against data transfers

'Personal data shall not be transferred to a country or territory outside the European Economic Area, unless that country or territory ensures an adequate level of protection for the rights and freedoms of data subjects in relation to the processing of personal data.'

The harmonisation of data protection rules in the EU aims to ensure the free movement of information including personal data between member states whilst at the same time ensuring a high level of protection for any person concerned. In the case of non-EEA countries, Directive 95/46/EC therefore requires member states to permit transfers of personal data only where there is 'adequate protection' in a particular country for such data, unless one of a limited number of specific exemptions applies. There are accordingly a number of ways available in order to facilitate transfers of personal data avoiding the prohibition of the eighth principle which are detailed below. A French ruling in May 2007 suggests that enforcement action against companies who fail to comply with such rules may be on the increase. In this case the French data protection authority imposed a fine on a company, Tyco, for sending human resources data to the US (a common practice) but without adequate protections. Companies should heed this warning.

However, it is first important to establish whether or not a transfer, subject to the default prohibition in fact arises. In some situations and particularly relevant in an Internet context, data may only *transit* or be routed through a third country and not be deemed to have transferred there.

In the case of *Bodil Lindqvist v Kammaraklagaren*,[100] the European Court of Justice held that the loading of data onto a website in a member state did not amount to a transfer of data to a third country, even though the website could be accessed potentially round the world. However the court did state that a transfer would have occurred if the data was then actually accessed in a third country. The fact was in this case that the local church website was not in a third country. The significant factor that the court distinguished, and which the UK Information Commissioner has subsequently emphasised, is that there was no intention for the data to be so accessed. The outcome of this case should prompt care rather than comfort on the part of website publishers. In many cases there will be an intention to access a worldwide audience. In such case it is immediately apparently that many of the options set out below to ensure that the eighth principle is not breached simply will not be possible. For example, on a basic level there simply may not be a processor or controller in a third country with whom to enter into model contract clauses. In these situations, it is essential to ensure that consent is obtained before placing pictures or other personal data on a website.

100   (2003)(Case C 101/01), ECJ.

6.2.5.8.1   EU publication of a country's adequacy

The European Commission has the authority to publish findings that a regime in a particular State ensures an adequate level of protection for the rights and freedoms of data subjects. Transfers to such states will therefore be treated in the same way as transfers to an EEA State. At the time of writing, Switzerland, Argentina, Guernsey, Isle of Man and Canada (although not in the case of the latter in relation to all types of personal data) have been approved in this manner.

6.2.5.8.2   US Safe Harbor Scheme

As for the countries listed above, the Information Commissioner has made a specific finding of adequacy where transfers of data are made to an entity in the IS which is subject to the US Safe Harbor Scheme. Under this self-regulatory scheme, US companies signed up to the scheme and complying with the rules issued by the US Department of Commerce are recognised[101] as offering adequate protection.

---

49. A UK-based advertising company is considering using a third party company to manage its personnel databases. It is choosing between companies based in Norway, Holland, Canada, the US and New Zealand. The transfer to the US will contravene the eighth principle unless the company has signed up to the Safe Harbor Scheme or one of the other exemptions applies. Another exemption must apply with respect to New Zealand, but an automatic assumption of adequacy exists in relation to the other jurisdictions.

6.2.5.8.3   Own assessment of adequacy

Data controllers are open to make their own findings as to whether the level of protection afforded by all the circumstances of a particular case is adequate (having regard to both legal and general adequacy criteria) when weighed against the potential risks to the rights and freedoms of data subjects which may arise.

Although this may sound an easy option it carries grave risks and will demand that each transfer is considered carefully on a case-by-case basis. Unsurprisingly, the Information Commissioner warns in official guidance on the subject[102] that a data controller is likely to consider the other options instead since self-assessment is a time-intensive exemption with no guarantee of being correct and significant sanctions if the conclusion is incorrect.

For businesses with branches in several different European jurisdictions, the key problem is that national data protection authorities apply their own interpretations of the concept of 'adequacy'. This makes it extremely problematic to establish a suitable and practical transfer procedure which can be used again and again from several countries within the EU.

101   European Parliament resolution of July 2000.
102   'The Commissioner's legal analysis and suggested good practice approach to assessing adequacy including consideration of the issue of contractual solutions' first issued in July 1999.

6.2.5.8.4   Standard contractual clauses

EU data protection authorities are obliged[103] to recognise that transfers have adequate protection where the model clauses approved by the EU Commission are used.

There are three different sets of model clauses:

(1) *Controller to Processor*, for the transfer of personal data from data controllers in the EU to processors (subcontractor) established in non-EU countries[104] under which the data exporter instructs its subcontractor to treat the data with full respect of the EU data protection requirements and guaranteeing that suitable technical and security measures are in place in the country to which they are sent.

(2) *Controller to Controller Set I,* for the transfer of data from a data controller in the EU to another data controller outside the EC.[105]

(3) *Controller to Controller Set II*, being an alternative set of model clauses for transfers between data controllers which provide greater flexibility and give more discretion to the data importer as to how they comply with data protection laws.[106] They also differ from the other model contract clauses in that a data subject is only able to enforce its rights against the breaching data controller, in contrast to Set I above, where exporter and importer are jointly and severally liable.

Use of the model clauses offers an attractive pan-European approach to businesses but does not offer room for flexibility. Parties are free to agree to *add* other clauses where they do not contradict, directly or indirectly the standard contractual clauses. The model contracts may not however be changed in other ways. Essentially, data controllers are required therefore to follow the clauses word-for-word 'filling in the blanks'. Where businesses may seek to amend the clauses to suit their own business needs (even where this does not alter the meaning or effect of any clause), the Information Commissioner has stated that this will not amount to authorised use under[107] the Act. In such a situation, it would then be up to the data controller to take its own view that either the transfer gives data subjects sufficient safeguards with the resulting risks that this brings. Alternatively, it should seek individual approval for that contract.

---

103   Except in exceptional circumstances e.g. where a competent authority has established that the data importer has not respected the contractual clauses or there is a substantial likelihood that the standard contractual clauses are not being or will not be complied with and the continuing transfer would create an imminent risk of grave harm to the data subjects.

104   The European Commission adopted a Decision on 29 December 2001 effective from 3 April 2002.

105   As contained in the European Commission Decision on Standard Contractual Clauses for the transfer of personal data to third countries under Directive 95/46/EC.

106   Commission Decision 2005/915/EC17 dated 27 December 2004.

107   Sch 4, para 9.

6.2.5.8.5   Approval on a case-by-case basis

Under art 26(2), Directive 95/46/EC, national authorities may authorise on a case-by-case basis specific transfers to a country outside the EEA where the data exporter in the EU is able to demonstrate that adequate safeguards are in place to protect the personal data protection rights of the data subjects. This is usually through a contractual arrangement made between the exporter and the importer which are then submitted to the national authority for approval.

This is a lengthy and difficult process which is not suitable for organisations which will be regularly sending data abroad. This option is particularly cumbersome since each EU data protection authority has a different procedure for granting such approval, different timescales, formalities and grounds for assessment.

6.2.5.8.6   Binding corporate rules

Binding corporate rules have been established to assist multinationals to transfer data outside of the EEA but still within the corporate group. Unlike the model contract clauses these rules must be submitted for prior-authorisation before the UK Information Commissioner. The Information Commissioner will only give authorisation if he believes that adequate safeguards are in place. Such a potentially costly and time-consuming process is therefore unattractive; only a few organisations were known to have taken such a path and obtained authorisation in the UK at the time of writing (Phillips and GE Capital being two such).

The advantage of binding corporate rules is that a multinational need not seek authorisation in every country in which it has a group-presence. Instead, the group is able to select one authority to act as the main point of contact which then co-ordinates with the other relevant bodies. The lead authority is likely to be the country in which the headquarters are or otherwise where most decisions relating to data transfers are taken.

6.2.5.8.7   Other derogations

Under art 26(1), Directive 95/46/EC, data may be transferred to a country outside of the EEA where:

(1)   the data subject has given his consent unambiguously to the proposed transfer; or

(2)   the transfers necessary for the performance of a contract between the data subject and the controller or the implementation of pre-contractual measures taken in response to the data subjects request; or

(3)   the transfer is necessary for the conclusion or performance of a contract concluded in the interests of the data subject between the controller and a third party; or

(4)   the transfer is necessary or legally required on important public interest grounds, or for the establishment, exercise or defence of legal claims; or

(5)   the transfer is necessary in order to protect the vital interests of the data subject; or

(6)   the transfer is made from a register which according to laws or regulations is intended to provide information to the public and which is open to consultation either by the public in general or by any person who can demonstrate a legitimate interest, to the extent that the conditions laid down by the law for consultation are fulfilled in the particular case.

In practice, the first two of these will be the most attractive to data controllers. It will be relatively straightforward for a data controller to incorporate consent provisions at the point of data capture and at the time that other consents are being obtained (e.g. for direct marketing). Careful attention will have to be had to properly informing individuals what they are consenting to, however, in order to ensure that their consent is 'unambiguous'. Data controllers must also remember that consent can always be revoked at any time and that a clear audit trail evidencing such consent will be needed. In practice, therefore, model contract clauses, or 'safe harbor' status, in the case of the US, will usually be a more prudent and robust approach.

Data controllers relying on derogation (b) must also remember that the threshold for demonstrating that processing is 'necessary' for the performance of a contract is a high one. In illustration, this may not always be an attractive option for multinational companies transferring employees' personal data to other branches.

---

50.   Mexican Bliss is an online travel agent. It specialises in honeymoons and arranges everything for the happy couple from transfers to and from the airports to champagne on arrival. It is obviously necessary that Mexican Bliss transfers the names of the honeymoon couple to the hotel in Mexico.

There is a clear message in this discussion. There is no obvious or automatic method for transferring personal data outside the EEA. Transfers are not impossible but the needs of a data controller, the purpose and scope of the transfer and therefore the exemptions to the eighth principle must be considered on a case-by-case basis.

6.2.6   Enforcement

The eight principles are enforced by the Commissioner serving an enforcement notice.[108] Unlike the bizarre situation under the 1984 Act, the Commissioner may now bring such enforcement proceedings against any data user, and not merely those who have registered (now 'notified'). In short, there is no longer a protective loophole for those who breach the principles. This said, the Commissioner must at least take into account whether the breach has caused or is likely to cause damage or distress to any person.[109] Non-compliance with an enforcement notice is an offence.[110] Subject to a limited defence of 'due diligence', non-compliance with such a notice can result in prosecution. The bad publicity generated by any

---

108   Data Protection Act 1998, s 40.
109   Data Protection Act 1998, s 40(2).
110   Data Protection Act 1998, s 47.

action taken against a company could, of course, be one of the most damaging effects.

6.3   DIRECT MARKETING

In addition to a data subject's underlying right to prevent the sending to them of direct marketing messages and the principle of fair collection under the Act, those wanting to send such mailshots must also comply with the consent and information requirements of certain other legislation. This includes the Electronic Commerce Regulations 2002 and The Privacy and Electronic Communications (EC Directive) Regulations 2003 ('PEC Regulations').

6.3.1   Transparency requirements

The Electronic Commerce Regulations place obligations on service providers to ensure that commercial communications provided by them (therefore including website content as well as marketing emails or text messages that may be sent) contain information to enable the recipient to identify them, clarify that the message is commercial in nature and clearly explain details of any promotion, game or competition that is the subject matter of the communication. Unsolicited communications sent by electronic mail must be 'clearly and unambiguously identifiable as such'.[111]

Similar obligations appear in the PEC Regulations which prohibit the concealment of the identity of the person sending or instigating the transmission of direct marketing emails or other electronic mail and require that the recipient be given a valid address to which they can send a request that such communications cease (reg 23).

It is also important to note that additional obligations in the PEC Regulations apply to the use of software devices (such as web beacons, clear gifs and cookies) which may be included in marketing communications or on websites to track the success of campaigns. As with cookies, providers must ensure that users are clearly alerted to the presence of such devices and what they are used for, and given an opportunity to disable them.

These provisions seek to protect consumers from unclear and misleading promotions whilst also ensuring that the sender is identifiable in the event of a problem arising. The principles and requirements are also to be found in certain UK marketing rules, for which see Chapter 9.

6.3.2   Consent requirements

In the UK, the consents required for the sending of unsolicited marketing messages by email are covered by the PEC Regulations which implement Directive

111   Regs 7 and 8.

2002/58/EC concerning the processing of personal data and the protection of privacy and electronic communications. This legislation fills the gap previously left by the Telecoms (Data Protection and Privacy) Regulations 1999 (implementing Directive 97/66/EC), which referred only to 'calls' and 'called lines' and therefore left ambiguity as to how email and text messages should be dealt with.

Ensuing differences of approach across member states, and lack of uniformity of trade practices, necessitated a change. Article 13 of the new Directive gave member states no option. Unsolicted emails are now not to be allowed 'without the consent of the subscribers concerned'.

The key rule to remember in terms of consent is that the form of consent that is required from the recipient depends on the medium by which the communication will be sent, not the medium through which the consent was captured. In this way, the consent that is needed to send a promotional flyer by post is different from that required to send competition details by text or for a cold call via telephone. Promoters need to be alert to this. They should also consider, in obtaining consents initially, whether cross-promotional campaigns may be considered in the future. If that is the intention, different tick boxes will be needed to obtain the different consents that may be required. Alternatively, a promoter may need to move to the highest common denominator of consent needed in order to capture all required.

In terms of email promotions, as will be considered here, the next step is to then consider to whom the communication will be sent and to whom it will be sent since this, in turn, will affect the consents which need to be obtained.

6.3.2.1 Marketing via electronic mail to individual subscribers: opt-in requirements

Regulation 22(2) provides that marketing communications may not be sent by email, video or text message[112] to individual subscribers unless 'the recipient of the electronic mail has previously notified the sender that he consents for the time being to such communications being sent by, or at the instigation of, the sender'. 'Individual subscriber' here means a living individual, but also includes an unincorporated body and therefore not just relating to consumers but also sole traders and non-limited liability partnerships. There is one exception to this general rule, detailed in section 6.3.2.2 below.

---

51. A US online fashion house launches a UK site run out of its London branch. To rely on the 'soft opt-in' marketing consent mechanisms, only the UK entity will be able to send marketing emails to UK customers about its products. Cross-marketing by the US company will not be possible unless express consent is obtained.

---

112 The PEC Regulations refer to 'electronic mail', defined as 'any text, voice, sound or image message sent over a public electronic communciations network which can be stored in the network or in the recipient's terminal equipment until it is collected by the recipient and includes messages sent via a short message service', which the Information Commissioner has stated in his November 2003 guidance to the PEC Regulations would also apply to voice-mail/answerphone messages although not to live phone calls.

The general rule is almost universally referred to as an 'opt-in' requirement, although this term is not used in any of the legislation itself. By 'Opt-in' it is meant that the individual must have actually done something positive to indicate their consent. Therefore, a failure to de-select a pre-ticked box, or a failure simply to state that they did not want to receive such communications,will not fulfil such criteria. A common way of capturing such consent will be the use of a tick box which the individual can choose to tick. Likewise, actively responding with a text message or email saying 'Yes' or otherwise to indicate that one wants to receive further communications would work.

This is not the only way, however. The Information Commissioner has stated in his guidance to the PEC Regulations[113] simply that 'there must be some form of communication whereby the individual knowingly indicates consent. This may involve clicking an icon, sending an email or subscribing to a service.' This last example may be key to providers. The use of a clear, unambiguous and strategically placed statement next to a subscribe button or signature for a service may be sufficient where the individual then knows that in taking a positive step to subscribe, they are also giving their consent to receive email marketing communications. This author believes that real caution must be taken with such an approach, not least in the positioning and choice of words used but also in view of the fact that the Information Commissioner's guidance is non-binding and it is possible to see an argument that a positive step in relation to a contractual commitment cannot fairly append other conditions. If this approach is taken then at the very least the provider should also provide a clear facility for the subscriber to choose not to take this option.

6.3.2.2   *Marketing via electronic mail to individual subscribers: the soft opt-in exception*

There is one key exception to the 'opt-in' requirement which is contained in reg 22(3) and is frequently referred to as the 'soft-opt in' option. This permits the sending of electronic mail marketing messages to individual subscribers, but only where the following conditions are all[114] met:

(i)   The recipient's contact details (i.e. email address) were obtained in the course of a sale or negotiations or the sale of a product or a service to that recipient (for example where a purchase was made online).

(ii)   Given that the wording of reg 22(3) applies the exemption to the person or instigator of the marketing message who collected the contact details under (i), this prevents the use of the exemption by any third party including, importantly, any group company. This means that a promoter will always have to seek 'opt-in' consent to either send marketing materials itself which

---

113   Information Commissioner guidance for marketers, dated November 2006.
114   There is a misconception that the exception may be relied upon where any of these conditions is satisfied. This is not the case. The Regulation specifically makes this a cumulative list.

relate to third party products, or pass its list to third parties for their use and it will not be able to rely on soft-opt consents acquired by a third party when using contact details obtained by them.

(iii) The marketing is in respect of similar goods and services. This is not defined, and therefore a pragmatic approach should be taken; for example, if the contact details were obtained in the context of a sale of, say, groceries online, permission would not extend to marketing in relation to insurance, even if offered by the same provider.

(iv) The recipient must have been given an opportunity (free of charge) to refuse the use of their contact details for marketing purposes when the details were collected, and each time a communication is sent. This requires the use of an 'opt-out' mechanism not just when the initial sale was made but each time a marketing email is sent, for example by providing a link or email to say no to further communications in the future.

6.3.2.3 Marketing via electronic mail to corporate subscribers

Where a recipient of a marketing communication is not an individual subscriber (therefore they are a corporate subscriber), the consent requirements do not apply and only the transparency requirements need be followed (see section 6.3.1 above).

This creates an odd position in which depending on whether one receives the same spam message seeking readers to enter into a dubious competition during the day whilst at work, or when one logs onto a personal home email account, differing rights may be available. This is the case even though the competition may be totally unrelated to the recipient's employment.

At the same time, however, one may have rights of redress, given that a work email address often contains personal data. However, here redress is not pursuant to the PEC Regulations but the Data Protection Act itself where one can rely on rights as a data subject and the controller's obligations under the sixth principle (for which see section 6.2.5.6.2 above).

6.3.3 Penalties and enforcement

52. Tunz4U sells games for mobile phones from its website. It cold-calls previous phone customers who have not expressed any objection to receiving such calls and intends to follow this up with a demo sent to them by email attachment. Tunz4U will need also to ensure that the customers have not objected to being contacted directly by email and that residents of countries with an opt-in requirement are asked directly whether they can be contacted in this way.

The PEC Regulation obligations apply to senders and instigators of commercial communications, the Data Protection Act to data controllers, and action against these persons may therefore be taken for any contravention.

There has been widespread cynicism as to the effectiveness of the PEC Regulations to tackle spam in the UK. The problems fall into two camps. Firstly, much spam comes from companies based outside the UK and even Europe. The Data Protection Act only imposes obligations on data controllers who are based in or have equipment for processing in the UK. The PEC Regulations do not have any specified jurisdiction (the marketing-specific requirements relating simply to 'a person'), but the difficulties of bringing an action outside of the UK are obvious.

The second concerns the enforcement action which may be taken itself. The PEC Regulations provide for the following form of redress.

6.3.3.1   PEC Regulations

A person who suffers damage may bring court proceedings compensation (and, pursuant to the Supreme Court Act 1981, for an injunction).

As with the Data Protection Act itself, the problem here is that damages claimed are unlikely ever to be substantive and the deterrent effect therefore limited. Three actions have been brought since the PEC Regulations came into force in 2003. The first was brought by Nigel Roberts in 2005 against Internet marketing company Media Logistics (UK), in which the judge of the Colchester small claims court found in Mr Roberts' favour, leading to a settlement award of just £270. The second was brought by an individual against Transcom, which resulted in an award of £750 by the Edinburgh Sherriff's Court (the maximum which could be claimed in the Scottish small claims courts).

Although not likely to be an attractive route for individuals, for network operators, there may be more appeal, not least given the potential availability of injunctions. In this respect the third, 2006, case provides an important precedent. The case concerned an action for summary judgment by Microsoft Corporation against Paul Martin McDonald who operated a website offering lists of emails for sale for marketing purposes, which the defendant claimed had opted in to receiving marketing communications, including a large quantity of hotmail addresses. Microsoft claimed that as a result of such actions it had suffered loss of goodwill and had also had to purchase additional servers to cope with the volume of spam which was sent via its networks to its subscribers. The court held that the policy underlying the PEC Regulations and the Directive was the protection of subscribers and electronic communications networks themselves. Therefore Microsoft had a direct action itself falling within the class of persons for whom the statute sought to benefit.

In addition, this case clarifies that the seller of such email lists can be a defendant, since such action will be deemed to constitute the 'instigation' of such commercial communications.

6.3.3.2   Data Protection Act

The Information Commissioner may exercise his enforcement functions pursuant to Part V of the Data Protection Act; this may be at the request of OFCOM or an aggrieved individual. The Information Commissioner imposed enforcement notices on several companies for making unsolicited calls to individuals who had specifically requested that they not be contacted. Initial action will first be a public warning, however. Until an enforcement notice is actually breached, no offence is made out.

In the UK, a potentially more likely route of enforcement is through the numerous self-regulatory and other codes which have adopted the PEC Regulation rules. For example, the Advertising Standards Authority took action against World Networks to require it to pre-clear future adverts, following complaints that its opt-out provisions contained in a text message promotion were unclear. The CAP Code which the ASA enforces has incorporated consent requirements which echo those of the PEC Regulations. Likewise, the ICSTIS code which regulates providers of premium rate telephone services, and the Direct Marketing Association policing of the consent requirements they have set out in their respective codes of practice.

6.4 DATA RETENTION AND DISCLOSURES FOR LAW ENFORCEMENT

Sitting alongside the provisions of the Data Protection Act which protect the privacy of individuals in respect of the processing of their personal data, is further legislation which contains prohibitions on access to and interception of communications made over electronic networks, except in prescribed circumstances. Many of the exceptions concern the access that law enforcement and government bodies may wish to have for the purpose of investigation of crimes and national security. The scope of what access is needed, and what data should be made available, has received greater focus in recent years in line with the attention on the growing threat of terrorism and international crime which may use or rely on such networks, at least in part.

All network operators and many website owners may therefore find themselves the recipient of a request for email or IP addresses or other information from official bodies which extends beyond the requests for data subject access or from solicitors acting for clients that they may be used to pursuant to the Data Protection Act or be concerned as to how the principles under this Act may tie-in with such requests and growing obligations under new statutes. This section sets out the high-level principles and obligations relevant to such issues.

6.4.1 Restrictions on interception of communications

The Regulation of Investigatory Powers Act 2000 ('RIPA') seeks to ensure that investigatory powers concerning electronic networks are conducted in accordance with human rights, but also concerns obligations and prohibitions which will be relevant on a day-to-day basis.

The key starting point in RIPA is Part 1. This makes it an offence for any person to intentionally and without lawful authority intercept communications in the course of their transmission via a public postal or public or private telecommunications system (unless they have consent for such interception). It also creates the right for a civil action by a sender or recipient of a communication that is intercepted by or with the consent of the controller of a private telecommunication system if such interception is without lawful authority.

A person will have lawful authority to intercept a communication (which can include any form of modification or interference or monitoring which makes any of the contents of such communication available to a person other than the recipient or sender and therefore does not impact on any actions taken solely in relation to traffic data[115]) in several ways. The most relevant reasons for providers are likely to be: (i) the consent of recipient and sender has been obtained; (ii) it is an interception undertaken in accordance with the Lawful Business Practice Regulations for purposes connected with the provision and operation of that system (i.e. day-to-day facilitation of the service itself); (iii) where the provider is expressly provided with a warrant to provide access to an authorised person to cause an interception. Access in this way is considered below.

6.4.2   Obligations to provide access to data

Although RIPA has detailed provisions in relation to encryption and surveillance, there are two key provisions which enable certain bodies to obtain access to data and place obligations on providers to provide such access which must be understood.

The first, under Part 1, Chapter I, relates to the warrants which may be obtained in order to secure an interception of communications, assistance in respect of such an interception or the disclosure of intercepted material and related communications data. These warrants are therefore required if the contents of communications may need to be intercepted or disclosed; as a consequence, the process for obtaining such a warrant is onerous, and most providers are unlikely to ever be provided with such a warrant. Warrants may only be issued if proportionate and also necessary, either in the interests of national security, for the purposes of preventing or detecting serious crime, safeguarding the economic wellbeing of the UK, or giving effect to a mutual agreement (i.e. pursuant to an international warrant). Such warrants are issued by the Secretary of State and may only be applied for by a very restricted list of persons and bodies (Director of GCHQ etc).

The second, under Part 1, Chapter II, relates to notices which may be issued in order to obtain access to communications data as opposed to the contents of communications. 'Communications data' means traffic data or other information which does not contain the contents but is about the use made by a person of the system in question or is otherwise held by the service provider. The circumstances in which such a notice may be obtained are wider and extend to purposes of the prevention and detection of crime or of preventing disorder (as

---

115   'Traffic data' is defined in ss 9 and 10, Part 1, and includes information for the purposes of identification of the apparatus, origination or location of the transmission, data comprised in signals which effect the transmission and identifying data as comprised in or attached to a communication.

opposed to 'serious' crime for a warrant), public safety or health, tax, preventing harm or injury to a person in an emergency. Such notices may also be issued by designated persons of a police force as well as by Commissioners of Customs and Excise, Inland Revenue, intelligence services and certain public authorities.

A provider in receipt of such a notice or warrant is obliged to comply with it and, in so doing, is exempted from obligations which might otherwise apply in relation to action or any processing of personal data which might otherwise apply pursuant to the Data Protection Act. It is important that such a provider should understand the limits of such devices, however, and not, for example, provide more data than is requested and, in particular, appreciate that a notice does not permit the provision of the transcripts of calls, emails or online communications.

6.4.3 Obligations to retain data

In addition to obligations to disclose data, there are various grounds upon which a service provider can find itself required to actually retain data, the common basis being that such data needs to be retained so that it can be made available to law enforcement authorities, regulatory authorities or government agencies.

There are three broad categories of data retention obligation which must be considered: (i) those that apply specifically because a service provider is in the business of providing Internet services or access or conducts business via the Internet; (ii) those which apply to their specific line of business (i.e. under financial services or health authority rules); and (iiii) those which apply following the receipt of a specific order, notice or warrant received from a relevant person (for example a court order, or pursuant to RIPA as considered above and as considered in further detail in Chapter 5. This section focuses on the first of these.

6.4.3.1   Voluntary retention of communications data

Currently, service providers are not legally required to systematically retain Internet-specific traffic or contents data (such as IP addresses or emails) for law enforcement purposes.

A Code of Practice has been developed pursuant to the Anti-Terrorism, Crime and Security Act 2001 (as outlined in section 6.1 of this chapter) which sets out suggested data retention periods for service providers. It also provides a framework for the Secretary of State may enter into voluntary agreements with individual public communication service providers (i.e. providers of any telecommunications service which is offered or provided to a substantial section of the public in any one or more parts of the UK). The purpose is to clarify the data retention practices which such communications provider agrees to adhere to so that those authorities seeking access to such data under RIPA have knowledge and comfort that data will be available to them and not deleted. The Code characterises this agreement as a kind of service level agreement which supplements and expands on the requirements under the Code.

6.4.3.1.1   Data types

The Code specifies the *minimum* of data that must be retained by providers. As a result, all providers must analyse their existing data capture to ensure that their data sets include *at least*: traffic data, service data and subscriber data.

6.4.3.1.2   Purposes of retention

Much of the communications data usually held by providers will be for business purposes. Under both human rights and data protection legislation it is rarely legitimate to retain data indefinitely. It follows that in the normal course of events, after a period of time, providers would be advised to destroy or anonymise data.

In contrast, under the Code, communications data must be retained for an extended period for the purposes of national security. It follows that at a point in time, communications data being held by providers will move from being classified as both business and national security data into merely national security data. At that point, a provider must *not* access the data for its own purposes. This older data therefore needs to be put in a 'silo' so that it may be accessed, but only for national security purposes.

6.4.3.1.3   Period of data retention

Unless otherwise directed, the following retention periods apply:

Subscriber information: 12 months

E-mail data: 6 months

ISP data: 6 months

Web activity logs: 4 days

Communications data (other than SMS, EMS and MMS data) shall be held for a maximum of 12 months unless either directed to retain for longer, or, where destroying that data would compromise the analysis of other data. Of course, as mentioned above, there may be good, legitimate business purposes for retaining the data for longer. If this is the case, the data may only be retained if justified under human rights and data protection legislation.

6.4.3.1.4   Costs of retention

Where for business purposes the same types of data are otherwise being retained for the same 12-month extendable period, the costs shall be borne by the communications provider. However, where new types of data are to be held or any data is to be retained for significantly longer than for business purposes, the Secretary of State will contribute a reasonable proportion of the marginal capital or running costs as appropriate. Clearly, 'significantly' longer in relation to a 12-month retention stipulation would mean that the data would otherwise have been retained for only a few months. The issue of costs can be negotiated to some extent, but these negotiations should take place prior to the signing of the contract.

6.4.3.2 Moving to compulsory data retention

As set out in section 6.1 of this chapter, the UK Government is currently in the process of consulting on Regulations which will introduce compulsory data retention for providers. The good news for Internet providers is that the provisions relating to Internet data are not likely to come into force until March 2009. Only the 12-month minimum data retention period for telephony (mobile and fixed) data will apply from its implementation, which was required by September 2007.

For the time being, therefore, obligations to retain IP, email and other Internet-related data remain subject to the voluntary requirements set out above. Having said this, it is clear that the voluntary Code does provide an important benchmark by which providers' compliance with the provisions of the Anti-Terrorism, Crime and Security Act 2001 may be judged by a court. Following the Code is therefore likely to be recommended for many providers, not least since it also provides a useful guide point and justification for the retention of data for a specific purpose under data protection rules. Providers must balance these incentives against the practical and financial risks involved in the holding of huge quantities of data for long periods, in terms of both storage and dealing with requests that may then need to be fulfilled for disclosure pursuant to RIPA and other legislation.

CHAPTER SEVEN

Taxation

'The big issue is that it will make it more difficult for government to collect taxes.'

Milton Friedman, on the Internet

Despite the Internet's global reach, and the technologies that it encompasses not having been envisaged when the underlying principles of tax law were developed, the UK's tax laws appear, to date, to have withstood the challenges of the online world.

Whilst the maturing online market continues to produce novel ways of doing business, commercial activities on the Internet can generally be distilled into one of the following broad category of supplies:

1. traditional mail order;
2. the sale and transfer of digital material;
3. advertising; and
4. the provision of 'other' services.

Business taxes are levied not by reference to the methods by which business is conducted, but by the financial results of business. The concepts of profit and loss apply equally to online businesses as to bricks and mortar business and, as a result, online businesses face similar tax concerns to their traditional counterparts.

Consequently, this chapter addresses the following questions:

1. What are the tax considerations of starting an Internet business? In particular, in what (legal) form should that business be set up?
2. Because the Internet is transnational, what international tax issues need to be considered? Or, more simply, in what countries will the business be liable to tax?
3. How does value added tax (VAT) apply to supplies made over the Internet?

Although tax laws which existed prior to the Internet can readily be applied to online businesses, the Internet has shaped the way in which tax laws have evolved in recent times. In the same way, evolving tax law has shaped online trading behaviour.

The more 'virtual' an online business, the more readily it can be set up in, or migrated to, a tax haven. This ability to transport an online business (when coupled with the requisite personnel being prepared to move with it) has seen online businesses in certain sectors move offshore. Such migration has been countered with changes to tax law with either anti-avoidance 'sticks' or promises of low-tax 'carrots' to 'beat' or 'tempt' taxpayers back to where certain governments consider they belong.

Thus, for example, prior to 2001 there was an explosion in offshore gambling sites intended to circumvent the imposition of UK betting duty and other UK taxes. A direct effect of this development was the 'carrot' of the replacement, in the March 2001 Budget, of the unpopular UK general betting duty on stakes paid by the betting public with a new form of general betting duty on bookmakers' gross profits. The government of the time agreed to this change on the strength of an understanding, reached between the UK's major retail bookmakers and the Treasury, that the former would bring their online bookmaking operations back within the UK's jurisdiction if the latter introduced the new regime. Thereafter, in the hope of keeping such gambling sites within the UK's tax net, the government continued to offer 'carrots' with the promise of a new regulated gambling regime in the UK (in the form of the Gambling Act 2005, discussed in Chapter 9) and the promise of a low rate of online gaming duty on its implementation in September 2007. When the latter failed to materialise in the Spring Budget of 2007, the gambling sites began to migrate offshore once more.

In terms of VAT, the changes to the VAT treatment of electronically supplied services were implemented as a result of the material difference in VAT treatment between UK-based and non-EU based suppliers of Internet access to UK customers. This was illustrated by the well publicised dispute between the UK-based company, then called Freeserve (now part of Orange Home UK plc), whose supplies of Internet access to UK customers were subject to UK VAT, and the US-based company, AOL (now part of TimeWarner Inc.), whose supplies to UK customers were free of UK VAT. The VAT on Ecommerce Directive (discussed below) was introduced to level the VAT playing field in this area as a consequence.

7.1   UK TAX – GENERAL

Liability to tax in the UK is, in the main, imposed by a series of Finance Acts following the Budget each year. Periodically Finance Acts and other taxing statutes are consolidated and, in recent years, much of the tax legislation has been rewritten in plain English as part of the tax law rewrite project. Recent Acts which form part of this project are the Income Tax (Earnings and Pensions) Act 2003 (ITEPA), the Income Tax (Trading and Other Income) Act 2005 (ITTOIA) and the Income Tax Act 2007 (ITA). All of this legislation is amended frequently.

Direct tax is administered by HM Revenue & Customs ('HMRC') under the Taxes Management Act 1970. The basic system is that a taxpayer (or his accountant) completes a self-assessment tax return in which the taxpayer calculates his own tax liability. Both individuals and companies are subject to a system of self-assessment.

Following submission of a taxpayer's self-assessment return, HMRC has a period of time within which to open enquiries into that return. Where HMRC considers that a taxpayer's self-assessment of his liability is incorrect, it will seek to agree or impose an appropriate change to the taxpayer's self-assessed liability. An appeal against an assessment or a decision of a tax officer may be made on any grounds. The appeal is heard by one of two tribunals: the General Commissioners or the Special Commissioners. A hearing before either body of Commissioners is similar to other legal proceedings in the UK, except that the strict rules of evidence do not apply, and usually each side bears its own costs. Decisions of the Commissioners are subject to a right of appeal to the High Court, and thereafter to the Court of Appeal and the House of Lords. It is sometimes possible to 'leapfrog', so as to omit either the High Court stage or the Court of Appeal stage.

Tax appeals tend to be on questions of law, usually ones of statutory construction. From such decisions, a body of judge-made law has evolved which complements the tax statutes. For example, the line of cases dealing with tax avoidance and statutory interpretation, culminating in the decisions in *Barclays Mercantile Business Finance v Mawson* and in *Scottish Provident Institution v Commissioners of Inland Revenue*,[1] are an important component of the UK's tax laws.

The tax year for individuals runs from 6 April to 5 April in the following year. For companies, it runs from 1 April to the following 31 March.

Individuals pay income tax on their year's income at the basic rate up to a threshold and, to the extent that such threshold is exceeded, a higher rate of income tax applies. In addition to income tax, individuals are liable to pay capital gains tax ('CGT') on capital profits.

Sole traders (i.e. individuals trading as such) are liable to income tax on the income profits, and to CGT on the capital profits, arising from their business. Partners in a partnership are also taxed as individuals, although some special rules apply.

Companies pay corporation tax on both income and capital profits. Corporation tax is calculated in respect of each accounting period of a company. Accounting periods usually last one year, but do not have to coincide with the tax year.

Where an individual derives income from being an employee or director, income tax is deducted at source under the PAYE scheme and, where appropriate, primary class 1 (or 'employee's') national insurance contributions ('NICs') are deducted from each payment of salary. It is mandatory for UK employers to operate the PAYE scheme. Employers are also liable to pay secondary class 1 (or 'employer's') NICs, which are payable in addition to the salary. From an employer's perspective, therefore, the total cost of paying a salary is the aggregate of the gross salary and the employer's NICs payable in addition to that salary. Such payments will ordinarily, however, be deductible from a business's taxable profits for the purposes of income or corporation tax (as applicable).

1   [2005] STC 1 and [2005] STC 15.

7.2 SOLE TRADER, PARTNERSHIP OR COMPANY?

When setting up a new business, a crucial decision will be the type of legal structure (or 'vehicle') to use. In general, the choice is threefold:

1. sole trader;

2. a company; or

3. a partnership.

Although there are a number of factors to be considered in choosing the appropriate vehicle, tax is generally a key driver.

A limited company is perhaps the most common vehicle for businesses. Of its principal attractions, the benefit of limited liability and the fact that it is such a familiar business vehicle are two of the strongest.

Sole traders and partners in a general partnership cannot rely on limited liability. Accordingly, they may be better served by setting up business as a limited liability partnership (or 'LLP'). An individual can achieve this by creating an LLP between himself and a company that he owns, with the latter participating in the partnership to only a small extent (e.g. 1 per cent of profits and gains). It should, of course, be borne in mind that the protection offered by limited liability may be illusory where shareholders of a company or partners of an LLP are, in practice, required to personally guarantee the debts of the business.

From a tax perspective, however, the relative attractiveness or otherwise of each vehicle should be considered in relative terms in light of the expected profits or losses of the business and the extent to which cash will be extracted from the business or reinvested.

A move from one vehicle to another is always a possibility. It is relatively easy to commence trading as a sole trader or a partnership and then 'incorporate' the business at a later date by transferring the business to a company. Whilst the reverse is possible, it is not so easy to achieve in a tax-efficient manner.

The principal difference between a company and a partnership is that the former is itself a taxable entity whilst the latter is not.

Since a company has separate legal personality, tax is potentially payable on two separate occasions. Corporation tax is payable by the company on its profits and, thereafter, the shareholders are charged to income tax on profits distributed to them as a dividend. If a company is very profitable (and so is liable to the higher rates of corporation tax) and all profits are extracted from it year-on-year and paid to individual shareholders who pay income tax at the higher rate, the combined effect of corporation tax (at company level) and income tax on dividend income (at shareholder level) can give an overall effective tax rate in excess of 45 per cent.[2]

In contrast, since a partnership is not a taxable entity, tax is only payable in the hands of the partners. The profits of the partnership are divided between the part-

---

2   At the rates in force at the time of going to press.

ners in accordance with the partnership agreement and taxed as the partners' income on an arising basis (i.e. regardless of whether the profits of the partnership are actually distributed to them). As a result, partners in a partnership pay income tax at a maximum of 40 per cent.[3] Partners in an LLP and a general partnership are taxed in the same way. Sole traders are taxed in broadly the same way also.

An advantage of a company is that retained profits are subject only to corporation tax, which is generally levied at a lower rate than income tax (i.e. if profits are to be retained in the company and reinvested, and so are not distributed to shareholders, those profits are only subject to tax once). Where profits are expected to be retained, therefore, a company may be more tax-efficient than a partnership.

Where profits are not of an amount sufficient for the top rates of corporation tax (on the company's profits) and income tax (on amounts distributed to shareholders) to be applicable and/or where a shareholder looks to extract income from a company by way of salary (which gives a corresponding deduction from taxable profits), the relative tax merits of the different legal structures can change. In addition, with recent Chancellors tinkering with the rates of tax on an annual basis, one structure may be the tax-efficient choice one year but not the next.

7.3 BUSINESS PROFITS

A taxation question commonly of concern to businesses is whether items of expenditure are deductible in computing the amount of taxable profits.

In general, income expenditure which is wholly and exclusively laid out or expended for the purposes of the trade will be deductible from the profits of the business for tax purposes.

Expenditure incurred on creating a website to advertise a business, or through which e-commerce is to be transacted, is likely to have been incurred wholly and exclusively for the purposes of the trade and thus should be deductible from a business's taxable profits. This should remain the case even where the material provided online is free of charge to users, if such expenditure has been incurred in order to market products or otherwise to provide publicity for the business.

Save where a 'capital allowance' is available, expenditure on capital items used in the business is not deductible from taxable profits. Accordingly, in determining the taxable profits of a business from the net accounting profit figure in the business's profit and loss account, accounting depreciation of capital assets has to be added back.

The system of capital allowances does permit certain deductions to be made from taxable profits, as a form of 'tax depreciation', in respect of expenditure on a capital asset over a period of years.

---

3   At the rates in force at the time of going to press.

Capital allowances are given in respect of expenditure on plant and machinery. These words are not defined in the legislation, but 'plant' has been held to include 'whatever apparatus is used by a businessman for carrying on his business'.[4] Allowances are most commonly given at a fixed rate, on an annual basis, on a pool of qualifying expenditure.

Expenditure on computers, servers, telecoms equipment and other electronic apparatus is likely to qualify for capital allowances. Expenditure on computer software is also eligible for capital allowances and, for such purposes, is treated as plant. This should apply to all software, whether an off-the-shelf package, software bundled with hardware or bespoke software.

Although not part of the capital allowances regime, if a UK company incurs expenditure on 'intangible fixed assets' it can obtain relief from corporation tax. This would include expenditure incurred on the creation, acquisition or licence of any patent, trade mark, registered design, copyright or design right. The tax relief available is given in line with the depreciation of such intangible assets in the company's accounts (in accordance with generally accepted accounting practice) or, by election, at the rate of 4 per cent per annum.

7.4   UK RESIDENCE

UK taxation is based on a person's place of residence.

Individuals who are resident in the UK are taxed on their worldwide income and gains. However, the UK has not, for many years, taxed individuals who are UK resident on income derived from a non-UK source to the extent that such income is not remitted to the UK unless they are also UK domiciled (i.e. broadly they have made the UK their permanent home).[5] For an individual, 'residence' means 'to dwell permanently or for a considerable time, to have one's settled or usual abode, to live in or at a particular place'.[6]

A company which is treated as being resident in the UK will be taxed on its worldwide income and gains. A company will be treated as resident in the UK for the purposes of taxation if either it is incorporated in the UK or if its central management and control is effected in the UK.

There is no statutory definition of central management and control. The UK courts have held that central management and control means the highest form of control and direction of a company's affairs, as distinct from the management of the company's day-to-day operations. The location of a company's central management and control is a question of fact in each particular case.

In *De Beers Consolidated Mines Ltd v Howe*,[7] it was held that a South African incorporated company was resident in the UK because a majority of the directors lived in London and the board meetings, by which the operations of the company

---

4   See *Yarmouth v France* (1887) 19 QBD 647.
5   Pursuant to the announcement made in the pre-Budget report of Autumn 2007, the UK tax treatment of non-UK domiciled individuals is likely to change on 6 April 2008.
6   *Levene v IRC* [1928] AC 217, HL.
7   [1906] AC 455, 5 TC 198, HL.

worldwide were controlled and managed, were held in London. This was held to be the case even though shareholders' meetings were held in South Africa and the registered office and head office were located in South Africa. More recently, the Court of Appeal in *Wood v Holden*[8] confirmed the test in *De Beers* as the relevant test, and went on to emphasise that in determining the place of a company's central management and control, it was necessary to decide whether effective decisions were taken by the company's board of directors or whether those decisions were taken by someone else.

In summary, therefore, it is the place where the people who take the company's key strategic decisions are physically located when they take those decisions that will determine the place of a company's central management and control.

Unlike common law countries (such as the UK), in civil law countries a company is usually taxable only in its country of domicile; namely, where it is incorporated. The US takes a similar approach. In such jurisdictions, the territory from which the company is managed and controlled becomes irrelevant.

7.5 THE SOURCE OF PROFITS AND TAXABLE PRESENCE

Since one can be resident or have a taxable presence in more than one country, it is thus possible for income to be potentially taxable in two countries simultaneously. This situation may be mitigated by a double taxation treaty between the two countries in question which aims to ensure that tax is charged only in one or other of the two countries that have agreed the treaty or, sometimes, that part only of the profits or gains in question are taxed in each country. The UK, which has treaties with more than one hundred countries, has the most extensive network.

A non-UK resident company will only be subject to UK tax on its profits and gains if such a liability arises under UK domestic law and a relevant double tax treaty does not override the UK domestic law position.

Under UK domestic law, a company not resident in the UK will be subject to income tax to the extent that it carries on a trade 'within' (rather than 'with') the UK; i.e. the business is actually carried on from within the UK rather than the business merely entering into transactions with UK customers. If a non-resident company's presence in the UK constitutes a 'permanent establishment' (see below), it will be within the charge to UK corporation tax (again pursuant to UK domestic law) to the extent that it carries on a trade through that UK permanent establishment.

Most of the UK's double tax treaties provide that the UK only has the right to tax the profits of a company (or other entity) resident in the other contracting state (i.e. the country with which the UK has signed the treaty), if that non-UK resident company is carrying on a trade or business through a 'permanent establishment' in the UK (thus the concept of 'permanent establishment' is found both in the UK's domestic legislation and in its double tax treaties). Accordingly, where a company, which is resident in a country with which the UK has a double tax treaty, is trading 'within' the UK (and so potentially has a UK income tax liability under UK domestic law) but its trading presence is something less than a UK permanent establishment (as defined in the applicable treaty), the UK domestic law may be overridden by the treaty with the result that no UK tax liability will arise.

7.6   UK PERMANENT ESTABLISHMENT

Although not identical, the definitions of a permanent establishment for UK domestic law purposes and the definition used in its double tax treaties are very similar.

A non-UK resident company will have a permanent establishment in the UK if it has a fixed place of business (i.e. something physical, such as an office) in the UK through which its principal business activities (being matters which are not merely ancillary to its business) are wholly or partly carried on (the 'physical test').

A non-UK company will also have a permanent establishment in the UK if a dependent agent acting on its behalf has, and habitually exercises, authority to enter into contracts, or otherwise does business, on its behalf while in the UK (the 'agency test').

In theory, therefore (and by way of example), the physical test could be applied to a server on which a website is hosted in circumstances where the website allows customers to download telephone ringtones for payments made via an online payment facility. If the server is owned by the foreign company and is both located and physically fixed (i.e. has a degree of permanence) in the UK then, since the business of the foreign company is carried on through it (e.g. the selling of ringtones), the server could (without more) arguably constitute a UK permanent establishment. Were this to be the case, all profits derived from the website hosted on the server would be subject to UK tax.

In the UK, HMRC's published practice is that a website, of itself, is not a permanent establishment and that a server is, of itself, insufficient to constitute a permanent establishment of a business that is conducting ecommerce through a website on that server.

Other jurisdictions (particularly other OECD member states) do not, however, take this view. Accordingly, the tax effects of the location of servers should be carefully determined when companies or other entities (wherever resident) are considering locating servers outside of their country of residence.

7.7   WITHHOLDING TAXES

In many jurisdictions, certain payments may be subject to deduction of income tax at source, otherwise known as withholding tax. The most common are payments of royalties, interest and dividends.

The UK levies no withholding tax on dividends paid by UK resident companies. The UK does, however, levy withholding taxes on certain payments of interest and royalties.

Some payments of annual interest between UK resident persons are subject to withholding tax. For example, where a UK resident company makes a payment of interest to an individual, tax at the basic rate is required to be withheld. In contrast, however, payments between UK resident companies are not subject to withholding tax.

Most payments of interest by UK borrowers to non-UK lenders are subject to withholding tax under UK domestic law. This can, however, be effectively overridden by the EC Interest and Royalties Directive or a relevant double tax treaty (both of which are discussed below) which may eliminate the UK withholding tax liability entirely or, in the case of a double tax treaty, reduce it to a lower amount.

Save in the case of certain patent royalties, withholding tax liabilities do not arise under UK domestic law in respect of royalty payments made by UK licensees to UK licensors.

In relation to royalties paid to non-UK licensors, however, a withholding tax liability will usually arise under UK domestic law in respect to royalties paid for the use of certain patents, copyrights, design rights and registered designs. Copyright royalties that are subject to withholding tax do not include video recordings, films or, where not separately exploited, their soundtracks.

Thus video on demand and video streaming services provided via the web are likely not to be caught, so long as it can be established that the copyright exploited is a copyright in a video recording or cinematograph film. In contrast, payments for audio streaming, the download of music tracks and software licences are potentially caught. HMRC's practice, however, has been that payment for a licence to give the user only a limited right to use the software in question should not be subject to withholding tax[9]. Accordingly, an obligation to withhold should only arise where payment is made to acquire a right of reproduction to make many copies or to otherwise exploit the original.

A requirement to withhold tax under UK domestic law may be removed or varied if either the EC Interest and Royalties Directive applies or if a relevant double tax treaty applies.

The EC Interest and Royalties Directive will apply where the payer is a UK company or a UK permanent establishment of an EU company and the recipient of the payment is a company in a different member state and both companies are 25 per cent associates (i.e. one company holds at least 25 per cent of the capital or voting rights in the other or a third company has such a holding in both companies). Where the Directive applies, the payment can be made free of withholding tax.

Where a withholding liability exists under UK domestic law and the EC Interest and Royalties Directive does not apply, a double tax treaty between the UK and the country of residence of the recipient of the royalty may reduce or eliminate the withholding liability. Some treaties (for example, the treaty between the UK and the US) provide that royalties and/or interest arising in

9   Although, at the time of going to press, the wording in HMRC's manuals which reflected this practice had been withdrawn.

one country which are beneficially owned by a resident of the other country are taxable only in that other country. This, in effect, reduces the withholding tax liability to zero. In other treaties, a reduced rate of withholding tax on payments is prescribed.

If the person paying a royalty in the UK has a reasonable belief that the non-UK payee is entitled to benefit under a double tax treaty, the reduced rate of withholding in the treaty can be applied without seeking advance clearance from HMRC. If this reasonable belief is misplaced, however, the payer remains liable for the full withholding liability and so seeking advance clearance often remains the prudent approach. Note that this rule does not apply to payments of interest.

Many multinational groups of companies implement structures to minimise taxes on royalty income. A typical structure would involve a group company based in a low-tax jurisdiction owning intellectual property and licensing that intellectual property to other companies in the group. Such a structure may route the royalty payments via an intermediary group company based in a country with an extensive network of treaties which impose beneficial rates of withholding tax so as to eliminate or materially reduce withholding tax liabilities on royalty payments flowing back to the owner of the intellectual property.

It is, however, becoming increasingly common for tax treaties to contain specific provision to counter 'treaty shopping'; namely, the practice of establishing an entity in a particular jurisdiction for the primary purpose of taking advantage of the favourable tax treatment offered by a treaty between that jurisdiction and another. In addition, the decision of the UK's Court of Appeal in *Indofood International Finance Limited v JP Morgan Chase Bank NA*[10] has cast doubt on the efficacy of certain international structures which use an intermediate finance entity. Although HMRC have published guidance on the decision, it remains to be seen whether they will use the decision to attack treaty-based structures where they can argue that an interposed entity does not have the requisite 'beneficial ownership' of the relevant payment to benefit from the treaty.

7.8   VAT

7.8.1   Introduction

Value added tax is an indirect tax on consumers imposed by all member states of the European Union.

The primary EU legislation is EC Council Directive 2006/112 of 28 November 2006 (the 'VAT Directive'). Member states are required to enact domestic legislation giving effect to the VAT Directive. Since in certain areas the VAT Directive permits member states to choose which of a number of provisions to adopt in their domestic legislation, the VAT laws across the member states are not completely aligned. An example is the standard rate of VAT itself, which is at the discretion of each member state so long as it is at least 15 per cent. As a consequence, VAT rates vary across the EU from 15 per cent to 25 per cent.

VAT is imposed on supplies of goods and services provided for a consideration (money or something of value exchanged for the goods or services) in the course

10   [2006] STC 1195.

of a business. Accordingly, VAT is not payable in respect of items supplied between unconnected parties for free (e.g. free downloads). Where payment is made in a non-cash form, VAT is payable on the value of the non-cash consideration provided.

The VAT system effectively taxes the final consumer of goods and services. In general terms, those businesses in the supply chain that create or add value to those goods or services merely collect and account for VAT to the tax authorities on the value added by them in the supply chain. Accordingly, save where the suppliers are exempt (see below), they do not bear the cost of VAT as they are able to recover any VAT which they have themselves been charged on any goods or services they have used to make their own supplies.

For an example, a company selling chart music in digital form and charging VAT on the services it provides to its customers would be able to reclaim any VAT incurred on buying computers necessary to run the business, on the cost of constructing, maintaining and hosting its website and on royalties that it has to pay to artists. In respect of any VAT accounting period, it would only be required to account to the tax authorities for the difference between the VAT arising in respect of supplies that it has made to its customers (its 'output tax') and the VAT which it had itself been charged on the goods and services it had consumed in order to make those supplies (its 'input tax').

Although the end consumer bears the burden of paying VAT on taxable goods and services, it is the supplier of goods or services who is legally responsible to account for the VAT charged. VAT is deemed included in a price unless expressly stated otherwise. Accordingly, if a supplier omits to charge his customers VAT he is nonetheless liable himself to account for the VAT to the tax authorities. In order to make supervision of the system of deducting input tax possible, a business can only reclaim VAT on its inputs if it holds an invoice from its supplier to show that VAT is payable.

7.8.2   Exempt and zero-rated supplies

There are two special categories of supplies:

1.   exempt supplies; and
2.   reduced and zero rated supplies.

The supplier of an exempt supply is not required to charge VAT on those goods or services. Categories of exempt supply include financial services, insurance services, certain supplies of land, betting and gaming and education.

A trader making exempt supplies cannot, however, recover as input tax any VAT charged to him on supplies which have been used as components of an exempt supply. Thus, he is effectively treated as the final consumer of those components. For example, since the services of an online bookmaker are exempt, he could not reclaim any VAT incurred on the setting up of a website to provide online betting services.

The supplier of a zero-rated supply is required to charge VAT, but at the reduced rate of 0 per cent. Reduced rates of VAT are applied differently in different member states. In the UK, categories for zero-rating include foodstuffs, passenger transport services, and books and newspapers.

Although for the purchaser of a zero-rated supply there is no practical difference from an exempt supply (because no VAT is in fact charged), zero-rating is advantageous to the supplier as he is able to deduct input VAT incurred in respect of the components of the supply. For example a publisher of physical works (note that the supply of digital works are not exempt) will often have no output tax to pay, due to all his supplies being zero-rated, but will nevertheless have incurred input tax in respect of purchases of paper, inks, binding materials, office equipment, etc. Accordingly, provided that he has registered for VAT, the publisher will actually receive repayments of VAT from HMRC at the end of each VAT period.

7.8.3   The VAT system in the UK

The rate of VAT in the UK is currently 17.5 per cent.

In the UK, VAT is imposed by the Value Added Tax Act 1994 (VATA 1994), as amended by annual Finance Acts following the Budget. Secondary legislation often contains important provisions; for example, the Value Added Tax Regulations 1995 contain much of the law relating to administration and collection of VAT in the UK.

Collection of VAT is the responsibility of HMRC. All persons making taxable supplies (i.e. supplies other than exempt supplies) whose turnover from taxable supplies which are not zero-rated exceeds a certain threshold[11] must register for VAT. In respect of each period (usually three months, but exceptionally one month or twelve months) the taxable person is obliged to complete a VAT return and to pay any VAT due. Businesses are also required to maintain proper records and to supply customers who are themselves registered or required to be registered with a VAT invoice in respect of taxable supplies.

There is a right of appeal from any decision of HMRC to a judicial body known as the VAT and Duties Tribunal. Further appeals from decisions of the Tribunal on questions of law may be made to the High Court, Court of Appeal and ultimately the House of Lords. Since VAT is a European tax, points of European law often arise and it is not uncommon for questions to be raised as to whether the UK legislation, or the way in which HMRC seek to implement it, exceed what is permitted under the European legislation. Both the VAT and Duties Tribunal and the higher courts hearing VAT appeals are, therefore, able to refer questions for decision to the European Court of Justice in Luxembourg.

7.8.4   VAT and supplies made via the Internet

As mentioned at the start of this chapter, commercial activities conducted via the Internet generally include one of the following:

1.   traditional mail order;

2.   advertising;

11   £64,000 for the 2007/08 tax year.

3.   the supply or download of digital products; or

4.   'other' services.

The principal difficulty surrounding the VAT treatment of supplies made via the Internet is jurisdictional or, more accurately, determining *where* the supplies in question are made for VAT purposes.

Supplies are treated as being subject to UK VAT if they are treated as being supplied 'in the UK'. If they are not treated as being supplied in the UK, they will not be subject to UK VAT but may be subject to VAT in another EU member state or other value added or goods and services taxes outside the EU (e.g. sales taxes in the US or GST in Australia).

Accordingly, in determining the VAT treatment of any particular supply, one must first determine where that supply is treated as being made.

There are specific rules which determine where, for VAT purposes, a supply is treated as being made with different rules applying to goods and different rules applying to services. As the next step, therefore, one must determine whether a specific supply is a supply of goods or a supply services.

For VAT purposes, with a few exceptions, goods are anything tangible. Services, therefore, are everything else.

7.8.4.1   Supplies of goods via the Internet

Where the Internet is simply used as a form of mail order for physical goods, one must consider the place of supply rules relating to goods; i.e. the normal VAT rules applicable to such transactions continue to apply regardless of the means of ordering them.

The VAT place of supply rules relating to goods differ depending upon:

1.   the place where the supplier belongs;

2.   the place where the recipient belongs; and

3.   whether the supply is a supply to a VAT registered person (i.e. 'business to business' or 'B2B') or a supply to a person who is not registered for VAT (i.e. 'business to consumer' or 'B2C').

7.8.4.1.1   UK to UK (B2B or B2C)

Where goods are ordered over the Internet by a UK purchaser (whether on a B2B or B2C basis) from a UK VAT-registered business, UK VAT will usually have to be accounted for in the normal way.

7.8.4.1.2   Outbound – UK to non-EU (B2B or B2C)

Supplies of goods made by UK businesses to customers outside of the EU are zero-rated provided that the UK supplier retains appropriate evidence that the goods have been exported outside of the EU. This is the case whether the supply is on a B2B or B2C basis. In these circumstances, the supplier would still be able to recover the input VAT on any component costs of the supply.

7.8.4.1.3   Outbound – UK to EU (B2B)

Supplies of goods made by UK VAT-registered businesses to customers within the EU are zero-rated if they are supplied to a person registered for VAT in another member state, the supplier obtains his customer's VAT registration number and shows this on his VAT invoice and if he holds appropriate documentary evidence that the goods have been removed from the UK.

7.8.4.1.4   Outbound – UK to EU (B2C)

If the EU-based customer is not registered for VAT, the UK registered supplier must charge VAT at the UK rate. However, once B2C supplies made by the UK registered supplier to any particular EU country exceed an annual threshold set by that country for VAT distance selling purposes (which can be either €35,000 or €100,000 or the relevant currency equivalent), the supplier must register for VAT in that country and then charge VAT at the rate applicable in the country of destination.

7.8.4.1.5   Inbound – non-EU to UK (B2C)

Where a non-VAT registered UK customer buys goods over the Internet from outside the EU, UK VAT is payable by the purchaser on the entry of those goods into the UK. For example, where goods are ordered by a UK private customer over the Internet from a non-EU website and sent by mail, the Post Office will require payment of the VAT due from the purchaser before delivery will be made. However, small value (less than £18) items are tax- and duty-free at import. This means, for example, that there is no VAT to pay on a single CD ordered over the Internet by a UK customer from a supplier based in the Channel Islands.

7.8.4.1.6   Inbound – EU to UK (B2C)

Where non-VAT registered UK customers acquire goods from suppliers in other EU member states, those private customers will be charged VAT at the rate applicable in the other member state, unless the supplier is also registered for VAT in the UK under the UK's distance selling rules referred to above, in which case UK rates of VAT would be charged. Under the UK's distance selling rules, EU suppliers must register for VAT in the UK if the annual value of supplies made to the UK exceeds £70,000.

7.8.4.1.7   Inbound – EU or non-EU to UK (B2B)

Acquisitions of goods from other member states and imports from non-EU member states are subject to VAT at the UK rate if the customer is VAT-registered in the UK. Thus, a VAT registered UK customer will have to account for UK VAT on such purchases.

7.8.4.2   *Supplies of services via the Internet*

As with the VAT rules which determine the place of supply of goods, the VAT place of supply of services rules depend upon:

1. the place where the supplier belongs;

2. the place where the recipient belongs; and

3. whether the supply is a B2B or B2C supply.

The place of supply of services rules are, however, made more complicated by subdividing services into three different categories. The categories are:

1. those which fall within Sch 5 VATA ('Sch 5') and which are not subject to the 'use and enjoyment rules' – e.g. advertising;

2. those which fall within Sch 5 and which are subject to the 'use and enjoyment rules' – e.g. electronically supplied services; and

3. those which do not fall within Sch 5.

Services falling within Sch 5 that are not subject to the use and enjoyment rules include supplies of: rights (e.g. copyright, trade marks, etc.); advertising; services of professionals (e.g. lawyers, accountants etc.); data processing and the provision of information; banking, financial and insurance services and the supply of staff. Depending upon the circumstances (e.g. if the supply is a cross-border B2B supply), such supplies are treated as being supplied where received (i.e. where the recipient belongs).

Supplies falling within Sch 5 which are potentially subject to the use and enjoyment rules include supplies of: telecommunication services; radio and television broadcasting services and electronically supplied services (see below). These supplies are treated in the same way as other Sch 5 services save that in certain circumstances (illustrated below), the 'supplied where received' treatment is overridden by the place of effective use and enjoyment.

Services not falling within Sch 5 (i.e. all other services) are subject to the general rule that the place of supply is that where the supplier belongs.

'Electronically supplied services' ('ESS') are defined to include, amongst other things, supplies of web-hosting, distance maintenance of programmes and equipment, the supply and updating of software, the supply of images, text, information, databases, music, film and games, the supply of political, cultural, artistic, sporting, scientific and entertainment broadcasts and events and the supply of electronic auctions, Internet service packages and some interactive distance teaching.

Prior to 1 July 2003, ESS made on a B2C basis were subject to the general rule that supplies of services are made where the supplier belongs. Accordingly, suppliers of such ESS based outside the EU could make supplies to non-business customers in the EU without charging VAT. This gave such non-EU suppliers a significant pricing advantage over their EU competitors who had to account for VAT at the standard rate applicable in the member state in which they were established on supplies of ESS made to non-business customers located in the EU. EU-based suppliers were at a further disadvantage in that they also had to charge VAT on some ESS made to non-EU based customers. The new rules relating to ESS, which removed these pricing differences, are discussed further below.

In the context of supplies of services made over the Internet, other than where the Internet is being used as a means of delivery, supplies of services are most likely to constitute either 'advertising' or fall within the definition of 'electronically supplied services'.

Where the Internet is merely being used as a means of delivery, the fact that this method of communication has been chosen will not alter VAT treatment of the underlying supply (e.g. a lawyer sending his legal advice via email must account for VAT on the basis that he is making a supply of legal advice and not a supply of an ESS). Supplies of services which are merely delivered by electronic means are outside the scope of this chapter.

The rules described below set out the different ways in which the place of supply of services rules can apply to supplies of online services that either constitute advertising or the supply of an ESS. The results below assume that the supplies being made are neither exempt nor zero-rated for UK VAT purposes and that advertising is only supplied on a B2B basis.

7.8.4.2.1   UK to UK (B2B or B2C)

An ESS or a supply of advertising made by a UK-based supplier to a UK-based customer will be treated as made in the UK and so is subject to UK VAT.

7.8.4.2.2   Outbound – UK to non-EU (B2B or B2C)

Supplies of advertising or ESS that are made by a UK supplier to a person outside of the EU (whether on a B2B or B2C basis) are not subject to UK VAT and are expressed to be 'outside the scope of VAT'. The exception is in relation to ESS that are supplied for business purposes (i.e. on a B2B basis) where those supplies are 'effectively used or enjoyed' within the UK, in which case they are subject to UK VAT.

7.8.4.2.3   Outbound – UK to EU (B2B)

Supplies of advertising or ESS that are made by a UK supplier to a business customer within the EU are allowed to be 'zero rated' provided that the UK supplier obtains and retains the EU VAT number of the customer.

7.8.4.2.4   Outbound – UK to EU (B2C)

Supplies of ESS made by a UK supplier to an EU-based non-business customer are treated as made in the UK and so are subject to UK VAT.

7.8.4.2.5   Inbound – EU or non-EU to UK (B2B)

Business customers established in the UK receiving supplies of advertising or ESS from suppliers in another country (whether or not a member state) have to account for UK VAT via the reverse charge mechanism. The reverse charge mechanism essentially requires the business customer receiving the services to self-assess for the input VAT and then, to the extent that he can (i.e. depending upon whether the services received are a component part of an exempt supply), seek to recover that input VAT.

The exception to this rule is in relation to ESS that are supplied for business purposes (i.e. on a B2B basis) where those supplies are 'effectively used or enjoyed' outside of the EU; in which case they are not subject to UK VAT.

7.8.4.2.6   Inbound – EU to UK (B2C)

Supplies of ESS that are made by EU suppliers to non-business customers within the UK are treated as being made where the EU supplier belongs and so will be subject to EU VAT at the rate applicable in the member state of the supplier.

7.8.4.2.7   Inbound – non-EU to UK (B2C)

Since 1 July 2003, supplies of ESS by non-EU suppliers to EU-based business are treated as being made where the recipient belongs and so are subject to VAT at the rate applicable in the country where the recipient belongs. These rules are discussed in more detail below.

7.8.5   ESS and the VAT on Electronic Commerce Directive

Council Directive 2002/38 of May 7, 2002 (referred to as the 'VAT on Electronic Commerce Directive') was formally adopted by the European Council on May 7, 2002 and came into force and was given effect in the UK on 1 July 2003. This Directive is now reflected in the VAT Directive, arts 357 to 369.

For businesses established outside the EU making supplies of ESS to non-business customers resident in a member state, the post-1 July 2003 rules introduced a completely new VAT regime.

The place of supply of ESS by businesses established outside of the EU to non-business customers resident in a member state was changed to the place where the non-business customer resides. This change of law was innovative since it created a VAT liability for suppliers who are outside the EU and, therefore, beyond the jurisdiction of the taxing authorities of the member states who collect and administer VAT.

So as to make compliance easier for non-EU-based suppliers making supplies of ESS to non-business customers in a member state, such suppliers are permitted, instead of registering for VAT in each member state where the registration threshold is exceeded (i.e. under the usual rules), to opt for a simplified scheme of registration and VAT accounting. Under this 'special accounting scheme', non-EU suppliers of ESS may register for VAT in just one member state of their choosing. They will then, in relation to each separate supply, be required to account (to the authorities in the member state in which they are registered) for VAT at the standard rate charged by the member state in which each of their non-business customers are resident.

The effect of the post-1 July 2003 rules and the 'special accounting scheme' is that, regardless of the member state in which such a non-EU-established business has registered, that business will need to account for VAT at up to 27 national rates. Whilst this special scheme is likely to be preferable to having to register separately in each member state in which their customers reside, in contrast to businesses located within the EU (see sections 7.8.4.2.4 and 7.8.4.2.6 above), the rules for non-EU-based businesses can be administratively burdensome and can result in those businesses being at a pricing disadvantage to their competitors established in member states with low rates of VAT. These disadvantages are a key reason why, since 1 July 2003, many non-EU suppliers of ESS have re-established their businesses in member states with low rates of VAT.

At the time of going to press, these rules were scheduled to continue in force until 31 December 2008.

7.8.6   Further changes to the place of supply of ESS

In December 2007, the Council of the EU reached agreement on further changes to the rules governing the place of supply of services. In broad terms, more supplies of services will be treated as taking place where the customer belongs. The new rules can be subdivided into two parts.

First, all services (and not just those within Sch 5) which are supplied cross-border on a B2B basis will be treated as supplied where received. Accordingly, all services will be subject to the reverse charge mechanism when supplied cross border to an EU-based VAT-registered recipient. This change in the rules will be introduced on 1 January 2010.

Second, supplies of telecoms, broadcasting and ESS that are made intra-EU on a B2C basis will be treated as made where they are received. In broad terms, this change is designed to align intra-EU supplies with the post-1 July 2003 treatment of B2C supplies of ESS when supplied into the EU from traders based outside the EU (thereby completely levelling the playing field and eliminating the potential price disadvantages for B2C suppliers of ESS based outside of the EU).

This second change is, once again, innovative in that the supplier will have to account for VAT at the rate applicable in a country other than his own; namely, that where his customer is established. So as to ease the administration of this change, a 'one-stop' system has been proposed so that EU-based service providers can register for VAT in their home states and comply with all their VAT obligations in that jurisdiction only. In practice, however, a supplier of relevant services to non-business customers throughout the EU will have to account for VAT at the rates applicable in up to 27 member states. Under the 'one-stop' system, VAT revenue not belonging to the supplier's home state will be transferred from that state to that of the customer.

These rules will not be brought into force until 1 January 2015 and will then be phased in over a four-year period to 2019. Under this regime, the member state where the supplier is established will be entitled, for an initial period, to retain a fixed proportion of the VAT receipts collected through the one-stop scheme; i.e. a 'halfway house' of sorts. The proportion will be 30 per cent from 1 January 2015 until 31 December 2016, 15 per cent from January 2017 until 31 December 2018 and 0 per cent from 1 January 2019.

The exact details of this new regime remain to be seen, but it represents a compromise to deal with concerns of member states with lower VAT rates, notably Luxembourg. These member states anticipated a loss of VAT receipts under the new general regime since many providers of B2C ESS have registered in those states; particularly those who were previously established outside of the EU and have re-established themselves in Luxembourg since the introduction of the VAT on Ecommerce Directive.

As discussed at the start of this chapter, the rules announced in December 2007 and referred to above are another example of the way in which tax laws continue to evolve to cope with the challenges created by transnational ecommerce.

CHAPTER EIGHT

Competition law and the Internet

'The Court has upheld a landmark Commission decision to give consumers more choice in software markets. That decision set an important precedent in terms of the obligations of dominant companies to allow competition, in particular in hightech industries. The Court ruling shows that the Commission was right to take its decision. Microsoft must now comply fully with its legal obligations to desist from engaging in anti-competitive conduct.'

Neelie Kroes, European Commissioner for Competition

'In light of the United States' own antitrust case and judgment against Microsoft, and the importance of the computer industry to consumers and to the global economy, the United States has a particular interest in today's CFI decision. . . . We are, however, concerned that the standard applied to unilateral conduct by the CFI, rather than helping consumers, may have the unfortunate consequence of harming consumers by chilling innovation and discouraging competition.'

Thomas O. Barnett, US Department of Justice Assistant Attorney General for Antitrust

In principle, the Internet should be enormously pro-competitive. It is highly innovative and constantly changing. It facilitates market entry and is a highly transparent sales channel which brings us closer to the economists' utopia of perfect competition. The application of competition law to Internet-related business should be considered against this background.

However, ordinary competition law still applies to Internet-related business just as it does to bricks and mortar business. As with any industry, there are ways in which Internet businesses develop or operate which may raise competition concerns. Anyone involved in the business of the Internet needs to know how competition law can affect them and how it can be used to their own advantage – Microsoft and Sun Microsystems can testify to that.

This chapter examines the impact of the following competition law provisions for Internet-related business.

Relevant legal provisions

Domestic provision	European provision	Focus
Competition Act 1998, Chapter I prohibition	EC Treaty Art 81	Anti-competitive agreements
Competition Act 1998, Chapter II prohibition	EC Treaty Art 82	Abuse of a dominant position
Enterprise Act 2002, Part 6	Not applicable	Cartel offence
Enterprise Act 2002, Part 3	EC Merger Regulation	Merger control
Enterprise Act 2002, Part 4	Council Regulation 1/2003 (Art 17)	Market investigations/ sector inquiries

8.1　INTRODUCTION TO COMPETITION LAW

Competition law can be seen as a sophisticated form of consumer protection. While unfair contract terms legislation tries to prevent consumers from being bound by unjust conditions, competition law tries to ensure that markets operate competitively, so that consumers benefit from lower prices, better service and wider choice. It assumes that the natural state of markets is not necessarily to move towards increasing competition. As Thurman Arnold, the one-time head of the US Department of Justice Anti-Trust Division,[1] explained: '[t]he maintenance of a free market is as much a matter of constant policing as the flow of traffic on a busy intersection. It does not stay orderly by trusting to the good intentions of the drivers or by preaching to them'.

However, just because competition law controls certain types of behaviour does not mean that it tries to make markets cosy places. On the contrary, a key aim of competition law is to prevent cosiness between competitors. Another important role of competition law is to ensure that companies that have market power do not use it to suppress competition. Nevertheless, it should not be assumed automatically that 'big is bad', in competition law terms. Although being big can give companies the power to be bullies, it can also simply be a sign of success. Companies grow big when they do things well.

Just as big is not necessarily bad, so small is not necessarily good. Although we might feel sympathy for small businesses who try hard and do not succeed against larger competitors, competition law should have no such sentiment. If larger organisations can deliver products and services more efficiently, then competition law should offer no protection to the small guys who suffer as a result. Competition law, as its name suggests, should protect competition, not competitors. When European regulators and courts take a more expansive view of competition law than their American counterparts (as in the case of the Microsoft investigation), they are often charged with straying beyond protection of competition and, ultimately, consumers, to protection of competitors.

1　1939–43.

8.2   THE LEGAL FRAMEWORK

8.2.1   Anti-competitive agreements and abuse of a dominant position

Articles 81 and 82 of the EC Treaty[2] are the foundation of European competition law. They had been in force for almost 50 years at the time of writing, since the inception of what is now the European Union. Arts 81 and 82 prohibit anti-competitive agreements and abuses of a dominant position respectively, provided that they have an appreciable effect on trade between EU member states.

Most member states also have national laws that prohibit anti-competitive agreements and behaviour that have an effect within member states. Most of these are based on Arts 81 and 82. Chapters I and II of the Competition Act 1998 replicate Arts 81 and 82 for restrictions of competition with an effect in the UK, such that companies face effectively the same set of rules whether a competition issue arises at a domestic or European level. Although the Competition Act has been in force only since 1 March 2000, s 60 of the Competition Act requires national competition authorities, sectoral regulators and courts to interpret the Competition Act so as to avoid inconsistency with European competition law. In other words, the Competition Act incorporates the long-standing jurisprudence of European competition law.

Articles 81 and 82 have historically been enforced principally by the European Commission. However, since the Modernisation Regulation[3] came into force on 1 May 2004, national competition authorities, sectoral regulators and courts have been empowered to enforce Arts 81 and 82 in full, in addition to national competition law. The European Commission has also retained jurisdiction to enforce Arts 81 and 82. Chapter IV of the Modernisation Regulation provides that the European Commission will co-operate with national competition authorities, sectoral regulators and courts regarding the application of Arts 81 and 82 and the European Commission has issued a Notice which sets out the principles for the allocation of cases between the Commission and national competition authorities and sectoral regulators.[4]

Since it is intended that Arts 81 and 82 of the EC Treaty and Chapters I and II of the Competition Act should be congruent, they are discussed alongside one another in this chapter. Only where there are specific differences between the regimes are they dealt with separately.

2   Prior to May 1999 and the coming into force of the Amsterdam Treaty, these were numbered Arts 85 and 86 respectively. This renumbering makes reading (and searching for) relevant European cases a rather frustrating experience.
3   Council Regulation 1/2003 on the implementation of the rules on competition laid down in Arts 81 and 82 of the EC Treaty (known as the 'Modernisation Regulation').
4   Commission Notice on cooperation within the Network of Competition Authorities (2004/C 101/03).

8.2.2   UK cartel offence

Separately from the Competition Act prohibitions (and with no parallel under European law), the Enterprise Act 2002 introduced a criminal cartel offence in the UK, which came into force on 20 June 2003. This is enforced by the UK Office of Fair Trading ('OFT') and Serious Fraud Office ('SFO').

8.2.3   Market investigations

In addition, the Enterprise Act introduced a new UK market investigation regime, replacing the previous regime under the Fair Trading Act 1973. Under the new regime, final decisions are taken by the UK Competition Commission rather than a member of the Government (other than in exceptional circumstances) and the test is based on competition law issues rather than a more general public interest. The Modernisation Regulation referred to above also formalised, from 1 May 2004, a regime for market investigations undertaken by the European Commission.[5]

8.2.4   Merger control

The final change to UK competition law introduced by the Enterprise Act was the replacement of the previous UK merger control regime under the Fair Trading Act 1973. Consistent with the changes to the market investigation regime, under the new regime final decisions are taken by the OFT or Competition Commission rather than a member of the Government (other than in exceptional circumstances) and the test is based on competition law issues rather than a more general public interest. In addition, the Enterprise Act introduced procedural changes to the UK merger control regime, which are considered in more detail below.

8.2.5   Sector-specific legislation

Although there is no Internet-specific competition law, there are specific regimes, at both domestic and European level, governing electronic communications and broadcasting. It is beyond the scope of this chapter to explore these regimes, but it is notable that in the electronic communications field, the UK Office of Communications ('OFCOM') has the power to control prices, set minimum quality and service standards and impose 'interconnection' obligations requiring infrastructure owners to allow third party access to their system (following a market review and a finding of market power). OFCOM can also, and has, set 'General Conditions of Entitlement' which include consumer protection

5   Art 17.

obligations, service requirements, technical obligations and numbering arrangements. These conditions may in some cases apply to Internet service providers. ISPs offering voice over Internet protocol ('VOIP')-based services, other than strictly peer-to-peer, may for example be subject to a number of consumer protection obligations. If any Internet-related agreement, merger or potentially anti-competitive behaviour involves issues of line pricing or access in a relevant market where so-called SMP (significant market power) obligations have been imposed, it is important to consider the effects of the relevant electronic communications legislation and the possible reactions of OFCOM. Also, as noted above, the Competition Act confers upon the sectoral regulators, including OFCOM as regards electronic communications and broadcasting, the power to apply the Chapters I and II prohibitions concurrently with the OFT.

8.3   ANTI-COMPETITIVE AGREEMENTS[6]

The most important operative part of the Competition Act Chapter I prohibition (s 2(1)) provides that:

'... agreements between undertakings, decisions by associations of undertakings or concerted practices which –

(a)   may affect trade within the United Kingdom, and

(b)   have as their object or effect the prevention, restriction or distortion of competition within the UK,

are prohibited unless they are exempt in accordance with the provisions of this Part...'

A prohibited agreement is void unless it is exempted. Article 81 is in almost identical terms – the key difference with Chapter I is that in order to be contrary to Art 81, an agreement or concerted practice must have a European dimension; more particularly it must have an appreciable actual or potential effect on trade between EU member states.[7] The following sections will consider the constituent parts of the Chapter I prohibition.

8.3.1   Undertakings

Any entity capable of carrying on commercial or economic activities in relation to goods or services will be considered an 'undertaking' for the purposes of the Competition Act. This means that either natural or legal persons can be under-

---

6   See also OFT Guideline 401 on Agreements and Concerted Practices.
7   Save for this difference between the Chapter I prohibition and Art 81, the interpretation of the two provisions is the same (in the light of s 60 of the Competition Act 1998). Throughout the remainder of the chapter, references to the Chapter I prohibition should be read as references to both it and Art 81 unless otherwise specified.

takings, whether they are companies, partnerships, sole traders, co-operatives or even charities.

Although a wide range of entities can be undertakings, where two undertakings form part of a single economic unit, for example parent and subsidiary companies, agreements between them are not relevant for the purposes of Chapter I. This means that arrangements between subsidiaries and parents can include provisions which, if they formed part of an agreement between independent companies, would fall foul of Chapter I.[8]

8.3.2   Agreements and concerted practices

Just as the term 'undertaking' is widely drawn, so is the term 'agreement'. In fact, it is hard to distinguish from the European case law what is an agreement and what is a concerted practice. Since nothing hinges on identifying arrangements as one or the other, trying to draw a clear distinction is a sterile exercise.

It is clear that for the purposes of Chapter I, 'agreement' includes far more than just enforceable contracts as defined by English law; gentlemen's agreements are also covered. More informal co-operation or understandings between undertakings also fall within the scope of the Chapter I prohibition, although they are usually referred to as concerted practices. The breadth of these terms reflects the fact that anti-competitive behaviour may be arranged by a 'nod and a wink', rather than through laboriously drafted contracts. As Adam Smith observed in his oft-quoted comment, 'people of the same trade seldom meet together, even for merriment and diversion, but the conversation ends in a conspiracy against the public, or in some contrivance to raise prices'.[9]

When the OFT considers whether there is a concerted practice between undertakings, it will look at whether there have been contacts between the parties; regular gatherings of competitors in obscure hotels, and frequent emails marked 'Private and Confidential', tend to raise suspicions rapidly. It will also consider whether the behaviour of the parties has affected the market in which they are operating in ways that might not be dictated by market forces. Deciding whether this is the case tends to depend on a relatively complex analysis of the nature of the market, the type and number of competitors, their cost structures and their overall pricing behaviour. Inferences can be drawn from competitor meetings followed by parallel actions.

8.3.3   Decisions of associations of undertakings[10]

Both 'association of undertakings' and 'decision' are broadly applied and the scope of the provision is not limited to any particular form of membership structure or to any particular type of resolution by the members. This element of the

---

8   See Case 22/71 *Beguelin Import v GL Import Export* [1972] CMLR 81.
9   Adam Smith, *The Wealth of Nations*, Book 1, Ch X.
10   See also OFT Guideline 408 Trade Associations, Professions and Self-Regulating Bodies.

prohibition covers trade associations and other standard-setting bodies that have trade members. The decisions in question may be parts of the constitutions of these associations or may be mere recommendations which, although not enforced, are generally applied. The key issue is whether the decision in question limits the freedom of the members in relation to some commercial matter.

In industries, such as those associated with the Internet, where standard-setting may be important and may be achieved by associations of companies which are otherwise direct competitors, it is important to note that competition law applies just as it would to bilateral agreements between the individual companies. Of course, agreements to create truly open standards are generally highly pro-competitive. Therefore, even if they fell within the scope of the Chapter I prohibition, they might well be exempted.

8.3.4   May affect trade

This requirement is often a key threshold over which small agreements do not pass in the context of European law, where it is necessary to show that trade between EU member states is affected and that the repercussions are not simply domestic. However, this is less significant since the introduction of the Competition Act for agreements with purely domestic effects.

8.3.5   Jurisdiction

Although the Chapter I prohibition is a domestic law provision, it applies to any agreement or arrangement which 'is, or is intended to be, implemented in the United Kingdom'[11] (or part of it). This means that even if the parties to the arrangement are not situated within the UK, or the agreement is not governed by UK law, it can still fall foul of the Chapter I prohibition.

If companies are based outside the UK but the anti-competitive arrangement relates to supplies of goods or services made in the UK, such an arrangement will be prohibited. In the context of the global Internet industry, the nature of the UK courts' jurisdiction is important. Even if you are based in California and you enter into an agreement with a company in Moscow, but which is implemented in the UK, your agreement may be caught. A similar approach to jurisdiction is adopted at European level – if the agreement in question affects trade within the EU, it can be caught by Art 81. This extended jurisdiction reflects the judgment of the European Court of Justice in the *Woodpulp* case.[12]

11   Competition Act 1998, s 2(3).
12   See Cases 114, 125-129/85 *Ahlstrom v EC Commission* (woodpulp) [1988] ECR 5193.

8.3.6   Object or effect

It is sufficient that an agreement have either an 'object' or an 'effect' that is anti-competitive: it need not have both. Consideration should first be given to the object of the agreement in the economic context in which it is to be operated. An agreement that is never implemented may still be held to infringe Chapter I if it has a clearly anti-competitive object, for example a price-fixing or market-sharing agreement.

Where, however, the analysis of the object of the agreement does not reveal an obvious anti-competitive objective, it is then necessary to look at its effect, taking account of all surrounding factors and, in particular, the economic context of the agreement. Factors in such an analysis include the market shares of the parties in the relevant markets, whether the agreement is part of a network of similar agreements, and the state of competition in the market in the absence of the agreement in question.

8.3.7   Prevention, restriction or distortion of competition

What constitutes an illegitimate constraint on competition is a question at the heart of all competition law systems. Most agreements are pro-competitive, in that they facilitate economic activity. The Chapter I prohibition and Art 81 provide identical lists of examples of behaviour which may be caught:

8.3.7.1   *Directly or indirectly fixing purchasing or selling prices*

Fixing purchasing or selling prices is almost certain to infringe the prohibition. Formation of a price cartel is a serious infringement under this head, but prices can also be fixed by, for example, agreement to adhere to published price lists or to forewarn competitors of intended price rises. Similarly, prices may be indirectly affected by agreeing to limit discounts or credit terms or charges for transportation.

Where companies exchange price information (or other relevant data such as their strategies) so that uncertainties in the market are removed, such arrangements may also be contrary to the prohibition. Whether such information-sharing has an anti-competitive effect will depend upon the nature of the market in question and the information exchanged – where there are a small number of competitors in a market for relatively undifferentiated products and sensitive sales information is exchanged, the authorities are likely to consider it unacceptable.

It has been suggested by some that Internet business-to-business ('B2B') marketplaces may be the 'smoke-filled rooms' of the twenty-first century – the places where competing undertakings get together, share information and collude, in particular, on pricing. In principle, the regulatory authorities treat the possibility of cartel-like behaviour in B2Bs in the same way as in any other industry. They consider the structure of the arrangement, the levels and types of information passing between the members and, in the context of price fixing, the levels of prices being charged and the basis upon which changes occur.

In none of the cases that has come before the European Commission in relation to B2Bs (whether under Art 81 or the EC Merger Regulation) has there been any finding of collusion between parties. That, of course, is not surprising since the European Commission was scrutinising the arrangements at their outset before they had been put into practice.[13] Nonetheless, in the *Volbroker*[14] case the European Commission required that conditions be complied with to prevent unnecessary risk of collusion or information-sharing before an agreement between major banks to establish a foreign exchange B2B could be approved.

Volbroker.com was created through an agreement between subsidiaries of six major banks which were market makers in the market for foreign currency options. It provided the first brokerage service to bring automated trading in foreign currency options for banks. The parent banks sought clearance under Art 81 from the European Commission (note that since the Modernisation Regulation came into force on 1 May 2004, notifications for clearance under Art 81 have not been available – contractual parties must generally 'self-assess' their agreements' compatibility with Art 81, assisted by their advisers). The parent banks secured a comfort letter (informal clearance) for the arrangements on the basis of the following assurances:

1. none of Volbroker.com's staff or management would have any contractual or other obligations towards any of the parent banks (and vice versa);

2. Volbroker.com's staff and management would be in a geographically distinct location;

3. the representatives of the parent banks who sat on Volbroker.com's board of directors would not have access to commercially sensitive information relating to each other or to third parties;

4. the parents would not have access to the information technology and communication systems of Volbroker.com; and

5. the parent banks would ensure that staff and management understood the importance of keeping commercially sensitive information confidential and that sanctions for breach were spelt out.

8.3.7.2   Limiting or controlling production, markets, technical development or investment

In economic terms, limiting output has a similar detrimental effect to raising prices. Output restrictions are, therefore, treated with similar severity to price fixing arrangements. In the context of high technology Internet-related business, agreements to restrict the development of new products and innovations could clearly inhibit competition and retard the development of the market. Although in many circumstances agreements between undertakings to set standards may

---

13   See, for example, COMP/M 1969 UTC/Honeywell/i2/myaircraft.com decision of 4 August 2000.
14   See Commission Press Release 31 July 2000, IP/00/896.

reduce waste and consumers' search costs, such agreements can restrict competition by reducing the scope for innovation.

8.3.7.3   Sharing markets or sources of supply

Competitors dividing up markets, whether into geographical sectors or by types of customer, means that there is in principle a loss of competition. A customer in a particular area (or particular group) has less choice and the incumbent supplier is insulated from competitive pressures which would drive down prices, increase levels of service or increase choice of products.

In the US, a challenge was brought (under US antitrust law) against the 'Baby Bell' telecoms companies[15] for their alleged formation of a cartel to dominate the Internet yellow pages market.[16] The key allegations were that: (a) the various telecoms companies had agreed amongst themselves to share geographical markets across the US and control essential points of access to the Internet; and (b) major ISPs had made agreements with the telecoms companies to exclude competitors, including GTE New Media, by giving prominence to their own yellow pages on the ISPs' guides. The matter was settled before it came to court, but it illustrates how market sharing arrangements may be challenged in the context of Internet-related activity.

8.3.7.4   Discriminating between customers

Whether on the basis of price or the conditions of sale, discriminating between customers may place certain customers at a competitive disadvantage and thereby distort the operation of the market. In particular, where a trade association or other association of undertakings sets prices or conditions for sales between its members different from those it sets for non-members, the arrangement may infringe the prohibition.

8.3.7.5   Attaching supplementary obligations unconnected to the subject of the agreement

This may also infringe the Chapter I prohibition. In other words, burdening companies with obligations which are irrelevant to the subject-matter of the principal transaction may be anti-competitive.

8.3.8   Appreciability

The arrangements in question must not just affect competition in the relevant market; they must affect competition to an appreciable extent.[17]

---

15   The regional companies which resulted from the break-up of certain parts of AT&T ordered in 1984.

16   *GTE New Media Services Inc v Ameritech Corpn* (DDC complaint filed 6 October 1997).

17   See, for example, *Volk v Vervaecke* Case 5/69 [1969] ECR 295.

The European Commission notice on agreements of minor importance[18] sets out a 'safe harbour' for appreciability based on the market shares of contracting parties: 10 per cent combined market share if they are actual or potential competitors, and 15 per cent market share for either party if they are not actual or potential competitors. The OFT follows the same approach to appreciability when applying Chapter I.[19] The thresholds are reduced to 5 per cent if there are parallel networks of similar agreements operating in a substantial part of the market. In addition, the safe harbours do not apply to agreements containing 'hardcore restrictions', i.e. (a) competitors directly or indirectly fixing prices, sharing markets or limiting production or (b) suppliers restricting resellers' ability to determine resale prices or the customers to, or territories in which, they sell. Furthermore, in applying these tests, it is often difficult to decide what is the 'relevant market'.

8.3.9 Market definition

Market definition is a vexed question which has bedevilled the application of competition law throughout the world. There is, however, a general consensus between US, European and UK competition authorities as to how the analysis should generally be carried out.[20]

A market has two key dimensions: product and geography. It is necessary to identify the group of products with which the products at issue compete, and the geographical area within which they compete. Formally, these dimensions are identified by applying what is known as the 'hypothetical monopolist' test. This works as follows: you define the smallest group of products (and geographical area) which, if it was controlled by a single (hypothetical) company, would allow that company to raise prices by a small but significant amount (5–10 per cent) for the foreseeable future.[21]

If the hypothetical monopolist can raise prices by 5–10 per cent for the foreseeable future that means that (a) consumers do not consider other products to be substitutes for the products over which there is a monopoly (demand-side substitution), and (b) new suppliers would not enter the market to produce the products which the monopolist controls (supply-side substitution). If consumers could switch to other products then the hypothetical monopolist could not sustain higher prices (and maintain his profits). Similarly, if new suppliers could enter the market, the new suppliers could charge lower prices and again, the hypothetical monopolist could not impose prices 5–10 per cent above competitive levels.

18 Notice on agreements of minor importance which do not appreciably restrict competition under Art 81, OJ [2001] C 368/13.
19 See OFT Guideline 401 on Agreements and Concerted Practices, paragraphs 2.16 to 2.21.
20 See OFT Guideline 403 market definition, Commission Notice on the definition of the market for the purposes of Community competition law [1997] OJ C 372/5; and the Department of Justice and Federal Trade Commission Horizontal Merger Guidelines 1992.
21 This test is sometimes referred to as the 'SSNIP' test – Small but Significant, Non-transitory Increase in Price.

In order to run the test it is necessary to consider whether there are any substitutes for the product or service at issue in the eyes of customers, and whether a rival supplier of similar products or services could enter the market if prices were raised so that the hypothetical monopolist was making excessive profits. This is where the nice neat test becomes rather difficult to apply, for two reasons: first, it is often difficult to gather evidence to support a particular result of the thought-experiment; second, if the company at issue is already charging monopoly prices then when you run the experiment you might consider that people are switching to substitute products when in fact they are just giving up on that product and turning to different activities. From the subject matter of the American case in which this latter problem first arose, this is known as the 'cellophane fallacy'.[22]

The European Commission has considered the nature of the relevant market in a number of cases involving the Internet, a number of them mergers. Although each case must be considered on its own merits and there is no formal system of precedents with competition authority decisions, the following examples are useful illustrations of how Internet-related markets have been defined.

The *Worldcom/MCI* merger[23] was only approved on the undertaking that MCI divest itself of its Internet business. Initially, the parties argued that other forms of data transmission were a substitute in the eyes of consumers for Internet services. The Commission quickly rejected this suggestion because customers purchasing an Internet access service do so in the expectation that they will be able to access the full range of services available on the Internet and make contact with all other users. While one-to-one data transmission systems might enable customers to perform certain tasks outside the Internet, it would not provide 'the permanent, unfettered access to the community of Internet users which is the main purpose of buying the service'.[24] Accordingly, on the demand-side there was no substitute for the Internet.

The Commission then went on to consider whether these two large telecoms companies, which had substantial fibre networks carrying Internet traffic, were in a narrower market than that for Internet access services. The Commission held that the structure of the market was in fact hierarchical: there was a tier of top-level ISPs, a group of ISPs with smaller networks and then ISPs who simply resell access to other ISPs' networks. If top-level ISPs raised the prices of their Internet connection services by 5 per cent, resellers would have to keep using their systems and so would pay the increase and, in due course, pass it on to consumers. Smaller ISPs would also have to continue to deal with the top-level ISPs if a price rise was imposed and so would not act as a competitive constraint on the top-level ISPs.

In terms of geography, the Commission found that for top-level ISPs the market was global because, although they were based in the US, they operated at an international level providing services throughout the world.

---

22   *United States v Dupont* (cellophane) (351 US 377 (1956)).
23   IV/M 1069 *Re Concentration between Worldcom Inc and MCI Communications Corpn* [1999] 5 CMLR 876.
24   IV/M 1069 *Re Concentration between Worldcom Inc and MCI Communications Corpn* [1999] 5 CMLR 876 at 894.

The Commission has recognised that different Internet-related services can constitute different product markets. In the *Telia/Telenor/Schibsted* case[25] it distinguished the market for Internet access from those for paid-content, e.g. games, special news services and for Internet advertising. It also recognised the weight of the parties' argument that website production services may be a sufficiently technical and specialised activity to constitute a separate market.

In addition to distinguishing between different Internet-related services, the Commission has also distinguished the Internet provision of services from other channels. The *Bertelsmann/Mondadori*[26] case concerned two major publishing enterprises wishing to create a joint venture to combine their respective book club activities.[27] Although the Commission did not have to reach a final conclusion on market definition, it considered that it might be possible to distinguish between 'distant selling' of books (including book club sales, mail order and Internet sales) and the retail sale of books. This reasoning follows the earlier decision in *Advent/EMI/WH Smith*,[28] where a similar distinction between the distant selling and retail selling of books was drawn. Were a distinction between Internet and traditional sales channels to be sustained, it could have a profound impact upon the competitive analysis of Internet retailers: if the Internet is a separate market from retail, Internet retailers will be considered to have far larger market shares than would otherwise be the case.

However, the above cases can be contrasted with the more recent views of the OFT and the Competition Commission in the UK on the *HMV/Ottakar's* merger – while the OFT noted only a limited degree of competitive constraint exercised by Internet retailers on traditional retailers, principally in relation to pricing, on referral the Competition Commission went significantly further in ruling that no separate market for online book retailing exists.[29] It is already apparent, both at UK and European level, that where price sensitivity is a particular feature of a market, it is becoming more likely that Internet sales channels may be found to exercise competitive restraints on traditional channels – see, for example, the Commission decision in *Karstadtquelle/Mytravel*[30] (package holiday retail), and the OFT decisions in *Staples/Globus Office World*[31] (office supplies) and *O2/The Link*[32] (mobile phone retailing). Conversely, where the consumer experience is

---

25 IV/JV 1 *Telia/Telenor/Schibsted* (27 May 1998, unreported). See also IV/JV 5 *Cegetel/Canal+/AOL/Bertelsmann* (4 August 1998, unreported); IV/JV 11 *@Home Benelux* (15 September 1998, unreported); and *DeTeOnline/Axel Springer/Holtzbrink/Internet Corpn* (12 October 1998, unreported).

26 IV/M 1407 *Bertelsman/Mondadori* OJ C 145 26/05/1999.

27 In relation to the geographical extent of the market, emphasis was placed on language barriers and the market limited to Italy. See also Case No IV/M 1459 *Bertelsmann/Havas/BOL* (6 May 1999, unreported).

28 IV/M 1112 Advent International/EMI/WH Smith OJ C 172 06/06/1998. See also, in the context of catalogue sales, IV/M 0070 *Otto/Grattan* OJ C 093 11/04/1991.

29 OFT, *Anticipated acquisition by HMV Group plc, through Waterstone's Limited, of Ottakar's plc*, 6 December 2005, and Competition Commission, *Proposed acquisition of Ottakar's plc by HMV Group plc through Waterstone's Booksellers Limited*, 12 May 2006.

30 COMP/M.4601 *Karstadtquelle/Mytravel*, 04/05/2007.

31 OFT, *Proposed acquisition by Staples Inc of Globus Office World plc*, 21 July 2004.

32 OFT, *Completed acquisition by O2 UK Limited of the Link Stores Limited*, 10 October 2006.

fundamentally different between the online and offline worlds, as the OFT has found in a number of gambling-related cases (see *William Hill/Stanley Leisure*[33] and *Gala Group/Coral Eurobet*[34]), distinctions between the different channels may endure.

In the *myaircraft.com* case,[35] which concerned the creation of a B2B market place for aircraft parts and attendant services, the parties argued that the provision of aircraft parts and services over the Internet was part of the general market for aircraft parts and services: 'e-commerce should be considered as one segment among the many modalities by which companies transact business'. Although the Commission did not find it necessary to make a definitive finding upon the relevant market, the competitive assessment of the arrangements takes into account the position of the participants in the general market for aircraft parts and services, not just Internet-based sales.

At the time of writing, Google's proposed acquisition of Internet advertising sales house DoubleClick had just been notified to the European Commission.[36] Whether or not the Commission identifies issues with that acquisition will depend on how the relevant market(s) are defined. Google argues its online search advertising business and DoubleClick's online graphical advertising activities belong to separate markets, and as such their merger would not alter the position in either of those markets. Conversely, a finding of a wider market for online search advertising in general might lead to the creation or strengthening of a dominant position by Google/DoubleClick.

8.3.10   Convergence

A particular manifestation of the way in which the Internet changes the competitive structure of other industries is seen in what is referred to in the jargon as 'convergence'. Televisions, computers and telephones are increasingly able to perform similar functions as digital technology develops. We can access the Internet through our televisions and mobile phones and equally access television and make phone calls through our computers.

From the competition law point of view, the key issue is that those people wanting to provide television programming, telecommunications links or online shopping will have a variety of routes by which they can reach the consumer. The result is that different infrastructure systems (or 'platforms') may be competing against one another for business.

When considering whether the activities of Internet businesses are anti-competitive it may be necessary to consider not just the market for Internet provision of the relevant services or products but also other distribution mechanisms.

---

33   OFT, *Completed acqusition by William Hill plc of the licensed betting office business of Stanley plc*, 1 August 2005.

34   OFT, *Completed acquisition by Gala Group of Coral Eurobet Group*, 10 January 2006.

35   COMP/M 1969 *UTC/Honeywell/i2/myaircraft.com* decision of 4 August 2000.

36   COMP/M.4731 *Google/DoubleClick*, notified 21 September 2007.

Equally, it means that agreements or mergers between businesses which have little or no overlap in their existing activities require close scrutiny because each set of activities reinforces the other in the convergent world.[37] A particular example of this was provided by the acquisition by BSkyB, nominally a satellite TV broadcaster and channel supplier, of retail broadband provider Easynet. The OFT noted the opportunity presented to BSkyB to begin to provide 'triple-play' services, and leverage its dominance in premium TV content to its advantage in the market for Internet service provision, in part by providing its content over the Internet.[38]

British Interactive Broadcasting (which traded as 'Open') was a joint venture whose parents were BSkyB, British Telecom, HSBC and Matsushita. It was established to provide digital interactive television services to consumers in the UK. Using BSkyB's digital satellite broadcasting system and BT's telecommunications network, consumers were able to access a range of interactive services, including home banking, home shopping and a limited 'walled garden' of websites. Upon review of the joint venture, the European Commission found that there was a separate market for the supply of interactive services via the television as distinct from via computers or indeed through high street retailers.[39] It is unsurprising that the supply of services (and goods) from high street retailers was not considered a substitute for interactive services accessible from the comfort of your own home using the television.

Rather more surprising is the distinction between interactive services accessed through a computer and those accessed through the television. The Commission concluded that a small but significant increase in the prices of interactive television services could be sustained. The possibility of accessing such services through a computer would not constrain prices for two reasons: first, only 25 per cent of households in the UK had computers; and secondly, the cost of switching between television and computer is high because a whole PC system had to be bought. A further reason adduced was that TVs are traditionally found in the living room and are a focal point of family life, whereas computers are tucked away elsewhere. The characteristics of the use of the television therefore meant that people would not start using computers as a substitute.

As convergence continues, this may be found to be an untenable distinction in future cases. The traditionally defined roles of the television and computers are rapidly eroding, and people are increasingly using computers for receiving films

37 The Time Warner/AOL merger is the most poignant example of this phenomenon. Time Warner had relatively limited Internet interests but was a major broadcaster with access to substantial valuable content. AOL had large numbers of people to whom they were ISP and to whom they wished to provide content. By merging, Time Warner was able to provide content which AOL lacked to AOL's subscribers using Internet technology. See below and Commission Press Release IP/00/1145 of 11 October 2000, 'Commission gives conditional approval to AOL/Time Warner merger'.

38 OFT, *Anticipated acquisition by BSkyB Broadband Services Limited of Easynet Group plc*, 30 December 2005.

39 IV/36.539 *British Interactive Broadcasting/Open* [1999] OJ L312/1. See also comment upon the decision by Andres Font Galarza in the Competition Policy Newsletter [1999] No 3 October.

and other entertainment. At a certain point, substitution will be sufficient to widen the relevant market. As above, the *BSkyB/Easynet* merger presages the possibility of premium content, e.g. a BSkyB sports channel, being delivered by a number of different delivery methods. Note also the interventions by the European Commission to break up the sale of football rights, including requiring the separation of broadcasting rights over the different platforms of traditional television, Internet and mobile phone and, in the case of the UEFA Champions League rights, enforcing the simulcasting of matches over the Internet.[40] The capacity for substitution between the different platforms is bound to grow as the technological capabilities of the new media develop and catch on among consumers.

A more sustainable distinction might be that which the Commission drew between interactive television services, pay television and free-to-air television.[41] The idea that free-to-air television does not constrain the pricing of pay television is widely accepted (although not uncontroversial) – it is easy to argue that if free-to-air TV was a substitute for pay TV, everyone would watch free TV because everyone prefers not to pay. The distinction drawn between pay TV services, which are principally entertainment services, and interactive TV services, which are largely transactional or information-providing, is perhaps more interesting. The Commission considered that interactive TV was a complement to pay TV, not a substitute.

Note also in the context of the pay television market that the Commission distinguished between the wholesale supply of films and sports channels and other pay TV content. Films and sports channels are often referred to as 'premium' channels due to their higher pricing as compared with basic channels. This higher pricing itself tends to indicate a separate market for such services.[42] It also vindicates the hackneyed new media saying that 'content is king'.

Finally, the Commission considered the infrastructure market. Commentators have suggested that cable networks have had a significant technological advantage over satellite broadcasting systems since satellite systems lack a simple 'return path' – a route by which the viewer can easily communicate with the broadcaster. By linking BSkyB's satellite broadcasting system to the narrowband telephone network, Open was able to compete against the UK cable system by providing a return path which enabled interactivity between consumers and the service providers. The Commission concluded that Open was, therefore, competing in an infrastructure market which included the BT copper wire network and the fibre cable network. Notably, mobile networks were excluded from the market definition.

---

40   See COMP/C.2-37.398 – Joint selling of the commercial rights of the UEFA Champions League, COMP/C.2-38.173 and 38.453 Joint selling of the media rights of the FA Premier League on an exclusive basis, and COMP/C.2/37.214 – Joint selling of the media rights to the German Bundesliga.

41   Free-to-air: programming that customers do not have to pay a subscription for such as ITV1 and BBC1.

42   A similar distinction was drawn by the UK Monopolies and Mergers Commission in its report on the proposed merger between BSkyB and Manchester United [1999] Cm 4305, in particular, paras 2.25–2.51.

8.3.11 Exemptions[43]

Article 81(3) provides that certain agreements which meet the above criteria, i.e. they appreciably prevent, restrict or distort competition, can be exempted from the adverse consequences of falling foul of the prohibition. There are two types of exemption available under European law: individual exemptions and block exemptions. The Chapter I prohibition has a parallel system of exemptions.

8.3.11.1 Individual exemptions

An agreement which appreciably prevents, restricts or distorts competition will nevertheless benefit from an individual exemption from Art 81 and Chapter I if it meets the following Art 81(3) criteria:

1. contributes to the improvement of production or distribution or promotes technical or economic progress;

2. provides consumers with a 'fair share' of these benefits;

3. does not impose on the parties restrictions which are not indispensable to the attainment of the objectives specified; and

4. does not eliminate competition in respect of a substantial part of the products in question.

Although this test is stringent, it is essentially carrying out a balancing exercise: do the pro-competitive aspects outweigh the restrictions of competition, and are all the restrictions included in the agreement necessary to achieve the pro-competitive ends?

As noted above, since the Modernisation Regulation came into force on 1 May 2004, it is no longer possible to apply to the European Commission or UK OFT for a formal or informal individual exemption (although they may give informal advice in cases resolving novel or unresolved questions of law) – contractual parties must generally 'self-assess' their agreements' compatibility with Art 81, assisted by their advisers.

The creation by several airlines of the online travel website Opodo generated complaints to the European Commission. As part of a settlement to close the case, the shareholders of Opodo gave various undertakings in order to satisfy the Art 81(3) criteria:[44]

1. they should not discriminate against other travel agents in favour of Opodo;

2. access to Opodo should not be restricted to shareholder airlines, and Opodo should treat all airlines equally: i.e. Opodo should not favour shareholder

---

43 These exemptions are subject to 'clawback' provisions which enable the relevant authorities to remove their protection in certain circumstances.
44 Comp/A.38.321 TQ3/OPODO.

airlines over non-shareholder airlines (unless there is an objective commercial basis for doing so); and

3.   the shareholders of Opodo should deal with Opodo on a strictly commercial basis, i.e. commercially sensitive information should not flow between the shareholders of Opodo through Opodo.

8.3.11.2   Block exemptions

There is a range of block exemptions covering, amongst other things, exclusive distribution, exclusive purchasing and franchising (all vertical agreements),[45] research and development,[46] specialisation[47] and technology transfer agreements.[48] These block exemptions provide 'safe harbours' as long as certain criteria are met. Most importantly, the agreements must not contain certain specified 'hardcore restrictions'. The block exemption will not apply to the agreement if such clauses are included. Furthermore, in most instances such clauses will be deemed to restrict competition and will not benefit from an exemption and therefore will infringe Art 81 or Chapter I.

The vertical agreements block exemption covers a wide range of agreements between parties at different levels in the production and distribution chain. Agreements containing restrictions on resale prices or 'passive sales' (sales where the customer approaches the supplier, rather than where the supplier has touted for the customer's business) are not covered by the block exemption and would be considered hardcore. Furthermore, where the supplier (or, in certain circumstances, the buyer) has 30 per cent or more of the relevant market for the products at issue, it cannot benefit from block exemption protection.

The guidelines accompanying the block exemption indicate that the use of the Internet to advertise or sell products is, in general, considered a form of passive sales insofar as the website is not directed towards a territory or customer group exclusively allocated to another distributor. Agreements which prevent any use of websites would therefore generally not benefit from the protection of the vertical restraints block exemption and such a restriction would be considered hardcore. However, there are exceptions: Internet sales can be banned if there is an objective justification, such as perhaps health and safety grounds; and the use of links or on-site advertising which specifically target customers allocated to other distributors are permissible.[49] In addition, a supplier may restrict Internet sales by imposing quality standards, particularly when it has established a 'selective distribution' system, i.e. where the supplier has selected its distributors on the basis of objective criteria, such as service quality or nature of premises. The Commission has in the past accepted a prohibition on Internet-only distributors

---

45   Commission Regulation on the application of Art 81(3) of the EC Treaty to categories of vertical agreements and concerted practices [1999] OJ L336/21 and accompanying guidelines, [2000] OJ C 291/1.
46   Reg 417/85.
47   Reg 418/85.
48   Reg 772/2004.
49   European Commission Vertical Agreements Guidelines, [2000] OJ C 291/1, para 51.

for luxury goods.[50] However, the Commission has also fined Yamaha €2.56 million for various infringements of competition law, including an obligation on its dealers to notify Yamaha before exporting any of its products via the Internet.[51]

8.4   ANTI-COMPETITIVE CONDUCT

Section 8.3 of this chapter considered the prohibitions against anti-competitive agreements contained in Art 81 of the EC Treaty and Chapter I of the Competition Act. This section considers the prohibitions against anti-competitive conduct contained in Art 82 and Chapter II. The Chapter II prohibition (s 18) provides that:

> 'any conduct on the part of one or more undertakings which amounts to the abuse of a dominant position in a market is prohibited if it may affect trade within the United Kingdom.'

The only significant difference between this provision and Art 82 is that Art 82 refers to a dominant position 'within the common market or in a substantial part of it', and requires an effect on trade between member states. Under domestic law, a dominant position means a dominant position within the UK or part of it.[52]

8.4.1   Dominance

The definition of a dominant position which has been applied in European case law and, by virtue of s 60 of the Competition Act, also applies under UK competition law, was given in the *United Brands* case,[53] where the European Court of Justice stated that a dominant position is:

> 'a position of economic strength enjoyed by an undertaking which enables it to prevent effective competition being maintained on the relevant market by affording it the power to behave to an appreciable extent independently of its competitors, customers and ultimately of its consumers'.

'Dominance' is assessed in the context of a particular market, therefore the issue of market definition raises its ugly head again. The market definition considerations discussed at section 8.3.9 above in the context of Chapter I/Art 81 apply equally in the context of Chapter II/Art 82.

8.4.1.1   Market share

OFT guidance notes the (rebuttable) presumption of dominance under both EU and UK law, where a market share remains persistently over 50 per cent. OFT

---

50   *Yves Saint Laurent Parfums*, European Commission press release of 17 May 2001, IP/01/713.
51   *PO/Yamaha*, COMP/37.975.
52   Competition Act 1998, s 18(3).
53   Case 27/76 *United Brands v EC Commission* [1978] ECR 207 at 277.

guidance also states that it is unlikely that a market share of below 40 per cent would amount to (single firm) dominance, although this also depends on other factors.[54] Much will depend upon the structure of the market in question – for example, if the undertaking in question is the only large player in the market and competition comes from far smaller players, it is more likely that a finding of dominance will be made. Countervailing buyer power and the existence of barriers to entry and expansion by competitors are also key factors.

8.4.1.2   Growth and innovation

In addition to considering market shares, it is important to look at the nature of the market for the products or services in question. If there are low barriers to entry for new competitors and there is a great deal of innovation in the market, a company with a large market share at any particular moment might quickly see it diminished.

Almost all sectors of Internet-related activity are highly innovative. The hardware and software which enables people to use the Internet evolves rapidly. Processor speeds have increased rapidly whilst prices have fallen. Routers and switching systems manage greater and greater volumes of traffic. Applications software from accountancy packages to browsers is constantly changing and improving.

This rapid change and rapid growth has significant implications for the application of any competition law system. Where products and services are constantly evolving, it tends to be more difficult for any one company to secure the sort of market power which will enable it to distort the proper functioning of the market. Although a product may be very popular at a particular time, the possibility of a new, more advanced, product coming in and replacing it in the near future is higher in dynamic high-technology markets. Although there may be concerns about the manner in which such markets operate from time to time, authorities should be slow to intervene because dynamic markets may well rectify their own problems within a short time.

In addition, there are major practical problems with intervention in dynamic markets. First, it is often hard to gather sufficient quantities of useful data to enable a regulator to gain an accurate picture of how the market is operating. Second, any regulatory intervention tends to take time for consideration and implementation. By the time a conclusion is reached that intervention is necessary, the market may have moved on and, whilst the proposed solution might have been appropriate months or years ago, it may be past its sell-by-date before it can be implemented.

8.4.1.2.1   Network effects

There are certain features of Internet-related industries which might incline authorities to intervene. The Internet is a network of networks which is dependent upon common language, protocols and applications in order to confer benefits on individuals. As more people adopt a particular standard, the more value it has to all those using it as a network grows. Each new potential user will have a greater incentive to adopt the standard. The phenomenon is referred to as Metcalfe's Law: the value of a network to its users grows exponentially with the addition of each new user. It is known by competition lawyers as a 'positive network effect'. In practice, it means that if you can be the first to get an application into the market so that you build up a base of users, it is more likely that your application, rather than a competing application, will become the industry standard. In other words, by getting a good start in the market, you can have significant advantages in securing a powerful market position.

Any competition regulator would prefer to stop competition problems before they start. Early intervention to prevent any individual or group of individuals getting undue power in the marketplace is better than waiting until they have market power and actually use it to distort competition. By that time, many potential competitors may have already suffered, and potential entrants will have been deterred. It tends to require government with a very heavy hand, to unravel monopolies. There is, therefore, a temptation for regulators to step in earlier on in the development of a market which exhibits network effects in order to prevent those effects maintaining a monster (in competition terms). The existence of network effects for operating systems was an important motivating factor for the European Commission in investigating Microsoft, which led to an abuse of dominance decision, subsequently upheld on substantive grounds by the European Court of First Instance ('CFI') – see section 8.4.2.8 below.[55]

Network effects in an Internet-related market may be reinforced where the market is in knowledge-based products or services. In such markets marginal costs may be zero. For example, once you have made the effort to produce some software, the cost of producing an additional copy is negligible. Developing the knowledge may have been expensive and the initial investment in exploitation may have been high, but once those investments have been made, further exploitation is cheap. It is therefore extremely easy to scale-up your operations quickly. Once a company in a market with network effects has a small advantage, it is able to attract new customers more easily than its nearest rival. The company's attractiveness to customers rapidly increases and so its advantage over its rivals extends, allowing it to bring in new customers easily without incurring significant cost.

8.4.1.2.2 Intellectual property rights

One particular matter which is important to the competition law analysis of so-called knowledge-based industries is the role played by intellectual property rights. Although the possession or use of an intellectual property right is not in and of itself anti-competitive, intellectual property law potentially enables companies to develop significant market power by ensuring that nobody else uses their unique hardware, software, ideas or branding.

---

55   COMP/C-3/37.792 *Microsoft*, and Case T-201/04 *Microsoft v Commission*.

The relationship between intellectual property rights and competition law is vexed. A patent, for example, may be seen as a sanctioned monopoly in relation to particular works, products or processes. It is justified on the basis that the prospect of winning such a monopoly encourages innovation and endeavour – if there were no such monopolies, writers and inventors would be unable to reap any benefit from their work, since it would be copied as soon as it became public. The extent of these mini-monopolies is limited by competition law. There is therefore a tension between what intellectual property rights can legitimately be used to achieve, and what is anti-competitive. This tension was at the heart of the *Microsoft* case.

8.4.1.3   Joint dominance

Both Art 82 and Chapter II refer explicitly to 'one or more undertakings' being dominant. This reflects the possibility that, in certain situations, distinct companies considered together are able to act independently of competitive pressures. This concept of joint or collective dominance has been endorsed by the European Courts[56]. In the *Almelo* case[57] the European Court of Justice held that '[i]n order for . . . a collective dominant position to exist the undertakings must be linked in such a way that they adopt the same conduct on the market'. It is clear that contractual links may be sufficient to give rise to a position of joint dominance.

However, other economic links between the parties within a tight oligopoly may be sufficient to result in collective dominance in a market with the appropriate characteristics, in particular in terms of market concentration, transparency and product homogeneity. Where parties are in a position to anticipate one another's behaviour and are therefore strongly encouraged to align their conduct in the market so as to maximise their joint profits by restricting production with a view to increasing prices then collective dominance may exist. In such a context, each trader is party to a 'game' where it is aware that highly competitive action on its part designed to increase its market share (for example a price cut) would provoke identical action by the others, so that it would derive no benefit from its initiative in the long run.[58] Although the possibility of collective dominance existing in markets is recognised, it is in practice difficult to prove[59] and there are very few cases where collective dominance has been found for the purpose of Art 82 or Chapter II.

8.4.2   Abuse

The concept of abuse of a dominant position covers a range of behaviour. As with Art 81 and Chapter I, Art 82 and Chapter II includes a (non-exhaustive) list of

---

56   See, in particular, Case T-68/89 *Societa Italiano Vetro v EC Commission* [1992] ECR II-1403.
57   Case C-393/92 [1994] ECR I-1477.
58   See, in particular, Case T-102/96 *Gencor Ltd v Commission* [1999] ECR II–753 where it was suggested that in certain circumstances companies in oligopolistic markets may have a jointly dominant position even without contractual links.
59   See Case T–342/99 *Airtours v EC Commssion* [2002] 5 CMLR 317.

examples of the types of behaviour which may fall foul of the prohibition.[60] Abuses fall into two broad categories: exploitation of customers ('exploitative abuses') and exclusion of competitors ('exclusionary abuses').

8.4.2.1 Excessive pricing

The classic exploitative abuse, and intuitively the most obvious form of abuse of a dominant position, is excessive pricing. Prices are excessively high where they are above the prices which would be charged by undertakings if the market was competitive.

In *Napp Pharmaceuticals v Director General of Fair Trading*[61] the Competition Commission Appeals Tribunal held that the following methods could be used in assessing whether prices were excessive:

• A comparison of prices against costs.

• A comparison of prices against the costs of the next most profitable competitor.

• A comparison of prices against the prices of competitors.

• A comparison of prices against the undertaking's own prices in other markets.

Precisely how much higher prices would need to be above costs to indicate excess is not clear. In fact, excessive pricing is one of the hardest forms of abuse to prove. Referring to profitability in assessing excessive pricing can be highly unreliable. In the OFT Economic Discussion Paper 377 'Innovation and Competition policy', Charles River Associates state: 'Measuring profitability is a poor way of conducting competition policy in standard industries. It is likely to be even worse in high technology industries. The very high ex ante risks of failure mean that the returns to "winners" in high technology markets should be very high.' At the time of writing, we are not aware of any decisions or judgments involving exclusionary abuses in the Internet/IT sector.

8.4.2.2 Predation

An alternative strategy that a dominant firm might adopt, rather than trying to secure higher profits in the short run by pricing excessively high, is to drop prices, to drive competitors out of the market (predatory pricing – an exclusionary abuse). The intention of this strategy is that once the competitors are driven out, the incumbent will be free to increase prices and recover the losses it incurred in dropping the prices and go on to make greater profits overall.

---

60   There is no system of exemption for breaches of Art 82/Chapter II. Limited exclusions are provided for in s 19 of the Competition Act 1998 – the key area excluded is mergers and concentrations.

61   [2002] Comp AR 13.

Again, predatory pricing is an abuse which is often difficult to prove. After all, where markets are competitive it would be expected that competitors would drop prices in order to increase market share. Lower prices may simply be a reflection of increased efficiency.

The general rule historically adopted under Art 82 and Chapter II is that where a company prices below its average variable cost of production, i.e. the average of those costs which vary according to the amount of the product produced, predation is to be presumed. The 2005 European Commission Staff Discussion Paper[62] proposed the slightly different cost benchmark of average avoidable costs, i.e. those additional costs that the producer incurs by producing the units at the lower price.

However, in high technology markets, standard price tests are likely to be unhelpful if fixed costs are high and marginal costs are close to zero. As OFT Discussion Paper No 377 points out: 'In one sense, such tests are likely to be far too permissive: they would allow pricing in response to a new entrant that could not possibly be the rational response except for the anti-competitive benefits of exclusion. In another sense such tests are not permissive enough: when competition is for the market, very low penetration pricing may be a perfectly rational and pro-competitive form of competition.'[63]

This 'rational' explanation is often the true state of affairs on the Internet. On the Internet, much content and software is available at no apparent cost to the end-user. What amounts to predation in such markets may, therefore, be more difficult to identify. It has been suggested that the relevant test should focus upon whether the alleged infringer only took the action because of the anti-competitive (often exclusionary) benefits.[64] Nevertheless, in the *Wanadoo* case,[65] the European Commission found Wanadoo (France Telecom) guilty of predation by reference to average variable costs (and average total costs) in the context of the provision of ADSL-based Internet services. Wanadoo was fined €10.35 million.

8.4.2.3   Discrimination

Price discrimination can be both exploitative and exclusionary. This is most easily identified where undertakings charge materially different prices to different categories of customer without a justification for the distinction. Customers might be divided into regional price categories or by type of activity. It should be noted, however, that the prohibition on discriminatory pricing does not mean that discounting structures are prohibited. Discounts are a form of price competition and so are to be encouraged. It is only where a discount structure is not justified by the economies of bulk buying, but is based on a formula which has the effect of rewarding exclusivity, that it is likely to be found to be abusive. Where a dis-

---

62   European Commission, DG Competition discussion paper on the application of Art 82 of the Treaty to exclusionary abuses, December 2005.
63   Para 1.11.
64   OFT Economics Discussion Paper No 377 at para 1.13.
65   COMP/38.233 *Wanadoo Interactive*.

count structure is put in place which is conditional upon customers buying all or a very large proportion of their needs from a dominant undertaking (what are known as 'fidelity discounts'), they will be prohibited because they foreclose the market for other sellers competing with the dominant undertaking. In addition to discrimination on the basis of price, discriminatory terms of sale including access to new developments or updates may constitute an abuse. At the time of writing, Intel has been sent a Statement of Objections by the European Commission in relation to the allegedly exclusionary effect of its rebate structure.[66]

Another form of price discrimination is known as a 'margin squeeze', i.e. where a dominant vertically integrated company sets a margin between its wholesale and retail prices that is insufficient in the sense that an efficient company competing downstream, which buys raw material at the wholesale price, could not make a reasonable return when competing with the dominant firm's downstream retail prices. This can be achieved by the dominant company overcharging its downstream competitors for the raw material and then using the profits achieved to subsidise a lower retail price for its own products in the downstream market than is sustainable by its competitors. In July 2007, the Commission found Telefónica guilty of a margin squeeze in relation to broadband access for competitors to its downstream retail broadband services.[67] Telefónica's competitors in the retail market were not able to operate profitably in the retail market and therefore faced the choice of incurring losses, exiting the market or choosing not to enter the market at all. Telefónica was fined €151,875,000.

8.4.2.4 Vertical restraints

As described above in the context of the Art 81/Chapter I prohibition, the authorities adopt a relatively beneficent approach to vertical restrictions. However, arrangements which might otherwise be exempted by a block exemption can still constitute an abuse of a dominant position. The market power of a dominant player can, for example, render exclusive purchasing and distribution arrangements anti-competitive. Where a dominant undertaking enters into such arrangements, they can foreclose the market to competitors.

8.4.2.5 Tying and bundling

Tying sales of one product or service to another may also constitute an abuse, particularly if the tie is intended to ensure that the customer takes the full range of the producer's goods when, in fact, the customer would prefer to be more selective. The tying together of products is often referred to as 'bundling'. In the *Microsoft* case, one of the findings was that Microsoft had abused its dominant position by bundling its media player product with Windows (see below).

---

66   COMP/37.990 *Intel.*
67   COMP/38.784 *Telefonica SA* (broadband).

8.4.2.6   Refusal to supply

Although it might be thought that anyone is free to do business, or not do business, with whomsoever they choose, dominance can limit this freedom. If a dominant undertaking wants to refuse to supply a customer there must be an objective justification for the refusal to supply. Examples of justifications for refusal to supply include a lack of capacity to make the supply, the cost of dealing making the supply unprofitable or the creditworthiness of the customer being extremely dubious. It is generally far harder to justify the termination of supply to an existing customer than it is to justify the refusal of supply to an entirely new one (save in the case of essential facilities, discussed below). In the *Microsoft* case, the other finding of abuse was the refusal by Microsoft to supply (license) source code information required by competitors to develop products that interoperate with Microsoft's Windows operating system (see below).

8.4.2.7   Access to essential facilities

It has been suggested that in certain circumstances access to facilities controlled by an undertaking are *essential* if someone is to compete in a particular market. It is argued that such access is indispensable where it is not possible (or extremely difficult) to duplicate the facility due to physical, geographic or legal constraints. Proving that a facility is essential tends to be a difficult task.[68]

Where an undertaking controls an essential facility, it is likely to be found to be in a dominant position and that refusal to allow access to the facility on fair terms is likely to constitute an abuse. In the context of the Internet it may be possible to argue (in certain circumstances) that telecommunications networks are essential facilities. In the *Worldcom/MCI* merger case, although the term 'essential facility' was not used, the reasoning of the Commission decision would tend to suggest that the provision of top-level Internet connectivity by ISPs could arguably be an essential facility.

In contrast, in the US, Cyber Promotions, who were sending millions of email advertisements to AOL subscribers, claimed that AOL monopolised the essential facility to advertise to AOL's subscribers using electronic mail.[69] The argument was given short shrift by the court: Cyber could send electronic adverts to AOL subscribers by other means and, in any event, Cyber was not even completely barred from the AOL network. There were no grounds whatsoever for suggesting that the facility was essential. In the *Microsoft* case, the interoperability information was not characterised by the European Commission or the Court of First Instance as an essential facility.

8.4.2.8   Microsoft

The most relevant case relating to abuse of a dominant position involving Internet-related activities is that brought by the European Commission against Microsoft. In 2004, the Commission found under Art 82 that Microsoft had

---

68   See, in particular, Case C-7/97 *Oscar Bronner v Mediaprint* [1998] ECR I-7791.
69   *Cyber Promotions Inc v America Online Inc* 948 F Supp 456 (ED Pa 1996).

abused its dominant position on the operating system market by: (1) refusing to release its interoperability information; and (2) bundling Windows media player ('WMP') with its Windows operating system. The Commission fined Microsoft a record €497 million and required Microsoft to license interoperability information and release a version of Windows without WMP (although it is free to sell this at the same price as the bundled version of Windows).[70] In September 2007, the European Court of First Instance ('CFI') rejected Microsoft's appeal against the Commission's decision, affirming all of the Commission's reasoning on the substance of the case.[71] Microsoft did not appeal against the CFI's decision.

8.4.2.8.1 Refusal to license interoperability information

As explained at section 8.4.2.6 above, failure to supply can be an abuse of a dominant position. The first claim against Microsoft was that it had excluded competitors from the market for work group server operating systems by refusing them interoperability information allowing them to interface with Windows operating system servers. Microsoft argued that the interoperability information was protected by intellectual property rights. For the Commission and the CFI this was debatable, but they took the cautious approach of assuming that the information was protected by intellectual property rights and applied the more stringent regime that applied in such cases (in order to balance the competing needs of protecting competition and stimulating innovation). That regime was established by the European Court of Justice in the cases of *Magill*[72] and *IMS Health*,[73] where it held that a refusal to license an intellectual property right is only an abuse in 'exceptional circumstances', articulated as follows by the CFI in the *Microsoft* case:

1.   The refusal relates to a product or service indispensable to the exercise of a particular activity on a neighbouring market. The 'extraordinary feature' of Microsoft's 90 per cent share of the PC operating systems market was central to the CFI's finding that Microsoft was therefore able to impose the Windows domain architecture as the de facto standard for work group computing. The Commission's market evidence suggested that interoperability with that de facto standard was the primary consideration for purchasers of work group server operating systems, notwithstanding that other products might offer enhanced features.

2.   The refusal is of such a kind as to exclude any effective competition on that neighbouring market. The CFI relaxed the *Magill* and *IMS Health* approach by equating *likelihood* of elimination of competition with *risk* of elimination of competition. Further, the CFI stated that all competition need not be

---

70   COMP/C-3/37.792 *Microsoft*.
71   Case T-201/04 *Microsoft v Commission*.
72   Joined cases C-241/91 P and C-242/91 P *Radio Telefis Eireann (RTE) and Independent Television Publications Ltd (ITP) v Commission (Magill)* [1995] ECR 743 para 55.
73   Case C-418/01, *IMS Health GmbH & Co. OHG v NDC Health GmbH & Co. KG* [2004] ECR I-5039.

eliminated: 'a marginal presence of competitors remaining on the market does not equate to effective competition'. The CFI was influenced by Microsoft's rapid growth, since a late entry into the market, to 65 per cent of market share by 2002 and concluded that its competitors were being confined to marginal positions on the market.

3.   The refusal prevents the appearance of a new product for which there is potential consumer demand. In both *Magill* and *IMS Health*, there was a specific new product, for which there was demonstrable consumer demand, and the emergence of which was rendered impossible by the refusal to license the relevant intellectual property. In response to Microsoft's submissions that the Commission had identified no specific new product, and therefore no corresponding consumer demand, the CFI was obliged to pursue a notably broader interpretation of the new product test. The CFI stated its view that the test includes situations where technical development is limited, i.e. consumer detriment is caused not just by the absence of a specific new product, but by the absence of innovation in general.

4.   There is no objective justification for the abusive behaviour. The CFI concluded that Microsoft's abusive behaviour could not be objectively justified, and disagreed that a requirement to supply would disincentivise innovation. Significant by its absence from the CFI's judgment is an explicit weighing of the 'value' of the relevant intellectual property rights against the need to protect competition, which was a feature of the *Magill* and *IMS Health* judgments, as was the particular effort in those cases to diminish the value of the intellectual property rights (copyright) at issue.

The Commission and Microsoft could not agree about the extent of information that competitors required in order to develop interoperating products. The Commission sought a licence of the operating system 'protocols', while Microsoft argued that this would enable competitors to 'clone' the Windows operating system. The CFI confirmed that the Commission had been correct to assess the required level of interoperability as that which was necessary for a competitor to remain viably on the work group operating systems market – fundamentally, competitors had to be able to interoperate with Windows domain architecture on an equal footing with Windows operating systems. For this, the CFI considered that they needed the protocols and reasoned that this would not enable them to clone the Windows operating system because they would not have the source code.

8.4.2.8.2   Bundling WMP

The second claim against Microsoft was that by bundling its WMP product with its Windows operating systems, the market for streaming media players was effectively foreclosed to its competitors. In its consideration of the bundling abuse, the CFI confirmed that the following five elements were present, and therefore that Microsoft had abused its dominant position under Art 82:

1.   Microsoft was dominant in the market for PC operating systems. This was not disputed by Microsoft.

2. PC operating systems and streaming media players are two separate products. Microsoft argued that media functionality is an integral part of a PC operating system. At trial, Microsoft's advocates brandished the unbundled version of Windows which had sold just 2,000 copies, mocking the notion that Windows and WMP were separable products. However, the CFI noted the presence of alternative, stand-alone media players such as QuickTime and RealPlayer, as well as Microsoft's development and independent marketing of WMP for other operating systems, as indications of the existence of a separate market for media players. The CFI also confirmed that the relevant date for assessment was May 1999 and acknowledged the possibility that changes in consumer expectations may lead consumers in future to expect an operating system to include native media streaming functionality, and as such the operating system and the media player functions may come to constitute one single product.

3. Customers were given no choice to obtain Windows without WMP automatically installed. This deterred OEMs and end users from installing another player, and encouraged the use of WMP at the expense of competing media players, notwithstanding that other players might have been superior.

4. The tying foreclosed competition from alternative streaming media players. Essentially, the CFI agreed with the Commission that the bundling and automatic installation of WMP with Windows guaranteed its ubiquity on personal computers, Windows being installed on 90 per cent of such machines. The effect was to give WMP automatic market penetration without having to compete on the merits with other products. The Commission and the CFI took particular account of RealPlayer's market share, which had been double that of WMP in 1999, and became roughly half that of WMP by 2003. Other media players had no access to a distribution system of comparable efficiency and effectiveness to counterbalance WMP's advantage. The Commission and the CFI also identified significant indirect network effects resulting from the bundling of WMP on the development decisions of content providers and software developers. The desire of such providers to maximise the reach of their own products would favour their writing to the WMP platform, and further consolidate WMP's position as the default streaming media player. The potential which the CFI identified for this to generate knock-on effects on adjacent markets is noted, such as those for media players on wireless devices, set-top boxes, DRM solutions and online music delivery.

5. There was no objective justification for the abusive conduct.

8.4.2.8.3 Commentary

Disputes of a similar nature in the United States (*United States of America v Microsoft Corporation*)[74] were the subject of a settlement in November 2002. In

---

74 *United States of America v. Microsoft Corporation*, Civil Action No. 98-1232 (CKK).

respect of both interoperability and bundling, the US settlement is notably less onerous to Microsoft than the subsequent Commission/CFI rulings in Europe. The difference in approach between Europe and the US to dominance/monopolisation cases in the Internet sector creates an issue for what are often by their nature global markets. The need to comply with local competition law in many different markets presents an unappetising choice: either (1) to pull out of commercially less attractive markets where restrictive enforcement is prevalent, or (2) in the case of restrictive enforcement in commercially critical markets such as Europe, to adopt a 'lowest common denominator' approach by ensuring compliance with the most restrictive jurisdiction in which it operates.

The *Microsoft* judgment is particularly important to technology markets and operators, given the tendency of such markets to coalesce around industry standards. In its response to the CFI ruling, Microsoft stated that the likes of Apple, Google and IBM, being allegedly dominant in other markets of their own, may now be subject to scrutiny by the European regulators, and may be susceptible to accusations of Art 82 abuses relating to their existing practices around proprietary software standards, application diversification and so on. At the very least, the *Microsoft* judgment has been a great boost to the European Commission's confidence, at the time of writing encouraging it to continue pursuing Art 82 cases against Rambus (for an alleged 'patent ambush' in relation to an industry standard for DRAM chips),[75] Intel (for its rebate scheme which is alleged to exclude AMD)[76] and Qualcomm (for its alleged failure to license on FRAND terms in relation to mobile phone chipsets).[77]

8.5   ENFORCEMENT PROCEDURE

8.5.1   Complaints

An interested party can make a complaint to the OFT or sectoral regulators in relation to alleged infringements of the Chapter I and II prohibitions and Arts 81 and 82. In the case of Arts 81 and 82, a complaint can alternatively be made to the European Commission. The European Commission has produced a pro forma for complaints,[78] which should include:

*   information regarding the complainant;

*   details of the alleged infringement and evidence;

*   decision sought and the complainant's legitimate interest; and

*   information about any proceedings before national courts or competition authorities.

---

75   COMP/38.636 *Rambus.*
76   COMP/37.990 *Intel.*
77   COMP/39.247 *Texas Instruments/Qualcomm.*
78   Form C, Annex to Commission Notice 2004/C 101/05.

8.5.2 Investigation

The competition and sectoral regulators have wide powers to pursue alleged anti-competitive activity. They can both request information from undertakings and conduct direct investigations. Where an investigation is made without prior notice to the relevant undertaking, it is known as a 'dawn raid'.

Three principles may act as a bulwark against the authorities' investigatory powers: relevance, legal professional privilege, and the privilege against self-incrimination. However, it is for the officials conducting the investigation to determine what the relevant documents to be examined are. They are entitled not only to examine but also to take copies of the books and other business records – undertakings will be reimbursed for reasonable photocopying costs. In particular, the investigating authorities have the power to interrogate computer databases and copy computer files, disks and drives.

An undertaking may consult a legal adviser during an investigation, but the presence of a lawyer is not a requirement for the validity of the investigation. It is extremely important, therefore, for companies to be well prepared to deal with the competition authorities in the event of a dawn raid.

8.5.3 Interim measures

The competition authorities and sectoral regulators have the power to order interim measures pending their final decisions. These may include positive measures (such as resumption of supply), as well as prohibitory orders. Interim measures can only be taken when it is necessary for the regulator to act urgently to prevent serious irreparable damage to competition.[79]

8.5.4 Orders to terminate infringements

The competition authorities and sectoral regulators have the power, by a decision, to require an undertaking or an association of undertakings to terminate infringements and to refrain from any similar conduct in future.[80]

8.5.5 Commitments

The competition authorities and sectoral regulators also have the power and discretion to accept binding commitments from undertakings as an alternative to

---

79   Modernisation Regulation, Art 8; Competition Act 1998, s 35; see also OFT Guideline 407 Enforcement.
80   Modernisation Regulation, Art 7; Competition Act 1998, ss 31 and 32; see also OFT Guideline 407 Enforcement.

reaching an infringement decision.[81] The OFT has indicated that it will only accept commitments for hardcore infringments in exceptional circumstances.

8.5.6   Fines

The competition authorities and sectoral regulators have the power to impose fines for infringements of Chapters I or II or Arts 81 or 82. Fines are intended to secure implementation of competition policy by suppressing illegal activity and preventing recurrence. They are also used as a general deterrent. Fines are capped at 10 per cent of group worldwide turnover in the preceding business year for the undertaking in question. However, fines rarely reach this cap. The starting point is up to 30 per cent of the revenue generated in the market where the infringement took place, depending upon the seriousness of the offence. This is then subject to many possible adjustments for duration, aggravating and mitigating circumstances that ultimately give the authorities a wide discretion in determining the ultimate level of fine.[82]

Aggravating factors include:

*   repeated infringements of the same type by the same undertakings ('recidivism');

*   refusal to co-operate with or obstruction of the investigation; and

*   instigating or leading the infringement.[83]

Mitigating factors include:

*   terminating the infringement immediately upon investigation (except for cartels);

*   limited role in the infringement; and

*   co-operation beyond legal requirements.[84]

8.5.7   Whistleblowing/leniency

The European Commission has published a notice on the non-imposition and reduction of fines[85] which is intended to give incentives to participants to blow

---

81   Modernisation Regulation, Art 9; Competition Act 1998, s 31A; see also OFT Guideline 407 Enforcement.
82   Modernisation Regulation, Art 23(2); Competition Act 1998, s 36(8); see also OFT Guideline 423 Penalties and European Commission Guidelines on the method of setting fines, 2006/C 210/02.
83   European Commission Guidelines on the method of setting fines, 2006/C 210/02.
84   European Commission Guidelines on the method of setting fines, 2006/C 210/02.
85   OJ [2002] C 45/3.

the whistle on cartels and co-operate with the Commission in its investigation. Those who co-operate will have their fines reduced. The key point to bear in mind is that if you are the first undertaking to approach the Commission and you co-operate fully, you can secure a 100 per cent reduction in any subsequent fine. The OFT operates a similar system, as set out in its guidelines.[86] The OFT's system was displayed recently when British Airways was fined £121.5 million for its part in fixing fuel surcharges on passenger and cargo flights, while Virgin Atlantic received total immunity from fines for blowing the whistle.[87] This illustrates the importance of approaching the OFT or the European Commission as quickly as possible if you are involved in anti-competitive activity (the 'grass first premium').

8.6   CARTEL OFFENCE

The Enterprise Act 2002 added a new dimension to the enforcement of competition law in the UK. Since 20 June 2003, the actions of an individual can be investigated and an individual can be subject to criminal prosecution for a substantive infringement of competition law. This 'cartel offence' applies only where the individual is involved in the most serious and damaging forms of anti-competitive behaviour (hardcore cartels).

The cartel offence operates alongside the existing Competition Act regime that imposes civil sanctions on companies that enter into agreements that restrict, distort or prevent competition in the UK or the EC. The cartel offence, however, applies to a much more limited and carefully defined range of activities. The main enforcement body is the OFT. However, when investigating and prosecuting the cartel offence the OFT will generally act under the direction of the Serious Fraud Office (SFO) and will use a new set of investigatory powers granted to it under the Enterprise Act 2002. In December 2007 the OFT initiated the first prosecutions and a number of other investigations were underway at the time of writing.

Under s 188 of the Enterprise Act 2002, an individual is guilty of an offence if he dishonestly agrees with one or more other persons to make or implement, or cause to be made or implemented, arrangements whereby at least two undertakings will engage in one or more prohibited cartel activity in the UK. The prohibited cartel activities are: direct or indirect (horizontal) price-fixing; limitation of production or supply; sharing customers or markets; and bid-rigging. A person who is guilty of the cartel offence is liable to imprisonment for up to five years and an unlimited fine.

The OFT's powers under the Enterprise Act 2002 operate in parallel with those under the Competition Act 1998 and Arts 81 and 82. It is quite possible that on the same set of facts the OFT/SFO will seek to prosecute

---

86   OFT Guideline 423 Penalties.
87   OFT press release 113/07.

individuals for the criminal cartel offence and that the OFT will wish to bring proceedings against the companies involved under the Competition Act 1998.

The OFT will be able to grant 'immunity' from prosecution for individuals in relation to the cartel offence. This is in keeping with the policy adopted in civil cases that there are significant benefits in encouraging cartel participants to come forward, to confess and to co-operate with an investigation. Unlike in civil cases, however, the application of this 'leniency policy' in criminal cases has statutory recognition.

8.7   MERGER CONTROL

Whilst the Competition Act 1998 and Arts 81 and 82 principally operate to prevent anti-competitive behaviour once it has started ('ex-post regulation'), merger control effectively gives regulatory authorities the chance to stop such behaviour before it starts ('ex ante regulation'). Essentially, the merger control regimes of the UK and EC provide the authorities with the opportunity to prevent the creation of such market power as would jeopardise the proper functioning of the market. Small mergers are not generally of interest to the OFT or Commission unless the merger gives the new entity significant power in a narrow market. For this reason both the domestic and European regimes contain 'threshold' tests for when a merger qualifies for scrutiny.

When considering whether a merger should be allowed, the factors taken into account will be similar to those considered when assessing whether an arrangement or certain behaviour is anti-competitive under the provisions referred to above. A number of illustrative examples given above in relation to anti-competitive agreements refer to merger decisions.[88] The fundamental test under both the EC and the UK regimes is whether a merger creates or enhances market power, although the substantive test is formulated differently under the two regimes.

It is beyond the scope of this chapter to give a detailed account of merger control in the UK and EC. The following sections indicate the basic tests which should be applied in deciding whether a merger will qualify for investigation and what broad principles are applied in assessing mergers.

8.7.1   EC Merger Regulation

The EC Merger Regulation[89] is intended to be a one-stop-shop for European merger control. If an arrangement falls within the scope of the Regulation it will not generally be scrutinised by member states' national merger control authori-

---

88   See, for example: *MCI/Worldcom;Telia/Telenor/Schibsted; Bertelsmann/Mondadori.*
89   Council Regulation 139/2004 on the control of concentrations between undertakings.

ties nor will the merger itself be separately scrutinised under Arts 81 and 82 or their national equivalents.

The Merger Regulation requires the prior notification to the European Commission of 'concentrations having a Community dimension'. A 'concentration' is defined by the Merger Regulation as being a situation where two or more independent undertakings merge, or where one or more undertakings acquire the ability to exercise 'decisive influence' over another undertaking. 'Undertaking' has the same meaning as under Arts 81 and 82 (and Chapter I and II). Generally, acquisition of under 20 per cent of the voting rights of a company will not give rise to decisive influence, although the position is more complicated in the case of joint ventures where veto rights over strategic decisions confer decisive influence.

Whether or not a merger has a Community dimension is determined by a series of complex turnover thresholds which relate to aggregate worldwide, EC and domestic turnover. If the aggregate worldwide turnover of the undertakings concerned exceeds €2.5 billion and the EC turnover of at least two undertakings exceeds €100 million, there may be a Community dimension unless each of the parties achieves more than two-thirds of its turnover in one and the same member state.

If a merger does constitute a concentration with a Community dimension, the merger must be notified to the European Commission in the manner prescribed by Form CO. The Commission will appraise the merger's compatibility with the Common Market on the basis of the following principle: a concentration which 'significantly impedes effective competition in the Common Market or in a substantial part of it, in particular as a result of the creation or strengthening of a dominant position' should be prohibited (or remedies sought to overcome the competition concerns).

8.7.2   UK Enterprise Act

The Enterprise Act 2002 is the legislative basis for the UK merger control regime. A transaction is reviewable under the Enterprise Act 2002 if a 'relevant merger situation' has been created in the preceding four months or will be created (and the EC Merger Regulation does not apply). There is a relevant merger situation if two or more enterprises 'cease to be distinct' and certain thresholds are met. Where enterprises cease to be distinct, the Chapter I and II prohibitions will not apply to that agreement.

The concept of enterprise under the Enterprise Act 2002 is similar to that of undertaking under EC competition law and the Competition Act. Enterprises cease to be distinct if one acquires at least the ability materially to influence the policy of another. This concept is not defined in the Enterprise Act 2002, but the OFT provides guidance. Material influence can occur with voting rights as low as 10 per cent, and will generally arise with voting rights of more than 25 per cent. It is generally recognised to be a lower threshold than the concept of decisive influence under the EC Merger Regulation. The additional thresholds referred to above are alternative (only one needs to be met). They are as follows: (i) the merger will create or enhance a 25 per cent or greater share of the purchase or supply of any goods or services in the UK or a substantial part of the UK; or (ii) the annual UK turnover of the target is £70 million or more.

The OFT, the Competition Commission and the Secretary of State for Business, Enterprise and Regulatory Reform (Secretary of State) have decision-making powers under the Enterprise Act merger control regime. The first phase of a merger investigation is carried out by the OFT. The OFT has a duty to refer mergers to the Competition Commission where it believes that there is, or may be, a relevant merger situation that has resulted, or may be expected to result, in any substantial lessening of competition ('SLC') in the UK. Alternatively, the OFT may accept undertakings from the merging parties in lieu of a reference. If a merger is referred to it, the Competition Commission must decide whether a relevant merger situation has been or will be created and, if so, whether the situation results or may be expected to result in an SLC within any market in the UK. If so, the Competition Commission must also decide what (if any) remedies (including prohibition or divestment) should be imposed. In cases involving public interest issues (limited to national security and media at the time of writing), the Secretary of State may refer a merger to the Competition Commission on public interest grounds and take the final decision based on the Competition Commission's report.

Notification of mergers under the UK regime is voluntary, and mergers may be completed without merger control clearance even if they are reviewable. Nevertheless, in practice many mergers are notified for reasons of legal certainty because the Competition Commission has the power to impose remedies even where the merger has been completed, including forced divestment. A notification to the OFT can be by informal submission or by a formal merger notice. In addition it is possible to seek confidential or informal guidance from the OFT.

8.8　MARKET INVESTIGATIONS

The European Commission and the UK competition authorities and sectoral regulators have the power to conduct investigations into markets or sectors that are perceived not to be functioning properly (as opposed to specific alleged infringements of competition law by particular undertakings or individuals).

The European Commission powers are contained in Art 17 of the Modernisation Regulation. However, this is in practice merely an information-gathering exercise, as the European Commission has no power to impose fines or remedies unless the sector inquiry also reveals an infringement of Arts 81 or 82. None of the European Commission sector inquiries at the time of writing has focused on Internet-related activities.

The position is different in the UK. The Enterprise Act 2002 allows the OFT and sectoral regulators to conduct investigations into the workings of a market, and for them, or, in certain cases, the Secretary of State, to refer a market to the Competition Commission for further detailed investigation and a decision on whether any features of the market have an adverse effect on competition. The Competition Commission may impose remedies in relation to markets which are not operating competitively but where this is not the result of a breach of either of the Chapter I or II prohibitions and/or Arts 81 or 82. Similarly, the OFT or sectoral regulators may accept remedies in lieu of a reference to the Competition Commission. Additionally, these provisions can be used where the only way to prevent continued breach of the Competition Act prohibitions is to require structural changes to the relevant market.

The Competition Commission has a wide discretion as to the type of remedies by which it may seek to address any adverse effects on competition that it identifies. The types of remedies that it might consider include:

- structural remedies designed to make a significant and direct change to the structure of the market, such as divestment of a business or assets;

- structural remedies that affect the market structure less directly by reducing entry barriers or reducing switching costs (for example, by requiring the licensing of know-how or intellectual property, introducing industry-wide technical standards or recommending changes to regulations which limit entry to the market);

- behavioural remedies directing companies to act in a certain way (for example, giving notices of price changes or displaying prices and terms and conditions of sale more prominently) or to restrain conduct (for example, the imposition of a price cap); and

- monitoring remedies, for example, a requirement to provide the OFT with information on prices or conduct.

At the time of writing, none of the market investigations under the Enterprise Act had focused on Internet-related activities.

CHAPTER NINE

Regulation and regulated activities

'So what we're seeing on the net is a reflection of the society that we live in ...
But you know, when you have a problem in the mirror you do not fix the mirror,
you fix that which is reflected in the mirror.'

Vint Cerf, founding father of the Internet,
29 August 2007, BBC Radio 4, *Today* Programme.

An all too familiar question from the uninitiated is 'how is the Internet regulated?', or 'what actually governs the Internet?' These are by no means naïve enquiries.

The fact is that the Internet has posed a unique challenge for governments, both on a national and international basis, over the last decade and, as it develops, will continue to do so. Having said this, much of the 'lost cause' pessimism has thankfully not borne fruit; it is clear that the Internet is not the lawless wilderness which it might once have appeared from some angles. There are rules and there are structures. There is enforcement and there has been progression towards a recognisable framework for regulation.

It may seem strange to conclude this book with a chapter on Internet regulation. Surely this should be the starting point? But, the truth is that the nature of this regulation is only understood by looking at the sum parts which have preceded this one, understanding how these come together and then identifying what is still left behind. This is how many laws develop, after all.

The Internet is not unique, but it certainly does present a special challenge for the lawyer, the legislator and the provider. It brings together nearly all of the areas of law: crime, tort, contract, intellectual property, competition, tax, each with its own rules, characteristics and mix of statute and case law. It then requires that many of the traditional bases upon which these have grown be looked at with new eyes and questions. How can a case based on physical property translate to the selling of digital goods? What can the ruling in an action concerning a pedler selling wares by lot from the back of a horse-drawn cart tell us about how a modern-day court might approach a case involving an international auction site?

In some scenarios, this becomes a stretch too far and legislation must be amended. In others, the legislative rules need shaping from scratch to master some common consensus and understanding.

This chapter seeks to fill in some of the missing pieces. All of the topics covered here are based on statutory developments concerning key Internet activities.

Of course this is not all-inclusive. Nor indeed could it be, since the Internet now allows for the sale and exchange of any type of good or service. Instead, it considers those issues which will be of most common interest and necessity to practitioners and providers alike. The chapter therefore leaps between the structure of regulation, to core rules in respect of certain common Internet content and services.

This chapter considers the following questions:

1. Do Internet service providers have to be licensed? How is their core business and service generally regulated?

2. Financial services are subject to separate regulation, but how does this translate into advertising or selling financial products over the Internet? What e-payments are regulated?

3. Is advertising on the Internet subject to self-regulation? Are there any controls?

4. How does the Gambling Act 2005 change things for those offering online gambling services? Can a website provide quizzes and competitions without concern?

5. What special rules apply when goods and services are sold to consumers via a website? What rights of return does a consumer have because they have not been able to see the product?

6. As television programmes increasingly become available on the Internet, how will traditional forms of regulation of television need to adapt, and what changes are already afoot?

9.1 INTERNET ACCESS AND ADMINISTRATION

9.1.1 Introduction

The Internet, being a network of computer networks linked by telecommunications circuits, naturally requires consideration of telecommunications regulation. Those involved in the provision of telephony, cable and other networks are regulated in respect of the access and related services which they supply. This section explains whether Internet service providers and voice over Internet protocol providers are regulated by this regime.

9.1.2 Ofcom regulation of ISPS

Internet service providers operate the backbone networks of the Internet, each of which must interconnect with others to allow traffic to reach its destination. To do this an ISP must either have a direct connection with its destination terminal, or interconnections with intermediary networks to allow the transmission of the message. Interconnect necessitates often complex commercial arrangements.

End-users of the Internet connect to their own ISP's network to send and receive messages and access the Internet more generally. ISPs provide access to their network through a variety of means. Broadly speaking, there are two different types. Dial-up uses standard telephone networks known as the public switched telephone network ('PSTN') and, although not tending to have the bandwidth to permit practical use of many services (including videoconferencing and gaming), this remains the usual option for many living in remote or rural areas. Broadband, on the other hand, has now become the norm, providing high speed access and bringing with it the added advantage of not disrupting telephone usage whilst in operation. Common forms of broadband access include cable and DSL (digital subscriber line technology, which uses local telephone networks but the modem applies filters so that telephone and the Internet can be used simultaneously).

ISPs are regulated under the same regime as other providers of electronic communications networks and services, regardless of the access technology used. Regulation in the UK no longer involves licensing and prior-authorisation, but compliance with conditions imposed on specific categories of person and behavioural requirements under the Communications Act 2003. These conditions apply to all providers of electronic communications services, being services which allow the conveyance of messages by means of an 'electronic communications network', essentially a transmission system for the conveyance of messages. It is the underlying service which is regulated in this way rather than, say, a content provider which provides messages and services through another provider's system. The provider is generally that person who has the contractual relationship with the user (whether that be a consumer, business or reseller). ISPs fall firmly within this category as providers.

The conditions comprise: general conditions (including those protecting the interests of end-users, service interoperability and network access); universal service conditions (which are imposed on specified persons such as BT and Kingston Communications); access-related conditions which cover network access and interoperability issues; privileged supplier conditions (imposed on persons granted special or exclusive rights in other industries); and significant market power conditions which apply to those who have been found to be dominant.

The regime is regulated by the Office of Communication (Ofcom) and failure to comply with the conditions can result in fines and even suspension of authorisation to supply.

9.1.3 Voice over Internet protocol

Voice over Internet protocol is fast becoming a popular means of voice communication for consumers and business alike. VOIP is a technology which allows telephone calls to be transmitted over the Internet, instead of using usual telephony networks which utilise PSTNs (for definition, see section 9.1.2 above). It works by digitalising and compressing the voice data and transmission of this data in packets (in the usual way with Internet traffic), the data then being reassembled at the other end.

Using IP-based networks, operators are able to avoid or reduce call origination and termination charges which apply to those using PSTNs. Many are therefore able to offer free subscription and calls and so the competitive advantage becomes clear.

In terms of regulation, given the abolition of the licensing regime for telecommunications in the UK, there is no requirement on VOIP providers to be licensed. However, the uncertainty as to whether they need to comply with the general conditions of entitlement established under the Communications Act 2003 has been put to bed through Ofcom's announcement and amendments to such conditions in the spring of 2007. OFCOM has confirmed that it will proactively monitor and enforce compliance with the rules and therefore all VOIP providers must carefully consider all general conditions of entitlement to ensure that they identify and implement the requirements which affect their business.

9.1.4   Self-regulation

In addition to Ofcom's oversight of the networks and underlying service arrangements for ISPs, regulation of content and services depends to a large degree on self-regulatory initiatives. A Code of Conduct was developed and adopted in 1999 by trade association body ISPA (the Internet Service Providers Association), with government support. Compliance is mandatory for all ISPA members and this therefore covers most major providers. The Code covers various topics, including privacy, spam, and illegal content and pricing rules.

Another initiative is the voluntary regulatory body, the Internet Watch Foundation, funded by providers, which operates in a similar manner to ICSTIS which regulates the premium rate telephony industry, although with less independence. The IWF runs a hotline for reporting illegal content, specifically in relation to images of child sexual abuse, obscenity and racial hatred. Once a complaint is made, the IWF locates the content and, if it is potentially illegal, traces the source of the server on which the content is contained. For servers based in the UK, the IWF then administers the sending of a take down notice to the relevant service provider (the key to lifting a provider's reliance on the Electronic Commerce Regulation defences by putting them on notice of the content, as discussed at length elsewhere in this book) and notifies it to the police. If the content is located on a non-UK server then a partner organisation is notified where relevant and, if the content relates to child pornography, Interpol is notified. The IWF also provides consumer information on filtering products. More details about the IWF and the law relating to pornography, obscenity and indecent images of children are contained in Chapter 5 (Crime).

9.2   FINANCIAL PRODUCTS AND SERVICES

Those undertaking regulated financial services using the Internet or websites and email to complement, market or facilitate such activities will be caught by the regime which regulates this. It is subject to enforcement by the Financial Services Authority in the UK. The scope of regulated financial services is defined in the Financial Services and Markets Act 2000 ('FSMA'), and ranges from banking, investments and deposits through to various intermediary activities in connection with insurance and mortgages.

Financial services were carved out of the Distance Selling Directive[1] (implemented in the UK in the form of the Consumer Protection (Distance Contracts) Regulations 2000, which are discussed in section 9.5.2 of this chapter), receiving separate treatment in a dedicated sector-specific Directive brought in in parallel to the general Directives – these rules have, where relevant, been translated by the FSA into its Handbook, the 'master rule book' that all regulated entities must consult and to which they must adhere.

Importantly, however, the carve-out in the Distance Selling Directive and corresponding UK Regulations for financial services, is picked up by the specific Financial Services (Distance Marketing) Regulations 2004.[2] This legislation extends beyond mere FSA regulated financial services to other, more general financial services (for example consumer credit arrangements, such as hire purchase arrangements). Providers of these products and services must therefore be careful to ensure they comply with its provisions when offering such services via a website or sending out email communications. This is particularly important, since the financial services-specific rules include greater cancellation rights for consumers than the general non-financial services distance selling and electronic commerce rules. The financial services rules also include far more onerous penalties (including criminal offences) if not followed.

This section sets out some of the key regulations which impact on financial services (FSA regulated or not) when offered and marketed via the Internet, including financial promotions rules, details on the regulation of electronic money, and requirements for contracting with consumers.

9.2.1   The Electronic Commerce (Financial Services and Markets) Directive and Financial Promotions

The provision and promotion of financial services over the Internet has grown in parallel with other forms of electronic commerce. Always a particularly tightly regulated sector, the unique opportunities, but also risks for consumers, represented by transacting over the Internet (including both in terms of security and the need for transparency and clarity of information), have necessitated the development of specific protections. Key legislation is considered below.

9.2.1.1   The Electronic Commerce Directive

The Electronic Commerce Directive 2002[3] is intended to remove restrictions on electronic commerce and to build consumer confidence in online activity.

---

1   Directive 97/7/EC of the European Parliament and of the Council of 20 May 1997 on the protection of consumers in respect of distance contracts. (OJ L1444, 4 June 1997, p 19).
2   SI 2004/2095.
3   European Parliament and Council Directive of 8 June 2002 and legal aspects of information society services, in particular electronic commerce, in the Internal Market (No 2000/31/EC). OJ L17811, 17 July 2000.

Providing a harmonised framework for the provision of cross-border services, the Directive follows a 'country of origin' approach. This means that financial service providers regulated in their 'home state' are not now subject to duplicate or separate regulation within other member states in to which they may wish to provide services.

As already discussed in Chapter 2 (Contract), the Directive's definition of 'Information Society Service' means that any services provided over the Internet are caught. The Directive has been implemented in the UK by way of various specific financial services regulations.[4] These regulations variously amend the FSMA so as to implement the country of origin principles in respect of matters within the scope of regulations by the FSA. This includes amendments to ensure that communications made from places of establishment in other EEA states are not restricted. The general regulations (Electronic Commerce (EC Directive) Regulations 2002) give effect to the Directive in other areas, as discussed in Chapter 2.

In practice this means that those entities which are undertaking regulated financial services in the UK and are thereby authorised here, need only adhere to the provisions of UK legislation, even though they may have a website which promotes their services to and seeks customers from other European countries.

9.2.1.2   Financial promotions

The general rules and principles brought in by the various financial services regulations extend not only to actual transactions for financial services but also to their promotion.

FSMA prohibits (as a criminal offence) any person from communicating in the course of business an invitation or inducement to engage in investment activity. This revised restriction replaces previous references to specific concepts such as advertisements. In so doing, it is specifically intended to be media-neutral in this way, so seeking to encapsulate technological developments such as the increase in web promotions and email.

The effect of this prohibition and the specific provisions of the Financial Services and Markets Act 2000 (Financial Promotion) Order 2001 (as amended), is significant for those who may be involved in the communication of advertisements and promotions for financial services using the Internet. This regulation impacts upon two main groups: first, those who provide financial services; second, those who provide online services used to promote the services.

For providers of financial services, the rules mean that promotions made from another EEA state into the UK (known as 'incoming electronic commerce communications') are permitted and not subject to FSA regulation. The services should of course comply with the equivalent rules with the territory from which

---

4   Specifically: the Electronic Commerce (Financial Services and Markets) Regulations 2002, Financial Services and Markets Act 2000 (Electronic Commerce Directive) Regulations 2002, Financial Services and Markets Act 2000 (Regulated Activities) (Amendment) (Electronic Commerce Directive) Order 2002 and the Financial Services and Markets Act 2000 (Financial Promotions) (Amendment) (Electronic Commerce Directive) Order 2002.

they originate. In contrast, 'outgoing electronic commerce communications' made by UK-regulated entities are subject to the full financial promotion rules of the FSA.

For providing the online services (for example an ISP), comfort is provided in the form of exemptions from liability where their involvement is only in providing hosting, caching or mere conduit services. It is important to note that the relevant financial services-specific Statutory Orders refer directly to the concepts and definitions contained in the Electronic Commerce Directive. The conditions in that Directive therefore must be met (for example, that such an intermediary does not knowingly modify a promotion and expeditiously removes it if a take down notice is received). The Orders also include specific exemptions for journalists preparing articles contained in qualifying publications; this comes as a relief to those providing online reviews of financial products or services, for example.

The exemptions operate in a way, however, meaning that a website which knowingly allows the provision of financial services advertising or even hyperlink arrangements on its site should seek legal guidance to ensure that it does not fall foul of the restrictions. The site should have in place the requisite procedural and contractual safeguards to protect it from unwitting liability.

9.2.2   Electronic money

The issuing of electronic money is an investment activity regulated by the FSA by virtue of the Financial Services and Markets Act 2000 (Regulated Activities) (Amendment) Order 2002 that implements the Electronic Money Directive.[5] This required the introduction of supervisory regimes for electronic money by member states. Any person who is not authorised to carry on the business of issuing e-money by the FSA is prohibited from doing so. In becoming an authorised 'electronic money institution' ('EMI'), an entity is able to avoid the need for, in some ways, more weighty regulation as a 'deposit taking' institution (another regulated activity, which is akin to being a regulated bank). An EMI authorised in one member state will also be able to operate in other member states (subject to the obtaining of relevant 'passporting') notifications from target authorisation authorities.

'Electronic money' is defined as monetary value represented by a claim on the issuer, which is stored on an electronic device, issued on receipt of funds and is accepted as means of payment by undertakings other than the issuer. Electronic cash value stored on a PC (therefore including e-wallet or e-purse services), mobile phone or other electronic device such as a smart device, is caught. The value is only caught by the rules if it fulfils certain key criteria. First, that the

---

5   Directive 2000/46/EC of 18 September 2000 of the European Parliament and of the Council on the taking up, pursuit of and prudential supervision of the business of electronic money institutions (OJ L 275, 27 October 2000, p.39) and Directive 2000/28/EC of 18 September 2000 of the European Parliament and of the Council amending Directive 2000/12/EC relating to the taking up and pursuit of the business of credit institutions (OJ L 275, 27 October 2000, p 37).

value relates to pre-paid products only. The customer must have paid for the facility in advance, which therefore precludes any credit facility that may be offered electronically but would include a debit card. The second criterion is that the customer must be able to use the facility to purchase goods and services from persons other than merely the issuer. Classic examples of an e-money type service include PayPal and WorldPay.

---

1. KoolMoosik.com offers its customers the ability to keep an online account which they can top up from time to time to pay for tracks and albums and earn additional 'points' into their account depending on the amount they spend. Although the value is stored electronically and is paid in advance, because a customer is only able to use their KoolMoosik account to buy goods off the site and not from third parties, the account facility does not constitute e-money. When Koolmusik.com starts allowing its accounts to be used to purchase concert tickets from individual bands' websites, it is then in the realm of e-money.

9.2.3   Financial contracts over the Internet

On 23 September 2002 a Directive on the distance marketing of consumer financial contracts was adopted.[6] The Directive had a hard passage through the European Commission and Council, and was eventually published in the Official Journal on 9 October 2002. Together with marketing prohibitions on inertia selling, cold calling and 'spamming', the Directive also introduced a requirement to provide comprehensive information to consumers before a contract is concluded. Like the more general Distance Selling Directive (applying to non-financial products and services and as considered in detail at section 9.5 below), it also includes a new consumer right to withdraw from the contract during a cancellation period – except in cases where there is a risk of price fluctuations in the financial market.

The Directive has been implemented in the UK by way of the Financial Services (Distance Marketing) Regulations 2004 ('Financial Distance Selling Regulations'). The FSA has updated its Handbook to incorporate the rules that are relevant for different FSMA regulated activities. It is important to understand however that, as discussed above, the Financial Distance Selling Regulations have a wider scope than merely regulated financial services caught by the FSA's ambit. One example is that certain consumer credit arrangements are subject to enforcement by the Office of Fair Trading rather than the FSA.[7]

The core issue addressed by the Financial Distance Selling Regulations are: what is a distance contract; what information should be provided prior to the contract's conclusion; what are the effects of cancellation rights; and, what are the risks of ignoring or breaching the Financial Distance Selling Regulations.

---

6   Directive 2002/65/EC of the European Parliament and of the Council concerning the distance marketing of consumer financial services and amending Council Directive 90/619/EEC and Directives 97/7/EC and 98/27/EC. OJ, 9 October 2002.

7   However, note that consumer hire agreements are still subject to the general Distance Selling Regulations and not the Financial Distance Selling Regulations.

9.2.3.1 Distance consumer contracts

There are three aspects to a contract falling within the Financial Distance Selling Regulations. First, it must be a contract concerning a certain type of transaction. The second aspect is that a means of distance communication has to have been used exclusively up to and including the moment that the contract was concluded. Finally, the contract must be between a supplier and a consumer. Fortunately the Financial Distance Selling Regulations borrow much of their language from the general Distance Selling Directive and UK implementing Regulations. As a consequence, where relevant, readers are referred to the analysis of the Distance Selling Directive in section 9.5.2 of this chapter.

9.2.3.1.1 Type of transaction

The Financial Distance Selling Regulations define the all-important 'distance contract' in the same way as the Distance Selling Regulations, but only one 'concerning financial services'[8] (and including schemes run by intermediaries as well as the supplier). These, in turn, are defined as 'any service of a banking, credit, insurance, personal pension, investment or payment nature'.[9]

9.2.3.1.2 Use of means of distance communication

The Financial Distance Selling Regulations define 'mean of distance communication' in a similar way to the Distance Selling Directive's definition of the same term. It is defined as being a means of communication which, 'without the simultaneous physical presence of the supplier and the consumer, may be used for the distance marketing of a service between those parties'.[10] Unlike the general Distance Selling Regulations, there is no non-exhaustive list of such possible means, but there is little doubt from reading the recitals that websites and organised email campaigns would be caught.

9.2.3.1.3 Suppliers and consumers

The definitions of 'supplier' and 'consumer' differ slightly to those in the general Distance Selling Regulations. It is submitted that these differences have little legal impact; readers are directed to the discussion below on these definitions.[11]

9.2.3.2 Information to be provided prior to conclusion of contract

As under the general Distance Selling Regulations, under the Financial Distance Selling Regulations, sellers of financial services and products are obliged to provide consumers with a comprehensive set of information before a distance contract is concluded. This information must include specific information about the supplier, the financial service itself, the contract and redress available to the

---

8   Art 2(a).
9   Art 2(b).
10   Art 2(e).
11 See 'Suppliers and consumers', at 9.5.2.1.3.

consumer in the event of a dispute. Information on the technical quality and nature of the financial service must be provide in accordance with the rules of the other directives on credit, insurance and investment services or with relevant national rules for services not currently subject to EU legislation.

9.2.3.2.1 Manner of providing information

Like the general Distance Selling Regulations, the information detailed above must be provided in a clear and comprehensible manner in any way appropriate to the means of distance communication used. In addition suppliers should have due regard to the principles of good faith in commercial transactions, and the principles governing the protection of those who are unable, because of the legislation of certain member states, to give their consent, such as minors.[12]

9.2.3.3 Cancellation rights

Cancellation rights are more complex under the Financial Distance Selling Regulations than under its sister regulations. There is an obvious reason for this. Financial services, often by their very nature, could not exist if consumers had a right to cancel them after a short period. For example, if a consumer were to purchase some foreign currency over the web from their bank, receive it and not spend it, can they return it if the exchange rate moves in their favour? Understandably, the financial services industry lobbied hard to eliminate these barriers to them providing online financial services. Indeed, it is apparent from the language of the Directive that the financial community has gained a very wide carve-out indeed.

9.2.3.3.1 Which financial services cannot be cancelled?

The right to cancel does not apply to financial services that may be subject to fluctuations in the financial market, such as sales of foreign currency and securities.[13] The Financial Distance Selling Regulations provide a non-exclusive list of these and similar services which will fall under this exemption. The Financial Distance Selling Regulations have also exempted contracts connected to contracts of insurance which cover travel risks and have a total duration of one month; credit secured by a legal mortgage on land; timeshare credit agreements; and, restricted use credit agreements.

In addition, in the event of fraudulent use of payment cards or other non-cash means of payment, consumers will be able to cancel transactions and be entitled to reimbursement of any sums charged.

9.2.3.3.2 How and when cancellation can occur

Consumers have the right to cancel a contract within 14 calendar days beginning on the day that the contract is concluded. In the case of life insurance and pension

---

12   Art 3(2).
13   Art 6(2).

plans, this increases to 30 calendar days.[14] Suppliers should note, in contrast, that the general Distance Selling Regulations provide a cancellation right of seven working days, which will often be the equivalent of nine calendar days. Over the Christmas period, however, it is possible that a period of 14 calendar days will be shorter than one of seven working days.

Like a cancelling consumer under the general Distance Selling Directive, a consumer can cancel by notifying the supplier on paper or on another durable medium available and accessible to the supplier. An email will suffice. The notification must be sent before the relevant deadline expires.[15]

9.2.3.3.3 Obligations on cancellation

Unlike cancelling under the Distance Selling Directive, under the Financial Distance Selling Regulations a consumer of financial services at a distance may be obliged to pay for 'part' of the financial services received if they choose to exercise their cancellation right. This amount must both be brought to the attention of the consumer prior to the contract being concluded and must not be a 'penalty'. In other words, it must be a genuine proportion of the full price to the extent that the service has already been provided.[16]

From the day on which a supplier receives notification of a withdrawal, they have no more than 30 calendar days to return to the consumer any sums due, less any proportional deduction described above.

9.2.3.4 Risks of breaching regulations

A supplier failing to comply with the information requirements of the Financial Distance Selling Regulations may be guilty of an offence and liable, on summary conviction, to a fine. Directors, managers, secretaries or other similar officers of a body corporate or partnership or unincorporated association in breach may also be guilty of the offence and punished separately. This personal sanction only sticks if the failing is committed by them or attributable to their negligence. This also applies to the restrictions on unsolicited communications in the Financial Distance Selling Regulations.

In addition, enforcement functions are shared between the FSA and the OFT. The FSA is responsible for activities deemed to be 'specified contracts' and which largely equate to those falling within its jurisdiction, the OFT assuming responsibility for any other breach. These enforcement bodies have powers to consider complaints and apply for stop now orders and publish notices of applications. Further, to the extent that the rules are incorporated by the FSA into its Handbook, additional action may be taken by the FSA for such a breach, including any which may have an impact on a person's authorisation and could lead to the imposition of far greater fines.

---

14   Art 6(1).
15   Art 6(6).
16   Art 7(1).

9.3   ADVERTISING

Many people are confused as to whether and how advertising on the Internet is regulated. There are no advertising regulations or statutes which apply specifically to the Internet. There are various forms of advertising that one may come across on the Internet, from banner adverts, pop-ups or even just the contents of websites, most of which act as sophisticated billboards advertising the products and services of their providers in ways which traditional marketing mediums simply cannot replicate. Establishing whether and how each different type and future types may be regulated can seem like a daunting task.

The single starting point is to break down the three different sets of rules which may apply. First, consider the extent to which the UK's advertising codes of practice apply to the Internet. Second, examine the general statutory requirements which apply to all advertising mediums and encompass trade descriptions and other rules many of which will come under the ambit of the Unfair Commercial Practices Directive[17] and its UK implementing legislation, the Consumer Protection from Unfair Trading Regulations 2007. Finally, third, analyse any specific rules which apply to the particular product or service which is being advertised, for example pharmaceuticals, consumer credit, alcohol, financial services or timeshares about which regulations have been developed and which apply to the product or service rather than to the medium by which it is advertised.

This section focuses on the first of these three as it relates to the Internet.

9.3.1   Voluntary advertising codes

Advertising in the UK is largely regulated by way of several voluntary codes of practice. The British Code of Advertising, Sales Promotion and Direct Marketing, known as the CAP Code (the new edition of which came into force on 4 March 2003), covers non-broadcast advertising. Broadcast advertisements are regulated either by the BCAP Radio Advertising Standards Code or the BCAP Television Advertising Standards Code, depending on the medium. It is the first of these which is relevant, at least in part, to the Internet.

9.3.1.1   Scope of regulation

Significantly, the CAP Code does not apply to all advertising or marketing material that one may view on the Internet, but covers only emails, online sales promotions and advertising which may appear online in paid for space. This means that banners and pop-ups are caught, but the general copy contained in the body of a website is not caught, regardless of whether or not it is specifically advertising products or services or just general editorial. This potential gap will, to a certain extent, be closed by the application of the Unfair Trading Regulations,

---

17   Directive 2005/29/EC of the European Parliament and of the Council of 11 May 2005 on unfair commercial practices in the internal market (OJ L 149/22).

considered below. Therefore, this (combined with the second and third rules described in the introduction to this section) does not mean that such general website content will always sit entirely in an unregulated void.

---

2. Fromcandletograve.com is running a promotion to drum up publicity for its new range of luxury aromatic candles for masses and celebrations. It puts a big promotional feature on its homepage, with knocked-down prices, and also pays for some banner ads on various online newspaper sites. Only the content of the banner adverts it uses will be caught by the CAP Code, and not the feature.

The CAP Code contains various rules and principles which should be noted. These include: ensuring that adverts are legal, decent, honest and truthful and not misleading, as well as more specific guidance on using terms such as 'free'. Examples of ASA findings in relation to online advertising include the 2005 complaint against Orange's 'double talk, double text' airtime promotion which was used across various media including the Internet. The ASA found that the advertisements were misleading and in breach of the CAP Code, and Orange agreed to amend the content of the advertisements. Another concerned a pop-up promotion by Mars which contained the phrase '70 wrappers = Xbox', which the ASA held to be misleading since consumers who collected 70 Mars bar wrappers were not necessarily entitled to a free Xbox.

9.3.1.2 Enforcement

The CAP Code is not a statutory code but is self-regulatory. The Advertising Standards Authority is an independent body which investigates complaints made about adverts and its Council makes adjudications on adverts which are published online on a weekly basis. The Committee of Advertising Practice (CAP) on the other hand is responsible for amendments to the CAP Code and also issues guidance and oversees sanction's which have been applied.

The ASA and CAP do have authority to apply sanctions to marketers who fail to comply with the Code. Sanctions include adverse publicity caused by publication of adverse findings, issuing of alerts to members which highlight failings of fellow marketers, and which can lead to the denial of further services. In addition, given that this system is recognised by the courts and the Office of Fair Trading, the ASA can refer matters to the OFT or trading standards bodies who can then take further action against those responsible as needed including application of stop now and other orders.

9.3.2 Unfair commercial practices

The Unfair Commercial Practices Directive is another quest by the European Commission to harmonise protections for consumers across the European Community. It is intended to provide both protections for consumers and some simplicity for sellers based in one member state who wish to promote and sell their wares to consumers based in others. The Directive applies to the Internet sales as well as other sales mediums.

In terms of implementation, the Directive gives member states a deadline of

December 2007 to ensure that implementing legislation takes effect. In the UK at the time of writing, it was confirmed that a draft of the Consumer Protection from Unfair Trading Regulations 2007 was not expected to come into force until 6 April 2008. However, it will cover certain rules which already apply under UK laws. In this respect, when the Regulations come into force, the UK will simultaneously repeal statutes such as the Trade Descriptions Act 1968, Part III of the Consumer Protection Act 1987 and various other legislation including those relating to price indications. These rules all currently apply to Internet-based as well as other adverts.

9.3.2.1   Scope of the Regulations

The Regulations apply to any commercial practices directly connected with the promotion and sale of products to consumers. Transactions between consumers are specifically excluded. 'Products' must be considered in the widest sense, however, thereby encompassing simple sales of goods as well as services. The rules will apply to every stage of the supply chain and therefore, unlike the Distance Selling Regulations, require consideration of all before and after sales practices which may be related to the sale (for example debt recovery and customer support).

---

3. Fred puts an advert on a local online e-listings site to sell some gym equipment he bought on a whim and hasn't used for years. Fred won't need to comply with the Unfair Trading Regulations. However, if Fred ran a shop or business selling gym equipment to consumers, then he would need to consider the rules in the promotion and sale of such equipment.

9.3.2.2   Unfair commercial practices

Regulation 3 contains a general prohibition on unfair commercial practices, stating that a practice will be unfair if it:

(i)   is not professionally diligent; and

(ii)   materially distorts, or is likely to materially distort, the economic behaviour of the typical customer.

In essence, a consumer must not be coerced or somehow tricked into making a purchase they would not otherwise have bought. The potential for uncertainty is apparent; for example, when does the influence of an overwhelming marketing campaign which grabs the attention of thousands of new potential customers actually verge on distorting consumer behaviour? It will be difficult to answer this properly until final supplementary guidance and some rulings are available. In the meantime, the draft Regulations contain some examples, as considered below.

9.3.2.3   General prohibition

Schedule 1 of the Regulations contains 31 different commercial practices which are considered to be unfair and therefore prohibited. This encompasses unfair trade descriptions that readers will be familiar with from exposé television shows and newspaper articles: the electrician who claims to be certified but endangers the life of a granny by inadequately rewiring her electrics; the farmers' market stall which falsely claims to sell organic produce. It also includes the use of misleading terms such as 'free', which will already be familiar from CAP and other advertising rules.

9.3.2.4 Misleading and aggressive practices

Regulations 5-7 prohibit commercial practices which are misleading or aggressive and which cause a typical consumer to take a different decision.

Misleading practices include giving false information to or deceiving consumers, generally giving misleading information, creating confusion as against competitors' products, failing to honour firm commitments made in a code of conduct, giving insufficient information about a product. Aggressive practices, on the other hand, include those which use coercion or harassment (physical or not), or which significantly impair the consumer's freedom of choice.

In an Internet context, actions such as the use of fake consumer testimonials in blogs or online reviews or products ratings would be caught. Companies must therefore resist the temptation to (and ensure that their employees do not) post such statements, in case they are then deemed to be misleading.

9.3.2.5 Typical consumer

Whether a commercial practice is in breach of any of the above prohibitions is judged in the context of the 'typical consumer' – a new slant on the previous concept of the 'average man' or 'man on the Clapham omnibus' with which readers will be familiar from English case law.

A typical consumer may fall into three categories, the Office of Fair Trading guidance states. These are 'average', 'average targeted' and 'average vulnerable' consumers. 'Average consumer' comes from European Court of Justice case law, meaning a person who is reasonably informed, observant and circumspect, taking into account social, cultural and linguistic factors. An 'average targeted' consumer is relevant where a commercial practice is directed at a particular group, therefore bringing into play factors such as age, knowledge and other characteristics of that particular group. 'Average vulnerable' relates to those who may be particularly vulnerable to a particular commercial practice which a trade could reasonably be expected to foresee. The test is objective.

9.3.2.6 Enforcement

The Unfair Trading Regulations allow the Office of Fair Trading to bring criminal prosecutions for various breaches. Civil proceedings are also available.

The Department for Business, Enterprise and Regulatory Reform (previously the Department of Trade and Industry) issued a further consultation to specifically seek responses on how criminal offences should be framed. The Department concluded that the offence relating to general prohibitions on unfair commercial practices should include a *mens rea* or 'knowledge' element (to be reviewed three years after the Directive enters into force); the offence of misleading actions, omissions, aggressive practices and prohibited practices will be strict liability. At the time of writing, the Regulations themselves had not been published and therefore the extent to which this has found its way into the text and the applicable fines related to such offences is uncertain.

9.4   ONLINE GAMBLING

The regulation of betting and gaming activities has been undergoing wide-reaching change within the last few years, culminating in the adoption in the UK of the Gambling Act 2005 and the US authorities' very public crackdown on those offering gaming services to American customers. The new legislation is hoped to bring new opportunities for those wanting to provide betting and gaming facilities in the UK, but with it some complex new licensing rules and implications for those offering related services such as providers of gambling software and online platforms.

A mammoth and specialised field in itself, this section simply seeks to provide Internet providers and their advisors with an overview of the regime and new developments. Such an understanding is particularly important for those who do not intend to be involved directly in such activities themselves, and have traditionally not been subject to regulation. One needs to appreciate how the impact of their customers or their own related activities could have an impact or lead to unwitting liability in the future.

9.4.1   Gambling

Under the Gambling Act 2005, 'gambling' encompasses betting, gaming, and participating in a lottery. The Act then creates new concepts of remote gambling and the provision of facilities for gambling. All such activities are now regulated and require a licence. Each of these concepts and the impact of the new regime are considered below.

9.4.1.1   Betting

Under the new Gambling Act 2005, 'betting' is defined as 'making or accepting a bet on: (a) the outcome of a race, competition or other event or process; (b) the likelihood of anything occurring or not occurring; or (c) whether anything is true or not true'.

Betting can of course be structured in different ways, for example pool, fixed odds/sportsbook and peer-to-peer betting. Each is caught by the regulatory regime. The uniting factor for all these variations and which makes them 'betting' is that a stake is placed on the outcome of a future or uncertain/unknown event or fact. Spread betting is an exception, since it remains subject to separate legislation by the Financial Services Authority pursuant to the Financial Services and Markets Act 2000.

A provider of betting services used to be required to obtain a bookmaker's permit under the Betting, Gaming and Lotteries Act 1963 and be liable for payment of betting duty as a form of gross profits fact in accordance with the Betting, Gaming Duties Act 1981. Since 1 September 2007, those previously holding or wishing to apply for a bookmaker's permit required licences from the Gambling Commission.

9.4.1.2 Gaming

In contrast to betting, gaming has traditionally been circumscribed by tighter control, but the new legislation brings a certain relaxation and new opportunities for UK gaming operators.

Part I, s 6 of the Act defines gaming as: 'playing a game of chance for a prize'. A game of chance includes:

'(a) (i) a game that involves both an element of chance and an element of skill,

   (ii) a game that involves an element of chance that can be eliminated by superlative skill, and

   (iii) a game that is presented as involving an element of chance, but

(b) does not include a sport.'

Games based purely on skill are not caught therefore because they do not rely on chance. To constitute gaming it is also necessary for some kind of payment to be made to enter and Schedule 2 of the Act contains useful guidance as to what will constitute 'payment' for these purposes.

The Act specifically recognises and ensures that games generated by computer images or data are not exempted.

---

4. A travel website runs a competition for a luxury weekend for two at a top London hotel and spa in order to promote its new hotel booking service. Entrants must answer correctly whether the capital city of England is: '(a) Timbuktu, (b) London, or (c) Mauritania'. Although the question is so easy as to be likely to fulfil the criteria of being for chance, because participation is free, it is not a lottery and will be permitted. Had users needed to enter by phoning and leaving their answer via a premium rate phone line however (without any real free entry route) then this would constitute payment and therefore a lottery.

This new definition is significant since it brings within the ambit of gaming certain competitions and games which any provider may seek to offer, whether on a website, television or otherwise. Unlawful prize competitions (which do not involve a requisite level of skill) have always been unlawful but rarely sanctioned. The new regime combined with much negative publicity in 2007 surrounding television phone in competitions is likely to see firmer regulation and enforcement moving forwards. The Act also provides clarity over the status of 'hybrid' competitions, such as those involving a skill-based entry criteria or question but followed by a tie-break for those qualifying. These competitions will now clearly fall within part (a) of the definition set out above. Those designing a promotional competition or game must therefore take real care to ensure that they do not inadvertently fall foul of the rules on gaming or on running lotteries as discussed below.

The biggest change for the gaming industry is that the Gaming Act 1968 (which previously regulated gaming) stipulated that gaming could only be provided in the UK on premises in respect of which there was either a gaming licence in place or which are registered as a club or miners' welfare institute. It further required that licensed gaming could only take place on such premises if the only people participating in such game were present and on those premises at the time when the gaming took place. Those provisions meant that any form of online or virtual gaming was, consequently, illegal.

This did not stop the activity. It simply led to the establishment of offshore only poker and other gaming websites offering services to UK and other customers. It was clear that some kind of regulatory development was needed. The ensuing Gambling Act 2005 therefore represents a new regime which recognises that online gaming is present and even on the increase but accepts that it can be permitted in the UK provided that such activities and providers established in the UK are licensed, as online betting services had been to date.

This approach rests in stark contrast to the response of the US government in 2007 which has sought to enforce prohibitions on offshore gaming providers from targeting US customers. This culminated in some high-profile actions taken against directors of such operations when stepping onto US soil and against payment providers involved in the accepting of gaming payments made by US customers.

9.4.1.3   Lotteries

Part I, s 14 of the Gambling Act defines a lottery as an arrangement which meets the criteria for either a simple or complex lottery as described in that section. A lottery has three key elements: participants pay for the opportunity to win a prize; there is a prize element; and the outcome depends entirely on chance (in this way including any competition which does not include any skill).

If such criteria are met, then a lottery operating licence may be needed. However, these may only be issued to non-commercial societies (such as charities), local authorities and external lottery managers. The National Lottery is subject to a separate exemption and is covered by separate regulations.

Other exemptions exist for:

(1)   Incidental non-commercial lotteries where no sum is intended to be raised for private gain.

(2)   Private lotteries, which include a wide range of privately organised raffles or draws which would otherwise be caught. This includes those organised by a society (established and conducted for purposes unconnected with gambling) only for the purposes for which the society is conducted and where tickets are sold to members of the society or on society premises. It also includes work or residential premises where persons to whom tickets are supplied also work or conduct business in or live in such work or residential premises.

(3)   Small society lotteries promoted on behalf of a non-commercial society and where the maximum prize is not more than £25,000 and the proceeds do not exceed £20,000 or, in aggregate over a year £250,000. These lotteries do however need to be registered with the relevant local authority.

9.4.1.4   Remote gambling

Unlike gaming operations, it has for a long time been possible to provide betting services from abroad to the UK using online media. The new Gambling Act 2005 does not remove this right but simply requires that remote providers obtain separate operating licences in respect of such authorised 'remote' activities. It also extends this right to gaming as considered above.

The definition of remote gambling incorporates communication using the Internet as well as the telephone, television, radio or any other kind of electronic or other technology for facilitating communication. In order to 'future proof' the legislation, the Act also provides that the Secretary of State may, by issuing regulations, provide that a particular method of communication is or is not to be considered as remote communication.

The Gambling Act 2005 therefore establishes, for the first time, a comprehensive system of regulation for remote gambling in Great Britain. Since 1 September 2007, all operators wishing to offer facilities for remote gambling require a licence from the Gambling Commission.

9.4.1.5   Providing facilities for gambling

Another key development for those who may be involved in the provision of gambling services over the Internet is that the legislation introduces new rules which impose licensing and other requirements on intermediaries who provide facilities for gambling or for remote gambling.

In this respect, under the definition set out in Part I, s 5(1), anyone who manufactures, supplies, installs, develops or adapts software which may be used for any type of gambling is deemed to provide facilities for gambling and therefore requires an appropriate licence.

The legislation does attempt to provide some comfort to those who are simply passive Internet service providers. It clarifies that the supply or installation of software does not capture those who make facilities for remote communication available to another person who uses such facilities themselves for the supply or installation of gambling software.

9.4.1.6   Licensing and enforcement

There are three broad categories of licences: operating, personal (attaching to persons who occupy specified management office or operational functions) and premises licences (which are issued by local authorities). Separate licences are then required in relation to the relevant gambling activity outlined above.

Failure to have a valid licence is a criminal offence enforceable by the Gambling Commission and local authorities. The Gambling Commission also has power to review and revoke licences and to impose financial penalties.

9.5 CONTRACTING WITH CONSUMERS

9.5.1 Introduction

Contracting with consumers over the Internet requires consideration of rules designed to protect their interests which lie dotted across various different statutes, legislative instruments and codes of practice.

Many of these rules, such as the Unfair Terms in Consumer Contracts Regulations 1999 and Unfair Contract Terms Act 1997, are not specific to the Internet. These rules apply to any contract with consumers (provisions of the latter also applying to certain business contracts) and are considered in Chapter 1 of this book. In addition, legislation has been developed at a European level and implemented by member states to protect consumers from unique problems presented by new sales channels such as the Internet, as opposed to traditional face-to-face transactions. The two key rules in this respect (as implemented in the UK) are the Electronic Commerce (EC Directive) Regulations 2002 (which specifically contains information rules which also apply in business-to-business scenarios and therefore are considered in the first chapter) and the Consumer Protection (Distance Selling) Regulations 2000, which are considered below.

The latest developments reveal a return to more general consumer protection rules with the passing of the Unfair Commercial Practices Directive,[18] which aims to bring in harmonised protections for consumers throughout the European Community against unfair, misleading or commercial practices. These rules transcend differences of platform or sales and marketing medium. Broad in scope, the Directive applies to any acts or omissions of businesses connected to the promotion, sale or supply of products to consumers, and therefore spans both advertising rules as well as the way in which contracts can be formed. Whilst applying to Internet and other sales mediums, this Directive does also seek to cover some new problems which would not exist were it not for the Internet. These rules are considered in section 9.3.2.2 of this chapter.

9.5.2 Selling goods and services at a distance

On 20 May 1997 Directive 97/7/EC on the protection of consumers in respect of distance contracts was adopted. The Directive[19] affects the practice of those who use the Internet to sell goods and non-financial services to European consumers.[20] It is implemented in the UK by the Consumer Protection (Distance Contracts) Regulations 2000.[21] The core issues are: what is a distance contract for the

---

18　Directive 2005/29/EC.
19　Choice of law clauses will not be effective in ousting the consumer's rights. See art 12.
20　This Directive has a similar cumulative effect as some of the US federal laws and regulations. See Federal Trade Commission 16 CFR 310, 16 CFR 435 and Federal Communication Commission Restrictions on Telephone Solicitations, 47 CFR 64.1200. Also Federal Trade Commission Mail or Telephone Merchandise Order Rule.
21　SI 2000/2334.

purposes of these Regulations; what information should be provided on websites prior to the contract's conclusion; what information should be provided in a durable medium on or before delivery or performance; what are the effects of cancellation rights; and what are the risks of ignoring or breaching the regulations?

9.5.2.1 Ambit of the Regulations

There are three aspects to a contract falling within the Regulations. First, it must be a contract concerning a certain type of transaction. The second aspect is that a means of distance communication has to have been used exclusively up to and including the moment that the contract was concluded. Finally, the contract must be between a supplier and a consumer. Each aspect is discussed below.

9.5.2.1.1 Exempted types of transactions

Not all contracts concluded using a website fall within these Regulations. Exempted contracts[22] include those for the sale or disposition of an interest in land, and construction contracts relating to the same.[23]

The Regulations do not apply to contracts concluded at a genuine auction,[24] although, given that 'auction' is undefined, there remains uncertainty as to whether this exemption covers all types of bidding-style transactions, or only those which use a traditional auctioneer-style process. Member states have applied different interpretations to date, and this ambiguity is just one of the problems highlighted in the European Commission's current review of the 'Consumer Acquis', various Directives which cover consumer protection.[25] The Department for Business Enterprise and Reform (previously the DTI) has clarified in its September 2006 publication 'A Guide for Business on Distance Selling' that, whether or not a bidding transaction constitutes an auction, and is therefore exempt from the Regulations, will depend on the specific circumstances. This includes the contractual relationship between the website provider and the seller, whether the seller is acting as a supplier and whether the buyer is acting as a consumer. In many common online transactions involving bidding, unlike traditional auctions, the site does not actually sell the goods on behalf of the seller and therefore does not act as an auctioneer but, rather, just provides a platform in which sellers and buyers can be introduced, put up for sale and bid for items.

The Regulations also carve out a wide, non-exhaustive list of financial services which are subject to their own distance contracts regime, discussed in section 9.2 of this chapter.[26]

---

22 Reg 5(1).
23 Reg 5(1)(a) and (b).
24 Reg 5(1)(f).
25 Green Paper on the Review of the Consumer Acquis, Brussels, 08.02.07 COM (2006) 744 Final. For further information on Internet 'auctions', see section 2.3.6 of Chapter 2 (Contract).
26 Reg 5(1)(c) and Sch 2.

9.5.2.1.2   Use of means of distance communication

The supplier must exclusively use, both prior to and for conclusion of the contract, a 'means of distance communication' as part of an organised distance sale or service provision scheme. The term 'distance communication' is very widely defined as any means which, without the simultaneous physical presence of the supplier and the consumer, may be used for the conclusion of a contract between the parties.[27]

It is rare for a contract to be concluded over the Internet *not* to be at a distance. The very nature and benefit of the Internet, and the e-commerce that it facilitates, is that parties no longer need to be in the same place to form a contract. There is no doubt that websites and email fall squarely within such a definition.[28]

The reference to an organised scheme means that one-off or occasional sales conducted via email or a website where the supplier usually does business with consumers face-to-face will not be caught, although a dedicated website or standard email or form would be.

9.5.2.1.3   Suppliers and consumers

The final trait of a 'distance contract' is that it is between a 'supplier' and a 'consumer'. Suppliers are any person, whether legal or natural, who is acting in his commercial or professional capacity, and this would include a public body not exercising a statutory function.[29] A consumer, by contrast, is any *natural* person acting outside his business.[30] Two issues become relevant here: one legal, the other commercial.

The legal issue, unlike the Brussels Regulation and the Rome Convention, is that a 'consumer' must be a natural person. Businesses ordering supplies are not therefore covered by these Regulations. It is a sign of success of e-commerce that more and more individuals as well as companies are choosing to harness online resources to sell or make available their own content, goods and services as well as, or perhaps at the same time as, being a consumer of content, goods and services from others. Such users want to have protections but also need to know where the demarcation of liability and responsibility falls and therefore what obligations they have to others, if any. Currently it is not anticipated that, for example, an individual selling the contents of their loft via an online exchange will be subject to the same rules (although the exchange itself will be when contracting with such seller and potential buyers to sign up to and use the service). This is also the case since, in this example, the individual's sale will not be an organised distance sale or service provision scheme (as discussed above).

The commercial issue is that it is sometimes difficult to tell, using a website, whether an order has been placed by a natural person acting as a consumer on

27   Reg 3(1).
28   See Sch 1 for a non-exhaustive list which at para 11 includes the term of art 'e-mail'. The Schedule does not refer to 'website' instead, somewhat amusingly, referring at para 10 to 'videotext (microcomputer and television screen) with keyboard or touch screen'.
29   Reg 3(1).
30   Reg 3(1).

their own behalf or by a natural person acting as an employee tasked by their business to place the order. In some situations it will be relevant to distinguish between the two. Website operators could include a query on the ordering page which simply asks the question whether the order is being placed on behalf of a business. In practice, however, most sites will simply want to adopt a 'one size fits all' approach, providing to all customers the higher level of protection required for consumers.

---

5. A hotel establishes a website to allow particular types of room to be searched for, reserved and paid for. A credit card must be used to reserve each room, for which a billing address is required. The website does not require the person reserving the room to specify whether it is a corporate or individual booking. As a result, to be safe, the hotel will need to assume that every user of the website is a natural person.

9.5.2.2   Information to be provided prior to conclusion of contract

Having determined that a contract falls within these Regulations, one must consider the textual changes needed to be made to the website being used as the means of distance communication. These changes fall mainly within the remit of providing certain information to the consumer prior to the conclusion of the contract.

In good time prior to the conclusion of the contract, the supplier needs to provide certain information to the consumer.[31] The scope of the information to be provided is enumerated below. This is followed by a discussion of the manner in which the information must be provided.

9.5.2.2.1   Information to be provided

The scope of the information to be provided (discussed below) is straightforward. It is[32]:

1. *the identity of the supplier and, where the contract requires payment in advance, the supplier's address;

2. a description of the main characteristics of the goods or services;

3. *the price of the goods or services including all taxes;

4. *delivery costs where appropriate;

5. the arrangements for payment, delivery or performance;

6. the existence of a right of cancellation where this applies;

7. the cost of using the means of distance communication where it is calculated other than at the basic rate;

8. the period for which the offer or the price remains valid;

---

31   Reg 7(1).
32   Reg 7(1)(a)(i)–(ix) and (b) and (c).

9.   where appropriate, the minimum duration of the contract, in the case of contracts for the supply of goods or non-financial services to be performed permanently or recurrently; and

10.   where appropriate, information that in the event of the goods or services ordered by the consumer being unavailable, the supplier will provide substitute goods or services (as the case may be) of equivalent quality and price; and information that the cost of returning any such substitute goods to the supplier in the event of cancellation by the consumer would be met by the supplier.

9.5.2.2.2   Manner of providing information

This information must be provided in a 'clear and comprehensible' manner appropriate to the means of distance communication.[33] On a website, therefore, it should be acceptable to use an obvious link from an ordering page to this prior information. In contrast, using a link from within any terms and conditions on the website may be burying the information too much.

Some of the information to be provided will also need to be provided under the Electronic Commerce Regulations. These items are preceded with an asterisk in the list above. These items of information are not required to be provided twice, but website designers should ensure that the *manner* in which the information is required to be provided for both statutes is met. For example, the Electronic Commerce Regulations require that the 'name of the service provider' is made available in a form and manner which is 'easily, directly and permanently accessible'. The Distance Contracts Regulations require the same information to be provided in a 'clear and comprehensible manner' prior to the conclusion of the contract. It is therefore prudent to observe the Electronic Commerce Regulation's stricter requirements relating to the manner of displaying this information.

---

6. A site's designer ensures that just before someone buys a particular product on his site they are shown a flashy animation summarising the price and delivery details. This cannot be printed but is rather impressive. Once the product is ordered one cannot see the price again. The designer may well have complied with the Distance Selling Regulations' requirement of providing the prices in a 'clear and comprehensible manner'. In contrast, being ephemeral, the animation is not likely to comply with the Electronic Commerce Regulations' requirement that the price be 'permanently accessible'.

9.5.2.3   *Information to be provided on or before performance of contract*

Either prior to the conclusion of the contract, or during performance of the contract, further information must be provided to the consumer. Unlike the information listed above, this information must be provided in a durable medium. The nature of this provision is discussed below the scope of the information in this section.

33   Reg 7(2).

9.5.2.3.1 Information to be provided

There are two sets of information which must be provided. First, those items listed from 1 to 6 (inclusive), above.[34] As has been described, this information must also be provided prior to the conclusion of the contract. Additional information is limited to the following[35]:

1. where appropriate, notification that the supplier intends that the consumer shall return the goods to the supplier in the event of cancellation;

2. where appropriate, information as to whether the consumer or the supplier is responsible for the cost of returning any goods to the supplier, or the cost of his recovering them, in the event of a cancellation (note that it is not possible to require that the consumer return the goods as a precondition of refund, as discussed below);

3. the geographical address of the place of business of the supplier, to which the consumer may address any complaints;

4. information about any after-sales services and guarantees;

5. the conditions for exercising any contractual right to cancel the contract, where the contract is of an unspecified duration or a duration exceeding one year; and

6. where appropriate, prior to the conclusion of a contract for the supply of services (and not therefore applicable in the case of sales of goods), a statement that unless the parties agree otherwise, the consumer will not be able to cancel the contract once the performance of the services has begun with his agreement.

9.5.2.3.2 Cost of cancellation

It is financially important that suppliers pay particular attention to the second item of information listed above. In the event of a cancellation of a contract relating to goods, discussed below, the supplier must specify whether he or the consumer should be responsible for the costs of returning the goods. Most suppliers will not wish to pay for goods to be returned to them. These suppliers should therefore ensure that they include a statement that the consumer pays.

9.5.2.3.3 Cancelling services

Services, such as the online provision of music, can also be cancelled. This is discussed below. Suppliers need to be aware that, unless they state otherwise (the sixth item of information listed above), consumers will be able to cancel a contract once performance of the services has begun. In contrast to rules in relation to the distance selling of financial services, this applies without the right for the

---

34   Reg 7(1)(a)(i)–(vi).
35   Reg 8(2)(a)–(e).

supplier to charge for those services already delivered and enjoyed by the consumer. For obvious reasons, therefore, suppliers are advised to include a statement that, once the services begin to be provided, the contract cannot be cancelled. Advisors are also warned to consider carefully the nature of the transaction between a supplier and a consumer. Many websites do not actually provide goods at all but rather perform a service. Some transactions however may involve the provision of goods and services simultaneously, such as the provision of a mobile phone and airtime contract, or parts plus maintenance services, and in such cases, careful consideration will be needed to identify the different contracts and cancellation periods which may run in parallel.

---

7. ToughSafe.co.uk runs a website that can be used to store documents and pictures on behalf of individuals. It is very secure and costs many hundreds of pounds each year, paid in advance. The website and online contract is silent as to whether the hosting can be cancelled after it has commenced. The site cannot prevent a user from lawfully using the site for a few days and then cancelling the contract. ToughSafe.co.uk will need then to refund the monies to the user, meaning it, in practice, becomes a free temporary storage service.

9.5.2.3.4   Manner of providing information

The information above must be provided to a consumer 'in writing, or another durable medium which is available and accessible to the consumer'.[36] It is important that the consumer is able to retain the information. An email containing the information is therefore acceptable. A website may not be acceptable because, unless it remains always available, it does not have the quality of permanence envisaged by the legislation. Similarly, it is not likely to include 'instant messaging' messages; the Directive's recital 13 warns against 'ephemeral' information not received 'on a permanent medium'. Suppliers are advised to use email as their preferred method of providing the information.

The written material containing the information, in the case of goods, should be received at latest by the time of delivery. Including the material inside the packaging will therefore be sufficient. In the case of services, the information must be provided during the performance of those services.

9.5.2.4   Cancellation rights

The Distance Selling Regulations introduce a new right for consumers buying products and services at a distance to be able to cancel their contract within a certain time period following the receipt of the goods or performance of the services. The rationale for this is simple. Even the best websites cannot accurately portray what an actual product will be like. Consumers in a shop, in contrast, put on a watch, try on clothes, flick through a book; they can check they are happy with what they are buying. The Regulation aims to level this playing field and so encourage the take-up of consumer e-commerce activity. It can materially impact suppliers, though. They should be aware of under what conditions goods and ser-

36   Reg 8(1).

vices may be cancelled and, for cash-flow and stock control purposes, when this cancellation can occur. Finally, they should be geared up to administer cancellations. These three critical ramifications are discussed below.

9.5.2.4.1 What can be cancelled?

All goods and services can be cancelled unless they fall within one of two categories. The first category exhaustively defines those goods and services which are *by their nature* exempted from the cancellation regime. The second category is those goods which, by virtue of the way that they have been *used by the consumer,* are not capable of being cancelled.

(i) Categories of goods that cannot be cancelled

Not all goods and services can be cancelled after a contract is formed with a consumer. The Regulations set out a limited number of exemptions.[37] For example, a contract for newspapers, periodicals or magazines cannot be cancelled after the goods are received.[38] This should be obvious; consumers could otherwise read them and then, within the allotted seven working days, send them back for a full refund.

Similarly a contract for the supply of sealed audio, video recordings or computer software cannot be cancelled if the consumer has unsealed the goods.[39] Again, there is a common-sense reason for this; consumers could watch the DVD a number of times over a weekend and then send it back for a full refund. This would end up being the cheapest way to rent DVDs! Again, for obvious reasons, goods which are made to a consumer's personal specification or are clearly personalised, cannot be returned for the full refund.[40]

---

8. MugMug.co.uk is a website which sells mugs onto which they will print a photograph supplied by a consumer. Apparently these are very popular for birthday presents and Mrs Jones sends a digital photograph of Mr Jones to MugMug.co.uk. Six mugs arrive a week later and Mrs Jones wraps them and gives them to Mr Jones as a present. He hates them. Mrs Jones cannot invoke her rights of cancellation; the goods were made to her specification.

There is also a set of goods and services which cannot be cancelled because their value is transitory. These include betting, gaming or lottery services[41] and goods or services whose price is dependent on fluctuations in the financial market, if this cannot be controlled by the supplier.[42] Similarly, consumers cannot return goods which are liable to deteriorate or expire rapidly, or those which, by their nature, cannot be returned, such as electricity.[43]

---

37 Reg 13(1).
38 Reg 13(1)(e).
39 Reg 13(1)(c).
40 Reg 13(1)(c).
41 Reg 13(1)(f).
42 Reg 13(1)(b).
43 Reg 13(1)(c).

> 9. A department store with a food hall establishes a website. The website includes a limited range of food for sale and delivery the next day. One Wednesday a consumer orders a wheel of Brie for a party at the weekend. The cheese arrives on the Thursday but, sadly, no one turns up for the party. To add to his woes, he cannot return the Brie, as it is perishable.

Finally, there is a category of services which cannot be cancelled. These are those which the supplier has, with the consumer's consent, started to provide before the end of the seven-working-day cancellation period. It is in the interests of most online providers of services to ensure that they therefore exclude the cancellation right in such circumstances in their contracts with consumers. Suppliers should also remember that this notice needs to be in a durable medium and delivered before conclusion of the contract.[44]

(ii)   Categories of goods which become unable to be cancelled

It has already been mentioned that a consumer can return for a full refund a *sealed* DVD, but not an unsealed DVD. Such goods are capable of being cancelled, but for their use by the consumer. In a much broader context, the Regulation stipulates that consumers are under a duty to retain possession of the goods and take reasonable care of them throughout the period prior to cancellation.[45] The Regulation is silent as to what the consequences are for the consumer in not retaining possession of or reasonable care of the goods, but government guidance has clarified that this offers the supplier an opportunity to sue the consumer for breach of statutory duty (hardly an attractive option).

Although untested by the courts, it is reasonable for suppliers to assume that they do not need to refund goods that have been treated unreasonably by consumers. It follows that suppliers should be clear to consumers as to what 'reasonable care' means in the context of the goods during the potential cancellation period and before return. Reasonable examples would be requiring a consumer not to remove hygiene strips from swimwear, or not trying on shoes other than inside on a carpeted or dirt-free surface. Related to this, suppliers should ensure that the goods are covered by an insurance policy until the expiry of the cancellation period.

9.5.2.4.2   How and when cancellation can occur?

There are three different deadlines within which consumers may give notice to cancel their distance contract and obtain a refund. The first deadline applies to goods; the second to services. A final deadline applies where a supplier has failed in its obligations to provide the consumer with the information in a durable medium.[46] Each deadline is set out below, after consideration of how such cancellation right may be exercised.

---

44   See Manner of Providing Information, at section 9.5.2.3.4 of this chapter.
45   Reg 17(2).
46   See 'Information to be provided on or before performance of the contract', at section 9.5.2.3.

9.5.2.4.3 How a consumer cancels

It is simple for a consumer to cancel a distance contract. All they need to do is to give the supplier a notice of their intention, in writing or another durable medium (including email).[47] A format for the notice cannot be prescribed; 'however expressed' an 'indicat[ion] of the consumer to cancel the contract' is sufficient.[48]

Consumers are not even obliged to send the notice by a certain means, such as email, to a particular person. The notice will be treated as properly given if the consumer leaves it, or posts it to the address last known by the consumer or to a company's registered address.[49] It should be made out for the attention of the supplier or other person by name. In these circumstances the notice will be deemed to have been given on the day it was left or posted.[50]

There is nothing to prevent a supplier from providing a recommended physical or email address to a customer or a phone number but a refund can not be made contingent on its use and cancellation notices otherwise lawfully received must still be acknowledged.

9.5.2.4.4 Cancellation deadline for goods

A consumer may cancel a contract for the supply of goods by giving notice within the seven working days commencing on the later of the day after the date on which the goods were received by the consumer, or the day after the date on which all the prior durable information was received.

> 10. Mark orders a book on Greek wines. It arrives on Monday morning. On the Tuesday of the following week he sends an email to the supplier expressing his intention to cancel the contract and return the goods for a full refund. The supplier replies to the email saying that it is too late as seven days have elapsed. The supplier is wrong to say this. The first working day of the seven was the day after the book's delivery: Tuesday. The following Tuesday was actually working day six. Mark gave notice a day before he needed to.

9.5.2.4.5 Cancellation deadline for services

A consumer may cancel a contract for the supply of goods by giving notice within the seven working days commencing on the later of the day after the date on which the contract is concluded, or the day after the date on which all the prior durable information was received. This will not apply of course if the consumer has agreed to the service starting before the end of the usual cancellation period and they have been given the required durable information in which case the cancellation right ends when performance of the service starts.

---

47 Reg 10(1) and (3).
48 Reg 10(3).
49 Reg 10(4)(a), (b) and 5(a).
50 Reg 10(4)(a) and (b).

9.5.2.4.6   Cancellation where supplier has not provided information in durable medium

Readers will note that for both goods and services, the cancellation deadline cannot occur until the prior durable information is received. What happens if the supplier never sends this; does the cancellation period extend forever? No, the Regulations impose a backstop date for any cancellation period. This is three months and seven working days from the consumer receiving the goods or the contract for services being concluded. Most businesses' balance sheets and stock control systems will not expect to reimburse and return three-month-old goods. It is therefore critical that suppliers send the necessary information to their consumers.

9.5.2.4.7   Effects of cancellation

There are two aspects to cancellation: the consumer's obligations and the supplier's obligations. As one would expect, a Directive strengthening consumer rights does not impose many new obligations on those consumers. Suppliers, in contrast, may find their new obligations quite onerous.

9.5.2.4.8   Consumer obligations on cancellation

Having provided a notice of cancellation, consumers must still look after the goods. If the contract is silent on the issue, the consumer simply needs to leave the goods at their premises to await collection. In the meantime, they must retain possession of the goods and take reasonable care of them.[51] Unfortunately for suppliers, if a consumer fails to do so, this does not remove their right to cancel, it only gives the supplier a right of action against them for breach of statutory duty.

Alternatively, the contract, or the supplier within 21 days of cancellation, can specify that the consumer must return the goods (although this does not apply if the order is incorrect or the goods are faulty, since the Regulations do not affect consumers' rights under general consumer law such as the Sale of Goods Act 1979). This is good practice from a supplier's point of view. The consumer becomes obliged to return the goods at their own expense. If they do not return them at all, or do so at the supplier's expense, the supplier may charge the consumer for their 'direct costs' of collecting the goods.[52] Where a third party is involved in this collection, say a parcel delivery company, this amount will be easy to calculate. There can be difficulties for a supplier where the supplier's own staff and facilities are used to collect the goods. In such a situation, the direct costs may be no more than the incremental costs of recovery; these may be no more than the extra petrol to collect from the consumer's premises. Suppliers may therefore tend to use third parties to collect the goods.

It is important to remember however that a consumer can not be required to return the goods as a precondition to receiving a refund.

---

51   Reg 17(3).
52   Reg 14(5).

9.5.2.4.9 Supplier obligations on cancellation

Having provided a notice of cancellation, suppliers are obliged to refund all the monies paid by the consumer within 30 days beginning with the date written notice of cancellation was given.[53] The supplier should also cancel any related credit agreement.[54] Suppliers should check the detailed provisions relating to withholding the portions of payment relating to interest paid in regs 15 and 16.

9.5.2.5 Risks of breaching Regulations

Should sites which breach the Regulations care? In short, yes. There are two types of sanctions for breaching the Regulations: extension of cancellation rights, and injunctions and 'stop now' orders.

9.5.2.5.1 Extension of cancellation rights

If a supplier fails to comply with the information requirements of the Regulations, the cancellation period is extended to a maximum of three months and seven working days until they do comply with the requirements. If the supplier never provides the information, the consumer may return the goods or cancel the services (where appropriate) within three months and seven working days starting the day after the goods are received, or the conclusion of the contract for services.

---

11. A website is established by a retailer to supply Christmas crackers. The website guarantees delivery by 23 December. A family orders four dozen crackers at a cost of £48. They arrive in eight sealed boxes on 23 December. Neither the website nor the delivery contains the necessary information under the Regulations. The family enjoy the crackers. At the end of March, they discover under a couch that they still have three boxes left. Because the website failed to comply with the information requirements, the family may serve their cancellation notice during March and still be within the three months and seven working days.

9.5.2.5.2 Injunctions and 'stop now' orders

The Director General of Fair Trading and the Trading Standards Departments have a duty to consider any complaint about a possible breach of the Regulations. Where they consider that a breach has occurred, they have the power to apply for an injunction in the courts or to apply for a 'stop now' order[55] against the supplier.

---

53   Reg 14(1) and (3).
54   Reg 15.
55   Stop Now Orders (EC Directive) Regulations 2001, reg 2(3)(i) and Sch 1, para 9.

9.6   AUDIOVISUAL MEDIA

9.6.1   The Communications Act

The Communications Act 2003 provided a considerable overhaul of the regulation of the communications industry in the UK including radio, television and telecommunications. By defining new media services under the same umbrella as traditional terrestrial services, as a 'television licensable content service' or 'radio licensable content service', the Act has created a single framework for regulation of television and radio like services delivered by cable, satellite and Internet as well as the previous wireless telegraphy means.

In drafting the legislation, government drew on the perception that audiences expect traditional television and radio broadcasting to be different and more highly regulated to other services such as video-on-demand or those received via the Internet. As a consequence, those services provided entirely online and accessed online remained outside the scope of regulation. This is achieved in the Act by the drawing of a distinction between 'push' services, where the decision is made by the provider as to when the particular broadcast signal is sent, and 'pull' services where the consumer makes this decision.

> 12. A digital channel broadcaster launches a new website to promote a new youth series. The site will run competitions, blogs and forums where viewers can log on and exchange comments and thoughts on the series and engage in live chats with cast members. Sneak preview clips will also be available to view to those who join. None of this content will be regulated.

The other determining factor for whether a service is regulated (and therefore required to be licensed), or not, is the source of the service or the context in which it is provided. In this respect, the government sought to exclude from regulation those services simply provided within the context of other non-broadcast services. In contrast, services which wholly or primarily are aimed at the provision of streamed television or radio programming do remain regulated.

This sounds somewhat simple in principle, but the Act creates long and complex chains of definitions which are often hard to follow. 'Television licensable content service' is defined in s 232 as any service (i) which is provided (whether in digital or analogue form) as a service to be made available for reception by members of the public (itself as defined in s 361) by being broadcast from a satellite, or distributed by an electronic communications network, and (ii) which consists of television programmes or electronic programme guides (or both). Section 233 then sets out those services which are excluded from this definition which crucially include website material provided as part of another service (for example by a non-broadcaster providing some content it has created), but also material comprised in a stand-alone site.

> 13. The success of the website considered in the previous example proves so great that the broadcaster decides to simultaneously live stream each episode to the site when it goes out on air so that users can discuss the show with each other whilst watching. In so doing, this streaming is likely to become a television licensable content service.

Some future flexibility is assured through s 234 which gives the Secretary of State power to modify ss 232 or 233 where considered appropriate. In so doing however, the Secretary of State must 'have regard to the level of protection expected by the public as regards the content of television programmes and text services, taking into account the means of reception; the ability of the public – having been made aware of the contents of a forthcoming programme – to control what they watch; technical innovation; the financial consequences of modification; and the relative ease or difficulty of setting different levels of regulation for different services.'[56]

9.6.2 The Audiovisual Media Services Directive

9.6.2.1 Background

The most important development in the regulation of Internet television and radio services will come with the adoption of the European Audiovisual Media Services Directive is adopted as expected. However, this will not be as fundamental a shift as first believed.

The Directive was tabled by the European Commission on 13 December 2005 as an amendment to the 1989 'TV without Frontiers' Directive[57] and subsequently named the Audiovisual Media Services Directive. It came into force on 19 December 2007. The Directive touches on many of the signature features of the 1989 Directive. It takes a country of origin approach to remove restrictions on the reception and retransmission of audiovisual media services across European territories (primarily intended to deal with satellite coverage) whilst still providing countries to block services in accordance with national laws where they harm minors or incite racial hatred. Both Directives also seek to preserve certain public interest objectives such as cultural diversity, the right to reply and consumer protection.

9.6.2.2 Regulation of non-linear services

The brave new step taken by the Audiovisual Media Services Directive is the attempt to tackle the rapid technological advances made in the audiovisual sphere in recent years. Prompted by various factors including the decline in traditional television advertising revenues and the ever-growing popularity of mobile and online forums, entertainment and other services, the expansion of broadcasters into the Internet and other new media has been significant. The Audiovisual Media Services Directive seeks to provide a framework of modernised rules to cover all audiovisual media services regardless of the transmission technology used – from traditional TV broadcasts to emerging, on-demand

---

56 Section 527, Explanatory Notes to the Communication Act 2006.
57 Council Directive 89/552/EEC of 3 October 1989 on the coordination of certain provisions laid down by law, Reg or administrative action in member states concerning the pursuit of televisual broadcasting (OJ L298, 17 October 1989), as amended by the Europen Parliament and Council Directive 97/36/EC of 30 June 1997 (OJ L202, 30 July 1997).

services. In this way the European institutions are seeking to address the concerns of some politicians that the current lack of regulation applied to the Internet creates a problem as more and more content specifically attractive to children becomes available online. If TV content is regulated to protect the vulnerable, promote pluralism, and uphold key public interest values, they argue, why then should TV and video over the net be exempt?

The drafts of the Directive came under widespread scrutiny and the final text continues to be controversial. Critics fear that regulation will lead to impractical and stifling rules unable to cope with future growth and developments. Many feel that self-regulation, the traditional means for policing the Internet, provides sufficient controls.

Some such fears were allayed with amendments made to the draft Directive in December 2006 which provide that regulation shall apply only to commercial 'television-like services', and not to user-generated content such as that found on popular sites such as YouTube. The implemented Directive distinguishes between TV broadcasts, or 'linear', and on-demand audiovisual media, or 'non-linear' services, essentially drawing on the push versus pull distinction that the UK's own Communications Act currently makes. Non-linear services are those where the user decides upon the moment in time when a specific programme is transmitted on the basis of a choice of content selected by the media service provider. Such non-linear services do not escape regulation, although they are subject only to a basic set of minimum principles (such as the protection of minors and preventing the incitement of racial hatred). As with the Communications Act, the TV/on demand, linear/non-linear or push/pull distinction ultimately depends upon who decides when a specific programme is transmitted and whether schedules exist. Linear services are those 'pushed' by broadcasters.

The Directive came into force on 19 December 2007. Member states have until 19 December 2009 to transpose its provisions into national law.

In the UK, it has been reported that implementation may involve giving formal powers to the self-regulatory body that oversees video-on-demand television. The Association of Television-On-Demand could be given a statutory role in relation to 'television-like' non-linear services which, through the Directive, will be regulated specifically for the first time. The Directive would not permit a self-regulatory body to continue supervising the video on demand sector, but a co-regulatory role, alongside Ofcom, is reportedly an option under consideration. The Association was set-up to oversee the emerging video-on-demand industry in 2002 on a self-regulatory basis, as an alternative to jurisdiction by Ofcom under the Communications Act. Under current UK law, VOD services do not need a specific licence and the Association's members voluntarily subscribe to a Code of Practice.

Index

[all references are to paragraph number]

A

Abuse of dominant position
and see COMPETITION LAW
abuse
  access to essential facilities, 8.4.2.7
  bundling, 8.4.2.5
  discrimination, 8.4.2.3
  excessive pricing, 8.4.2.1
  introduction, 8.4.2
  Microsoft case, 8.4.2.8
  predation, 8.4.2.2
  refusal to supply, 8.4.2.6
  tying, 8.4.2.5
  vertical restraints, 8.4.2.4
dominance
  growth and innovation, 8.4.1.2
  intellectual property rights, 8.4.1.2.2
  introduction, 8.4.1
  joint dominance, 8.4.1.3
  market share, 8.4.1.1
  network effects, 8.4.1.2.1
enforcement
  commitments, 8.5.5
  complaints, 8.5.1
  fines, 8.5.6
  interim measures, 8.5.3
  investigations, 8.5.2
  orders to terminate infringements,
    8.5.4
  whistleblowing, 8.5.7
introduction, 8.4
legal framework, 8.2.1

Acceptance
acknowledgement, and, 2.1.4.1.1
authentication, 2.1.4.5
"battle of the forms", 2.1.4.3
communication of, 2.1.4.1.1

Acceptance – *contd*
conduct, by, 2.1.4.1.1
consumers, by, 2.1.4.1.1
digital signatures
  advanced, 2.1.4.5.2
  basic, 2.1.4.5.1
e-mail, by
  generally, 2.1.4.1.2
  timing, 2.1.4.2.2
ignorance of offer, 2.1.4.1.1
intention, and, 2.1.4.1.1
introduction, 2.1.4
means, 2.1.4.1
mistake, and, 2.1.4.4
post, by, 2.1.4.2.1
telephone, by, 2.1.4.2.1
timing, 2.1.4.2
website, through
  generally, 2.1.4.1.1
  timing, 2.1.4.2.3

Access to the Internet
introduction, 9.1.1
OFCOM regulation, 9.1.2
self-regulation, 9.1.4
VOIP, 9.1.3

Acquiescence
trade marks, and, 4.4.8.1

Applicable law
trade marks, and, 4.8.5

Advertising
introduction, 9.3
unfair commercial practices
  aggressive practices, 9.3.2.4
  enforcement, 9.3.2.6
  general prohibition, 9.3.2.3
  generally, 9.3.2.2
  introduction, 9.3.2

Advertising – *contd*
  unfair commercial practices – *contd*
    misleading practices, 9.3.2.4
    scope of regulation, 9.3.2.1
    typical consumer, 9.3.2.5
  voluntary codes
    enforcement, 9.3.1.2
    introduction, 9.3.1
    scope of regulation, 9.3.1.1
Audiovisual media
  EC Directive
    background, 9.6.2.1
    next steps, 9.6.2.3
    non-linear services, 9.6.2.2
  legislative framework, 9.6.1
Acknowledgement
  acceptance, and, 2.1.4.1.1
Actus reus
  unauthorised access, and
    alteration of programs or data,
      5.1.2.1.3
    automatic causation of function,
      5.1.2.1.2
    computer, 5.1.2.1.1
    copying programs and data, 5.1.2.1.3
    data, 5.1.2.1.1
    erasure of programs or data, 5.1.2.1.3
    function on any computer, 5.1.2.1.2
    held in any computer, 5.1.2.1.1
    introduction, 5.1.2.1
    moving programs and data, 5.1.2.1.3
    output of programs or data, 5.1.2.1.3
    performing any function, 5.1.2.1.2
    program, 5.1.2.1.1
    securing access, 5.1.2.1.3
    unsuccessful attempts, 5.1.2.1.2
    using a program, 5.1.2.1.3
  unauthorised acts to impair or to
    prevent or hinder access, and,
      5.1.4.1.1
Adapting articles for commission for an
  offence
  generally, 5.1.5.1
  introduction, 5.1.5
  sentencing, 5.1.5.4
Anonymous data
  data protection, and, 6.2.1.3
Anti-competitive agreements
  and see COMPETITION LAW
  agreements, 8.3.2
  appreciability, 8.3.8
  concerted practices, 8.3.2

Anti-competitive agreements – *contd*
  decisions of associations of
    undertakings, 8.3.3
  discriminating between customers
    attaching supplementary
    unconnected obligations,
      8.3.7.5
  control of production, markets,
    development or investment,
      8.3.7.2
  fixing purchase or sale prices,
      8.3.7.1
  introduction, 8.3.7
  sharing markets or sources of supply,
      8.3.7.3
  effect on trade, 8.3.4
  enforcement
    commitments, 8.5.5
    complaints, 8.5.1
    fines, 8.5.6
    interim measures, 8.5.3
    investigations, 8.5.2
    orders to terminate infringements,
      8.5.4
    whistleblowing, 8.5.7
  exempt agreements, 8.3.11
    block exemptions, 8.3.11.2
    individual exemptions, 8.3.11.1
    introduction, 8.3.11
  geographic market, 8.3.9
  introduction, 8.3
  jurisdiction, 8.3.5
  legal framework, 8.2.1
  market definition, 8.3.9
  object or effect, 8.3.6
  prevention, restriction or distortion of
    competition, 8.3.7
  product market, 8.3.9
  undertakings, 8.3.1
Anti-competitive conduct
  and see COMPETITION LAW
  abuse
    access to essential facilities, 8.4.2.7
    bundling, 8.4.2.5
    discrimination, 8.4.2.3
    excessive pricing, 8.4.2.1
    introduction, 8.4.2
    Microsoft case, 8.4.2.8
    predation, 8.4.2.2
    refusal to supply, 8.4.2.6
    tying, 8.4.2.5
    vertical restraints, 8.4.2.4

Anti-competitive conduct – *contd*
dominance
  growth and innovation, 8.4.1.2
  intellectual property rights,
    8.4.1.2.2
  introduction, 8.4.1
  joint dominance, 8.4.1.3
  market share, 8.4.1.1
  network effects, 8.4.1.2.1
enforcement
  commitments, 8.5.5
  complaints, 8.5.1
  fines, 8.5.6
  interim measures, 8.5.3
  investigations, 8.5.2
  orders to terminate infringements,
    8.5.4
  whistleblowing, 8.5.7
introduction, 8.4
legal framework, 8.2.1
Anti-terrorism
defences
  hosting, 5.4.2.3.2
  mere conduit, 5.4.2.3.2
  take down notices, 5.4.2.3.1
dissemination of terrorist publications,
  5.4.2.2
introduction, 5.4
publication of terrorist statements,
  5.4.2.1
threat to electronic systems, 5.4.1
Archives
data protection, and, 6.2.3.2.1
ARPANET
background, 1.2–1.3
Artistic works
copyright, and, 4.9.2.1
Auctions
intellectual property rights, and, 2.3.6
Authorship
copyright, and, 4.9.4.2
Automated processing
data protection, and, 6.2.5.6.3
Automatic-answer modems
data protection, and, 6.2.5.7.2

B
Back-up
data protection, and, 6.2.5.7.1
websites, and, 4.15.1
"Battle of the forms"
acceptance, and, 2.1.4.3

Breach of duty
generally, 3.1.1.2
harm to website user, 3.1.2.2.2
viruses, 3.1.2.1.2
Broadcasts
and see COPYRIGHT
generally, 4.9.2.1
qualification for protections, 4.9.4.3
Browsers
generally, 1.5.9.2
Brussels Regulation
civil and commercial matter, 2.4.1.1
consumer contracts
  direct activities to several member
    states, 2.4.1.6.2
  introduction, 2.4.1.6
  pursuing activities in consumer's
    member state, 2.4.1.6.1
contract, and
  civil and commercial matter, 2.4.1.1
  consumer contracts, 2.4.1.6
  domicile of defendant, 2.4.1.2
  express choice of clause, 2.4.1.7
  introduction, 2.4
  meaning of 'contract', 2.4.1.3
  other obligations, 2.4.1.5
  place of performance, 2.4.1.4
defamation, 3.7.2.2.4
digital damage, 3.7.2.2.1
domicile of defendant
  company domicile, 2.4.1.2.2
  EFTA state domicile,
    2.4.1.2.1–2.4.1.2.2
  individual, 2.4.1.2.1
  introduction, 2.4.1.2
  legal person's domicile, 2.4.1.2.2
  member state domicile,
    2.4.1.2.1–2.4.1.2.2
  non-member state domicile,
    2.4.1.2.1–2.4.1.2.2
  UK domicile, 2.4.1.2.1–2.4.1.2.2
express choice of clause, 2.4.1.7
location of harmful events, 3.7.2.2
negligent misstatement, 3.7.2.2.3
place of performance, 2.4.1.4
secondary damage, 3.7.2.2.2
tort, and
  defamation, 3.7.2.2.4
  digital damage, 3.7.2.2.1
  generally, 3.7.2
  introduction, 3.7.1
  location of harmful events, 3.7.2.2

Brussels Regulation – *contd*
tort, and – *contd*
meaning of 'tort', 3.7.2.1
negligent misstatement, 3.7.2.2.3
secondary damage, 3.7.2.2.2
Bulletin boards
generally, 1.5.5
Hedley Byrne v Heller, and, 3.4.1.3.2

C

Cancellation rights
cancellable goods and services,
9.5.2.4.1
consumer obligations, 9.5.2.4.8
effects, 9.5.2.4.7
financial contracts with customers, and
cancellable services, 9.2.3.3.1
introduction, 9.2.3.3
manner of cancellation, 9.2.3.3.2
obligations, 9.2.3.3.3
introduction, 9.5.2.4
manner of cancellation, 9.5.2.4.3
supplier not provided information in
durable medium, where, 9.5.2.4.6
supplier obligations, 9.5.2.4.9
time limits for goods, 9.5.2.4.4
time limits for services, 9.5.2.4.5
Cartel offence
and see COMPETITION LAW
generally, 8.6
legal framework, 8.2.2
Causation
harm to website user, 3.1.2.2.4
intervening acts, 3.1.1.4.3
introduction, 3.1.1.4
'thin-skull' rule, 3.1.1.4.1
type of damage, 3.1.1.4.2
viruses, 3.1.2.1.4
Choice of law
absence of choice
characteristic performance, 2.5.3.1
consumer contracts, 2.5.3.3.1
course of trade or profession,
2.5.3.2.1
generally, 2.5.3
location, 2.5.3.2
modifications to, 2.5.3.3
outside trade or profession, 2.5.3.2.3
website's place of business, 2.5.3.2.2
contract, and
absence of choice, 2.5.3
express choice, 2.5.2

Choice of law – *contd*
contract, and – *contd*
introduction, 2.5
Rome Convention, 2.5.1
double actionability test, 3.8.1.1
express choice
consumer contracts, 2.5.2.2.4
demonstration of, 2.5.2.1
generally, 2.5.2
modifications to, 2.5.2.2
UCTA, and, 2.5.2.2.3
websites, and, 2.5.2.2.4
introduction, 2.5
Rome Convention, 2.5.1
tort, and
common law, at, 3.8.1
double actionability test, 3.8.1.1
introduction, 3.8
statute, under, 3.8.2
Codes of conduct
pre-contract information, and, 2.1.2.3.1
Competition law
abuse of dominant position
abuse, 8.4.2
access to essential facilities, 8.4.2.7
bundling, 8.4.2.5
discrimination, 8.4.2.3
dominance, 8.4.1
excessive pricing, 8.4.2.1
growth and innovation, 8.4.1.2
intellectual property rights, 8.4.1.2.2
introduction, 8.4
joint dominance, 8.4.1.3
legal framework, 8.2.1
market share, 8.4.1.1
Microsoft case, 8.4.2.8
network effects, 8.4.1.2.1
predation, 8.4.2.2
refusal to supply, 8.4.2.6
tying, 8.4.2.5
vertical restraints, 8.4.2.4
anti-competitive agreements
agreements, 8.3.2
appreciability, 8.3.8
attaching supplementary
unconnected obligations, 8.3.7.5
block exemptions, 8.3.11.2
concerted practices, 8.3.2
control of production, markets,
development or investment,
8.3.7.2
convergence, 8.3.10

Competition law – *contd*
anti-competitive agreements – *contd*
decisions of associations of
undertakings, 8.3.3
discriminating between customers,
8.3.7
effect on trade, 8.3.4
exempt agreements, 8.3.11
fixing purchase or sale prices, 8.3.7.1
geographic market, 8.3.9
individual exemptions, 8.3.11.1
introduction, 8.3
jurisdiction, 8.3.5
legal framework, 8.2.1
market definition, 8.3.9
object or effect, 8.3.6
prevention, restriction or distortion
of competition, 8.3.7
product market, 8.3.9
sharing markets or sources of supply,
8.3.7.3
undertakings, 8.3.1
cartel offence
generally, 8.6
legal framework, 8.2.2
enforcement
commitments, 8.5.5
complaints, 8.5.1
fines, 8.5.6
interim measures, 8.5.3
investigations, 8.5.2
orders to terminate infringements,
8.5.4
whistleblowing, 8.5.7
introduction, 8.1
legal framework, 8.2
market investigations
generally, 8.8
legal framework, 8.2.3
merger control
Enterprise Act, 8.7.2
generally, 8.7
legal framework, 8.2.4
Regulation, 8.7.1
sector-specific legislation, 8.2.5
Computer misuse
extradition
generally, 5.1.6.2
introduction, 5.1.6
hacking for further criminal purpose
further offence, 5.1.3.1
future intention, 5.1.3.3

Computer misuse – *contd*
hacking for further criminal purpose –
contd
impossible further offence, 5.1.3.4
intention, 5.1.3.2
introduction, 5.1.3
sentencing, 5.1.3.5
introduction, 5.1.1
jurisdiction
double criminality, 5.1.6.1.2
generally, 5.1.6.1
introduction, 5.1.6
location of accused, 5.1.6.1.1
location of victim computer,
5.1.6.1.1
section 1, under, 5.1.6.1.1
section 2, under, 5.1.6.1.2
section 3, under, 5.1.6.1.3
significant link, 5.1.6.1.1
making, adapting, supplying or offering
to supply articles for commission
for an offence
generally, 5.1.5.1
introduction, 5.1.5
sentencing, 5.1.5.4
obtaining an article for supply or
assistance in commission of an
offence
generally, 5.1.5.3
introduction, 5.1.5
sentencing, 5.1.5.4
supply of article to commit or assist in
commission of an offence
generally, 5.1.5.2
introduction, 5.1.5.2
sentencing, 5.1.5.4
unauthorised access
actus reus, 5.1.2.1
conduct, 5.1.2.1
for further criminal purpose, 5.1.3
intention, 5.1.2.2
introduction, 5.1.2
mens rea, 5.1.2.2
sentencing, 5.1.2.3
unauthorised acts to impair or to
prevent or hinder access
actus reus, 5.1.4.1
conduct, 5.1.4.1
intention, 5.1.4.2
introduction, 5.1.4
mens rea, 5.1.4.2
sentencing, 5.1.4.3

508   *Index*

Computer software
trade marks, and, 4.2.4.1
websites, and, 4.9.6.3.7
Conduct
acceptance, and, 2.1.4.1.1
Consent
negligence, and
generally, 3.1.1.5.2
viruses, 3.1.2.1.5
trade marks, and, 4.4.8.1
Consideration
introduction, 2.1.5
web-wrap, 2.1.5.1
Consumer contracts
see also CONTRACTING WITH
CONSUMERS
jurisdiction, and
direct activities to several member
states, 2.4.1.6.2
introduction, 2.4.1.6
pursuing activities in consumer's
member state, 2.4.1.6.1
Contract
acceptance
authentication, 2.1.4.5
"battle of the forms", 2.1.4.3
digital signatures, 2.1.4.5
e-mail, by, 2.1.4.1.2
introduction, 2.1.4
means, 2.1.4.1
mistake, and, 2.1.4.4
timing, 2.1.4.2
website, through, 2.1.4.1.1
choice of law
absence of choice, 2.5.3
express choice, 2.5.2
introduction, 2.5
Rome Convention, 2.5.1
consideration
introduction, 2.1.5
web-wrap, 2.1.5.1
digital signatures, 2.1.4.5
formation of contract
And see FORMATION OF CONTRACT
acceptance, 2.1.4
consideration, 2.1.5
general approach, 2.1.1
intention, 2.1.6
introduction, 2.1
invitations to treat, 2.1.3
offers, 2.1.3
pre-contract information, 2.1.2

Contract – *contd*
intellectual property rights
auctions, 2.3.6
exhaustion of rights, 2.3.1
express licence, 2.3.5
implied licence, 2.3.4
introduction, 2.3
retention of title, 2.3.2
use as copying, 2.3.3
intention
introduction, 2.1.6
programmed intention, 2.1.6.1
invitations to treat
introduction, 2.1.3
location, 2.1.3.5
misrepresentations, 2.1.3.4
shops, 2.1.3.2
timing, 2.1.3.5
web invitations, 2.1.3.3
webvertisements, 2.1.3.1
jurisdiction
civil and commercial matter, 2.4.1.1
common law, at, 2.4.1.8
consumer contracts, 2.4.1.6
contract, and, 2.4.1.3
domicile of defendant, 2.4.1.2
express choice of clause, 2.4.1.7
introduction, 2.4
other obligations, 2.4.1.5
place of performance, 2.4.1.4
misrepresentations, 2.1.3.4
offers
introduction, 2.1.3
location, 2.1.3.5
misrepresentations, 2.1.3.4
shops, 2.1.3.2
timing, 2.1.3.5
web invitations, 2.1.3.3
webvertisements, 2.1.3.1
payment
credit card, 2.2.2
digital cash, 2.2.3
generally, 2.2.1
performance
payment, 2.2
pre-contract information
establishment of providers, 2.1.2.1
general information, 2.1.2.2
introduction, 2.1.2
transactional information, 2.1.2.3
stipulation by parties, 2.1.1.1
type, 2.3

Contracting with customers
distance sales of goods and services
and see DISTANCE SALES OF GOODS AND
SERVICES
cancellation rights, 9.5.2.4
exempt transactions, 9.5.2.1.1
introduction, 9.5.2
means of distance communication,
9.5.2.1.2
pre-contract information, 9.5.2.2–
9.5.2.3
risks of breach of regulations,
9.5.2.5
scope of regulation, 9.5.2.1
suppliers and consumers, 9.5.2.1.3
financial products and services
and see FINANCIAL PRODUCTS AND
SERVICES
cancellation rights, 9.2.3.3
distance consumer contracts, 9.2.3.1
introduction, 9.2.3
pre-contract information, 9.2.3.2
risks of breach of regulations, 9.2.3.4
introduction, 9.5.1
Contributory negligence
generally, 3.1.1.5.1
viruses, 3.1.2.1.5
Conversation threads
copyright, and, 4.9.6.2.1
Copyright
adaptation, 4.11.6
artistic works, 4.9.2.1
authorship, 4.9.4.2
broadcasts
generally, 4.9.2.1
qualification for protections, 4.9.4.3
communication to the public, 4.11.5
conversation threads, 4.9.6.2.1
copying, 4.11.1
database rights
and see DATABASE RIGHTS
infringement, 4.12
introduction, 4.9.7
nature, 4.9.7.1
scope, 4.9.8.1
term of protection, 4.9.8.2
dramatic works, 4.9.2.1
electronic mail, 4.9.6.1
films, 4.9.2.1
fixation, 4.9.2.2
forums
conversation threads, 4.9.6.2.1

Copyright – *contd*
forums – *contd*
introduction, 4.9.6.2
UGC forums, 4.9.6.2.2
infringement
adaptation, 4.11.6
communication to the public, 4.11.5
copying, 4.11.1
examples, 4.13
introduction, 4.11
issuing copies to the public, 4.11.2
lending to the public, 4.11.3
performing in public, 4.11.4
playing in public, 4.11.4
renting to the public, 4.11.3
showing in public, 4.11.4
Internet examples
electronic mail, 4.9.6.1
forums, 4.9.6.2
introduction, 4.9.6
web links, 4.9.6.4
websites, 4.9.6.3
introduction, 4.9
issuing copies to the public, 4.11.2
jurisdiction over infringement, 4.16
lending to the public, 4.11.3
literary works, 4.9.2.1
moral rights
and see MORAL RIGHTS
infringement, 4.10.4
integrity, 4.10.2
introduction, 4.10
paternity, 4.10.1
waiver, 4.10.3
musical works, 4.9.2.1
originality, 4.9.2.3
performers' rights, 4.9.2.1
performing in public, 4.11.4
place of publication, 4.9.4.1
playing in public, 4.11.4
prohibited acts
adaptation, 4.11.6
communication to the public, 4.11.5
copying, 4.11.1
examples, 4.13
introduction, 4.11
issuing copies to the public, 4.11.2
lending to the public, 4.11.3
performing in public, 4.11.4
playing in public, 4.11.4
renting to the public, 4.11.3
showing in public, 4.11.4

Copyright – *contd*
protected works
fixation, 4.9.2.2
generally, 4.9.2.1
originality, 4.9.2.3
skill, labour or judgment, 4.9.2.4
protection
generally, 4.9.1
qualification, 4.9.4
relevant works, 4.9.2
scope, 4.9.3
term of protection, 4.9.5
qualification for protection
authorship, 4.9.4.2
broadcasts, 4.9.4.3
introduction, 4.9.4
place of publication, 4.9.4.1
renting to the public, 4.11.3
scope of protection, 4.9.3
search engines, 4.14
showing in public, 4.11.4
skill, labour or judgment, 4.9.2.4
sound recordings, 4.9.2.1
term of protection, 4.9.5
typographical arrangements, 4.9.2.1
web links
generally, 4.9.6.4
infringement, 4.14
websites
backup copies, 4.15.1
commercial issues, 4.9.6.3.6
computer programs, as, 4.9.6.3.7
creation, 4.9.6.3.1
deep links, 4.15.4
framing, 4.15.2
generally, 4.9.6.3
graphics, 4.9.6.3.4
infringement, 4.15
joint authorship, 4.9.6.3.9
jurisdiction over infringement, 4.16
'look and feel', 4.9.6.3.8
making an unlicensed article, 4.15.3
music, 4.9.6.3.5
preparatory material, 4.9.6.3.2
sounds, 4.9.6.3.5
spiders, 4.15.4
text, 4.9.6.3.3
Corporation tax
and see TAXATION
generally, 7.1
Correction of input errors
pre-contract information, and, 2.1.2.3.1

Credit card
payment, and, 2.2.2
Crime
anti-terrorism
defences, 5.4.2.3
dissemination of terrorist
publications, 5.4.2.2
introduction, 5.4
publication of terrorist statements,
5.4.2.1
threat to electronic systems, 5.4.1
computer misuse
extradition, 5.1.6.2
hacking for further criminal purpose,
5.1.3
introduction, 5.1.1
jurisdiction, 5.1.6.1
making, supplying or obtaining
articles for used in computer
misuse, 5.1.5
unauthorised access, 5.1.2
unauthorised acts to impair or to
prevent or hinder access, 5.1.4
cyberstalking, 5.5
dissemination of terrorist publications,
5.4.2.2
evidence
burden, 5.6.2
common law presumption, 5.6.1
introduction, 5.6
extradition, 5.1.6.2
fraud, 5.2
hacking for further criminal purpose
further offence, 5.1.3.1
future intention, 5.1.3.3
impossible further offence, 5.1.3.4
intention, 5.1.3.2
introduction, 5.1.3
sentencing, 5.1.3.5
harassment
Communications Act, under, 5.5.3
introduction, 5.5
Malicious Communications Act,
under, 5.5.2
Protection from Harassment Act,
under, 5.5.1
making, adapting, supplying or offering
to supply articles for commission
for an offence
generally, 5.1.5.1
introduction, 5.1.5
sentencing, 5.1.5.4

Crime – *contd*
obscene material
  indecent material, 5.3.2
  introduction, 5.3
  liability of ISPs, 5.3.4
  publication over the Internet, 5.3.1
  transmission, retrieval and
    downloading, 5.3.3
obtaining an article for supply or
  assistance in commission of an
  offence
  generally, 5.1.5.3
  introduction, 5.1.5
  sentencing, 5.1.5.4
publication of terrorist statements,
  5.4.2.1
stalking
  Communications Act, under, 5.5.3
  introduction, 5.5
  Malicious Communications Act,
    under, 5.5.2
  Protection from Harassment Act,
    under, 5.5.1
supply of article to commit or assist in
  commission of an offence
  generally, 5.1.5.2
  introduction, 5.1.5.2
  sentencing, 5.1.5.4
threat to electronic systems, 5.4.1
unauthorised access
  actus reus, 5.1.2.1
  conduct, 5.1.2.1
  for further criminal purpose, 5.1.3
  intention, 5.1.2.2
  introduction, 5.1.2
  mens rea, 5.1.2.2
  sentencing, 5.1.2.3
unauthorised acts to impair or to
  prevent or hinder access
  actus reus, 5.1.4.1
  conduct, 5.1.4.1
  intention, 5.1.4.2
  introduction, 5.1.4
  mens rea, 5.1.4.2
  sentencing, 5.1.4.3
Cyberstalking
Communications Act, under, 5.5.3
introduction, 5.5
Malicious Communications Act, under,
  5.5.2
Protection from Harassment Act, under,
  5.5.1

D
Damage
defamation, and, 3.6.4.1
negligence, and
  generally, 3.1.1.3
  harm to website user, 3.1.2.2.3
  viruses, 3.1.2.1.3
trespass, and, 3.2.3
Data controllers
'actual or potential processed data',
  6.2.3.1.2
'determines', 6.2.3.1.1
generally, 6.2.3.1
introduction, 6.2.3
jurisdictional scope, 6.2.3.1.3
Data processors
archives, 6.2.3.2.1
data warehousing, 6.2.3.2.1
generally, 6.2.3.2
introduction, 6.2.3
remote manipulation, 6.2.3.2.3
servers, 6.2.3.2.2
Data protection
accurate and up-to-date data
  'accuracy', 6.2.5.4.1
  Internet data sources, 6.2.5.4.1
  introduction, 6.2.5.4
  notification of inaccuracy, 6.2.5.4.1
  'up-to-date', 6.2.5.4.2
adequate, relevant and not excessive
  data
  future business models, 6.2.5.3.3
  introduction, 6.2.5.3
  living individual, 6.2.5.3.1
  P3P, 6.2.5.3.2
anonymous data, 6.2.1.3
archives, 6.2.3.2.1
automated processing, 6.2.5.6.3
automatic-answer modems, 6.2.5.7.2
back-up of data, 6.2.5.7.1
data, 6.2.1.1
data controllers
  'actual or potential processed data',
    6.2.3.1.2
  'determines', 6.2.3.1.1
  generally, 6.2.3.1
  introduction, 6.2.3
  jurisdictional scope, 6.2.3.1.3
data processors
  archives, 6.2.3.2.1
  data warehousing, 6.2.3.2.1
  generally, 6.2.3.2

Data protection – *contd*
  data processors – *contd*
    introduction, 6.2.3
    remote manipulation, 6.2.3.2.3
    servers, 6.2.3.2.2
  data subject access, 6.2.5.6.1
  data warehousing, 6.2.3.2.1
  definitions
    data controllers, 6.2.3
    data processors, 6.2.3
    introduction, 6.2
    personal data, 6.2.1
    processing, 6.2.2
  deletion of data, 6.2.5.7.1
  destruction of data, 6.2.5.7.1
  direct marketing, and
    and see DIRECT MARKETING
    consent requirements, 6.3.2
    enforcement, 6.3.3
    introduction, 6.3
    penalties, 6.3.3
    process in accordance with data
      subject's rights, 6.2.5.6.2
    transparency requirements, 6.3.1
  duration of retention of data, 6.2.5.5
  electronic mail marketing, 6.2.5.6.2
  enforcement, 6.2.6
  fair and lawful processing
    additional conditions, 6.2.5.1.4
    consent to processing, 6.2.5.1.4
    disingenuous consent, 6.2.5.1.1
    freely given, 6.2.5.1.4
    identity of data user, 6.2.5.1.1
    information obligations, 6.2.5.1.1
    informed consent, 6.2.5.1.4
    introduction, 6.2.5.1
    non-obvious purposes, 6.2.5.1.1
    obtaining data fairly, 6.2.5.1.1
    obtaining information fairly,
      6.2.5.1.2
    prior consent, 6.2.5.1.1
    processing data fairly, 6.2.5.1.3
    processing data lawfully, 6.2.5.1.5
    processing necessary, 6.2.5.1.4
    surreptitious obtaining, 6.2.5.1.1
  interception of communications, and
    and see INTERCEPTION OF
      COMMUNICATIONS
    data access obligations, 6.4.2
    data retention obligations, 6.4.3
    introduction, 6.4
    restrictions, 6.4.1

Data protection – *contd*
  keep no longer than necessary
    historical data, 6.2.5.5.2
    introduction, 6.2.5.5
    multiple purposes, 6.2.5.5.1
    'purge rule', 6.2.5.5.3
  keep secure
    'appropriate', 6.2.5.7.1
    automatic-answer modems, 6.2.5.7.2
    back-up of data, 6.2.5.7.1
    deletion of data, 6.2.5.7.1
    destruction of data, 6.2.5.7.1
    e-mail transactions, 6.2.5.7.2
    Internet security, 6.2.5.7.2
    introduction, 6.2.5.7
    networks, 6.2.5.7.2
    'organisation, adaptation or
      alteration', 6.2.5.7.1
    outsourcing, 6.2.5.7.1
    'processing', 6.2.5.7.1
    remote access, 6.2.5.7.2
    social authority, 6.2.5.7.1
    technical authority, 6.2.5.7.1
    'unauthorised', 6.2.5.7.1
    viruses, 6.2.5.7.2
    web servers, 6.2.5.7.2
  lawful obtaining, 6.2.5.2.2
  legislative provision
    Anti-Terrorism, Crime and Security
      Act 2001, 6.1.5
    Data Protection Act 1998, 6.1.2
    Data Retention Directive, 6.1.6
    introduction, 6.1
    Regulations, 6.1.3
    RIPA 2000, 6.1.4
  notification
    contents, 6.2.4.2
    exemptions, 6.2.4.1
    introduction, 6.2.4
  obtaining for lawful purposes, 6.2.5.2.2
  obtaining for specified purposes,
    6.2.5.2.1
  opinions on individuals, 6.2.1.2.4
  outsourcing, 6.2.5.7.1
  P3P, 6.2.5.3.2
  "personal"
    introduction, 6.2.1.2
    living individual, 6.2.1.2.2
    opinions on individuals, 6.2.1.2.4
    possession of other information,
      6.2.1.2.3
    relate to an individual, 6.2.1.2.1

Data protection – *contd*
personal data
anonymous, 6.2.1.3
data, 6.2.1.1
personal, 6.2.1.2
principles
accurate and up-to-date, 6.2.5.4
adequate, relevant and not excessive,
6.2.5.3
fair and lawful processing, 6.2.5.1
introduction, 6.2.5
keep no longer than necessary,
6.2.5.5
keep secure, 6.2.5.7
process in accordance with data
subject's rights, 6.2.5.6
prohibition of data transfer, 6.2.5.8
specified and lawful purposes,
6.2.5.2
Privacy and Electronic
Communications (EC Directive)
Regulations 2003, 6.1.3
process in accordance with data
subject's rights
automated processing, 6.2.5.6.3
data subject access, 6.2.5.6.1
direct marketing, 6.2.5.6.2
electronic mail marketing,
6.2.5.6.2
introduction, 6.2.5.6
processing, 6.2.2
prohibition of data transfer
assessment of adequacy, 6.2.5.8.3
case-by-case approval, 6.2.5.8.5
contractual clauses, 6.2.5.8.4
corporate rules, 6.2.5.8.6
EC Directive derogations,
6.2.5.8.7
EU determination of adequacy,
6.2.5.8.1
introduction, 6.2.5.8
US Safe Harbor Scheme, 6.2.5.8.2
Regulation of Investigatory Powers Act
2000, 6.1.4
remote access, 6.2.5.7.2
remote manipulation, 6.2.3.2.3
servers, 6.2.3.2.2
specified and lawful purposes, 6.2.5.2
value of personal data database,
6.2.5.2.3
viruses, 6.2.5.7.2
web servers, 6.2.5.7.2

Data retention
and see INTERCEPTION OF COMMUNICATIONS
compulsory scheme, 6.4.3.2
costs, 6.4.3.1.4
duration, 6.4.3.1.3
introduction, 6.4.3
purposes, 6.4.3.1.2
types of data, 6.4.3.1.1
voluntary scheme, 6.4.3.1
Data warehousing
data protection, and, 6.2.3.2.1
Database rights
and see COPYRIGHT
caching, 4.12.4.3
Creative Commons licences, 4.12.4.2
dealings
course of business, 4.12.3.3
exhibit, distribute and possess,
4.12.3.4
introduction, 4.12.3.2
knowledge, 4.12.3.5
reason to believe, 4.12.3.5–4.12.3.6
hosting, 4.12.4.4
infringement
dealings, 4.12.3
defences, 4.12.4
'extracts', 4.12
introduction, 4.12
secondary, 4.12.2
'substantial part', 4.12.1
'utilises', 4.12
introduction, 4.9.7
licences
Creative Commons, 4.12.4.2
generally, 4.12.4
temporary licence, 4.12.4.1
scope, 4.9.8.1
secondary infringement, 4.12.2
term of protection, 4.9.8.2
Databases
and see DATABASE RIGHTS
copyright, and, 4.9.7.1
Deep linking
websites, and, 4.15.4
Defamation
caching defence, 3.6.3.2.2
damages
extent of publication, 3.6.4.2
presumption of damage, 3.6.4.1
reductions and recommendations,
3.6.4.3
defamatory statements, 3.6.2.1

Defamation – *contd*
defences
  caching defence, 3.6.3.2.2
  hosting defence, 3.6.3.2.1
  introduction, 3.6.3
  mere conduit defence, 3.6.3.2.2
  s.1 defence, 3.6.3.1
designing websites, 3.6.3.1.3
e-mails, and, 3.6.3.1.3
extent of publication, 3.6.1.3
forums, 3.6.3.1.3
hosting defence, 3.6.3.2.1
identity of defendant, 3.6.1.2
introduction, 3.6
mere conduit, 3.6.2.5
mere conduit defence, 3.6.3.2.2
mirror sites, 3.6.3.1.3
newsgroups, 3.6.3.1.3
publication, 3.6.2.4
s.1 defence, 3.6.3.1
similar interests, 3.6.2.2
statutory provision
  defamatory material, 3.6.2.3
  defamatory statements, 3.6.2.1
  introduction, 3.6.2
  mere conduit, 3.6.2.5
  publication, 3.6.2.4
  similar interests, 3.6.2.2
  storage providers, 3.6.2.6
storage providers, 3.6.2.6
strategy, 3.6.5
technicalities
  extent of publication, 3.6.1.3
  identity of defendant, 3.6.1.2
  introduction, 3.6.1
  third party, 3.6.1.1
third party, 3.6.1.1
types of defamatory material, 3.6.2.3
websites, 3.6.3.1.3
Defences
anti-terrorism, and
  hosting defence, 5.4.2.3.2
  mere conduit defence, 5.4.2.3.2
  take down notices, 5.4.2.3.1
defamation, and
  caching defence, 3.6.3.2.2
  hosting defence, 3.6.3.2.1
  introduction, 3.6.3
  mere conduit defence, 3.6.3.2.2
  s.1 defence, 3.6.3.1
negligence, and
  consent, 3.1.1.5.2

Defences – *contd*
negligence, and – *contd*
  contributory negligence, 3.1.1.5.1
  Electronic Commerce Regulations,
    in, 3.1.1.5.3
  harm to website user, 3.1.2.2.5
  introduction, 3.1.1.5
  viruses, 3.1.2.1.5
Delay
offers, and, 2.1.3.5.1
Digital cash
introduction, 2.2.3
'pure', 2.2.3.2
third party, 2.2.3.1
Digital signatures
advanced, 2.1.4.5.2
basic, 2.1.4.5.1
Dilution
due cause, 4.4.6.1
introduction, 4.4.6
unfair advantage or detriment,
  4.4.6.2
Direct marketing
see also DATA PROTECTION
consent requirements
  e-mail marketing, 6.3.2.1–6.3.2.3
  introduction, 6.3.2
data subject's rights, and, 6.2.5.6.2
e-mail marketing
  corporate subscribers, to, 6.3.2.3
  individual subscribers, to, 6.3.2.1–
    6.3.2.2
enforcement, 6.3.3
introduction, 6.3
opt-in requirements
  generally, 6.3.2.1
  soft exception, 6.3.2.2
penalties
  Data Protection Act, 6.3.3.2
  introduction, 6.3.3
  PEC Regulations, 6.3.3.1
soft opt-in exception, 6.3.2.2
transparency requirements, 6.3.1
Disclaimers
exclusions
  digital damage, 3.5.1.1
  effectiveness, 3.5.2
  incorporation, 3.5.2.1
  limitations, 3.5.2.2
  negligent links, 3.5.1.3
  negligent misstatement, 3.5.1.2
  UCTA 1977, and, 3.5.2.2.1

Disclaimers – *contd*
exclusions – *contd*
UTCCR 1999, and, 3.5.2.2.2
introduction, 3.5
Dissemination of terrorist publications
generally, 5.4.2.2
Dispute resolution (trade marks)
confusingly similar to mark, 4.7.3.2
disclaimers, 4.7.3.2.1
factual issues, 4.7.2
formal issues, 4.7.1
identical to mark, 4.7.3.2
introduction, 4.7
irrelevant changes, 4.7.3.2.2
legal issues, 4.7.3
nature of mark, 4.7.3.1
no rights or interest in domain name,
4.7.3.3
other matters, 4.7.3.5
registration companies, and, 4.7.5
registration in bad faith, 4.7.3.4
timing of arbitration, 4.7.4
Distance sales of goods and services
cancellation rights
cancellable goods and services,
9.5.2.4.1
consumer obligations, 9.5.2.4.8
effects, 9.5.2.4.7
financial contracts with customers,
and, 9.2.3.3
introduction, 9.5.2.4
manner of cancellation, 9.5.2.4.3
supplier not provided information in
durable medium, where,
9.5.2.4.6
supplier obligations, 9.5.2.4.9
time limits for goods, 9.5.2.4.4
time limits for services, 9.5.2.4.5
exempt transactions, 9.5.2.1.1
financial contracts with customers, and
introduction, 9.2.3.1
means of distance communication,
9.2.3.1.2
suppliers and consumers,
9.2.3.1.3
transaction types, 9.2.3.1.1
introduction, 9.5.2
means of distance communication,
9.5.2.1.2
pre-contract information
and see PRE-CONTRACT INFORMATION
durable medium, in, 9.5.2.3

Distance sales of goods and services –
contd
pre-contract information – *contd*
financial contracts with customers,
9.2.3.2
introduction, 9.5.2.2
manner of provision, 9.5.2.2.2
performance, prior to, 9.5.2.3
relevant information, 9.5.2.2.1
Regulations, 2.1
risks of breach of regulations
extension of cancellation rights,
9.5.2.5.1
financial contracts with customers,
9.2.3.4
injunctions, 9.5.2.5.2
introduction, 9.5.2.5
'stop now' orders, 9.5.2.5.2
scope of regulation
consumers, 9.5.2.1.3
exempt transactions, 9.5.2.1.1
introduction, 9.5.2.1
means of distance communication,
9.5.2.1.2
suppliers, 9.5.2.1.3
suppliers and consumers, 9.5.2.1.3
Distance Selling Regulations
generally, 2.1
Distinctiveness
trade marks, and, 4.4.5.1
Domain names
generally, 1.5.1
Domain names (trade marks)
availability, 4.6.1
descriptive, 4.2.2.1
generally, 4.1.3–4.1.4
identifying ownership, 4.3.1
misrepresentation, 4.5.2.1
protection, 4.6.4
protective measures
availability of name, 4.6.1
dispute rules, 4.6.5
introduction, 4.6
protection of name, 4.6.4
registration of name, 4.6.2
use of name, 4.6.3
registration, 4.3
use of sign in course of trade, 4.4.1.3
Domicile of defendant
company domicile, 2.4.1.2.2
EFTA state domicile
companies, 2.4.1.2.2

Domicile of defendant – *contd*
EFTA state domiciled – *contd*
individuals, 2.4.1.2.1
individual, 2.4.1.2.1
introduction, 2.4.1.2
legal person's domicile, 2.4.1.2.2
member state domicile
companies, 2.4.1.2.2
individuals, 2.4.1.2.1
non-member state domicile
companies, 2.4.1.2.2
individuals, 2.4.1.2.1
UK domicile
companies, 2.4.1.2.2
individuals, 2.4.1.2.1
Dramatic works
copyright, and, 4.9.2.1
Duty of care
generally, 3.1.1.1
harm to website user, 3.1.2.2.1
viruses, 3.1.2.1.1

E

Economic loss
negligence, and, 3.1.2.1.3
Economic torts
generally, 3.3.4
Electronic Commerce Regulations
generally, 2.1
obscene material, and, 5.3.4.2
Electronic mail marketing
data protection, and, 6.2.5.6.2
Electronic money
and see FINANCIAL PRODUCTS AND
SERVICES
regulation, 9.2.2
Electronic signatures
advanced, 2.1.4.5.2
basic, 2.1.4.5.1
E-mail
acceptance, and
generally, 2.1.4.1.2
timing, 2.1.4.2.2
copyright, and
generally, 4.9.6.1
infringement, 4.13.1
data protection, and
marketing, 6.2.5.6.2
security, 6.2.5.7.2
defamation, and, 3.6.3.1.3
direct marketing, and
corporate subscribers, to, 6.3.2.3

E-mail – *contd*
direct marketing, and – *contd*
individual subscribers, to, 6.3.2.1–
6.3.2.2
generally, 1.5.2
infringement of copyright, and
ISP, by, 4.13.1.2
recipient, by, 4.13.1.1
jurisdiction, and, 2.4.1.8.1
marketing, and, 6.2.5.6.2
offers, and, 2.1.3.5.1
E-mail contracts
jurisdiction, and, 2.4.1.8.1
Enforcement
competition law, and
commitments, 8.5.5
complaints, 8.5.1
fines, 8.5.6
interim measures, 8.5.3
investigations, 8.5.2
orders to terminate infringements,
8.5.4
whistleblowing, 8.5.7
data protection, and, 6.2.6
Establishment of providers
introduction, 2.1.2.1
location of servers, 2.1.2.1.1
multiple establishments, 2.1.2.1.2
Evidence (criminal)
burden
continuity of access evidence, 5.6.2.1
generally, 5.6.2
common law presumption, 5.6.1
continuity of access evidence
false identification, 5.6.2.1.2
fragmentation of Internet hacking,
5.6.2.1.1
generally, 5.6.2.1
spoofing, 5.6.2.1.2
introduction, 5.6
Exclusions
digital damage, 3.5.1.1
effectiveness, 3.5.2
incorporation, 3.5.2.1
limitations
introduction, 3.5.2.2
UCTA 1977, 3.5.2.2.1
UTCCR 1999, 3.5.2.2.2
negligent links, 3.5.1.3
negligent misstatement, 3.5.1.2
Exhaustion of rights
intellectual property rights, and, 2.3.1

Express licence
intellectual property rights, and, 2.3.5
Extradition
generally, 5.1.6.2
introduction, 5.1.6

F
Fair and lawful processing
see also DATA PROTECTION
additional conditions, 6.2.5.1.4
consent to processing, 6.2.5.1.4
disingenuous consent, 6.2.5.1.1
freely given, 6.2.5.1.4
identity of data user, 6.2.5.1.1
information obligations, 6.2.5.1.1
informed consent, 6.2.5.1.4
introduction, 6.2.5.1
non-obvious purposes, 6.2.5.1.1
obtaining data fairly, 6.2.5.1.1
obtaining information fairly, 6.2.5.1.2
prior consent, 6.2.5.1.1
processing data fairly, 6.2.5.1.3
processing data lawfully, 6.2.5.1.5
processing necessary, 6.2.5.1.4
surreptitious obtaining, 6.2.5.1.1
False identification
criminal evidence, and, 5.6.2.1.2
Fax
offers, and, 2.1.3.5.1
File transfer protocol (FTP)
generally, 1.5.8
Films
copyright, and, 4.9.2.1
Financial contracts with customers
cancellation rights
cancellable services, 9.2.3.3.1
introduction, 9.2.3.3
manner of cancellation, 9.2.3.3.2
obligations, 9.2.3.3.3
distance consumer contracts
introduction, 9.2.3.1
means of distance communication,
9.2.3.1.2
suppliers and consumers,
9.2.3.1.3
transaction types, 9.2.3.1.1
introduction, 9.2.3
pre-contract information
introduction, 9.2.3.2
manner of provision, 9.2.3.2.1
risks of breach of regulations, 9.2.3.4

Financial products and services
contracts with customers
cancellation rights, 9.2.3.3
distance consumer contracts, 9.2.3.1
introduction, 9.2.3
pre-contract information, 9.2.3.2
risks of breach of regulations, 9.2.3.4
electronic money, 9.2.2
financial promotions rules
Electronic Commerce Directive,
9.2.1.1
general rules, 9.2.1.2
introduction, 9.2.1
introduction, 9.2
Fixation
copyright, and, 4.9.2.2
Formation of contracts
acceptance
authentication, 2.1.4.5
"battle of the forms", 2.1.4.3
digital signatures, 2.1.4.5
e-mail, by, 2.1.4.1.2
introduction, 2.1.4
means, 2.1.4.1
mistake, and, 2.1.4.4
timing, 2.1.4.2
website, through, 2.1.4.1.1
consideration
introduction, 2.1.5
web-wrap, 2.1.5.1
digital signatures, 2.1.4.5
Distance Selling Regulations, 2.1
Electronic Commerce Regulations, 2.1
general approach, 2.1.1
intention
introduction, 2.1.6
programmed intention, 2.1.6.1
introduction, 2.1
invitations to treat
introduction, 2.1.3
location, 2.1.3.5
misrepresentations, 2.1.3.4
shops, 2.1.3.2
timing, 2.1.3.5
web invitations, 2.1.3.3
webvertisements, 2.1.3.1
misrepresentations, 2.1.3.4
offers
introduction, 2.1.3
location, 2.1.3.5
misrepresentations, 2.1.3.4
shops, 2.1.3.2

Formation of contracts – *contd*
offers – *contd*
timing, 2.1.3.5
web invitations, 2.1.3.3
webvertisements, 2.1.3.1
pre-contract information
establishment of providers, 2.1.2.1
general information, 2.1.2.2
introduction, 2.1.2
transactional information, 2.1.2.3
stipulation by parties, 2.1.1.1
web invitations, 2.1.3.3
webvertisements, 2.1.3.1
Forums
copyright, and
conversation threads, 4.9.6.2.1
infringement, 4.13.1.3
introduction, 4.9.6.2
UGC forums, 4.9.6.2.2
defamation, and, 3.6.3.1.3
generally, 1.5.6
Framing
websites, and, 4.15.2
Fraud
generally, 5.2

G

Gambling
betting, 9.4.1.1
enforcement, 9.4.1.6
facilities provision, 9.4.1.5
gaming, 9.4.1.2
generally, 9.4.1
introduction, 9.4
licensing, 9.4.1.6
lotteries, 9.4.1.3
meaning, 9.4.1
remote gambling, 9.4.1.4
Graphics
websites, and, 4.9.6.3.4

H

'Hacking'
actus reus
alteration of programs or data,
5.1.2.1.3
automatic causation of function,
5.1.2.1.2
computer, 5.1.2.1.1
copying programs and data, 5.1.2.1.3
data, 5.1.2.1.1
erasure of programs or data, 5.1.2.1.3

'Hacking' – *contd*
acus reus – *contd*
function on any computer, 5.1.2.1.2
held in any computer, 5.1.2.1.1
introduction, 5.1.2.1
moving programs and data, 5.1.2.1.3
output of programs or data, 5.1.2.1.3
performing any function, 5.1.2.1.2
program, 5.1.2.1.1
securing access, 5.1.2.1.3
unsuccessful attempts, 5.1.2.1.2
using a program, 5.1.2.1.3
alteration of programs or data, 5.1.2.1.3
automatic causation of function,
5.1.2.1.2
computer, 5.1.2.1.1
conduct, 5.1.2.1
copying programs and data, 5.1.2.1.3
data, 5.1.2.1.1
erasure of programs or data, 5.1.2.1.3
for further criminal purpose, 5.1.3
function on any computer, 5.1.2.1.2
held in any computer, 5.1.2.1.1
intention, 5.1.2.2
introduction, 5.1.2
mens rea
insiders, 5.1.2.2.4
intention to secure access, 5.1.2.2.1
introduction, 5.1.2.2
outsiders, 5.1.2.2.3
unauthorised, 5.1.2.2.2
moving programs and data, 5.1.2.1.3
output of programs or data, 5.1.2.1.3
performing any function, 5.1.2.1.2
program, 5.1.2.1.1
securing access, 5.1.2.1.3
sentencing, 5.1.2.3
unauthorised, 5.1.2.2.2
unsuccessful attempts, 5.1.2.1.2
using a program, 5.1.2.1.3
'Hacking' for further criminal purpose
further offence, 5.1.3.1
future intention, 5.1.3.3
impossible further offence, 5.1.3.4
intention, 5.1.3.2
introduction, 5.1.3
sentencing, 5.1.3.5
Harassment
Communications Act, under, 5.5.3
introduction, 5.5
Malicious Communications Act, under,
5.5.2

Harassment – *contd*
Protection from Harassment Act, under
causing fear of violence, 5.5.1.2
introduction, 5.5.1
relevant conduct, 5.5.1.1
Harm to website user
breach of duty, 3.1.2.2.2
causation, 3.1.2.2.4
damage, 3.1.2.2.3
defences, 3.1.2.2.5
duty of care, 3.1.2.2.1
introduction, 3.1.2.2
Hedley Byrne v Heller
bulletin boards, 3.4.1.3.2
finding or requesting, 3.4.1.4.2
identity, 3.4.2
instant messaging, 3.4.1.3.1
introduction, 3.4.1
reasonable reliance
information, on, 3.4.1.4
Internet, on, 3.4.1.3
tailored websites, 3.4.1.4.1
website, 3.4.1.3.3
Hosting defence
anti-terrorism, and, 5.4.2.3.2
defamation, and, 3.6.3.2.1
Hypertext Markup Language (HTML)
generally, 1.5.9.1

I

Identification of input errors
pre-contract information, and, 2.1.2.3.1
Implied licence
intellectual property rights, and, 2.3.4
Income tax
and see TAXATION
generally, 7.1
Indecent material
introduction, 5.3.2
photographs, 5.3.2.1
Infringement of copyright
adaptation, 4.11.6
communication to the public, 4.11.5
copying, 4.11.1
e-mail, and
ISP, by, 4.13.1.2
recipient, by, 4.13.1.1
examples
e-mail, 4.13.1.1–14.3.1.2
forums, 4.13.1.3
peer-to-peer networks, 4.13.1.4
forums, and, 4.13.1.3

Infringement of copyright – *contd*
introduction, 4.11
issuing copies to the public, 4.11.2
lending to the public, 4.11.3
peer-to-peer networks, and, 4.13.1.4
performing in public, 4.11.4
playing in public, 4.11.4
renting to the public, 4.11.3
showing in public, 4.11.4
Infringement of database rights
dealings, 4.12.3
defences, 4.12.4
'extracts', 4.12
introduction, 4.12
secondary, 4.12.2
'substantial part', 4.12.1
'utilises', 4.12
Infringement of trade marks
defences, 4.4.8
dilution, 4.4.6
identical sign to registered mark,
4.4.4
in relation to goods and services, 4.4.3
introduction, 4.4
jurisdiction
applicable law, 4.8.5
basic rules, 4.8.3.2
EC domiciles, and, 4.8.3
E-Commerce Directive, 4.8.3.1
exclusive jurisdiction, 4.8.3.3
generally, 4.8.2
introduction, 4.8
non-EC domiciles, and, 4.8.4
unregistered rights, of, 4.8.3.4
metatags, 4.4.7
similar or identical sign with similar or
identical goods or services, 4.4.5
use as trade mark, 4.4.2
use of sign in course of trade, 4.4.1
Instant messaging (IM)
generally, 1.5.4
Hedley Byrne v Heller, and, 3.4.1.3.1
Intellectual property rights
auctions, 2.3.6
contracts, and
auctions, 2.3.6
exhaustion of rights, 2.3.1
express licence, 2.3.5
implied licence, 2.3.4
introduction, 2.3
retention of title, 2.3.2
use as copying, 2.3.3

Intellectual property rights – *contd*
copyright
  and see COPYRIGHT
  database rights, 4.9.7
  general protection, 4.9.1
  infringement, 4.11
  infringement examples, 4.13
  Internet examples, 4.9.6
  introduction, 4.9
  jurisdiction over infringement,
    4.16
  moral rights, 4.10
  prohibited acts, 4.11
  protected works, 4.9.2
  qualification requirements, 4.9.4
  scope of protection, 4.9.3
  term of protection, 4.9.5
  web links, 4.14
  websites, 4.15
database rights
  and see DATABASE RIGHTS
  infringement, 4.12
  introduction, 4.9.7
  nature, 4.9.7.1
  scope, 4.9.8.1
  term of protection, 4.9.8.2
exhaustion of rights, 2.3.1
express licence, 2.3.5
implied licence, 2.3.4
introduction, 2.3
moral rights
  and see MORAL RIGHTS
  infringement, 4.10.4
  integrity, 4.10.2
  introduction, 4.10
  paternity, 4.10.1
  waiver, 4.10.3
retention of title, 2.3.2
search engines, 4.14
trade marks
  and see TRADE MARKS
  dispute resolution, 4.7
  domain names, 4.1.3–4.1.4
  infringement, 4.4
  introduction, 4.1
  jurisdiction over infringement, 4.8
  nature of rights, 4.1.1–4.1.2
  passing off, 4.5
  protective measures, 4.6
  registration, 4.2–4.3
use as copying, 2.3.3
web links, 4.14

Intellectual property rights – *contd*
websites
  backup copies, 4.15.1
  deep links, 4.15.4
  framing, 4.15.2
  introduction, 4.15
  jurisdiction over infringement, 4.16
  making an unlicensed article, 4.15.3
  spiders, 4.15.4
Intention
acceptance, and, 2.1.4.1.1
introduction, 2.1.6
programmed intention, 2.1.6.1
Interception of communications
see also DATA PROTECTION
data access, 6.4.2
data retention
  compulsory scheme, 6.4.3.2
  costs, 6.4.3.1.4
  duration, 6.4.3.1.3
  introduction, 6.4.3
  purposes, 6.4.3.1.2
  types of data, 6.4.3.1.1
  voluntary scheme, 6.4.3.1
introduction, 6.4
restrictions, 6.4.1
Internet
concepts, 1.5
cost, 1.4
historical background, 1.1–1.3
Internet access
introduction, 9.1.1
OFCOM regulation, 9.1.2
self-regulation, 9.1.4
VOIP, 9.1.3
Internet payment
credit card, 2.2.2
digital cash
  introduction, 2.2.3
  'pure', 2.2.3.2
  third party, 2.2.3.1
generally, 2.2.1
Internet service providers (ISPs)
obscene material, and, 5.3.4
Internet Watch Foundation
obscene material, and, 5.3.4.1
Intervening acts
negligence, and, 3.1.1.4.3
Invitations to treat
introduction, 2.1.3
location, 2.1.3.5
misrepresentations, 2.1.3.4

Invitations to treat – *contd*
post, by, 2.1.3.5.1
shops, 2.1.3.2.1
timing, 2.1.3.5
web invitations, 2.1.3.3
webvertisements, 2.1.3.1
IP addresses
generally, 1.5.1
trade marks, and, 4.1.3

J

Jurisdiction
anti-competitive agreements, and, 8.3.5
Brussels Regulation (contract), under
civil and commercial matter, 2.4.1.1
consumer contracts, 2.4.1.6
contract, and, 2.4.1.3
domicile of defendant, 2.4.1.2
express choice of clause, 2.4.1.7
introduction, 2.4
other obligations, 2.4.1.5
place of performance, 2.4.1.4
Brussels Regulation (tort), under
defamation, 3.7.2.2.4
digital damage, 3.7.2.2.1
generally, 3.7.2
introduction, 3.7.1
location of harmful events, 3.7.2.2
meaning of 'tort', 3.7.2.1
negligent misstatement, 3.7.2.2.3
secondary damage, 3.7.2.2.2
civil and commercial matter, 2.4.1.1
common law (contract), at
contract sub-rule, under, 2.4.1.8.1
introduction, 2.4.1.8
service out, 2.4.1.8.1
staying actions, 2.4.1.8.2
common law (tort), at
extent of circulation, 3.7.3.3
introduction, 3.7.3
service out, 3.7.3.1
staying actions, 3.7.3.2
tort sub-rule, under, 3.7.3.1.1
computer misuse, and
double criminality, 5.1.6.1.2
generally, 5.1.6.1
introduction, 5.1.6
location of accused, 5.1.6.1.1
location of victim computer,
5.1.6.1.1
section 1, under, 5.1.6.1.1
section 2, under, 5.1.6.1.2

Jurisdiction – *contd*
computer misuse, and – *contd*
section 3, under, 5.1.6.1.3
significant link, 5.1.6.1.1
consumer contracts
direct activities to several member
states, 2.4.1.6.2
introduction, 2.4.1.6
pursuing activities in consumer's
member state, 2.4.1.6.1
contract, and
Brussels Regulation, 2.4.1.1–2.4.1.7
common law, at, 2.4.1.8
introduction, 2.4
contract sub-rule, under, 2.4.1.8.1
copyright infringement, and
examples, 4.13
generally, 4.11
defamation, 3.7.2.2.4
digital damage, 3.7.2.2.1
domicile of defendant
company domicile, 2.4.1.2.2
EFTA state domicile,
2.4.1.2.1–2.4.1.2.2
individual, 2.4.1.2.1
introduction, 2.4.1.2
legal person's domicile, 2.4.1.2.2
member state domicile,
2.4.1.2.1–2.4.1.2.2
non-member state domicile,
2.4.1.2.1–2.4.1.2.2
UK domicile, 2.4.1.2.1–2.4.1.2.2
e-mail contracts, 2.4.1.8.1
express choice of clause, 2.4.1.7
extent of circulation, 3.7.3.3
location of harmful events, 3.7.2.2
negligent misstatement, 3.7.2.2.3
other obligations, 2.4.1.5
place of performance, 2.4.1.4
secondary damage, 3.7.2.2.2
tort, and
Brussels Regulation, 3.7.1–3.7.2
common law, 3.7.3
introduction, 3.7
tort sub-rule, under, 3.7.3.1.1
trade mark infringement, and
applicable law, 4.8.5
basic rules, 4.8.3.2
EC domiciles, and, 4.8.3
E-Commerce Directive, 4.8.3.1
exclusive jurisdiction, 4.8.3.3
generally, 4.8.2

Jurisdiction – *contd*
    trade mark infringement, and – *contd*
        introduction, 4.8
        non-EC domiciles, and, 4.8.4
        unregistered rights, of, 4.8.3.4
    website contracts, 2.4.1.8.1

L

Language of contract
    pre-contract information, and, 2.1.2.3.1
Links
    generally, 1.5.9.1
Literary works
    copyright, and, 4.9.2.1
    databases, and, 4.9.7.1
'Look and feel'
    websites, and, 4.9.6.3.8
Lugano Convention
    And see JURISDICTION
    contract, 2.4.1
    tort, 3.7.1

M

Madrid Protocol
    trade marks, and, 4.2
**Making articles for commission for an
    offence**
    generally, 5.1.5.1
    introduction, 5.1.5
    sentencing, 5.1.5.4
Market investigations
    and see COMPETITION LAW
    generally, 8.8
    legal framework, 8.2.3
Merger control
    and see COMPETITION LAW
    Enterprise Act, 8.7.2
    generally, 8.7
    legal framework, 8.2.4
    Regulation, 8.7.1
Mens rea
    unauthorised access, and
        insiders, 5.1.2.2.4
        intention to secure access, 5.1.2.2.1
        introduction, 5.1.2.2
        outsiders, 5.1.2.2.3
        unauthorised, 5.1.2.2.2
    unauthorised acts to impair or to
        prevent or hinder access, and
        computer, program or data. 5.1.4.2.1
        intent to impair or prevent or hinder
            access, 5.1.4.2.1

Mens rea – *contd*
    unauthorised acts to impair or to prevent
        or hinder access, and – *contd*
        introduction, 5.1.4.2
        recklessness as to act, 5.1.4.2.2
        temporarily, 5.1.4.2.1
Mere conduit defence
    anti-terrorism, and, 5.4.2.3.2
    defamation, and, 3.6.3.2.2
Metatags
    generally, 4.4.7.1
    introduction, 4.4.7
    keywords, 4.4.7.2
Mirror sites
    defamation, and, 3.6.3.1.3
Misrepresentations
    offers, and, 2.1.3.4
Mistake
    acceptance, and, 2.1.4.4
Moral rights
    and see COPYRIGHT
    attribution as author, 4.10.1
    false attribution as author, 4.10
    infringement, 4.10.4
    integrity, 4.10.2
    introduction, 4.10
    objection to derogatory treatment,
        4.10.2
    paternity, 4.10.1
    waiver, 4.10.3
**Multipurpose Internet Mailing
    Extensions (MIME)**
    generally, 1.5.2
Music
    websites, and, 4.9.6.3.5
Musical works
    copyright, and, 4.9.2.1

N

Navigation aids
    generally, 1.5.9.3
Negligence
    application
        harm to website user, 3.1.2.2
        introduction, 3.1.2
        viruses, 3.1.2.1
    breach of duty
        generally, 3.1.1.2
        harm to website user, 3.1.2.2.2
        viruses, 3.1.2.1.2
    causation
        harm to website user, 3.1.2.2.4

Negligence – *contd*
causation – *contd*
intervening acts, 3.1.1.4.3
introduction, 3.1.1.4
'thin-skull' rule, 3.1.1.4.1
type of damage, 3.1.1.4.2
viruses, 3.1.2.1.4
consent
generally, 3.1.1.5.2
viruses, 3.1.2.1.5
contributory negligence
generally, 3.1.1.5.1
viruses, 3.1.2.1.5
damage
generally, 3.1.1.3
harm to website user, 3.1.2.2.3
viruses, 3.1.2.1.3
defences
consent, 3.1.1.5.2
contributory negligence, 3.1.1.5.1
Electronic Commerce Regulations,
in, 3.1.1.5.3
harm to website user, 3.1.2.2.5
introduction, 3.1.1.5
viruses, 3.1.2.1.5
duty of care
generally, 3.1.1.1
harm to website user, 3.1.2.2.1
viruses, 3.1.2.1.1
economic loss, 3.1.2.1.3
Electronic Commerce Regulations
defence
generally, 3.1.1.5.3
viruses, 3.1.2.1.5
elements
breach of duty, 3.1.1.2
causation, 3.1.1.4
damage, 3.1.1.3
duty of care, 3.1.1.1
introduction, 3.1.1
harm to website user
breach of duty, 3.1.2.2.2
causation, 3.1.2.2.4
damage, 3.1.2.2.3
defences, 3.1.2.2.5
duty of care, 3.1.2.2.1
introduction, 3.1.2.2
intervening acts, 3.1.1.4.3
introduction, 3.1
standard of care
generally, 3.1.1.2
harm to website user, 3.1.2.2.2

Negligence – *contd*
standard of care – *contd*
viruses, 3.1.2.1.2
'thin-skull' rule, 3.1.1.4.1
viruses
breach of duty, 3.1.2.1.2
causation, 3.1.2.1.4
consent, 3.1.2.1.5
contributory negligence, 3.1.2.1.5
damage, 3.1.2.1.3
defences, 3.1.2.1.5
digital damage, 3.1.2.1.3
duty of care, 3.1.2.1.1
economic loss, 3.1.2.1.3
Negligent misstatement
exclusions, and, 3.5.1.2
generally, 3.4
Hedley Byrne v Heller, 3.4.1
identity, 3.4.2
reasonable reliance, 3.4.3–3.4.4
Networks
data protection, and, 6.2.5.7.2
generally, 1.1
Newsgroups
defamation, and, 3.6.3.1.3

O
Obscene material
Electronic Commerce Regulations,
5.3.4.2
indecent material
introduction, 5.3.2
photographs, 5.3.2.1
Internet Watch Foundation, 5.3.4.1
introduction, 5.3
liability of ISPs, 5.3.4
photographs, 5.3.2.1
publication over the Internet
abroad, 5.3.1.2
generally, 5.3.1
transmission or retrieval, 5.3.1.1
transmission, retrieval and
downloading, 5.3.3
**Obtaining an article for supply or
assistance in commission of an
offence**
generally, 5.1.5.3
introduction, 5.1.5
sentencing, 5.1.5.4
Occupiers' liability
generally, 3.3.1

Offering to supply articles for commission for an offence
generally, 5.1.5.1
introduction, 5.1.5
sentencing, 5.1.5.4
Offers
consumers, by, 2.1.3.5.1
delay, and, 2.1.3.5.1
e-mail, by, 2.1.3.5.1
fax, by, 2.1.3.5.1
introduction, 2.1.3
location, 2.1.3.5
misrepresentations, 2.1.3.4
post, by, 2.1.3.5.1
shops
  invitations, 2.1.3.2.1
  offers, 2.1.3.2.2
timing, 2.1.3.5
web invitations, 2.1.3.3
webvertisements, 2.1.3.1
Online gambling
betting, 9.4.1.1
enforcement, 9.4.1.6
facilities provision, 9.4.1.5
gaming, 9.4.1.2
generally, 9.4.1
introduction, 9.4
licensing, 9.4.1.6
lotteries, 9.4.1.3
meaning, 9.4.1
remote gambling, 9.4.1.4
Originality
copyright, and, 4.9.2.3
Outsourcing
data protection, and, 6.2.5.7.1

P
P3P
data protection, and, 6.2.5.3.2
Partnerships
taxation, and, 7.3
Passing off
BT v One in a Million decision, 4.5.4.1
damage, 4.5.3
disclaimer, 4.5.2.2
domain name misrepresentation, 4.5.2.1
goodwill of plaintiff, 4.5.1
instrument of fraud claim, 4.5.4
introduction, 4.5
misrepresentation by defendant, 4.5.2
remedies, 4.5.5

Payment
credit card, 2.2.2
digital cash
  introduction, 2.2.3
  'pure', 2.2.3.2
  third party, 2.2.3.1
generally, 2.2.1
Peer-to-peer networks
infringement of copyright, and, 4.13.1.4
Performance
payment, 2.2
Performers' rights
and see COPYRIGHT
generally, 4.9.2.1
Permanent establishment
taxation, and, 7.7
Personal data
and see DATA PROTECTION
anonymous, 6.2.1.3
data, 6.2.1.1
personal, 6.2.1.2
Photographs
obscene material, and, 5.3.2.1
Place of performance
jurisdiction, and, 2.4.1.4
Portals
navigation aids, and, 1.5.9.3
Post
acceptance, and, 2.1.4.2.1
offer, and, 2.1.3.5.1
Pre-contract information
codes of conduct, 2.1.2.3.1
correction of input errors, 2.1.2.3.1
distance selling, and
  and see PRE-CONTRACT INFORMATION
    (DISTANCE SELLING)
  cancelling services, 9.5.2.3.3
  cost of cancellation, 9.5.2.3.2
  durable medium, in, 9.5.2.3
  financial contracts with customers,
    9.2.3.2
  introduction, 9.5.2.2
  manner of provision, 9.5.2.2.2
  performance, prior to, 9.5.2.3
  relevant information, 9.5.2.2.1
establishment of providers
  introduction, 2.1.2.1
  location of servers, 2.1.2.1.1
  multiple establishments,
    2.1.2.1.2
filing concluded contract, 2.1.2.3.1

Pre-contract information – *contd*
  financial contracts with customers, and
    introduction, 9.2.3.2
    manner of provision, 9.2.3.2.1
  general information
    disclosable information, 2.1.2.2.1
    form, 2.1.2.2.2
    introduction, 2.1.2.2
    manner, 2.1.2.2.2
  identification of input errors, 2.1.2.3.1
  introduction, 2.1.2
  language of contract, 2.1.2.3.1
  technical steps to conclude contract,
    2.1.2.3.1
  terms and conditions for storage and
    reproduction, 2.1.2.3.1
  transactional information
    clear, comprehensible and
      unambiguous, 2.1.2.3.1
    introduction, 2.1.2.3
**Pre-contract information (distance
  selling)**
  cost of cancellation, 9.5.2.3.2
  durable medium, in
    cancelling services, 9.5.2.3.3
    cost of cancellation, 9.5.2.3.2
    introduction, 9.5.2.3
    manner of provision, 9.5.2.3.4
    relevant information, 9.5.2.3.1
  financial contracts with customers, and
    introduction, 9.2.3.2
    manner of provision, 9.2.3.2.1
  introduction, 9.5.2.2
  manner of provision, 9.5.2.2.2
  performance, prior to
    cancelling services, 9.5.2.3.3
    cost of cancellation, 9.5.2.3.2
    introduction, 9.5.2.3
    manner of provision, 9.5.2.3.4
    relevant information, 9.5.2.3.1
  relevant information, 9.5.2.2.1
Processing
  and see DATA PROTECTION
  generally, 6.2.2
Product liability
  generally, 3.3.2
Protocols
  generally, 1.1
Pseudo-anonymity
  generally, 1.5.3
Publication of terrorist statements
  generally, 5.4.2.1

R
Regulated activities
  access to the Internet
    introduction, 9.1.1
    OFCOM regulation, 9.1.2
    self-regulation, 9.1.4
    VOIP, 9.1.3
  advertising
    introduction, 9.3
    unfair commercial practices, 9.3.2
    voluntary codes, 9.3.1
  audiovisual media
    EC Directive, 9.6.2
    legislative framework, 9.6.1
  cancellation rights
    cancellable goods and services,
      9.5.2.4.1
    consumer obligations, 9.5.2.4.8
    effects, 9.5.2.4.7
    financial contracts with customers,
      9.2.3.3
    introduction, 9.5.2.4
    manner of cancellation, 9.5.2.4.3
    supplier not provided information in
      durable medium, where,
      9.5.2.4.6
    supplier obligations, 9.5.2.4.9
    time limits for goods, 9.5.2.4.4
    time limits for services, 9.5.2.4.5
  contracts with customers
    distance sales of goods and services,
      9.5.2
    financial products and services, 9.2.3
    introduction, 9.5.1
  distance consumer contracts
    introduction, 9.2.3.1
    means of distance communication,
      9.2.3.1.2
    suppliers and consumers, 9.2.3.1.3
    transaction types, 9.2.3.1.1
  distance sales of goods and services
    cancellation rights, 9.5.2.4
    exempt transactions, 9.5.2.1.1
    introduction, 9.5.2
    means of distance communication,
      9.5.2.1.2
    pre-contract information,
      9.5.2.2–9.5.2.3
    risks of breach of regulations, 9.5.2.5
    scope of regulation, 9.5.2.1
    suppliers and consumers, 9.5.2.1.3
  electronic money, 9.2.2

Regulated activities – *contd*
  financial contracts with customers
    cancellation rights, 9.2.3.3
    distance consumer contracts, 9.2.3.1
    introduction, 9.2.3
    pre-contract information, 9.2.3.2
    risks of breach of regulations, 9.2.3.4
  financial products and services
    contracts with customers, 9.2.3
    electronic money, 9.2.2
    financial promotions, 9.2.1
    introduction, 9.2
  financial promotions rules
    Electronic Commerce Directive,
      9.2.1.1
    general rules, 9.2.1.2
    introduction, 9.2.1
  online gambling
    betting, 9.4.1.1
    enforcement, 9.4.1.6
    facilities provision, 9.4.1.5
    gaming, 9.4.1.2
    generally, 9.4.1
    introduction, 9.4
    licensing, 9.4.1.6
    lotteries, 9.4.1.3
    meaning, 9.4.1
    remote gambling, 9.4.1.4
  pre-contract information
    and see Pre-contract information
    durable medium, in, 9.5.2.3
    financial contracts with customers,
      9.2.3.2
    introduction, 9.5.2.2
    manner of provision, 9.5.2.2.2
    performance, prior to, 9.5.2.3
    relevant information, 9.5.2.2.1
  risks of breach of regulations
    extension of cancellation rights,
      9.5.2.5.1
    financial contracts with customers,
      9.2.3.4
    injunctions, 9.5.2.5.2
    introduction, 9.5.2.5
    'stop now' orders, 9.5.2.5.2
  unfair commercial practices
    aggressive practices, 9.3.2.4
    enforcement, 9.3.2.6
    general prohibition, 9.3.2.3
    generally, 9.3.2.2
    introduction, 9.3.2
    misleading practices, 9.3.2.4

Regulated activities – *contd*
  unfair commercial practices – *contd*
    scope of regulation, 9.3.2.1
    typical consumer, 9.3.2.5
  voluntary codes
    enforcement, 9.3.1.2
    introduction, 9.3.1
    scope of regulation, 9.3.1.1
Remote access
  data protection, and, 6.2.5.7.2
Remote manipulation
  data protection, and, 6.2.3.2.3
Residence
  taxation, and, 7.5
Retention of title
  intellectual property rights, and, 2.3.2
Risks of breach of regulations
  extension of cancellation rights, 9.5.2.5.1
  financial contracts with customers, and
    9.2.3.4
  injunctions, 9.5.2.5.2
  introduction, 9.5.2.5
  'stop now' orders, 9.5.2.5.2
Rome Convention
  And see Choice of law
  generally, 2.5.1
Rylands v Fletcher liability
  generally, 3.3.3

S

Search engines
  copyright, and, 4.14
  navigation aids, and, 1.5.9.3
**Secure Multipurpose Internet Mailing
  Extensions (S/MIME)**
  generally, 1.5.2
Sentencing
  making, supplying or obtaining articles
    for use in computer misuse, and,
    5.1.5.4
  unauthorised access, and, 5.1.2.3
  unauthorised access for further criminal
    purpose, and, 5.1.3.5
  unauthorised acts to impair or to
    prevent or hinder access, and,
    5.1.4.3
Servers
  data protection, and, 6.2.3.2.2
Shops
  offers, and
    invitations, 2.1.3.2.1
    offers, 2.1.3.2.2

Software
trade marks, and, 4.2.4.1
Sole traders
taxation, and, 7.3
Sound recordings
copyright, and, 4.9.2.1
Sounds
websites, and, 4.9.6.3.5
Spiders
websites, and, 4.15.4
Spoofing
criminal evidence, and, 5.6.2.1.2
Stalking
Communications Act, under, 5.5.3
introduction, 5.5
Malicious Communications Act, under,
5.5.2
Protection from Harassment Act, under,
5.5.1
Standard of care
generally, 3.1.1.2
harm to website user, 3.1.2.2.2
viruses, 3.1.2.1.2
**Supplying articles for commission for
an offence**
generally, 5.1.5.1
introduction, 5.1.5
sentencing, 5.1.5.4
**Supplying articles to commit or assist in
commission of an offence**
generally, 5.1.5.2
introduction, 5.1.5.2
sentencing, 5.1.5.4

T

Take down notices
anti-terrorism, and, 5.4.2.3.1
Taxation
business profits, 7.4
companies, 7.3
general, 7.2
introduction, 7.1
partnerships, 7.3
permanent establishment, 7.7
residence, 7.5
sole traders, 7.3
source of profits, 7.6
taxable presence, 7.6
value added tax
electronically supplied services,
7.9.3.2
EU Directive, 7.9.4

Taxation – *contd*
value added tax – *contd*
introduction, 7.9.1
supplies made via Internet, 7.9.3
supplies of goods, 7.9.3.1
supplies of services, 7.9.3.2
system in UK, 7.9.2
withholding taxes, 7.8
Technical steps to conclude contract
pre-contract information, and, 2.1.2.3.1
Telephone
acceptance, and, 2.1.4.2.1
Terms and conditions
storage and reproduction, 2.1.2.3.1
'Thin-skull' rule
negligence, and, 3.1.1.4.1
Threat to electronic systems
generally, 5.4.1
Tort
choice of law
common law, at, 3.8.1
double actionability test, 3.8.1.1
introduction, 3.8
statute, under, 3.8.2
defamation
caching defence, 3.6.3.2.2
damages, 3.6.4
defamatory statements, 3.6.2.1
defences, 3.6.3
extent of publication, 3.6.1.3
hosting defence, 3.6.3.2.1
identity of defendant, 3.6.1.2
introduction, 3.6
mere conduit, 3.6.2.5
mere conduit defence, 3.6.3.2.2
publication, 3.6.2.4
s.1 defence, 3.6.3.1
similar interests, 3.6.2.2
statutory provision, 3.6.2
storage providers, 3.6.2.6
strategy, 3.6.5
third party, 3.6.1.1
types of defamatory material, 3.6.2.3
disclaimers
exclusions, 3.5.1–3.5.2
introduction, 3.5
economic torts, 3.3.4
exclusions
digital damage, 3.5.1.1
effectiveness, 3.5.2
incorporation, 3.5.2.1
limitations, 3.5.2.2

Tort – *contd*
  exclusions – *contd*
    negligent links, 3.5.1.3
    negligent misstatement, 3.5.1.2
    UCTA 1977, and, 3.5.2.2.1
    UTCCR 1999, and, 3.5.2.2.2
  jurisdiction
    Brussels Regulation, 3.7.1
    common law, 3.7.3
    generally, 3.7.2
    introduction, 3.7
    location of harmful events,
      3.7.2.2
    meaning of 'tort', 3.7.2.1
  negligence
    application, 3.1.2
    breach of duty, 3.1.1.2
    causation, 3.1.1.4
    consent, 3.1.1.5.2
    contributory negligence, 3.1.1.5.1
    damage, 3.1.1.3
    defences, 3.1.1.5
    duty of care, 3.1.1.1
    elements, 3.1.1
    harm to website user, 3.1.2.2
    intervening acts, 3.1.1.4.3
    introduction, 3.1
    standard of care, 3.1.1.2
    'thin-skull' rule, 3.1.1.4.1
    viruses, 3.1.2.1
  negligent misstatement
    generally, 3.4
    Hedley Byrne v Heller, 3.4.1
    identity, 3.4.2
    reasonable reliance, 3.4.3–3.4.4
  occupiers' liability, 3.3.1
  product liability, 3.3.2
  Rylands v Fletcher, 3.3.3
  trespass
    damage, 3.2.3
    introduction, 3.2
    physical interference with goods,
      3.2.1
    possession, 3.2.2
Trade marks
  absolute grounds of refusal
    descriptive domain names, 4.2.2.1
    introduction, 4.2.2
    www. and .com, etc, 4.2.2.2
  acquiescence, 4.4.8.1
  applicable law, 4.8.5
  average consumer, 4.4.5.3

Trade marks – *contd*
  classification of goods and services
    computer software, 4.2.4.1
    generally, 4.2.4
  .com, 4.2.2.2
  Community trade marks, 4.2
  computer software, 4.2.4.1
  consent, 4.4.8.1
  defences to infringement
    acquiescence, 4.4.8.1
    consent, 4.4.8.1
    introduction, 4.4.8
    own name, 4.4.8.2
    remedies, 4.4.9
  descriptive domain names, 4.2.2.1
  dilution
    due cause, 4.4.6.1
    introduction, 4.4.6
    unfair advantage or detriment,
      4.4.6.2
  dispute resolution
    confusingly similar to mark,
      4.7.3.2
    disclaimers, 4.7.3.2.1
    factual issues, 4.7.2
    formal issues, 4.7.1
    identical to mark, 4.7.3.2
    introduction, 4.7
    irrelevant changes, 4.7.3.2.2
    legal issues, 4.7.3
    nature of mark, 4.7.3.1
    no rights or interest in domain name,
      4.7.3.3
    other matters, 4.7.3.5
    registration companies, and,
      4.7.5
    registration in bad faith, 4.7.3.4
    timing of arbitration, 4.7.4
  distinctiveness, 4.4.5.1
  domain names
    and see DOMAIN NAMES
    availability, 4.6.1
    descriptive, 4.2.2.1
    generally, 4.1.3–4.1.4
    identifying ownership, 4.3.1
    misrepresentation, 4.5.2.1
    protection, 4.6.4
    protective measures, 4.6
    registration, 4.3
    use of sign in course of trade, 4.4.1.3
  due cause, 4.4.6.1
  electronic communications, 4.2.4.1

Trade marks – *contd*
goods and services
classification, 4.2.4
generally, 4.2.3
grounds of refusal
descriptive domain names, 4.2.2.1
introduction, 4.2.2
www. and .com, etc, 4.2.2.2
identical sign to registered mark
identical goods, 4.4.4.1
introduction, 4.4.4
infringement
defences, 4.4.8
dilution, 4.4.6
identical sign to registered mark,
4.4.4
in relation to goods and services,
4.4.3
introduction, 4.4
jurisdiction, 4.8
metatags, 4.4.7
similar or identical sign with similar
or identical goods or services,
4.4.5
use as trade mark, 4.4.2
use of sign in course of trade, 4.4.1
introduction, 4.1
IP addresses, 4.1.3
jurisdiction over infringement
applicable law, 4.8.5
basic rules, 4.8.3.2
EC domiciles, and, 4.8.3
E-Commerce Directive, 4.8.3.1
exclusive jurisdiction, 4.8.3.3
generally, 4.8.2
introduction, 4.8
non-EC domiciles, and, 4.8.4
unregistered rights, of, 4.8.3.4
legal rights, 4.1.1
Madrid Protocol marks, 4.2
metatags
generally, 4.4.7.1
introduction, 4.4.7
keywords, 4.4.7.2
nature of rights, 4.1.1–4.1.2
opposition, 4.2.5
own name, 4.4.8.2
passing off
BT v One in a Million decision,
4.5.4.1
damage, 4.5.3
disclaimer, 4.5.2.2

Trade marks – *contd*
passing off – *contd*
domain name misrepresentation,
4.5.2.1
goodwill of plaintiff, 4.5.1
instrument of fraud claim, 4.5.4
introduction, 4.5
misrepresentation by defendant,
4.5.2
remedies, 4.5.5
protective domain names measures
availability of name, 4.6.1
dispute rules, 4.6.5
introduction, 4.6
protection of name, 4.6.4
registration of name, 4.6.2
use of name, 4.6.3
registrability, 4.2.1
registration
goods and services, 4.2.3–4.2.4
grounds of refusal, 4.2.2
introduction, 4.2
opposition, 4.2.5
registrability, 4.2.1
similar or identical sign with similar or
identical goods or services
average consumer, 4.4.5.3
distinctiveness, 4.4.5.1
introduction, 4.4.5
similarity of goods, 4.4.5.2
technical rights, 4.1.1
unfair advantage or detriment
advantage, 4.4.6.2.1
detriment, 4.4.6.2.2
introduction, 4.4.6.2
unregistered marks, 4.2
use as trade mark, 4.4.2
use of sign in course of trade
determining factors, 4.4.1.2
domain names, 4.4.1.3
introduction, 4.4.1
use on Internet as use in UK, 4.4.1.1
well-known marks, 4.2
www. and .com, etc, 4.2.2.2
Transactional information
clear, comprehensible and
unambiguous, 2.1.2.3.1
introduction, 2.1.2.3
Trespass
damage, 3.2.3
introduction, 3.2
physical interference with goods, 3.2.1

Trespass – *contd*
possession, 3.2.2
US examples, 3.2.3.1
Typographical arrangements
copyright, and, 4.9.2.1

U
Unauthorised access
actus reus
alteration of programs or data,
5.1.2.1.3
automatic causation of function,
5.1.2.1.2
computer, 5.1.2.1.1
copying programs and data, 5.1.2.1.3
data, 5.1.2.1.1
erasure of programs or data, 5.1.2.1.3
function on any computer, 5.1.2.1.2
held in any computer, 5.1.2.1.1
introduction, 5.1.2.1
moving programs and data, 5.1.2.1.3
output of programs or data, 5.1.2.1.3
performing any function, 5.1.2.1.2
program, 5.1.2.1.1
securing access, 5.1.2.1.3
unsuccessful attempts, 5.1.2.1.2
using a program, 5.1.2.1.3
alteration of programs or data, 5.1.2.1.3
automatic causation of function,
5.1.2.1.2
computer, 5.1.2.1.1
conduct, 5.1.2.1
copying programs and data, 5.1.2.1.3
data, 5.1.2.1.1
erasure of programs or data, 5.1.2.1.3
for further criminal purpose, 5.1.3
function on any computer, 5.1.2.1.2
held in any computer, 5.1.2.1.1
intention, 5.1.2.2
introduction, 5.1.2
mens rea
insiders, 5.1.2.2.4
intention to secure access, 5.1.2.2.1
introduction, 5.1.2.2
outsiders, 5.1.2.2.3
unauthorised, 5.1.2.2.2
moving programs and data, 5.1.2.1.3
output of programs or data, 5.1.2.1.3
performing any function, 5.1.2.1.2
program, 5.1.2.1.1
securing access, 5.1.2.1.3
sentencing, 5.1.2.3

Unauthorised access – *contd*
unauthorised, 5.1.2.2.2
unsuccessful attempts, 5.1.2.1.2
using a program, 5.1.2.1.3
**Unauthorised access for further
criminal purpose**
further offence, 5.1.3.1
future intention, 5.1.3.3
impossible further offence, 5.1.3.4
intention, 5.1.3.2
introduction, 5.1.3
sentencing, 5.1.3.5
**Unauthorised acts to impair or to
prevent or hinder access**
act, 5.1.4.1.1
actus reus, 5.1.4.1.1
conduct, 5.1.4.1
intention, 5.1.4.2
introduction, 5.1.4
mens rea
computer, program or data. 5.1.4.2.1
intent to impair or prevent or hinder
access, 5.1.4.2.1
introduction, 5.1.4.2
recklessness as to act, 5.1.4.2.2
temporarily, 5.1.4.2.1
modification, 5.1.4.1.1
sentencing, 5.1.4.3
unauthorised, 5.1.4.1.1
Unfair advantage or detriment
advantage, 4.4.6.2.1
detriment, 4.4.6.2.2
introduction, 4.4.6.2
Unfair commercial practices
aggressive practices, 9.3.2.4
enforcement, 9.3.2.6
general prohibition, 9.3.2.3
generally, 9.3.2.2
introduction, 9.3.2
misleading practices, 9.3.2.4
scope of regulation, 9.3.2.1
typical consumer, 9.3.2.5
User- generated content
generally, 1.5.7

V
Value added tax
and see TAXATION
electronically supplied services, 7.9.3.2
EU Directive, 7.9.4
introduction, 7.9.1
supplies made via Internet, 7.9.3

Value added tax – *contd*
supplies of goods, 7.9.3.1
supplies of services, 7.9.3.2
system in UK, 7.9.2
Viruses
breach of duty, 3.1.2.1.2
causation, 3.1.2.1.4
consent, 3.1.2.1.5
contributory negligence, 3.1.2.1.5
damage, 3.1.2.1.3
data protection, and, 6.2.5.7.2
defences, 3.1.2.1.5
digital damage, 3.1.2.1.3
duty of care, 3.1.2.1.1
economic loss, 3.1.2.1.3
Voluntary codes of advertising
enforcement, 9.3.1.2
introduction, 9.3.1
scope of regulation, 9.3.1.1

W

Web invitations
offer, and, 2.1.3.3
Web links
generally, 4.9.6.4
infringement, 4.14
Web servers
data protection, and, 6.2.5.7.2
Website contracts
jurisdiction, and, 2.4.1.8.1
Websites
acceptance, and
generally, 2.1.4.1.1
timing, 2.1.4.2.3
backup copies, 4.15.1
copyright, and
commercial issues, 4.9.6.3.6
computer programs, as, 4.9.6.3.7
creation, 4.9.6.3.1
generally, 4.9.6.3
graphics, 4.9.6.3.4
infringement, 4.15–4.16
joint authorship, 4.9.6.3.9

Websites – *contd*
copyright, and – *contd*
'look and feel', 4.9.6.3.8
music, 4.9.6.3.5
preparatory material, 4.9.6.3.2
sounds, 4.9.6.3.5
text, 4.9.6.3.3
deep links, 4.15.4
defamation, and, 3.6.3.1.3
framing, 4.15.2
Hedley Byrne v Heller, and, 3.4.1.3.3
infringement of copyright, and
backup copies, 4.15.1
deep links, 4.15.4
framing, 4.15.2
generally, 4.15
jurisdiction, 4.16
making an unlicensed article, 4.15.3
spiders, 4.15.4
jurisdiction, and, 2.4.1.8.1
making an unlicensed article, 4.15.3
spiders, 4.15.4
Webvertisements
offer, and, 2.1.3.1
Web-wrap
consideration, and, 2.1.5.1
Wide area networks (WANs)
generally, 1.1
Withholding taxes
and see TAXATION
generally, 7.8
World wide web (www)
browsers, 1.5.9.2
generally, 1.5.9
links, 1.5.9.1
navigation aids, 1.5.9.3
Wrongful interference with goods
damage, 3.2.3
introduction, 3.2
physical interference, 3.2.1
possession, 3.2.2
www. and .com, etc
trade marks, and, 4.2.2.2